Powers of the Pres

D0472421

DATE DUE

FEB 2 6 1999			
MAR 1 6 1999			
MAY 2 7 1999			
APR 0 8 2000			
NOV 2 0 [illegible]			
JUN 1 0 2005			
JAN 2 3 2006			
FEB 1 1 2008			
APR 0 8 2009			
JUN 1 7 2009			

PRINTED IN U.S.A.

DISCARDED

Powers of the Presidency

SECOND EDITION

CONGRESSIONAL QUARTERLY INC.
WASHINGTON, D.C.

27.00

JK
511
P75
1997

EL CAMINO COLLEGE
LIBRARY

Copyright © 1997 Congressional Quarterly Inc.
1414 22nd Street, N.W., Washington, D.C. 20037

All rights reserved. No part of this publication may be reproduced or transmitted in any form or by any means, electronic or mechanical, including photocopy, recording, or any information storage and retrieval system, without permission in writing from the publisher.

Book design and production by Kachergis Book Design,
Pittsboro, North Carolina

Printed and bound in the United States of America

The paper used in this publication meets the minimum requirements of the American National Standard for Information Science—Permanence of Paper for Printed Library Materials, ANSI Z39.48-1984.

Cover illustration credits (clockwise from top right): Library of Congress; Library of Congress; no credit; White House; Pete Souza—White House; Library of Congress; Library of Congress

Illustration credits and acknowledgments appear on page 281, which is to be considered an extension of the copyright page.

LIBRARY OF CONGRESS CATALOGING-IN-PUBLICATION DATA
Powers of the presidency.—2nd ed.
p. cm.
Includes bibliographical references and index.
ISBN 1-56802-310-3 (alk. paper)
1. Executive power—United States—History. 2. Presidents—United States—History. I. Congressional Quarterly, Inc.
JK511.P75 1997
352.23'0973—dc21 97-503

Table of Contents

Preface

At the top of the U.S. government, the president wields tremendous power. The president appoints high-ranking officials of the federal government, signs or vetoes congressional legislation, concludes agreements with foreign nations, commands the armed forces in war and in peace, presides over the nation's most cherished celebrations, and guides the formation of the nation's economic policy. *Powers of the Presidency,* second edition, examines the constitutional origins, the historical developments, and contemporary understanding of the various formal and inherent powers of the presidency.

Presidents, in fulfilling their constitutional duty to "take Care that the Laws be faithfully executed," have broad discretionary powers as head of the executive branch. Chapter 1, Chief Executive, explores presidential powers in running the federal bureaucracy and all that entails. A president is chief administrator of the executive branch, chief personnel officer in making appointments, chief financial officer in budgeting matters, and chief law enforcement officer. In each role there are checks and balances with the other branches of government.

Chapter 2, Legislative Leader, analyzes the president's role in shaping the nation's laws. The president, although not part of the legislative branch, is paradoxically the nation's top legislator. This standing is primarily by virtue of the president's constitutional power to say "no," to veto legislation. The American citizenry has also come to expect presidential leadership over the direction of public policy. The ability to tap into public support gives the president considerable influence in promoting or opposing legislation.

Presidents historically have formulated and implemented the nation's foreign policy. Chapter 3, Chief Diplomat, evaluates the president's powers in recognizing foreign governments, initiating and concluding treaties and executive agreements with foreign nations, appointing diplomatic personnel, overseeing intelligence gathering activities, and representing the United States within alliances and at summit meetings with world powers. Although formal consent of the Senate is often required for White House actions in foreign affairs, the president's foreign policy leadership is rarely effectively challenged by Congress.

Chapter 4, Commander in Chief, focuses on the president as commander of the U.S. armed forces. This chapter reviews the development of presidential war powers through American history, especially noting the expanded powers of President Abraham Lincoln, who suspended *habeas corpus* during the Civil War and even directed the battlefield movements of his generals, and President Franklin D. Roosevelt, who assumed vast authority during World War II. The landmark War Powers Resolution of 1973 reasserted congressional authority to approve military actions begun by the president, influencing modern-day presidential commitments of the U.S. military forces in the Persian Gulf, Haiti, and Bosnia.

Presidents are afforded powers and responsibilities in addition to those stated specifically in the Constitution. Chapter 5, Chief of State, looks at how the ceremonial duties of the presidency enhance presidential authority. Presidents are symbols of the nation at home and abroad. They proclaim the nation's holidays and celebrations, present the nation's highest awards, and mourn the deaths of notable Americans or foreign heads of states. These and other ceremonial roles imbue presidents with cultural and symbolic power. This chapter also examines the heavy burdens placed on presidents, especially in the modern era.

Although the Constitution does not grant the presidency specific economic powers, presidents clearly exert some influence over the economy. Chapter 6, Chief Economist, assesses the president's role in formulating economic policy, creating and overseeing the nation's budget, negotiating trade agreements, and responding with emergency powers in periods of economic distress. Although presidents throughout history have always promoted the nation's prosperity, the American public has come to demand a more activist presidential role in managing the economy.

Tables of historical data supplement the discussions in *Powers of the Presidency.* Each chapter concludes with a note section and a selected bibliography for further reading. A comprehensive index is also provided.

Contributors

W. CRAIG BLEDSOE is professor of political science and chair of the Department of History and Political Science at David Lipscomb University. His teaching interests include political theory, methodology, and American government, including the presidency and presidential elections. He has written extensively on the presidency and is the editor of *Historical Encyclopedia of Presidential Commissions* (forthcoming).

CHRISTOPHER J. BOSSO is associate professor of political science and department chair at Northeastern University, where he specializes in American politics and public policy. He is the author of *Pesticides and Politics: The Life Cycle of a Public Law* (1987), winner of the 1988 Policy Studies Organization award for the best book in policy studies. He also has written on the intersection of environmental values and American democratic institutions, on trends within the environmental community, and on public policymaking dynamics generally.

DANIEL C. DILLER is a freelance writer on presidential history and international governments. He has contributed to several Congressional Quarterly books, including *Guide to the Presidency* (1996), *Russia and the Independent States* (1993), and *The Middle East* (1995)

DEAN PETERSON is assistant professor of economics in the Albers School of Business and Economics at Seattle University. His teaching interests include macroeconomics and statistics, and his current research concentrates on the history of economic thought. His recent article on organizing a history of economics course is forthcoming in the *Journal of Economic Education.*

MARK J. ROZELL is associate professor of political science at American University and the author of six books including *Executive Privilege: The Dilemma of Secrecy and Democratic Accountability* (1994). His research interests include the presidency, media politics, and Christian right politics.

STEPHEN H. WIRLS is assistant professor of political science at Rhodes College. He has published articles on the judiciary, the presidency, and liberalism. He is currently writing a book on the theory and practice of the Senate and bicameralism.

CHAPTER 1

Chief Executive

BY W. CRAIG BLEDSOE, CHRISTOPHER J. BOSSO, AND MARK J. ROZELL

ARTICLE II of the Constitution lists the president's powers. Although it grants far fewer explicit powers to the president than Article I grants to Congress, the ambiguity and vagueness of Article II have made it possible for presidents to expand their powers. Section 1 of the article clearly grants executive power to the president: "the executive Power shall be vested in a President. . . ." Section 3 makes the president responsible for the execution of federal laws: the president "shall take Care that the Laws be faithfully executed. . . ."

In theory, these directives make the president responsible for carrying out or executing the laws of the federal government. In practice, however, the ambiguity of this mandate often has increased the power of the presidency. For example, by broadly interpreting the authority to execute the law, Grover Cleveland used federal troops to break a labor strike in the 1890s and Dwight D. Eisenhower sent troops to help integrate a public school in Little Rock, Arkansas, in 1957.

At the beginning of the Constitutional Convention, the Framers expressed a great deal of uncertainty over the exact nature of the executive. They derived many of their political ideals from seventeenth- and eighteenth-century European writers such as John Locke, Jean Jacques Rousseau, and Baron de Montesquieu, whose theories emphasized both popular sovereignty and individual liberty. If the Framers had fully adopted the political beliefs of these writers, the chief executive would be a directly elected public official responsible only to the people. The presidency would not be set up as a monarchy, not even a limited one, but instead would represent the popular will.

Still, the Framers feared the effects of an unrestrained democracy. They were afraid that the chief executive might be too inclined to accede to popular demands in ways harmful to minority rights. Consequently, they attempted to insulate the office of president by having the public participate in presidential selection only indirectly through the electoral college.

The debate on the strength of the executive spilled over into the effort to define the exact nature of the president's administrative duties. Influenced by classical liberal writers, such as Montesquieu, the Framers dispersed power by structuring an executive branch separate and independent from the legislature. In doing so, they gave the presidency sweeping administrative responsibilities to "faithfully execute" the laws. But to keep the presidency from becoming too powerful, they subjected it to certain constraints by giving Congress immense powers of its own. The president has the power to appoint officials of the executive branch, but the Senate must confirm many of the appointments. And the president is in charge of administering the federal laws and programs, but Congress creates them, and it may change them at any time. Specifically, Congress can create and destroy agencies, and it determines whether they are going to be located in the executive branch or outside it. In other words, if it chooses, Congress can make an agency completely independent of the president.

The legislature also has the power of appropriation, which gives it ultimate control over federal agencies. Congress can define exactly what an agency has the power to do and not do. Consequently, as political scientist Peter Woll has observed, "Congress has virtually complete authority to structure the administrative branch and determine where formal lines of accountability shall be placed. It may or may not decide to let the President exercise various types of control."[1]

In *The Federalist Papers,* Alexander Hamilton defined the president's administrative activities as "mere execution" of "executive details." His was a narrow interpretation, for he in no way understood what would develop later. Hamilton, however, saw the president as the person solely responsible for administrative action. In *Federalist* No. 72 he wrote,

> The persons, therefore to whose immediate management these different [administrative] matters are committed, ought to be considered as the assistants or deputies of the chief magistrate, and on this account they ought to derive their offices from his appointment, at least from his nomination, and ought to be subject to his superintendence. This view of the subject will at once suggest to us the intimate connection between the duration of the executive magistrate in office and the stability of the system of administration.[2]

> The executive power shall be vested in a president of the United States of America.
>
> *—from Article II, section 1*

> The President shall be Commander in Chief of the Army and the Navy of the United States, and of the Militia of the several States, when called into the actual Service of the United States. . . .
>
> *—from Article II, section 2*

Since the 1930s Congress has delegated to the president the broad authority to achieve several general goals. Congress will often pass laws, leaving to the president and the executive branch the discretion to define the regulations and programs to be put into effect. This practice has come into being through political events, not by design. Americans increasingly look to the president for leadership in times of crisis and in everyday affairs, making the chief executive responsible for a growing portion of the nation's successes and failures. Consequently, the administrative responsibilities of the presidency have grown tremendously. As the presidency evolved, presidents found themselves serving as chief administrators, chief personnel officers, chief financial officers, and chief law enforcers—all part of the job of "chief executive."

Political scientist Clinton Rossiter was so impressed with the demands on the presidency that he introduced his classic book, *The American Presidency,* with a quotation from Shakespeare's *Macbeth:* "Methought I heard a voice cry 'Sleep no more!' "[3] A few days before he was assassinated on November 22, 1963, President John F. Kennedy wrote Rossiter to comment on the use of the quote from *Macbeth.* Kennedy believed the quote to be apt but thought an even more appropriate one could be found in Shakespeare's *King Henry IV, Part I,* in which Glendower boasts, "I can call spirits from the vasty deep," and Hotspur replies, "Why so can I, or so can any man; but will they come when you do call for them?" Kennedy pointed to the difference between presidents' calling for action and actually accomplishing their desired goals. After almost three years in office, he understood the paradoxical nature of presidential power and its limitations.

The President as Chief Administrator

Although the Founders placed a high priority on the presidency's executive duties, the Constitution provides very few instructions about the president's tasks as head of the executive branch. Specific presidential administrative powers have evolved as the presidency has matured.

The Constitution does not make direct provisions for the vast administrative structure that the president must oversee. It does, however, authorize the president to demand written reports from the "principal Officer in each of the executive Departments, upon any Subject, relating to the Duties of their respective Offices" (Article II, section 2). This clause implies a division of labor within the executive branch and clearly establishes an administrative hierarchy with the president as the chief administrative officer.

Similar to chief executives in private corporations, the chief executive in the White House tries to persuade subordinates in government to conform to presidential objectives. The chief executive tries to give direction to the administration. Presidents do not have time to follow through on every action taken by the bureaucratic departments and agencies directly under their control. They sit atop a federal executive structure that has approximately three million civilian employees. They must develop techniques that give them control over this vast administrative organization. Because this organization has grown tremendously since the early days of the Republic, analysis of the president's power as chief executive entails discussion of the structure of the executive branch.

STRUCTURE OF THE EXECUTIVE BRANCH

Often the term *bureaucracy* is considered pejorative, for to many it suggests red tape, inflexibility, and confusion. Opposition to "big government" has become almost synonymous with opposition to bureaucracy. Political candidates from both major political parties usually decry the evils of the burgeoning U.S. bureaucracy, denouncing it for removing Americans from the decision-making process of their federal government.

Those who work in the federal bureaucratic structure—"bureaucrats"—are often criticized for being unproductive and obstinate. Political scientist Charles Goodsell has written that "the employee of bureaucracy, that 'lowly bureaucrat,' is seen as lazy or snarling, or both. The office occupied by this pariah is viewed as bungling or inhuman, or both. The overall edifice of bureaucracy is pictured as overstaffed, inflexible, unresponsive, and power-hungry, all at once."[4]

Bureaucracy, however, has a technical meaning. The German sociologist Max Weber saw the bureaucratic model of organization as one distinguished by its large size, its formulation of rules and procedures, the presence of a clear hierarchy, the systematic maintenance of records, and the employment of a full-time appointed staff who perform specific duties using technical knowledge.[5]

By this definition, a large corporation or university is a bureaucracy, and so is the federal government. The departments, agencies, bureaus, commissions, and offices of the executive branch make up most of the federal bureaucracy. Although not as large and usually not as visible as the executive branch, Congress and the courts have their own bureaucracies.

Despite the negative connotations of the term, a *bureaucrat* is simply an administrator who carries out the policies of the elected officials of government. The structure of the federal bureaucracy under the president's control can be broken down into the Executive Office of the President (EOP), the cabinet departments, the executive agencies, and the regulatory commissions.

Executive Office of the President

In 1939 Executive Order 8248 created the Executive Office of the President to advise the president and to help manage the growing bureaucracy. The EOP includes the White House Office, the Council of Economic Advisers, the National Security Council (NSC), and the Office of Management and Budget (OMB)—agencies conceived to help the president control the expanding executive branch.

Since then the EOP has grown tremendously, employing approximately sixteen hundred people in the early 1990s. Its most

On January 21, 1993, his first full day in office, President Bill Clinton meets with his top White House aides in the Roosevelt Room of the West Wing.

important components are the White House Office, the NSC, and the OMB.

The White House Office consists of the president's closest assistants. Their actual titles vary from one administration to another, but under each new president it is this group who oversees the political and policy interests of the administration. Serving as a direct extension of the president, they do not require Senate confirmation. The creation of the White House Office has allowed the president to centralize executive power within the White House at the expense of the cabinet secretaries. For example, Henry A. Kissinger, Richard Nixon's assistant for national security affairs, forged such a strong power base in foreign affairs that his authority eclipsed that of the secretary of state.

In 1947, early in the cold war, Congress passed the National Security Act, which created the NSC to help coordinate military and foreign policies. Responsible for coordinating activities between the State Department and the Defense Department, the NSC has four statutory members: the president, the vice president (added in 1949), the secretary of state, and the secretary of defense. The act further names the chairman of the Joint Chiefs of Staff and the director of the Central Intelligence Agency (CIA) as advisers to the NSC. In addition to the NSC but distinct from its formal membership is the NSC staff. Made up of foreign policy advisers and headed by the national security adviser, the NSC staff has evolved into an apparatus used by many presidents to implement their own foreign policy goals. Because the role of the NSC and its staff is purely advisory, presidents have used it to varying degrees. President Kennedy, preferring his own close advisers, used the NSC infrequently. President Nixon, however, gave the NSC formal authority in formulating and executing foreign policy.

In 1970 President Nixon created the Office of Management and Budget to replace the Bureau of the Budget (BOB), established in 1927. OMB is the largest of the EOP agencies—in 1995 it operated with about 550 employees. Its staff members help presidents achieve their policy objectives by formulating and administering the federal budget. Departments and agencies of the executive branch must submit annual budget requests to OMB. Besides preparing the budget, OMB serves as an important managerial tool of the president by reviewing the organizational structure and management procedures of the executive branch, assessing program objectives, and developing reform proposals. OMB has tremendous power within the federal government. In the early 1980s President Ronald Reagan relied heavily on OMB Director David Stockman for the technical expertise necessary to implement his political objective of cutting the budget.

Cabinet Departments

The cabinet is made up of the heads—or "secretaries"—of the major departments of the government. Originally, there were only three cabinet departments—State, War, and the Treasury. By 1989 the number had grown to fourteen. (In 1995 the Republican 104th Congress considered legislation that would have dismantled four cabinet departments: the Departments of Commerce, Education, Energy, and Housing and Urban Development. The only bill to advance was one to eliminate the Commerce Department, and President Bill Clinton vetoed it during his successful 1995–1996 budget battle with Congress.) Lacking any constitutional or statutory base, the cabinet is primarily an advisory group. Although presidents may work closely with individual cabinet officers, they rarely use the collective cabinet for advice. Once President Abraham Lincoln, opposed by his entire cabinet on an issue, remarked, "Seven nays, one aye; the ayes have it." President Eisenhower, who held regular cabinet meetings and listened to opinions of others, came closer than any other modern president to making the cabinet a truly deliberative body.

Each cabinet secretary is appointed to head a specific department with a specific constituency. Although presidents make their own appointments, with Senate confirmation, the power they have over a specific department is limited. One reason is that the president can appoint only a limited number of a department's employees. When President Clinton came into office in 1993, for example, he could appoint only about one hundred people to positions in the Department of Transportation—less than 1 percent of its employees.

Executive Agencies

Executive agencies are agencies or commissions that are not considered a part of the cabinet and that often have quasi-independent status by law. Examples of these executive agencies include the National Aeronautics and Space Administration, the Peace Corps, and the CIA.

The difference between a "presidential" agency and an "independent" agency often is vague. Generally, heads of presidential agencies and commissioners serve at the discretion of, and may be removed by, the president. Independent agency heads and commissioners are appointed for fixed terms of office and have some independence from the president in their operations.

Government corporations, such as the Tennessee Valley Authority (TVA), also fall under the category of executive agencies. Similar to private corporations, these organizations perform business activities such as operating a transportation system (Amtrak) or selling electricity (TVA). Government corporations are generally controlled by boards of directors and are run like businesses. Because the president appoints these boards and their chairs, they have come increasingly under the control of the presidency.

Regulatory Commissions

Regulatory commissions are responsible for regulating certain segments of the economy. Many of them, such as the Food and Drug Administration (FDA) and the Occupational Safety and Health Administration (OSHA) are located within the cabinet departments. FDA is a part of the Department of Health and Human Services, and OSHA is in the Labor Department. Other regulatory agencies, such as the Consumer Product Safety Commission and the Federal Trade Commission, are independent in their relationship to the executive branch and so are insulated from regular presidential control and policy direction.

By statutory law each independent regulatory agency is governed by a bipartisan board of commissioners, who serve overlapping terms of five years or more. Although presidents have the power to appoint board members, they do not have the power to remove these appointees from office unless they can prove reasons of incompetence. This regulation ensures a certain amount of independence from executive control. Presidents cannot fire commission members simply because they do not like the policy direction of the agency, nor can they veto agency actions.

Still, presidents influence regulatory commission policies by choosing the commissioners and the chairs. Bipartisanship rarely means much in the composition of these boards, for presidents always have been able to name board members who share their views regardless of political party affiliation. Many conservative Democrats share the same policy beliefs as Republicans, and many liberal Republicans share the same policy beliefs as Democrats. Although commissioners serve long, overlapping terms, presidents still have the opportunity to place a majority of their appointees in any given agency.

BUREAUCRATIC GROWTH AND REFORM

In 1789 President George Washington's administration consisted primarily of the three cabinet departments (State, Treasury, and War) and employed only a few hundred people. By 1816 the number of federal civilian employees had grown to a little more than 4,800. Only about 500 of these worked in Washington. Most of the rest were scattered throughout the country providing mail service as employees of the Post Office Department. By 1931, however, the number of federal civilian employees had reached slightly more than 600,000, and by 1953 the number had expanded to approximately 2.5 million.

Although the number of federal employees has remained relatively constant since the 1950s (topping out at 3.1 million in the 1990s), federal expenditures have continued to increase. From 1965 to 1996, annual federal expenditures jumped from $118 billion to more than $1.5 trillion. This period also saw an increase in the number of people working for the federal government as either contractors or consultants or through grant-in-aid programs administered by state or local governments. Federal employment figures usually overlook the large and growing number of people who work indirectly for the federal government as employees of private firms and state and local governments that are largely, or entirely, funded by U.S. taxpayers. In 1978 Secretary of Health, Education and Welfare Joseph Califano observed that although his department employed almost 144,000 people, it indirectly paid the salaries of about 980,000 more in state and local governments through numerous grant-in-aid programs.[6]

Every president, eventually frustrated by the large and often unresponsive bureaucracy, talks of federal bureaucratic reform. Reform-minded presidents must move carefully, however. They must convince key members of the bureaucracy that proposed changes are worth making for the country as a whole and that they will not hurt individual bureaucrats. Thus, presidents try to persuade bureaucracies to favor their reforms. In addition, and far more important, presidents are subject to the same private interest pressures that afflict an individual agency. By the time they reach office, presidents have become indebted to people who have contributed to their election campaigns and helped them achieve their political stature. Rarely do presidents bite the hands that feed them. Presidents are very reluctant to undermine an agency that might serve one of their clientele groups.

Few presidents are successful in achieving the reforms they seek. When President Jimmy Carter came into office, he vowed to make a wholesale overhaul of the ninety-five-year-old civil service system, but the Civil Service Reform Act (1978) that finally passed Congress in Carter's second year in office had little effect. Campaigning for office, Carter promised to reduce the nineteen hundred existing federal agencies to two hundred. After he took office, however, the campaign promise was quickly forgotten and never appeared in the civil service reform law. In fact, in attempting to win their support for the reform measure, Carter promised civil service employees, "No one will be demoted, have their salaries decreased, or be fired as a result of reorganization. You need not fear that."[7]

Some presidential reforms have been more successful. In 1993 President Clinton promised to reduce the number of federal employees and cut bureaucratic waste, and in the process, improve the efficiency and effectiveness of the workforce by "reinventing government." After a six-month study, the National Performance Review, under the direction of Vice President Albert Gore Jr., offered several recommendations to save $108 billion and cut 252,000 jobs, mostly managerial, from the 2.9 million-person federal workforce. On the first anniversary of the National Performance Review in 1994, the Clinton administration claimed that its efforts had already saved $47 billion by removing more than 70,000 workers from the federal payroll. By the end of 1996 the administration estimated that the equivalent of more than 200,000 civilian federal jobs had been cut, and that the federal workforce was the smallest it had been in 30 years. The Clinton initiative enjoyed widespread support from the public and from both Republicans and Democrats in Congress. Since initial cuts were achieved through attrition, early retirements, and buyouts, and by cutting paperwork, the National Performance Review proposals also had widespread support among government employees' unions.

Carter's and Clinton's efforts are typical—in fact, the evolution of the federal bureaucracy has been largely a history of presidential attempts at reform. Although these efforts were aimed at reducing the power of the bureaucracy, instead they gradually increased it. In examining these recurring efforts, presidency scholar Michael Nelson has pointed out the irony in bureaucratic reform: the disparity between what the reforms have intended and the actual results has led to increases rather than reductions in the power and scope of bureaucracy.[8]

The Founders were ambivalent about the exact nature of the government's administrative structure and about who was to control it. The subject was not mentioned in convention debates; consequently, it was not mentioned in the Constitution. Nelson has argued that this ambivalence helped create the rapid growth that later characterized the American bureaucracy. By not spelling out the exact nature of the government's administrative structure, the Founders created a situation that allowed the bureaucracy to come under the simultaneous control of both the president and Congress in the nineteenth century. The system of dual control allowed administrators to increase their own independence by playing one institution off the other. Nelson observed:

> The Constitutional Convention, in loosing the agencies from their old legislative moorings (politically necessary if the support of executive power adherents was to be won) without tying them securely to the presidency (equally politic if anti-federalist support was to be kept) forced agencies to find and exercise relatively independent power. Agencies began to learn to play one branch off of another; if neither president nor Congress was supreme, then law was, and the agencies interpreted and implemented the law.[9]

Nelson concluded that the power of bureaucracy has grown in part because of the attempts to control it. For example, reformers, intent on controlling the bureaucracy by making it less susceptible to corruption, actually made it less efficient and responsible. To make it harder for public employees to defraud the government, agencies developed elaborate systems of internal checks and balances. These checks and balances took time to operate. Efficiency, responsiveness, or some other value often was sacrificed for the sake of preventing official cheating.

Nelson's historical account of bureaucratic reform points out that bureaucratic power usually endures even throughout the most challenging of reforms. Although the historical record indicates that reformers have unintentionally increased the power and scope of bureaucracy, attempts at reform will undoubtedly continue. Future presidents, like their predecessors, will become frustrated with the sluggishness and unresponsiveness of their administrations. Efforts at deregulation, civil service reform, and cutbacks in government expenditures that aim at removing the financial support for various agencies therefore will continue. Political scientist Robert Sherrill has outlined the problem: "Because so many portions of the bureaucracy are no longer responsive to the needs of the general public, and because they do their narrowly selfish work without fear of reprisal from the public, it may seem useless to talk of reform. But it isn't useless to talk of reform; it is only naive to expect much."[10]

CONTROL OF THE BUREAUCRACY

Presidents often complain that they lack sufficient control over the executive branch bureaucracy. They are quick to blame the bureaucracy for the many problems that hinder the implementation of presidential programs. Franklin Roosevelt provided one of the best-known illustrations of a president's lack of control over the bureaucracy. He is reported to have had the following exchange with one of his aides:

> "When I woke up this morning, the first thing I saw was a headline in the *New York Times* to the effect that our Navy was going to spend two billion dollars on a shipbuilding program. Here I am, the Commander in Chief of the Navy having to read about that for the first time in the press. Do you know what I said to that?"
>
> "No, Mr. President."
>
> "I said: 'Jesus Chr-rist!'"[11]

Other presidents faced similar frustrations later. Contemplating what it would be like for Eisenhower to be president rather than a general, Harry S. Truman once said, "He will sit here and he will say, 'Do this! Do that!' And nothing will happen. Poor Ike—it won't be at all like the Army! He'll find it very frustrating."[12] In office nineteen months, Clinton was surprised to find that a $310 million spy complex was being built without his administration's knowledge. The budget for the National Reconnaissance Office was buried in the budget for intelligence discretionary funds, known as the "black budget." Cost overruns brought the building to the attention of the Senate Intelligence Committee, which eventually disclosed the project to the Clinton administration.

Chief executives expect to have their orders obeyed and their programs set in motion. Yet upon assuming office, they often find that their programs rarely are implemented as promptly or as efficiently as they would like. They must face, and learn how to manage, an obstinate and unruly bureaucracy. Frank Carlucci, President Nixon's chief assistant for bureaucratic reorganization, stated that it takes "from six to eight months for a presidential directive to be translated into agency guidelines and reach the action level." In some cases, Carlucci maintained, it could take the policy two to three years to be put into action.[13] Controlling the bureaucracy has become a major priority for most presidents. All presidents after Franklin Roosevelt, whether liberal or conservative, have shared the desire to make the bureaucracy more responsive to their program objectives. Historian Arthur M. Schlesinger Jr. commented, "As any sensible person should have known, the permanent government has turned out to be, at least against innovating presidents, a conservatizing rather than a liberalizing force."[14]

Presidents face a tremendous task when they try to manage the bureaucracy and make it work for them. To control a specific agency, the chief executive must know what the agency does and what it did in the past. The president must know the preferences and inclinations of its members and the pressures being put on the agency from clientele groups. In addition, the president must anticipate the political implications of the agency's actions. Ideally, the chief executive should be able to do this for the hundreds of departments, bureaus, boards, commissions, independent commissions, and public corporations under White House supervision. But even with the help of the Executive Office of the President, it is an almost impossible task. Presidential scholar Richard Pious wrote, "It takes a few weeks for a new administration to learn how to intervene in the affairs of a bureau; it may take a few years for the president to know enough to stay out of them."[15] Instead of being intimately involved in every little detail of an agency's affairs, a president must learn to delegate; that is, the president must be a manager. Presidential scholar Thomas E. Cronin wrote:

> He must constantly delegate, he must be most precise about what he is delegating, and he must know whether and for what reasons the agencies to which he is delegating share his general outlook. He must be sensitive to bureaucratic politics, to the incentives that motivate bureaucrats, and to the intricacies of their standard operating procedures. He must have some assurance (and hence an adequate intelligence system) that what he is delegating will be carried out properly.[16]

Unfortunately, most presidents have not done well in this respect. They often have misunderstood the bureaucracy and have concentrated on the goals rather than the implementation of policy. Political scientist Richard Rose has argued that "once in office, a president is much more concerned with choosing what to do than he is with how these decisions are implemented (that is, how choices are turned into routine government activities) or the conduct of program activities on a continuing basis."[17]

In addition to the problems of understanding the exact nature of the bureaucracy, presidents must face problems inherent in the political process itself that make it difficult to control their administrations. Upon entering office, presidents find that most bureaucratic institutions are already fixed. If they want to reorganize, as did Nixon, they run the risk of a confrontation with Congress. Few presidents want to risk an outcry of disapproval from a Congress that tries to protect the interests of its constituencies, who are often the clients of the existing bureaucratic agencies. Instead, newly elected presidents attempt to do the best they can with the bureaucratic structures already at their disposal. Constitutional inhibitions also make it difficult for the chief executive to fashion the bureaucracy into a more responsive institution. Presidential programs require legislative approval and appropriations, and they are subject to review, and possible nullification, by the courts. Even with statutory and constitutional authority, the president often faces untold difficulty in making the bureaucracy more responsive. Although the Constitution charges presidents with the execution of the laws, the formal authority to take that action is often statutorily vested in a cabinet secretary or the head of a specific agency. In theory, such presidential appointees will carry out the president's objectives. In practice, however, heads of departments and agencies often operate independently of the president and are more attuned to their clientele groups than to the administration's goals.

Instruments of Presidential Control

Although the obstacles to effective management of the bureaucracy are great, presidents do have two tools that afford them at least a small measure of influence: their authority to appoint top officials and their own centralized management staff—the Executive Office of the President.

Appointments. Presidents appoint fourteen cabinet heads and some 5,200 other executive officials, including all members of the independent and regulatory agencies. In other words, presidents may hire or fire almost all of their top officials at will, except the board members of independent regulatory commissions. This authority gives them great control over their immediate aides and department and agency heads, but not over the vast majority of the executive branch.

In addition to the power of removal, presidents may also attempt to make appointments that are ideologically compatible with their policies. President Reagan attempted to transform departments and agencies by appointing officials who shared his desire to curb the size and influence of the federal establishment. For example, Reagan appointed Thorne Auchter, an opponent of "unnecessary" federal rules, to head the Occupational Safety and Health Administration and Robert F. Burford, who helped lead a movement to return greater control of federal lands to the states, as director of the Interior Department's Bureau of Land Management.

Similarly, President Clinton attempted to place his stamp on the bureaucracy by keeping control of appointments firmly within the White House. Early in his administration, Clinton demanded that cabinet secretaries seek prior White House approval before making subcabinet appointments. In an effort to ensure that the policies bureaucracies carried out were those of the White House, Clinton wanted loyal appointees in key bureaucratic leadership positions.

Centralized Executive Power. In 1933 Franklin Roosevelt found himself facing a bureaucracy staffed by holdovers from preceding conservative Republican administrations. He feared that his New Deal programs, if left to the discretion of these bureaucrats, would never be put into effect, at least not in the way they were intended. To ensure compliance with the intent of the New Deal legislation, he established numerous new agencies, such as the short-lived National Emergency Council, to coordinate directives through new and old agencies committed to his liberal programs. By adding on to the existing bureaucracy, Roosevelt created an organizational monster.

Roosevelt found it difficult to get the information he needed to implement his policies. Frustrated by the bureaucratic mess of his administration, he asked Congress to expand his supervisory staff. Congress agreed, and on September 8, 1939, Roosevelt issued Executive Order 8248, which established the Executive Office of the President (EOP). In so doing, Roosevelt created a miniature bureaucracy to help him control the vast executive apparatus and thus expanded the modern presidency. Clinton Rossiter described the creation of the EOP as a "nearly unnoticed but nonetheless epoch-making event in the history of American institutions."[18]

Roosevelt maintained that only a strong, well-staffed presidency could provide unity and direction to the federal government. Later presidents agreed and continued trying to centralize power within the White House to control the bureaucracy. More often than not, however, such attempts overloaded the White House staff and undermined the effectiveness of the presidency. By the early 1970s, the presidency was attempting to centralize all policy at the White House by using White House staff to oversee programs of high presidential priority.[19] In attempting to centralize power within the White House, Nixon structured his staff in a way that limited his associates to those over whom he had the most control. This attempt at centralization isolated him and put him out of touch with the rest of the government.

However interested presidents might have been in centralizing power, it did not work. The White House staff was simply not large enough to control the massive executive branch, which in the early 1970s comprised nearly five million military and civilian employees and spent more than $300 billion annually. This points to the reality that no presidential mechanism has ever been large enough or powerful enough to control the bureaucracy. Some scholars maintain that presidents should not be in complete control of the bureaucracy.[20] They contend that the president's role in overseeing the success or failure of federal programs should be relinquished to the executive departments. Most federal laws, they argue, deliberately provide for discretion to be given to top departmental and agency officials. Richard Rose has pointed out that the work of the executive branch is carried out by operating departments granted specific powers and responsibilities by acts of Congress, and not by presidential delegation.[21] Therefore, both appointed and career executives should have the liberty to apply standards, revise regulations, and interpret legislative intent to fit specific situations. The president and the EOP should not be involved in most situations. These scholars hold the view that Congress is as much in charge of administration as the president, for it is Congress that creates the laws, funds the programs, and confirms the executive branch appointments.

Most presidents oppose this view. They argue that only the president can provide the coordination necessary to master the complexity of the federal bureaucracy. Cronin summarized the presidential perspective: "Only the president should have discretion over budget choices and the administration of federal policies. He is the one charged with faithfully executing the laws. . . . a strong presidency makes a major difference in the way government works, and . . . this difference will be in the direction of a more constructive (desirable) set of policy outcomes."[22]

This is the position that Hamilton advocated in *Federalist* No. 70: "A feeble Executive implies a feeble execution of the government. A feeble execution is but another phrase for a bad execution; and a government ill-executed, whatever it may be in theory, must be, in practice, bad government."[23]

At the heart of this argument is the idea that the government bureaucracy has become so large and diverse that the White House itself spends more time reacting to the whims of the bureaucracy than controlling it. Former presidential adviser McGeorge Bundy maintained that the executive branch often "more nearly resembles a collection of badly separated principalities than a single instrument of executive action."[24] The answer, according to this logic, is more hierarchy. An accountable president must be able to control the bureaucracy.

Information Management

Part of the problem of management is the control of information. The maxim "Knowledge is power" is never truer than in the executive branch. Presidents must deal with a highly specialized and expert bureaucracy.

Obtaining Information. How does a president gather the information necessary to make informed decisions? One way is to rely on information supplied by bureaucratic agencies

Former Maine senator Edmund S. Muskie, former Texas senator John Tower, and former national security adviser Brent Scowcroft were members of the Tower Commission, established to investigate the Iran-contra affair.

themselves. But if this is the chief executive's only source of information, then the presidency runs the risk of being dominated by, or dependent on, the bureaucracy. To a large extent this dependence on the bureaucracy is unavoidable. Compared with the rest of the executive branch, the president's management staff—the Executive Office of the President—is quite small, usually comprising about 1,700 employees. Thus the president and the EOP must make decisions on the facts and opinions supplied by the agencies themselves. But even if the EOP were enlarged to give the presidency greater information-gathering capability, it could never become large enough to provide the president with relevant information for *all* policy decisions for every agency. As Woll has written, "The scope and technical complexity of administrative legislation and adjudication alone precludes this, even if there were no legal and political obstacles to presidential control. What is of greater importance is the fact that the president alone cannot personally comprehend these areas."[25]

Those who insist upon expansion of the EOP argue that presidents need larger staffs to channel information from the multitude of agencies for which they are responsible. Since the offices within the EOP, such as the Office of Management and Budget (OMB), are not dependent on any clientele or constituency group but serve as the president's staff, they are viewed as being independent of the political pressures that other agencies endure. But the EOP suffers from political tensions just like any other executive bureaucracy. In examining the effects of information within the EOP, Woll described the need for presidents to be sensitive also to other major departments and agencies, such as the Department of Agriculture, which have powerful support from Congress. He has observed, "Such political support has a way of showing up in the White House sooner or later, and if OMB were continually at odds with the agencies it supposedly supervises, its job would be made impossible both politically and practically."[26] Not only do agencies outside the EOP constantly seek to channel their points of view to the White House, but EOP offices inevitably become advocates of particular viewpoints of their own. Such advocacy within the president's own management staff poses a serious problem for chief executives who attempt to remain detached from many of their top advisers in the EOP. This detachment allows key EOP staffers to make decisions based on their own particular interests and without presidential supervision. Thus, it becomes increasingly difficult for presidents to maintain the type of information surveillance necessary to remain knowledgeable and up-to-date. According to the *Tower Commission Report,* the involvement of Reagan aides Oliver North and John Poindexter in the Iran-contra scandal was the result of a lack of presidential control of key advisers. Their strong advocacy of support for the Nicaraguan contras coupled with the president's lack of direction in the activities of his aides resulted in a policy disaster for the Reagan administration.[27]

Transmitting Information. Not only the gathering of information but also its transmission can be a big obstacle for presidents. The transmission of information from one level of the administrative hierarchy to another provides those who receive it with the opportunity to screen out a portion of the information before sending it on. Screening out information may be deliberate on the part of those who wish to frustrate the efforts of a president, or it may be unintentional. Economist Anthony Downs estimated that as much as 98 percent of information can be lost or distorted in this way.[28] With as large a bureaucratic structure as the president must attempt to control, the task of disseminating information is particularly formidable. Presidents cannot simply assume that their instructions, statements of policy, or program directives are traveling down the bureaucratic hierarchy as they intended. To ensure that presidential communications from the EOP have been received and accurately understood, presidents must do follow-up; that is, they must check for agency compliance and require regular feedback. Since administrative agencies resist supplying feedback in the same way that they resist sending information through regular channels, presidents must conscientiously monitor bureaucratic activity to maintain control at the top of the bureaucracy. This monitoring requires extra personnel; it is one reason why most presidents have called for a larger EOP.

Permanent versus Presidential Government

Beneath this desire to manage the transmission of information throughout the federal bureaucracy more deliberately is an equally important motivation for greater presidential control of the bureaucracy—an antipathy toward, and a contempt for, the bureaucracy because of its ability to frustrate presidential policy. Most presidents never completely trust civil servants and are not completely at ease with their own political appointees. They fear that bureaucrats and department appointees develop loyalties that may obstruct presidential policy objectives. With this view comes a widely accepted belief among presidential scholars that an administration's failures result from ineffective management of the bureaucracy. Or, more specifically, an administration's failures result from the attempts of careerists (career civil servants who have made their careers in a particular department or agency) to supplant the policies of the president with those of their own agencies.

Arthur M. Schlesinger Jr., a former Kennedy staffer, said of the Kennedy administration:

> Our real trouble was that we had capitulated too much to the existing bureaucracy. Wherever we have gone wrong . . . has been because we have not had sufficient confidence in the New Frontier approach to impose it on the government. Every important mistake has been the consequence of excessive deference to the permanent government. . . . The problem of moving forward seemed in great part the problem of making the permanent government responsive to the policies of the presidential government.[29]

Consequently, many presidents have sought to reform the executive branch to make the bureaucracy more responsive to their policy initiatives. They want to provide the EOP with a larger staff and greater resources for coordination of the various departments and agencies and their programs. According to Cronin, these presidents see themselves as "the recipients of endless special-interest pleas and narrow-minded agitation, even from many of their own cabinet members. In its crudest form, their goal is to presidentialize the executive branch."[30] To gain control over what they perceive to be hostile environments, they push for strong bureaucratic reform measures.

Presidential scholar Louis Koenig has argued for reforms that would give presidents powerful administrative control over the bureaucracy:

> The strong presidency will depend on the chief executive's capacity to control and direct the vast bureaucracy of national administration. Ideally, the president should possess administrative powers comparable to those of business executives. What the president needs most can be simply formulated: a power over personnel policy, planning, accounting, and the administration of the executive branch that approaches his power over the executive budget.[31]

Nixon stands out among recent presidents for the depth of his animosity toward the bureaucracy and his suspicion that it sought to sabotage his administration. In line with his view of a hostile bureaucracy, Nixon attempted to adopt strategies of governance designed to decrease the role of bureaucracy and increase the power of the White House staff. After abandoning a legislative strategy to put his stamp on domestic policy, Nixon turned to an administrative strategy that would take over the bureaucracy and concentrate on achieving policy objectives through administrative action.

Public administration scholar Richard P. Nathan referred to the Nixon administration as the "anti-bureaucracy administration." He noted that over the course of Nixon's tenure in office "there was no reduction in mistrust of the bureaucracy. On the contrary, these attitudes hardened to the point where unprecedented reorganizational steps were planned for the second term to take control of the machinery of domestic government."[32] Hostility toward the bureaucracy could be found in several statements of Nixon's aides. One staff member referred to the "White House surrounded"—apparently by a bureaucracy more attuned to the policies of interest groups than to those of the president. Another Nixon aide, former White House staff assistant Michael P. Balzano, described the federal bureaucracy in June 1972 in the following terms: "President Nixon doesn't run the bureaucracy; the civil service and the unions do. It took him three years to find out what was going on in the bureaucracy. And God forbid if any president is defeated after the first term, because then the bureaucracy has another three years to play games with the next president."[33] This view of a hostile bureaucracy probably contributed greatly to some of Nixon's later difficulties in the Watergate affair.

Nathan pointed out that Nixon's 1973 decision to develop an administrative strategy for his second term brought up an important question. What should be the role of the elected chief executive in influencing the career professionals of the executive branch agencies? Should Congress, the courts, interest groups, the press, and the public be as powerful in controlling the executive branch, or even more so? Nathan argued that the president "should have the most important role in this area of modern government. Purely as a practical matter, the chief executive is in a much better position than a large group of people in a legislative body or the courts to give cohesive policy direction and guidance to the work of large public bureaucracies."[34]

THE PRESIDENT'S ADMINISTRATIVE STYLE

How the chief executive organizes the EOP affects the success of any administration. Eisenhower, pointing to the necessity of a president giving considerable thought to administrative organization, wrote, "Organization cannot make a genius out of an incompetent. On the other hand, disorganization can scarcely fail to result in inefficiency and can easily lead to disaster."[35]

Presidents have used different styles in running their administrations. Some are comfortable with a system that is tidy and neat; others prefer a chaotic system that allows them to be innovative. In choosing their administrative styles, they determine how much advice and information they want to receive from within government and how much they want to receive from outside. Their decisions on administrative style determine whether they will give competing assignments and have overlapping jurisdictions or rely on aides with specific and narrowly defined responsibilities. Presidential scholars have traditionally divided these patterns of presidential organization and management into two systems: circular and hierarchical.

The Circular System

Some presidents, such as Franklin Roosevelt and John Kennedy, did not adopt a system with rigid lines of responsibility. They gave staffers different jobs over time and nurtured a competitive spirit. In this way they hoped to find the best person for any given task. Political scientist Stephen Hess described this style of staff organization as "circular," with the president at the hub of the wheel.[36] With no chief of staff to filter out less important information or decide who can and cannot see the president, this system permits large numbers of people—staffers, cabinet secretaries, members of Congress—to have relatively easy access to the Oval Office. Top staffers report directly to the chief executive.

Roosevelt is the clearest example of a hub-of-the-wheel president. Choosing a wide-open, free-wheeling, conflict-loaded system, Roosevelt delighted in encouraging and cultivating chaos in his staff. Although it was seldom clear either to outsiders or insiders where the lines of authority ran, there was never the slightest doubt that Roosevelt was in charge. It was not unusual for Roosevelt to assign two of his top assistants to work on the same problem without informing either of them that the other had the same task. For example, Roosevelt pitted Secretary of State Cordell Hull against Assistant Secretary of State Raymond Moley at the International Monetary and Economic Conference held in London in 1933. The two men, both assigned the responsibility of working out a policy on protective tariffs, had widely differing views. Hull considered protective tariffs a terrible mistake, and Moley was convinced that they were indispensable to industrial recovery at home during the New Deal. Hull, who was chairing the U.S. delegation at the conference, was surprised when Roosevelt sent Moley as his personal liaison when the conference stalled. Who had more authority? Which view was closer to Roosevelt's? No one knew until Roosevelt sided with Hull. Infuriated by the whole episode, Moley resigned.

At whatever cost, Roosevelt had no intention of being isolated in the White House. He was determined to get as much information from as many people as he could, even if doing so meant duplicating assignments or bruising egos. Political scientist Frank Kessler described the Roosevelt system:

> One hundred or so persons could get to him directly by telephone without being diverted by a secretary. He employed no chief of staff and permitted few of his staffers to become subject matter specialists. Except for Harry Hopkins, to whom he turned almost exclusively for foreign policy assignments, staffers were assigned problems in a variety of areas. He wanted to be sure that no staffer would become so steeped in an issue area that he would be forced to lean on that person for advice. Everyone but FDR had to be expendable.[37]

The Hierarchical System

Other presidents, such as Dwight Eisenhower and Richard Nixon, valued formal, hierarchical relationships. They felt more comfortable with an arrangement that placed greater coordinating and integrating responsibilities upon a chief of staff. According to Hess, these presidents designed a highly structured pyramidal system with themselves at the pinnacle.[38]

Leaning heavily on his experience in the army, Eisenhower set up a pyramid with himself at the top and delegated as much responsibility to his staff as possible. The key to the operation was Chief of Staff Sherman Adams, who served, in effect, as a deputy president. Adams, a former member of Congress and governor of New Hampshire, came to the Eisenhower administration with a great deal of government experience. Eisenhower placed much confidence in Adams and would not read memos or reports coming across his desk unless his chief of staff had seen them first. Adams wrote, "Eisenhower simply expected me to man a staff that would boil down, simplify and expedite the

Chief of Staff H. R. Haldeman, left, was called the "Berlin Wall" because he jealously guarded the entrance to the Oval Office. He is shown here meeting with President Nixon and aide C. Stanley Blair.

urgent business that had to be brought to his attention and keep . . . work of secondary importance off of his desk."[39]

The Nixon administration epitomized the pyramid staffing pattern. Similar to the Eisenhower system, Nixon constructed a highly stratified organization with himself at the top and a chief of staff standing between him and the rest of the executive branch. Because he preferred to make decisions from option papers rather than through face-to-face communications, Nixon allowed papers to get through to him more easily than people. Nixon's chief of staff (before the Watergate scandal forced his resignation), H. R. Haldeman, became known as the "Berlin Wall" because he jealously guarded the entrance to the Oval Office. Few staff members could get around Haldeman to see the president. Kessler has told the following story: "Once Federal Reserve Board Chairman Arthur Burns met Nixon for his allotted ten minutes but, on his way out, he remembered something else he wanted to tell the president. Haldeman reportedly thrust his arm across the doorway telling Burns to make another appointment."[40]

Although Nixon's operation was successful in freeing the president to think out broad policy initiatives, Haldeman often was criticized for keeping too tight control over who got in to see the president. Critics argued that Haldeman took too much responsibility upon himself. But two other chief Nixon aides, speechwriter William Safire and National Security Adviser Henry A. Kissinger, contended that Haldeman was performing the very role that the president assigned him. They maintained that Nixon wanted to be protected from the "unnecessary" intrusions of his lower staff.[41] Haldeman himself reportedly once insisted, "Every president needs an S.O.B., and I'm Nixon's."

Patterns of Organizational Change

Not all presidential organizational styles fit neatly into the circular or hierarchical systems exemplified by Roosevelt and Nixon respectively. Political scientist Charles O. Jones, in *The Presidency in a Separated System,* finds that neither the circular nor the hierarchical system adequately reflects how presidents do their work.[42] Relying on these systems to explain the ways in which presidents organize their administrations may oversimplify the vast differences in presidential organization and management. Presidents face different concerns and obstacles when it comes to organizing their administrations. Jones writes, "The process of designing a presidency at the top is allowed to be quite personal, suited to the perception of needs and responsibilities of the occupant. As a consequence, there is an astonishing lack of accepted wisdom as to how it should be done."[43] Consequently, presidents often resort to trial and error when organizing and staffing their administrations.

Rather than relying on the circular or hierarchical system to describe presidential organization and management, Jones looks at organizational changes that take place within individual administrations. These changing patterns of management better portray how presidents go about their work. Jones identifies four organizational patterns of change that describe presidential administrative styles: stable, adjustable, renewable, and transitional. A stable pattern reflects a high degree of continuity in the organizational structure of a president and a high degree of continuity in the personnel serving throughout a president's term. An adjustable pattern reflects ordinary organizational adaptation and ordinary personnel changes through a president's term. A renewable pattern reflects major organizational restructuring and substantial personnel changes during a presidency. A transitional pattern occurs when one president succeeds another.

Presidents reflect more than one organizational pattern throughout their tenure in office. For example, neither Jimmy Carter's, Ronald Reagan's, nor George Bush's administrative style fits neatly into the hub-of-the-wheel or the pyramid administrative system; instead, their administrations reflect changing patterns of management.

The Carter Administration

The first two and one-half years of the Carter administration were stable, but shortly after midterm the Carter presidency undertook a renewal. This renewal reflected a change in Carter's administrative philosophy. When Carter entered office, he put in place a cabinet government and a decentralized system of administration, one in which great amounts of authority were to be delegated to the department secretaries. He proclaimed, "I believe in cabinet administration. There will never be an instance while I am president where members of the White House staff dominate or act in a superior position to the Cabinet."[44]

Carter originally organized his staff along functional lines rather than strict lines of command. He devised three administrative levels: the president at the top, nine key aides on the next level, and the rest of the staff below. He planned no pecking order. All of his aides, especially those on the level right below him, would have equal access to the president. As Carter's term progressed, the role of the White House staff increased at the expense of the various departments and agencies in the executive branch.

Part of the reason Carter's commitment to cabinet government did not last can be found in a personal work style that proved cumbersome in the White House. Carter had a passion for details that often obscured larger policy goals. Kessler wrote, "Often he overlooked the big picture because he was bogged down in particulars. Memos that crossed his desk in the Oval Office were often returned to the sender with Carter's comments penciled in the margin. He went so far as to correct his young staffer's grammar."[45] Because of his predilection for immersing himself in detail, Carter spent much time consuming large amounts of factual information. Early in his administration, senior career civil servants from OMB were astounded to learn that they were to brief Carter personally rather than his top aides on the defense budget. Once, in a meeting that lasted from three o'clock in the afternoon to eleven o'clock at night, the president devoured every piece of information that OMB could feed him. This commitment to detail pushed the adminis-

Even though President Jimmy Carter organized his White House staff with no formal pecking order, Hamilton Jordan, right, and Jody Powell, left, became his closest advisers. By Carter's third year in office, Jordan had become his official chief of staff.

tration away from a hub-of-the-wheel approach to a more structured pattern. Political scientist Colin Campbell has suggested, "Every fiber of Carter's personal makeup had actually been conspiring all along to run a highly centralized administration. Here the president's tendency to engross himself in details served as the fifth column."[46]

In 1979, after thirty months in office, Carter renewed his presidency. In an unusual Camp David retreat with some of his most trusted political advisers, Carter reviewed his cabinet and White House staff. The group recommended that some of the cabinet resign and that the White House staff be strengthened. The recommended personnel changes led to the resignation of six cabinet secretaries and the appointment of Hamilton Jordan as chief of staff.

Under Jordan's direction, the White House began to solidify its control over bureaucratic operations. In the first few months of the Carter administration, cabinet secretaries and the heads of many other agencies had enjoyed great latitude in appointing people to fill vacancies. Personnel officers in each of the departments eventually were told, however, that the White House wanted to be consulted on all appointments to high government positions—a major blow since the departments had been promised great flexibility and control over their own affairs.

The Reagan and Bush Administrations

The twelve years of the Reagan and Bush administrations represent a "transitional" presidency, moving through periods of adjustment, renewal, and finally, transition. The Reagan administration itself moved from an early period of normal adjustment with several changes in cabinet secretaries to a period of renewal as political events unfolded during Reagan's eight years in office. As a vice president elected to follow his own party's immensely popular president, Bush faced some special problems in setting up his administration during the transition period.

Reagan cared little for the details of the presidency. Throughout his administration, he conveyed almost a nonchalance about the specifics of presidential organization and management. Preferring one-page mini-memos that boiled down even the most complex issues to the bare essentials, Reagan operated largely through massive delegation of duties. He maintained a "nine-to-five" schedule characteristic of pyramid presidents who prefer delegation to detail.

Although Reagan had certain broad policy goals he wanted to see accomplished, he left it to others to organize his administration to achieve these goals. The responsibility for organizing the Reagan presidency fell to James A. Baker III, Michael Deaver, and Edwin Meese III, all key Reagan political advisers in the 1980 presidential campaign. The result was a modified pyramid form of staffing in which authority was divided between Baker, who served as chief of staff, and Meese, who served as counselor to the president. Baker was charged with handling political matters and selling the president's programs to the public, the press, Congress, and interest groups. Meese was charged with policy formulation. In addition, Michael K. Deaver became part of the inner circle of advisers who had easy access to Reagan. Deaver's responsibilities included scheduling, appointments, and travel.

Dividing power among Baker, Meese, and Deaver, Reagan gave these three aides almost unlimited access to him in his first term. This arrangement kept him from becoming completely isolated, as Nixon had become by having only a single chief of staff in Haldeman. Meese served as Reagan's political conscience, keeping him true to his conservative policy goals. Baker and Deaver helped him undertake the practical aspects of policy implementation. It was a system that suited Reagan's personality and one with which he was quite comfortable.

Once in office, Reagan exercised great control over the appointment process in the departments and agencies, thereby imposing exceptional discipline on his administration. By ensuring the ideological compatibility of his nominees, Reagan could delegate and not worry about subordinates sabotaging his programs. Reagan's most effective source of discipline early in his administration, however, was OMB under the direction of David Stockman (1981–1985). By mastering the intricacies of the budget process and controlling the budgets of the various departments and agencies, Stockman was able to impose a stringent regimen on the departments and agencies and bring them under the policy directions of the Reagan administration.

The Reagan administration's pattern of renewal roughly corresponded with a changing White House staff and cabinet and events relating to the Iran-contra affair. Although Reagan had one chief of staff during his first administration, he had three during his second: Donald Regan, Howard Baker, and Kenneth Duberstein. In addition, after the 1984 election, Reagan's cabinet

In the early years of Ronald Reagan's White House, authority was divided among these advisers: from the left, James A. Baker III, chief of staff; Edwin Meese III, counselor to the president; and Michael K. Deaver, White House aide who scheduled appointments.

underwent five changes. Although there were no mass firings, the changes after the election represented a natural point for renewal. The initial Reagan appointments drew heavily from those outside Washington circles of power. At the point of renewal, Reagan's new appointees often reflected more experience in federal government.

Reagan attempted to maintain a modified pyramid with a tight system of discipline in formulating and implementing presidential initiatives throughout most of his administration. The success of this kind of system depends on the president's knowing when to become involved in details and which issues merit concentrated attention. Many who served in the Reagan administration give the president credit for involving himself energetically in important issues such as tax reform and contra funding. One aide stated: "He [Reagan] has a ruthless sense of priorities. He really knows that he can accomplish a few things. He's going to pick some good people and let them handle the rest."[47]

David Stockman, Reagan's first director of the Office of Management and Budget, imposed strict budgetary discipline on the administration's departments and agencies.

Yet the success of the type of system Reagan used requires that the president have a certain amount of knowledge even to decide which issues not to concentrate on. In several instances Reagan lacked the depth of knowledge in a specific policy area to make this determination. Political scientist Paul Quirk argues that presidents, such as Reagan, who adopt a "minimalist" approach that relies heavily on the advice of subordinates often have difficulties making intelligent decisions. He writes, "By never paying attention to the complexities of careful policy arguments, one never comes to understand the importance of thorough analysis."[48] In 1987 the *Tower Commission Report* charged that President Reagan relied too much on a bottom-up administrative system. The report noted that Reagan, by delegating too much responsibility to the NSC, did not give enough attention to important details of security policy. His inattention resulted in the secret sale of military equipment to Iran and the diversion of funds to assist U.S.–backed forces in Nicaragua during 1985 and 1986. This ill-fated undertaking became the subject of much public attention and embarrassment to the Reagan administration. The *Tower Commission Report* concluded that Reagan's management style put too much responsibility for policy review and implementation on the shoulders of his advisers. It stated, "The president should have ensured that the NSC system did not fail him. He did not force his policy to undergo the most critical review of which the NSC participants and the process were capable. . . . Had the president chosen to drive the NSC system, the outcome could well have been different."[49]

The Bush presidency reflected a period of transition from one administration to another within the same political party. Although Bush had to live up to expectations arising from the legacy of the popular Reagan administration, he attempted to put his own stamp on his administration by appointing staffers and cabinet members who reflected his priorities. Some of those appointees, however, were holdovers from the Reagan administration. Several cabinet appointments made in the waning months of the Reagan administration appeared to be transitional appointments. Bush called on three members of the last Reagan cabinet and two others who had served in earlier Reagan cabinets to serve in his administration.

Many of those appointed to the Bush administration were longtime political associates and friends of George Bush. One of those longtime political friends proved to be an embarrassment in the early days of the Bush presidency. Former senator John Tower was not confirmed by the Senate as secretary of defense because of problems with alcohol and women. Most Bush appointees, however, were highly regarded. Their competence allowed the president a certain amount of confidence to grant his staff and cabinet the freedom to provide direction and control over his administration.

There was never any question about the type of management system Bush would use. Bush chose a chief-of-staff system similar to Reagan's. His years of service in the Reagan administration and his close association with James Baker, Reagan's former chief of staff, contributed to Bush's understanding of presidential management and the ways in which he desired to organize his presidency.

Bush modified the pyramid system, however. Unlike Reagan, Bush wanted to be somewhat involved in the day-to-day operations of his staff. With many friends and close associates on his cabinet and staff, Bush had no desire to be isolated. Although his personality and close friendships among his appointees might point to an administration organized along a hub-of-the-wheel model, Bush saw the need for a chief of staff who would keep the administration in line. For chief of staff, he choose John Sununu, a former governor of New Hampshire and a Washington outsider who was not afraid to offend those who disagreed with him. Although vigorous in his pursuit of Bush's objectives, Sununu could not stand between Bush and his close associates within the administration. Too many staffers retained access to the president.

After the transition period, most of the Bush presidency was stable, with few adjustments and no wholesale firing of cabinet members that had characterized other administrations. Sununu met a premature demise as chief of staff—due partly to accusations that he had used air force jets at taxpayers' expense. Otherwise, many staffers and cabinet members remained in their positions until the end of the administration. Six of Bush's fourteen cabinet secretaries served until the next administration. Four of those who left took other jobs in the administration. The Bush presidency was one of few traumas in personnel and organization.

The Clinton Administration

The way in which President Clinton set up his administration for his first term exemplified another organizational pattern not found within traditional geometric models. As is the case with all presidents, the organization of the Clinton administration directly reflects the president's personality. Clinton had run a "hands-on" campaign in 1992 and wanted to extend that approach to the organization and governing of his presidency. Thus, the staffing and organizing of the Clinton presidency took place in Little Rock, Arkansas, the headquarters of the Clinton campaign, under the watchful eye of the president-elect and his wife, Hillary Rodham Clinton. The result of their efforts was a loosely structured and accessible presidency, staffed largely with inexperienced Washington outsiders.

Initially, the Clinton White House was largely unstructured. Elizabeth Drew, in *On the Edge: The Clinton Presidency,* describes Clinton's governing style in the early months of his administration:

> The unhierarchical structure and the collegial style of the Clinton White House seemed, at first, wonderful. Clinton himself contributed to the informality, often wandering the halls and dropping in on aides or on the Vice President. Aides felt fairly free to drop in on him. In March, Bruce Lindsay said, "More people tend to walk in on him than probably any of his predecessors." A peephole in the door leading from the back corridor to his office enabled an aide to see if he was on the phone, or talking with people, before going in.[50]

Clinton enjoyed the informal structure. He encouraged a large number of meetings with a large number of people attending. His desire was to get as much information from as many people as possible. This allowed him to place himself in the middle of his administration, participating directly in the formulation of policy.

Clinton had no desire for either a strong chief of staff, such as Sununu, or the highly structured White House organization that a strong chief of staff would necessitate. During the transition, Clinton chose Thomas F. "Mack" McLarty III as his chief of staff. McLarty, a business executive and Clinton boyhood friend had no Washington experience. He was to serve as an "honest broker" rather than a strong chief of staff who had unchallenged control over access to the president. Although many were critical of McLarty's lack of experience and easygoing management style, Clinton was very comfortable with him. Since McLarty did not impose a specific view or try to take charge, Clinton had the freedom he wanted to circulate among his staff in search of different views.

This nonhierarchical system with a weak chief of staff was complicated by the informal policy role assigned to Hillary Clinton. During the campaign, it was generally assumed that Mrs. Clinton would have a significant role in the new administration. At the beginning of the Clinton presidency, Mrs. Clinton was put in charge of domestic policy—excluding economic policy—although she was never given a title, nor was the decision to place her in charge of domestic policy ever formally announced. Mrs. Clinton's influence was represented by the loca-

Hillary Rodham Clinton, greatly expanding the role of the first lady, managed the Clinton administration's attempt at reforming the nation's health care system and acted unofficially as key domestic policy adviser to the president.

tion of her office in the West Wing of the White House near the president's office. Traditionally, first ladies' offices had been located in the East Wing. Especially because of her responsibility for developing a national health care plan, Mrs. Clinton exerted significant influence over the president.

Hillary Clinton participated in most of President Clinton's policy decisions. She was heavily involved in the staffing and organization of the Clinton administration, and she continued her involvement through key policy-making roles in the administration. Drew reports that some Clinton aides saw Mrs. Clinton as a de facto chief of staff, since aides had to make their policy arguments to the president through her. One White House aide reportedly said: "[Mrs. Clinton] concerns herself with the overall management of the White House and what she feels is a failure to integrate the president's politics into the workings of the White House. She expresses frustration about the loose management of the White House and the inability to hold some people accountable."[51] The strong influence of Mrs. Clinton, coupled with the weak chief of staff system under McLarty, proved to be troublesome for the administration.

The Clinton White House made its first real adjustment five months after the inauguration. In an effort to improve the management of the White House, and thus Clinton's approval rating, which had fallen steadily since he had taken office, McLarty was vested with more authority. McLarty in turn brought David Gergen into the administration as director of communications to give the Clinton presidency a more mature and moderate image. Gergen, who had served in the Nixon and Reagan White Houses, was experienced in Washington and was generally known as a political centrist. In addition, McLarty attempted to shore up lines of responsibility and to limit access to the president. The purpose was to structure the president's time better, freeing him to work more on larger policies rather than the details of policy. Despite McLarty's attempts to tighten control within the administration, it was not apparent that any real organizational change took place. There was little coordination of policy making among various groups within the White House and little clear responsibility. One Clinton aide said: "It's a floating crap game about who runs what around here. The last person who has an idea can often get it done, whether it's part of the strategy or not. The situation hasn't improved."[52]

By mid-1994 the public approval rating of Clinton's presidency and his ability to govern reached another low. Realizing that his presidency was in serious trouble, Clinton once again made significant changes in his White House staff. Acquiescing to advice from his closest advisers, Mrs. Clinton and Vice President Gore, Clinton replaced his longtime friend McLarty as chief of staff with Leon Panetta, the budget director. Panetta was given great latitude to rearrange the White House staff. He attempted to tighten the White House organization. He controlled access to Clinton much more closely by reducing the number of meetings staffers had with the president and drastically reducing walk-in privileges to the Oval Office. Panetta tightened lines of authority and generally attempted to return management of the White House to a more traditional, strong chief-of-staff model. McLarty stayed on the White House staff as a counselor to the president. Because his main ally no longer held a position of significant power, Gergen was sent to the State Department.

Throughout the turmoil in the White House staff, there were few changes in the cabinet during Clinton's first term. With few exceptions, the Clinton cabinet was chosen for its diversity, not for experience or loyalty to Clinton. Most cabinet members had little Washington experience. Only one, Mike Espy, secretary of agriculture, could be considered a Clinton loyalist from the early days of the campaign. In late 1994 Espy was forced to step down in the wake of accusations that he accepted gratuities from firms regulated by his department.

One of the ways Clinton attempted to ensure loyalty, and thus control, was to insist on his right to approve subcabinet appointments. His transition team believed that not ensuring loyalty among subcabinet positions was a fatal organizational mistake made by the Carter administration. Halfway through the Clinton administration, there was some indication that not ensuring loyalty from his cabinet secretaries may have also been a mistake. A few cabinet members, such as Attorney General Janet Reno, often took public positions that differed from Clinton's. This created a public perception of lack of respect for the president among some of his cabinet members.

CONGRESSIONAL OVERSIGHT

Article I, section 1, of the Constitution states that "all legislative powers herein granted shall be vested in a Congress of the

United States, which shall consist of a Senate and a House of Representatives." Section 8 lists specific congressional powers and gives Congress all powers "necessary and proper" to implement them. Over the years these provisions have been used to establish administrative agencies such as the General Accounting Office to implement congressional policies. The constitutional grants of authority have given Congress the power of life and death over these administrative agencies.

Because Congress has the power to enact laws and create and abolish executive branch agencies without presidential consent, members of Congress have significant opportunities to tell the bureaucracy what to do and how to do it. Most programs enacted into law by Congress are technical and complex, however. In an ideal world, statutes are precise and the legislature's intent is clear. But Congress, starting especially in the 1920s, began to use broader statutory language that, in the process, often delegated substantial discretionary authority to executive branch departments and agencies. Congress did so for several reasons: it did not possess the technical capacity for greater precision, it could not reach consensus on the minutiae of increasingly complex policy questions, or it concluded that the fluidity of circumstances required a degree of executive flexibility in policy implementation. As a result, Congress usually states general goals to be achieved by programs administered through bureaucratic agencies.

The Economic Opportunity Act of 1964, for example, states that the poor should have "maximum feasible participation" in the administration of the programs of the Office of Economic Opportunity (OEO). The interpretation of the act was left entirely to OEO and its local branches. Occasionally Congress specifies very precise standards that eliminate bureaucratic discretionary power, as it did in the Securities Act of 1933, which requires that investors receive financial and other significant information concerning securities being offered for public sale.

The very size of the *Federal Register,* a journal published each weekday in which agencies announce and publicize all the new rules and regulations used in administering programs, indicates the amount of freedom agencies have in interpreting congressional intent. Delegating this authority to the bureaucracy allows Congress to keep its workload manageable. Otherwise, the volume and complexity of its work would allow Congress to accomplish little.

By giving agencies considerable leeway in realizing their objectives, however, Congress abrogates a certain amount of control over the bureaucracy. Thus, a great deal of public policy is made by the bureaucracy, without any specific direction from Congress. Because administrative agencies have wide latitude in promulgating regulations and establishing policies, the burden of reconciling conflicts among competing interest groups often falls on the bureaucracy rather than on Congress. Peter Woll has written, "Theoretically, Congress still retains the primary legislative power, and is merely appointing an agent to act for it; in fact, however, virtually complete legislative discretion is given to the designated agency or to the President."[53]

Although Congress delegates to executive branch agencies much of its authority to make and implement policy, it retains considerable influence through a variety of activities known collectively as *congressional oversight.* Through laws and precedents, Congress has developed procedures that allow it to monitor the way the bureaucracy exercises its delegated authority.

The Legislative Reorganization Act of 1946 requires congressional committees to oversee continuously those agencies that they create or that fall under their jurisdiction. For many years after passage of this act, members of Congress were more interested in creating new laws than in monitoring ones they had already made; oversight, therefore, was not a major concern of the committees. With the growth in the 1960s and 1970s of grant-in-aid programs, which gave state and local governments federal funds to administer specific programs in areas such as highways, hospitals, and welfare services, interest groups and state and local officials encouraged legislative oversight of agencies providing goods and services to constituents.

The Legislative Reorganization Act of 1970 increased the capability of Congress to oversee federal programs by giving committees additional staffing and funds to retain outside experts. In addition, the 1970 legislation increased the resources of the General Accounting Office (GAO)—created by Congress in 1921 to oversee the expenditures of the executive branch—and gave it power to review and analyze government programs whenever a congressional committee ordered it to do so. As a consequence GAO hired economists, systems analysts, engineers, and management consultants to help monitor and analyze programs as requested by Congress. Despite the Pentagon's objections, during the 1970s approximately twelve hundred of GAO's 2,700 professional staff spent their time auditing and evaluating Department of Defense programs.[54]

Since legislation can allow considerable latitude in an agency's interpretation of congressional intent, the tools provided by GAO improve committees' capacities to monitor agency actions. In addition to GAO monitoring, committees can hold either regular hearings or special investigations on specific aspects of a program. They also can monitor an agency's actions through informal means, such as phone calls and visits with bureaucrats, lobbyists, and constituents. Program evaluations, conducted by either the committee's staff or GAO, often provide ways in which the agency's actions can be changed to bring it into line with what Congress intended.

Legislative oversight has become increasingly important in recent years. According to Joel D. Aberbach, the number of days of oversight hearings conducted by House and Senate committees increased almost fourfold from 1961 to 1983.[55] One reason for the increase in oversight hearings is the tension resulting from divided party control of Congress and the presidency. As divided government has tended to dominate the political landscape since the early 1950s, Congress has become more assertive in its oversight function. In 1987 a Democratic Congress formed a joint committee to investigate the Reagan administration's secret sales of military equipment to Iran and its policy of using the proceeds from these sales to aid the rebel forces in Nicaragua. In the mid-1990s, a Republican Congress exerted its oversight power to investigate the investment activities of the Clintons, known as the Whitewater affair.

The Legislative Veto

Fearing that federal bureaucrats—or the president—might abuse the authority delegated by Congress, congressional committees frequently attach to new statutes provisions that allowed the committees to pass preemptive judgment on new regulations or other bureaucratic actions. Such provisions are known as *legislative vetoes.* These provisions typically require that no regulatory action can go into effect for a prescribed length of time (such as ninety days), during which Congress can vote to disallow the regulation or action through a simple resolution of both houses, one house singly, or even one congressional committee, depending on the provision in question. These requirements provide committees a formal veto over executive actions and give them authority to approve or disapprove specific actions of an agency.

The legislative veto was first written into legislation used by President Herbert C. Hoover in his attempt to reorganize the executive branch. In 1932 Congress passed a joint resolution that allowed Hoover to reorganize executive agencies but specified that his changes would not take effect for ninety days. During this time either house of Congress by a simple resolution could veto his reorganizations, but neither did.

Perhaps the best example of the use of a legislative veto comes from the Joint Committee on Atomic Energy (JCAE) in the 1950s. In setting up the Atomic Energy Commission, Congress required that agency to keep the JCAE informed on the development of its nuclear reactor programs. As Richard M. Pious concluded, "In effect that provision made the committee a 'board of directors' that supervised the peaceful development of atomic energy. The committee determined what technology would be advanced, the location of experimental facilities, and policies relating to the private development of commercial power plants."[56]

Controversy over legislative vetoes blossomed through the 1970s as use of the device mushroomed. Notable congressional attempts to rein in the executive branch by use of the legislative veto include provisions of the War Powers Resolution of 1973, which restricted the president's power to deploy troops without a formal declaration of war, and the Budget and Impoundment Control Act of 1974, which allowed the president to rescind expenditures only if both houses of Congress approved. Congress resorted increasingly to legislative veto provisions at this time in no small part because of the partisan, ideological, and political conflicts between Richard Nixon and a Congress dominated by Democrats. Put simply, Congress and the executive were locked in a state of mutual distrust, with Congress particularly loath to allow the president more discretion than necessary in carrying out the legislature's will. Describing the effects of legislative control over the bureaucracy, political scientist Allen Schick noted that by 1983 "Congress had adopted more than 250 veto provisions; of these, more than half were enacted during the 1970s."[57]

If Congress saw the legislative veto as the most effective tool possible to ensure that the president and the bureaucracy conformed to the intent of legislation, many presidents viewed the legislative veto as a violation of the doctrine of the separation of powers and as an unconstitutional encroachment on the powers of the presidency. Worse, at least from a presidential perspective, there was no formal way for a president to respond to legislative vetoes because simple resolutions do not go to the president for approval. Legislative vetoes could not themselves be vetoed.

Although the legislative veto has been challenged by various presidents and their attorneys general, not until June 1983 did the Supreme Court rule on this congressional power. In *Immigration and Naturalization Service v. Chadha,* the Supreme Court held the legislative veto to be unconstitutional. It found that the Constitution positively requires in Article I that "every order, resolution, or vote to which the concurrence of the Senate and House of Representatives may be necessary . . . shall be presented to the president of the United States" who must either approve it or veto it.[58] In other words, the president must concur in any action that Congress takes that has the force of law, including the legislative veto. If Congress wishes to prevent the executive branch from undertaking some action, the Court's majority ruled, Congress must either legislate in greater detail to begin with or pass a regular bill—subject to presidential review—to redress an action it deems unacceptable.

The decision in *Chadha* left unanswered the question of whether the laws to which the veto provisions were attached were also unconstitutional. To date, the Court has been reluctant to go that far. Congress for its part has adapted to life after *Chadha* in two ways. On the one hand, Congress has gone back to using more explicit statutory language, which of course raises complaints about congressional micromanagement. On the other hand, Congress has resorted to adding even more language in appropriations bills forbidding funding for some specific bureaucratic or presidential actions. This language provides the functional equivalent of a legislative veto if the president accepts the appropriations bill as a whole. The Court has yet to rule on this strategy. However, the passage in April 1996 of the "line-item" veto—the constitutionality of which is also in doubt—may enable the president to wrest control of the budgetary process from Congress. *(See "Line-item Veto, p. 94, in Chapter 2.)*

Critics of congressional oversight and the legislative veto argue that rather than allowing committees to oversee agencies effectively, the legislative veto gives too much influence to interest groups. They contend that "alliances" between the agency, its constituent group, and its congressional committee compromise the ability of the committee to monitor agency activities objectively. According to this theory, because the congressional committee is "captured" by the interest groups it serves, its oversight of agencies and programs will be biased to benefit the constituent groups.

Since the *Chadha* decision, Congress has passed more than 140 laws containing legislative vetoes. Thus, presidential expert Louis Fisher argues that the legislative veto continues to survive "by open defiance and subtle evasions" of *Chadha*.[59] For example, in 1989 President George Bush entered into an informal agreement with Congress, known as the Baker Accord, that restricted the executive branch in its efforts to aid the contras in Nicaragua by requiring that four congressional committees agree to the aid.

Problems of Presidential Control

Congressional oversight and the legislative veto make it much more difficult for the president to control the bureaucracy. Through a variety of oversight techniques, Congress has made significant gains in controlling both foreign and domestic bureaucratic agencies. Congressional oversight helped thwart the efforts of the executive branch in its bombing of Cambodia in 1973 and inhibited various other covert intelligence activities during the Nixon years. In fact, political scientists Thomas Franck and Edward Weisband argued that executive dominance in foreign policy has been replaced by a system of policy codetermination in which power is shared by the president and Congress.[60]

As a result, presidents have learned to live with congressional efforts at bureaucratic control, often signing bills that include oversight and veto provisions not completely to their liking. Franklin Roosevelt signed the Lend-Lease Act under which he lent American destroyers to Great Britain before the United States officially entered World War II, and other wartime measures that gave him extensive war powers, despite the constraints that Congress put on him. Nixon signed the 1974 Impoundment Control Act granting him authority to defer the spending of funds already appropriated by Congress, although either house could veto his actions. Almost any statute that delegates congressional authority to the executive branch will contain provisions for legislative review.

Presidential control of the bureaucracy, however, has not been replaced by congressional control. Congress is much too large and much too overworked to provide effective control of the bureaucracy. According to Pious, "Although Congress' oversight role has increased in recent years, it should not be exaggerated. It is still intermittent, especially in the Senate, where members are spread too thin, serving on too many committees and subcommittees to develop expertise in agency operations."[61]

REORGANIZATION POWER

Because the president and Congress often find themselves opposing each other for control of the bureaucracy, presidents frequently look to reorganization as a means of gaining the upper hand and increasing their ability to manage their administrations. Presidents have attempted countless reorganization plans, however, only to find that the affected agencies are strongly protected by their sponsoring congressional committees. Without the cooperation of Congress, it is extremely difficult for presidents to effect any reorganization plan for making the bureaucracy more efficient.

Every president wants to coordinate policy-making efforts as much as possible, but because the number of federal programs has increased rapidly, coordination of the many agencies and departments is difficult. In the area of transportation policy alone, the president must work not only with the Department of Transportation but also with the National Transportation Safety Board and the Federal Maritime Administration, as well as other agencies. This overlap among the agencies means that the executive branch often wastes time and effort trying to manage the development and implementation of public policy.

Brownlow Committee

The first real effort at administrative reorganization recognized these problems of inefficiency in the executive branch. Franklin Roosevelt wanted to establish a line of command that ran directly from the White House through the department secretaries to their subordinates. In March 1936 he created the Committee on Administrative Management and gave it the task of planning the overhaul of the executive branch. With Louis D. Brownlow as its chairman and political scientists Charles E. Merriam and Luther Gulick as the other members, the Brownlow Committee concluded in 1937 that the executive branch under Roosevelt had become so complex that "the president needs help."[62]

The Brownlow Committee specifically recommended that the president receive increased administrative support. It proposed the creation of six new presidential assistants, "possessed of high competence, great physical vigor, and a passion for anonymity," who would be assigned at the president's discretion. In addition, it recommended that discretionary funds be put at the president's disposal to allow him to acquire more help as needed. Finally, the committee proposed a major organizational addition to the presidency, consisting of the Executive Office of the President, with the Bureau of the Budget as its centerpiece.[63]

Along with placing the Civil Service Commission under the control of the White House, Roosevelt won approval from Congress in 1939 for some of the Brownlow Committee's recommendations. He was given reorganization authority for a two-year period. In addition, Roosevelt was permitted to hire the six assistants that the Brownlow Committee recommended.

In Reorganization Plan No. 1, the president moved three EOP offices—the Bureau of the Budget, the Central Statistical Board, and the National Resources Planning Committee—into the State, War, and Navy Building next door to the White House. Soon after Reorganization Plan No. 1, Roosevelt issued an executive order that delineated the organization and responsibilities of the newly expanded presidency. This order detailed the formal relationships in the EOP among the White House Office, BOB, and the remaining agencies of the executive branch.

Although Roosevelt got much of what the Brownlow Committee had recommended, the reorganization bill that finally passed Congress in 1939 was less than what he had hoped. The original bill was introduced in 1937 and became embroiled in Roosevelt's attempt to modify the composition of the Supreme Court. The final bill was a compromise and lacked most of Roosevelt's initial proposals. Peri E. Arnold has written, "It [the Reorganization Act of 1939] was on its face a congressional product, drafted under the guidance of Representative Lindsay Warren (D-N.C.) as a way of short-circuiting the intense, negative connection between presidential strength and the reorganization program."[64] Even so, the main thrust of the Brownlow Committee's recommendations was preserved, with regard both to structural changes and the intent to strengthen the president's control over the administration. Although Congress has been reluctant to go along completely with presidential recommendations to extend top-level management, it has allowed presidents gradually to centralize control over the bureaucracy in the EOP.

First Hoover Commission

The next major effort at centralizing presidential control occurred during the Truman administration. After large gains in the congressional elections of 1946, Republicans anticipated the end of the Truman presidency in 1948. The Republican-controlled Congress approved legislation to help a new president grapple with the problems of executive branch organization by setting up the Commission on the Organization of the Executive Branch of the Government. In 1947 Truman appointed former president Herbert Hoover as chairman.

Hoover set about the task of evaluating the effectiveness of executive branch organization with much enthusiasm. Truman, who could have viewed the commission as a means of criticizing his administration, also was enthusiastic about the project and gave it his full cooperation. It is one of the ironies of the U.S. presidency that Truman was the one to benefit from the Hoover Commission's efforts when the Republicans failed to capture the presidency in 1948.

The Hoover Commission report recommended 277 specific measures that would institute "a clear line of control from the president to these departments and agency heads and from them to their subordinates . . . cutting through the barriers that have in many cases made bureaus and agencies practically independent of the chief executive."[65] The commission's report charged that the executive branch was unmanageable; its lines of communication and authority were confusing, and there were too few tools at the top for the development of effective policy.

The commission suggested three major areas of reform. First, department heads should assume the major authority within their departments rather than allowing it to reside in the bureau chiefs. This recommendation was aimed at overcoming the congressional practice of vesting statutory powers directly in agency chiefs. With department heads more easily held responsible to the president, the lines of authority and responsibility would be more distinct. Second, the commission wanted to achieve greater clarity of direction and greater control by grouping the executive branch agencies into departments "as nearly as possible by major purposes in order to give a coherent mission to each department."[66] Third, the commission recommended that the EOP be strengthened by giving the president a stronger staff, including a staff secretariat in the White House. The president should have absolute freedom in dealing with this staff, giving it shape, and appointing its members.

Truman enthusiastically supported the commission's recommendations. In addition, both Congress and the public gave their support to most of the report's proposals. The most important recommendations were realized. Recommendations for increased presidential staff and discretion in the use and organization of the EOP were implemented. And, following the commission's proposals, the Post Office, and the Departments of Interior, Commerce, and Labor were reorganized. The NSC and a number of independent agencies, including the Civil Service Commission and the Federal Trade Commission, also were reorganized.

By and large, the success of the reforms reflected the nonpolitical nature of the report. Hoover and his commission approached the presidency solely in managerial terms without engaging in political ideology. Arnold has observed, "At one and the same time, reorganization planning aimed at strengthening the presidency while presenting the issue of enhanced presidential capacity as merely managerial and irrelevant to politics. Herbert Hoover and his commission of 1947–1948 present perhaps the most successful application of that logic within reorganization planning's history."[67]

Second Hoover Commission

When Dwight D. Eisenhower came to office in 1952, he faced a bureaucracy that had grown tremendously since Hoover, the last Republican president, had left office in 1933. After twenty years of Democratic control of the presidency, few Republicans had experience in running the federal government. In fact, after years of opposing big government and big spending, Republicans now found themselves in charge of the same government they had criticized. Further complicating things for Eisenhower was a bureaucracy composed mostly of Democrats appointed under Democratic presidents. Searching for a way to make the executive branch more responsive to his leadership, Eisenhower in 1953 called once more on Hoover—at that time seventy-nine years old—to head the Commission on the Organization of the Executive Branch of Government (the Second Hoover Commission).

The First Hoover Commission had been interested primarily in improving the administrative management of the executive branch; the Second Hoover Commission focused on issues of policy and function. At the heart of its recommendations was the idea that the executive branch should reduce its scope, saving money, reducing taxes, and eliminating competition with the private sector. The Second Hoover Commission had a specific conservative ideological agenda that aimed at reducing the growth of the government since the New Deal. It argued that many of the Roosevelt era programs and agencies had become counterproductive.[68] The commission was more concerned with prescribing what government should do rather than how it should be organized and managed.

Most of the commission's recommendations were of only indirect value to the Eisenhower administration as it wrestled with the problems of a massive executive bureaucracy. For the first time, however, a major reorganization report dealt with the relations between political appointees and career public servants. Among its specific recommendations was the creation of a "Senior Civil Service" comprising approximately three thousand upper-level career executives serving in administrative positions. The commission proposed that these senior civil servants be able to transfer from one agency to another if their particular skills and competencies suited those agencies. These senior civil servants would constitute a personnel pool that would be rotated regularly to improve management quality. The idea finally became incorporated into general personnel practices in the executive branch with the establishment of the Senior Executive Service in 1978.

Ash Council

In April 1969, Richard Nixon sought to simplify the domestic side of policy making in the executive branch by creating the Advisory Council on Executive Organization. Intending to use private-sector strategies in reorganization planning for his administration, Nixon appointed industrialist Roy Ash, president of Litton Industries, as chair and named four other private citizens to the council. Known as the Ash Council, the reorganization group set out to address three problems. First, it examined the executive branch's response to increasing demands on the federal government. Second, it gave attention to the organizational problems of the more than 150 departments, offices, and agencies in the executive branch. Third, the council evaluated the organizational complications resulting from intergovernmental relations.[69]

The Ash Council recommended that the executive branch's domestic programs be directed by a small number of major-purpose superdepartments. The council believed that this reorganization not only would save the government money but also would increase the effectiveness of executive branch management. Specifically, the council proposed that departments be set up in which the secretary would be assisted by a small number of secretarial officers holding department-wide responsibilities. Secretarial officers would include a deputy secretary who would serve as an alter ego and department manager for the secretary, two undersecretaries, several assistant secretaries, and a general counsel. The recommendations pointed to a desire to "facilitate decentralized management while simultaneously providing for effective secretarial control and department cohesion."[70]

President Nixon sent four departmental reorganization proposals to Congress on March 25, 1971. These proposals would have abolished seven existing departments and replaced them with four new superdepartments. The new Department of Natural Resources would have merged the Interior Department with parts of Agriculture, Defense, and Commerce. The Department of Health, Education, and Welfare would have become the Department of Human Resources. The Department of Community Development would have combined Housing and Urban Development with some of the remaining parts of Agriculture. The Department of Economic Affairs would have combined Labor with parts of Commerce. But none of the departmental bills ever got out of their congressional committees, and Nixon eventually lost interest in the superdepartments.

Some of the Ash Council's recommendations did become important to executive branch reorganization, however. In its recommendations on the EOP, the council proposed the creation of a Domestic Council and the conversion of the Bureau of the Budget into the Office of Management and Budget. Nixon incorporated these proposals into his Reorganization Plan No. 2, which he submitted to Congress on March 12, 1970.

The Ash Council intended for the Domestic Council to serve as a domestic counterpart to the NSC. It would be a cabinet-level advisory group composed of the president, the vice president, the attorney general, and the secretaries of Treasury, Interior, Agriculture, Commerce, Labor, Transportation, Housing and Urban Development, and Health, Education, and Welfare. The important changes to the Bureau of the Budget included expanding its managerial, policy coordination, and program information functions in its reincarnation in OMB. Both President Nixon's reorganization efforts and the Ash Council's recommendations sought through reorganization to centralize executive branch policy formation in EOP.

Under the authority granted by Congress through the periodic extension of the Reorganization Act of 1949, presidents could reorganize executive branch entities as they pleased. Congress retained oversight of such reorganizations through a legislative veto provision in the reorganization act.

President Carter used this method several times while in office. In 1978, for example, he ordered four thousand workers involved in border inspection to move their operations from the Justice Department to the Treasury Department. He also shifted 3500 people from the firearms and explosives division of the Treasury Department to the Justice Department. In 1977 Carter exerted his reorganization powers to their fullest when he established a whole new Energy Department, absorbing two independent agencies—the Federal Power Commission and the Atomic Energy Commission. In 1979 he divided the Department of Health, Education, and Welfare into two new departments, the Department of Education and the Department of Health and Human Services. Congress, however, refused to renew the reorganization act after the Supreme Court declared legislative vetoes unconstitutional in 1983. As a result, executive branch reorganizations must now be achieved through normal legislative procedures. As part of Vice President Gore's National Performance Review to "reinvent government" by making it more efficient, President Clinton reorganized the Department of Agriculture by legislation. In 1994 Congress passed his proposal to merge or eliminate a number of the department's forty-three agencies and reduce staff and personnel.

The Appointment Power

As the size of the federal government has grown, presidents have been forced to delegate more and more of their administrative responsibilities to a growing number of political executives. No single chief executive can make all the important policy and administrative decisions necessary to carry out the functions of the U.S. government. Consequently, one of the most important administrative powers that presidents have is their ability to recruit and appoint people to fill high-level positions in their administrations.[71]

Article II, section 2, of the Constitution gives the president the power to appoint top political executives. The language of the Constitution separates the appointment process of major executive officers into a two-step procedure shared by the president and the Senate. The president recruits and nominates potential appointees, and the Senate either confirms or rejects the president's appointments. The Constitution also gives Congress the ability to place other appointments within the prerogative of the president (such as the White House staff), of the courts (such as special independent counsels), or of the department heads without Senate confirmation.

Although the Constitution gives the chief executive the responsibility for selecting the approximately 2.9 million civilian employees (as of 1995) of the executive branch, over the years the chief executive has given up much direct participation in the process to the federal civil service system. Until the 1880s most executive branch jobs were apportioned through *patronage*, the system of granting favors and filling jobs as political rewards. Nineteenth-century presidents placed their friends and allies in federal government positions. Beginning with the passage in 1883 of the Pendleton Act, which created the Civil Service Commission, the civil service system has grown to the point where most agencies must now choose their employees according to their qualifications and ability to do the job.

> [H]e shall nominate, and by and with the Advice and Consent of the Senate shall appoint Ambassadors, other public Ministers and Consuls, Judges of the supreme Court, and all other Officers of the United States, whose Appointments are not herein otherwise provided for and which shall be established by Law; but the Congress may by Law vest the Appointment of such inferior Officers as they think proper in the President alone, in the Courts of Law, or in the Heads of Departments.
>
> —*from Article II, section 2*

Because more than 90 percent of executive branch positions are covered by the civil service, only the most senior executive positions are filled by presidential appointees. For example, the Clinton administration could appoint only 222 (less than 1 percent) of the 37,485 employees of the Department of Commerce. By choosing personnel for these positions, presidents articulate their political goals to the bureaucracy.

At the beginning of a new administration, Congress publishes *Policy and Supporting Positions*—known as the "plum book"—which lists the top executive branch positions available for direct presidential appointment, many of which require Senate confirmation. Each new presidential administration must appoint approximately 200 members of the White House staff, fourteen department heads, 400 to 500 members of the subcabinet, ninety-three U.S. attorneys, and approximately 150 ambassadors.

In addition, agency and department heads appoint 600 to 800 members of the Senior Executive Service and about 1,800 special aides in Schedule C positions, which are exempted from the testing and qualification requirements of the civil service merit system. Altogether, presidents and their subordinates must appoint about 5,200 people to the executive branch.[72] Of these, political scientist Hugh Heclo estimates that presidents are most interested in approximately three hundred top political executive posts—cabinet secretaries, undersecretaries, assistant secretaries, and bureau chiefs.[73]

Because executive appointees link the president to the vast organizational components of the executive branch, the right to recruit and appoint these people is extremely important to the chief executive's ability to control the disparate components of the federal government. To ensure effective leadership, presidents look for competence and loyalty in their appointees.

The sixteenth-century political theorist Niccolo Machiavelli observed, "The first opinion that is formed of a ruler's intelligence is based on the quality of men he has around him."[74] This observation suggests that an administration is only as good as the people the president appoints to fill it. The immense size of the executive branch makes it impossible, however, for presidents to know most of the people they appoint, much less to make personal assessments of their quality. Upon winning the presidency after several months of campaigning, John Kennedy complained about trying to fill many of his top positions: "People, people, people! I don't know any people. All I know is voters! How am I going to fill these 1,200 jobs?"[75] Kennedy knew less than half of his final cabinet appointments.

Some new appointees come to their positions well qualified, but others do not. What occupational and educational characteristics do presidential appointees have? Between 1982 and 1985 a National Academy of Public Administration survey found that 40 percent of federal appointees are transferred or promoted from other positions in the government. Sixty percent, however, come from occupations outside the federal government: 24 percent from business, 16 percent from academic and research communities, 12 percent from the legal profession, 7 percent from state and local governments, and 1 percent from other organizations. The educational level of presidential appointees is relatively high: 19 percent hold bachelor's degrees, 21 percent hold master's degrees, 17 percent hold Ph.D.s, and 34 percent hold law degrees.[76]

In addition to competence and loyalty, presidents must consider other factors when they make their selections. Most presidents have accumulated quite a few political debts on their way to the White House. Numerous groups and individuals have contributed both money and votes to their victories, and presidents look for ways to reward their chief supporters with major political appointments. Although these selections usually do not constitute the majority of a president's appointments, they are an important consideration. President Truman, for example, appointed banker John Snyder and Democratic National Committee Chairman Robert Hannegan, both old friends from Missouri, to the positions of Treasury secretary and postmaster general, respectively. Early in his administration, President Clinton appointed Thomas F. "Mack" McLarty as chief of staff and Mickey Kantor as U.S. trade representative. Both were friends and longtime supporters.

Presidents also make many appointments for purely political reasons. The very first presidential personnel selections are the most important politically. In fact, the appointments that presidents make as they establish their administrations generally set the tone and priorities of their presidencies. These selections are important for symbolic reasons and are subject to very close public scrutiny. In his study of presidential cabinets, political scientist Richard Fenno commented: "The presidential decisions leading to the composition of a new 'official family' are taken during the peak period of public interest which attends the national election campaign. As executive decisions go, they are pre-eminently concrete and visible. Among the earliest of presidential moves, they are treated as symbolic acts of considerable significance."[77] In addition, presidents consider in what ways future political relationships will be affected by their early choices. An administration's success often depends on the ability of the president to forge political alliances and broaden the presidency's base of support. The president's circle of political allies frequently can be expanded through the appointment process. In addition to rewarding those who have supported them in the past, presidents often use appointments to get on the good side of members of their own political party, interest groups whose support they seek, and, often, members of Congress.

This strategy can backfire, however. William Howard Taft, quoting Thomas Jefferson, used to lament, "Every time I make an appointment I create nine enemies and one ingrate." As political scientist Calvin Mackenzie wrote: "The selection process, particularly in the early stages of a new administration is governed by scarce resources and multiple, competing demands. Opportunities exist for gaining some political advantage from these early personnel choices, but, if used unwisely, those opportunities are easily squandered."[78]

Another important consideration in presidential appointments is the presidency's managerial needs. As the bureaucracy has become more technologically complex, presidents have had to choose appointees who bring with them managerial and administrative capabilities. The larger the department or agency, the greater the need for management expertise. Departments such as Defense and Health and Human Services and agencies such as the U.S. Postal Service are examples of large government organizations requiring administrative competence in their top leadership.

Although many presidents desperately seek better management, rarely are appointments made on the basis of objective consideration such as management ability. Most jobs are filled immediately after the presidential election, when presidents have the largest number of appointments to make and the least amount of time to consider them. Ironically, at this point in their administrations, when they are best able to lure potential appointees, presidents often are unable to take full advantage of one of their greatest administrative powers. The ability to manage may be one of the last considerations applied to a potential appointee, both because the administration is unable to judge its management needs and because political considerations outweigh managerial skill. Characteristics such as an appointee's geographic or ethnic background are often much more obvious and easy to consider than administrative ability.

No matter how well intentioned they may be in trying to fill their appointments, most presidents rarely succeed in accomplishing their objectives in the appointment process. For example, President Clinton started the staffing process during his 1992 campaign. Wishing to instill loyalty and new ideas in his administration, he developed an appointment strategy that emphasized centralizing power in the White House by appointing loyal but qualified individuals. This philosophy of controlling all appointments from the White House, which reflected Clinton's tendency to micromanage, resulted in serious problems for his administration. The White House transition team was very slow filling positions below the secretary rank. Since subcabinet positions had either to be filled or approved by the White House to ensure loyalty, the process was quite cumbersome. Clinton would sometimes question a cabinet member's entire slate of nominations because it was not diverse enough or because a single nominee's credentials looked suspect. This had the effect of sending the entire slate back to the secretary. As a result, secretaries often complained that they were understaffed and overworked in the first year or so of the administration. In addition, the emphasis on personal loyalty to Clinton meant that few appointees had any Washington experience. In fact, many appointees felt hostile to Washington and were determined to keep the Clintons out from under its spell.[79]

CONSTRAINTS ON THE APPOINTMENT PROCESS

The postelection rush to fill vacancies in the new administration places a number of constraints on the appointment process. Between the election and the inauguration, the president works to establish the policy objectives of the administration. While still forming their policy objectives, presidents or their subordinates must make the vast majority of their most important appointments. Cronin has noted: "Too frequently appointees are not carefully related to policy. Many subcabinet appointments, for example, are made by subordinates, with the president hardly aware of whether the appointee is matched with the position. . . ."[80] Once in office many appointees adopt new attitudes as a result of new institutionalized responsibilities; or some, perhaps ill-suited for institutional management, may become rigidly wedded to the views of the interest groups with which they most frequently interact.

Presidents often find it difficult to persuade their potential nominees to give up high-paying positions in the private sector and move to Washington, D.C. Since the early 1970s, the gap between the salaries paid to private executives and the salaries paid to those in the federal government who perform equivalent work has grown wider. In 1980 the Commission on Executive, Legislative, and Judicial Salaries concluded: "There is growing evidence that low salaries are a major reason for highly talented people declining appointment to key positions in the federal government."[81]

Sometimes presidents have found it difficult to persuade potential nominees to disclose their financial background and income. Because the American public expects executive branch officials to perform their duties without undue regard for special interests, Congress passed strict financial disclosure laws in 1965. Certain top executive branch employees were required to report information about their personal finances to the head of the Civil Service Commission, who could report this information to the president if there seemed to be a conflict of interest. Title II of the Ethics in Government Act of 1978 broadened disclosure provisions by requiring all presidential appointees to complete the Executive Personal Financial Disclosure Report, which publicly discloses their personal financial information. These provisions have been a source of great concern for many potential appointees. E. Pendleton James, President Reagan's assistant for personnel, stated that "literally hundreds" of potential presidential nominees lost interest as a result of demanding disclosure provisions.[82]

Similarly, presidents must sometimes pass up potential nominees because of the person's involvement with a past administration, a scandal, or even the appearance of wrongdoing. For example, in 1989 former senator John Tower was nominated by George Bush as secretary of defense but was forced to withdraw under opposition from Congress over charges of womanizing and excessive drinking. In the *The Confirmation Mess,* law professor Stephen Carter argues that the current system for approving presidential nominations demands that more attention be paid to the "disqualifications" than to the qualifications of a nominee. He writes, "We presume the nominees to be entitled to confirmation absent smoking guns, and then we look for the smoke in order to disqualify them."[83] In short, presidents face enormous difficulties in finding appropriate candidates in a shrinking pool of potential nominees who are willing to go to Washington. The difficulties in finding those willing to serve are exacerbated by the fact that appointees must face intense, and often excessive, public scrutiny.

THE ROLE OF THE SENATE

The Senate is an integral part of the appointment process and serves as one of the most important limits to the presidential appointment privilege. Constitutionally, presidents share the appointment of many political executives with the Senate in that the Senate must confirm most of the president's major appointments. As a result, the Senate has come to view the appointment procedure as a process in which its members should have a considerable say. As Mackenzie has observed, "For Senators and Senate committees, the confirmation process is both a responsibility and an opportunity."[84] It is a constitutional responsibility and a political opportunity. Senators view the appointment process as a way to influence government policy. Cronin has noted that senators even try to influence presidential policy by getting the president to nominate their choices: "They . . . often have candidates of their own. This is especially the case in recent years, for as the staffs of Congress have expanded . . . there are more and more aides to Congress who seek top executive branch appointments."[85]

The number of presidential nominations sent to the Senate for confirmation is staggering. The Senate must process between 90,000 and 170,000 nominations during each Congress (two-year period). Usually, the vast majority of these nominations are routine military commissions and promotions that require very little of the Senate's time. Although the number of civilian appointments is much lower, the Senate must still spend a great deal of time and energy processing them. In 1989, the first year of the Bush administration, the Senate received more than 48,000 nominations. The majority of those—about 45,000—consisted of routine military commissions and promotions. About 3,000 were routine nominations to such civilian organizations as the Foreign Service, the Public Health Service, and the National Oceanic and Atmospheric Administration. However, more highly scrutinized nominations to top-level policy-making positions in the executive branch—averaging only about 600 per session—require much attention from the Senate.

Like most other matters before Congress, the nomination process is handled almost entirely by standing committees. Although each committee has different sets of procedures for managing appointments referred to them, most committees have developed their own standard sets of structured proceedings. Usually, these procedures require additional background checks and financial disclosures, other than those already required by the president's personnel director and the Ethics in Government Act of 1978, and extensive hearings. The average length of time required by the Senate to confirm presidential nominees during the Reagan administration was 14.6 weeks. The result of this rigorous and lengthy investigative process has been an increase in demands on potential appointees. In his study of the Senate's role in the presidential appointment process, political scientist Christopher J. Deering pointed out that this demanding investigatory process has made the Senate's role in the nomination process not only more thorough but also more demanding: "Unfortunately, the process has . . . become more tedious, time-consuming, and intrusive for the nominees. For some the price is too high. . . ."[86]

The Founders intended the Senate's constitutional role in the presidential appointment process to serve as a check on executive power. To what extent has the Senate checked presidential power through its confirmation power? All presidents have been successful in getting the majority of their nominees confirmed. For example, more than 92 percent of all civilian presidential nominations were confirmed by the Ninety-eighth Congress. Most nominations that are defeated are defeated in committees. Since 1960 only six nominees have been defeated on the floor of the Senate.

Many presidents, however, have had a few of their potential appointees rejected. The Senate regularly thwarted the efforts of James Madison and Ulysses S. Grant to nominate their choices for executive branch positions freely. John Tyler perhaps had the most difficulty with the Senate in attempting to fill vacancies. His appointees were frequently rejected by the Senate, including four cabinet and four Supreme Court appointees. In one day in 1843, the Senate rejected Tyler's nomination of Caleb Cushing as secretary of the Treasury three times. In 1984 President Reagan's nominee for associate attorney general, William Bradford Reynolds, was turned down by the Senate Judiciary Committee. His opponents argued that Reynolds had been negligent in enforcing antidiscrimination laws during his tenure as chief of the Justice Department's Civil Rights Division.

Nominations are often withdrawn it if becomes apparent that the Senate opposes a particular candidate. In the early months of the Clinton administration, two nominations to the Justice Department were withdrawn when it became obvious that the Senate would not confirm the president's nominees. Although the Senate does not often reject a presidential nominee, the thoroughness of its investigations of those who are confirmed, and its occasional threats of rejection indicate that the Senate does exert some control over the president's prerogative to appoint key members to the administration.

In some cases, however, the Senate may use its confirmation power more as a political bargaining chip than anything else. It will often "hold" the nominee in limbo until the president agrees to support a particular political position. For example, President Reagan's nomination of Edwin Meese as attorney general was used by the majority leader as leverage to exact a promise to support farm aid legislation. During the periods in which the Republicans controlled the Senate in the 1980s and 1990s, Sen. Jesse Helms (R-N.C.) repeatedly held up nominations because he found them politically unacceptable or because he wished to force political opponents to compromise on policy issues. Deering has written, "On numerous occasions in recent years, members of the Senate of both parties have placed holds on particular individuals. In some cases, the nominee is the target, in other cases merely a pawn, but in either case the use of nominees as, in effect, hostages has undermined the integrity of the system."[87]

THE PRESIDENTIAL PERSONNEL SYSTEM

The process by which presidents select their top political appointees remained relatively unchanged throughout the first 150 years of U.S. history. Presidents had little, if any, staff to help them make their appointments; political parties usually controlled personnel selection for the president. Even when chief executives did become actively involved in the selection process, they often used the existing political party structure. Other nominees were usually suggested to the president by party leaders or members of Congress from the president's party. Too often this White House dependence on the party resulted in administrations filled with top-level appointees with little loyalty to presidential objectives.

Roosevelt and Truman Administrations

Since Franklin Roosevelt entered the White House, newly elected presidents have needed significant staff support and a centralized procedure for choosing personnel because of the vast number of appointments that must be made in a short period of time. Perhaps more important, a centralized appointment process under the president's control ensures faithfulness to White House policies and objectives.

Until the 1940s, the selection of presidential appointees was haphazard and unfocused. Presidential personnel operations relied heavily on chance to place the right people in the right positions. During the 1940s, however, President Roosevelt attempted to alleviate much of the problem by introducing a number of governmental reforms that removed presidential patronage from the national political parties. For example, Roosevelt appointed a White House assistant to handle personnel matters in an effort to improve presidential control over the appointment process. In the following decades the presidency's administrative powers increased, allowing it more discretion in personnel selection.

Dom Bonafede has attributed the growth of a more centralized selection procedure within the White House after 1940 to three factors. First, political reforms that increased the number of state primaries and emphasized grassroots politics "hastened the decline of the national parties and minimized their brokerage role as conduit and clearinghouse for appointments." Presidents were no longer obligated to party leaders for their election and, therefore, had less need to reward them with government jobs. Second, the movement toward a strong administrative presidency, which centralized power in the White House, further strengthened the president's hand vis-à-vis Congress and the bureaucracy. Third, "the complexity of domestic and foreign issues, such as arms control, tax reform, federal deficits, and trade imbalances, necessitated elaborate institutional support, placing a premium on substantive knowledge and managerial competence."[88]

Specific recommendations by the Committee on Administrative Management, headed by Louis D. Brownlow, and the two Hoover Commissions helped centralize more power in the presidency. *(See "Reorganization Power," p. 18.)* In 1939, acting on Brownlow Committee recommendations, Congress created the Executive Office of the President and brought the Bureau of the Budget under the control of the president within the EOP. These measures began what has become known as the "institutional presidency."[89] The first and second Hoover Commissions further increased the administrative power of the presidency by giving it more control over the vast federal bureaucracy and substantial authority over the appointment process.

President Truman appointed the first full-time staff member responsible only for personnel matters. Although this aide, Donald Dawson, addressed mostly routine concerns and spent a good deal of time in contact with the Democratic National Committee, the new position signaled the growing importance of staffing issues.

Eisenhower Administration

Dwight D. Eisenhower came to office in 1953 with a strong desire to improve the management of the executive branch but with a dislike for personnel matters. He frequently wrote in his diary that patronage was one of the great banes of his administration and one of the things most likely to cause him to lose his temper. Consequently, he delegated personnel concerns to members of his staff, primarily to Sherman Adams, his chief of staff. Adams, however, soon found the job of personnel director too demanding when added to his other responsibilities. The president then approved the position of special assistant for executive appointments, which several people held during the eight years Eisenhower was in office. These special assistants did not choose the president's appointees. Rather, they managed the appointment process by narrowing the president's choices to candidates with the best qualifications and the fewest political liabilities. More than anything else, Eisenhower sought appointees who were loyal to his political philosophy and his programs.

Kennedy and Johnson Administrations

Shortly after his election, President-elect Kennedy put together a personnel selection staff called "Talent Hunt." Comprising some of the best people from the campaign, Talent Hunt was a loosely organized operation with two objectives. First, it tried to determine the president-elect's political obligations—supporters who helped him win the election—and find appropriate jobs to pay off those debts. Second, it attempted to identify the most important jobs the president would have to fill and to find the best people for those positions. After the inauguration, Talent Hunt broke up, and its members went to their own jobs in the administration.

Dan Fenn, President John F. Kennedy's personnel aide, created a White House appointment process that gave the president recruiting ability independent of the political parties.

In mid-1961 Kennedy appointed Dan Fenn of the Harvard Business School faculty to take over the day-to-day personnel responsibilities of the White House. Asked to recommend changes in the traditional method of filling executive positions, Fenn concluded that the procedure was too limited. The most important jobs in the federal government were being filled by a very unsophisticated "Whom do you know?" system—a process he called "BOGSAT," that is, a "bunch of guys sitting around a table."

Fenn attempted to correct this problem by creating a systematic White House appointment operation that involved three major stages. First, he and his staff developed reliable job descriptions that allowed them to match candidates with positions, something most administrations had not been able to do. Second, Fenn offered the president a wider selection of candidates from whom to choose. He believed that the range of people with whom presidents normally come into contact was too narrow to provide the talent necessary for a successful administration. Third, since he could offer a wider range of choices only by reaching beyond traditional political sources for appointments, Fenn established a network of well-positioned people throughout the country whose opinions the president trusted and who could provide Kennedy with candid information about potential nominees. Although prevailing partisan considerations kept the system Fenn established from working as well as it might have, Fenn's efforts nonetheless marked the first time a president had significant independent recruiting ability, separate from the influence of the political parties.

During Lyndon B. Johnson's administration, the centralization of presidential personnel selection took a giant leap forward. Although Kennedy had put together a significant staff for selecting nominees, he would often bypass the process by selecting appointees without using the system Fenn had established. Johnson, too, would sometimes circumvent his personnel staff, but he always maintained the appearance that the selection had been made through the White House personnel system. The authors of one study of the presidential selection process concluded:

> Those who wanted to influence Johnson's appointment decisions quickly got the message that their contact point for this was the personnel staff and that efforts to evade the established personnel selection procedures would be difficult to pull off. This focused more attention on the White House and significantly strengthened its role at the hub of the appointment process.[90]

The Kennedy and Johnson presidencies brought about three important long-term changes in presidential personnel management. First, a full-time personnel staff became a regular component of the White House Office. Second, presidents have attempted to maintain their independence from traditional political party pressures by recruiting their own candidates. Third, each administration has developed and followed routine procedures for scrutinizing the background, competence, integrity, and political loyalty of each potential appointee.

Nixon Administration

When Richard Nixon took office in 1969, he at first failed to incorporate in his presidency many of the advances made in personnel selection in preceding administrations. He had little interest in personnel matters and delegated most of the responsibility for filling offices to his staff. His initial appointment process was slow and cumbersome, and too many times the White House appointed people who had little loyalty to the president's programs. As a result, in 1970 Nixon appointed Frederic V. Malek to study the personnel selection process and recommend improvements. Malek called for a personnel system similar to those of Nixon's predecessors: centralization of the recruiting process in the White House, recruitment outreach beyond traditional political party sources of potential nominees, and a more rigorous clearance process.

In 1971 Nixon appointed Malek director of his personnel operation. Malek, acting on his own recommendations, set up the White House Personnel Office (WHPO). Following the examples of the organizations set up by Fenn and John W. Macy, personnel assistant to President Johnson, Malek made the WHPO a tightly organized operation that employed a highly professional staff. The WHPO employed professional headhunters whose sole responsibility was to find the right person for the right job in the administration. In addition, the WHPO developed a much more sophisticated evaluation system than had ever been

Frederic V. Malek, President Richard Nixon's personnel director, established the White House Personnel Office in 1971.

used in the White House. Thus, after two years of haphazard personnel selection, the Nixon White House emerged with a firm commitment to centralized personnel decision making for almost all noncareer positions in the federal government. Yet eventually, the WHPO lost much of its professionalism and some of its members went beyond the limits of propriety in attempting to control the appointment process. The WHPO outlined ways in which the civil service could be manipulated by the administration. One way was to write job descriptions to fit specific applicants loyal to Nixon. Those unsympathetic were to be transferred to undesirable locations or assignments requiring a great deal of travel. The press and Congress finally intervened, forcing the WHPO to retreat from its continued efforts at centralization.

Ford and Carter Administrations

Gerald R. Ford's personnel staff spent much of its time trying to clean up the image of the aggressive WHPO under Nixon. The first thing that Ford changed was the name. The WHPO became the Presidential Personnel Office. In addition, Ford reduced the size of the personnel operation and narrowed the focus of its activities to positions traditionally viewed as presidential appointments rather than most noncareer appointments.

Jimmy Carter was the first president who began planning for his presidency while still running for election. In the summer of 1976, he set up a small staff in Atlanta to begin working on the staffing of his administration. Carter chose Jack Watson to head up the operation, which became known as Talent Inventory Program (TIP). After Carter won the election, Watson moved his operation to Washington. Once there he became locked in a power struggle with Carter's campaign manager, Hamilton Jordan, over who would control the appointment process. As a result of this struggle, the Presidential Personnel Office floundered for almost two years. Although a personnel staff was established in the White House, its ability to manage the appointment process effectively was hampered by the rivalry between

Watson and Jordan. Throughout the Carter administration, there was no central coordination of appointments in the White House, and much of the early work of TIP was ignored.

Carter contributed to the disorder in the appointment process by insisting that cabinet heads be given almost total discretion in choosing their subordinates. At various times in the campaign, he had proclaimed: "There will never be an instance while I am president where members of the White House staff dominate or act in a superior position to the members of our Cabinet."[91] This promise made good campaign rhetoric, but it diminished Carter's ability to control his administration by decentralizing the decision-making process outside of the White House. Some departments made appointments after a rigorous search procedure. Others resorted to "politics as usual" and used political networks to select potential nominees whose main qualifications were friendship and loyalty to department secretaries. As Dom Bonafede described the results, "In an unseemly brief period it became clear to the president's top lieutenants—and only later to Carter himself—that he had made a major mistake in giving secretaries carte blanche authority to handpick their assistants."[92]

E. Pendleton James, Ronald Reagan's assistant to the president for personnel, saw to it that all appointees shared Reagan's political philosophy.

Reagan and Bush Administrations

Reagan viewed the appointment process as an integral part of his plans for changing the direction of the federal government. Determined to avoid the mistakes of the Carter administration, he centralized the appointment process within the White House.

Reagan also made a determined effort to appoint only persons who shared his political philosophy. E. Pendleton James, Reagan's postelection talent search manager and eventual assistant to the president for personnel, declared, "You can't separate personnel from policy."[93] This outlook pervaded the administration's appointment efforts. From the "kitchen cabinet" made up of Reagan's elite, conservative California advisers who chose politically acceptable potential nominees before his election, to the personnel office, which managed appointments during the administration, the strategy was to choose nominees whose political philosophy matched the president's.

The Reagan appointment process benefited from some of Carter's mistakes. James gave the process a consistency it lacked under Carter. During the transition and throughout the first eighteen months of the Reagan administration, James presided over the day-to-day operation of the administration's personnel selection. As a result, there was very little confusion about the process itself or who was in charge. Also, Reagan visibly involved himself in the appointment process. He made the final decision on all of the important appointments during the transition and the first year. The authors of one study noted:

> This proved to be an effective deterrent to those in the departments and agencies and in Congress who might try and wrest control of appointment decisions away from the White House. It is one thing to attempt that when low-level White House staff members are making appointment decisions; it is quite another when those decisions are being made in the Oval Office.[94]

As had Carter, Vice President Bush began planning for staffing his administration while running for the presidency. Early in his 1988 campaign, Bush named Charles Untermeyer to begin organizing his personnel operation. But because Bush wished to avoid appearing overconfident, Untermeyer was not allowed to set up a formal office or recruit any nominees until after the election. When Bush won the presidential election, his personnel management team moved rapidly into action. Although Bush anticipated no major policy shifts from his Republican predecessor, he did insist that his administration have his stamp on it, promising to replace 90 percent of Reagan's political appointees.

Bush played a much less visible role than Reagan in selecting appointees for his administration. Those charged with making most of the staffing decisions were given two major criteria by the president-elect: loyalty and experience. Where Reagan had sought ideological loyalty, Bush sought personal loyalty in his appointments. Personal friends of the president and those who had played a major role in Bush's campaign were given priority in the new administration. As one who had been around Washington a long time, Bush also sought experience. The resulting appointments made his administration one of the most experienced and thus one of the most competent in recent history.

Clinton Administration

During the 1992 fall presidential campaign, Mickey Kantor, Bill Clinton's campaign chair, set up a formal organization—the Clinton-Gore Presidential Transition Planning Foundation—

for staffing a potential administration. This early attempt at centralization promised a disciplined staffing process. After the election, however, Kantor ran afoul of other campaign officials and was blocked from heading the transition, and the formal responsibility for finding personnel for the new administration fell largely to Harold Ickes, a New York attorney and close friend of Hillary Clinton.

President-elect Clinton, however, abandoned a highly centralized transition operation. Instead, he opted for a kitchen table approach to staffing his first term. Ickes, Mrs. Clinton, Susan Thomases, an attorney and close friend of Mrs. Clinton, and Bruce Lindsay, an attorney and a longtime Clinton loyalist, made most of the actual decisions about staffing the new presidency around a six-foot table at Clinton headquarters in Little Rock, Arkansas. Operating under the dictum that they had been voted to go to Washington to change things, the personnel team chose executive branch staffers who were largely inexperienced in Washington politics. In addition, appointees were young and geographically, ethnically, and racially diverse, as compared with previous administrations.

Although Clinton abandoned his early attempt at a centralized transition, he clearly wanted to keep personnel functions within the White House. Clinton based his personnel appointment system on a memo, "Transition Workplan for Reviewing the Staffing and Organization of the White House and Executive Office of the President," written at the direction of Harrison Wellford, a former Carter budget official. The memo urged the centralization of political power within the White House by ensuring that appointments to the White House, the Executive Office of the President, the cabinet, and the subcabinet be controlled squarely by the president. This approach contrasted with the Carter system, in which the absence of central coordination of appointments reduced Carter's ability to effectively control his administration.

One of the most distinctive features of the Clinton personnel system was the slowness with which it responded to the need for filling positions in the new administration. After eight months in office, Clinton still had not nominated political appointees for more than 40 percent of policy-making positions, and about one-third of the posts on independent agencies, regulatory boards, and commissions remained unfilled. Clinton was well behind the pace of nominations set by both Carter and Reagan. He was ahead of Bush, but as a Republican succeeding another Republican, Bush was in no real hurry to replace personnel. Clinton's slowness in making his initial appointments was the result of both his desire for diversity and his system requiring White House approval for executive branch appointments.

Since Franklin Roosevelt's administration, presidents have relied on increasingly sophisticated methods of centralizing the appointment power in the White House in their attempts to strengthen control over their administrations. The personnel office is now a permanent part of the White House organizational structure. Succeeding presidents have significantly increased the number of staff assigned to find competent and loyal political executives. And presidential personnel operations have come to rely on professional recruiting techniques. Yet, as important as the office is to presidential control, it is not at the top of the executive branch hierarchy. Bonafede has concluded that, in most administrations, the presidential personnel office

> lacks institutional stability; the process varies from one presidency to another, and it even varies in the zeal and orderliness with which it is conducted within the same administration. Each incoming administration, distrustful of past personnel procedures, feels compelled to reinvent its own system. Few presidents have been willing to lend their prestige to the office.[95]

THE REMOVAL POWER

The ability of presidents to control their administrations often depends on their authority to remove subordinates from office. This issue lies at the very heart of the chief executive's power over the bureaucracy. The power of presidents to remove officials who are not doing their jobs properly or who disagree with presidential goals and programs is, however, controversial and has been significantly limited by the Supreme Court. Because the Constitution does not explicitly grant presidents power to remove officials from office, the legitimacy of the power often has rested on court interpretations of specific presidential removal actions.

The Tenure of Office Act of 1867 provided much debate about whether a president could remove executive branch officials. On the suspicion that President Andrew Johnson intended to fire Secretary of War Edwin Stanton, Congress passed the act that made it a high misdemeanor to remove without the Senate's approval any government official whose nomination had been confirmed by the Senate. Congress's intention was to protect incumbent Republican officeholders from retaliation if they did not support Johnson. President Johnson vetoed the bill on the grounds that it was unconstitutional to restrict the president's power of removal, but Congress overrode the veto. When Johnson immediately tested the Tenure of Office Act by attempting to remove Stanton, the House voted 126 to 47 to impeach him. Tried by the Senate, Johnson was acquitted by one vote. The Tenure of Office Act was virtually repealed early in President Grant's administration, once Republicans regained control of the appointment power. It was entirely repealed in 1887 when public opinion forced Congress to introduce legislation to repeal it.

Preferring to avoid the issue as long as possible, the Supreme Court refused to make a definitive ruling on the issue of presidential removal of public officeholders until 1926. In *Myers v. United States* the Court ruled that an 1876 law that limited the president's removal power over postmasters was unconstitutional. In 1917 President Woodrow Wilson had appointed Myers to be a postmaster in Portland, Oregon, for a term of four years. Attempting to make his administration responsive to his policy goals, Wilson removed Myers from office in 1920 without the consent of the Senate, although the 1876 statute provided that postmasters should be appointed and removed by the president by and with the advice and consent of the Senate. Myers sued for his salary in the U.S. Court of Claims. When he received an adverse judgment, he took his case to the Supreme Court.

In delivering the opinion of the Court, Chief Justice William Howard Taft, a former president, strongly argued that presidents cannot effectively administer the executive branch unless they can control their subordinates with the threat of removal for political and other reasons. He stated that the power of removal was implied in the constitutional provision in Article II, which gives the presidency the responsibility to see that the laws are faithfully executed. Furthermore, Congress could not constitutionally restrain or limit that power. Taft, referring to the Tenure of Office Act and declaring it had been unconstitutional, contended that presidents cannot carry out their constitutional responsibilities if Congress interferes with their ability to control the executive branch.[96]

The *Myers* case arguably gave presidents sweeping authority to remove not only immediate executive subordinates but also members of independent regulatory commissions, such as the Interstate Commerce Commission and the Federal Trade Commission. Independent regulatory commissioners are appointed under the provisions of statutes that confer upon them a certain amount of independence and freedom from the political control of the president. In creating these agencies, Congress had carefully outlined the provisions by which a commissioner could be removed in an attempt to free these executives from political control. If the *Myers* case applied to all political executives, then the regulatory commissions would lose their political independence. Sooner or later the question of unlimited presidential power of removal would be challenged.

The question of the president's ability to remove independent regulatory commissioners came up quickly during Franklin Roosevelt's administration and was settled in 1935 by the Supreme Court in *Humphrey's Executor v. United States.* President Herbert C. Hoover had nominated William E. Humphrey to the Federal Trade Commission (FTC) in 1931. Under the terms outlined by Congress in the Federal Trade Commission Act of 1914, FTC commissioners were supposed to serve a term of seven years. The act stated that commissioners could be removed by the president only for "inefficiency, neglect of duty, or malfeasance in office." After his election to office, Roosevelt wrote Humphrey and requested his resignation from the FTC so that "the aims and purposes of the administration with respect to the work of the Commission can be carried out most effectively with personnel of my own selection." After Humphrey's initial reluctance to resign, Roosevelt again wrote him, this time stating: "You will, I know, realize that I do not feel that your mind and my mind go along together on either the policies or the administering of the Federal Trade Commission, and frankly, I think it is best for the people of the country that I should have full confidence."[97] When Humphrey refused to resign, Roosevelt notified him that he had been removed. Humphrey died in 1934, never having agreed to his removal. The executor of Humphrey's estate decided to sue for salary he believed was due Humphrey but never paid him.

The court of claims asked the Supreme Court to answer two questions before it could render a judgment. First, did the Federal Trade Commission Act limit the president's power to remove commissioners except for reasons stated in the act? Second, if the act did indeed limit the president's power to remove commissioners, was it constitutional?

Roosevelt had made clear that the removal of Humphrey was for political reasons. Justice George Sutherland delivered the Court's opinion that the *Myers* case did not apply to Humphrey because the FTC was "an administrative body created by Congress to carry into effect legislative policies." Therefore, it could not "in any sense be characterized as an arm or an eye of the Executive." Sutherland continued:

> Whether the power of the president to remove an officer shall prevail over the authority of Congress to condition the power by fixing a definite term and precluding the removal except for cause will depend upon the character of the office; the Myers decision, affirming the power of the president alone to make the removal, is confined to purely executive officers.[98]

The *Humphrey* decision not only invalidated Roosevelt's removal of Humphrey but also generally limited presidential removal power to officials who could be classified as "purely executive officers." Except for appointees immediately responsible to the president and those exercising nondiscretionary or ministerial functions, such as White House aides, the president's power of removal could be limited by Congress.

The Supreme Court attempted to make a distinction between "executive" and "administrative" functions within the federal bureaucracy. Presidents have complete control over executive functions, or those that deal with the execution of the policy of the administration and are under the direction of the president, such as the functions of the EOP staff and cabinet members. The Court ruled that presidents do not, however, have complete control over administrative functions, or those that have quasi-judicial or quasi-legislative roles, such as those of the independent regulatory commissions. Only when Congress chooses specifically to give presidents control over these agencies can they remove officials for merely political reasons.

In 1958 the Supreme Court further clarified the removal power of presidents. In *Wiener v. United States,* the Court held that if officials are engaged in adjudicative functions presidents may not remove them for political reasons. In 1950 President Truman had appointed Wiener to serve on the War Claims Commission. When Eisenhower assumed office, he requested Wiener's resignation. When Wiener refused, Eisenhower removed him from office. Similar to Roosevelt's removal of Humphrey, Eisenhower's removal of Wiener rested on purely political reasons. Congress had created the War Claims Commission to adjudicate damage claims arising from World War II. It made no provisions for removing commissioners. Wiener sued for his lost salary.

Noting the similarity between the *Wiener* and *Humphrey* cases, the Supreme Court ruled in favor of Wiener. The Court argued that in both cases presidents had removed persons from quasi-judicial agencies for political purposes. Calling the War Claims Commission a clearly adjudicative body, Justice Felix Frankfurter concluded for the Court:

> Judging the matter in all the nakedness in which it is presented, namely, the claim that the President could remove a member of an adjudicative body like the War Claims Commission merely because he wanted his own appointees on such a Commission, we are compelled to conclude that no such power is given to the President directly by the Constitution, and none is impliedly conferred upon him by statute simply because Congress said nothing about it. The philosophy of Humphrey's Executor, in its explicit language as well as its implications, precludes such a claim.[99]

In 1988 the Supreme Court further limited the president's removal power in *Morrison v. Olson* by upholding the independent counsel provisions of the Ethics in Government Act of 1978. In the aftermath of the Watergate scandal, Congress created the independent counsel system to investigate and possibly prosecute high-level executive officers accused of serious crimes. Arguing for the majority, Chief Justice William Rehnquist defended the creation of an independent counsel within the executive branch who would not be responsible to the president. Rehnquist asserted that the president's inability to remove an independent counsel in no way damaged the president's ability to govern.[100] By implication, some scholars have argued that this rationale may in the future be extended beyond the independent counsel law to other administrators who could be viewed as operating independently of the president in such areas as economic, health, or safety regulation.

Generally, presidents may remove all heads of cabinet departments and all political executives in the Executive Office of the President. In addition, they may remove at any time the directors of the following agencies: ACTION, the Arms Control and Disarmament Agency, the Commission on Civil Rights, the Environmental Protection Agency, the Federal Mediation and Conciliation Service, the General Services Administration, the National Aeronautics and Space Administration, the Postal Service, and the Small Business Administration.

The Budgeting Power

The power to control the budget process is one of the most important administrative prerogatives of the presidency. The chief executive is an important participant in the budget process, for often it is the president who decides how and on what money is spent. As presidential scholar Richard Pious has noted, "To budget is to govern. In a system of separated institutions that share power, the question is which institution, and by what authority, determines spending levels for the departments?"[101] In the last part of the twentieth century, the presidency has assumed an increasingly important role in determining federal spending and thus more responsibility in governing. Although Congress constitutionally controls the purse strings, the president oversees the formulation and development of the budget.

The Constitution does not clearly establish a budgetary process or spell out the presidency's role in such a process. Because of this ambiguity, presidents have been able to bring much of the process under their control. Article I of the Constitution gives Congress the powers to tax and spend. Article II, section 3, gives presidents the power to recommend to Congress such measures as they deem appropriate. ("He shall from time to time give to the Congress Information of the State of the Union, and recommend to their Consideration such Measures as he shall judge necessary and expedient.") Implicit in this power is the idea that presidents may present to Congress a financial program.

Historically, presidents have not taken part in budget planning. Even in modern times, presidential involvement in the process has varied from one administration to another. For many presidents, preparing a budget is a tedious and time-consuming job. President Lyndon Johnson once wrote, "The federal budget is a dry, unfathomable maze of figures and statistics—thicker than a Sears-Roebuck catalogue and duller than a telephone directory."[102] Some presidents have been able to maintain consistent interest in the budget's complexities throughout their terms in office; others have not. Political scientist Lance T. LeLoup examined the roles that past presidents played in the budget process and found that shortly after the first year in office, Dwight D. Eisenhower and Richard Nixon tired of the tedious budget process. Harry S. Truman and Gerald R. Ford, however, were able to maintain their enthusiasm throughout their administrations.[103]

Budgeting gives the presidency a tremendous amount of administrative power, and most presidents have recognized the importance of the budget in controlling their administrations. They usually approach their first budget optimistically, excited about the potential power to eliminate or cut back programs that they feel have outlived their usefulness. Describing his involvement in his first budget, Lyndon Johnson wrote, "I worked as hard on that budget as I have ever worked on anything. . . . Day after day I went over that budget with the Cabinet officers, my economic advisers, and the Budget Director. I studied almost every line, nearly every page, until I was dreaming about the budget at night."[104]

Although their enthusiasm may fade, presidents continue to seek to control the budget process. They see their participation in the process as a way of doing things that can benefit the national economy and their own political fortunes. In the words of President Ford, "The budget is the president's blueprint for the operation of government in the year ahead."[105] According to Dennis S. Ippolito in his study of the budget process, presidents become involved in the budget process to achieve a means of administrative management and control: "By affecting the resources available for agencies and programs, the president can seek to promote better planning of what is done, more effective supervision of how it is done, and more systematic evaluation of how well various objectives are accomplished." In addition, Ippolito has pointed out that budget decisions can affect political support. He has written, "By emphasizing particular programs or criticizing others, by challenging Congress' spending preferences, by trumpeting the need for fiscal responsibility, or by reiterating commitments to greater economy and efficiency, a president can attempt to dramatize his leadership role and to generate public support for his economic policies and program preferences."[106]

Attempts to control the budget process often force presidents to play a public relations game. Most presidents want to be considered fiscal conservatives. The overwhelming majority of Americans want a balanced budget and want the president to curtail the growth of federal expenditures. Yet presidents must continue to fund existing programs for various groups and for the American public in general. In addition, presidents are expected to present new initiatives, some of which benefit groups to whom presidents have political obligations. The dilemma is one of holding down public expenditures while trying to solve public problems. It is not an easy task, and it makes presidential participation in the budget process much more demanding and important. For example, the 1995–1996 budget battle between President Clinton and a Republican Congress proved to be more than a public relations game. It became a marathon discussion about the size and role of government in American life. Although Clinton emerged victorious, tough decisions on how to overhaul the nation's entitlements programs were postponed.

THE PRESIDENT'S ROLE IN THE BUDGET PROCESS

Presidents had little influence in managing executive branch funds before passage of the Budget and Accounting Act of 1921. Previously, budget requests went directly from each department to the House of Representatives without much interference from the White House. There was very little budget coordination by presidents or their staffs. Congress believed it could handle the budget without much help from the president. By the end of World War II, however, both the executive and legislative branches had developed an awareness that the massive growth of the federal government needed better fiscal management.

The Budget and Accounting Act of 1921

The Budget and Accounting Act of 1921 gave presidents important managerial controls over the budgeting process and made them the dominant participants in budgetary politics. Ironically, this act was passed by Congress in an attempt to bring order into its own chaotic budget process. An earlier House committee pointed to the haphazard nature of a budget process that lacked a coherent review of the executive branch's budget request. But in attempting to alleviate the problem, the act placed the presidency squarely in the budgetary process by requiring presidents to submit to Congress annual estimates of how much money it would take to run the federal government during the next fiscal year. (A fiscal year is the twelve-month span in which financial accounting is made. This period for the federal government runs from October 1 to September 30.)

The annual budget messages delivered by the president contain recommendations on how much federal money should be appropriated by Congress for each department of the federal government. The White House first evaluates all agency budget requests and decides which to accept or alter before submitting the annual budget message. Consequently, presidents become very much involved in the process. They receive more information about the budget than most members of Congress, allowing them to initiate budget discussions on their own terms.

In addition, the Budget and Accounting Act created the Bureau of the Budget (BOB) and placed it under the control of the Treasury Department. Its role was to "assemble, correlate, revise, reduce, or increase the estimates of the several departments or establishments."[107] In 1939, as a result of a growing need for coordination of New Deal programs and recommendations from the Committee on Administrative Management (the Brownlow Committee), President Roosevelt moved BOB into the Executive Office of the President.

BOB began instituting a form of "budget clearance" so that the departments could not bypass its budget review process either for statutory authorizations or for annual appropriations. No longer were the departments on their own in requesting funds from Congress. Bureaus and agencies made requests for funds to their departments, and the departments sent their budgets through BOB for consideration by the president. From 1939 to 1969, BOB evolved into a highly influential component of the EOP.

Office of Management and Budget

In 1970 President Richard Nixon changed the name and modified the function of BOB. Emphasizing the management roles of the budget agency, Nixon renamed it the Office of Management and Budget (OMB). As the word *management* implies, new emphasis was placed on providing departments with advice on ways to improve their efficiency to reduce the costs of their operations.

Nixon specifically assigned four major roles to OMB. First, it was to continue many of BOB's functions, especially writing the federal budget. Second, it was to serve as a clearinghouse for new programs and legislation. Third, Nixon wanted some part of the Executive Office of the President to have the ability to track legislation as it moved through Congress. OMB was vested with this capacity. Fourth, OMB was given the specific authority to provide management advice to the various departments and agencies. Since its inception, OMB has served as the centerpiece of presidential budgeting.

Although the president's budget is not submitted to Congress until the February before the first day of the new fiscal year (October 1), the presidential budget process begins at least nineteen months before the submission of the finished budget proposal. *(See Table 1-1, p. 32.)* The budget cycle begins in early spring with OMB informing the departments of the fiscal outlook and the spending priorities of the president. During the

TABLE 1-1 Budget Timetable in the Executive Branch and Congress

Executive branch	*Timing*	*Congress*
Agencies subject to executive branch review submit initial budget request materials.	September 1	
Fiscal year begins.	October 1	Fiscal year begins.
President's initial appropriation order takes effect (amounts are withheld from obligation pending issuance of final order).	October 1	
	October 10	Congressional Budget Office (CBO) issues revised report to Office of Management and Budget (OMB) and Congress.
OMB reports on changes in initial estimates and determinations resulting from legislation enacted and regulations promulgated after its initial report to Congress.	October 15	
President issues final sequester order, which is effective immediately, and transmits message to Congress within 15 days of final order.	October 15	
Agencies not subject to executive branch review submit budget request materials.	October 15	
	November 15	Comptroller general issues compliance report.
Legislative branch and the judiciary submit budget request materials.	November–December	
President transmits the budget to Congress.	1st Monday in February	Congress receives the president's budget.
OMB sends allowance letters to agencies.	January–February	
	February 15	CBO reports to the budget committees on the president's budget.
	February 25	Committees submit views and estimates to budget committees.
OMB and the president conduct reviews to establish presidential policy to guide agencies in developing the next budget.	April–June	
	April 1	Senate Budget Committee reports concurrent resolution on the budget.
	April 15	Congress completes action on concurrent resolution.
	May 15	House may consider appropriations bills in the absence of a concurrent resolution on the budget.
	June 10	House Appropriations Committee reports last appropriations bill.
	June 15	Congress completes action on reconciliation legislation.
	June 30	House completes action on annual appropriations bills.
President transmits the midsession review, updating the budget estimates.	July 15	Congress receives midsession review of the budget.
OMB provides agencies with policy guidance for the upcoming budget.	July–August	
Date of "snapshot" of projected deficits for the upcoming fiscal year for initial OMB and CBO reports.	August 15	
	August 20	CBO issues its initial report to OMB and Congress.
OMB issues its initial report providing estimates and determinations to the president and Congress.	August 25	
President issues initial sequester order and sends message to Congress within 15 days.	August 25	

SOURCE: Office of Management and Budget, Circular No. A-11 (1988).

summer, the OMB director issues specific revenue projections and imposes specific guidelines for departmental spending. On September 1 agencies submit their initial budget requests to OMB. OMB then holds formal hearings on these requests at which departmental officials justify their proposed budgets before OMB examiners.

OMB's director examines the entire budget from November 1 to December 1. Often the director will invite the National Security Council (NSC), the Council of Economic Advisers, and several White House aides to participate in the review. The OMB director makes final decisions subject to the economic forecast for the coming fiscal year and communicates these decisions to the departments. The departments may appeal the decisions directly to the president. Usually, however, each department will revise its formal budget to coincide with the budget director's wishes, for presidents rarely reverse their budget directors' decisions.

Congress receives the first official hint of what the president wants in the State of the Union address at the end of January, and specifics are then spelled out in the president's budget message in February. Pending approval by Congress, the budget goes into effect with the new fiscal year, October 1.

Not all agency requests are treated equally. Until the Nixon administration, the Defense Department's budget requests were exempt from control by the president's budgeting organization. During the administrations of John Kennedy and Lyndon Johnson, the Pentagon submitted its budget directly to the president without review by the Bureau of the Budget. If BOB believed budget items to be too high, it could appeal to the president. This practice, a reversal of the traditional procedure, placed the burden of proof on the budget office rather than on the department. President Nixon changed the procedure for the Pentagon by leaving final decisions with the NSC and OMB and giving the Defense Department the right of appeal. Subsequent presidents have continued to use OMB as a counterbalance to the Pentagon's budget requests.

Current Services Budget

Under the provisions of the 1974 Congressional Budget and Impoundment Control Act (PL 93-344), presidents must submit two budget proposals. When they submit their budget for the upcoming fiscal year, they must also submit, through the supervision of OMB, a *current services budget.* The current services budget provides Congress with an indication of the cost of existing budget obligations and a guide for evaluating additional budget proposals. Specifically, the current services budget includes the "proposed budget authority and estimated outlays that would be included in the budget for the ensuing fiscal year . . . if all programs were carried on at the same level as the fiscal year in progress . . . without policy changes."[108]

Although this procedure was intended to provide Congress with a basis for determining the overall size and direction of existing budget commitments and for assessing and evaluating the president's budget proposals, it has never quite lived up to its potential. Political scientist Howard E. Shuman has noted that the current services budget has little significance or meaning: "Only budget buffs and perennial budget watchers pay much attention to it. It is, however, a useful document in assessing whether any or how much fundamental change has been made in the old budget to produce the new one."[109]

Uncontrollable Spending

In any given year, much of OMB's current service estimates can be classified as *uncontrollable spending,* expenditures mandated by current law or some previous obligation. To change the spending on these mandated programs would require congressional action. By 1995, 64 percent of the federal budget could be classified as uncontrollable spending. These expenditures can be broken down into three major categories.

The first category, fixed costs, consists of legal commitments made by the federal government in previous years. These commitments require the government to spend whatever is necessary to meet these expenses. The largest and most important component of this category is interest on the national debt. Another fixed-cost expenditure is public housing loans. Fixed costs are virtually "uncontrollable" because they can be eliminated only by such extreme measures as default.

The second category is large-scale government projects that require long-term financing. These multiyear contracts and obligations include the building of dams, weapons systems, aircraft, and the space shuttle. Many of these projects are reviewed annually, and expenditure levels are occasionally modified. For example, in 1994 funding was curtailed for the space program and eliminated for the supercollider. Historically, however, most are not.

The third category of expenditures officially designated as uncontrollable is the largest. These programs, called "entitlements," commit the federal government to pay benefits to all eligible individuals. Any attempt at controlling these expenditures would require changing the laws that created them. Entitlements include Social Security, Medicare, Medicaid, Supplemental Security Income, food stamps, public assistance, and federal retirement. *(See Table 1-2.)* In some cases, the federal government pays individuals directly; in other cases, the states deter-

TABLE 1-2 Entitlement Spending, 1975–2000
(billions of dollars)

Category	*1975*	*1985*	*1994*	*1995*	*2000*[a]
Social Security and railroad retirement	67.3	190.3	321.1	337.0	425.4
Federal employees' retirement and insurance	18.4	49.8	79.4	82.2	100.1
Unemployment assistance	12.8	16.2	27.2	21.9	27.7
Medical care, including Medicare and Medicaid	26.2	104.2	264.6	289.7	395.1
Assistance to students	6.2	9.2	8.6	14.8	11.1
Housing assistance	2.1	11.2	22.4	25.5	25.0
Food and nutrition assistance	6.6	18.5	36.7	37.5	42.3
Public assistance and related programs	12.2	24.6	57.9	61.8	79.3
All other payments for individuals	2.0	3.3	4.3	4.2	3.4
TOTAL PAYMENTS FOR INDIVIDUALS	153.8	427.3	822.2	874.6	1109.6

SOURCE: Office of Management and Budget, *The Budget of the United States, Fiscal Year 1997,* Historical Tables (Washington, D.C.: Government Printing Office, 1996), 182–190.
NOTE: a. Estimate.

BUDGETING THEORIES

One of the most important functions served by the budget is to increase presidential administrative control and management of federal agencies and programs. However, the budget process has always been the subject of criticism aimed at improving the efficiency of government management. Over the years, critics, both within the presidency and outside it, have complained about the lack of coordination and centralization in the executive branch's efforts to control the federal administration. Consequently, since the early 1960s various presidents have introduced reforms aimed at making budgeting more efficient, rational, and comprehensive. Rarely, however, have they been as successful as they have hoped.

PLANNING-PROGRAMMING-BUDGETING

In 1961 Secretary of Defense Robert S. McNamara introduced a planning-programming-budgeting (PPB) system into the Pentagon. McNamara brought PPB from the private sector and used it to improve the quality of decision making and budget planning for national security policy. In 1965 President Johnson announced that PPB would also be applied to domestic operations.

PPB was designed to allow budget decisions to be made by focusing on program goals and on quantitative comparisons of costs and benefits. Once budget officials established priorities among their objectives, they then determined the best expenditure mix in the annual budget to achieve the largest future benefits.

By 1971 PPB had fallen into disfavor with executive budget makers. Although many people had looked to PPB to reform budgeting in the executive branch by making it more rational and less "political," PPB failed to gain a permanent place in the budget process for a variety of reasons. It never achieved any great degree of popularity within the departments and agencies in part because it required a very formal structure.

In addition, PPB suffered major resistance from Congress. Advocates of PPB apparently forgot that Congress had an important and jealously guarded role in the budget process. Members of Congress who had spent years building up their contacts and knowledge of agency budgets resented a new budget system that disrupted their channels of influence and information in an effort to make budgeting more rational and less political.

MANAGEMENT BY OBJECTIVE

In the late 1950s, economist Peter Drucker developed a management technique for business called management by objective (MBO). In the early 1970s, OMB adopted the system. Similar to PPB, it was an attempt to make budget decisions more rational. Not quite as ambitious in its comprehensiveness as PPB, MBO simply stated that agencies should specify goals and alternative means of achieving those goals. It was a system much less centralized than PPB, with less emphasis on long-range planning, but it still was based on agencies making rational choices about their policy goals.

Despite its simplification, MBO also had a short life in the federal government. By the beginning of Jimmy Carter's administration, it had passed from use. Lance LeLoup pointed out that many of the problems with PPB remained with MBO. He wrote, "It was difficult to specify and agree on objectives, and to quantify benefits. MBO was not supported at middle and lower levels of agency management because it was still perceived as a system that increased control at the upper levels."[1]

ZERO-BASE BUDGETING

The most recent attempt at presidential control over the national budgeting process was zero-base budgeting (ZBB). Developed in the private sector (like PPB and MBO) by Peter Pyhrr of Texas Instruments, Inc., ZBB was first applied to state governments.

Under Pyhrr's direction, Jimmy Carter first implemented it in Georgia while he was governor. In 1977, several months after he became president, Carter instructed OMB to implement ZBB. Carter promised that "by working together under a ZBB system, we can reduce costs and make the federal government more efficient and effective."[2] ZBB was primarily designed to avoid "incremental" budgeting in which some arbitrary percentage is more or less blindly added to the preceding year's budget. Instead ZBB aims to force agencies to identify and analyze goals and objectives, making them an integral part of the budget process.[3]

Like PPB and MBO, the appeal of a comprehensive budgeting program such as ZBB is tremendous, but its success has been limited. Budget scholar Allen Schick concluded that the effect of ZBB on the budgeting activities of the executive branch had been almost negligible. Under ZBB most budget items have been funded at or slightly above past current services levels.[4]

1. Lance T. LeLoup, *Budgetary Politics,* 2d ed. (Brunswick, Ohio: King's Court, 1980), 271.

2. Quoted in Joel Haveman, "Zero-Base Budgeting," *National Journal,* April 2, 1977, 514.

3. Peter A. Pyhrr, *Zero-Base Budgeting: A Practical Management Tool for Evaluating Expenses* (New York: Wiley, 1973), 10.

4. Allen Schick, "The Road from ZBB," in *Contemporary Approaches to Public Budgeting,* ed. Fred A. Kramer (Cambridge, Mass.: Winthrop, 1979), 216.

mine eligibility and administer the programs. Most of these programs have no limit on the amount of spending they may entail. As more people become eligible for benefits, expenditures increase.

As uncontrollable spending has pushed federal budget deficits higher, presidents have tried to decrease these so-called uncontrollable expenditures. Nixon and Ford, for example, attempted to decrease entitlement expenditures by restricting eligibility and establishing a limit on benefit increases on several programs. In his first full budget year, Reagan proposed an entitlement cut of $11.7 billion. His budget proposal reflected the frustration that many presidents have felt in attempting to deal with uncontrollable expenditures. It said in part, "The explosion of entitlement expenditures has forced a careful reexamination of the entitlement or automatic spending programs. . . . When one looks behind the good intentions of these programs, one finds tremendous problems of fraud, waste, and mismanagement. Worse than this, the truly needy have not been well served."[110] From 1995 to 1996 President Clinton fought Congress over the future growth of Medicare. Congress sought a $270 billion cut in Medicare funding over seven years while Clinton sought only $124 billion. The final 1996 fiscal budget reflected Clinton's priorities but it did not address the long-term issue of the solvency of Medicare's trust fund, which was scheduled to go broke by 2001.

Controllable Spending

The president does have some control over several categories of expenditures. Sixty percent of expenditures that can be classified as controllable are used for salaries and fringe benefits for both civilian and military personnel. Although these expenses technically fit the category of controllable expenditures, the practical problems surrounding spending on salaries and fringe benefits make it difficult for a president to control them completely. Seniority and civil service rules protect so many federal employees that it is futile to attempt real cutbacks in expenditures going to salaries.

A second category of controllable federal expenditures is the general operating expenses of the various departments and agencies. Spending for operating expenses constitutes 22 percent of the budget. Although conservational measures can be undertaken on such things as heating, cooling, electricity, transportation, and supplies, expenses will always continue if operations continue. Inflation also increases operating expenses.

The third category of controllable expenditures, research and development of new programs, makes up 18 percent of the controllable portion of the federal budget. Medical research, weapons research, and grants to state and local governments encompass a large proportion of this category. Again, budget cuts can be made in this category, but only within limits. As a result, even the controllable categories of the federal budget give the president little latitude in budget decisions.

Early in his presidency, however, President Clinton attempted to trim some controllable spending in an effort to cut the deficit. He proposed cutting $6.6 billion over five years from the federal budget, eliminating 100,000 bureaucrats and freezing federal pay levels to save $47.2 billion over the same period, cutting back agriculture benefits in order to save $9.9 billion in five years, and cutting veterans' programs by $4.8 billion over the period. Although the cuts sounded large, they actually represented just a small percentage of the projected budget, adding up to less than $70 billion over five years. The modest cuts represented the little latitude Clinton found in his attempts to cut spending.

CONGRESSIONAL RESPONSE TO THE PRESIDENT'S BUDGET

Because the presidency traditionally has controlled the compilation and production of the budget, Congress frequently complained that it could get only superficial information from the president on technical budget matters on which it would eventually have to make important decisions. It argued that it did not possess adequate professional staff to evaluate independently the details, proposals, and estimates of the president's budget. Congress had become dependent on OMB and the presidency for all its budgetary information. In recent years, however, Congress has become increasingly aggressive in its desire to function equally with the executive branch in its budgetary role.

Congressional Budget Office

To improve its ability to evaluate the budget, Congress in 1974 created the Congressional Budget Office (CBO) through the Congressional Budget and Impoundment Control Act. CBO was a major innovation for Congress and a major challenge for the presidency. Designed to provide congressional budget committees with a variety of budget and policy information, CBO's professional staff incorporates several functions performed in the executive branch by OMB.

CBO activities fall into five categories. First, CBO prepares an annual report on budget alternatives, including fiscal policy options, levels of tax revenues, and budget priorities. Second, it issues five-year budget projections for spending and taxation. Third, CBO projects the long-term costs of bills approved by House and Senate committees and sent to the full Congress for consideration. Fourth, CBO performs a "scorekeeping" function by comparing pending and enacted legislation with targets and ceilings specified by Congress. Fifth, CBO provides Congress with special reports on economic and budgetary issues.

CBO's independent database allows Congress to evaluate presidential budget proposals more effectively. In measuring the success of CBO after its first five years of operation, political scientist Aaron Wildavsky wrote, "The Congressional Budget Office has improved the accuracy of budget numbers by providing a competitive source of expertise, and it has made competent analysis more widely available to those that want it."[111] CBO has allowed Congress to become more independent from the executive branch in its budget-making powers. In his book, *The Power Game,* political journalist Hedrick Smith wrote, "CBO represents the most important shift of power on domestic issues between the executive branch and Congress in several decades."[112]

This competition in the budget process, however, has irritated more than one president. CBO's economic forecasts usually counter OMB's optimistic and more moderate projections, leading to numerous congressional-presidential confrontations over budget proposals. Shuman notes that in the past CBO "angered President Carter because it disputed his energy program savings and angered President Reagan by saying that his economic assumptions about inflation, interest rates, and unemployment were unrealistic, overly optimistic, and wrong."[113] President Bush disagreed with various CBO projections on his administration's budget proposals, including affordability of proposed weapon systems and estimates of the likely effect on economic growth of capital gains tax reductions. Part of the

1995 budget battle between President Clinton and Congress centered around different economic forecasting data produced by OMB and CBO. OMB's numbers were more optimistic than CBO's. After several weeks of negotiations, the White House and Congress agreed that CBO's economic forecast (after consultation with OMB) would serve as a basis for fiscal projections for any budget agreement. CBO then revised its figures slightly upward, but Congress and the White House still remained apart on other budget issues.

Gramm-Rudman-Hollings

With budget deficits growing throughout the 1980s and President Reagan's refusal to support tax increases, Congress believed that additional budget reform was necessary to control spending. In 1985 Congress passed the Balanced Budget and Emergency Deficit Control Act of 1985, also known as Gramm-Rudman-Hollings for its primary sponsors: Sens. Phil Gramm, Warren Rudman, and Ernest Hollings. Although several budget control measures were discussed, including a line-item veto for the president and a constitutional amendment to balance the budget, a strategy of mandatory spending cuts was the alternative chosen by Congress.

Gramm-Rudman-Hollings represented a major revision in the budgetary process by providing for deficit reduction targets during six years. By imposing declining deficit ceilings, it would bring the budget into balance by 1991. If the budget process exceeded these guidelines, the president could order across-the-board spending cuts, or sequestration. (Some programs, such as Social Security and veterans' benefits, were exempt from these mandatory cuts.) The act failed to live up to its billing, however. In the 1986 budget process, Gramm-Rudman-Hollings achieved some modest success. In early 1987, when the CBO announced that the deficit for fiscal 1988 would be well above the target for that year, Congress changed the targets. It moved back the budget deficit targets two years so that the federal budget would be balanced in 1993.

In 1987 President Reagan invoked a $23 billion sequestration under Gramm-Rudman-Hollings. On October 19, one day before Reagan was to begin the procedure for automatic spending cuts, the stock market suffered its worst single-day loss ever. In a deal reached between Congress and the president, the sequestration order was repealed and a budget agreement was reached that was supposed to save $75 billion during the next two years. This agreement included spending cuts and some tax increases to ensure compliance with Gramm-Rudman-Hollings targets. The actual deficit reduction was less than the proposed targets. By 1990 deficits stood at record levels. Facing a widening deficit gap, President Bush and Congress made a budget control agreement for fiscal years 1991 through 1995 that abandoned the Gramm-Rudman-Hollings deficit reduction timetable. In doing so, Bush broke his 1988 campaign promise of "Read my lips, no new taxes" by agreeing to some tax increases to help bring down the budget deficit.

The mammoth U.S. budget for fiscal 1981 rolls off the presses.

The 1990 budget agreement, known as the Budget Enforcement Act (BEA), was amended in 1993 to run through 1998. The BEA sought to lower budget deficits by imposing limits on annual appropriations for discretionary spending in three broad areas: defense, domestic programs, and foreign aid. Under the BEA, OMB determines whether the annual caps have been exceeded and, if so, by how much. It then reports those amounts to the president, who may issue sequestration orders that prevent agencies from spending in excess of the limits set by Congress. In addition, BEA requires Congress to either raise taxes or reduce other entitlements if it creates any new entitlement programs.

Early in his administration President Clinton had to deal with the accumulated deficits of the Reagan and Bush administrations and the new caps on spending imposed by the BEA. The promise to cut the budget deficit was an important part of Clinton's presidential campaign. Under optimistic economic projections, Clinton's initial budget plan proposed to cut the budget deficit by a combined $473 billion by 1998. The Clinton budget was enacted by close votes in Congress in 1993, and the federal deficit declined during the first three years of the Clinton administration. Although Clinton's 1995 budget deficit of $164 billion was the lowest since 1989, a balanced budget was a long way off.

In 1994 Republicans took control of Congress in part on a promise to balance the budget. Throughout most of 1995 and into 1996, President Clinton and Congress debated the appropriate path to a balanced budget. Republicans sought to decrease the size of government significantly and turn over many of its responsibilities to the states. After months of budget stalemate, congressional Republicans failed in their effort to convert broad public support for a balanced budget into specific program cutbacks. President Clinton and congressional Democrats found greater public approval for their more modest deficit-reduction efforts. After two government shutdowns resulting from a failure on the part of Congress and the president to reach budget agreements, congressional Republicans in 1996 gave up their more strident demands for downsizing government. Boosted by his budget stand against the Republicans in Congress and buoyed by continued good economic news, Clinton won a convincing reelection in 1996. Immediately after the election Clinton said his top priority for his second term would be balancing the budget. The budget deficit had declined to $107 billion in fiscal year 1996, however tough decisions remained for Clinton (once again facing a Republican-controlled Congress in 1997) before a balanced budget could be reached by the targeted year 2002.

Congress and Presidential Lobbying

Because an almost adversarial relationship exists between Congress and the president over development of the budget, presidents must actively lobby Congress for their budget recommendations to become public policy. This difficult task is complicated by the dispersal of congressional budget authority among the House and Senate Appropriations committees and the various standing (ongoing) committees. After the president submits the budget plan, Congress gives different committees jurisdiction over different aspects of it. The House Ways and Means and Senate Finance committees consider revenue proposals. The various standing committees consider proposals for changes in laws that affect the uncontrollable expenses. The Joint Economic Committee studies the fiscal implications of the president's proposals. The House and Senate Budget committees obtain budget information and prepare the budget resolution. The House and Senate Appropriations committees consider expenditure requests. Presidents must exert influence on these different committees if their proposals are to become grants of spending authority for their departments and agencies.

Probably the most important committees with which presidents have to deal are the Appropriations committees. These are also the most difficult for presidents to influence because they are among the most powerful and the most isolated from White House control. Appropriations committees have several independent sources of information from which to work when they consider presidential budget requests. They have the figures prepared by OMB, estimates from the substantive committees of possible expenditures of programs under their jurisdiction, program estimates and options prepared by CBO, and tentative spending guidelines prepared by the various budget committees.

In addition to having sources of information besides OMB, the Appropriations committees are free from the political control of the president. Their members enjoy tremendous electoral freedom, especially those in the House. In the 1980s and 1990s, more than 90 percent of House members have been reelected. Although the percentages are not as large in the Senate, the number of incumbents reelected has been well above the 80 percent range in recent years. Richard Pious has written, "Each committee member can maintain his position in his district through delivery of goods and services and patronage, from agencies eager to please him. The president cannot oust these members from his party, the committee, or the House by purging them if they cross him."[114]

Still, the initiative usually remains with the president. A determined president, who exerts the full force of the presidency, can overcome many congressional objections. The president represents one view. Congress often speaks with many confused and chaotic partisan voices. It is therefore difficult for Congress to defeat presidential budget initiatives. Consequently, the momentum in the budget proceedings belongs to the presidency, which usually speaks with unanimity. As Shuman has pointed out, because of this consensus the White House can control the debate: the president's "budget and . . . views are the subjects of the lead paragraphs in the early budget stories. Congressional criticism trails as an afterthought at the end of the article."[115] After introducing his first budget in Congress, for example, President Reagan went on the offensive by explaining his budget before friendly audiences. Before a joint session of the Iowa legislature he said, "The budget we have proposed is a line drawn in the dirt. Those who are concerned about the deficits will cross it and work with us on our proposals or their alternatives. Those who are not . . . will stay on the other side and simply continue their theatrics."[116]

In 1995 Congress seized the initiative from President Clinton in balancing the budget and seemed to be speaking with one voice. Under the energized leadership of newly elected House Speaker Newt Gingrich, the Republican-controlled Congress promised to deliver on its 1994 campaign promise of a balanced budget. In the early stages of the budget negotiations, Republicans were united behind plans to force President Clinton to side with their proposals to downsize the federal government. As government shutdowns occurred and public opinion swung toward the White House, however, Congress became less unified in its budget strategy and goals. President Clinton remained firm in his refusal to capitulate to congressional demands for sharper cuts in programs such as Medicare and Medicaid. As a result of a waning consensus in Congress and a growing determination in the White House, some of the budgeting initiative returned to the president by early 1996.

Sometimes presidents can use the advantages of their office to pressure recalcitrant members of Congress to go along with their budget proposals. Often these tactics are not so subtle.

When Vice President Gore telephoned Sen. Richard Shelby, then a conservative Democrat from Alabama, to urge his support of the Clinton administration's first budget, Shelby had television cameras present and publicly challenged the Clinton budget as being too high on taxes and too low on spending cuts. The Clinton White House did not think this rebuff to the vice president and the president's budget should go unchallenged. Clinton promptly retaliated by moving a NASA project worth $380 million a year and involving ninety jobs from Huntsville, Alabama, to Houston, Texas. The administration then leaked the story to the media to send a message to other Democrats who might be thinking of abandoning Clinton's budget proposal.[117] The strategy eventually backfired on the Clinton administration, however. A year later, Shelby became a Republican.

PRESIDENTIAL SPENDING

Although Congress has power over the appropriations process, presidents always have a certain amount of *discretionary power* over spending, that is, they may spend certain funds as they please within broad areas of responsibility. Often Congress delegates discretionary power to the president. In a crisis, for example, especially during wartime, Congress has given the president "lump sum," or very broadly defined, appropriations so that the president and executive branch officials who represent presidential wishes may devote funds as they deem appropriate within the congressional limit. For example, Congress set up the Disaster Relief Fund to be administered by the EOP without restrictions. Although the discretionary power does not give presidents unlimited spending authority, it does give them some budget flexibility and some latitude in the actual spending of funds as well as a final opportunity to make policy. As political scientist Louis Fisher has observed, "What is done by legislators at the appropriations stage can be undone by administrators during budget execution."[118]

Sometimes presidents exercise discretionary spending power that Congress has not delegated specifically by interpreting spending authorizations and appropriations as permissive rather than mandatory. In 1959, for example, President Eisenhower simply did not establish a food stamp program that Congress had passed into law. Presidents also can delay setting up appropriated programs in their efforts to frustrate congressional initiatives. In 1975, after Congress had developed a summer employment program, the Ford administration successfully stymied the program by setting it up so slowly that the appropriated funds could not be spent during the fiscal year. Similarly, OMB can delay funding from the Treasury to an agency in an attempt to eliminate the agency or its programs. In 1975 the Ford administration undermined the Community Services Administration by delaying the agency's funds until after the agency's authority expired.[119]

Confidential Funding

Occasionally, Congress grants the president confidential funding for urgent, highly sensitive, or secretive matters. Presidents have complete discretion over such annually funded budget items. For example, during his 1974 visit to Egypt, President Nixon used a presidential contingency fund to give Anwar Sadat a $3 million helicopter as a gift.

Fisher has reported that several confidential accounts are noted in public record but are not audited by Congress, including four in the White House, six for diplomatic agencies, and one each for atomic energy, space, the Federal Bureau of Investigation (FBI), and the Central Intelligence Agency (CIA).[120] One of the most notorious confidential funds was President Nixon's Special Projects Fund, which was used to finance a massive spying and sabotage campaign against Nixon's "political enemies."

Secret Funding

In addition to the various confidential funds, presidents may ask Congress for a general appropriation for secret projects. Secret funds do not require either the appropriation (the amount of money granted by Congress) or the expenditure (the amount of money spent by the executive branch) to be a matter of public record.

Secret funding was used for the Manhattan Project during World War II. The development of the atomic bomb required more than $2 billion, which Congress approved with very little scrutiny of the purpose of the appropriation.

Secret funding also is used for intelligence organizations such as the CIA. The CIA's expenditures are drawn on requests from the agency's director and are not made public or audited by Congress. CIA activities are financed by secret transfers of funds from the appropriations accounts of other agencies, primarily the Defense Department. This process keeps the CIA budget hidden not only from the public, but also from many members of Congress.

In recent years Congress has attempted to restrict the use of confidential and secret funds and bring existing funds under greater congressional scrutiny. In 1974, after revelations of covert operations overseas, Congress prohibited the CIA from funding operations other than activities intended solely for obtaining necessary intelligence.[121] More recently, there has been a move to make the funding of the CIA and other intelligence agencies a matter of public record. Congress has the power either to control or to limit this type of discretionary power, but so far it has chosen to impose only moderate limitations. As Ippolito has pointed out, "[Congress] can insure, as it has done with respect to the CIA, that more of its members participate in the oversight activities. Congress can also provide for review and audit by the Government Accounting Office to insure that confidential or secret funds are expended in accordance with legislative intent."[122]

Transfers

Another method of bypassing the congressional appropriations process is the transfer and reprogramming of funds. In these cases, presidents attempt to use appropriated funds for purposes other than what Congress originally intended. Such transfers occur when Congress permits the executive to shift funds from one appropriation account to another, allowing officials to use appropriated funds for different purposes. As noted earlier, intelligence agencies frequently are funded with transfer funds. The Central Intelligence Agency Act of 1949 allows the CIA to transfer funds to and from other agencies to perform its functions.

In 1970 the Nixon administration used transfer authority to finance the Cambodian intervention with a $108.9 million transfer from military aid accounts for Greece, Turkey, Taiwan, the Philippines, and South Vietnam. In 1972 Congress prohibited transfers of military aid from one nation to another unless the president gave Congress notice. Yet, despite the Nixon administration's agreements to submit transfers to Congress for approval, the war in Cambodia in 1972 and 1973 was financed by more than $750 million in transfer authority already given the president.

Reprogramming

Presidents may also reprogram funds, that is, move funds within an appropriation account from one budget item to another. In some cases, presidents have used reprogramming to frustrate congressional intent by shifting funds for projects that had been approved to projects that had not been approved.

Presidents most frequently reprogram funds within the defense budget. The Pentagon often reprograms funds in an attempt to develop new weapons systems after the House and Senate Appropriations committees have cut the defense budget. In the 1960s, for example, as many as one hundred reprogramming actions moved several billion dollars in a single year. Between 1956 and 1972, average annual reprogramming in the Pentagon totaled $2.6 billion. In the past, congressional committees allowed departments to reprogram first and inform them afterwards. But because some departments maneuvered around the intent of appropriations measures, Congress now requires at least semiannual notification and, in some cases, prior clearance with the committees.

IMPOUNDMENT POWERS

Until 1974, the most powerful presidential tool in overcoming the congressional funding prerogative was the power of impoundment—the president's refusal to spend funds that Congress had appropriated for a particular purpose. Historically, presidents have claimed both constitutional and statutory authority to impound funds either by treating the funding as permissive, that is, optional, rather than mandatory and rescinding spending authority or by deferring spending to future years. The impoundment power is similar to the veto power in that both are attempts to block or thwart congressional actions.

One of the most famous early examples of a president's use of the impoundment power was Thomas Jefferson's refusal in 1803 to spend a $50,000 appropriation for gunboats on the Mississippi River to protect the western frontier. Jefferson carefully informed Congress that the money should be used for the purchase of more advanced boats the following year. Similarly, President Ulysses S. Grant refused to spend fu had appropriated for public works projects, a could be completed for less money than had been In both cases Congress eventually accepted the pres er to refuse to spend congressionally appropriated mo

Congress eventually gave impoundment authority a statutory basis by passing the Anti-Deficiency Acts of 1905 and 1906. These laws allowed presidents to withhold funds for a period of time to prevent deficiencies or overspending in an agency. In 1921 the Bureau of the Budget established impoundment authority when its director, Charles Dawes, announced that "the president does not assume . . . that the minimum of government expenditures is the amount fixed by Congress in its appropriations."[123]

Under the New Deal, President Roosevelt occasionally used impoundments for budgetary or policy purposes. In some cases, the president acted with at least the implied consent of Congress. During the Great Depression, for example, spending bills were sometimes treated as ceilings, allowing Roosevelt to refuse to spend money that he believed to be unnecessary. During World War II, Roosevelt argued that his war powers gave him the power to cut spending that was not essential to national security. Presidents Truman, Eisenhower, and Kennedy all used impoundments to cut military spending.

President Johnson, however, used impoundments to curtail domestic spending during the Vietnam War. As the war progressed and inflation rose, Johnson impounded funds designated for agriculture, conservation, education, housing, and transportation. These impoundments were usually temporary, and the funds eventually were released. Although Johnson did not use the power of impoundment to cripple congressionally appropriated programs (many of them were his own programs), his actions did set an example of impoundment power being used to combat inflation—a power later adopted and expanded by Nixon.

Both Johnson and Nixon used impoundment to control spending, but Nixon's use was unprecedented in its scope and effects. Whereas Johnson relied on temporary deferrals rather than permanent cuts and worked personally with Congress to soothe tempers, the Nixon administration's impoundments seemed designed to eliminate or to curtail particular programs favored by the Democratic Congress. Between 1969 and 1974 the administration made a determined effort to redistribute the emphasis of governmental services. When Congress overrode Nixon's veto of the Federal Water Pollution Control Act Amendments of 1972, for example, the Nixon administration impounded half of the $18 billion that had been allotted for fiscal years 1973 through 1975, thereby handicapping the program. In addition, the Nixon administration undertook major impoundment reductions in low-rent housing construction, mass transit, food stamps, and medical research programs.

By 1973 Nixon had impounded more than $20 billion, and his budget for fiscal 1974 contained a list of 109 reductions he wanted to make, 101 of which he said would require no congressional approval. Ippolito concluded, "While administration spokesmen advanced a variety of justifications in support of these impoundments—including precedent, statutory responsibilities, and general executive authority—it was apparent that impoundment was being used to enforce the president's policy preferences and budgetary priorities."[124] More than thirty lower court cases overturned Nixon impoundments. The Supreme Court eventually tackled Nixon's impoundment of funds for water pollution control. In *Train v. City of New York,* the Court ruled that once water pollution control funds had been appropriated by an act of Congress, funds could not be withheld at a later stage by impoundment.[125]

Eventually, public pressure began to build for Congress to do something about Nixon's use of the impoundment power. At first, individual members attempted to intervene personally with the president in an effort to restore funds to certain projects. By 1970 many subcommittees had become concerned over the impoundment pattern that was beginning to emerge—a pattern that threatened their control of the policy-making process. In 1973 House and Senate Appropriations committees began holding hearings on the impoundment of funds for low-income housing, and Congress began inserting mandatory language in certain spending bills to eliminate the discretionary authority that had allowed presidential impoundment.

In 1974 Congress adopted the Congressional Budget and Impoundment Control Act. Besides setting up the Congressional Budget Office to improve congressional monitoring of, and deliberation on, the budget, the act also aimed at controlling presidential impoundment. It stipulated two new procedures, *rescissions* and *deferrals,* by which presidents could temporarily override or delay congressional appropriations decisions. If presidents wish to rescind (that is, cancel) all or part of the appropriated funds, they also must tell Congress. Unless Congress passes a rescission bill within forty-five days permitting the cancellation of funding, presidents must spend the funds. As the Congressional Budget and Impoundment Act was originally written, either house of Congress could block a deferral (that is, delay) of spending. In 1983 the Supreme Court, in *Immigration and Naturalization Service v. Chadha,* ruled the one house legislative veto unconstitutional.[126] The effect of *Chadha* was to require a resolution by a majority vote of both houses directing that appropriated funds be spent immediately.

Since Nixon resigned in 1974, a few months before the implementation of the impoundment control provisions of the budget act, he never felt the force of the act. The first administration to be confronted with these statutory impoundment limitations was the Ford administration. Of the $9 billion in rescissions requested by President Ford during his term in office, 86 percent of his requests were denied by Congress. Only 24 percent of his deferral requests were rejected, however. This pattern has been followed fairly consistently since the Ford administration. Congress usually grants deferrals; in most years, it allows 90 percent of them. Rescissions are a different matter, however. In recent years, congressional approvals have ranged from 80 percent in 1979 to none in 1980. Usually, Congress approves fewer than half of presidential rescissions.[127] Both the Reagan and Bush administrations called for increased rescission authority in their efforts to reduce the deficit. In March 1996 the Republican-controlled Congress ended months of negotiation to grant to the president "enhanced rescission" authority—a type of line-item veto. *(See "Line-item Veto, p. 94, in Chapter 2.)* President Clinton signed the bill on April 9, 1996. The law gives the president (beginning in 1997) the power to "cancel" individual items in spending and tax bills unless overturned by a two-thirds vote of both houses of Congress. Many anticipated that the Supreme Court would rule on the doubtful constitutionality of the measure.

Executive Orders

Article II of the Constitution assigns to the president the "executive power," probably one of the document's least specific but potentially most far-reaching grants of power. Before 1787 state legislatures generally defined executive power for their respective governors, who were kept on rather short leashes in most cases.[128] However, the drafters of the Constitution, learning from their experiences with the state legislatures as well as with the Articles of Confederation, shied away from having Congress dictate the boundaries of presidential action. Instead they left the range of executive powers undefined, open-ended, and ripe for reinterpretation by later presidents.

This silence proved critical. When paired with the Article II provision requiring presidents to "take Care that the Laws be faithfully executed," the executive power clause today provides for a range of "implied" powers whose extent and potency have grown beyond anything the Founders could have foreseen.[129] The Constitution actually grants to the president a limited array of explicit "express" powers, leaving the clear impression that Congress is dominant on almost all other matters. But the powers implied in the Constitution and given substance by years of continuous reinterpretation are the sources of the president's ability to act alone, often without specific congressional statute. Much of U.S. history has involved a struggle between presidents claiming the power to act without clear constitutional mandates and their critics arguing to the contrary.

On its face, the "take care" clause directs the president to administer statutes in a manner faithful to legislative language and intent. Like so many constitutional provisions, however, the clause is vague in meaning and elastic in potential ramifications. In an 1890 case, for example, the Supreme Court ruled that the clause pertained not only to statutes enacted by Congress but to any "rights, duties, and obligations growing out of the Constitution itself, our international relations, and all the protection implied by the nature of the government under the Constitution."[130]

This decision seemed to suggest that the president possessed a range of discretionary power broader than any expressed specifically in the Constitution. These powers were derived from the president's dual roles as chief executive and commander in chief. By this reasoning, presidents theoretically can undertake any action deemed necessary to carry out their constitutional duties, to provide for the nation's defense, or to protect the common good. To make matters murkier, the Constitution is mute on what the "common good" entails—one of those "great silences" that makes the potential of implied powers so controversial.

An offspring of the implied powers doctrine is the *executive order.* This instrument of presidential power is defined nowhere in the Constitution but generally is construed as a presidential directive that is intended to carry out other executive powers. As such, an executive order's legal authority derives either from existing statutes or from the president's other constitutional responsibilities, not from any specific congressional approval. Executive orders usually pertain directly to government agencies and officials. They are used most frequently by presidents to establish executive branch agencies, modify bureaucratic rules or actions, change decision-making procedures, or give substance and force to statutes.[131] However, their effects often extend to average citizens. For example, one of the first actions by President Clinton was to sign an executive order on January 22, 1993, ending a "gag rule" that had, under the Reagan and Bush administrations, prohibited abortion counseling and referrals at family planning clinics that received federal funding.

The Constitution does not specify procedures for issuing executive orders. During the nation's first hundred or so years they were issued without any system of publication or recording. The numbering of executive orders began only in 1907, with numbers assigned retroactively to the time of Abraham Lincoln. More than 13,000 executive orders have been officially recorded through 1996 *(see Table 1-3),* though haphazard record keeping throughout much of history—even after 1907—leads scholars to estimate that between 15,000 and 50,000 directives never were recorded.[132] To respond to growing concerns that these lax conditions undermined democratic accountability, Congress in the Administrative Procedures Act of 1946 mandated that the number and text of all executive orders, executive branch announcements, proposals, and regulations must be published in the *Federal Register,* the official U.S. government record. There are exceptions to this rule specifically for "classified" executive orders pertaining directly to sensitive national security matters, which are entered into the *Federal Register* by number only.[133]

TABLE 1-3 Executive Orders, by President, 1789–1996

President	*Years in office*	*Number of orders*	*Average per year*
Washington	8.00	8	1.00
J. Adams	4.00	1	0.25
Jefferson	8.00	4	0.50
Madison	8.00	1	0.13
Monroe	8.00	1	0.13
J. Q. Adams	4.00	3	0.75
Jackson	8.00	12	1.50
Van Buren	4.00	10	2.50
W. H. Harrison	0.08[a]	0	—
Tyler	4.00	17	4.25
Polk	4.00	18	4.50
Taylor	1.25	5	4.00
Fillmore	2.75	12	4.36
Pierce	4.00	35	8.75
Buchanan	4.00	16	4.00
Lincoln	4.00	48	12.00
A. Johnson	4.00	79	19.75
Grant	8.00	217	27.13
Hayes	4.00	92	23.00
Garfield	0.50	6	—[b]
Arthur	3.25	96	29.50
Cleveland (1st term)	4.00	113	28.25
Harrison	4.00	143	35.75
Cleveland (2d term)	4.00	140	35.00
McKinley	4.75	185	38.95
T. Roosevelt	7.25	1081	149.10
Taft	4.00	724	181.00
Wilson	8.00	1803	225.38
Harding	2.60	522	200.77
Coolidge	5.40	1203	222.77
Hoover	4.00	968	242.00
F. Roosevelt	12.33	3522	285.64
Truman	7.67	897	116.96
Eisenhower	8.00	478	59.75
Kennedy	3.00	228	76.00
L. Johnson	5.00	316	63.20
Nixon	5.60	355	63.39
Ford	2.40	152	63.33
Carter	4.00	311	77.75
Reagan	8.00	409	51.13
Bush	4.00	165	41.25
Clinton[c]	4.00	200	50.00

SOURCES: Calculated by the author from Lyn Ragsdale, *Vital Statistics on the Presidency* (Washington, D.C.: Congressional Quarterly, 1996), 337–343; *Weekly Compilation of Presidential Documents,* various 1996 issues.

NOTES: Includes both numbered and unnumbered executive orders.
a. W. H. Harrison died after only one month in office. b. Garfield was assassinated after six months in office, during which he issued six executive orders. At that rate his average would have been twelve per year. c. Through 1996.

THE DISCRETIONARY PRESIDENCY

Executive orders are critical to the legislative role of the contemporary presidency precisely because Congress frequently (though not always) finds itself unable or unwilling to respond to complex national problems with highly specific statutory language. Instead, Congress copes with legislative language that sets goals, timetables, and standards, delegating to the executive branch the power to hammer out the frequently arcane technical matters, regulatory procedures, and rules that carry out a statute's legislative intent. Any such administrative rules and regulations carry the force of law.

In the Budget and Accounting Act of 1921, for example, Congress directed the president to coordinate all executive branch budget requests and package them together in a single annual budget document. But Congress never said how the president should do so, nor did it set any clear limits to that authority. As a consequence, presidents over time have used executive orders to

PROCESSING EXECUTIVE ORDERS

Proposed executive orders can originate from almost anywhere in the executive branch. A few are composed directly in the White House, but most originate from within the various executive departments and agencies. Some orders, such as those imposing trade sanctions on another nation, may be composed at the express instruction of the president. Most, however, are devised by career staff personnel in the departments and agencies to implement federal regulations, propose new rules or procedures, or to add technical language to congressional statutes. In any case, and because executive orders have the force of law, they are crafted largely by professional legal counsel at the instruction of the president's appointees. Rarely does a president take a direct hand in writing an order's actual language.

Because it has the force of law, each proposed executive order is composed and submitted according to precise procedures laid out in the U.S. Code. It must be prepared in a specific format and style (for example, on certain types of paper, in certain language) and must contain language explaining its nature, purpose, background, and effects, along with an assessment of how it relates to existing law. The proposed order is then sent, with seven copies, to the director of the Office of Management and Budget (OMB), where it is examined for adherence to the administration's overall policy and budgetary goals. If approved, the order and its copies are sent next to the attorney general, whose office scrutinizes it for potential legal problems. Since both the attorney general and the director of OMB typically are among the president's closest personal advisers, clearance by these offices normally can be assumed to signify presidential approval.

Following these steps, the proposed order is transmitted to the director of the Office of the Federal Register, a part of the National Archives and Records Services that is itself part of the General Services Administration, the federal government's housekeeping arm. The order is reviewed once more for stylistic and typographical errors, after which it and three copies are submitted to the president for final approval. If signed by the president, the order and two copies go back to the director of the Federal Register for publication in the *Federal Register*, the official publication of the executive branch. It is only upon the moment of publication in the *Federal Register* that an executive order takes force.

Not all executive orders follow these precise steps. Those relating to some natural emergency or international crisis may bypass much of the lengthy review process and go directly to the president for final approval. What is more, the text of an order that encompasses some aspect of national security may be treated as confidential, in which case only the order's number is published in the *Federal Register*. The overwhelming number of executive orders do not fit into these categories, however, so the process for creating and implementing an order typically follows a pattern set by law.

expand the scope and power of the Office of Management and Budget from a relatively minor bookkeeping agency to a central oversight body that screens virtually all policy-related activities within the executive branch. In one important case, Ronald Reagan in 1981 (Executive Order 12291) dramatically expanded the OMB's role in policy making by requiring that it formally approve all new bureaucratic rules and regulations before they go into effect. The effects of this order were seen immediately in such areas as environmental policy, where the Environmental Protection Agency increasingly found its regulatory actions overruled by the OMB for budget or policy reasons.[134] Reagan's successors naturally retained the OMB's enhanced clearance power—no president, regardless of party or philosophy, cedes power readily. The cumulative effect of Reagan's action has been greater centralization of decision making in the Executive Office of the President. Congress passed no specific law to accomplish this reorganization in executive branch procedures, nor was the president required to gain prior congressional approval to do so.

Even when Congress is reasonably precise in its instructions to the executive branch, as it usually is in tax legislation, there are often policy contradictions, unforeseen circumstances, or technical considerations that require executive branch officials to exercise their judgment in implementing legislative intent. The Tax Reform Act of 1986, for example, spawned approximately forty-two new Internal Revenue Service regulations, sixty-five announcements, thirty-two rulings, and forty-eight new tax forms within the first thirteen months after passage.[135]

Congress also consciously delegates broad discretionary authority to the president in the name of flexibility, effectiveness, or efficiency.[136] The Smoot-Hawley Tariff Act of 1930 is remembered in part because it ran more than 170 pages as Congress tried to codify into law virtually every known type of tariff and trade matter. Smoot-Hawley proved a spectacular nightmare, and the 1934 Reciprocal Trade Agreements Act, by contrast, ran but two pages. This time Congress simply authorized the president to do whatever was necessary to achieve the law's intent.[137] Congress in this case had decided that executive branch personnel were better positioned to act flexibly on issues with broad domestic and international effects, a view that would dominate legislating for decades.

On paper, administrative actions must conform with legislative intent. Yet there rarely is a precise line between "making" and "administering" law.[138] The reality is that executive branch agencies make law constantly when they interpret the intent of the law, giving lie to the fiction that presidents only administer the will of Congress. This confusion occurs even more noticeably in international affairs, executive branch operations, and national security matters where the Constitution gives the president primary authority.

Some scholars argue that it is unwise or illegitimate for Congress to delegate broad discretionary authority to the president, but executive orders usually are not controversial when based clearly on existing statutory authority.[139] They do, however, spark disputes when based on vaguely defined implied powers. The first such dispute between a president and Congress came in 1793, when President George Washington unilaterally declared U.S. neutrality in the war between France and England. Washington argued that his constitutional responsibility to represent the nation included the implied power to keep the United States out of war. This rationale did not convince James Madison, who retorted that the proclamation was invalid because only Congress could decide issues of war and peace.[140] The dispute has simmered since, erupting most when presidents take actions that Congress deems to be unconstitutional intrusions into its domains.

Presidents also generate controversy when they base executive orders on implied legislative consent; that is, when Congress has not legislated against some action. Federal courts tend to judge each case individually, but usually give presidents the benefit of the doubt when Congress has failed to decide an issue during a prolonged period of time. Making matters still more complex, Congress often gives presidents retroactive authority for their unilateral actions, particularly during emergencies. In the aforementioned case, Congress reluctantly approved Washington's proclamation of neutrality a year after he made it, a pattern repeated enough that presidents often proceed on the assumption that Congress will acquiesce eventually.

Finally, presidents maintain that they have the constitutional authority to act unilaterally because they possess inherent "war" or "emergency" powers during periods of apparent crisis. *(See "Emergency Powers," p. 49.)*

GROWTH IN EXECUTIVE DISCRETION

Federalists like Alexander Hamilton wanted a national government that "left substantial freedom of action to high officials and kept Congress out of most administrative details."[141] As secretary of the Treasury under Washington, Hamilton argued that Congress should legislate and appropriate revenues in broad categories, but then it should grant the executive branch wide latitude to administer programs. Washington's years in office in fact witnessed a remarkable degree of deference to presidential authority, particularly in the areas of fiscal policy and trade. This did not prevent controversies from arising, particularly over Hamilton's aggressive claims to executive branch discretion, but Congress generally trusted the revered first president to get the new nation on its feet.

Such deference had eroded by 1800 as Jefferson's Democratic-Republicans took control and established a more assertive view of legislative dominance. Jefferson and his allies, notes historian Leonard White, "emphasized the responsibility of the executive branch and the administrative system to Congress." Congress in the nineteenth century held tight reins over executive branch actions through highly detailed statutes, strict budget controls, and reviews of even the most mundane administrative matters.[142] Executive orders in these years usually supplemented acts of Congress and carried out rather minor matters like salary increases for individual employees. With the exception of Abraham Lincoln's dramatic assumption of emergency power during the Civil War, presidents and legislators alike accepted the view that presidents mostly administered the law.

A shift toward greater executive discretion began forcefully with Theodore Roosevelt at the turn of the century. Roosevelt's "stewardship" theory of the office hinged on the claim that the president enjoyed a range of residual executive powers implied in the Constitution. This view may have been controversial only a few years earlier, but by the early 1900s Americans expressed a growing acceptance of federal (and presidential) responsibility in the United States and abroad.[143] Such residual powers, Roosevelt argued, were neither enumerated in the Constitution nor assigned broadly to a specific branch; instead, they resided simply in concepts like national sovereignty or the public good. Thus, Roosevelt wrote, "my view was that every officer, and above all every executive officer in high position, was a steward of the people. . . . My belief was that it was not only his right but his duty to do anything that the needs of the Nation demanded unless such action was forbidden by the Constitution or by the laws."[144] The president was to represent the nation as a whole, a view of the office at sharp contrast to the traditional notion that presidents were mere "clerks" who carried out congressional dictates.

But the Constitution says very little about what powers might be available to a stewardship presidency. As political scientist Richard Pious suggests, "to use prerogatives effectively the president must first stake out his claims to them. Like Excalibur's sword, he must wrest his powers from the Constitution before he can wield them."[145] In this respect Abraham Lincoln and Theodore Roosevelt were exceptions to the "clerkship" presidency of the nineteenth century. The image of a truly discretionary presidency did not begin to gain real shape until World War I, when Woodrow Wilson issued almost two thousand executive orders and wielded expansive emergency powers to direct the war and domestic economic production. The powers Wilson asserted in wartime did not dissolve once hostilities ceased. They endured for the benefit of later presidents—a ratchet-like expansion of executive power that was to be repeated time and again.

RISE OF THE DISCRETIONARY PRESIDENCY

Franklin Roosevelt gave permanence to the stewardship view of the presidency during the New Deal and World War II. Elected as depression raged, and given wide latitude by Congress and the American people, Roosevelt relied heavily on executive initiatives to attack the economic crisis and rally the nation. He issued 654 executive orders in 1933 alone.[146] These included his inauguration-day proclamation closing all banks for four days to restructure the crumbling banking system and the creation of mechanisms for implementing New Deal programs. In most cases Roosevelt got quick and often retroactive congressional approval. Congress also uncharacteristically appropriated massive discretionary funds in order to allow the executive branch to develop programs more quickly and, maybe, more effectively than might be possible via normal legislative procedures.[147] The crisis prompted support for decisive action, and enabled Roosevelt to stretch the boundaries of his constitutional powers to the limit.

Roosevelt's highly muscular view of presidential discretion was buttressed by the sheer growth in federal government during the 1930s, which brought with it an explosion in executive branch responsibility. Congress found it increasingly difficult to grapple with the size and complexity of new national programs and began the widespread delegation of authority that marks contemporary government. What is more, scholars and politicians began openly to support the idea that broad executive discretion leads to more efficient and effective administration, arguments that redefined the concept of chief executive away from the more traditional views of the president as a mere agent of Congress.[148] For Congress to delegate broad authority to the president made pragmatic sense but also meshed with emerging views within the scholarly community that more executive discretion offered unalloyed benefits to a fragmented and decentralized system of government. Constitutional constants like separation of powers and federalism, long defended as essential for safeguarding citizens' rights and liberties, were now seen as impediments to effective government. Short of major constitutional reform, only strong presidential leadership could overcome the systemic flaws in the nation's structure of governance.[149]

Like Wilson a generation earlier, Roosevelt during World War II seized broad authority to prosecute the war and manage the domestic economy. Roosevelt moved unilaterally in many instances without the benefit of even vague statutory authority, basing his actions instead on powers that he claimed derived from his constitutional duties as commander in chief and chief executive. In 1941, for example, Roosevelt ordered the seizure of manufacturing plants, shipyards, and coal mines to prepare the nation for war. In this and other cases Congress provided the requisite statutory authority afterward, and even then it gave Roosevelt tremendous discretionary spending authority because of the national emergency.

But there were limits to congressional acquiescence, even in wartime. Roosevelt's tendency to use executive orders to create wartime agencies and fund them with moneys appropriated for other purposes eventually provoked a backlash. Congress in 1944 barred use of any appropriations for an agency created through executive order unless the funds were authorized specifically for that agency.[150]

Roosevelt's use of executive orders frequently stirred controversy. Perhaps the most controversial was Executive Order 9066, issued in 1942, which authorized the forced removal of Americans of Japanese ancestry from the West Coast and their confinement to camps in the southwestern desert for the duration of the war. This order later came to be viewed as a gross violation of the civil liberties of U.S. citizens, but at the time was defended as a safeguard against potential sabotage—though this logic was not applied to citizens of German or Italian descent. Though no citizen of Japanese descent ever was convicted of espionage or sabotage, the Supreme Court in 1944 ruled that Roosevelt had acted legally to protect the nation during wartime.[151]

National security became the primary justification for unilateral executive action in the years after World War II. The cold war between the United States and the Soviet Union expanded U.S. commitments around the world, and a consensus on the need for assertive executive leadership prompted Congress through the 1960s to accede to presidential dictates across a wide spectrum of domestic and international policy domains. Congress so generously delegated foreign policy-making power, in sharp contrast to the tight reins on executive discretion it maintained before World War II, that many scholars characterize the era between the late 1940s and early 1970s as one of relative congressional decline.

In its reluctance to hobble presidential flexibility in international affairs, Congress appeared to surrender many of its traditional prerogatives. As political scientist Allen Schick noted, "when Congress controls, it legislates the particulars; when Congress withdraws, it legislates in general terms."[152] Indeed, statutes in both domestic and foreign policy areas became far less detailed and constraining compared to laws passed before Roosevelt became president. The presidency that evolved from the New Deal through the cold war was the presidency at its least constrained.[153]

Ironically, postwar presidents did not need to rely on executive orders as heavily as their prewar counterparts. For one thing, the accumulation of a large body of administrative law replaced the need for unilateral presidential action in routine matters, such as personnel administration and regulatory procedures. What is more, of almost two thousand executive orders issued between 1945 and 1965, more than 80 percent were based on existing statutory authority, indicating in part the breadth of the statutory web woven after World War II.[154]

Although the frequency with which presidents issue executive orders has declined in the past three decades, the tendency of presidents to use them to bypass or confront Congress has made them even more controversial. Lyndon Johnson, for example, issued an executive order to create minority hiring guidelines for federal contracts after Congress failed to embody affirmative action in the Civil Rights Act of 1964.[155] As with the use of the veto, this tendency is most pronounced among presidents facing a Congress controlled by the other party. Nixon used executive orders to restructure and gain tighter presidential control over the executive branch after Congress turned down his reorganization proposals, Reagan used an executive order to preempt congressional action mandating drug testing for federal employees, and Bush sidestepped Congress to give a new White House Council on Competitiveness the power to assess the economic consequences of new regulations. This council later was abolished by Clinton, whose strategic use of executive orders became more noticeable after the Republican Party took control of Congress in 1994.

EXECUTIVE ORDER 12836
February 1, 1993
Revocation of Certain Executive Orders Concerning Federal Contracting

By the authority vested in me as President by the Constitution and the laws of the United States of America, and in order to eliminate Executive orders that do not serve the public interest, it is hereby ordered as follows:

SECTION 1. Executive Order No. 12818 of October 23, 1992 (prohibiting the use of project agreements on Federal construction contracts), and Executive Order No. 12800 of April 13, 1992 (requiring Federal contractors to post a notice that workers are not required to join unions), are revoked.

SECTION 2. The heads of executive agencies shall promptly revoke any orders, rules, or regulations implementing Executive Order No. 12818 of October 23, 1992 or Executive Order No. 12800 of April 13, 1992, to the extent consistent with law.

William J. Clinton
The White House,
February 1, 1993

SOURCE: Office of the Federal Register, *Weekly Compilation of Presidential Documents,* February 8, 1993 (Washington, D.C.: Government Printing Office, 1993), 120.

ORDERS AS EXECUTIVE LAWMAKING

Postwar presidents issued executive orders for a wide range of purposes, but they tended to use them most strategically in three particular areas: to combat various forms of discrimination against citizens, to increase White House control over the executive branch, and to maintain secrets.

Combating Discrimination

Beginning with Franklin Roosevelt, who eased racial segregation of defense plants during World War II, presidents have used executive orders to safeguard or promote the civil rights of minorities and women. Many orders were applied to operating procedures and rules within executive branch agencies, while others reshaped the implementation of entire federal programs when Congress proved unable or unwilling to act. For example, Harry Truman in 1948 used Executive Order 9981 to integrate the armed forces, an action that, combined with calls within the Democratic Party for stronger civil rights protection, split Democrats during the 1948 election. Dwight Eisenhower in 1957 sent federal troops into Little Rock, Arkansas, to enforce Supreme Court decisions forbidding racial segregation in public schools,[156] while John Kennedy similarly ordered greater federal protection for blacks seeking admission to southern state universities.

Kennedy in 1963 also used Executive Order 11063 to bar racial discrimination in federally subsidized housing after finding the legislative route blocked by southern conservatives. As noted earlier, Lyndon Johnson in 1965 used Executive Order 11246 to direct firms contracting with the federal government to create minority hiring programs after Congress refused to do so in the Civil Rights Act of 1964.[157] Johnson's creation of "affirmative action" was redefined somewhat by Nixon's "Philadelphia Plan," a 1969 executive order instituting racial hiring quotas on federal projects. Nixon's action ran contrary to the 1964 Civil Rights Act, which forbade quotas of any kind, but his order was upheld by a federal court of appeals based partly on the implied power of the president to set federal procurement policies.[158]

Not surprisingly, a great deal of controversy erupts when presidents use executive orders to bypass Congress on issues involving discrimination. Each of the aforementioned cases created considerable public debate, and not a little conflict. A telling example involves a prospective executive order never actually signed: President Clinton's 1993 promise to lift a long-standing ban on homosexuals serving in the military. The proposal erupted into a major political controversy that threatened to overtake Clinton's domestic agenda at a critical time in his young presidency, so he abandoned the idea of an executive order and sought an unofficial compromise with congressional and military leaders that eventually took the form of a directive issued by the military. Clinton's experience suggests that there are limits to the discretionary presidency, at least in peacetime.[159]

Controlling Executive Bureaucracies

The Constitution nowhere spells out the relationship between presidents and employees of the executive branch. Presidents thus have made vigorous use of executive orders to mold and control the activities of federal employees. Such efforts accelerated sharply as the sheer growth in federal responsibilities brought with it an explosion in executive branch size and complexity. One of the contemporary presidency's greatest tasks is to control the federal establishment itself, and the executive order has become an instrument for government management.[160]

Presidents may be vexed most by the tenacity of linkages forged between the professional bureaucracy and Congress. Taken together, the power of Congress over lawmaking and budgets, the tenure offered by civil service rules, and the relatively temporary nature of presidential terms of office make it incredibly hard for presidents and their political appointees to prevent lower-level career employees from bypassing their putative superiors and dealing directly with sympathetic congressional committees. William Howard Taft as early as 1909 (Executive Order 1142) prohibited agency officials from applying to Congress for funds without prior consent from their cabinet secretaries, but it was Franklin Roosevelt who relied most heavily on executive orders to start the first great effort to centralize presidential control over agencies and their expenditures. Executive Order 6166 in 1933, for example, transferred all executive branch budget-making authority from department heads to the Bureau of the Budget. Perhaps more important, Roosevelt in 1939 (Executive Order 8248) moved BOB from the Treasury Department to the newly created Executive Office of the President, thus imposing even greater direct presidential control over bureaucratic actions.

Richard Nixon directed the next powerful effort to centralize presidential control over the bureaucracy. After Congress in 1970 approved the reorganization of the Bureau of the Budget into the Office of Management and Budget, Nixon in Executive Order 11541 directed the new bureau to engage in a more forceful monitoring of all agency programs and budgets. This order effectively began the transformation of OMB from a low-profile budget office into a powerful and controversial policy-making arm of the presidency. Ronald Reagan went further in Executive Order 12291 (1981), which prohibited federal agencies from proposing or issuing a new rule until OMB ensured that the rule's benefits exceeded its costs. Even more important, Executive Order 12498 in 1985 extended OMB's reach to agency "prerulemaking activities," defined as almost any activity that could lead to consideration of the need for a regulation. This order also required OMB to approve an annual "regulatory program" submitted by each agency and prohibited actions not in that program unless cleared by OMB observers.

These directives have had the cumulative effect of endowing OMB with great power to supervise the policy development process in all agencies, stop any rules or policies that are in conflict with the president's agenda, and insert the president's own priorities more squarely into the routines of agency life. Congress in particular criticizes this tendency toward the "centralization" of executive branch power, but most complaints seem to come from those opposing the policies of particular presidents. Future presidents are unlikely to reverse this trend, since the desire to control the bureaucracy is common to Democratic and Republican presidents alike. Whether Congress will continue to acquiesce in this area will be a major question. After all, how much control presidents *should* have over policy implementation is a source of conflict between the branches.[161]

There is even less agreement about presidential efforts to control the personal views or behavior of executive branch employees, efforts that usually derive from desires to ensure "loyalty" or "proper" lifestyles. These efforts have always sparked heated debates about the erosion of civil servants' fundamental civil rights and civil liberties. Woodrow Wilson, for example, used an April 1917 executive order to give agency heads the power to fire any employee judged "inimical" to the public welfare. The order was a way to dismiss anyone alleged to hold socialist or other "un-American" views as the nation prepared for World War I. Later, as the nation became caught in the grip of the cold war between the United States and the Soviet Union, Truman's Executive Order 9825 in 1947 instituted loyalty oaths for all federal employees to root out possible Communist sympathizers. This order later was codified into law by the Summary Suspension Act of 1950.[162]

Contemporary presidents have been less concerned about employees' personal views than with their personal habits, particularly as the nation became concerned about drug and alcohol use. Ronald Reagan in September 1986 (Executive Order 12564) ordered all executive branch agencies to establish random drug-testing programs for all personnel in "sensitive" positions. The order was controversial, even within the Reagan White House, because it was not confined to military or intelligence agencies that already used such tests. Civil libertarians asserted that random tests violate the privacy rights of public employees, but the Supreme Court in 1989 ruled that mandatory drug tests were constitutional under certain conditions.[163]

Maintaining Secrets

The use of executive orders to create a system for classifying government documents or other information in the name of national security has been especially controversial. Governments always have pursued secrecy in sensitive diplomatic or military matters, but the idea that the United States should maintain a formal classification system did not take hold until the eve of World War II, when Franklin Roosevelt in March 1940 authorized the classification of military intelligence information. The test of what constitutes secrets worth classifying, Roosevelt said, "is what the Commander in Chief of the Army and Navy thinks would be harmful to the defense of this country to give out."[164]

Subsequent orders extended classification beyond its original confines as the war progressed, and the trend did not end once hostilities ceased. The exigencies of the cold war instead led presidents to expand the categories of information deemed essential to national security. Truman used two executive orders to extend classification to any executive branch agency when secrecy was deemed essential. Where Roosevelt based his 1940 executive order on the vague authority provided by a 1938 statute classifying military charts, Truman's expansion of secrecy was based simply on an assertion that inherent executive powers gave him the responsibility to do whatever was "necessary and proper" to protect the general welfare.[165] Constitutional scholars debated the legality of Truman's claim but worried even more about the effects of pervasive secrecy on democratic accountability. The government could now classify virtually anything, and there were few mechanisms to guard against the tendency toward overclassification, which is inevitable when agencies consider information a valuable resource, when they break the law in pursuit of other ends, or when they simply wish to hide their mistakes. As presidential scholar Richard Pious noted, "The new system could be used in the conduct of diplomacy to keep Congress uninformed or misinformed."[166]

Dwight Eisenhower in 1953 (Executive Order 10501) similarly asserted a general claim of inherent presidential authority when he attempted to streamline the classification system and narrow secrecy to information critical to "national defense." Despite the outward appearance of reining in overclassification, historian Arthur M. Schlesinger Jr. argued, Eisenhower's order actually gave greater discretionary power to a secretive Interagency

Committee on Internal Security, a panel composed of security officials from various agencies. These officials generally supported extensive classification, and thereafter they would play decisive roles in narrowing public access to government information. Kennedy, who certainly did not shy away from using secrecy in military and diplomatic ventures when it suited his purposes, nonetheless fought against bureaucratic tendencies toward blanket classification of all information. Executive Order 10964, issued in 1962, set up procedures for declassifying or downgrading the classification of information no longer essential to national security, but his efforts were undermined by hardliners within both Congress and the bureaucracy. In fact, notes Schlesinger, the classification system itself eventually was classified.[167]

Secrecy expanded even further under Nixon, who in 1972 (Executive Order 11652) stretched the boundaries of "national security" to encompass any information in "the interest of the national defense or foreign relations of the United States," including information about domestic intelligence activities. Nixon's order was a reaction to the publication of the *Pentagon Papers,* an internal Pentagon study of how the United States became enmeshed in the Vietnam conflict. Civil liberties advocates and Nixon's opponents in Congress charged the White House with broadening secrecy rules and strangling freedom of the press.

Issues of secrecy have changed noticeably with the end of the cold war and the collapse of the Soviet Union. In general, the post–cold war trend has been toward greater declassification, especially of documents dating back to World War II. A particularly interesting and highly charged political twist to this effort concerns documents possibly related to military personnel missing in action or held as prisoners of war during the Vietnam War. President Bush in 1992 issued an executive order expediting the declassification of Vietnam-era documents, and President Clinton expanded this effort with his executive order of November 11, 1993—Veterans' Day.

However, another Clinton executive order may have potentially momentous effects on the long trend toward ever-greater secrecy. Executive Order 12598, which took effect in October 1995, mandates the *automatic* declassification of all government files more than twenty-five years old unless the relevant government agency can show which information should be kept secret for another ten years.[168] In theory, at least, Clinton's order should dramatically limit the range and scope of classification, but, as with any executive order, the actual outcome will depend on how well the order is enforced in the future.

POTENTIAL FOR ABUSE

Not surprisingly, executive orders are controversial because of their great potential for overuse by presidents who are unwilling or unable to work with Congress, frustrated by career bureaucrats and other domestic opposition, or overeager to impose strict secrecy. The discretionary presidency brings with it fears that presidents have become less accountable to congressional oversight, especially in matters of foreign policy, where the president already enjoys significant constitutionally supported leverage.

Potential Threats to Civil Liberties

Besides secrecy, another major controversy since the early 1970s has been the use of executive orders to inaugurate domestic surveillance of persons opposed to presidential foreign policy initiatives. Nixon, for example, in 1971 (Executive Order 11605) unilaterally created sweeping new executive authority to investigate Americans and determine if they were threats to national security. Most of the domestic surveillance was aimed at groups opposed to U.S. action in Vietnam, and included secret wiretapping, breaking into offices, and using informers to infiltrate groups. Details of past activities came to light when Congress held investigative hearings in the mid-1970s, and the ensuing controversies forced Ford and Carter to narrow the range of permissible domestic surveillance actions and to impose stricter control over federal agents.

However, in 1981 Ronald Reagan issued Executive Order 12333, which, in the name of combating possible domestic terrorism, loosened considerably the restrictions put in place by Ford and Carter. Civil libertarians were alarmed because the order sanctioned covert domestic surveillance activities based merely on suspicion that there was "probable cause" to believe that some group might be engaged in terrorist actions, as opposed to the more stringent suspicion of actual crimes applied in criminal law. Critics were even more troubled because the precise guidelines for initiating and conducting investigations themselves were classified.[169] Revelations in 1988 that the Federal Bureau of Investigation had relied on this sweeping authority to conduct an extensive covert surveillance program against groups opposed to U.S. policy in Central America sparked tremendous controversy. Particularly troubling to many was the sheer breadth of the investigation, which had spread to religious groups and labor unions, and the fact that it was based on information allegedly fabricated by an FBI informant. The episode embarrassed the Reagan administration just as it was seeking to generate greater public support for its Latin American policies.

Secret Orders

Problems also can arise when an executive order is based on information that is classified for national security purposes. Federal law mandates the publication of executive orders and proclamations, but it also allows for secret orders in the name of the public interest. For example, Truman's 1952 executive order creating the National Security Agency, the largest and most secretive of the nation's intelligence organizations, itself remained officially classified for more than forty years after the fact.

Another notable example of the problem is Reagan's secret order of September 1986 retroactively authorizing arms shipments to Iran despite an official U.S. embargo against that nation.[170] Reagan did not notify congressional intelligence oversight committees of the arms sales, asserting later that notification was "deferred" to prevent leaks of information that might harm hostages being held in Lebanon by groups allied with Iran. Trouble for the president came when news of the arms sales came to light in the foreign press. Americans reacted with shock and anger to the dealings with Iran, and to the use of the proceeds from the arm sales as financial support for rebels fighting the Nicaraguan government, in apparent violation of a congressional ban on such aid. Whatever the political or strategic merits of the arms sales or of the use of their profits to aid the Nicaraguan rebels, the political damage to the administration grew out of its secrecy and the questionable legality of the whole affair.

The penchant for executive secrecy and, particularly, for keeping Congress completely excluded from foreign policy decision making seems to have lessened a bit since the Iran-contra scandal and since the end of the cold war with the former Soviet Union. George Bush turned noticeably away from the strongly confrontational strategy of his predecessor and tended to seek compromise. Bush also saw to it that congressional leaders were at least notified in advance of major actions, such as U.S. interventions in Panama (1989) and in the Persian Gulf after the Iraqi invasion of Kuwait (1990–1991).[171] Bill Clinton similarly kept congressional leaders informed prior to sending American troops to Haiti in 1994 and Bosnia in 1995.

Compared to the pre-Vietnam period, Congress today also is far more assertive in exercising its oversight responsibilities. Indeed, although the president is likely to retain significant discretion in foreign policy making, the extent to which that discretion can be exercised in secrecy may be far more constrained today than in many years.[172] Still, temptations for secrecy will never subside entirely.

Inertia and Accountability

Heavy reliance on executive orders can take on a life of its own. Presidents may use them instead of seeking congressional action, for example, simply because executive orders have become a "normal" way of operating. What is more, political scientist Phillip Cooper argues, "as orders move from administration to administration within any given issue area, they tend to spin off more policy elements more widely distributed across the policy space than their predecessors."[173] For example, the sheer accumulation of successive orders affecting civil rights and government secrecy over time constructed ever more encompassing policy domains, which Congress found increasingly difficult to influence. Equally important, federal courts usually grant legitimacy to such policies because they are the products of long and consistent practice. The result is lawmaking by executive decree, a reality antithetical to the belief that Congress alone has power to make law, or that Congress at least should be included in executive decision making.

Whether the policies that result from executive orders are good or bad is immaterial. The real question of government by decree is one of democratic accountability. Executive orders by nature exclude Congress—and, by extension, the public—from the process of decision making, often leaving the legislature to catch up after the fact. Few scholars of any political persuasion argue that presidents should not enjoy at least some discretionary authority to administer laws and carry out executive functions. The problem with unilateral presidential actions lies in their tremendous influence, lack of consistent congressional participation, and prospects for ever greater centralization of policy making in the executive branch.

REINING IN THE DISCRETIONARY PRESIDENCY

The period between the start of the New Deal in 1933 and the end of the Watergate era in 1974 probably marked the apogee of what historian Arthur Schlesinger Jr. called the "imperial presidency."[174] By the early 1970s Congress had begun to seek ways to limit what was perceived widely as a gradual but systematic aggregation of expansive executive power and its apparent abuses in both domestic and foreign policy spheres. The war in Vietnam and the "incursion" into Cambodia, excessive use of impoundment, domestic surveillance and other abuses of civil liberties, and, finally, Watergate suggested to many a presidency out of control.

Not surprisingly, the reaction to the "imperial presidency" was to rein in the discretion enjoyed by the chief executive. During the 1970s Congress enacted a wide range of laws and provisions limiting executive discretion, including the 1974 Budget and Impoundment Control Act, legislative vetoes *(see "The Legislative Veto," p. 17)*, shorter term authorization for federal programs or policies to ensure more frequent reviews of executive agencies as the statutes expired, greater use of provisions in appropriations bills dictating how funds were to be spent, freedom of information rules, and additional executive branch reporting responsibilities. Congress also dramatically expanded its own institutional capacities for overseeing the executive branch by hiring thousands of additional staff and by creating or expanding congressional support agencies such as the General Accounting Office and Congressional Budget Office.

In short, Congress since the early 1970s has sought to retake much of the control over governance that it had ceded to the president in previous decades. Congress in the 1990s is involved more forcefully in the routines of federal policy making, and in many ways the power of Congress in the 1990s is far greater relative to that of the presidency than since before Franklin Roosevelt. The decline in presidential discretion can also be attributed to external factors: the end of the sense of crisis that characterized the cold war, constraints on government imposed by the federal budget deficit, and a set of broad political dynamics at work in the United States and abroad that militate against unilateral American action. For many reasons, then, presidents in the 1990s probably have much less discretionary power than even a decade earlier.

But Congress, even a Congress suspicious of executive power, will not abolish the discretionary presidency. Contemporary governance cannot return to the halcyon days of nineteenth-century congressional dominance because Congress cannot legislate in the detail necessary to carry out most government functions. There also remains a great reluctance, even on the part of those members of Congress most critical of executive discretion and bureaucratic policy making, to place too many or too strict limitations on the ability of the president to act quickly or flexibly when conditions require. Congress can no more dictate every nuance or rule of the North American Free Trade Agreement of 1994 than of the Smoot-Hawley Tariff Act of 1930. What is more, the greater fluidity of global politics in the post–cold war world demands a degree of presidential discretion in a broad range of policy realms, be they the use of American troops for humanitarian reasons, the imposition of trade sanctions as an extension of foreign policy, or the capacity to negotiate international environmental agreements.[175] The discretionary presidency is not about to go away.

The Constitution guarantees tension between Congress and the presidency, but the intensity of the friction between the branches tends to run in cycles. As political scientist Allen Schick has pointed out, "The president and other executive officials try to stretch the authority given them by Congress more broadly than might have been intended. Congress responds by narrowing executive discretion. But the new restrictions hobble executive performance and lead to demands for relaxation."[176] Neither branch can achieve complete dominance, because the other always retains a range of constitutional and political resources that ensure both independence and a degree of countervailing power.

Emergency Powers

In times of crisis presidents frequently assert claims to extraordinary unilateral power to preserve the nation, promote the general welfare, or provide for the common good of the people. But the Constitution does not grant express "emergency" powers either to the president or to Congress. Instead, such powers are judged to reside purely in the fundamental need for a nation to protect its sovereignty and to preserve domestic order. To many constitutional scholars the "great silences" in the Constitution imply the existence of an array of residual powers for each branch to draw upon in times of crisis.

The doctrine of emergency powers is a variation of what the Framers knew as the Lockean Prerogative. John Locke, the early eighteenth-century English philosopher, believed strongly in a government of laws. But he also argued that, in dire emergencies, "the laws themselves. . . . give way to the executive power, or rather to this fundamental law of nature and government . . . [namely] that, as much as may be, all the members of society are to be preserved." Limited government was the ideal at all other times, but in emergencies, responsible leaders might have to resort to extraordinary actions simply because legislatures usually are slow to move and the imperative for national self-preservation is superior to legal niceties. Of equal importance, wrote Locke, is "the people's permitting their rulers to do several things of their own free choice, where the law is silent, and sometimes, too, against the direct letter of the law, for the public good, and their acquiescing in it when so done."[177] Locke's views were echoed by the French philosopher Jean Jacques Rousseau who, despite disagreements with Locke on a great many other matters, in the 1760s warned, "It is advisable not to establish political institutions so strongly as to prevent a possibility of suspending their operation."[178]

The Framers of the Constitution were well versed in the writings of philosophers such as Locke and Rousseau, but nowhere in the Constitution did they indicate explicitly that the national government, much less the president, could wield unspecified emergency powers. In fact, the only possible such authority granted to the president was the ability to grant reprieves and pardons (Article II, section 2), which the Framers believed might be useful in resolving domestic insurrections such as Shays's Rebellion of 1786 (which in many ways had prompted the Constitutional Convention in the first place). The Constitution also provided for suspending writs of *habeas corpus* in cases of rebellion or invasion, which would allow for arrest without due cause, but this power was enumerated to Congress in Article I, section 9.[179]

Even so, the notion that government can wield emergency powers is arguably implied in the document. For example, Article II mandates that the president shall "preserve, protect and defend" the Constitution and uphold its provisions. This duty could require the president to bring to bear the commander-in-chief and chief executive powers from which many implied powers arise. What is more, in *The Federalist Papers,* Alexander Hamilton and James Madison both argued that national preservation might be cause for superseding constitutional restrictions.[180] Nonetheless, as Arthur Schlesinger Jr. noted, Hamilton and Madison also warned that those claiming emergency powers did so at their own risk and, having acted, would have to gain support from Congress and the people if constitutional government was to survive.[181]

The debate over emergency powers is a highly practical one. The structure of the U.S. system of government is designed to fragment political power in the name of safeguarding the rights of the states and the people. It is therefore prone to tremendous inertia, even stalemate, since no branch of the national government can easily or quickly overpower the others. These structural constraints might be maddening to participants in "normal" times, but they could be fatal to the Republic when crisis or war intrudes, particularly in a world of intercontinental ballistic missiles and a highly integrated world economy. That the president might have to act quickly and with flexibility when the situation demands was a reality the Framers apparently acknowledged when they created the single executive and endowed it with powers as chief executive and, particularly, as commander in chief.

CATEGORIES AND EXAMPLES OF EMERGENCY POWERS

When emergencies are declared, or during times of crisis, the president has at hand a broad array of potential powers. These emergency powers can be grouped into three categories of actions the president may take:

Powers over Individuals

Confine individuals seen to be threats to national security

Restrict travel of Americans to other nations (such as Cuba) or travel of some foreigners to the United States

Restrict movement of citizens within the United States

Require persons, because of their backgrounds, associations with certain groups, or ownership of particular articles (such as weapons), to register with government officials

Restrict certain persons from working in industries critical to national security

Remove federal employees regarded as threats to national security

Suspend writs of *habeas corpus*

Declare martial law

Assign armed forces to conflicts in foreign nations

Powers over Property

Order stockpiling of strategic materials (such as uranium)

Impose restrictions on exports (such as computer equipment)

Allocate materials in ways necessary to aid national defense

Require industries to give priority to government contracts and seize industries failing to comply with such orders

Fix wages and prices

Powers over Communications

Withhold information from Congress and the public deemed potentially sensitive to national security

Monitor and censor communications between United States and other nations

Require foreign representatives to register with U.S. government.

SOURCES: U.S. Congress, House of Representatives, Subcommittee on Administrative Law and Governmental Relations, Committee on the Judiciary, Hearings on H.R. 3884, *National Emergencies Act*, 94th Cong., 1st sess., March 6–April 9, 1975, 22–23; Robert E. DiClerico, *The American President* (Englewood Cliffs, N.J.: Prentice-Hall, 1979), chap. 8.

Thus, in times of crisis the question is not who should lead. Rather, it is how to preserve the nation and the Constitution when the future of the Republic is threatened. Abraham Lincoln, in defending his remarkable usurpation of power during the early months of the Civil War, asked simply, "Is there in all republics this inherent and fatal weakness? Must a government of necessity be too strong for the liberties of its people, or too weak to maintain its own existence?" Or, as Lincoln later asked, "Was it possible to lose the nation and yet preserve the Union?"[182]

Lincoln's experiences during the Civil War were unique, but history is dotted with other moments when this dilemma emerged powerfully. Few doubt the need for presidents to wield extraordinary powers in times when the crisis is apparent to all, but debates rage when a "crisis" is not so apparent or when claims to emergency powers seem overstated.

That is the problem of emergency powers. "Whether intentionally or not," political scientists Erwin Hargrove and Michael Nelson have written, "the Constitution conferred prerogative power in times of emergency on the president. Efforts to define 'emergency' by legislation and thus limit the president in such cases have run up against Locke's warning of the futility of trying to legislate for cases yet unknown."[183] The nation's history has been marked by recurrent tensions between presidential claims to extraordinary powers and the right of Congress to impose its constitutional will. It is a struggle that probably will never be resolved entirely.

POWERS IN WARTIME

The United States has entered into five declared wars, one civil war, and numerous undeclared hostilities in its history. In each instance presidents invariably have asserted claims to some type of emergency powers to deal with the threat, but as presidential scholar Louis Koenig argues, the justifications have differed starkly. The "Lincolnian Pattern" asserts an aggressively broad view of the president's inherent war powers, based largely on wedding the presidential oath of office with the commander-in-chief and "take care" clauses. The decision by President George Bush in 1989 to send troops into Panama to capture General Manual Noriega, Panama's leader and a reputed leader in the international drug trade, could be seen in this light. The "Joint President-Congress Pattern," by contrast, involves broad congressional grants of executive authority to prosecute the war but maintains an official argument that presidential powers are statutory as opposed to inherent.[184] Woodrow Wilson and Franklin Roosevelt, during World Wars I and II respectively, followed this pattern.

Neither pattern is a pure type, of course, and every president exercises a mix of inherent and delegated war powers simultaneously. For example, Bush requested official congressional approval for armed action against Iraq during the Persian Gulf War of 1990–1991, but he nonetheless claimed an inherent power as commander in chief to carry out military actions should Congress not approve.[185] The difference between the two rationales lies in the specific claims presidents make to justify their actions when hostilities loom. These distinctions have become increasingly important as war itself has changed from the relatively stately styles of the eighteenth century to the more sudden and violent spasms typical of armed conflict today.

The Supreme Court throughout history has upheld presidential claims to some range of emergency powers when the nation was involved in hostilities. The earliest important test came during the War of 1812, when several New England governors challenged President James Madison's request that their state militias take up specific defense responsibilities. Madison's order was based on authority granted by Congress in the Militia Act of 1795, but the governors' resistance was upheld by their respective state high courts. However, in 1827, long after the end of hostilities with England, the Supreme Court ruled that Madison could overrule state governors because the president alone defines emergencies when the nation is at war or is faced with imminent hostilities.[186]

The Madison case was the exception to pre–Civil War claims of presidential emergency powers. In most instances, presidents deployed U.S. forces against pirates abroad or Indian uprisings at home to protect American citizens and their property. Their actions usually were based on a specific congressional grant of authority, such as the power that Congress gave James Monroe to protect American merchant ships against pirates, or the congressional declaration of war on Mexico in 1846. In general, early presidents—even the headstrong Andrew Jackson—exhibited a great deal of restraint in exercising their commander-in-chief responsibilities.

Lincoln and Inherent War Powers

Such presidential restraint was abandoned during the Civil War. Faced with secession by the states of the Confederacy, Abraham Lincoln claimed such an extensive array of emergency war powers to preserve the Union that he became, in the words of presidential scholar Clinton Rossiter, a "constitutional dictator."[187] On the other hand, Lincoln did run for reelection in 1864. However one characterizes Lincoln, there is little doubt that he used extraordinary and often unconstitutional means to quell the rebellion.

Congress was not in session when Fort Sumter fell in April 1861. With the onset of hostilities, Lincoln unilaterally proclaimed a blockade of Southern ports, mobilized state militias, increased the size of the army and navy, sent weapons to unionists in Virginia who established the state of West Virginia, authorized construction of ships for the navy, and appropriated funds for purchases of war materiel. Lincoln conveniently failed to call Congress into session for eleven weeks; when he did, he claimed his actions were justified by the inherent prerogative powers of the presidency, especially as commander in chief. Congress ultimately gave Lincoln retroactive authority for his actions, even though some (such as expanding the army and spending unappropriated funds) clearly were unconstitutional. Legal nuances paled before the emergency at hand, however, and Lincoln continued to assume and exercise independent war powers even with Congress in session.

This same sense of emergency led the Supreme Court to support many of Lincoln's claims. In the *Prize Cases* (1863), shipowners whose vessels were seized trying to run the Union blockade of Southern ports sued on the grounds that the blockade itself was unconstitutional because Congress had not declared war.[188] This was technically true but, the Court ruled, the South nonetheless was enemy territory and Lincoln was required to preserve the Union. However, as Arthur Schlesinger Jr. points out, the justices endorsed such executive power only in cases of domestic rebellions or invasions, and not, as some later presidents asserted, for use against other sovereign nations.[189]

The Union also faced insurrection behind its own lines. The problems were keenest around Washington, D.C., with secessionist Virginia on one side and Maryland filled with rebel sym-

PROCEDURES FOR EMERGENCY ORDERS

The National Emergencies Act of 1976 (PL 94–412) terminated all states of emergency legally in effect until that time, including some dating as far back as the 1930s. The act also set in place procedures for declaring and, equally important, terminating future states of emergency. As this brief overview suggests, the provisions of the National Emergencies Act were intended to force Congress and the president, acting singly or together, to ensure that any state of emergency does not outlive the conditions upon which it was based.

The president by law cannot declare a state of national emergency without also specifying the provisions of existing law or constitutional provisions under which the proposed action falls. Furthermore, any proclamation of a national emergency must be transmitted immediately to Congress and published in the *Federal Register*.

During a declared national emergency the president and all relevant executive branch agencies or departments must maintain files on all rules, regulations, executive orders, or any other activities carried out to address the emergency. This information must be transmitted promptly to Congress. Matters requiring confidentiality are to be handled in a prescribed manner (for example, restricted to members of congressional intelligence committees and those staff members with security clearances). All expenditures made by the executive branch to address the emergency also must be reported to Congress within ninety days after each six-month period following the declaration of the emergency.

The law also specifies how states of emergency are to be terminated. No later than six months after an emergency is declared, the two houses of Congress must meet to consider a concurrent resolution to determine whether the emergency should be terminated. The resolution must go through the normal congressional procedures, but according to a specific schedule to avoid delays. Should Congress be unable or unwilling to terminate the emergency (perhaps because of some disagreement between the House and the Senate), it must consider another such resolution within the next six-month period.

The president can terminate unilaterally a declared state of emergency when it is deemed that the conditions mandating the emergency have passed. But, to avoid another situation where states of emergency endure legally for decades, the law calls for automatic termination of an emergency upon the anniversary of its declaration, unless the president previously notifies Congress (and publishes in the *Federal Register*) of the need to continue the emergency. One way or another, states of emergency are to be terminated.

pathizers on the other. The mayor of Baltimore was decidedly pro-Confederate; mobs attacked federal troops; bridges were sabotaged; and the Maryland legislature was about to convene with the real possibility of voting to secede. Lincoln responded by declaring martial law and suspending writs of *habeas corpus* behind the Northern lines, thus allowing military authorities to arrest without warrants members of the Maryland legislature and other rebel sympathizers. Lincoln also suppressed opposition newspapers and ordered censorship of postal and telegraph communications. Some of these actions provoked clashes with the judiciary. In *Ex parte Merryman* (1861), Chief Justice Roger B. Taney, sitting as a circuit court judge, ruled that Lincoln had usurped the sole power of Congress to suspend writs of *habeas corpus* during an emergency.[190] Lincoln flagrantly ignored Taney, whose majority opinion in the controversial *Dred Scott* decision five years earlier was widely reviled in the North, and Congress later affirmed Lincoln's actions in the Habeas Corpus Act of 1863.

But Lincoln's continued reliance on preemptive arrests and use of military courts to try civilians set in motion another confrontation. In *Ex parte Milligan* (1866), the Supreme Court ruled that Lincoln lacked the constitutional authority to use military courts behind Northern lines so long as the civil judicial system remained intact. The Constitution worked "equally in war and in peace," said the justices, and national preservation was not cause enough to violate its principles.[191]

However, Lincoln was already dead and the Civil War over by the time the Court ruled. *Milligan* thus joined a number of judicial decisions that over time would create doubts about whether the Court would challenge a sitting president during national crises. These doubts reemerged during World War II when Franklin Roosevelt ordered some 112,000 Japanese-Americans from their homes on the West Coast to internment camps in the southwestern desert. The forced relocation was challenged in the courts, but with no great effect on Roosevelt's actions.[192]

World War and Delegated Powers

Unlike Lincoln, both Woodrow Wilson and Franklin Roosevelt fought wars on foreign soil based largely on powers at least broadly delegated to them by Congress. By the twentieth century, the nature of war itself had changed. Both World War I and World War II were "total wars," in which the lines between combatants and civilians were blurred; struggles involved not only armies but the entire social, economic, and industrial capacities of nations; and control over national populations was key to success. Total war thus required swift, massive, and sustained national organization and mobilization, the capacities for which lay mostly in the executive branch.

In both cases Congress recognized these realities and delegated broad powers to the presidency to carry out military functions and to regulate the domestic economy. In 1917 Congress passed a spate of laws granting Wilson a range of war-related powers: the Lever Food and Fuel Control Act empowered the president to seize defense-related facilities, to regulate food production, manufacturing, and mining, and to fix prices on commodities; the Selective Service Act enabled the president to raise an army; the Espionage Act gave Wilson the power to restrict exports; the Trading with the Enemy Act authorized the president to regulate and censor external communications. Wilson also was granted broad authority to monitor actions by resident aliens, to regulate or operate transportation and communications facilities, and to reorganize executive branch agencies where necessary. In effect, Wilson was granted almost free rein to conduct the war and to maintain the domestic economy. This pattern of congressional delegation was repeated a little more than two decades later for Franklin Roosevelt.[193]

Even with generous congressional delegation of emergency powers, neither Wilson nor Roosevelt shied away from asserting inherent prerogatives as commander in chief. Both claimed the right to go beyond the scope of congressional authorization and to create wartime agencies, to enforce "voluntary" press censorship, and to coordinate private industry. Roosevelt in particular claimed emergency powers to sidestep congressional declarations of neutrality as Europe fell into war. In 1939 he declared a "limited" state of emergency, which allowed him to invoke existing statutes (many of which had been enacted in Wilson's day) to prepare the nation militarily. In early 1941 he declared an "unlimited" state of emergency under which he reorganized the executive branch and prepared to deal with the domestic economy once the United States entered into hostilities. In neither instance did Roosevelt get prior congressional authorization for his actions, although he usually tried to cloak his actions in existing statutory powers.

Once Congress declared war, however, Roosevelt dropped even the pretense of delegated powers. His seizure of defense plants immediately after Pearl Harbor, for example, was based on claims of authority given to him by the Constitution and "the laws," although he never made clear which ones. His most intriguing claim came in 1942, when he asked Congress to repeal legislation regulating farm prices. If Congress did not do so, Roosevelt warned, he would repeal the provisions himself because "the president has the powers, under the Constitution and under congressional acts, to take measures necessary to avert a disaster which would interfere with the winning of the war."[194] Congress quickly gave in, so whether Roosevelt would have acted on his threat was never tested.

Truman and the Limits of Emergency Powers

Neither Wilson nor Roosevelt made sweeping claims to *inherent* emergency powers during either world war. Both made at least an effort to base their actions on broad statutory authority. Subsequent presidents operated differently, however, as the United States in the late 1940s began a period of prolonged confrontation with the Soviet Union. Conventional war gave way to indeterminate friction, with the potential for catastrophic thermonuclear war at one extreme and localized wars of containment at the other. This period also would be characterized by a permanent military establishment and the "imperial presiden-

JUSTICE JACKSON'S TEST OF PRESIDENTIAL EMERGENCY POWERS

Justice Robert Jackson's concurring opinion in *Youngstown Sheet and Tube Co. v. Sawyer* (1952) remains a classic analysis of the conditions under which a president may in fact possess extraordinary powers.[1] More important, Jackson's dispassionate examination suggests when those emergency powers may not exist.

Mr. Justice Jackson, concurring:

The actual art of governing under our Constitution does not and cannot conform to judicial definitions of the power of any of its branches based on isolated clauses or even single Articles torn from context. While the Constitution diffuses power the better to secure liberty, it also contemplates that practice will integrate the dispersed powers into a workable government. It enjoins upon its branches separateness but interdependence, autonomy but reciprocity. Presidential powers are not fixed but fluctuate, depending upon their disjunction or conjunction with those of Congress. We may well begin by a somewhat oversimplified grouping of practical situations in which a President may doubt, or others may challenge, his powers, and by distinguishing roughly the legal consequences of this factor of relativity.

1. When the President acts pursuant to an express or implied authorization of Congress, his authority is at its maximum, for it includes all that he possesses in his own right plus all that Congress can delegate. In these circumstances, and in these only, may he be said (for what it may be worth) to personify the federal sovereignty. If his act is held unconstitutional under these circumstances, it usually means that the Federal Government as an undivided whole lacks power. A seizure executed by the President pursuant to an Act of Congress would be supported by the strongest of presumptions and the widest latitude of judicial interpretation, and the burden of persuasion would rest heavily upon any who might attack it.

2. When the President acts in absence of either a congressional grant or denial of authority, he can only rely upon his own independent powers, but there is a zone of twilight in which he and Congress may have concurrent authority, or in which its distribution is uncertain. Therefore, congressional inertia, indifference or quiescence may sometimes, at least as a practical matter, enable, if not invite, measures on independent presidential responsibility. In this area, any actual test of power is likely to depend on the imperatives of events and contemporary imponderables rather than on abstract theories of law.

3. When the President takes measures incompatible with the expressed or implied will of Congress, his power is at its lowest ebb, for then he can rely only upon his own constitutional powers minus any constitutional powers of Congress over the matter. Courts can sustain exclusive presidential control in such a case only by disabling the Congress from acting upon the subject. Presidential claim to a power at once so conclusive and preclusive must be scrutinized with caution, for what is at stake is the equilibrium established by our constitutional system.

Into which of these classifications does this executive seizure of the steel industry fit? It is eliminated from the first by admission, for it is conceded that no congressional authorization exists for this seizure. That takes away also the support of the many precedents and declarations which were made in relation, and must be confined, to this category.

Can it then be defended under flexible tests available to the second category? It seems clearly eliminated from that class because Congress has not left seizure of private property an open field but has covered it by three statutory policies inconsistent with this seizure. In cases where the purpose is to supply needs of the Government itself, two courses are provided: one, seizure of a plant which fails to comply with obligatory orders placed by the Government; another condemnation of facilities, including temporary use under the power of eminent domain. The third is applicable where it is the general economy of the country that is to be protected rather than exclusive governmental interests. None of these were invoked. In choosing a different and inconsistent way of his own, the President cannot claim that it is necessitated or invited by failure of Congress to legislate upon the occasions, grounds, and methods for seizure of industrial properties.

This leaves the current seizure to be justified only by the severe tests under the third grouping, where it can be supported only by any remainder of executive power after subtraction of such powers as Congress may have over the subject. In short, we can sustain the President only by holding that seizure of such strike-bound industries is within his domain and beyond control of Congress. Thus, this court's first review of such seizures occurs under circumstances which leave presidential power most vulnerable to attack and in the least favorable of possible constitutional postures.

1. *Youngstown Sheet and Tube Co. v. Sawyer*, 343 U.S. 579 (1952).

cy."[195] Boundaries between war and peace no longer were clear, and the sheer scope of the meaning of national security (defense, intelligence, economic health, scientific advances—to name a few dimensions) gave presidents greater potential power than ever before in virtually every aspect of national affairs.

The cold war era debate over inherent powers first emerged in 1952. Harry Truman had put the nation on a war footing in 1950 after the invasion of South Korea by North Korea, and in late 1951 he ordered the seizure of strike-threatened steel mills to avoid shortages. Truman based his action not on his statutory authority to resolve labor disputes but "on the authority vested in me by the Constitution and laws of the United States, and as President of the United States and Commander in Chief of the armed forces of the United States."[196] When challenged on this rationale Truman argued simply, "The President has very great inherent powers to meet national emergencies."[197]

Congress did not respond, despite broad antipathy to Truman's action, because of the perceived exigencies of wartime. But the Supreme Court, in *Youngstown Sheet and Tube Co. v. Sawyer* (1952), declared the seizure of the steel mills unconstitutional because Congress in passing the 1947 Taft-Hartley Labor Act had not given presidents any right to take over industrial facilities shut down by strikes.[198] The majority suggested that presidents did not possess emergency powers, yet four out of the five justices concurring in the majority decision did not reject this notion outright. Their concurring opinions suggested that emergency prerogatives might exist when presidents act in accordance with the express or implied will of Congress, or in the absence of congressional action. *(See box, Justice Jackson's Test of Presidential Emergency Powers, p. 53.)* Congressional opposition places the presidency in its weakest constitutional position, these justices argued, and Truman's action could not be supported because it so clearly violated congressional intent.

Truman's greatest problem in the steel seizure case probably came from overstating the gravity of the situation. If Congress and the people had backed Truman—as they had backed Roosevelt in the internment of Japanese-Americans—it is doubtful that the Court would have challenged his claims. As Clinton Rossiter argues, "the Court's power of judicial review is least useful when most needed," since actions that may violate constitutional safeguards are likeliest to occur during perceived emergencies.[199] Indeed, the cold war period spawned a generation of scholars concerned that the nation's strategic commitments and ongoing readiness for war created conditions ripe for unfettered claims to inherent presidential war powers and for sudden executive action even in the absence of clear and broadly perceived emergencies. Whether such concerns will continue in the post–cold war world is as yet uncertain, if for no other reason than the nation's global role is as active as in the past.

POWERS IN ECONOMIC CRISES

Presidents also wield emergency powers during periods of serious economic instability outside of actual wartime. During such times it appears that presidential power emanates exclusively from statutes, although presidents have shown ingenuity in stretching the boundaries of that authority. For example, the Trading with the Enemy Act of 1917 gave the president the authority to impose an array of economic measures in times of war or national emergency. This law was intended as a wartime measure, but it was not repealed at war's end. Subsequent presidents discovered, usually to their delight, the apparent statutory justification for emergency actions to manage a faltering economy.

The best lesson on how to rely on "old" statutory authority came in 1933, when the newly inaugurated Franklin Roosevelt faced the imminent collapse of the nation's financial system. The day after his inauguration, Roosevelt declared a national state of emergency and closed the banks, basing his actions on the Trading with the Enemy Act. Roosevelt's interpretation of an old wartime statute was hotly debated, but it nonetheless reflected his desire to cloak his action in legal authority. Congress sanctioned his move three days later when it passed the Emergency Banking Act, and in the following months it granted Roosevelt a wide range of new powers to address the economic emergency. In fact, the single greatest outpouring of major legislation in peacetime U.S. history took place between March 9 and June 16, 1933, known to history as the "First Hundred Days."

Roosevelt's actions had been taken in response to a stark crisis, but Richard Nixon's August 1971 declaration of emergency in response to a growing imbalance in the U.S. balance of payments struck many observers as overly dramatic. Nixon used this declared emergency to disconnect the value of the dollar from the gold standard, levy a 10 percent surtax on imports, and freeze domestic prices for ninety days. The overall effect was to devalue the dollar, drive down the prices of American goods overseas, and temporarily halt inflation. Nixon based his actions on the Economic Stabilization Act of 1970, which authorized the president to "issue such orders as he may deem appropriate to stabilize prices, rents, wages and salaries," although he had signed the law only because it also had contained provisions affecting national defense.[200] Whatever the merits of Nixon's actions, they nonetheless showed the capacity of a determined president to stretch the boundaries of congressional authorization.

POWERS DURING DOMESTIC UNREST

Presidential emergency powers also include the authority to call out federal troops or to take control of state national guards (descendants of the state militias) to quell domestic unrest or to deter violence. Such authority has been used in the United States to put down illegal labor strikes, ensure delivery of the mail, impose order during natural disasters and urban riots, and prevent volatile situations from exploding.

Before the 1940s, and particularly during the late nineteenth century, presidential involvement in domestic disorders came most frequently during labor strikes. Until the passage of the Wagner Act of 1933, which ensured the right to collective bargaining and which established procedures for labor negotiations, strikes usually were considered illegal and often resulted in dramatic outbreaks of violence between strikers and company security forces. This was true particularly in the coal mining, steel, railroad, and, later, automobile industries—sectors in which relations between companies and workers were adversarial in the best of times. The presidential use of troops to break the 1894 Pullman strike in Chicago was but one famous example of a practice that virtually had ended by the 1950s.

During the 1950s and 1960s presidents relied on federal troops or state national guards to ensure calm in situations involving racial desegregation. The first and perhaps most notable case came in 1957, when Dwight Eisenhower sent troops into Little Rock, Arkansas, to enforce desegregation of the public schools in the face of resistance from state officials and angry mobs. John Kennedy in 1961 "federalized" the Mississippi National Guard to ensure the peaceful integration of the University of Mississippi, and in 1963 he confronted Alabama governor George Wallace when he sent federal troops to enforce the integration of the University of Alabama. Kennedy, and Lyndon Johnson after him, also used troops to protect civil rights marchers on several occasions.

During the late 1960s troops were used frequently to quell urban riots or to maintain order during demonstrations against U.S. involvement in Vietnam. For example, the April 1968 assassination of civil rights leader Martin Luther King Jr. sparked widespread rioting throughout more than one hundred cities and forced Lyndon Johnson and various governors to call out some 55,000 troops.[201] President Nixon in May 1970 called out troops to maintain order on a number of college campuses following the deaths of students at Kent State University in Ohio and at Jackson State University in Mississippi during protests against the U.S. incursion into Cambodia.

Nixon also figured in a different kind of military mobilization. In March 1970 he responded to a postal strike in New York, which threatened to cripple postal service nationally, by declaring a state of emergency and calling out federal troops to take over the postal system and keep mail deliveries flowing. Nixon's use of troops to sort and deliver the mail was unusual, but it showed how presidents can react to potential disturbances.

POWERS DURING NATURAL DISASTERS

Presidents rely on statutory authority to declare states of emergency in areas of the country hit by hurricanes, floods, earthquakes, or other natural disasters. By declaring a place a "natural disaster area," the president sets in motion the government machinery that can provide immediate aid, such as food, shelter, and police protection, not to mention longer-term assistance such as federally guaranteed low-interest home and business loans. In doing so, the federal government ensures that the economic effects of the disaster will be softened somewhat.

Not surprisingly, even governors who normally decry federal meddling in state affairs are quick to request such a presidential designation when natural disasters strike. In recent years such billion-dollar disasters as Hurricane Andrew, which in 1992 devastated south Florida, the massive floods along the Mississippi River in 1993, and the Northridge earthquake in southern California in 1993 prompted state calls for federal assistance, which was given in short order.

THE PERMANENT EMERGENCY

Most Americans probably never realized that the United States officially lived under a state of declared national emergency from 1933 to 1975. While President Truman in 1952 terminated Roosevelt's pre–World War II emergencies (declared in 1939 and 1941) that had granted the president greater discretion to direct defense preparations, organize the executive branch, and mobilize the nation for potential hostilities, four other states of emergency were still in force as of 1975: Roosevelt's bank emergency (1933), Truman's mobilization following North Korea's invasion of South Korea (1950), Nixon's use of troops to maintain mail deliveries (1970), and Nixon's response to international economic conditions (1971).

In none of these cases had Congress specified a termination date for the emergency, nor had it written into most of the statutes provisions for terminating the president's emergency authority. The reasons for such omissions lie in the nature of the emergencies themselves. Emergency declarations usually are drafted in the White House and rushed through Congress in the heat of crisis. In 1933, for example, legislators approved the law authorizing Roosevelt's emergency powers to alleviate the bank crisis after only eight hours of debate.[202] Critics of unrestrained presidential power worried that these unexpired states of emergency gave the president the technical authority to invoke a wide range of emergency powers when no crisis seemed imminent. These powers included the right to seize private property and regulate private enterprise, to organize and control all means of production and transportation, to call up reservists and assign military forces overseas, to institute martial law, and to restrict travel.[203]

The potential gravity of this condition of permanent emergency hit home in 1972 as a result of friction between Congress and the Nixon administration following the 1970 U.S. incursion into Cambodia. Members of the Senate Foreign Relations Committee asked Secretary of Defense Melvin R. Laird what would happen if Congress cut off all funds for continued U.S. involvement in Indochina. They were understandably surprised when Laird argued that the president could bypass Congress entirely and spend unappropriated funds through authority granted in a 1799 "feed and forage" statute. This law, enacted during a time when Congress met only half a year at a time, allowed the Secretary of War to get advance funding to provide supplies to American soldiers in remote outposts without having to await congressional appropriation. This provision was still on the books almost 170 years later and, at least theoretically, so too was the president's emergency power.[204]

Congressional Democrats, bruised after years of fights with Nixon, were greatly disturbed by this assertion, and they became concerned that other such laws might still apply years after their passage. Senate leaders created a Special Committee on National Emergencies and Delegated Powers to investigate the possible extent of presidential emergency powers. This committee discovered the continued existence of approximately 470 statutes dealing with emergency situations, and it learned that the aforementioned four states of emergency technically remained in effect.[205]

These findings prompted Congress to pass the National Emergencies Act of 1976, which officially terminated all of these states of emergency as well as the presidential powers stemming from the initial declarations of emergency. The law also established presidential authority to declare future states of national emergency in ways that clearly defined presidential powers during the emergency, provided for congressional review, and mandated that states of emergency would lapse after six months unless renewed.[206] The law does not require the president to consult with Congress before initially declaring a state of emergency, which everyone knew might not be feasible, but does mandate that the president specify clearly the nature of the emergency and the statutory powers to be invoked in response. Congress did not try to legislate for all emergencies but sought to ensure presidential accountability after declarations of emergency.[207]

The National Emergencies Act must be seen as part of a broader effort by Congress during the 1970s to rein in the discretionary aspects of the "imperial presidency" that had taken shape since the 1930s. In 1977 Congress amended the World War I era Trading with the Enemy Act, curbing executive authority to impose economic controls during presidentially declared states of emergency. The revised law defined a limited range of economic controls that presidents could employ without calling an actual state of national emergency, including the power to regulate foreign currency transactions, set embargoes against other nations, and freeze foreign assets. But Congress also confined the act's broader authority to actual wartime, making more explicit what had been implied.

ASSESSING PRESIDENTIAL POWER

There is an understandable tendency to examine the presidency in a context of crisis. Crises, after all, compel presidents to respond quickly and forcefully, and some have done so in ways that expanded presidential power thereafter. Lincoln, for example, claimed for the office a range of inherent war powers that endure in some form to this day. Franklin Roosevelt established the president's capacity to address economic problems, to aid allies in times of trouble, and to prepare the nation for war. The actions taken by contemporary presidents, whether George Bush's mobilization of American armed forces in response to Iraqi aggression against Kuwait, or Bill Clinton's use of presidential powers to mobilize a response to massive flooding in the Mississippi River system, are but variations on an older theme.

However, to study the presidency exclusively through the lens of crisis response is to introduce systematic inaccuracies into one's understanding of how the institution works and how it relates to the other parts of the national government. After all, episodes like the 1962 Cuban Missile Crisis, the subject of innumerable studies of presidential leadership, remain the exception to the rule. Emergencies are extraordinary times, and to use a crisis as the archetype of presidential leadership fosters the impression of greater presidential power and discretion than may in reality exist in a system in which political authority is shared among separate branches. Indeed, in many ways contemporary presidents, even popular ones like Reagan, always end up confronting a gap between public expectations of presidential power and the reality of what presidents actually can attain in ordinary times.

The crisis model of presidential leadership also may foster in the White House a view of leadership that can exist only during crises: the need to respond quickly to problems with little or no consultation with Congress, the temptation to resort to extraconstitutional (even unconstitutional) means to achieve important ends, and the tendency to function as if the president were above the law. Such attitudes—which some observers saw in Nixon's 1970 decision to invade Cambodia and Reagan's efforts to support rebels in Nicaragua—ultimately may do the institution of the presidency more harm than good if they invite congressional and public backlash. The ultimate lesson of emergency powers is to know when they are appropriate, not merely expedient.

The President as Chief Law Enforcement Officer

"All is gloom in the eastern states," wrote John Marshall in January of 1787.[208] Farmers, many of them veterans of the American Revolution, sought and were denied legislative or judicial relief from their debt. Under the leadership of Daniel Shays, a former officer of George Washington's army, farmers had revolted in Massachusetts. Would, as Marshall plainly worried, the American experiment survive?

It did survive. Shays's Rebellion was suppressed by Massachusetts militia, though not without considerable effort. The national government, such as it existed at the time, was powerless to assist.

Debtors, however, remained resentful, and property owners had become apprehensive. The political leadership of the United States sought a more durable remedy, and a more durable remedy was found.

In February 1787, the thirteen states of the United States were invited by Congress to send delegates to a May convention for the purpose of amending the Articles of Confederation. At the urging of leaders such as James Madison and Alexander Hamilton, however, the convention summarily rejected the Articles as a basis for continued political union among the thirteen states. The convention's new formula for government was proposed by Congress on September 17, 1787, and ratified by the requisite nine states the following year. On June 21, 1788, the U.S. Constitution became the supreme law of the land.

It would be excessive to say that Shays's Rebellion was the single or even the most significant event leading to the adoption of the Constitution; serious defects in the Articles had been generally known well before the Massachusetts farmers revolted. The contribution of Shays to the Constitution, rather, was to force the political leadership of the various states to do what they already knew had to be done. Shays aroused "an emotional surge" in favor of a new constitution.[209]

Thus, "We the People of the United States" sought, among other things, to "form a more perfect Union, establish Justice, [and] insure domestic Tranquility."[210] The people would not repeat the mistake of the Confederation; Americans would not render the national government powerless to promote domestic tranquility and justice.

The president, said the Constitution, would "take Care that the Laws be faithfully executed" and would preside as chief executive over what would become a vast law enforcement apparatus. The president could invoke the authority of "commander in chief" and deploy the armed forces, including units of state militia, to enforce the law. And, since mercy may be a more effective means of promoting domestic tranquility than the sword, the president would be given extensive clemency authority—the power to grant pardons and reprieves. The president would become the chief law enforcement officer of the United States.[211]

Presidential law enforcement power has grown in rough proportion to enlargements in the responsibilities and power of the national government itself. In 1789, the year Washington was inaugurated as the nation's first president, the national government generally restricted itself to activities such as collecting customs duties, suppressing domestic insurrections, enforcing federal court orders, and regulating American Indian tribes, the mails, and the army and navy. The law enforcement responsibility and power of the national government was potentially great, but actually weak.

This has changed, as Congress has added substantially to the law enforcement responsibility and power of the national government. Throughout most of the nineteenth century, direct federal enforcement of the law remained limited in scope. Congress generally left enforcement to state and local authorities. The states consequently had great discretion in deciding whether to enforce a federal statute. The move toward greater federal enforcement of the law was hastened in the final two decades of the nineteenth century and during the presidential administrations of Theodore Roosevelt, William Howard Taft, and Woodrow Wilson. Increased federal regulatory power was a fundamental element of Franklin D. Roosevelt's New Deal. With the peace following the World War II came novel and renewed demands for national regulation, demands that have been largely met.

As Congress added to the "police power" of the national government, that is, the power to regulate the health, safety, morals, and general welfare of the nation, it also increased the enforcement power of the executive branch. It supplemented the authority already vested directly in the president by the Constitution, or prior congressional act, and it gave the president additional resources to exercise these grants more effectively and with more power.

Congress has not relinquished its own considerable power over law enforcement. To the contrary, it has insisted that power in law enforcement be shared between the president and Congress. The role of each actor, and the relationship of each to the other, must be understood. So must the unique contribution of the judicial branch to the power of the president in law enforcement.

LAW ENFORCEMENT BY THE U.S. GOVERNMENT

The U.S. Constitution delegates limited power to the government of the United States. This means, essentially, that the U.S. national government possesses only those powers that are specifically granted to it by the Constitution, or those that can be fairly implied from specific grants and that are not limited by any other constitutional provision.

The Constitution itself does not give any branch of the national government explicit authority to regulate the health, safety, morals, or general welfare of the community.[212] Nonetheless, that result has been obtained. Although the Constitution does not make a grant of general police power to the national government, it does grant or enumerate a variety of powers that have been shaped, constitutionally and politically, into what now resembles a general national police power.

Article I, section 8, of the Constitution enumerates a variety of powers that may be exercised by Congress. To name only a few such powers: Congress may impose and collect taxes, regulate immigration, print currency and punish counterfeiters, provide postal service, and regulate the armed forces and military bases of the United States. Congress may also regulate commerce "among the several States" (the "commerce clause" of the Constitution). These powers constitute just a portion of the significant law enforcement authority of the national government. The basis for an expansive federal law enforcement power is found in the final clause of Article I, section 8, the "necessary and proper clause" of the Constitution: "The Congress shall have Power . . . To make all Laws which shall be necessary and proper for carrying into Execution the foregoing Powers, and all other Powers vested by this Constitution in the Government of the United States, or in any Department or Officer thereof." The U.S. Supreme Court has interpreted the necessary and proper clause of the Constitution to enlarge the enumerated powers of Congress so that it can exercise expansive police or regulatory powers.

In the 1819 case *McCulloch v. Maryland*,[213] the Court was asked to determine whether the Constitution gave Congress authority to charter a national bank when such a power was not among those specifically granted the legislative branch. If the national government was to be a government of limited, enumerated powers, the state of Maryland argued, then the Court must find that Congress had exceeded its authority.

Writing on behalf of a unanimous Court, Chief Justice John Marshall agreed completely with Maryland's contention that Congress is granted only limited regulatory power by the Constitution. He also conceded that chartering a national bank is not listed in Article I, section 8. Marshall was too clever a legal logician, however, and too ardent a supporter of national power to allow congressional regulatory authority to be curbed by such a restrictive interpretation of the Constitution.

The constitutional authority of Congress, Marshall wrote, consists of those powers that are expressly granted by the Constitution, plus (here is where he tied the necessary and proper clause to the enumerated powers of Congress) those powers that are necessary and proper to the exercise of its expressly granted powers. If the end (for example, collecting taxes or supporting an army) is legitimate (that is, authorized by an enumerated power), then the means chosen by Congress to promote that end (chartering a national bank) will be upheld judicially, as long as those means are not prohibited by some other constitutional provision.

The attention of the Court then shifted to giving meaning to the enumerated powers. Granted, Congress is authorized to enact any law that helps it, for example, to promote the regulation of interstate commerce, but what exactly does "commerce among the several States" mean? Is the Constitution referring to actual transportation of goods between two or more states? Or does the commerce clause imply more?

Again, the antecedents of modern constitutional doctrine were established during the tenure of Marshall.[214] But more than a century of judicial review was required before the modern rule became established: Congress has constitutional authority to regulate anything that *affects* interstate commerce, no matter how slight the effect.[215] Little imagination is required to find an affecting relationship between a specified activity and interstate commerce.[216]

The Supreme Court's expansive interpretation of the Constitution did not mandate a particular national role in law enforcement. It did not in any sense require Congress to exercise its police power to the fullest lawful extent. The Court, rather, conferred constitutional legitimacy on an expansive national police power. It was up to Congress to exercise that power.

Periodically responding to the perceived need and popular demand for national regulation, Congress has added incrementally to the police power of the federal government. The Interstate Commerce Commission (ICC) Act of 1887 provided for federal regulation of the railroads. This was followed by the Sherman Antitrust Act of 1890, Pure Food and Drug Act of 1906, Federal Reserve Act of 1913, and Federal Trade Commission Act of 1914. The basis for an extensive federal police power was firmly in place by the time Franklin Roosevelt was inaugurated as president in 1933.

The Great Depression was the singular fact faced by Roosevelt and Congress. Congress deferred to the president, and Roosevelt responded with the New Deal, a collection of programs adding directly to the regulatory authority of the federal government. The banking industry became more thoroughly regulated with the enactment of the Banking Act of 1933. Enactment of the Securities Acts of 1933 and 1934 placed the sale of stocks under direct federal supervision; the National Labor Relations Act of 1935 did the same for labor-management relations, and the Civil Aeronautics Act of 1938 for civilian aviation. Wages and hours of employment became the subject of extensive federal regulation with the passage of the Fair Labor Standards Act of 1938.

Roosevelt and Congress had inherited the rudiments of a federal police power in 1933. By the time the New Deal had effectively ended, with the 1941 entry of the United States into the World War II, the regulatory jurisdiction and power of the federal government had become even more inclusive, intensive, and extensive. Regulating the health, safety, morals, and general welfare of the nation had become a major preoccupation of the federal government.

This role has expanded in the years following the conclusion of World War II. The Federal Housing Act of 1949, and multiple amendments, made Washington the principal source of money to finance inner-city public housing construction and urban renewal. Money received from the federal government, whether in the form of loans, grants, or payments for goods and services, is accompanied by a plethora of regulations and contractual obligations. Various pieces of legislation—the most important being the employment, housing, and public accommodations provisions of the Civil Rights Act of 1964—banned discrimination based on race, color, religion, sex, and national origin. In response to nine Supreme Court decisions from 1986 to 1991 that had made it difficult for workers charging discrimination to win lawsuits, Congress enacted, and President Bush signed, the Civil Rights Act of 1991.[217] The law reaffirmed and strengthened the antidiscrimination provisions of the 1964 Civil Rights Act and also amended Title VII to allow for monetary damages for victims of discrimination.

Examples of other federal measures enacted during this period are the Federal Aviation Act of 1958, Consumer Credit Policy Act of 1968, National Environmental Protection Act of 1969, Occupational Health and Safety Act of 1970, Consumer Product Safety Act of 1972, Endangered Species Act of 1973, Americans with Disabilities Act of 1990, and Freedom of Access to Clinic Entrances Act of 1993.

Critics of federal law enforcement often charge that the implementation standards enacted by Congress are too vague, leading to abuses. A frequently cited example is the 1970 Racketeer Influenced and Corrupt Organizations Act (RICO). Congress intended this law to be used as a tool against the activities of organized crime. But provision for triple damage awards—intended as a deterrent to organized crime and an incentive to plaintiffs—gave an incentive to private businesses to sue competitors using RICO. The law is broad enough to allow them to do so. The broad language of the law also has resulted in charges against nonviolent demonstrators—for example, antiabortion groups—for engaging in "racketeering activity." The Supreme Court has refused to narrow the scope of RICO, maintaining that only Congress can rewrite the law. Several efforts to do so have not succeeded.

This summary points out that the police power of the national government has expanded greatly in the past century. Still, the summary indicates only some of the ways in which power has grown. It does not mention, for example, the many and frequent amendments to the Internal Revenue Code (annual amendments that are sometimes mockingly called "Lawyers and Accountants Relief Acts") or to the criminal code. Nor does it touch on more "traditional" exercises of federal police power: immigration, national security, regulation of Native American tribes, imposition of ethical standards on government employees, import restrictions and taxes, and operation of the postal system.

A policy of selective business "deregulation" initiated by President Jimmy Carter, and supported and furthered by his successors, Ronald Reagan, George Bush, and to a lesser extent Bill Clinton, deserves special mention. Supporters of deregulation argued that it would reduce consumer costs by fostering competition among businesses and by reducing the costs of regulation (that is, the costs of record keeping, administrative monitoring, and legal advice) borne by businesses and passed on to consumers.

Congress has directed deregulation efforts at a limited number of industries—primarily transportation, communications, and commercial credit—and only at selected business practices. Deregulation has reduced but not eliminated the national police power over economic activity. American businesses remain thoroughly regulated by the national government.

After enacting laws, members of Congress do not, of course, pin badges on their chests and act as enforcement officers. Rather, Congress makes the laws of the United States and then delegates enforcement jurisdiction and power to agencies and personnel of the executive branch. These agencies are also the creation of Congress.

Development of the federal civilian bureaucracy, and its power, has almost paralleled these diverse bursts of congressional energy. Civilian personnel employed by the federal government in nondefense capacities numbered 4,279 in 1816. Almost 80 percent of these were postal workers. By 1901 the number of such employees had increased to 186,532. Civilian personnel of the national government employed by nondefense agencies in 1993 totaled 2.09 million.[218]

Not all of these increases can be attributed to the growth of the police power of the national government. The workforce has grown in areas that have little to do with law enforcement, such as space exploration, agricultural advice, and maintenance of national parks. Nonetheless, most of the expansion of the federal civilian workforce is associated with the increased law enforcement role of the national government.

As chief executive and chief law enforcement officer of the United States, the president has been the most direct and most frequent beneficiary of this expansion of the national government.

PRESIDENTIAL LAW ENFORCEMENT AUTHORITY AND POWER

John F. Kennedy exercised the legal power of the president when, in September 1962, he deployed first U.S. marshals (and an assortment of other federal civilian law enforcement officers), and then regular army troops to Oxford, Mississippi. Kennedy was acting as chief law enforcement officer of the United States; he was, as Article II, section 3, of the U.S. Constitution requires, "tak[ing] Care that the Laws be faithfully executed."

Enforcing the law, in this case, meant backing a federal court order. In 1961 James Meredith applied for admission to the University of Mississippi ("Ole Miss"). Meredith was a Mississippi citizen, a veteran of the air force, and an African American. Ole Miss did not admit blacks at the time.

Denied admission by the university, Meredith appealed to the federal courts for assistance. His complaint was initially dismissed by a federal district court, but this decision was reversed by the U.S. Court of Appeals for the Fifth Circuit. A panel of Fifth Circuit judges found that Meredith had been denied admission to the university solely because of his race, and they ordered his enrollment.

Prolonged negotiations between Ross Barnett, the governor of Mississippi, Kennedy, and Kennedy's lieutenants, principally Attorney General Robert F. Kennedy, failed to produce an agreement for the orderly admission of Meredith. Mississippi, it became clear, would not use its own force to protect Meredith and maintain order on the campus. Protection and the maintenance of law and order, if they were to be supplied at all, would have to come from Washington.

Federal protection was provided initially by a contingent of U.S. marshals. A mob formed, however, and the original federal force had to be reinforced. Additional marshals were sent to Oxford, as were almost any federal law enforcement officers who could be spared—game wardens, border patrol personnel, and prison guards. Even this augmented force was threatened by the persistent and violent mob attacks.

On September 30, 1962, President Kennedy ordered the mob to disperse. He backed his order (and the original court order) with the deployment of regular army troops to the Ole Miss campus. Meredith was registered. *(See box, John F. Kennedy, the Law, and the "Ole Miss" Campaign, pp. 60–61.)*[219]

Kennedy enforced the laws of the United States when he ordered U.S. marshals and troops onto the Ole Miss campus. In doing so, however, he—as the president of the United States—was also acting according to law. In other words, he was acting according to and within the limitations set by the U.S. Constitution and Congress.

Presidential law enforcement power may be defined by either or both sources. Article II, section 1, of the Constitution vests in the president the "executive Power" of the United States. Section 2 of the second article designates the president as commander in chief of the armed forces, including, when ordered into national service, the National Guard of the various states. It also gives the president authority to appoint the principal officers of the executive and judicial branches, with Senate confirmation.

Finally, Article II, section 3, of the Constitution lays responsibility on the president to "take Care that the Laws be faithfully executed."

The Constitution also confers on Congress authority to delegate to the president and executive branch officers extensive enforcement powers. Article I, section 8, of the Constitution gives Congress authority to make all laws "necessary and proper" to execute its own enumerated authority as well as any other authority conferred by the Constitution on the government or any branch of the government of the United States.

Consequently, Congress has the authority "necessary and proper" to "provide for the Punishment of counterfeiting" the currency of the United States. Congress has used this authority to make counterfeiting a crime, to create the Secret Service of the Treasury Department, and to give the Secret Service authority to arrest suspected violators.

Although the Constitution and Congress vest considerable law enforcement authority in the president, both also limit that authority. The Constitution provides generally for shared decision making in many aspects of law enforcement. Presidential appointment of officers of the federal government having major

U.S. CONSTITUTION

The confrontation between President John F. Kennedy and Gov. Ross Barnett is remembered today as an instance in which federal power overwhelmed state resistance to a judicial order. Because Kennedy faithfully executed the laws of the United States, James Meredith enrolled as a freshman at the University of Mississippi.

But the judicial branch did not just order Meredith's admission to "Ole Miss," and the president did not just enforce that order. The courts and the president acted according to the laws of the United States. Certain of these laws are reproduced here to illustrate how law is connected with the exercise of presidential power.

A number of constitutional provisions also were involved in the Ole Miss controversy. These pertained to individual rights, the powers of the president, the powers of Congress, and the power of the national government in general.

Individual Rights. The Fourteenth Amendment, section 1, of the Constitution provides that no state may "deny to any person within its jurisdiction the equal protection of the laws." In 1954 the U.S. Supreme Court interpreted this passage to mean that segregated public educational facilities were constitutionally impermissible.[1] The U.S. Court of Appeals for the Fifth Circuit applied this rule when it ordered the University of Mississippi to admit James Meredith.[2]

Presidential Power. Article II, section 1, of the Constitution vests the "executive Power" of the United States in the president. Section 2 of this article designates the president "Commander in Chief" of the armed forces of the United States and, when called into federal service, of the several state militias. Finally, section 3 of Article II says that the president "shall take Care that the Laws be faithfully executed."

Congressional Power. Congress, under Article I, section 8, of the Constitution, is given power to "make all Laws which shall be necessary and proper for carrying into Execution" its own enumerated constitutional powers "and all other Powers vested by this Constitution in the Government of the United States, or in any Department or Officer thereof." Among the enumerated powers of Congress are the power "To raise and support Armies," "To make Rules for the Government and Regulation of the land and naval Forces," "To provide for calling forth the Militia to execute the Laws of the Union, suppress Insurrection. . . ," and "To provide for organizing, arming, and disciplining the Militia, and for governing such Part of them as may be employed in the Service of the United States. . . ."

National Power. The "supremacy clause" of the Constitution provides that the "Constitution, and the Laws of the United States which shall be made in Pursuance thereof . . . shall be the supreme Law of the Land." State and local officials are bound by interpretations of the Constitution made by federal courts.[3]

CONGRESSIONALLY ENACTED LEGISLATION

According to its constitutional authority to make all laws "necessary and proper" to carry out the powers of Congress and of the president that are enumerated above, Congress enacted the following laws.

Section 332. Use of Militia and Armed Forces to Enforce Federal Authority. "Whenever the President considers that unlawful obstructions, combinations, or assemblages, or rebellion against the authority of the United States, make it impracticable to enforce the laws of the United States in any State or Territory by the ordinary course of judicial proceedings, he may call into Federal service such of the militia of any State, and use such of the armed forces, as he considers necessary to enforce those laws or to suppress the rebellion."[4]

Section 333. Interference with State and Federal Law. "The President, by using the militia the armed forces, or both, or by any other means, shall take such measures as he considers necessary to suppress, in a State, any insurrection, domestic violence, unlawful combination, or conspiracy, if it—(1) so hinders the execution of the laws of that State, and of the United States within the State, that any part or class of its people is deprived of a right, privilege, immunity, or protection named in the Constitution and secured by law, and the constituted authorities of that State are unable, fail, or refuse to protect that right, privilege, or immunity or to give that protection; or (2) opposes or obstructs the execution of the laws of the United States or impedes the course of justice under those laws. In any situation covered by clause (1), the State shall be considered to have denied the equal protection of the laws secured by the Constitution."[5]

Section 334. Proclamation to Disperse. "Whenever the President considers it necessary to use the militia, or the armed forces under this chapter, he shall, by proclamation, immediately order the insurgents to disperse and retire peaceably to their abodes within a limited time."[6]

PRESIDENTIAL PROCLAMATION AND EXECUTIVE ORDER

Acting on his constitutional and congressionally delegated authority, President Kennedy ordered federal enforcement of the court desegregation order. First, a force of U.S. marshals and other federal law enforcement personnel were dispatched to the Ole Miss campus. Next, when a mob threatened to overwhelm this force, and when it became apparent that state law enforcement personnel would not assist the beleaguered federal force, the president commanded the secretary of defense to deploy regular army troops to the campus. The following excerpts are from Kennedy's September 30, 1962, proclamation ordering the mob to disperse and from his executive order of the same day, mobilizing the army to enforce the law:

PROCLAMATION 3497
Obstructions of Justice in the State of Mississippi
By the President of the United States of America
A Proclamation

WHEREAS, the Governor of the State of Mississippi and certain law enforcement officers and other officials of that State, and other persons, individually and in unlawful assemblies, combinations and conspiracies, have been and are willfully opposing and obstructing the enforcement of orders entered by the United States District Court for the Southern District of Mississippi and the United States Court of Appeals for the Fifth Circuit; and

WHEREAS, such unlawful assemblies, combinations and conspiracies oppose and obstruct the execution of the laws of the United States, impede the course of justice under those laws and make it impracticable to enforce those laws in the State of Mississippi by the ordinary course of judicial proceedings; and

WHEREAS, I have expressly called attention of the Governor of Mississippi to the perilous situation that exists and to his duties in the premises, and have requested but have not received from him adequate assurances that the orders of the courts of the United States will be obeyed and that law and order will be maintained:

NOW, THEREFORE, I, JOHN F. KENNEDY, President of the United States, under and by virtue of the authority vested in me by Constitution and laws of the United States, . . . do command all persons engaged in such obstructions of justice to cease and desist therefrom and to disperse and retire peacefully forthwith.[7]

Executive Order 11053

Providing Assistance for the Removal of Unlawful Obstructions of Justice in the State of Mississippi

WHEREAS on September 30, 1962, I issued Proclamation No. 3497 reading in part as follows:

[The portions of the proclamation quoted above are reprinted.] and

WHEREAS the commands contained in that proclamation have not been obeyed and obstruction of enforcement of those court orders still exists and threatens to continue:

NOW, THEREFORE, by virtue of the authority vested in me by the Constitution and laws of the United States, . . . , it is hereby ordered as follows:

SECTION 1. The Secretary of Defense is authorized and directed to take all appropriate steps to enforce all orders of the United States District Court for the Southern District of Mississippi and the United States Court of Appeals for the Fifth Circuit and to remove all obstructions of justice in the State of Mississippi.

SECTION 2. In furtherance of the enforcement of the aforementioned orders of the [specified courts], the Secretary of Defense is authorized to use such of the armed forces of the United States as he may deem necessary.

SECTION 3. I hereby authorize the Secretary of Defense to call into the active military service of the United States, as he may deem appropriate to carry out the purposes of this order, any or all units of the [national guard] of the State of Mississippi to serve in the active military service of the United States for an indefinite period and until relieved by appropriate orders. In carrying out the provisions of Section 1, the Secretary of Defense is authorized to use the units, and members thereof, ordered into the active military service of the United States pursuant to this section.[8]

1. *Brown v. Board of Education*, 347 U.S. 483 (1954).
2. *Meredith v. Fair*, 306 F2d 374 (5th Cir. 1962)
3. *Cooper v. Aaron*, 358 U.S. 1 (1958).
4. 10 United States Code section 332.
5. 10 United States Code section 333.
6. 10 United States Code section 334.
7. Proclamation 3497, 3 Code of Federal Regulations, 225–226 (1959–1963 compilation).
8. Executive Order 11053, 3 Code of Federal Regulations, 645–646 (1959–1963 compilation).

law enforcement responsibilities is often subjected to Senate approval. Presidents must obtain Senate approval for their appointments to the office of attorney general, for instance, as well as for the deputy and various assistant attorney generals, the director of the FBI, and the U.S. attorney for each judicial district.

The Constitution and Congress place direct restrictions on presidential power. The Constitution prohibits the president from spending money for law enforcement unless Congress first authorizes an appropriation for that expenditure.[220] Congress has limited the authority of the president to use military force for law enforcement.

A final characteristic of presidential power must be considered. This is the distinction between *discretionary* and *ministerial* authority.

Discretionary authority involves the exercise of judgment and choice. Ministerial authority does not. It involves, rather, the faithful implementation of decisions made by others.

The Constitution, for example, gives the president authority to nominate and, with Senate consent, to appoint justices to fill vacancies on the U.S. Supreme Court. Whom the president appoints, if anyone, is a matter left constitutionally to the discretion of the president; neither Congress nor the courts may compel the president to nominate a particular person.

Paying the salary of the person eventually appointed, however, is a purely ministerial act (with the constitutional proviso that the salary of a sitting federal judge may not be reduced). Congress sets the salary and authorizes payment; the job of the president (actually a subordinate of the president in the Department of the Treasury) is to write the check. Writing the check is a ministerial act.

Where discretionary authority is at issue, presidents act as policy makers, exercising their best judgment about law enforcement. Since this authority is bestowed on the president by the Constitution or Congress, a court cannot compel the president to make a particular decision. The issue is considered political, not legal.[221] A court, for example, cannot compel the president to grant a pardon to a criminal offender; the decision is entrusted to the discretion of the president.

Much of the law enforcement authority of the president is discretionary. The president sets law enforcement priorities and appoints senior law enforcement officials of the executive branch to implement those priorities. These officials, in turn, have been delegated considerable discretion by Congress and the president to set additional law enforcement policies—what types of offenses merit the greatest attention, what resources will be allocated, and what cases will be prosecuted.

Merely because a power is discretionary does not mean that external political pressure cannot be brought to bear on the president. A sufficiently aroused public can force the president to be more or less aggressive in enforcing a particular law, as can a sufficiently aroused Congress. Congressional and public dissatisfaction with enforcement of the nation's environmental laws in the early years of the Reagan administration, for example, led eventually to the almost wholesale replacement of the

President Grover Cleveland's suppression of the Pullman Railroad Strike of 1894 is an example of presidential enforcement authority. Here, a meat train leaves the Chicago stockyards under escort of U.S. Cavalry.

top management of the Environmental Protection Agency. The agency became more aggressive in its enforcement efforts as a result. A disappointed public may turn to a presidential candidate from the opposing party. Congress is equipped to retaliate in a variety of ways, escalating from mere public denouncements, to public investigation, to removal by impeachment. The uncompleted impeachment proceedings against President Richard Nixon (who resigned "voluntarily") remain a dramatic reminder of the ultimate measure of congressional retaliation.

The Constitution reveals four general categories of presidential authority in law enforcement. The three best recognized categories are the executive, military, and clemency powers of the president.

The fourth category stems from the "take care" clause of the Constitution.

The "Take Care" Power of the President

The U.S. Constitution provides in Article II, section 3, that the president "shall take Care that the Laws be faithfully executed." Two principal interpretations of that clause often are asserted.

One interpretation holds that the "take care" clause imposes an obligation on the president. The text itself is imperative in mood; it is a command to the president to obey and enforce the law. No separate and independent grant of authority to the president is stated; none can be implied.

Supreme Court Justice Oliver Wendell Holmes Jr. urged this interpretation in his dissent in *Myers v. United States:* "The duty of the President to see that the laws be executed is a duty that does not go beyond the law or require him to achieve more than Congress sees fit to leave within his power."[222]

No one disputes that the president is obligated to obey the law and to enforce the law with the authority that he is granted. Such a view is certainly supported by rulings of the U.S. Supreme Court.[223] The Court, however, has gone further. It has fashioned a power-granting interpretation of the "take care" clause, one that does not conform to Holmes's more restrictive interpretation.

The primary ruling resulted from an appeal to the Supreme Court in the case of *In re Neagle.*[224] A deputy U.S. marshal was assigned by the attorney general to guard an associate justice of the Supreme Court, Stephen J. Field. The marshal shot and killed an assailant and was prosecuted for murder by the state of California.

The marshal argued that inasmuch as he was performing official law enforcement duties as an officer of the United States at the time the assailant was shot, he was cloaked with immunity from state prosecution.

California did not dispute that U.S. marshals generally are not answerable in state courts for their official actions. It contended, however, that the marshal could not have been acting officially when he was guarding Field since Congress had not expressly given marshals that authority. Without congressional authorization, the marshal was acting merely in the capacity of a private citizen. He was, therefore, subject to the jurisdiction of the California courts.

The Court rejected California's argument and rendered an expansive interpretation of the "take care" clause in the process. The president's power to enforce the law, wrote Justice Samuel Miller, is not limited to enforcing specific acts of Congress. It also involves enforcing the Constitution and the general peace of the land. The Court ordered California to release its prisoner.

Another notable Supreme Court interpretation of presidential enforcement authority arose in response to President Grover Cleveland's suppression of the Pullman Railroad Strike of 1894. Arguing that the strike was interfering with interstate commerce and delivery of the mails, two activities assigned by the Constitution to the national government, the president sought and obtained a federal court injunction ordering the strikers to desist. The president dispatched federal troops to Chicago to enforce the injunction; those resisting were prosecuted for contempt of court.

The defendants challenged both the injunction and the use of military force to enforce the court order. Congress, they argued, had not given the federal court the authority to issue the injunction, nor had it authorized the use of military force by the president to enforce the injunction. The Court rebuffed both challenges.[225]

Neither Supreme Court decision should be read as giving the president power to override or ignore Congress. Rather, the Court invoked the "take care" clause in both instances when Congress had been silent.

Executive Powers of the President

Presidents are elected by the people, presumably to make policy and supervise its implementation. Presidents are not expected to involve themselves in the details of implementation. With few exceptions, they do not.

The same might be said of the attorney general, the secretary of the Treasury, or even the director of the Federal Bureau of Investigation (FBI) or the commissioner of the Internal Revenue Service (IRS). Considerable discretion to act is and must be delegated to the men and women who actually enforce the law: special agents of the FBI who witness a violation of federal law, IRS auditors who discover irregularities in tax filings, assistant U.S. attorneys who uncover evidence of criminal activity in the files of investigative reports.

The law enforcement power of the president, therefore, depends substantially on the president's ability to affect the behavior of subordinates within the executive branch. And the ability of the president to affect the behavior of these subordinates depends in part on the president's legal authority.

The Constitution says little about presidential authority over officers of the executive branch. The first sentence of Article II, section 1, states that the "executive Power shall be vested in a President of the United States of America." This appears to give the president great power; however, the Constitution does not define "executive Power." A narrow reading of this provision means that the Constitution merely confers on the president those powers contained in Article II. A more liberal interpretation is that Article II confers authority on the president that is not explicitly defined in the Constitution.

Appointment and Removal of Law Enforcement Officers. The executive power of the president embraces authority to appoint senior law enforcement officers of the executive branch and judges of the federal judiciary. *(See also "The Appointment Power," p. 21.)* That authority is conferred by the "appointments clause" of Article II, section 2, of the Constitution. *(See text from Article II, section 2, in box, p. 21, and "Instruments of Presidential Control," p. 6.)*

The appointment power of the president applies generally to the senior officers of the executive branch charged with law enforcement responsibility. All cabinet members serve by virtue of presidential appointment, as do agency heads and members of the so-called subcabinet: policy-making officers immediately subordinate to a cabinet officer and at the level of under secretary, deputy secretary, and assistant secretary. This means that the president appoints not only the attorney general and the principal officers of the Department of Justice, for example, but also the principal political officers of all federal departments and agencies involved in law enforcement.

These appointees generally serve at the pleasure of the president, which means simply that they may be fired by the president—for good reason, bad reason, or no reason at all. Such a move may be costly politically, but it lies within the legal discretion (that is, authority) of the president, and this discretion may not be curbed by Congress.[226]

Less senior but still high-ranking law enforcement officers may also be subject to presidential appointment. The director of the FBI, the commissioner of the IRS, and the administrator of the Drug Enforcement Administration (DEA) are examples. Other examples include the U.S. attorney for each judicial district of the United States, the chief U.S. marshal, and the commissioner of the U.S. Customs Service.

Presidential authority to fire these officers varies. U.S. attorneys may be removed at the will of the president. Since 1973 the director of the FBI has been appointed to a ten-year term and may not be fired without cause. In July 1993 President Clinton removed the FBI director, William S. Sessions, because of revelations in a Justice Department investigation of improper use of office. Sessions was the first FBI director in the department's seventy-year history to be fired by the president.

Two other classes of presidential appointees deserve special note: board members and other high-ranking officers of independent regulatory boards and commissions, and federal judges.

Independent regulatory boards and commissions are largely the product of the "good government" movement of the late nineteenth and early twentieth centuries. These boards and commissions are an outgrowth of the belief that certain aspects of policy implementation could and should be separated from ordinary partisan politics. If the organization implementing policy is legally separated from politics, then the decision makers in that organization will faithfully implement policy created by Congress and will not act to promote the partisan advantage of the incumbent president.

Congress created the Interstate Commerce Commission (ICC) in 1887 to regulate the nation's growing railroad industry and later assigned it jurisdiction over trucking as well. (Congress eliminated the ICC in 1996 but transferred some of its regulatory authority to the Transportation Department.) After establishment of the ICC, Congress created other independent boards and commissions to regulate business trade practices (Federal Trade Commission, or FTC), labor-management relations (National Labor Relations Board, or NLRB), television and radio broadcasting (Federal Communications Commission, or FCC), sales of stocks and bonds (Securities and Exchange Commission, or SEC), banking (Federal Reserve Board, or FRB), and the nuclear power industry (Nuclear Regulatory Commission, or NRC).

The exact authority of these agencies varies. They generally possess power to make law through what is called "rule making" and to adjudicate disputes about the application of the law through quasi-judicial methods. They also have authority to investigate unlawful conduct and, in some cases, actually to prosecute civil violations. (Criminal violations are prosecuted only by the Justice Department.) Their authority may extend to rate setting and licensing of businesses and individuals.

Congress has given the president authority to appoint the principal officers of these agencies. Presidential authority to fire them, however, has been limited to reasons specified by law. These limitations have been upheld by the U.S. Supreme Court.[227] *(See "The Removal Power," p. 28.)* Federal judges, including justices of the Supreme Court, are appointed by the president. That ends the president's formal authority over the judicial branch. By explicit constitutional provision, federal judges have life tenure and may not be removed from office except by the impeachment process.[228]

Presidential Authority to Command. In addition to the appointment and removal authority, the president possesses the authority to control the official behavior of certain officers of the government who are charged with law enforcement duties.

Federal judges are an exception in that they enjoy independent status from the chief executive. Similarly, presidents lack command authority in most instances over officers of independent regulatory boards and commissions. *(See "Regulatory Commissions," p. 4.)* Command authority over officers of the executive branch who do not enjoy independent status is greater, although still not absolute. If the presidential command is lawful, then failure of a subordinate to obey could constitute neglect or insubordination. The president could remove such an officer and justify the decision to do so. Presidents themselves, however, must obey the law, and they have no authority to command their subordinates to commit a violation.

Occasionally a disagreement exists about what the law requires or prohibits. Laws are often stated ambiguously and are subject to different interpretations. The president may fire a subordinate for insubordination when such a disagreement arises.

The great majority of federal law enforcement personnel are not appointed by the president. They are, rather, career civil servants, who obtain their positions through a competitive and nonpartisan selection process. These personnel may be fired only for causes specified by statute or administrative regulation, and only following a neutral and procedurally rigorous judicial-type hearing.

Special agents of the FBI, Secret Service, and Bureau of Alcohol, Tobacco, and Firearms belong to this category. So do deputy U.S. marshals, assistant U.S. attorneys, IRS auditors, and customs inspectors. In fact, just about all investigating and enforcement officers, supporting staff, and many policy-making officers of the executive branch belong to the civil service.

This makes presidential appointment authority especially important to presidential law enforcement power. Civil servants are not obliged to share the same law enforcement goals and priorities as the president. Their goals and priorities, rather, are shaped by their personal values and perceptions of what will promote their own interests. The official behavior of civil servants, therefore, should not be expected to conform in all cases with the goals and priorities of the president.

Civil servants, to be sure, are obliged to obey all lawful commands of the president and of their own bureaucratic superiors. Willful failure to comply will normally constitute legal cause for discipline, including being fired from the job. To be successful, therefore, bureaucratic resistance to the president must be displayed in a less direct, more subtle way. More than a century of accumulated experience has provided civil servants with a variety of such methods.

Seasoned bureaucrats know well, for example, the difference between complying with lawful orders and going through the motions of complying. A president might direct federal law enforcement agents to be especially aggressive in investigating members of Congress for corruption. Such a presidential order lies within the discretionary power of the president and is entirely lawful.

Most federal agents would comply. That is their job. Other agents, however, may not share the president's enthusiasm for investigating members of Congress. These agents may be concerned that an angry Congress would slice their budgets, or that particularly powerful members of Congress might retaliate in the future by blocking their appointments to high-level agency positions. In such a case, agents may examine documents (but not too thoroughly), and follow leads (but not too many). They will document their efforts and pronounce the absence of evidence justifying further investigations, thereby "complying" with the president's order.

The executive power of the president in law enforcement, then, depends substantially on the president's ability to choose trusted appointees who are able to influence the behavior of subordinates. Ideally, subordinates will share the president's values pertaining to law enforcement. Experience shows, however, that at least a degree of bureaucratic resistance may be expected.

Military Power

The significance of the armed forces of the United States to presidential law enforcement power should not be measured by

The President shall be Commander in Chief of the Army and the Navy of the United States, and of the Militia of the several States, when called into the actual Service of the United States. . . .

—*from Article II, section 2*

the frequency of their use. The significance, rather, lies in the fact that military power is available to the president to enforce the law when civilian power is unable to do so.

Presidents have used military power to enforce the law in several notable instances. George Washington used military force to quell the Whiskey Rebellion. His precedent was followed by Abraham Lincoln, who used a more powerful military force to suppress the Southern rebellion. Both presidents were, legally speaking, enforcing the law.

Defiance of court injunctions against labor strikes in the nineteenth century prompted both Rutherford B. Hayes and Grover Cleveland to deploy troops to enforce the law. In the twentieth century, Dwight D. Eisenhower and John F. Kennedy used force when court desegregation orders were met by local resistance. Lyndon B. Johnson used his military power in 1968 to put down rioting in Detroit. In December 1989 George Bush ordered the deployment of U.S. forces abroad to enforce federal drug laws. The U.S. military invaded Panama, ousted its drug-trafficking president, Manuel Noriega, and brought him to Florida to stand trial, where he eventually was convicted on drug and racketeering counts.

The military power of the president is derived from the Constitution and Congress.

The U.S. Constitution states in Article II, section 2, that the "President shall be Commander in Chief of the Army and the Navy of the United States, and of the Militia of the several States, when called into the actual Service of the United States." Article IV, section 4, provides that the United States, "on Application of the [state] Legislature, or of the Executive [governor] (when the Legislature cannot be convened)" shall guarantee "against domestic Violence."

The commander-in-chief clause of the Constitution gives the president authority to command the men and women of the armed forces. It is authority, however, that is itself shaped by law. The president and Congress share authority over the armed forces of the United States.

Congress, according to its authority to enact laws "necessary and proper" to "make Rules for . . . Regulation of the land and naval Forces" and "[t]o provide for calling forth the Militia to execute the Laws of the Union, suppress Insurrections and repel Invasions," has enacted legislation that both authorizes and places limitations on presidential use of the military to enforce the law.[229] *(See box, John F. Kennedy, the Law, and the "Ole Miss" Campaign, pp. 60–61, for a reprinting of these laws.)*

The Constitution does not seriously impede the ability of the president to use military force to assist civil authorities in enforcing the law. To the contrary, wrote Justice David Brewer: "There is no such impotency in the national government. . . . If the emergency arises, the army of the nation, and all its militia, are at the service of the nation to compel obedience to the laws."[230]

Nor does Congress impede the president in law enforcement. Although Congress has specified the conditions in which such force may be deployed, it leaves to the president considerable discretion in deciding if those conditions have been met.

A different situation arises, however, should the president attempt to declare martial law and supplant civil with military authority within the boundaries of the United States. The Supreme Court has ruled that for such an action to be maintained constitutionally, the situation must be so desperate that the civil courts are closed.[231] The military might of the United States must support, not supplant, the law.

Clemency Power

Article II, section 2, of the U.S. Constitution delegates to the president "Power to grant Reprieves and Pardons for Offenses against the United States, except in Cases of Impeachment." It gives to the president the ability to be merciful as well as vengeful.

But mercy was not necessarily what the Framers had in mind when they included clemency in the enumerated powers of the president. Alexander Hamilton explained in *Federalist* No. 74: "But the principal argument for reposing the power of pardoning . . . in the Chief Magistrate [president] is this: in seasons of insurrection or rebellion, there are often critical moments when a well-timed offer of pardon to the insurgents or rebels may restore the tranquility of the commonwealth."[232] Hamilton urged that the president—"a single man of prudence and good sense"—alone be given the authority to exercise this power because the legislature was not well suited to both weighing the national interest against other considerations and acting quickly.[233]

The pardon power was first used in 1792 when President George Washington "most earnestly admonish[ed] and exhort[ed]" whiskey manufacturers of western Pennsylvania to cease their disobedience and obstruction of the law. They were, the president's proclamation continued, not only refusing to pay taxes on the whiskey produced, they were also resisting enforcement of the tax law with violence.[234]

Washington tried demands to end the "Whiskey Rebellion," and he tried force. Law and order in the western counties of

[H]e shall have Power to grant Reprieves and Pardons for Offenses against the United States, except in Cases of Impeachment.

—*from Article II, section 2*

PRESIDENTIAL PARDONS

The presidential power to pardon is an absolute one granted by the Constitution. When President Gerald R. Ford granted a full and unconditional pardon to his predecessor, Richard Nixon, controversy arose not over Ford's authority, but his timing. Questions were asked whether it was wise to circumvent the judicial processes already at work by pardoning someone before he had been charged with a crime. Ford was never able to shake criticism of the Nixon pardon, which contributed to his defeat to Jimmy Carter in 1976. The following is an excerpt from Ford's pardon on September 8, 1974:

> It is believed that a trial of Richard Nixon, if it became necessary, could not fairly begin until a year or more has elapsed. In the meantime, the tranquility to which this nation has been restored by the events of recent weeks could be irreparably lost by the prospects of bringing to trial a former President of the United States. The prospects of such trial will cause prolonged and divisive debate over the propriety of exposing to further punishment and degradation a man who has already paid the unprecedented penalty of relinquishing the highest elective office in the United States.
>
> Now, therefore, I, Gerald R. Ford, President of the United States, pursuant to the pardon power conferred upon me by Article II, Section 2, of the Constitution, have granted and by these presents do grant a full, free and absolute pardon unto Richard Nixon for all offenses against the United States which he, Richard Nixon, has committed or may have committed or taken part in during the period from January 20, 1969 through August 9, 1974.

Outgoing President George Bush in December 1992 pardoned six former Reagan administration officials, including former Defense Secretary Caspar Weinberger, who had been involved in the Iran-contra scandal. All six had been accused of withholding information or lying to Congress. When Bush issued his pardon on Christmas Eve, four had already been convicted and three had served prison time; Weinberger was scheduled to go on trial in January. The following excerpts are from Bush's pardon proclamation:

> Today, I am exercising my power under the Constitution to pardon former Secretary of Defense Caspar Weinberger and others for their conduct related to the Iran-Contra affair. . . .
>
> Caspar Weinberger is a true American patriot. . . . I am pardoning him not just out of compassion or to spare a 75-year-old patriot the torment of lengthy and costly legal proceedings, but to make it possible for him to receive the honor he deserves for his extraordinary service to our country. . . .
>
> I have also decide to pardon five other individuals for their conduct related to the Iran-Contra affair. . . . First, the common denominator of their motivation—whether their actions were right or wrong—was patriotism. Second, they did not profit or seek to profit from their conduct. Third, each has a record of long and distinguished service to this country. And finally, all five have already paid a price—in depleted savings, lost careers, anguished families or errors of judgment they may have committed. . . .
>
> Now, therefore, I, George Bush, President of the United States of America, pursuant to my power under Article II, Section 2, of the Constitution, do hereby grant a full, complete, and unconditional pardon to Elliott Abrams, Duane R. Clarridge, Alan Fiers, Clair George, Robert C. McFarlane, and Caspar Weinberger for all offenses charged or prosecuted by Independent Counsel Lawrence E. Walsh or other members of his office, or committed by these individuals and within the jurisdiction of that office.

Pennsylvania, however, were not restored until the president promised and granted the offenders a full and absolute pardon.[235]

A reprieve reduces a sentence already imposed by a tribunal. A person sentenced to death by a U.S. district court or military court martial, for example, may have his or her sentence reduced to a long term of imprisonment by presidential reprieve. The guilt is not wiped out, but the severity of the punishment inflicted on the guilty person may be reduced.

Presidential pardons wipe out both guilt and punishment. They restore the person pardoned to his or her full civil rights, as if the offense had never been committed. President Gerald Ford, for example, granted a full and unconditional pardon to his predecessor, Richard Nixon, and relieved the former president of the possibility of being prosecuted for any involvement he may have had in the crimes associated with Watergate. In late December 1992 President George Bush issued controversial pardons to several key figures who had been implicated in the Iran-contra scandal during the Reagan administration. *(See box, Presidential Pardons, above.)*

Reprieves and pardons may be granted to individuals or to classes of people in the form of "amnesties." For example, Presidents Abraham Lincoln and Andrew Johnson signed amnesties for Confederate soldiers and political leaders, as did Presidents Gerald Ford and Jimmy Carter for draft evaders during the Vietnam War.

The president may attach conditions to either form of clemency. President Nixon, for example, pardoned labor leader Jimmy Hoffa on the condition that Hoffa would never again become involved in union activities.

The clemency authority of the president is extensive. It applies to any federal process or offender, except, by express constitutional language, those persons tried (or being tried) and convicted through congressional impeachment. Moreover, it is one of the few constitutional powers of the president that does not require legislative assent. Congress, in fact, may not interfere with presidential clemency authority in any manner, including, the U.S. Supreme Court has held, the imposition of restrictions on those pardoned.[236]

Hamilton's argument in favor of extensive presidential clemency authority received its strongest validation in the events following the Civil War. Harmony among the people of the United States was not restored immediately. In fact, hostility, anger, and resentment on both sides of the conflict made an amicable reunion of the two sides impossible for many decades. Healing took time and the passing of many generations.

However, the successful reintegration of Southerners into the American political process nourished the healing process. Not only did white Southerners regain the right to vote, they also ascended to high political office. And although no former Confederate soldier or political officer was ever elected president, many later served in the legislative, executive, and judicial branches of the United States.

President Cleveland, for example, appointed Augustus Garland as attorney general. President William Howard Taft appointed Edward Douglas White to the position of chief justice of the United States. Both appointees had previously served the Confederate cause.

The pardon process today is handled by the Office of the Pardon Attorney, created by Congress in 1891.[237] The pardon attorney reviews petitions for clemency and makes a recommendation to the attorney general, who then considers the petition and advises the president. Many presidents have not been reluctant to use this authority. Truman pardoned more than 1,500 people who had violated the Selective Service Act during World War II. Reagan issued nearly four hundred pardons during his two terms in office.[238]

THE LAW ENFORCEMENT BUREAUCRACY

The president commands a vast law enforcement bureaucracy, comprising scores of departments and agencies. Perhaps the most familiar element of this bureaucracy is the Federal Bureau of Investigation. Its historical feats (and faults) have been well chronicled. But the FBI is not the national police force of the United States. In fact, the United States has no national police force. Rather, the law enforcement power of the United States is distributed throughout the executive branch.

The FBI is part of the Department of Justice, itself the repository of several other important law enforcement agencies, including the Immigration and Naturalization Service (INS), the U.S. Marshals Service, the Drug Enforcement Administration, and the Criminal Division.

The Justice Department must be considered the lead law enforcement agency at the disposal of the president. The attorney general is the statutory head of the department. Initially, the attorney general served as a part-time legal adviser to the president and the department heads. For example, William Wirt served in that capacity (1817–1829) while maintaining a private law practice. Wirt represented the U.S. government to trial courts as a private counselor and charged a fee for his services, as he would for private clients. The enforcement activities of the federal government were not then so extensive as to require a full-time attorney general.[239]

Today the attorney general commands a variety of important investigatory and enforcement agencies, of which the FBI is only one. He or she also commands the principal prosecutorial agencies of the national government, the various U.S. attorneys across the United States, and the centralized prosecutorial divisions in Washington. Finally, the attorney general traditionally serves as the principal legal adviser to the president and supervises for the president the selection of nominees for federal judicial posts and clemency. *(See box, Attorneys General of the United States, p. 68.)*

Law enforcement responsibility and power are divided and allocated even further. They are allocated in significant respects to the Treasury Department, which contains the Secret Service, the Customs Service, the Bureau of Alcohol, Tobacco, and Firearms, and the Internal Revenue Service; to the Department of Labor, which enforces laws regulating labor unions, wages, and occupational health and safety; to the Department of Defense, which contains both civilian and military investigative and enforcement agencies; and to various regulatory agencies.

In one respect, applying the term "chief law enforcement officer of the United States" to the president is misleading. Beginning with the Interstate Commerce Commission in 1887, and continuing with the creation of such agencies as the Federal Trade Commission, the National Labor Relations Board, and the Securities and Exchange Commission, Congress has periodically allocated various law enforcement powers to independent boards and commissions within the executive branch but outside the supervisory authority of the president. The power of the president over these agencies generally is limited to appointing board members and other important agency officers when vacancies occur. These officials may not be fired by the president except for cause, which is defined by Congress.[240]

Categories of Federal Law Enforcement

Agencies of the executive branch are involved in at least eight categories of law enforcement. These categories overlap in many instances and oversimplify a highly complex regulatory scheme, but they do provide an overview of the law enforcement activities of the executive branch.

Economic. Agencies of the executive branch implement a variety of laws seeking to foster economic growth, stability, and competition. Also included in this category are laws designed to advance fairness in business practices and harmonious labor-management relations. The Antitrust Division of the Justice Department enforces laws promoting fair trade practices and proscribing monopolies. Financial institutions are subjected to regulation by the comptroller of currency and by the IRS of the Treasury Department. Employment is subject to enforcement actions by the Occupational Safety and Health Administration (OSHA) and by the Employment Standards Administration of the Department of Labor. Despite deregulation, substantial regulation of the transportation industry is still administered by the Federal Aviation Administration of the Department of Transportation. Energy, a relative newcomer to the federal regulatory scheme, is under the jurisdiction of the Departments of Energy and Interior.

Social. Congress has enacted laws that promote a mélange of social goals: equality, fairness, and material comfort. Antidiscrimination laws, such as the equal employment and fair hous-

ATTORNEYS GENERAL OF THE UNITED STATES

The attorney general of the United States is the chief legal adviser to the president and is the head of the U.S. Department of Justice. Because virtually every official decision made by the president is governed by law, and such a large percentage of the work of the federal government is devoted to enforcing the law, the nature of the attorney general's job almost ensures influence with the president. The attorney general usually is considered one of the "inside members" of the president's cabinet. The position has considerable power.

President George Washington turned to a fellow Virginian, Edmund Jennings Randolph, as his (and the nation's) first attorney general. Randolph had two qualities that have often characterized the individuals who have held that office ever since: talent and controversy.

Before serving with Thomas Jefferson, Alexander Hamilton, and Henry Knox in Washington's first cabinet, Randolph had distinguished himself through his service as a military aide to General Washington, as an attorney general and governor of Virginia, as a delegate to the Virginia constitutional convention of 1776, as a delegate from Virginia to the Continental Congress, and as a delegate to the U.S. Constitutional Convention of 1787. Although Randolph refused to sign the convention's final product, the U.S. Constitution, because, among other reasons, he opposed vesting the executive power in a single president, he did urge its ratification by Virginia.

When Thomas Jefferson resigned in 1794 as Washington's first secretary of state, Washington picked Randolph to succeed him. Randolph resigned the following year, however, amid false charges of soliciting bribes and giving secret information to the French government. Although stripped of his public standing by the charges, the capable Randolph led the successful legal defense in the treason trial of Aaron Burr.

Talent and controversy have followed the successors of Randolph. Roger Taney, attorney general to President Andrew Jackson, and Harlan Fiske Stone, attorney general to President Calvin Coolidge, became chief justices of the United States (in Stone's case, after serving sixteen years as an associate justice). Other former attorneys general who became Supreme Court justices were Nathan Clifford, Joseph McKenna, James C. McReynolds, Francis W. Murphy, Robert H. Jackson, and Thomas C. Clark.

Harry M. Daugherty was attorney general to President Warren G. Harding and was implicated in the Teapot Dome Scandal. Many people thought that Ramsey Clark, the last attorney general to President Lyndon B. Johnson, should have been indicted for treason, but he was not. Clark remains controversial for visiting Hanoi during the Vietnam War after he left office. Two of President Richard Nixon's attorneys general, John N. Mitchell and Richard G. Kleindienst, went to prison after leaving office and being convicted of crimes. President Reagan's controversial attorney general, Edwin Meese, spent much of his tenure fighting ethics charges stemming from inconsistencies and omissions in his financial disclosure forms.

One attorney general, Charles Joseph Bonaparte, had an unusual family history for an American leader. Bonaparte was the grandson of Jerome Bonaparte, king of Westphalia and marshal of France. Jerome, in turn, was the younger brother of Napoleon I, emperor of France. The American Bonaparte first distinguished himself as a leader of the good-government movement of the late nineteenth and early twentieth centuries, serving consecutively as president of the National Civil Service Reform League in 1904 and as president of the National Municipal League in 1905. This commitment appealed to President Theodore Roosevelt, who rewarded Bonaparte with appointments first as secretary of the navy and then as attorney general.

In 1993 President Bill Clinton wanted to appoint the nation's first woman attorney general. His first two choices for the position, Zoë Baird and Kimba Wood, had to withdraw from consideration because of revelations that they had employed illegal immigrants as nannies. Clinton's next choice for the job, Florida prosecutor Janet Reno, was confirmed by the Senate in March 1993. The selection of Reno was symbolically important and enormously popular. Her reputation for integrity was untarnished, and she was known as a straight-speaking, law-and-order prosecutor.

Although she initially was the most celebrated and highly regarded Clinton appointee, Reno soon faced controversy. After members of a religious cult refused to surrender to federal authorities, Reno authorized the FBI to inject nonlethal tear gas into the cult's Waco, Texas, compound. A fire erupted at the compound leading to the deaths of eighty-five people, many of whom were children. Reno testified to Congress that she was responsible for the disaster. Reno's candor earned her immediate praise, and she persevered to win the respect of many during Clinton's first term. In 1996 Reno argued one case (supporting the right of police officers to ask passengers to get out of a car) before the Supreme Court. Although some in the White House questioned her loyalty and felt that she was too quick to call for independent counsels to investigate alleged wrongdoings by high-ranking members of the administration, Clinton ask Reno to stay on for his second term.

---

ing provisions of the Civil Rights Act of 1964, the Age Discrimination in Employment Act, the Civil Rights Restoration Act of 1988, the Americans with Disabilities Act of 1990, the Civil Rights Law of 1991, and the Family and Medical Leave Act of 1993, belong in this category. Their enforcement generally is accomplished by the combined efforts of the Civil Rights Division of the Justice Department, the Equal Employment Opportunity Commission, and the Department of Education. Each agency of the federal government also has an office charged with enforcing internal compliance with these laws, as well as compliance by firms contracting with the agency. A multitude of retirement, medical care, and educational assistance acts are administered by the Social Security Administration of the Department of Health and Human Services, the Department of Veterans Affairs, and the Department of Education.

Political. Political decisions are made according to a complex system of procedural laws. The often-stated purpose of these laws is to promote fairness and integrity in government. The Voting Rights Act of 1965, for example, forbids racial discrimination in voting and is enforced by the FBI and the Civil Rights Division of the Department of Justice. Bribery of and extortion by federal government officials of all branches also fall under the jurisdiction of the FBI. Violations that the FBI uncovers are prosecuted by the Criminal Division of the Justice Department.

Judicial. Most judicial orders are complied with voluntarily. Judgment is entered against the defendant, and the defendant complies: that is, the defendant makes payment, stops the unlawful activity, or turns himself or herself over to authorities for completion of a jail sentence. Behind every instance of voluntary compliance, however, is at least the implicit backing of armed force. Armed force may also be necessary on occasion to enforce judicial orders and to protect judges, jurors, witnesses, and other participants in a trial. The U.S. Marshals Service of the Justice Department is the agency that usually enforces the authority of the judicial branch. Its power may, in extreme circumstances, be backed by the armed forces of the United States, principally by the army and by Army National Guard units nationalized by presidential order.

Public Health and Safety. The national government oversees many issues of public health and safety. They include transportation safety, a concern of the Federal Aviation Administration (FAA) of the Department of Transportation; occupational safety and health, consigned by Congress to the aptly named Occupational Safety and Health Administration of the Department of Labor; and food purity, which falls under the jurisdiction of the Food and Drug Administration (FDA) of the Department of Health and Human Services, the Environmental Protection Agency, and the Food Safety and Inspection Service of the Department of Agriculture.

Public health and safety activities of the executive branch also entail enforcement of more commonly known criminal laws, such as those prohibiting interstate kidnapping, prostitution, and transportation of stolen property. Finally, federal laws attempting to stem drug and alcohol abuse in the United States are enforced by the FBI, DEA, FDA, Customs Service, Coast Guard, Border Patrol, and Bureau of Alcohol, Tobacco, and Firearms. Prosecutions are the responsibility of the Criminal Division of the Justice Department and local U.S. attorneys.

In 1984 Congress passed an anticrime bill that revamped federal sentencing procedures to reduce disparities in the sentencing of criminals. The law reduced judicial discretion by creating a ranking system for crimes and requiring judges to follow sentencing guidelines adopted by a presidential commission. The law also eliminated parole for certain federal offenses, increased penalties for drug trafficking, provided expanded government authority to seize the assets of drug traffickers, and made it more difficult to use the insanity defense.

National Security. Treason and espionage are crimes, as are assorted other activities that jeopardize the military and diplomatic interests of the United States. Protection of national security is associated most often with the FBI, but the efforts of the FBI constitute only a part of the whole. A number of agencies of the Department of Defense—such as the Defense Investigative Service, the Naval Investigative Service, the Office of Special Investigations (air force), and the Intelligence and Security Command (army)—have law enforcement duties to protect national security, as do the Coast Guard, Border Patrol, Immigration and Naturalization Service, and Office of Security at the Department of State. The Central Intelligence Agency is *not* given domestic law enforcement authority by Congress, but it may pass to the FBI intelligence it gathers abroad about American national security breaches.

Public Resources. The public resources of the national government consist of money, property, and people. Almost every law enforcement agency of the national government is involved in the protection of one or all of these resources. The better known of these agencies are the FBI and the Secret Service. Others include the Postal Inspection Service, Park Police of the Department of Interior, U.S. Marshals Service, and Federal Protective Service of the General Services Administration. Each department and agency of the executive branch investigates theft, fraud, and personal security through an office of inspector general.

Public Revenue. Enforcing the nation's tax laws falls primarily under the jurisdiction of three agencies of the Department of Treasury: the Bureau of Alcohol, Tobacco, and Firearms (for taxes on alcohol and tobacco products), the Customs Service (for import tariffs and fees), and the Internal Revenue Service (for personal, corporate, and estate taxes). The Tax Division of the Justice Department prosecutes violations of the various tax laws. The 1994 anticrime bill gave the Customs Service authority to stop and search, without warrant, persons entering or leaving the United States whom a customs official suspects of violating a currency transaction law.

Law Enforcement Functions of the Bureaucracy

The bureaucracy performs four general law enforcement functions: investigation, enforcement, prosecution, and custody.

Investigation. Investigation entails fact finding, that is, a search for facts that may assist an agency in the discharge of its assigned law enforcement responsibilities. The search for facts may be directed toward enactment of new laws or the enforcement of existing laws with more effective strategies, policies, and priorities. Most agencies of the executive branch conduct fact-finding activities.

For an assortment of reasons—the need for impartiality, prestige, or outside expertise—the president may prefer on occasion that a particular issue in law enforcement be investigated by persons not affiliated with existing agencies. In such instances, the president may appoint a presidential investigatory commission.

The presidential commission normally comprises a bipartisan panel of Americans who may or may not be employed by the federal government but who have distinguished themselves publicly. The commission receives a presidential mandate to answer a question, or a series of questions, and is supported by a professional staff paid for by the president.

The National Advisory Commission on Civil Disorders, better known as the "Kerner Commission," is a good example. In July 1967, Detroit, Michigan, was torn by urban rioting. Unable to control the rioting with state and local forces, including the Michigan National Guard, the governor of Michigan requested the assistance of the president.

The president responded with airborne troops, and order soon was restored. But the president wanted to know the causes of the rioting, and he wanted to know what could be done to eliminate or control them.

To answer these questions, President Johnson established the Kerner Commission on July 29, 1967.[241] He appointed Otto Kerner, then governor of Illinois, to chair a panel composed of four members of Congress, one mayor, a state official, a local police chief, and one representative each from labor, business, and civil rights.[242] Two advisory panels, a large investigative staff, and outside consultants and witnesses assisted the panel.

The commission's findings followed months of public hearings, statistical analyses, and review of programs, policies, and procedures. Almost all the applied and theoretical disciplines of the social sciences influenced the final product: sociology, psychology, political science, economics, criminology, urban planning, and education. Participants speculated on the causes of the unrest and offered possible solutions.[243]

Some of the recommendations found their way into national policy; others were considered but never implemented. The timing of the Detroit riot, and the timing of the resulting report, were not good because President Johnson devoted much of his remaining and limited time in the White House to managing the Vietnam War. Richard Nixon, his successor in 1969, was not receptive to the proposals contained in the report.

The more routine form of law enforcement investigation is directed at enforcing rather than changing policy. This is fact finding aimed at determining whether an unlawful act has been committed, who the perpetrators are, and whether evidence can be gathered that is both admissible in court and sufficient to obtain a favorable verdict.

Most enforcement agencies of the executive branch are involved in this phase of law enforcement. The investigation may consist simply of witnessing a crime in progress and interrogating the suspect, in hopes of obtaining a signed confession.

Other investigations take more time, more effort, and considerably more resources. Investigation by the FBI of a national security breach, for example, may require months of investigative work, including surveillance of potential suspects, installation and monitoring of wiretaps, and rigorous background checks.

Certain investigations involve crimes so complex that the resources of multiple agencies from different departments may be mobilized into single task forces. Organized crime falls under this category; agents from the FBI, the IRS, and the DEA often join with their counterparts from state and local police forces and with federal and state prosecutors, to try to control this persistent problem.

Enforcement. Law enforcement involves more than arrest and conviction of criminal suspects. It also involves protection of federal resources and execution of judicial orders. Among the many federal agencies participating in enforcement (most often the same ones that conduct investigations), some of the most prominent are the following:

FOOD SAFETY AND INSPECTION SERVICE (AGRICULTURE DEPARTMENT). President Theodore Roosevelt is reputed to have been reading Upton Sinclair's *The Jungle* while eating breakfast one morning in the White House. Disturbed by Sinclair's description of the meat-packing industry in Chicago, the president threw his sausage out of the White House window and began working toward enactment of the Pure Food and Drug Act of 1906. Conditions have improved considerably since Roosevelt's day. Meat-packing and other food production and processing industries now are subjected to standards adopted and enforced by the Department of Agriculture. The job of the Food Safety and Inspection Service is to enforce these standards. In fiscal year 1995, this agency employed an estimated 10,150 persons and administered a budget of $542 million.[244] In October 1994 President Clinton signed legislation to reorganize the Department of Agriculture. The reorganization plan called for the elimination of thousands of staff positions over a five-year period. President Clinton and Congress undertook this reorganization as part of a broader mission to downsize the bureaucracy.

U.S. DEPARTMENT OF DEFENSE. By order of the president, units of the armed forces of the United States may be used to suppress domestic violence and to remove obstructions to the enforcement of the law. National Guard units of the states may be "nationalized" for this purpose by presidential order. When they are, they are placed under the operational command of the secretary of defense. The Defense Department and its component Departments of the Army, Navy, and Air Force include a number of internal agencies with law enforcement responsibility and authority. These agencies include both civilian and military personnel and provide protective services to the property and personnel of the department. They also enforce laws pertaining to fraud, corruption, and national security. For example, in 1988 investigations conducted by the Naval Investigative Service uncovered the Pentagon procurement scandal.

FEDERAL BUREAU OF INVESTIGATION (JUSTICE DEPARTMENT). In almost fifty years of leadership, J. Edgar Hoover, the consummate bureaucratic chief, shaped the FBI into a modern, professional, and semi-autonomous law enforcement agency. The bureau gained notoriety in the 1930s by apprehending or killing marauding and overly romanticized criminals, such as John Dillinger. The favorable image Hoover and his agents enjoyed was only enhanced by the agency's successful apprehension of enemy spies during World War II and the ensuing cold war. Always sensitive to public opinion, Hoover insisted that his agents conform to rigid dress and behavioral standards. He also initiated programs cultivating the bureau's reputation for effectiveness—the FBI's "ten most wanted list" is the outstanding example.

The mystique surrounding and protecting the FBI began to decay somewhat in the 1960s. Critics charged that Hoover was insensitive to civil rights issues and had refused to commit his resources to the investigation of organized crime. Additional blows to the agency came in the wake of Watergate, when its acting director, L. Patrick Gray, admitted to destroying documents important to the initial investigation and when high bureau officers were convicted and imprisoned for illegal activities.

The FBI is the closest thing the United States has to a general police agency in the national government. Its jurisdiction includes investigation and enforcement of laws pertaining to national security, fraud, corruption, civil rights, elections, kidnapping, and robbery of federally insured banks. In fiscal year 1995, the FBI employed an estimated 24,129 persons and had a budget of $2.2 billion.

DRUG ENFORCEMENT ADMINISTRATION (JUSTICE DEPARTMENT). Agents of the DEA have perhaps the most dangerous law enforcement job in the federal government: they enforce national drug laws. Most of the work of the DEA is conducted within the boundaries of the United States. Yet agents may and often do carry their investigations to foreign countries—the drug production, refinement, and transportation centers in Latin America, Europe, Asia, and the Middle East. Here they may advise and exchange intelligence information with their foreign counterparts and, depending on arrangements with their host countries, conduct their own investigations. Although they are subject to reprisals by foreign drug dealers, they are not always authorized to arm themselves. The $961 million budget and 6,653 employees authorized by Congress for the DEA in fiscal year 1995 reflect the agency's importance to federal law enforcement policy.

BORDER PATROL (JUSTICE DEPARTMENT). The Border Patrol, the uniformed component of the Immigration and Naturalization Service, does just what its name implies: it patrols the borders of the United States. As an agency of the INS, the principal task of the Border Patrol is to detect and apprehend illegal entrants. Performing this task, of course, exposes officers of the Border Patrol to an assortment of other crimes, the most notable of which is drug smuggling across the U.S. border. They have the authority to make arrests in such circumstances and are expected to do so.

U.S. MARSHALS SERVICE (JUSTICE DEPARTMENT). U.S. marshals have been a law enforcement resource of the president since the administration of George Washington. In the nineteenth century, marshals acted as the general police force for much of the American West; large sections of the West had not yet achieved statehood and were organized by Congress as territories of the United States. Television and films have taught us that the U.S. marshals of this period, of whom Wyatt Earp and Matt Dillon were only two, single-handedly stood between the ordinary law-abiding citizen and a host of predators—gunslingers, horse thieves, and the local cattle baron, all aided, apparently, by corrupt local sheriffs, mayors, and judges.

The job of the marshal in contemporary American society is less romantic but still important. Marshals enforce court orders, serve court papers, maintain security and order in courtrooms, protect witnesses, escort federal prisoners, and suppress domestic disturbances. Marshals possess general law enforcement power and are an all-purpose force at the disposal of the president and attorney general. In fiscal year 1995 the budget for the U.S. Marshals Service was comparatively small—$397 million. The service employed an estimated 3,757 persons.

SECRET SERVICE (TREASURY DEPARTMENT). The men and women wearing business suits, sunglasses, and earplugs who surround the president on every occasion are the best-known

Secret Service agents surround President Gerald R. Ford as he works the crowd on a 1976 campaign swing through Louisiana. The Secret Service provides security for the president and the first family as well as for past presidents and their families.

component of the Secret Service. But guarding the president is just one of the duties of this agency of the Treasury Department. It also provides security for the vice president, former presidents, immediate family members of current and former presidents, the president- and vice president-elect, presidential and vice-presidential candidates, and visiting heads of state. A uniformed branch of the Secret Service guards foreign embassies and missions and assists in guarding the White House. The Secret Service also has primary jurisdiction in enforcing laws pertaining to counterfeiting, credit card fraud, and defrauding of federally insured banks. Congress appropriated $482 million for the Secret Service in fiscal year 1995, a large portion of which was used to pay the salaries of the estimated 4,688 men and women it employs.

INTERNAL REVENUE SERVICE (TREASURY DEPARTMENT). The IRS has an enviable reputation in Washington for efficiency and impartiality, although many Americans view it apprehensively as the nation's tax collector. Consider its assignment from Congress: the IRS not only collects taxes owed the federal government from individuals and corporations but also processes tax returns from almost every American adult, corporation, partnership, and nonprofit organization. It also calculates and returns any amount previously overpaid by the taxpayer. Certain of these returns are selected for audit (usually by computer), a process designed to detect tax fraud and to deter intentional understatement of future tax liabilities. The IRS includes a criminal investigative division, whose agents are authorized to carry firearms, investigate possible criminal violations of the tax code, make arrests, and serve search warrants. In fiscal year 1995, the IRS employed an estimated 115,378 persons and was appropriated a budget of $7.7 billion for operating expenses.

CUSTOMS SERVICE (TREASURY DEPARTMENT). The men and women of the Customs Service inspect the baggage of persons—citizens and visitors—entering the United States. They are searching chiefly for goods subject to federal tax or prohibited by law from being imported into the United States, such as drugs, weapons, and certain agricultural products. Customs agents board and search incoming ships, airplanes, pleasure boats, trucks, buses, and automobiles, as well as their passengers, baggage, and cargo. Although the Customs Service is principally a tax collection and enforcement agency, it has assumed a lead role in the enforcement of the nation's drug laws by intercepting shipments on the borders of the United States. In fiscal year 1995, the Customs Service had an estimated 19,153 employees and a budget of $2.2 billion.

BUREAU OF ALCOHOL, TOBACCO, AND FIREARMS (BATF) (TREASURY DEPARTMENT). The BATF has authority to combat illegal firearms use as well as illegal trade practices involving alcoholic beverages and tobacco products. A spate of controversy and bad publicity attended the bureau's disastrous February 1993 raid on the compound of a religious cult in Waco, Texas. Critics charged that the BATF had acted improperly in the raid, which resulted in the deaths of four BATF officers and several cult members. The FBI was called in and the resulting standoff ended two months later in a fire that killed many of the remaining cult members and their children. Later that year, President Clinton proposed that the BATF be merged into the Justice Department. Congress opposed the idea and the Clinton administration dropped it. In fiscal year 1995, the BATF had an estimated 4,210 employees and a budget of $386 million.

EMPLOYMENT STANDARDS ADMINISTRATION (LABOR DEPARTMENT). The Fair Labor Standards Act mandates that employees engaged in interstate commerce not otherwise exempted must be paid a minimum hourly wage—$4.25 per hour as of January 1996. The same act also requires that compensation at the employee's usual hourly rate be paid for any work exceeding forty hours in a given work week. Enforcing these laws is the primary responsibility of the Employment Standards Administration (ESA). In fiscal year 1995, the ESA employed an estimated 3,677 persons and had a budget of $279 million.

OCCUPATIONAL SAFETY AND HEALTH ADMINISTRATION (LABOR DEPARTMENT). Health and safety in the workplace are the concerns of OSHA. In accordance with legislation passed by Congress, OSHA has put into effect detailed regulations governing such matters as protective clothing for workers, the handling of hazardous substances, and protective shields on industrial equipment. Inspectors from local OSHA offices inspect work sites and have authority to cite employers who violate or permit violations of the regulations. OSHA employed an estimated 2,323 persons in fiscal year 1995 and administered a budget of $315 million.

FEDERAL AVIATION ADMINISTRATION (TRANSPORTATION DEPARTMENT). The FAA administers and enforces laws pertaining to commercial air travel. Its jurisdiction includes pilot licensing, airport safety and security, air traffic control, and airplane safety. It employed an estimated 49,474 persons in fiscal year 1995 and administered a budget of $9.0 billion.

COAST GUARD (TRANSPORTATION DEPARTMENT). The Coast Guard traces its origins to the nation's first secretary of the Treasury, Alexander Hamilton, who created a service of revenue cutters (small, armed ships) to help prevent smuggling and the resulting evasion of customs taxes. The Coast Guard still performs this function. It also enforces regulations pertaining to maritime safety, licenses boat captains, patrols waterways for hazards (such as icebergs), and rescues people from sunken or disabled vessels. The Coast Guard has an important role in the current efforts to suppress drug smuggling and to intercept persons attempting to enter the United States illegally by sea. During war, operational command of the Coast Guard is transferred to the navy. In fiscal 1995, Congress gave the Coast Guard a budget of $3.7 billion, part of which was used to pay its estimated 44,500 uniformed and civilian personnel.

OFFICES OF THE INSPECTOR GENERAL. All federal departments and most federal agencies contain an office of the inspector general. The functions vary somewhat by agency but generally in-

A Coast Guard crew unloads bails of marijuana seized off the Florida coast.

clude investigations of fraud, abuse, bribery, waste, and personal misconduct within the agency.

Prosecution. U.S. attorneys filed an estimated 118,700 civil and criminal actions during fiscal 1995. This added to their existing workload of an estimated 146,000 docketed cases.[245]

The U.S. attorney is the workhorse of the federal prosecutorial system. Appointed by the president, and located within the Department of Justice, the U.S. attorney assumes the lead responsibility for representing the government in court. One U.S. attorney is appointed for each of the ninety-four judicial districts in the United States. Each is supported by a professional legal staff.

Although the U.S. attorney represents the government in most cases, there are other prosecutorial resources in the executive branch. The Department of Justice itself comprises different divisions that may, at times, be involved in litigation. Each division is headed by an assistant attorney general. Their jurisdiction is indicated by their division title: Antitrust Division, Civil Division, Civil Rights Division, Criminal Division, Environment and Natural Resources Division, and Tax Division.

One other component of the Justice Department is involved in the prosecution phase of law enforcement. This is the Office of the Solicitor General. The solicitor general determines which decisions of federal or state appellate courts will be appealed by the United States to the U.S. Supreme Court. He or she represents the government in the appeal. Owing to the considerable influence the Supreme Court has in interpreting the law, including laws allocating power to the president and presidential agencies, this function is particularly critical to the president.

Occasionally Congress gives limited prosecutorial authority and resources to departments and agencies outside of the Justice Department. The solicitor of labor, for example, has authority to initiate civil actions in federal court to enforce wage-and-hour and occupational health and safety laws.

Custody. Conviction of a crime in federal court may lead to a sentence of imprisonment. When it does, the prisoner is usually remanded to the custody of the Bureau of Prisons for punishment. The Bureau of Prisons is an agency of the Department of Justice and has responsibility for administering the federal prison system. This responsibility includes guarding the inmates (often from one another) as well as supplying them with housing, food, recreation, medical care, and rehabilitation services such as education and counseling. The bureau employed an estimated 25,662 people and administered a budget of $2.4 billion in fiscal 1995.

LAW ENFORCEMENT WITHIN THE U.S. POLITICAL SYSTEM

Law enforcement responsibility and power are shared in the U.S. political system, first of all by the national government and the fifty states and their units of local government. Responsibility and power for law enforcement are also shared by the three branches of the national government. With the notable exception of the president's constitutional authority to grant reprieves and pardons, all incidents of presidential law enforcement power may be checked by at least one of the two other branches.

Sharing within the Federal System

Federalism refers to a form of constitutional structure whereby at least two levels of government exercise sovereign power over geographically defined and overlapping jurisdictions. The two levels of sovereign government in the United States are the national government and the fifty independent state governments.

Allocation of law enforcement responsibility and power within the U.S. federal system has evolved significantly since George Washington and members of the First Congress took office in 1789. This evolution generally has increased the power and responsibility of the national government at the expense of state power and independence.

National law enforcement responsibility and power were slight in 1789 and remained so until the Civil War. States, however, had significant law enforcement responsibility and power during this period. Legislating to promote the public's health, safety, morals, and general welfare was the business of the state legislatures, and it was the business of local sheriffs, state militia, and state judges to enforce those laws.

A number of things changed this balance in favor of the national government. First, led by Chief Justice John Marshall, the U.S. Supreme Court handed down rulings in the first decades of the nineteenth century that interpreted expansively the constitutional grants of power to the national government. Congress, the Court ruled, has ample constitutional power to enact any law necessary and proper to carry out its enumerated powers, as long as that law is not proscribed by the Constitution itself.[246] Contrary provisions of state law must yield to laws enacted by Congress in accordance with its constitutional power,[247] and state court interpretations of federal law are susceptible to review and possible reversal by federal courts.[248]

The assumption of significant and broader law enforcement responsibility and power by the national government cannot be attributed to Marshall and his Court alone. Marshall and the Supreme Court legitimized an extensive and pervasive national role in law enforcement. Nonetheless, a workable consensus among the American people and their elected representatives in Congress that such a role ought to be exercised was not achieved until the latter part of the nineteenth century.

Business in the early decades of the American Republic was largely a local activity and was regulated primarily by state and local governments. By the latter two decades of the nineteenth century, however, it became increasingly apparent that many business activities either could not or would not be regulated effectively by state and local governments. The public eventually pressured Washington to assume the burden. Interstate rail transportation came under federal regulatory jurisdiction with enactment of the Interstate Commerce Act of 1887. Today, virtually no business activity is untouched by federal regulation.

The current relationship between the national government and the fifty state governments in law enforcement is complex. Some activities are regulated extensively and simultaneously by both levels of government. Retail sales, occupational health and safety, and banking, for example, are subject to a host of national and state laws and regulations.

Other activities tend to be regulated predominantly by either one or the other level of government. The national government regulates interstate and international airline travel, radio and television broadcasting, and nuclear power production. Most automobile speed limits, assault and battery, marriage and divorce, and medical licensing are principally matters for state regulation.

The current breakdown of state-national law enforcement responsibility reflects the will of Congress. Although Congress is empowered to exert a far-ranging regulatory reach, it traditionally has left the regulation of most activities to state government. Congress leaves the definition and enforcement of most crimes to state governments. Yet Congress may exercise its enforcement authority directly when a special federal connection exists, such as when the crime is committed by a member of the armed forces and on the premises of a military base. Or it may exercise its authority indirectly by mandating that the states adopt national enforcement standards.

When Congress enters a new regulatory field, the reason for such a move can usually be traced to the support of politically powerful interest groups, or to the American public, or both. Conversely, lack of congressional interest in a regulatory field is understandable when such a move is supported neither by powerful interest groups nor by a significant segment of the American public. This is especially true when a contemplated law is actively opposed.

Substantial public interest in enacting handgun control led to congressional passage of the 1993 "Brady Bill." President Bill Clinton had strongly backed the measure—the most significant gun control law enacted in the United States since 1968. The Brady Bill instituted a five-day waiting period for the purchase of handguns, raised licensing fees for gun dealers, and stipulated that police be informed of multiple gun purchases.

Little public interest is aroused by the notion of professional licensing by the national government. But the idea arouses strong opposition from well-organized and assertive interest groups such as national and state bar and medical associations. Attorneys and physicians are licensed by state government.

One way in which Congress has sought to ensure that states adopt certain regulatory and enforcement actions has been through the use of unfunded mandates. The 1994 anticrime bill, for example, requires states to take certain law enforcement actions, although the federal government provides no money.

The use of unfunded mandates became pervasive in the late 1980s and early 1990s when the federal government, in response to budgetary restraints, sought to pass on to the states the costs of enforcement activities. State governments protested these federal impositions, and in 1995 the Republican-controlled Congress passed restrictions on the use of unfunded mandates. In so doing, Congress sought to reduce the federal government's regulatory role and to give more autonomy to states and localities.

The relationship between national law enforcement agencies of the executive branch and their counterparts in state and local governments can be characterized most aptly as competitive but cooperative. Federal law enforcement agencies may request, and often receive, investigatory and enforcement assistance from state and local police forces. Such assistance, for example, may be given to locate and arrest a military deserter, an armed robber of a post office, or a counterfeiter, or it may be given in the form of security for a visiting president or foreign dignitary.

Former presidential press secretary James Brady (injured in the assassination attempt on President Ronald Reagan), left, his wife Sarah, and New York Rep. Charles Schumer were major advocates of the Brady Bill, which instituted a waiting period for the purchase of handguns.

The president and the principal law enforcement officers of the national government will be reluctant to deny a reasonable request from a state governor for law enforcement assistance. The request may be for troops to put down a riot, as occurred when President Lyndon Johnson sent airborne troops to Detroit in the summer of 1967. More commonly, though, it will involve special federal attention to local problems that either are beyond the competence of state and local resources to resolve or can be resolved more effectively and efficiently with federal assistance.

In April 1995, after the bombing of a federal office building in Oklahoma City, the FBI coordinated a massive effort involving other governmental departments as well as state and local authorities to identify and apprehend those responsible for the disaster. In addition to the FBI, the Secret Service, Department of Defense, Drug Enforcement Agency, Bureau of Alcohol, Tobacco, and Firearms, Oklahoma National Guard, Oklahoma Department of Public Safety, and Oklahoma City Police Department all assisted the criminal investigation.[249]

State and local agencies also receive routine assistance from federal law enforcement agencies. Federal agencies distribute law enforcement assistance grants to state and local governments, offer training in modern law enforcement techniques and technology to state and local enforcement officials, and provide intelligence about local criminal activity.

The federal government may also provide assistance to states and localities to carry out extensive crime fighting programs. The landmark 1994 anticrime bill, signed into law by President Clinton, provided $30.2 billion in federal assistance to states and localities to hire new police officers, build prisons and boot camps, and initiate crime prevention programs, among other measures. *(See box, Presidential Response to Crime, p. 76.)*

Sharing within the National Government

High school students in civics classes learn that laws are made by Congress, enforced by the president, and applied by the courts. It is by this means that tyranny in the United States is averted: political power in the national government is divided and allocated to separate and independent branches. Each branch, therefore, has some check on the goings-on (and possible abuses) of the others.

Article I, section 1, of the U.S. Constitution does assign the legislative power to Congress. And Article II vests the executive power of the United States in the president and imposes on the president the obligation to "take Care that the Laws be faithfully executed." Finally, Article III, section 1, delegates the judicial power of the United States to the Supreme Court and to such other courts as Congress chooses to create.

Still, there is more to this arrangement than the division and allocation of power to separate and independent branches. Power is also shared. Congress, the legislative arm of the national government, makes law according to its constitutional grant of power, but it does so subject to presidential approval or veto, and often at the president's urging. Congress also delegates practical lawmaking power—authority to promulgate binding administrative rules and regulations—to the president and officers of the executive branch who may or may not report to the president.

Furthermore, although the president has the authority to enter into treaties with foreign nation-states, he shares veto power with the Senate, which must ratify the agreements. The president similarly possesses the authority to appoint federal judges and high executive branch officers, but only with the advice and consent of the Senate.

Congress and Presidential Law Enforcement Power

Article I, section 1, of the Constitution states that "[a]ll legislative Powers" of the United States belong to Congress. This power bears directly, extensively, and frequently on the law enforcement obligations and powers of the president. Four categories of power are available to Congress, which, when exercised, may either increase or restrict the law enforcement power of the president. These are lawmaking, investigation, review of presidential appointments, and impeachment.

Lawmaking. Under its lawmaking power, Congress decided that railroads, airlines, and television ought to be regulated by the national government, and Congress determined that national standards ought to apply to the production of food and drugs. The expansion of the national police power is the product of congressional action.

The legislative work of Congress does not end with asserting the regulatory power of the national government. A system and a process must be set in place for enforcing the law. Agencies must be created and empowered. They must employ men and women to enforce the law. Finally, law enforcement officers of the executive branch must be granted specific law enforcement authority.

PRESIDENTIAL RESPONSE TO CRIME

The president occasionally sets about to bolster the federal government's law enforcement activities in response to public pressures—usually resulting from highly publicized events or persisting problems with crime. For example, in the 1980s public opinion polls frequently identified the drug scourge as one of the nation's leading problems. First Lady Nancy Reagan led a national campaign to stigmatize drug use among the youth. With the national elections looming, in 1988 Congress authorized $2.7 billion for antidrug law enforcement. President Ronald Reagan signed the bill on November 18, 1988. Among the law's provisions were:

1988 Antidrug Bill

- Creation of a cabinet-level position for coordinating a national antidrug strategy
- Harsher penalties for drug dealers
- Federal death penalty for major drug traffickers
- Increased funding for drug interdiction
- Denial of federal benefits to repeat drug-use offenders
- Increased funding for drug treatment, prevention, and education

In the 1990s numerous highly publicized incidents of violence outside abortion clinics, some resulting in the murders of abortion providers, emboldened pro-abortion activists to pressure a sympathetic Democratic Congress and President Bill Clinton to enact the Freedom of Access to Clinic Entrances (FACE) Act of 1993. This law made it a federal crime to block access to an abortion clinic; it prohibited intimidation of either women seeking abortions or clinic employees; and it gave similar protections to pregnancy counseling centers and places of worship. Violators became subject to both criminal and civil penalties.

Supporters of the measure framed the issue as one of law and order. They maintained that local authorities were unable to provide adequate protection, thereby requiring a federal response. Abortion protesters objected that the law constituted an infringement on their freedom of speech rights. In *Madsen v. Women's Health Center, Inc.*, a Supreme Court majority came down in favor of FACE, ruling that the government's interest in preserving order and protecting the constitutional right of abortion permits restrictions on protest activities outside of abortion clinics.

With the reported increase in all types of crime in the 1990s, especially the most violent type, opinion polls continually identified crime as one of the nation's leading problems. In his 1994 State of the Union address, President Clinton brought the issue to the national forefront as he endorsed a substantial increase in the reach of the federal law enforcement authority. This presidential attention to the issue helped to mobilize public support and prod Congress to pass a far-reaching anticrime bill that established a $30.2 billion trust fund to pay for various anticrime programs. Among the initiative funded were:

1994 Crime Bill

- Hiring 100,000 new police officers
- Constructing new prisons and boot camps
- Providing formula grants for local crime reduction programs
- Banning manufacture and possession of nineteen assault weapons
- Authorizing the death penalty for federal crimes that result in death or murder of federal law enforcement officials
- Allowing juveniles thirteen and older accused of certain crimes to be tried as adults in federal court
- Mandating life imprisonment for conviction of third violent felony (popularly referred to as "three strikes and you're out")

Congress provides the people necessary to staff the president's law enforcement agencies through authorizing legislation, and it provides for payment of their salaries through separate appropriations bills. Through a similar process, it provides enforcement officers with the personnel and material support necessary to do a satisfactory job.

Federal law enforcement agencies and personnel receive two principal forms of authority from Congress: jurisdictional and enforcement authority. The former determines the types of laws a given agency is supposed to enforce; the second provides enforcement officers with the specific powers to make their enforcement effective.

Congress, for example, has defined the jurisdiction of the Secret Service to include protection of the current and former presidents and vice presidents of the United States and the members of their immediate families; candidates for the presidency and vice presidency meeting certain conditions; and visiting foreign dignitaries. The Secret Service also has jurisdiction over laws pertaining to currency, enumerated sections of various banking laws, and various forms of electronic and credit card fraud.[250]

One agency's jurisdiction occasionally overlaps with another's. The Drug Enforcement Administration has primary jurisdiction over enforcement of the nation's narcotics laws. But that jurisdiction overlaps considerably with the jurisdiction given the FBI, the Customs Service, the Coast Guard, and the Food and Drug Administration. Congress has given all these agencies, and many more, the authority to enforce various aspects of the nation's drug laws.

In an effort to coordinate a federal antidrug strategy, Congress established in 1988 the executive branch Office of National Drug Control Policy, headed by a director and two deputies. The legislation also created a bureau of state and local affairs, led by an associate director for drug-control policy.

For the first time ever, Congress had created a cabinet-level position to coordinate the nation's antidrug effort. Congress gave the director, or "drug czar," authority to coordinate the antidrug activities of more than thirty governmental agencies, including the Central Intelligence Agency and the Departments of Justice, Treasury, Defense, State, Labor, and Education. The law requires the drug czar to submit a national drug control strategy to Congress annually. *(See box, Presidential Response to Crime, p. 76.)*

Special agents and other FBI personnel have congressional authority to "carry firearms, serve warrants and subpoenas issued under the authority of the United States." Congress has also given them authority to "make arrests without warrant for any offense against the United States committed in their presence, or for any felony cognizable under the laws of the United States if they have reasonable grounds to believe that the person to be arrested has committed or is committing such felony."[251]

Congress has made similar grants of authority to U.S. marshals, agents of the Secret Service and Drug Enforcement Administration, and a host of other federal law enforcement personnel.[252]

Congress may limit the authority that it confers on federal law enforcement agencies and personnel. Postal inspectors, for example, have authority to "make arrests without warrant for offenses against the United States committed in their presence,"[253] but only if the offense is related to the property or use of the Postal Service.[254]

Congress may affect the law enforcement power of the president through the exercise of its inherent authority to investigate. Investigations may be conducted for the purpose of determining whether new laws are needed, or to determine whether existing laws are being properly enforced.

Investigations. Congressional investigations frequently are conducted through the device of a committee hearing. Witnesses give their views on the issue before the committee and subject themselves to questions from committee members and counsel. The testimony may be given voluntarily or under compulsion (subpoena). In most instances a witness will be placed under oath, subjecting him or her to the possibility of prosecution for giving false testimony intentionally.

Impressive resources are available to Congress to assist in these investigations. These may include personal and committee staff, researchers of the Library of Congress, economists of the Congressional Budget Office, auditors of the General Accounting Office, and analysts of the Office of Technology Assessment. The staffs of each of these congressional agencies have established reputations for objective and competent work.

Television has enhanced the significance of congressional investigations. The specter of organized crime in the United States was revealed starkly in the televised investigations of the Kefauver Committee (Special Committee to Investigate Organized Crime in Interstate Commerce) in the 1950s. The American people heard, for the first time, mention of the "mafia" and "la cosa nostra" from witnesses who testified to the power and pervasiveness of these organizations in American society.

Separate Senate and House committees investigated alleged criminal activities committed during the Nixon administration, after burglars traced to the White House were arrested during a break-in of the Democratic National Committee headquarters at the Watergate complex in Washington, D.C. In 1987 a joint committee of Congress investigated the circumstances surrounding the Iran-contra affair.

Most congressional investigations lack such spectacular quality, but they are important nevertheless. A subcommittee of the House Committee on Interior and Insular Affairs, for example, conducted an investigation into the enforcement of federal law by the Nuclear Regulatory Commission. Its findings were critical, as is indicated by the title of its report: *"NRC Coziness with Industry: Nuclear Regulatory Commission Fails to Maintain Arms' Length Relationship with the Nuclear Industry."*[255]

Review of Presidential Appointments. The importance of presidential appointment authority to presidential law enforcement power has already been discussed. Congress exercises an important restraint on presidential law enforcement power by saying (within constitutional limitations) *which offices are subject to presidential appointment* and what limitations are imposed on the presidential authority to remove commissioned appointees.

Congress also influences presidential appointment authority by specifying the appointments that must receive Senate confirmation before the appointees may take office. Although most presidential appointees to law enforcement and judicial positions have been approved by the Senate, there is less deference to the president in this area today than there used to be. Refusal to confirm is usually based on judgments about the candidate's professional or ethical fitness. Nonetheless, partisan and ideological considerations often play an important role in considering whether to confirm presidential appointees.

In 1985 the Senate refused to confirm William Bradford Reynolds as President Reagan's appointee to associate attorney general. A sufficient number of senators were not satisfied that Reynolds had performed with sufficient vigor in his previous post as assistant attorney general in charge of the civil rights division.

In 1987 the Senate refused to confirm Judge Robert H. Bork for the U.S. Supreme Court. Bork's professional and ethical fitness for the position were beyond question. In a highly charged political campaign against his appointment, critics maintained that Bork was unfit to serve based on his earlier controversial academic writings and judicial opinions.

The effect of Senate approval on the presidential appointment power, however, cannot be measured solely by reference to the number of times the Senate refuses to confirm. Knowing that appointees must be examined and confirmed by the Senate may well cause presidents to make their selections carefully. Moreover, knowing that nominees will be subjected to Senate scrutiny should cause the president to insist that backgrounds be subjected to searching investigation before names are announced and submitted.

It does not always work that way. President Reagan's hastily chosen replacement for Bork, Douglas Ginsberg, soon withdrew from consideration after it was revealed that Ginsberg had engaged in illegal drug use. The day after his 1993 inauguration, President Clinton had to withdraw his first nominee for attorney general, Zoë Baird, because of revelations that she had hired an illegal immigrant as a nanny. Clinton admitted that he and his transition staff had failed to scrutinize Baird's background adequately. Yet soon afterward Clinton's top contender for the position, Kimba Wood, had to withdraw for similar reasons. (Wood was never officially nominated for the post; she withdrew at the conclusion of her background check.)

Senate examination of presidential nominees, usually conducted in public hearings, may result in promises being made by the nominee to Congress. A notable instance occurred when the Senate Judiciary Committee exacted a promise from Elliot Richardson that if confirmed as attorney general, he would not fire the special prosecutor investigating the Watergate improprieties except for misconduct. Richardson was confirmed and kept his promise. He resigned rather than obey President Nixon's order to fire Archibald Cox, the special prosecutor.

Impeachment. The ultimate congressional check on executive law enforcement power is removal from office through the impeachment process. Article II, section 4, of the Constitution gives Congress power to remove from office the president, vice president, "and all civil Officers of the United States," upon impeachment for and conviction of "Treason, Bribery, or other high Crimes and Misdemeanors."

The removal process is conducted in two stages: impeachment and trial. The first stage, which is assigned by the Constitution to the House of Representatives, is concerned with determining whether probable cause exists to believe that misconduct warranting removal has occurred and that the accused is culpable.[256] Acting much like a grand jury in a criminal case, the House considers charges of misconduct, hears evidence concerning the alleged acts of misconduct, and makes a preliminary determination of whether the alleged misconduct, if true, warrants removal, and whether the evidence supports the charges. If the House, by a majority vote, considers the allegations of misconduct sufficiently serious to warrant removal, and supported by the evidence, then it reports one or more articles of impeachment to the Senate for trial.

The House functions as a grand jury; the Senate acts much like a trial jury in a criminal case. With the chief justice of the Supreme Court presiding, its function is to convict or acquit for each article of impeachment, based on evidence heard in a trial conducted in the Senate chambers. Guilt or innocence of the charges contained in the articles of impeachment is determined by a two-thirds vote of the senators present.[257]

"Treason, Bribery, or other high Crimes and Misdemeanors," the constitutionally stated grounds for removal through by impeachment, do not have a meaning that is agreed upon universally. Alexander Hamilton described the impeachment power as political, for it would be applied to persons committing "injuries done immediately to society itself."[258]

Such injuries would include not only treason and bribery, but also such criminal acts as murder, rape, and mayhem. It is not clear that "high Crimes and Misdemeanors" include a violation of the Constitution; or of a statute not providing criminal penalties; or even a *failure* to enforce the law.

Only one president has been impeached (that is, charged) to date. In 1868 the House charged President Andrew Johnson with violating the Tenure of Office Act of 1867.[259] Specifically, the House charged the president with violating his constitutional obligation to take care that the laws are executed faithfully by firing Edwin M. Stanton, his secretary of war, without cause and without prior Senate consent. The Senate, however, failed by one vote to muster the two-thirds majority necessary to convict Johnson.

The precedent furnished by Johnson's ordeal is primarily negative. A narrow interpretation of the precedent would hold that the Senate merely confirmed that violation of the Tenure of Office Act, a legislative measure of dubious constitutional validity, did not constitute a sufficient basis for removal of the president.[260] A broader reading of the Senate's action would find significant the failure of the Senate to remove a president for what was really political incompatibility.

A more contemporary example of the impeachment power being used against a president is furnished by the events leading to the resignation of President Nixon in 1974. In 1972, employees of the Committee to Re-elect the President, Nixon's personal campaign organization, were arrested by District of Columbia police during a burglary of the Democratic Party headquarters in Washington's Watergate complex.

Investigations by local and federal law enforcement agencies, a federal grand jury, a Senate investigative committee, and a special prosecutor, as well as newspaper and broadcast journalists, revealed evidence not only of involvement by high- and mid-level members and former members of the Nixon administration in the burglary but also of various other allegedly unlawful activities. In 1974 an impeachment bill was introduced on the House floor and referred to the House Committee on the Judiciary.

Following televised hearings, the committee voted to recommend three articles of impeachment to the House. Each one of the three articles charged the president with violating his oath of office and his constitutional obligation to take care that the laws be faithfully executed. The three articles then enumerated specific allegations of misconduct, which, a majority of the committee believed, warranted Nixon's removal: obstruction of justice, abuse of power, abuse of individual rights, misprision (concealment) of felony, and failure to comply with congressional subpoenas.

Rather than face certain impeachment, Nixon resigned from office on August 9, 1974. Still, the committee action remains a

Only one president has been impeached to date—Andrew Johnson in 1868. Congress failed by one vote to remove him from office.

powerful reminder that the removal power of Congress is not entirely dormant. The circumstances warranting its use must be serious, and the charges must be backed by compelling evidence—a "smoking gun" was the phrase often used by some committee members. But the power remains, and it can be used.

The Judiciary and the President. The judiciary arbitrates and resolves legal disputes according to the law. In doing this, the judiciary both supports and checks presidential law enforcement authority. It also creates law enforcement opportunities and burdens for the president and makes law through the process of interpreting law.

The judiciary supports presidential law enforcement power by holding that presidential claims of authority are in accord with the U.S. Constitution and laws of the United States. Such pronouncements usually settle any immediate disputes between the president and Congress or the states over the existence and extent of specific presidential law enforcement powers, and they offer reassurance to the American people that their president acted within the law.

The judiciary also supports presidential law enforcement power by invalidating efforts by other political actors, usually Congress and the states, to restrict presidential authority unduly.

Americans witnessed the first type of support for presidential power when the U.S. Supreme Court upheld assertions of presidential power to deploy military forces to suppress a domestic insurrection (the Civil War) and to quell strikes inhibiting interstate movement of railroads and delivery of the U.S. mail.[261] Similarly, the Supreme Court upheld presidential discretion to use U.S. marshals to maintain peace in situations neither contemplated nor prohibited by legislation.[262] The Court has protected the president from congressional interference with the power to grant pardons, reprieves, and amnesties.[263]

American judges, however, are an independent lot, constitutionally and in fact. They are not appointed to be mere supporters of the president, and they do not define their own roles in that manner. They have authority to check presidential claims of law enforcement power, and they have the power to make their own authority felt.

The judiciary most often checks presidential law enforcement authority when judges rule against the government in civil or criminal cases. The ruling may be on an important interpretation of law, the admissibility in trial of a critical piece of evidence, or on the facts of the case. An assortment of judicial rulings can lead to the government losing. The result is the same.

When the rulings involve an interpretation of constitutionally or legislatively delegated authority of the president, then the effect may well limit the executive law enforcement capability in future cases as well as in the immediate case. Federal law enforcement agents know well, for example, that a confession obtained through coercion cannot be used as evidence in a trial.

NOTES

1. Peter Woll, *American Bureaucracy,* 2d ed. (New York: Norton, 1977), 63.
2. Alexander Hamilton, *Federalist* No. 72, in *The Federalist Papers* (New York: Tudor, 1937), 64.
3. Clinton Rossiter, *The American Presidency,* 3d ed. (New York: Harcourt Brace Jovanovich, 1963).
4. Charles T. Goodsell, *The Case for Bureaucracy* (Chatham, N.J.: Chatham House, 1983), 2.
5. H. H. Gerth and C. Wright Mills, *From Max Weber* (New York: Oxford University Press, 1946), 196–199.
6. George J. Gordon, *Public Administration in America,* 2d ed. (New York: St. Martin's Press, 1982), 297.
7. Quoted in Robert Sherrill, *Why They Call It Politics,* 4th ed. (New York: Harcourt Brace Jovanovich, 1984), 260.

8. Michael Nelson, "The Irony of American Bureaucracy," in *Bureaucratic Power in National Policy Making,* ed. Francis E. Rourke, 4th ed. (Boston: Little, Brown, 1986), 163–187.

9. Ibid., 169.

10. Sherrill, *Why They Call It Politics,* 259.

11. Quoted in ibid.

12. Quoted in Richard Neustadt, *Presidential Power* (New York: Wiley, 1960), 22.

13. Quoted in Mike Causey, "Trying to Activate Bureaucracy," *Washington Post,* May 30, 1972, B-9.

14. Arthur M. Schlesinger Jr., *The Crisis of Confidence* (Boston: Houghton Mifflin, 1969), 291.

15. Richard M. Pious, *The American Presidency* (New York: Basic Books, 1979), 212.

16. Thomas E. Cronin, *The State of the Presidency,* 2d ed. (Boston: Little, Brown, 1980), 333.

17. Richard Rose, *Managing Presidential Objectives* (New York: Free Press, 1976), 23.

18. Rossiter, *American Presidency,* 129.

19. Stephen Hess, *Organizing the Presidency* (Washington, D.C.: Brookings, 1988), 6.

20. David Truman, *The Governmental Process* (New York: Knopf, 1951); Hess, *Organizing the Presidency;* George Reedy, *The Twilight of the Presidency* (New York: World, 1970).

21. Rose, *Managing Presidential Objectives,* 147.

22. Cronin, *State of the Presidency,* 225.

23. Alexander Hamilton, *Federalist* No. 70, in *The Federalist Papers* (New York: Tudor, 1937), 49–50.

24. McGeorge Bundy, *The Strength of Government* (Cambridge, Mass.: Harvard University Press, 1968), 37.

25. Woll, *American Bureaucracy,* 241.

26. Ibid., 240.

27. Executive Office of the President, President's Special Review Board 1987, *Report of the President's Special Review Board (Tower Commission Report)* (Washington, D.C.: Government Printing Office, 1987).

28. Anthony Downs, *Inside Bureaucracy* (Boston: Little, Brown, 1967), 116–118.

29. Arthur M. Schlesinger Jr., *A Thousand Days: John F. Kennedy in the White House* (Boston: Houghton Mifflin, 1965), 683.

30. Cronin, *State of the Presidency,* 226.

31. Louis W. Koenig, *The Chief Executive* (New York: Harcourt Brace and World, 1968), 417.

32. Richard P. Nathan, *The Plot That Failed: Nixon and the Administrative Presidency* (New York: Wiley, 1975), 82.

33. "President Nixon Finds a Real Garbageman to Woo Garbagemen," *Wall Street Journal,* June 21, 1972, 1, 25.

34. Richard P. Nathan, "The Administrative Presidency," in Rourke, *Bureaucratic Power,* 216. See also Richard P. Nathan, *The Administrative Presidency* (New York: Macmillan, 1986).

35. Dwight D. Eisenhower, *The White House Years: Mandate for Change, 1953–1956* (Garden City, N.Y.: Doubleday, 1963), 114.

36. Hess, *Organizing the Presidency,* 2.

37. Frank Kessler, *The Dilemmas of Presidential Leadership: Of Caretakers and Kings* (Englewood Cliffs, N.J.: Prentice-Hall, 1982), 60.

38. Hess, *Organizing the Presidency,* 3–4.

39. Quoted in Koenig, *Chief Executive,* 193.

40. Kessler, *Dilemmas of Presidential Leadership,* 72.

41. William Safire, *Before the Fall* (Garden City, N.Y.: Doubleday, 1975); Henry Kissinger, *The White House Years* (Boston: Little, Brown, 1979).

42. Charles O. Jones, *The Presidency in a Separated System* (Washington, D.C.: Brookings, 1994).

43. Ibid., 103.

44. *Congressional Quarterly Weekly Report,* July 21, 1979, 1432.

45. Kessler, *Dilemmas of Presidential Leadership,* 68.

46. Colin Campbell, *Managing the Presidency: Carter, Reagan, and the Search for Executive Harmony* (Pittsburgh: University of Pittsburgh Press, 1986), 61.

47. Quoted in Campbell, *Managing the Presidency,* 71.

48. Paul Quirk, "Presidential Competence," in *The Presidency and the Political System,* 2d ed., ed. Michael Nelson, (Washington, D.C.: CQ Press, 1988).

49. *Tower Commission Report,* IV-10.

50. Elizabeth Drew, *On the Edge: The Clinton Presidency* (New York: Simon and Schuster, 1994), 98.

51. Ibid., 102.

52. Ibid., 241.

53. Woll, *American Bureaucracy,* 11.

54. Pious, *American Presidency,* 222.

55. Joel D. Aberbach, *Keeping a Watchful Eye: The Politics of Congressional Oversight* (Washington, D.C.: Brookings, 1990), 35.

56. Pious, *American Presidency,* 224.

57. Allen Schick, "Politics Through Law: Congressional Limitations on Executive Discretion," in *Both Ends of the Avenue: The Presidency, the Executive Branch, and the Congress in the 1980s,* ed. Anthony King (Washington, D.C.: American Enterprise Institute, 1983), 176.

58. *Immigration and Naturalization Service v. Chadha,* 462 U.S. 919 (1983).

59. Quoted in Martin Tolchin, "The Legislative Veto, an Accommodation That Goes On and On," *New York Times,* March 31, 1989, 8.

60. Thomas Franck and Edward Weisband, *Foreign Policy by Congress* (New York: Oxford University Press, 1979).

61. Pious, *American Presidency,* 229.

62. Executive Office of the President, President's Committee on Administrative Management, *Brownlow Commission Report* (Washington, D.C.: Government Printing Office, 1937), 5.

63. Ibid., 6–7.

64. Peri E. Arnold, *Making the Managerial President: Comprehensive Reorganization Planning, 1905–1980* (Princeton, N.J.: Princeton University Press, 1986), 114–115.

65. Commission on the Organization of the Executive Branch of Government, *General Management of the Executive Branch* (Washington, D.C.: Government Printing Office, 1949).

66. Ibid., 34.

67. Arnold, *Making the Managerial President,* 159.

68. Ibid., 177–193.

69. Ibid., 277.

70. Tyrus G. Fain, ed., *Federal Reorganization: The Executive Branch,* Public Document Series (New York: Bowker, 1977), xxxi.

71. See, for example, Koenig, *Chief Executive,* chap. 8.

72. James P. Pfiffner, "Strangers in a Strange Land: Orienting New Presidential Appointees," in *The In-and-Outers: Presidential Appointees and Transient Government in Washington,* ed. G. Calvin Mackenzie (Baltimore: Johns Hopkins University Press, 1987), 141. The total number of appointees is based on data from the Center for Excellence in Government, February 1989.

73. Hugh Heclo, *A Government of Strangers: Executive Politics in Washington* (Washington, D.C.: Brookings, 1977), 94.

74. Niccolo Machiavelli, *The Prince* (Harmondsworth, Middlesex, England: Penguin, 1961), 124.

75. Quoted in Schlesinger, *Thousand Days,* 127.

76. Pfiffner, "Strangers in a Strange Land," 142.

77. Richard F. Fenno Jr., *The President's Cabinet* (New York: Vintage, 1958), 51.

78. G. Calvin Mackenzie, *The Politics of Presidential Appointments* (New York: Free Press, 1981), 6.

79. Drew, *On the Edge,* 33–34, 99–101.

80. Cronin, *State of the Presidency,* 164.

81. U.S. Commission on Executive, Legislative, and Judicial Salaries, *Re-*

port of the Commission on Executive, Legislative, and Judicial Salaries (Washington, D.C.: Government Printing Office, 1980), ix, 1.

82. Quoted in Dick Kirschten, "Why Not the Best?" *National Journal,* June 12, 1982, 1064.

83. Stephen L. Carter, *The Confirmation Mess* (New York: Basic Books, 1994), 7.

84. Mackenzie, *Politics of Presidential Appointments,* 95.

85. Cronin, *State of the Presidency,* 165.

86. Christopher J. Deering, "Damned If You Do and Damned If You Don't: The Senate's Role in the Appointments Process," in Mackenzie, *The In-and-Outers,* 119.

87. Ibid., 117.

88. Dom Bonafede, "The White House Personnel Office from Roosevelt to Reagan," in Mackenzie, *The In-and-Outers,* 32.

89. See John P. Burke, *The Institutional Presidency* (Baltimore: Johns Hopkins University Press, 1992), chap. 4.

90. John W. Macy, Bruce Adams, and J. Jackson Walter, *America's Unelected Government: Appointing the President's Team* (Cambridge, Mass.: Ballinger, 1983), 32.

91. Quoted in Edward D. Feigenbaum, "Staffing, Organization, and Decision-Making in the Ford and Carter White Houses," *Presidential Studies Quarterly* (summer 1980): 371.

92. Bonafede, "White House Personnel Office."

93. Quoted in ibid., 48.

94. Macy, Adams, and Walter, *America's Unelected Government,* 39.

95. Bonafede, "White House Personnel," 57.

96. *Myers v. United States,* 272 U.S. 52 (1926).

97. Quoted in Woll, *American Bureaucracy,* 224.

98. *Humphrey's Executor v. United States,* 295 U.S. 602 (1935).

99. *Wiener v. United States,* 357 U.S. 349 (1958).

100. *Morrison v. Olson,* 487 U.S. 654 (1988).

101. Pious, *American Presidency,* 256.

102. Lyndon Baines Johnson, *The Vantage Point* (New York: Holt, Rinehart and Winston, 1971), 34.

103. Lance T. LeLoup, "Fiscal Chief: Presidents and the Budget," in *The Presidency: Studies in Policy Making,* ed. Stephen A. Shull and Lance T. LeLoup (Brunswick, Ohio: King's Court, 1979), 211.

104. Johnson, *Vantage Point,* 36.

105. Gerald Ford, "Budget Message of the President," *The Budget of the United States Government, Fiscal Year 1978* (Washington, D.C.: Government Printing Office, 1977), M-3.

106. Dennis S. Ippolito, *The Budget and National Politics* (San Francisco: Freeman, 1978), 40.

107. 42 Stat. 20, sec. 206.

108. Office of Management and Budget, *Preparation and Submission of 1977 "Current Services" Budget Estimates,* Bulletin No. 76–4 (Washington, D.C.: Government Printing Office, 1975), 1.

109. Howard E. Shuman, *Politics and the Budget: The Struggle Between the President and the Congress* (Englewood Cliffs, N.J.: Prentice-Hall, 1984), 225.

110. *Budget of the United States, Fiscal Year 1983: Major Themes and Additional Budget Details* (Washington, D.C.: Government Printing Office, 1982), 37.

111. Aaron Wildavsky in *The Congressional Budget Process After Five Years,* ed. Rudolph G. Penner (Washington, D.C.: American Enterprise Institute, 1981), 99.

112. Hedrick Smith, *The Power Game* (New York: Random House, 1988), 290.

113. Shuman, *Politics and the Budget,* 287.

114. Pious, *American Presidency,* 272.

115. Shuman, *Politics and the Budget,* 60.

116. *New York Times,* February 10, 1982, A1.

117. Drew, *On the Edge,* 109.

118. Louis Fisher, *Presidential Spending Power* (Princeton, N.J.: Princeton University Press, 1975), 7.

119. Pious, *American Presidency,* 278.

120. Fisher, *Presidential Spending Power,* 207.

121. 88 Statute 1804, sec. 32 (1974).

122. Ippolito, *Budget and National Politics,* 135.

123. Quoted in Pious, *American Presidency,* 278.

124. Ippolito, *Budget and National Politics,* 138–139.

125. *Train v. City of New York,* 420 U.S. 35 (1975).

126. *Immigration and Naturalization Service v. Chadha,* 462 U.S. 919 (1983).

127. John Ellwood and James Thurber, "The Congressional Budget Process Re-examined," in *Congress Reconsidered,* 2d ed., ed. Lawrence C. Dodd and Bruce I. Oppenheimer (Washington, D.C.: CQ Press, 1981), 266.

128. See Willi Paul Adams, "The State Constitutions as Analogy and Precedent: The American Experience with Constituent Power before 1787," in *The United States Constitution: Roots, Rights, and Responsibilities,* ed. A. E. Howard, (Washington, D.C.: Smithsonian Institution Press, 1992).

129. Edward S. Corwin, *The President: Office and Powers, 1789–1957,* 4th ed. (New York: New York University Press, 1957), 7; Pious, *The American Presidency,* 38.

130. *In re Neagle,* 135 U.S. 1 (1890). By contrast, see the Court's opinion in *Myers v. United States,* 272 U.S. 52 (1926), in which Justice Oliver Wendell Holmes argued, "The duty of the President to see that the laws be executed is a duty that does not go beyond the laws or require him to achieve more than the Congress sees fit to leave within his power." This view of executive discretion is generally superseded by the view propounded in *Neagle.* See Corwin, *President: Office and Powers,* 169.

131. *Proclamations* are mostly directed at private individuals or matters. Proclamations generally encompass such hortatory matters as Thanksgiving Day or National Black History Month, but some involve substantive issues that carry the force of law. The Supreme Court in *Wolsey v. Chapman,* 101 U.S. 755 (1879), ruled that there is no material difference between proclamations and executive orders, so this section makes no distinction between the two. This discussion focuses primarily on executive orders.

132. Phillip J. Cooper, "By Order of the President: Administration by Executive Order and Proclamation," *Administration and Society* 18 (August 1986): 239.

133. Ibid.

134. See Christopher J. Bosso, *Pesticides and Politics: The Life Cycle of a Public Issue* (Pittsburgh: University of Pittsburgh Press, 1987), 208–218.

135. *Newsweek,* February 29, 1988, 40.

136. Supreme Court decisions supporting congressional delegation of authority to the executive branch include *Field v. Clark,* 143 U.S. 649 (1891); *Butterfield v. Stranahan,* 192 U.S. 471 (1904); *United States v. Grimaud,* 220 U.S. 506 (1911); and *Clark Distilling Co. v. West Maryland Railway Co.,* 242 U.S. 311 (1917).

137. Schick, "Politics Through Law," 162.

138. See Corwin, *President: Office and Powers,* 126. In *United States v. Grimaud* the Court did distinguish between "legislative" and "administrative" powers but noted also that it was impractical for Congress to provide for every detail or possible occurrence.

139. See, for example, Theodore Lowi's indictment in *The End of Liberalism,* 2d ed. (New York: Norton, 1989).

140. Corwin, *President: Office and Powers,* 178–179.

141. Leonard White, *The Federalists* (New York: Macmillan, 1948), 512.

142. Leonard White, *The Jeffersonians* (New York: Macmillan, 1951), 552.

143. Corwin, *President: Office and Powers,* 152.

144. Theodore Roosevelt, *An Autobiography* (New York: Scribner's, 1931), 388.

145. Pious, *The American Presidency,* 49.

146. House Committee on Government Operations, *Executive Orders and Proclamations,* 85th Cong., 1st sess., December 1957, 36.

147. See Fisher, *Presidential Spending Power,* 61–64.

148. Schick, "Politics Through Law," 160.

149. A contemporary version of this argument can be found in James

Sundquist, *Constitutional Reform and Effective Government* (Washington, D.C.: Brookings, 1986).

150. Fisher, *Presidential Spending Power,* 36.

151. *Korematsu v. United States,* 323 U.S. 214 (1944).

152. Schick, "Politics Through Law," 161.

153. On the regulatory nature of the New Deal regime see, among others, George Hoberg, *Pluralism by Design: Environmental Policy and the Regulatory State* (New York: Praeger, 1992); and Michael J. Lacey, ed., *Government and Environmental Politics: Essays on Historical Developments Since World War Two* (Baltimore: Johns Hopkins University Press, 1991).

154. See Ruth Morgan, *The President and Civil Rights* (New York: St. Martin's Press, 1970), 5.

155. Cooper, "By Order of the President," 238.

156. *Brown v. Board of Education of Topeka,* 349 U.S. 483 (1954); *Brown v. Board of Education of Topeka,* 349 U.S. 294 (1955).

157. Cooper, "By Order of the President," 238.

158. Louis Fisher, *The President and Congress* (New York: Free Press, 1972), 51.

159. See Bob Woodward, *The Agenda: Inside the Clinton White House* (New York: Simon and Schuster, 1994); and Randy Shilts, *Conduct Unbecoming: Lesbians and Gays in the U.S. Military: Vietnam to the Persian Gulf* (New York: St. Martin's Press, 1993).

160. See Fisher, *Presidential Spending Power.*

161. On the tensions between Congress and the presidency over the direction of public policy, see Jones, *The Presidency in a Separated System;* David Mayhew, *Divided We Govern: Party Control, Lawmaking, and Investigations, 1946–1990* (New Haven, Conn.: Yale University Press, 1991); and James A. Thurber, ed., *Divided Democracy: Cooperation and Conflict between the President and Congress* (Washington, D.C.: CQ Press, 1991).

162. Corwin, *President: Office and Powers,* 100.

163. *Skinner v. Railway Labor Executives Association,* 489 U.S. 602 (1989) and *National Treasury Employees Union v. Von Raab,* 489 U.S. 656 (1989). See Jack W. Peltason, *Understanding the Constitution,* 12th ed.(New York: Holt, Rinehart, and Winston, 1992), 239–240.

164. Arthur M. Schlesinger Jr., *The Imperial Presidency* (New York: Popular Library, 1974), 324.

165. Ibid., 325.

166. Pious, *American Presidency,* 348.

167. Schlesinger, *The Imperial Presidency,* 325.

168. "The Struggle Against Secrecy," *New York Times,* January 3, 1996, A4.

169. *New York Times,* February 13, 1988, 33.

170. On the "Iran-contra" controversy see, among many works, Jane Mayer and Doyle McManus, *Landslide: The Unmaking of the President, 1984–1988* (Boston: Houghton Mifflin, 1988); Bill Moyers, *The Secret Government: The Constitution in Crisis* (Washington, D.C.: Seven Locks Press, 1988); *Report of the Congressional Committees Investigating the Iran-Contra Affair, with Supplemental, Minority, and Additional Views, November 1987* (Washington, D.C.: Government Printing Office, 1987); and Bob Woodward, *Veil: The Secret Wars of the CIA, 1981–1987* (New York: Simon and Schuster, 1987).

171. See Colin Campbell and Bert A. Rockman, eds., *The Bush Presidency: First Appraisals* (Chatham, N.J.: Chatham House, 1991).

172. Paul E. Peterson, ed., *The President, Congress, and the Making of Foreign Policy* (Norman: University of Oklahoma Press, 1994).

173. Cooper, "By Order of the President," 254.

174. Arthur M. Schlesinger Jr., *The Imperial Presidency.*

175. See James Rosenau, *Turbulence in World Politics: A Theory of Change and Continuity* (Princeton, N.J.: Princeton University Press, 1990).

176. Schick, "Politics Through Law," 157, 181.

177. John Locke, *The Second Treatise on Government* (Indianapolis: Bobbs-Merrill, 1952), 91–96. See also Peltason, *Understanding the Constitution,* 104–108.

178. Jean Jacques Rousseau, *The Social Contract* (New York: Hafner Press, 1947), 110.

179. A writ of *habeas corpus* (Latin for "you have a body") is a court order requiring that authorities must present a prisoner in court and show cause for that person's detention. The Constitution otherwise generally forbids detention of prisoners without due cause.

180. See, in particular, *Federalist* Nos. 28 and 41 in Alexander Hamilton, James Madison, and John Jay, *The Federalist Papers,* ed. Clinton Rossiter (New York: New American Library, 1961).

181. Schlesinger, *Imperial Presidency,* 27–28.

182. Quoted in ibid., 69; see also Clinton Rossiter, *Constitutional Dictatorship* (Princeton, N.J.: Princeton University Press, 1948), 19.

183. Erwin C. Hargrove and Michael Nelson, *Presidents, Politics, and Policy* (Baltimore: Johns Hopkins University Press, 1984), 26.

184. Louis W. Koenig, *The Chief Executive,* 5th ed. (New York: Harcourt Brace Jovanovich, 1986), 235–237.

185. On Bush and the Persian Gulf War see, among others, Campbell and Rockman, *The Bush Presidency: First Appraisals;* and Peterson, *The President, Congress, and the Making of Foreign Policy.*

186. *Martin v. Mott,* 12 Wheat. 19, 23–33 (1827).

187. See Rossiter, *Constitutional Dictatorship.*

188. *Prize Cases,* 2 Black 635, 17 L.Ed. 459 (1863).

189. Schlesinger, *Imperial Presidency,* 75.

190. *Ex parte Merryman,* 17 Fed. Cas. 144 (C.C.D. Md. 1861).

191. *Ex parte Milligan,* 71 U.S. (4 Wall.) 2, 18, L.Ed. 281 (1866); see also Schlesinger, *Imperial Presidency,* 78–79.

192. See *Hirabayashi v. United States,* 320 U.S. 81 (1943); *Korematsu v. United States,* 323 U.S. 214 (1944); and *Ex parte Endo,* 323 U.S. 284 (1944). In *Hirabayashi,* the Court narrowed but did not overturn the power of military officials to impose special curfews on Japanese Americans. In both *Korematsu* and *Endo,* the Court reluctantly upheld internment. In 1988 Congress formally apologized and granted $20,000 tax-free to each of the survivors of the internment.

193. Corwin, *President: Office and Powers,* 235–236.

194. See John Roche, "Executive Power and the Domestic Presidency: The Quest for Prerogative," *Western Political Quarterly* 5 (December 1952): 607.

195. See Schlesinger, *The Imperial Presidency.*

196. J. Malcolm Smith and Cornelius Cotter, *Powers of the President During Crises* (Washington, D.C.: Public Affairs Press, 1960), 134.

197. Robert DiClerico, *The American President,* 3d ed. (New York: Prentice-Hall, 1989), 322.

198. *Youngstown Sheet and Tube Co. v. Sawyer,* 343 U.S. 579 (1952).

199. Rossiter, *American Presidency,* 53.

200. William Manchester, *The Glory and the Dream: A Narrative History of America, 1932–1972,* vol. 2 (Boston: Little, Brown, 1974), 1535–1536.

201. Ibid., 1382.

202. Frank Church, "Ending Emergency Government," *American Bar Association Journal* 63 (February 1977): 198.

203. *Congress and the Nation,* vol. 4 (Washington, D.C.: Congressional Quarterly, 1977), 802.

204. See Fisher, *Presidential Spending Power,* 240.

205. *Congress and the Nation,* vol. 4, 801.

206. PL 94–412; see House Subcommittee on Administrative Law and Governmental Relations, Committee on the Judiciary, Hearings on H.R. 3884, *National Emergencies Act,* 94th Cong., 1st sess., March 6–April 9, 1975.

207. See DiClerico, *American President,* 327–329.

208. Letter of John Marshall to James Wilkinson, January 5, 1787, reprinted in *The Papers of John Marshall, 1775–1788,* vol. 1, ed. Herbert A. Johnson (Chapel Hill: University of North Carolina Press, 1974), 200.

209. Samuel Eliot Morison, Henry Steele Commager, and William E. Leuchtenburg, *The Growth of the American Republic,* vol. 1 (New York: Oxford University Press, 1969), 242. See generally this volume, pp. 227–261, for a description of the events immediately preceding and during the Constitutional Convention.

210. U.S. Constitution, preamble.

211. See generally U.S. Constitution, Article II, for an enumeration of presidential powers.

212. The U.S. Constitution does, in Article I, section 8, give Congress authority to "pay the Debts and provide for . . . the general Welfare of the United States." This is interpreted as a grant of authority for Congress to *spend money* to promote the general welfare of the nation. It is *not* interpreted as a grant of authority to enact any regulatory scheme that Congress believes will promote the general welfare.

213. *McCulloch v. Maryland,* 17 U.S. (4 Wheat.) 316 (1819).

214. *Gibbons v. Ogden,* 22 U.S. (9 Wheat.) 1 (1824).

215. *Wickard v. Filburn,* 317 U.S. 111 (1942).

216. What, for example, is the relationship between home-grown food for purely household consumption and interstate commerce? The Supreme Court gave its answer in *Wickard v. Filburn*: If a household grows and harvests food on its own land, and for its own use, then it will be less likely to purchase food products on the commercial market. The effects of this isolated instance of self-sufficiency will eventually be felt across state lines.

217. The most controversial of the nine cases was *Wards Cove Packing Co. v. Antonio,* 109 S.Ct. (1989).

218. U.S. Department of Commerce, Bureau of Census, *Historical Statistics of the United States: Colonial Times to 1970,* vol. 2 (Washington, D.C.: Government Printing Office, 1975), table Y 308–317, pp. 1102–1103; U.S. Department of Commerce, Bureau of the Census, *Statistical Abstract of the United States,* 115th ed. (Washington, D.C.: Government Printing Office, 1995), table 527, "Federal Civilian Employment by Branch, Agency, and Area."

219. Accounts of the "Ole Miss" incident may be found in Schlesinger, *A Thousand Days,* and in Theodore C. Sorensen, *Kennedy* (New York: Harper and Row, 1965).

220. U.S. Constitution, Article I, section 9.

221. The most famous discussion of this distinction is found in Chief Justice John Marshall's opinion for the U.S. Supreme Court in *Marbury v. Madison,* 5 U.S. (1 Cranch) 137 (1803).

222. *Myers v. United States,* 272 U.S. 52, 177 (1926).

223. See, for example, *Kendall v. United States,* 37 U.S. (12 Pet.) 524 (1838); *Youngstown Sheet and Tube Co. v. Sawyer,* 343 U.S. 579 (1952) (also known as the *Steel Seizure Case)*; and *United States v. Nixon,* 418 U.S. 683 (1974).

224. *In re Neagle,* 135 U.S. 1 (1890).

225. *In re Debs,* 158 U.S. 564 (1895).

226. *Myers v. United States.*

227. *Wiener v. United States,* 357 U.S. 349 (1958); *Humphrey's Executor v. United States,* 295 U.S. 602 (1935).

228. U.S. Constitution, Article III, section 1.

229. U.S. Constitution, Article I, section 8.

230. *In re Debs,* 158 U.S. 564, 582 (1895).

231. *Ex parte Milligan,* 71 U.S. (4 Wall.) 2 (1866).

232. Alexander Hamilton, *Federalist* No. 74, in *The Federalist Papers* (New York: Mentor, 1961), 449.

233. Ibid., 448.

234. Proclamation of September 15, 1792, George Washington, *Messages and Papers of the Presidents, 1789–1897,* vol. I, ed. James D. Richardson (Washington, D.C.: Government Printing Office, 1897), 124–125.

235. See Proclamation of July 10, 1795, George Washington, in *Messages and Papers of the Presidents, 1789–1897,* vol. I, 181.

236. *Ex parte Garland,* 71 U.S. (4 Wall.) 333 (1866). See generally *Schick v. Reed,* 419 U.S. 256 (1974).

237. 26 Stat. 946 (1891).

238. David G. Adler, "The President's Pardon Power," in *Inventing the American Presidency,* ed. Thomas E. Cronin, (Lawrence: University Press of Kansas, 1989), 212, 218–219.

239. Forrest McDonald, *The American Presidency* (Lawrence: University Press of Kansas, 1994), 282.

240. *Wiener v. United States* and *Humphrey's Executor v. United States.*

241. Executive Order 11365, July 29, 1967.

242. Kerner was later rewarded by the president with appointment to the U.S. Court of Appeals for the Seventh Circuit. The judge resigned after being indicted and convicted of a felony.

243. Office of the President, National Advisory Commission on Civil Disorders, *Report of the National Advisory Commission on Civil Disorders* (Washington, D.C.: Government Printing Office, 1968).

244. Estimates for employment and budget data for fiscal year 1995 in this section are taken from Office of the President, Office of Management and Budget (OMB), *Appendix: Budget of the U.S. Government—Fiscal Year 1996* (Washington, D.C.: Government Printing Office, 1995).

245. Ibid., A-631.

246. *McCulloch v. Maryland.*

247. *Gibbons v. Ogden,* 22 U.S. (9 Wheat.) 1 (1824).

248. *Martin v. Hunter's Lessee,* 14 U.S. (1 Wheat.) 304 (1816); *Cohens v. Virginia,* 19 U.S. (6 Wheat.) 264 (1821).

249. David Johnston, "Just Before He Was to Be Freed, Prime Bombing Suspect Is Identified in Jail," *New York Times,* April 22, 1995, 10.

250. 18 United States Code, section 3056 (a) and (b).

251. 18 United States Code, section 3052.

252. See 18 United States Code, sections 3053 (U.S. marshals) and 3056 (Secret Service); and 21 United States Code, section 878 (Drug Enforcement Administration).

253. 18 United States Code, section 3061 (a) (2).

254. 18 United States Code, section 3061 (b).

255. U.S. Congress, House, Committee on Interior and Insular Affairs, Subcommittee on General Oversight and Investigations, *NRC Coziness with Industry: Nuclear Regulatory Commission Fails to Maintain Arms' Length Relationship with the Nuclear Industry,* Committee Print No. 5, 100th Cong., 1st sess., 1987.

256. U.S. Constitution, Article I, section 2.

257. U.S. Constitution, Article I, section 3.

258. Hamilton, *Federalist* No. 65, in *The Federalist Papers* (Mentor edition), 396.

259. 14 Stat. 430 (1867).

260. Compare *Myers v. United States.*

261. The *Prize Cases,* 67 U.S. (2 Black) 635 (1863); *In re Debs.*

262. *In re Neagle.*

263. *Ex parte Garland.*

SELECTED BIBLIOGRAPHY

Aberbach, Joel D. *Keeping a Watchful Eye: The Politics of Congressional Oversight.* Washington, D.C.: Brookings, 1990.

Arnold, Peri E. *Making the Managerial President: Comprehensive Reorganization Planning, 1905–1980.* Princeton, N.J.: Princeton University Press, 1986.

Baker, Nancy V. *Conflicting Loyalties: Law and Politics in the Attorney General's Office, 1789–1990.* Lawrence: University Press of Kansas, 1992.

Bundy, McGeorge. *The Strength of Government.* Cambridge, Mass.: Harvard University Press, 1968.

Burke, John P. "The Institutional Presidency." In *The Presidency and the Political System,* ed. Michael Nelson, 4th ed. Washington, D.C.: CQ Press, 1995.

Campbell, Colin. *Managing the Presidency: Carter, Reagan, and the Search for Executive Harmony.* Pittsburgh: University of Pittsburgh Press, 1986.

Carter, Stephen L. *The Confirmation Mess: Cleaning Up the Federal Appointments Process.* New York: Basic Books, 1994.

Cronin, Thomas E. *The State of the Presidency.* 2d ed. Boston: Little, Brown, 1980.

Dodd, Lawrence C., and Richard L. Schott. *Congress and the Administrative State.* New York: Macmillan, 1986.

Drew, Elizabeth. *On The Edge: The Clinton Presidency.* New York: Simon & Schuster, 1994.

Fain, Tyrus G., ed. *Federal Reorganization: The Executive Branch.* Public Document Series. New York: Bowker, 1977.

Fenno, Richard F., Jr. *The President's Cabinet.* New York: Vintage, 1958.

Fisher, Louis. *The Politics of Shared Power: Congress and the Executive.* 3d ed. Washington, D.C.: CQ Press, 1993.

Heclo, Hugh. *A Government of Strangers: Executive Politics in Washington.* Washington, D.C.: Brookings, 1977.

Hess, Stephen. *Organizing the Presidency.* Washington, D.C.: Brookings, 1988.

Ippolito, Dennis S. *The Budget and National Politics.* San Francisco: Freeman, 1978.

Jones, Charles O. *The Presidency in a Separated System.* Washington, D.C.: Brookings, 1994.

Koenig, Louis W. *The Chief Executive.* 5th ed. New York: Harcourt Brace Jovanovich, 1986.

Kramer, Fred A. *Contemporary Approaches to Public Budgeting.* Cambridge, Mass.: Winthrop, 1979.

LeLoup, Lance T. *Budgetary Politics.* 2d ed. Brunswick, Ohio: King's Court, 1980.

Mackenzie, G. Calvin. *The Politics of Presidential Appointments.* New York: Free Press, 1981.

——, ed. *The In-and-Outers: Presidential Appointees and Transient Government in Washington.* Baltimore: Johns Hopkins University Press, 1987.

Macy, John W., Bruce Adams, and J. Jackson Walter. *America's Unelected Government: Appointing the President's Team.* Cambridge, Mass.: Ballinger, 1983.

McDonald, Forrest. *The American Presidency: An Intellectual History.* Lawrence: University Press of Kansas, 1994.

Nathan, Richard P. *The Administrative Presidency.* New York: Macmillan, 1986.

Nelson, Michael. *The Presidency and the Political System.* 2d ed. Washington, D.C.: CQ Press, 1988.

Nichols, David K., *The Myth of the Modern Presidency.* University Park: Pennsylvania State University Press, 1994.

Rossiter, Clinton L. *The American Presidency.* 3d ed. New York: Harcourt Brace Jovanovich, 1963.

Rourke, Francis E., ed. *Bureaucratic Power in National Policy Making.* 4th ed. Boston: Little, Brown, 1986.

Rozell, Mark J. *Executive Privilege: The Dilemma of Secrecy and Democratic Accountability.* Baltimore: Johns Hopkins University Press, 1994.

Smith, Hedrick. *The Power Game: How Washington Works.* New York: Random House, 1988.

Spitzer, Robert J. *President and Congress: Executive Hegemony at the Crossroads of American Government.* New York: McGraw-Hill, 1993.

CHAPTER 2

Legislative Leader

BY CHRISTOPHER J. BOSSO

THE CONSTITUTION "blends" power among the three branches of government. Yet, despite the popular notion that the branches are equal, only the legislative branch has the legal power to make laws. The Framers of the Constitution believed that only Congress could reflect the diversity of opinions bound to exist in a free society. By contrast, the Framers limited the president's ability to influence legislation to two enumerated or "express" powers: the power to recommend to Congress measures deemed "necessary and expedient" (Article II, section 3) and the power to veto bills passed by Congress (Article I, section 7). Presidents have the sole authority to negotiate treaties with other nations, but treaties gain the force of law only when "two-thirds of the Senators present concur" (Article II, section 2). Presidents also can convene "emergency" sessions of Congress (Article II, section 3), but these are extraordinary events.

The Constitution's terseness notwithstanding, the relationship between Congress and the presidency is the defining fulcrum of the U.S. system of government. The nation's history is marked by continual and immeasurable expansion in the array of resources and powers that presidents can deploy to influence public policy. Some of these powers were "implied" in the Constitution, awaiting only time and reinterpretation as unforeseen conditions and cases arose. Others were delegated officially by Congress to meet new economic or social circumstances, emerging government responsibilities, or new public demands. Still others have been shaped by new technologies such as television, or new international responsibilities such as the defense of Western Europe during the cold war.

The formal brevity of the executive's legislative role thus masks the considerable influence that presidents can wield over the congressional agenda and the direction of public policy. Despite this influence, the presidency's relationship with Congress remains fluid, ambiguous, and frustrating. Much of what presidents desire or need, particularly in the domestic sphere, still demands congressional cooperation. Presidents may ask Congress to enact new laws, appropriate funds, or, in the case of the Senate, approve treaties and executive and judicial branch appointments. In short, the president needs Congress. The legislature, for its part, often proves so stubbornly independent and uncooperative—even hostile—that residents of the White House rarely take its support for granted, even when both branches are controlled by the same political party.[1] New presidents may understand this intellectually, but the reality of the relationship with Congress must come as a shock.

The Veto

The veto is the president's primary formal tool for affecting legislation. All other means for influencing the shape and direction of lawmaking must be understood with reference to this formal power, because only the president's legal capacity to stop legislation gives the other instruments for shaping public policy their teeth.

CONSTITUTIONAL FOUNDATIONS

The ability to block acts passed by Congress finds its origins in the 1787 debate over the Constitution. The Framers of the Constitution are revered for their effort to create a national government that could foster unity and stability while safeguarding the rights and liberties of both the people and the respective states. Their concerns are reflected in the checks and balances woven into a system where separate institutions share power—a system designed ultimately to prevent any single branch (and, by extension, any individual or group) from gaining tyrannical political power.

Readers of the Declaration of Independence know well the colonists' complaints against King George III and their understandable fear of powerful executives. Yet lost too often in textbook treatments of the Constitution was the colonists' equal dread of unchecked legislative power. Thomas Jefferson's second villain in the Declaration of Independence was the English Parliament, a legislature unobstructed by written constitutional limits and loathed widely in the colonies for its apparent disregard for due process of law. These general fears about strong national government power were reflected in the Articles of Confederation, the Republic's first constitution. The Articles, which went into effect in 1781, essentially created a league of friendship among the thirteen nearly sovereign states that made the national government a creature of the states and dependent on them for its powers and funds.

But the national government under the Articles ultimately proved unable to promote either national unity or effective gov-

> He shall from time to time give to the Congress information of the State of the Union, and recommend to their Consideration such Measures as he shall judge necessary and expedient. . . .
>
> —*from Article II, section 3*

ernment. One problem, at least in the eyes of those who agitated for major changes in the Articles, was the lack of an independent national executive strong enough to administer the laws and resist legislative tyranny.[2] Not only was Congress unable to govern by itself, but the excesses of state legislatures during the 1780s led many political thinkers of the time to regard the legislature as being as dangerous to liberty as an unrestrained monarch.

Jefferson, reflecting on his experiences as governor of Virginia, wrote, "All the powers of government . . . result to the legislative body. The concentrating of these in the same hands is precisely the definition of despotic government."[3] These experiences were shared by many of the delegates at the Constitutional Convention of 1787, and it was clear that any new national executive would need some way to check legislative power and foster government efficiency.

The concept of a *veto* (Latin for "I forbid") was well known to the Framers. Indeed, in ancient Rome the veto was used by the plebeians to protect the common people against the excesses of a senate dominated by aristocrats. It later surfaced in medieval Europe as a royal check on newly developing legislatures. In preseventeenth-century England the monarch had an *absolute* power to deny acts by Parliament, a weapon that Queen Elizabeth I for one used quite frequently.[4] Closer to home, by 1787 a few state constitutions (such as that of Massachusetts) contained a form of executive veto.[5]

Not surprisingly, then, the Framers included some form of an executive check on laws passed by Congress in virtually every plan they considered for the new constitution. The Virginia Plan called for a "council of revision" of members from both the executive and the judicial branches that would keep the legislature from drawing "all power into its impetuous vortex."[6] But critics of this idea argued that such a "plural" veto would be too weak, since disputes within the council would undermine decisive executive action. Furthermore, George Mason of Virginia argued, the veto should be more than a check against legislative intrusion. It also was a necessary tool to discourage demagogy and prevent "unjust and pernicious" laws.[7] Other delegates also expressed discomfort with having judges act on bills before they came up as legal cases, so the convention eventually granted the veto to the president alone.

Some proponents of a strong executive initially supported an absolute veto, giving Congress no opportunity to respond, but such a weapon seemed too powerful to delegates who also worried about unresponsive and capricious executives. After much debate, the Framers gave the new executive a "partial negative." The president could reject bills or joint resolutions passed by Congress, but Congress in response could *override* a veto by extraordinary majorities of two-thirds of the members present in each chamber. Presidents could not veto constitutional amendments, concurrent resolutions, or resolutions passed by only one chamber.[8]

The veto was to be the constitutional core of executive independence. As defended during the battle over ratification by Alexander Hamilton in *Federalist* No. 73, "the primary inducement to conferring this power in question upon the executive is to enable him to defend himself; the second one is to increase the chances in favor of the community against the passing of bad laws, through haste, inadvertence, or design."[9] The legislature is not infallible, Hamilton argued, and, unless checked, its love of power would ultimately betray both it and the ability of government to function effectively. Additionally, argued James Madison in *Federalist* No. 48, only by giving each branch some control over the others could power be restrained and rights and liberties be protected—a theme he continued in *Federalist* No. 51 with his famous statement, "Ambition must be made to counteract ambition."[10]

> Every Bill which shall have passed the House of Representatives and the Senate, shall, before it become a Law, be presented to the President of the United States; If he approve he shall sign it, but if not he shall return it, with his Objections to that House in which it shall have originated, who shall . . . proceed to reconsider it.
>
> —*from Article I, section 7*

Opponents of the veto, although also worried about unrestrained legislative power, nonetheless argued that Congress alone represented the people. The veto might undermine democratic values by allowing the president to block "good" laws or simply to thwart majority rule. But, Hamilton retorted in *Federalist* No. 73, unrestrained majorities are equally as dangerous as unchecked elites, and "the injury which might possibly be done by defeating a few good laws will be amply compensated by the advantage of preventing a number of bad ones."[11] What is more, allowing the executive to threaten a veto might induce legislative moderation, making actual use of the veto unnecessary.

The Constitution gives the president three choices when presented with a bill passed by Congress: sign the bill into law; veto the bill and return it to the chamber where it originated within ten legislative days after presentation (Sundays excluded); or, finally, do nothing.[12] If the president does nothing, the bill becomes law automatically after ten legislative days. This provision prevents presidents from thwarting the majority will of Congress through simple inaction. The exception to this rule occurs when Congress passes a bill and then adjourns before ten legislative days elapse. Any bill not signed by the president when Congress so adjourns dies automatically. It cannot become law. This condition is called a *pocket veto*, which is discussed later in this section.

Several things can happen once a president vetoes a bill and returns it to Congress. If the legislature fails to act at all, the bill dies. If two-thirds of the members present in each chamber pass the bill once again, it becomes law automatically despite presidential disapproval.[13] Such "supermajorities" in each chamber combine to produce a veto *override*. Overrides are rare—only 105 of 2,524 presidential vetoes issued between 1789 and 1995

TABLE 2-1 Vetoes and Vetoes Overridden, All Bills, 1789–1996

President	*All bills vetoed*	*Regular vetoes*	*Pocket vetoes*	*Vetoes overridden*
Washington	2	2	0	0
J. Adams	0	0	0	0
Jefferson	0	0	0	0
Madison	7	5	2	0
Monroe	1	1	0	0
J .Q. Adams	0	0	0	0
Jackson	12	5	7	0
Van Buren	1	0	1	0
W. H. Harrison	0	0	0	0
Tyler	10	6	4	1
Polk	3	2	1	0
Taylor	0	0	0	0
Fillmore	0	0	0	0
Pierce	9	9	0	5
Buchanan	7	4	3	0
Lincoln	7	2	5	0
A. Johnson	29	21	8	15
Grant	93 [a]	45	48 [a]	4
Hayes	13	12	1	1
Garfield	0	0	0	0
Arthur	12	4	8	1
Cleveland (1st term)	414	304	110	2
B. Harrison	44	19	25	1
Cleveland (2d term)	170	42	128	5
McKinley	42	6	36	0
T. Roosevelt	82	42	40	1
Taft	39	30	9	1
Wilson	44	33	11	6
Harding	6	5	1	0
Coolidge	50	20	30	4
Hoover	37	21	16	3
F. Roosevelt	635	372	263	9
Truman	250	180	70	12
Eisenhower	181	73	108	2
Kennedy	21	12	9	0
L. Johnson	30	16	14	0
Nixon	43	26 [b]	17	7
Ford	66	48	18	12
Carter	31	13	18	2
Reagan	78	39	39	9
Bush [c]	44	29	15	1
Clinton [d]	17	17	0	1
TOTAL	2,530	1,555	1,065	105

SOURCES: *Presidential Vetoes, 1989–1994,* compiled by the Senate Library (Washington, D.C.: Government Printing Office, 1994), viii; *Congressional Quarterly Weekly Report,* various 1995 and 1996 issues.

NOTES: a. Veto total listed for Grant does not include a pocket veto of a bill that apparently never was placed before him for his signature. b. Two pocket vetoes, later overturned in court, are counted as regular vetoes. c. Two pocket vetoes, attempted by Bush during an intra-session period, are not counted since Congress considered the two bills enacted into law because of Bush's failure to return them to legislation. d. Through 1996.

were overridden—because to sustain a veto the president needs to gain only one-third plus one of the votes of those present in one chamber. *(See Table 2-1.)* Barring an override, Congress can either rewrite the legislation to meet the president's demands (as Hamilton foresaw) or simply can give up and start from scratch.

Bills vetoed by the president normally are returned to Congress accompanied by a message that states reasons for the president's opposition. *(See box, A Veto Message, p. 90.)* Sometimes the president will cite constitutional concerns, at other times political or issue disagreements, but veto messages are always aimed at advancing the president's views on the bill in question. Whatever their other purposes, veto messages ultimately are political statements directed not only at Congress but also at the public at large. In this sense, the veto message is an additional resource in the president's effort to influence public policy.

HISTORICAL DEVELOPMENT

Early presidents, whatever their other political beliefs, conformed to the Framers' view that Congress best represented the public will. Vetoes were confined to bills deemed unconstitutional—the idea that a president should veto a bill simply because it was "bad" politics or policy was not yet widely accepted. Indeed, the few vetoes issued by the first six presidents between 1790 and 1830 were usually based on constitutional grounds.

This narrow interpretation of the president's right (and, perhaps, duty) to use the veto was expanded significantly during the presidency of Andrew Jackson (1829–1837) of Tennessee—hero of the War of 1812, foe of eastern business and banking interests, and self-styled "Tribune of the People." Jackson actively engaged in intense partisan warfare with Congress and, as political scientist Clinton Rossiter suggests, "revived the veto and purified it of the niceties that had grown up around it" by making it an overtly political instrument.[14] Indeed, in eight years Jackson issued twelve vetoes, more than all of his predecessors combined. No veto was overridden. Perhaps most controversial of all was Jackson's rejection of an 1832 bill rechartering the Bank of the United States, which was opposed bitterly by Jackson's supporters among the frontier settlers and farmers because of its high interest rates.

Jackson's immediate successors professed renewed allegiance to the traditional doctrine of congressional supremacy, but they too proved surprisingly resolute when challenged by the legislature. John Tyler (1841–1845) vetoed two major bank bills supported by his party, and his 1842 veto of a controversial tariff measure sparked the first formal attempt in Congress to impeach a president. The effort failed. Tyler's successors showed equally notable bursts of independence. Even so, only fifty-nine bills were vetoed between 1789 and 1865, more than half of them by Presidents Jackson, Tyler, and Franklin Pierce (1853–1857).

Post–Civil War Era

The period between the Civil War and the late 1890s saw some of history's most acrid partisan battles, which often spilled over into conflict between the branches of government. Presidents and Congresses immediately after Abraham Lincoln (1861–1865) clashed with one another increasingly within a national political arena rife with sharp regional and partisan antagonisms, deep social and economic changes, and sharp disputes over the fundamental role of government. This era, although marked generally by congressional dominance, nonetheless saw surges in the use of the veto as successive presidents attempted to grapple with massive numbers of bills spawned by an often antagonistic Congress.

Lincoln's successor, Andrew Johnson (1865–1869) of Tennessee, suffered the most, in no small part because he was a former Democrat in the post–Civil War period facing a Congress controlled by Radical Republicans. Johnson was the first president to have Congress override a veto of an important bill, and, among all presidents, he had the greatest percentage of regular vetoes overridden (fifteen out of twenty-one, or 71 percent). What is more, Johnson's refusal to abide by the Tenure of Office Act, a law passed over his veto prohibiting presidents from firing political appointees without congressional approval, led directly to his impeachment by the House. Johnson was acquitted in the Senate by one vote, and Congress repealed the Tenure of Office Act (which most scholars view as unconstitutional) in 1887.[15]

The sheer visibility of Johnson's veto battles was more the exception than the rule. Most vetoes issued during the late nineteenth century were aimed at "private" bills, actions by Congress that benefited specific individuals, companies, or municipalities. *(See Table 2-2.)* Private bills in the late 1800s usually provided pensions for Civil War veterans, but many of them were fraudulent or excessive claims, often rushed through late in the congressional session. Grover Cleveland (1885–1889, 1893–1897) vetoed 482 private bills during his eight years in office—43 during one three-day period in 1886 alone.[16] Many of these were pocket vetoes, and only three of Cleveland's vetoes of private bills were overridden.

Contemporary Use

Franklin D. Roosevelt (1933–1945) used the veto more vigorously and strategically than all presidents to date. He was the first to veto major tax legislation and openly used the threat of the veto in his legislative strategy. Roosevelt in many ways created the contemporary presidency, and the veto became yet another instrument of executive influence within an environment of expansive federal government action and power.

Roosevelt's conscious use of the veto as a political tool for shaping legislation endures, particularly because contemporary U.S. presidents so frequently find themselves facing a Congress in which one or both chambers are under the control of another political party. Vetoes are used most frequently when such partisan splits occur and become part of larger political struggles. For example, Harry S. Truman (1945–1953) in 1947 vetoed the controversial Taft-Hartley Labor-Management Relations Act, which limited the political power of labor unions.[17] The Republican-controlled Congress overrode his veto, an action that Tru-

TABLE 2-2 Private Bills Vetoed, 1789–1996

President	*Regular vetoes*	*Pocket vetoes*	*Vetoes overridden*
Washington	0	0	0
J. Adams	0	0	0
Jefferson	0	0	0
Madison	2	0	0
Monroe	0	0	0
J .Q. Adams	0	0	0
Jackson	0	0	0
Van Buren	0	1	0
W. H. Harrison	0	0	0
Tyler	0	0	0
Polk	0	0	0
Taylor	0	0	0
Fillmore	0	0	0
Pierce	0	0	0
Buchanan	2	0	0
Lincoln	0	1	0
A. Johnson	0	2	0
Grant	29	37	3
Hayes	1	0	0
Garfield	0	0	0
Arthur	1	8	0
Cleveland (1st term)	271	82	1
B. Harrison	5	23	0
Cleveland (2d term)	30	99	2
McKinley	4	32	0
T. Roosevelt	27	31	0
Taft	10	7	0
Wilson	7	2	0
Harding	3	0	0
Coolidge	3	17	0
Hoover	4	6	0
F. Roosevelt	317	180	0
Truman	137	38	1
Eisenhower	43	64	0
Kennedy	8	4	0
L. Johnson	12	4	0
Nixon	0	3	0
Ford	3	2	0
Carter	0	2	0
Reagan	2	6	0
Bush	0	1	0
Clinton [a]	0	0	0
TOTAL	921	652	7

SOURCES: *Guide to Congress,* 4th ed. (Washington, D.C.: Congressional Quarterly, 1991), 366; *Congressional Quarterly Weekly Report,* various issues.

NOTES: The official distinction between public and private bills was rather hazy through the 1930s, although private bills generally were classified as those benefiting a single individual rather than a large segment of society (for example, a private pension bill). Beginning in 1936, however, a Library of Congress publication has listed all private bills. a. Through 1996.

man used to great political effect in rallying labor voters to the Democrats in the 1948 presidential and congressional elections.

Republican Dwight D. Eisenhower (1953–1961) wrestled with a Congress controlled by Democrats during all but two of his eight years in office. Eisenhower used the veto to kill new social programs and relied on a "conservative coalition" of Republicans and southern Democrats to prevent overrides. One notable example of the veto's power came in 1959, after liberal Democrats had made large gains in the previous congressional election. These Democrats ignored Eisenhower's veto warnings and tried to push a vigorous new domestic agenda. Eisenhower vetoed a succession of bills authorizing new spending for urban housing, rural electrification, and other domestic programs. The vetoes were upheld by the conservative coalition, and threats of further vetoes persuaded Democrats to cut back drastically on their efforts.[18]

Democrats John F. Kennedy (1961–1963) and Lyndon B. Johnson (1963–1969), blessed with friendly majorities in Congress, seldom used the veto, but Republicans Richard Nixon (1969–1974) and Gerald R. Ford (1974–1977) fared differently. Both Nixon and Ford faced off against Congresses dominated by Democrats, so the veto by necessity became central to their legislative strategies. Nixon vetoed several major bills he deemed inflationary, and once he even appeared on national television to sign a veto of a major appropriations bill. As with Eisenhower, a bipartisan conservative coalition in Congress often proved large enough to sustain Nixon's vetoes.

But the ultimate success of the veto as a tool for shaping legislation is tied inextricably to a president's overall political "strength." Nixon's growing political troubles eventually weakened his national popularity and influence in Congress. In 1973 Congress soundly overrode his veto of the War Powers Resolution, which aimed at limiting presidential ability to commit U.S. armed forces abroad without congressional approval. Congress also overrode Nixon's veto of the 1974 Budget Impoundment and Control Act, which Nixon opposed because it limited presidential ability not to spend funds appropriated by Congress. *(See "Line-item Veto," p. 94.)*

Gerald Ford became president upon Nixon's resignation in August 1974 and, faced with a Congress dominated by liberal Democrats, used the veto frequently and to great effect. Ford was sustained on all but four of the seventeen vetoes he issued in 1975 alone, and he used the threat of a veto to stop a popular consumer protection bill from ever passing in the first place. Ford's short tenure in office showed how the veto could be used to compensate partially for the severe political weaknesses that came with being an unelected chief executive succeeding a disgraced president.

Jimmy Carter (1977–1981), like Kennedy and Johnson, relied on the veto less frequently than his Republican predecessors because his fellow Democrats controlled Congress. A notable exception was his veto of a 1977 energy bill that included funds for a nuclear reactor he thought dangerous and expensive.[19] Congress chose not to challenge Carter on that veto, since many in his party also opposed the reactor. On the other hand, in Carter became the first president since Truman to suffer a veto override at the hands of a Congress controlled by his party.[20] Carter had vetoed a bill limiting the national debt because it also had a provision eliminating import fees on foreign oil. Congress overrode this veto in part because the fees were unpopular and in part because of an apparent weakening in Carter's general public support as the Iran hostage situation dragged on.

The role of the veto during the presidency of Ronald Reagan (1981–1989) was even more telling, since Congress was split between a Republican Senate and a Democratic House during Reagan's first term. Thus, partisan divisions made it unlikely that Congress would override a veto. Reagan in his first term aggressively vetoed spending bills contrary to his program and often publicly warned, "My veto pen is inked up and ready to go," when Congress was about to pass legislation he opposed.[21] His veto of a 1981 continuing appropriations bill was so potent that Congress reworked the measure to his satisfaction. However, Reagan found it harder to make veto threats work to his advantage after he was elected to his second term, and particularly after Democrats regained full control over both chambers of Congress following the 1986 elections. Indeed, in early 1987 bipartisan majorities in Congress easily overrode Reagan's vetoes of major water pollution and highway bills, signaling a palpable shift in the president's influence over national policy.

The two most recent presidents offer an especially useful contrast in the use of the veto as a means for influencing legislation. George Bush (1989–1993) issued forty-four vetoes in all but had only one overridden by a Congress controlled by Democrats. His successor, Bill Clinton (1993–), issued no vetoes at all during his first two years in office, relying instead on Democratic leaders in Congress to forestall legislative challenges. But in 1994 Republicans gained control over both chambers of Congress for the first time since 1954. It seemed only a matter of time before Clinton, faced with an especially energetic Republican congressional agenda, finally made use of the veto power. Clinton's first veto came on June 7, 1995, when, twenty-nine months after taking office, he returned to Congress with his disapproval a major bill that cut spending of funds already appropriated for that fiscal year. *(See box, A Veto Message, p. 90.)* This veto, which was not overridden, foreshadowed a struggle between Clinton and congressional Republicans for control over the federal budget. Several vetoes later, and with the support of the majority of Americans, Clinton emerged in April 1996 as victor in the 1995–1996 budget battle with Congress.

AN INSTRUMENT OF PRESIDENTIAL POWER

James Bryce, the nineteenth-century English observer of American government, argued that the veto "conveys the impression of firmness."[22] Contemporary scholars of the presidency agree with Bryce only to a point. Most see the veto as a clumsy instrument of executive power, one whose frequent use dis-

A VETO MESSAGE

A bill passed by Congress is formally vetoed when the president returns it to Capitol Hill unsigned and accompanied by a message stating the reasons for disapproval. Presidents today rarely write their own veto messages. Instead, the messages typically are composed by professional staff in the Executive Office of the President with input from experts in the Office of Management and Budget (OMB) and other executive branch agencies. The president may scan the final draft and on occasion may pen major parts of controversial veto messages, but the overall process of opposing Congress on a piece of legislation largely is a collective one.

Whether the reasons given for a veto are constitutional, fiscal, substantive, or "merely" political—or a combination of reasons—a veto message is designed with more than Congress in mind. In today's media-saturated political atmosphere any message from the White House to Congress is scrutinized closely for its potential political ramifications. Veto messages thus are crafted carefully, designed above all to sell the president's views on a bill to national opinion makers and to the public, not simply to Congress.

Most veto messages are signed in the relative privacy of the Oval Office and sent by courier to Capitol Hill. They then are delivered to the chamber from whence the bills in question originated, which normally takes the lead in any efforts to override the veto. On vetoes of major bills, however, a president may use the opportunity to convene a public ceremony, complete with supporters and members of the national press, to attack the bill and to generate public sentiment against Congress.

In the following excerpt, President Bill Clinton explains his objections to legislation cutting $16.5 billion in monies already appropriated for the 1995 fiscal year. The legislation also would have provided $7.3 billion for additional spending, some of it to provide funds for natural disaster relief. HR 1158 was Clinton's first veto. Congress made no attempt to override it, since the bill had passed by small majorities in either chamber.

TO THE HOUSE OF REPRESENTATIVES:

I am returning herewith without my approval HR 1158, a bill providing for emergency supplemental appropriations and rescissions for fiscal year 1995.

This disagreement is about priorities, not deficit reduction. In fact, I want to increase the deficit reduction in this bill.

HR 1158 slashes needed investments for education, national service, and the environment, in order to avoid cutting wasteful projects and other unnecessary expenditures. There are billions of dollars in pork—unnecessary highway demonstration projects, courthouses, and other Federal buildings—that could have been cut instead of these critical investments. Indeed, the Senate bill made such cuts in order to maintain productive investments, but the House-Senate conference rejected those cuts. . . .

In the end, the Congress chose courthouses over education, pork-barrel highway projects over national service, Government travel over clean water.

At my instruction, the Administration has provided alternatives to the Congress that would produce greater deficit reduction than HR 1158, cutting even more in fiscal year 1995 spending than is included in HR 1158. But the spending reductions would come out of unnecessary projects and other spending, not investments in working families. . . .

My Administration has provided the Congress with changes that would enable me to sign revised legislation. I urge the Congress to approve a bill that contains the supplemental funding included in HR 1158—for disaster relief activities of the Federal Emergency Management Agency, for the Federal response to the bombing in Oklahoma City, for increased anti-terrorism efforts, and for providing debt relief to Jordan in order to contribute to further progress toward a Middle East peace settlement—along with my Administration's alternative restorations and offsets.

I will sign legislation that provides these needed supplemental appropriations and that reduces the deficit by at least as much as this bill. However, the legislation must reflect the priorities of the American people. HR 1158, as passed, clearly does not.

Bill Clinton
The White House
June 7, 1995

plays political weakness, not strength.[23] Political scientist Thomas Cronin argues that to see the veto as a tool of "strong presidents" is illusory, because presidents historically have used vetoes predominantly against private bills and seldom have vetoed major tax and appropriations measures.[24] Another scholar of the presidency, George Edwards III, argues that the veto is a negative instrument, good for stopping legislation, but its frequent use shows that the president has failed to sway Congress from its course.[25] A veto override underscores a president's political weakness, particularly if Congress is controlled by the president's party.

Almost any discussion of the veto's potential as an instrument of presidential power brings up the experience of Gerald Ford, who scholars think was dealt the weakest political hand of any contemporary president. After succeeding Nixon, Ford faced a fiercely independent Congress dominated by liberal Democrats. Lacking a congressional majority, or the personal popularity with the general public necessary to cajole members into agreement, Ford used the veto more frequently against public bills than any other twentieth-century president because political circumstances gave him no option. That so many of his vetoes were sustained by a largely hostile Congress suggests the raw power of the veto to stop legislation.

Ford's record and the experiences of other presidents suggest that actual use of the veto is a measure of the last resort. Harry Truman's crafty use of the veto as a political weapon against congressional Republicans did not hide the fact that he often lost important override battles. Ronald Reagan's defeat on successive overrides in early 1987 resulted from his weakened political leverage in light of renewed Democratic dominance in Congress, his own troubles concerning secret arms sales to Iran, and the reality that Reagan was in the "lame duck" phase of his second term of office. For that matter, the only override battle that George Bush (1989–1993) lost came in the last months of his presidency on a bill regulating the cable television industry that was popular with Democrats and Republicans alike. Congressional Republicans in this case were more concerned with their reelection prospects than with upholding a veto issued by an unpopular president.[26]

When presidents veto legislation, the move may be seen as a sign of relative weakness; but when they successfully head off unwanted legislation by threatening to use the veto, the tactic is seen as an indicator of presidential strength. Veto threats are useful bargaining tools in the hands of a popular and wily executive. Presidential scholars often point to Franklin Roosevelt, who was known to beg his aides to "find something I can veto" as both a lesson and a reminder to Congress of his potential power.[27] The strength of Ronald Reagan's popularity during his first term more than once allowed him to challenge Congress with the veto and get legislation reworked to his liking. Even Gerald Ford, despite his problems, effectively used the threat of a veto to deter legislation, although he usually did so when Congress was about to adjourn to maximize the chance that his threat would have an impact.

The use of the veto is not always the best indicator of the strength or weakness of the president, however. A good example is Bill Clinton, who issued no vetoes of any kind during his first two years in office. Clinton faced a Congress where his party controlled both chambers, a rare condition for contemporary presidents, and he worked with Democrats in Congress on legislative compromises that avoided the need for vetoes. Yet Clinton after his first two years of office was widely regarded as having failed to deliver on some of his major campaign promises. Clinton's troubles came about in no small part because his party's majorities in Congress were not large enough to overcome sharp partisan and ideological divisions within the Democratic Party as well as unified opposition by Republicans. Especially telling was the fate of Clinton's plan for major reforms in the nation's health care system. The health care bill was the only piece of legislation that Clinton actually publicly threatened to veto if it did not contain key elements of his plan. But Clinton's threat did not matter: congressional Democrats were unable to come up with a bill that would satisfy enough members of their own party, much less get past almost unanimous Republican opposition. Congress adjourned in 1994 without passing health care legislation of any sort.

In general, Congress finds ways to undermine vetoes or threats of vetoes made even by popular presidents. Even with the "line-item" veto authority granted to the president by Congress in 1996—the constitutionality of which is in doubt—members of Congress often will load up major pieces of legislation with amendments on completely different subjects (known as "riders") or with pet spending programs that the president will be obliged to swallow in order to ensure passage of the bill. *(See "Line-item Veto," p. 94.)* Congress also may wait until late in each session to pass critical spending bills. The lateness of the hour narrows a president's range of possible responses, because a veto may not be feasible if Congress has adjourned and the funds needed to run the federal government are contained in the legislation. To make matters more complicated, Congress in recent years also has relied on massive omnibus (or "catch-all") bills to pass the budget, appropriate funds, and levy new taxes simultaneously.

Presidents Reagan and Bush each had to accept omnibus bills containing provisions they detested simply because they needed other items contained in the same bill. Reagan had to swallow the Boland Amendment restricting U.S. aid to rebels opposing the Nicaraguan government because it was tacked onto a 1984 appropriations bill. The administration's subsequent efforts to get around the Boland Amendment got it into deep political and legal trouble. Bush, to gain passage of the 1990 budget act, accepted new taxes, a compromise that angered many in his party and possibly hurt his chances at reelection in 1992.

A president also cannot rely automatically on fellow party members in Congress for support on veto threats, or even during override battles, since most members of Congress resist being seen by constituents as mere rubber stamps for the president's wishes. This is true especially when the bill in question benefits a member's district or state, as happened when Congress overrode Reagan's vetoes of water treatment and highway bills in 1987, or when it overrode a veto by Bush of a 1992 bill that promised to lower cable television rates. So popular were these measures that Republicans abandoned their presidents in droves, sacrificing a presidential agenda for their constituents' interests.

The veto is best seen as a powerful weapon for stopping legislation when all other means have failed. As a tool for crafting policy, however, its usefulness is less clear. Personal political skills certainly matter, insofar as the president can convince Congress that the veto is real and will have serious consequences. However, personal skills are not enough: a president's overall popularity, whether and to what extent the president's party controls Congress, the nature of the issue at hand, broad external political conditions, timing, and even luck, combine to determine whether a veto threat can reshape legislation more to the president's liking. As every president seems to discover at some point, these factors are beyond the control of the White House. Even Reagan, who used the veto threat effectively to shape an important 1986 tax reform act, discovered that his threats carried much less weight only a year later as even members of his party overrode his veto of a bill providing federal grants for local water pollution control projects. As a means for shaping legislation, the veto is a blunt and often unpredictable instrument.

POCKET VETO

The veto is mentioned specifically in the Constitution, as is the method for congressional override. But, as often is the case with the Framers' handiwork, minor provisions have evolved over time into major constitutional battles between Congress and the presidency. One of the most heated of these battles has been over what has come to be known as the *pocket veto.*

Constitutional Provision

The Constitution gives the president ten legislative days (excluding Sundays) to sign a bill into law or return it to Congress with a veto message. A bill not approved or vetoed by the president becomes law after ten days "unless the Congress by their adjournment prevent its return, in which case it shall not be law" (Article 1, section 7). This provision apparently was meant to ward off last-minute actions by Congress that might prove dangerous or foolhardy. The president cannot possibly veto and return bills to Congress as prescribed in the Constitution if Congress already has left for home after adjournment, so the Framers determined that under such circumstances it was better that any bill left unapproved at adjournment simply die.

A *pocket veto* results from executive inaction, not anything the president actively does, and the term reflects the notion that the president "pocketed" a bill rather than acted on it.[28] A president technically cannot "issue" a pocket veto: the entire situation occurs simply because Congress has adjourned and the bill cannot be returned with a regular veto message. Even so, many presidents have asserted a "right" to use the pocket veto as if it were an active power of the office.

The first president to rely on a pocket veto was James Madison, in 1812, and only twice more did a president use a pocket veto before 1830. The incidence of pocket vetoes increased thereafter, especially against the many private pension bills passed by Congress in the second half of the nineteenth century. The champion of the pocket veto in absolute numbers is Franklin Roosevelt (263), but Grover Cleveland used the device more frequently (averaging 30 per year in office, compared with Roosevelt's 22), largely against private Civil War veterans' pension bills.

> If any Bill shall not be returned by the President within ten Days, (Sundays excepted) after it shall have been presented to him, the Same shall be a Law, in like Manner as if he had signed it, unless the Congress by their Adjournment prevent its Return, in which Case it shall not be a Law.
>
> *—from Article I, section 7*

Constitutional Issues

The pocket veto is controversial because Congress and the president often disagree over what constitutes congressional adjournment. The Constitution, as so often is the case, is not clear on this point except for adjournment *sine die* (Latin for "without a day," meaning "without a day being set for meeting again"). Adjournment *sine die* marks the end of a two-year Congress, which itself runs the course of the two-year term of the House of Representatives.

There is no disagreement that the pocket veto is constitutional upon adjournment *sine die.* The controversy concerns whether the use of the pocket veto is constitutional with other types of recesses or adjournments. Any interpretation narrowing its use to adjournment *sine die* alone tends to benefit Congress. A more expansive definition magnifies executive power over legislation, because presidents might be able to defeat bills through inaction whenever Congress takes a recess, such as between sessions of the same Congress or during holidays occurring within any single session.

This question was not an issue during the nineteenth century, because Congress sat in session, on average, only half a year, and calling members back to Washington to override vetoes could take weeks of travel. But as Congress began to stay in session almost full time and as new technology made communications to and recall of Congress far easier than the Framers ever envisioned, the issue of when the president legally can use the pocket veto grew in importance.

The first real shot in this battle came with the 1929 *Pocket Veto Case,* in which the Supreme Court ruled that President Calvin Coolidge could pocket veto an Indian claims bill passed just before a four-month recess.[29] The justices ruled that the term *adjournment* applied to any break in the congressional calendar that prevented the return of a bill within the required ten-day period, in this case adjournment between sessions. The ruling, as historian Arthur M. Schlesinger Jr. noted, "was based in part on the idea that, if Congress was in adjournment, no officer or agent was authorized to receive on behalf of Congress a bill rejected by the President."[30] To close this apparent loophole, particularly as Congress began to convene year-round and to recess for only very short periods, both chambers started to appoint "agents"—usually the clerk of the House and secretary of the Senate—to receive presidential veto messages while members were away, thus theoretically negating a president's rationale for a pocket veto. After all, once Congress returned it could deliberate and perhaps override a presidential veto at any time before adjournment *sine die.*

Franklin Roosevelt, in declaring a pocket veto against a bill passed before Congress went on a three-day recess, asserted that this strategy was unconstitutional, but the Supreme Court in 1938 ruled that pocket vetoes could not occur during such brief recesses if the appropriate agents had been so named.[31] Regular veto procedures, the justices argued, gave the president enough time to consider a bill *and* gave Congress the opportunity to respond, so the use of agents to receive veto messages was deemed constitutional. Congress, not surprisingly, made this practice commonplace thereafter.

The issue lay dormant until the early 1970s, when Richard Nixon's application of the pocket veto again sparked controversy about what kind of congressional adjournment "prevents" regular veto procedures. Despite the 1938 ruling, Nixon in 1970 declared that he would use a six-day holiday recess to pocket veto the Family Practice of Medicine Act, which provided funds for medical training. Congress had passed the bill unanimously, had appointed agents to receive presidential messages, and arguably would have overridden a regular veto, but Nixon did not give Congress the chance to respond. Nixon created a furor when he asserted that the short recess was analogous to adjournment *sine die.* Members of Congress countered that the bill had indeed become law because Nixon could not exercise a pocket veto during the recess, and Sen. Edward M. Kennedy (D-Mass.) subsequently brought suit against the administration.[32] Kennedy's case was upheld by a U.S. court of appeals, which in 1974 ruled that pocket vetoes were disallowed during short recesses so long as Congress established procedures to receive veto messages in its absence.[33] The Nixon administration chose not to make an appeal of this decision to the Supreme Court.

Senator Kennedy figured in a similar lawsuit after President Ford declared a pocket veto against a bill passed just before the intersession break of the Ninety-third Congress. Once again, a federal court of appeals overturned a lower court decision and ruled that the pocket veto cannot be used except after adjournment *sine die* so long as both chambers appoint agents.[34] The Ford administration subsequently announced that it would abide by the ruling.[35]

Despite these rulings, Ronald Reagan in 1983 reasserted a more expansive view when he declared a pocket veto against a bill barring U.S. aid to El Salvador. The legislation had been passed just before the end of the first session of the Ninety-eighth Congress. As with Nixon and Ford, Reagan administration officials argued that the pocket veto applied to any congressional recess longer than three days. And, just as before, many in Congress declared that the device applied only to adjournment *sine die.* Thirty-three House Democrats sued the administration, and a U.S. court of appeals in 1984 again reversed a lower court decision and reaffirmed the standard set in 1976.[36] The administration appealed the decision to the Supreme Court, which in January 1987 declared the particulars of the case moot (since the dispute over aid to El Salvador had long passed) and upheld the decision of the court of appeals.[37] Both sides voiced disappointment that the high court had not settled the matter conclusively.

President Bush confused the issue further. In August 1989, with Congress out on a summer recess, Bush declared a pocket veto of a minor bill that would have expedited the signing of legislation to bail out the nation's failing savings and loan industry. In doing so, Bush became the first president since Nixon to use a pocket veto within a legislative session. In November 1989,

Stymied often by vetoes by President George Bush, House Democratic leaders at a 1991 press conference display their view of the president's veto pen.

Bush declared a pocket veto of a bill to allow dissident Chinese students to remain in the United States, but nonetheless returned the bill with a "memorandum of disapproval" outlining his objections. The Senate failed to override this "veto."

The Bush administration defended its actions on the basis of the *Pocket Veto Case* of 1929, which had upheld the use of the pocket veto during short congressional recesses. However, many in Congress—especially Democrats—looked instead to more recent federal appeals court cases that had limited the pocket veto to adjournment *sine die,* and in 1990 they responded to Bush's actions with legislation that would codify these rulings. This bill (HR 849) was approved along party line votes by the House Judiciary Committee and the House Rules Committee, but the legislation failed to get to the floor of either chamber because of sharp partisan disagreements over "codifying" rules governing the pocket veto's use.[38]

To add to this legal confusion, Bush in 1991 declared a pocket veto against a bill passed prior to a holiday recess. The legislation honored retiring House member Morris K. Udall (D-Ariz.) by setting up a foundation to promote environmental education. Although Bush supported the thrust of the legislation, he disagreed about how members of the foundation board were to be appointed. This bill was not returned to Congress, but it was not formally vetoed, so legal scholars argued that the bill should be considered a law. However, the Bush administration did nothing to publish or otherwise implement the law, so its legal status was in dispute. Congress, meanwhile, passed another version of the same bill that revised the appointment procedures, and Bush signed this revised version into law, leaving the issue of the pocket veto unsettled.[39]

What constitutes constitutional application of the pocket veto thus remains a point of contention between Congress eager to protect legislative prerogatives and presidents equally keen to find way to kill unwanted legislation. The issue of the pocket veto may not be settled until the Supreme Court acts.

LINE-ITEM VETO

The veto is a blunt tool for executive influence precisely because it is an all or nothing matter. A president (up through 1996) could not pull out items deemed wasteful within an otherwise acceptable spending bill. Many who supported greater strategic power for the president, particularly in an era of federal budgetary constraint, considered this a major flaw in the veto process. Proposals to give presidents the capacity to pick and choose among specific appropriations, called a *line-item veto* (or *item veto*) emerged periodically throughout history; but the effort had been continually thwarted by legislators fearful of even greater executive leverage within their constitutionally prescribed domain.

In 1996, governors from forty-three states had some form of line-item veto. Most of these provisions pertain primarily to spending bills, but others also extend the governor's power to substantive laws. At least ten states allow governors actually to amend spending bills and send them back to the legislature for reconsideration.[40]

The Framers appear to have given no attention to a line-item veto during the drafting or ratification of the Constitution, which seems surprising until we recall that even the regular veto proved highly contentious. The granting to Congress of full power over appropriations and revenues certainly showed the Framers' bias. However, the idea that the president should be able to excise specific parts of spending bills has enjoyed some popularity throughout American history. The states of the Confederacy included a clause in their constitution allowing the president to "approve any appropriation and disapprove any other appropriation in the same bill" (Article 1, section 7, clause 2), and efforts to pass a constitutional amendment creating similar executive power in the U.S. Constitution have been frequent since the 1870s.

A number of mid-twentieth-century presidents expressed strong support for a line-item veto, most notably Franklin Roosevelt and Eisenhower. Roosevelt came closest to realizing his wish when the House in 1938 voted to give the president that power, but the effort died in the Senate.[41] The issue was set aside through the 1970s, but arose again in the 1980s as the federal budget deficit became a major problem. Like the budget, however, the line-item veto quickly became enmeshed in partisan politics, with Republican presidents Reagan and Bush in favor and congressional Democrats generally opposed. Supporters argued that the line-item veto would give presidents greater control over federal spending, especially on programs and projects where Congress may lack the political will to make cuts. Opponents for their part expressed fears that a line-item veto would give the president excessive power over an area where Congress traditionally—and constitutionally—took the lead.

This clash of partisan and institutional perspectives kept proposals for the line-item veto from getting very far during the 1980s. In 1985 Reagan and congressional Republicans pushed for a two-year trial run, but the proposal was rebuffed both then and a year later. Even if the Senate in 1986 had approved the line-item veto, it was unlikely that the House, which is highly protective of its power of the purse, would have gone along. President Bush also pushed publicly for a line-item veto, but also had little success with Congress.

By the mid-1990s, however, the political dynamics surrounding the line-item veto had changed dramatically. President Clinton, who retained a line-item veto as governor of Arkansas, openly supported one for the president. However, key congressional Democrats still fought against any action that might infringe on Congress's control over the budget. But Clinton was to find strange bedfellows with congressional Republicans, who in 1994 gained control over both chambers of Congress for the first time since 1954. The line-item veto was a key part of the Republicans' "Contract with America," and prospects for passing some kind of line-item veto improved dramatically. However, efforts to pass a constitutional amendment creating a line-item veto soon fell victim to resistance in the Senate, so proponents took another tack. After months of negotiation a bipartisan majority voted to grant to the president "enhanced rescission" authority, the power to "cancel" automatically individual items in spending and tax bills unless overturned by a two-thirds vote of both houses of Congress. President Clinton signed this bill into law on April 9, 1996, but its effects are still uncertain. For one thing, it is not clear whether Congress can grant this kind of power to the president without a constitutional amendment, an issue which the Supreme Court could not review until after the new law went into effect in 1997.[42]

"Quasi-item Vetoes"

Presidents have compensated for the lack of formal line-item veto power through other means. One mechanism has been to "impound"—or *not* to spend—money appropriated by Congress for fiscal or administrative reasons. The concept of impoundment has not been controversial when presidents could show that the expenditure was no longer needed—as when Thomas Jefferson impounded funds earmarked for new naval ships because the hostilities that had prompted the appropriation were no longer going on—or when unforeseen circumstances delayed spending. But when presidents try to use impoundment for obvious fiscal or policy reasons, sharp conflict with Congress is guaranteed.

Impoundments were infrequent until the 1970s, largely because presidents sought to avoid major fights with Congress over control of the purse.[43] However, Richard Nixon relied boldly on impoundment to "veto" specific congressional budgetary allocations, even for entire agencies. These efforts proved so controversial that Congress in 1974 passed (over Nixon's veto) the Budget and Impoundment Control Act, which forbade impoundments unless approved by both houses of Congress.

Subsequent presidents have continued to "defer" or "rescind" funds under the auspices of the law, although the actions deemed most controversial have had difficulty getting congressional acquiescence. In 1986, for example, President Reagan attempted to defer $5 billion for housing and urban development programs because Congress had appropriated more money than he had requested, but a federal appeals court ruled that his actions violated the intent of the 1974 law.[44]

Presidents also on occasion refuse to abide by specific provisions in laws they sign, or they issue their own interpretations of the law when they think Congress has acted unconstitutionally. For example, in 1959 President Eisenhower announced that he would disregard a provision for congressional access to secret documents because it would violate the president's need to protect national security. In 1971 Nixon insisted that he was not bound by a provision requiring the president to state a specific time period for withdrawal from Vietnam.[45] In both cases the president effectively undermined the force of the provision in question, yet the constitutionality of these actions has not been tested in court.[46] President Bush likewise objected to provisions in appropriations bills that he nevertheless signed into law. In particular, Bush complained about what he saw as unconstitutional congressional interference in executive branch prerogatives, and he expressed his desire for a line-item veto.[47]

Line-item Veto Debate

Proponents of the line-item veto argue that such an instrument would help to limit federal spending, allow presidents to excise "wasteful" congressional appropriations, and give chief executives greater opportunities to promote their overall budget priorities. Political commentator George Will called it an "effective instrument of allocation" to help presidents carry out their electoral "mandates" and to strengthen presidential responsibility over the budget and the general direction of the federal government.[48]

Critics argue that a presidential line-item veto would not affect federal spending profoundly, particularly because it could not apply to the massive "entitlement" programs (like Social Security) that make up so much of the total budget and which can be reduced only by changing the laws that mandate these programs.[49] Critics also point out that presidents are no less responsible than Congress for budgetary growth, because they can use the regular veto to force legislative compliance if they have the political will to do so. Still others point out that any reference to line-item veto provisions in state constitutions ignores the very real differences between state legislatures and the U.S. Congress.[50]

Practical questions aside, the debate over the line-item veto ultimately is a debate over power, over which branch will be supreme when it comes to federal spending. Promoters of the line-item veto favor expanded executive power to control spending and the direction of national policy. Those opposing the line-item veto fear the effect of such enhanced power on congressional control of the purse and argue that the line-item veto provision would become yet another way for a president to reward friends, hurt enemies, and dominate the legislative process. The debate over the line-item veto promises to sizzle as long as the federal budget deficit continues to be a major political issue.

The President's Program

The president's second express constitutional duty in the legislative process is to "from time to time give to the Congress information of the State of the Union, and recommend to their consideration such measures he shall judge necessary and expedient" (Article II, section 3). This ability to "recommend . . . measures" has become the primary mechanism by which chief executives seek to shape the nation's political agenda, because the presidency's array of formal mechanisms for directing national policy is relatively weak, particularly when the nation is not in crisis. To shape the agenda of government—to decide what is or is not a priority—is in essence to influence what government will or will not do.[51] As the political scientist E. E. Schattschneider long ago concluded, "He who determines what politics is all about runs the country, because the definition of the alternatives is the choice of conflicts, and the choice of conflicts allocates power."[52]

Presidents naturally would love to have complete control over the agenda of government, particularly at the very start of their terms in office. In reality, a president's control over the agenda is tenuous. At times it is overwhelmed by unforeseen crises such as natural disasters, war, or sudden shifts in the economy. When crises occur, the existing agenda is thrown aside and presidential "success" or "strength" is judged by the pace and suitability of the response. Franklin Roosevelt's reaction to the virtual collapse of the banking system on the eve of his inauguration in 1933 often is cited as an example of strong presidential leadership. Within days of taking office Roosevelt led Congress in reorganizing the entire federal banking system. Even more important, he went on national radio to persuade citizens to return their savings to the banks, instilling renewed faith in the financial system and taking the first steps toward economic recovery.[53]

Ronald Reagan, by contrast, received a great deal of criticism in October 1987 for his apparently belated and passive response to a sudden plunge in the stock market. Financial analysts argued that the downturn reflected investors' unease with the deadlock between Reagan and Congress over resolving the federal budget deficit. Whether the "crisis" over the budget caused the market crash or whether Reagan responded inadequately is hard to say, yet common perceptions that he had not dealt forcefully with the situation eroded confidence in his leadership.

Crises aside, the presidency has a singularly unique institutional capacity to shape the nation's political debate and action. No other government institution can subject Congress to so

One of the most important means of communicating presidential goals to Congress and to the public is the annual State of the Union address before a joint session of Congress. Here Vice President Albert Gore Jr. and Speaker of the House Newt Gingrich listen to President Bill Clinton's 1995 address.

much pressure in so organized a manner, and no other political figure regularly commands so much attention from the public regardless of the issue. The presidency always has been a focal point of American politics because it is the only political office in the United States chosen through a purely national election, but its psychological and political importance has mushroomed in the second half of the twentieth century. The sheer growth in the scope and influence of the federal government, the emergence of the United States as a world economic and military power—which amplified the president's role as commander in chief—and the emergence of modern telecommunications have converged to place the presidency squarely in the public eye both at home and abroad.

The president, political scientist Bruce Miroff suggests, commands the "public space" in contemporary U.S. politics, largely forcing other participants in the political process to respond to issues as the president defines them.[54] That reality powerfully influences success or failure on policy initiatives, particularly in issue areas where most Americans have no direct experience. Reagan, for example, in the early 1980s consistently portrayed right-wing rebels fighting the left-wing Nicaraguan government as "freedom fighters," a picture so compelling to so many Americans that critics of Reagan's policies toward Nicaragua were forced continually to refute the president's definition before they could begin to attack his policy. It may be said, in fact, that Reagan alone carried the rebels along through the sheer power of his office to dominate the discussion.

Yet the president did not enjoy such an institutional capacity to define the national agenda throughout most of the nineteenth century. Congress dominated government, the White House was occupied by a succession of largely forgettable figures, and the technologies of mass communication did not yet exist. Presidents were not expected to formulate legislative agendas, prepare and present executive budgets, or do much else except oversee the executive branch, conduct foreign policy (such as it was when the United States was relatively isolated), and keep a check on Congress whenever necessary and possible. Nor did the dominant public view of government hold that presidents should actively initiate or influence public policy. Not until Franklin Roosevelt did the presidency become a strong institution, one that remained potent regardless of the person sitting in the Oval Office.

CONGRESS AND THE PRESIDENCY: TWO CULTURES

It is impossible to discuss the president's influence over legislation without first recognizing the essential differences between the branches. It is necessary, above all, to recall that the Constitution grants to Congress the preponderance of power over national policy. Only Congress has the power to make the law, generate revenues, and appropriate funds. The Constitution also establishes governing roles and sets of policy-making dynamics that set Congress fundamentally far apart from the presidency. These structural factors have remained remarkably constant throughout history and are important to understanding why presidents succeed or fail in achieving their legislative goals.[55]

Presidents and members of Congress reach office through entirely separate and distinct paths. Presidents (and vice presidents) are the only political figures elected through a nationwide election. That process, combined with the national responsibilities of the office, inevitably gives the president a broader perspective on issues. Members of Congress come to national government out of more localized constituencies, whether districts for the House of Representatives or states for the Senate, which by themselves help to ensure that for members of Congress "all politics is local," as the late Speaker of the House Thomas P. "Tip" O'Neill was fond of saying.[56] Members of Congress can and do think broadly on policy questions, but their constitutionally assigned roles as representatives of a specific set of citizens require that they tend to their constituents' needs first, even if they do not care much about getting reelected.

Presidents and members of Congress also serve for different terms of office. While a president serves for four years, members of the House have only two-year terms, which the Framers intended to keep representatives sensitive to the momentary needs and opinions of the people. House members thus tend to focus more on short-term concerns, which can cause problems for a president's agenda. And, because all House members (and one-third of all senators) are up for reelection in the second year of the president's term, midterm elections frequently are construed as public judgments on presidential performance. The president's party almost invariably loses House and Senate seats in midterm elections, and members of Congress from the president's party are keenly aware that public disenchantment with their leader may cause them serious electoral problems. The opposition party, for its part, naturally tries to use these contests to its advantage.

In 1980, for example, Republicans picked up thirty-four new House seats in the wake of Ronald Reagan's victory over Jimmy Carter.[57] Although House Democrats still outnumbered Republicans by a margin of fifty-one seats, a coalition of House Republicans and conservative Democrats gave Reagan the working majority to push through his dramatic tax reduction and budget bills. But a steep economic recession and Democrats' effective attacks on administration plans to tinker with the Social Security system saw Republicans lose more than two-thirds of those new seats in the 1982 midterm elections. The effects on Reagan's influence were noticeable: the Democratic majority in the House was larger and more unified against the president's agenda, and conservative Democrats no longer readily joined Republicans against their party.

The 1994 midterm elections, in which Republicans gained control of both chambers of Congress for the first time since 1954, were also particularly dramatic, perhaps even historic. Whereas President Clinton from 1993 to 1994 could at least count on Democratic control over both chambers of Congress to help him pass much of his legislative program, Republican control over Congress in 1995 effectively altered the political equation for both Congress and the president. The 1994 election effectively shifted control over the legislative agenda from the White House to the new and assertive GOP House majority. The long-term question of whether an organization of 435 semi-autonomous individuals could maintain control over the agenda in the face of the contemporary presidency's institutional capacity to dominate the nation's attention remained unanswered by 1996. House Republicans were soon seen by many as being too strident in the pursuit of their conservative goals. Clinton won reelection in 1996, regaining some presidential control over the national agenda.

The problem posed by the Senate is a bit different. Members of the Senate serve for six years, with only one-third of the body up for reelection every two years. Thus, most senators are not affected directly by a presidential election, and they have much greater freedom to oppose presidential initiatives without as much concern about short-term constituent pressures. The Senate also retains constitutional leverage over the executive through its power to approve presidential nominees to the federal judiciary and to high-level executive branch positions, and through its power to approve or reject treaties with other nations. These characteristics of the Senate guarantee problems for presidents, even with senators of the same party. Jimmy Carter failed to obtain Senate approval for the 1978 Strategic Arms Limitation Treaty despite Democratic dominance in the chamber, and Ronald Reagan faced the greatest opposition on the 1987 Intermediate Nuclear Force Treaty from conservative Republicans.

The two branches also have distinct decision-making cultures and processes that emerge from their fundamentally different governing responsibilities. The president, whose primary constitutional responsibilities are to implement the laws and act as commander in chief of the armed forces, sits atop an executive branch hierarchy that generally speaks with one official voice on policy matters. Debate over policy options may be vigorous within the executive branch, but final decisions are based usually on the president's overall ideology and political agenda. Loyalty to the president's program is a paramount virtue among all executive branch appointees: those who dissent openly find their access to the president severely limited, if not cut off completely.[58]

Congress, by contrast, speaks with many voices simultaneously, one for each of the 535 members of the House and Senate—not to mention the territorial delegates, staff members, and professionals in the congressional agencies. Congress as an institution rarely (if ever) presents a coherent sense of direction. Members of Congress both represent their constituents and make national policy. These dual roles often conflict, because what is good for any member's constituents (such as new services or public facilities) may bode ill for the nation (in the form of massive budget deficits, for example). Each member wields one vote, regardless of seniority or party position, and no member can be expelled from the legislature simply because of voting behavior or personal opinion. Only constituents have the right to "fire" their representatives.

This constitutionally generated egalitarianism forces Congress as an institution to operate according to relatively nonhierarchical decision-making processes. To do otherwise would appear antidemocratic. Decisions, whether in the form of new pieces of legislation or agreements on appropriations bills, among other things, are achieved only by building coalitions of members large enough to win a succession of committee and floor votes. Consensus is a hallowed norm of behavior, and successful legislating depends on knitting together enough diverse interests and demands to overcome opposition, using whatever tactics seem reasonable or necessary. This is especially true in the even less hierarchical Senate, where norms of courtesy, reciprocity, and consensus allow even a single member to obstruct the majority—or the president—until agreement surfaces.

This clash of cultures powerfully shapes the way in which the branches interact with each other. Presidents always want to move quickly to make the most of their limited opportunities through dramatic and often comprehensive policy initiatives. This is true particularly in the first year, as every president knows that the personal popularity so critical to overcoming the normal inertia of the political system inevitably fades. But Congress usually prefers a more cautious weighing of the consequences. Each member's constituency must be treated fairly, and coalitions of support must be constructed. Such considerations usually are more important to Congress, particularly to the Senate, than speed or ideological purity. Many a president has chastised Congress for its glacial pace of deliberation, but the legislature by design marches to its own drummer.

These fundamental differences invariably produce clashes between presidents, who theoretically act on behalf of the national interest, and members of Congress, who promote their constituents' needs. Presidents routinely accuse Congress of waste or inertia, but they also find that cumulative local and state interests often overcome any supposed national good. Carter, for example, early in his administration attacked spending for public works projects (such as dams and irrigation canals), but he discovered quickly that these projects are "sacred cows" to legislators eager to serve their constituents.[59] Reagan in 1987 vetoed a popular reauthorization of the Clean Water Act because he felt that its $20 billion appropriation for water and sewage treatment projects was wasteful, but Congress overrode his veto by overwhelming bipartisan margins. Clinton's effort to push a comprehensive overhaul of the nation's health care system ultimately fell prey to the tug of special interests, with members of his party unable—and often unwilling—to push the president's plan through determined Republican opposition.

Compare these dynamics with those of parliamentary systems, where prime ministers are selected by the majority party (or party coalition) in the legislature. There is no separation of powers in the American sense, and strong party cohesion is essential to maintaining control over government. Margaret Thatcher, to cite one example, in 1979 gained her position as British Prime Minister after the Conservative Party won control over the British House of Commons. A solid party majority allowed her to push through major legislation far more easily and quickly than any American president could imagine. In the United States, by contrast, members of Congress can and do go against their party and president when constituent interests are on the line. What the Constitution splits apart, party loyalty cannot easily bind together.[60]

The relationship between the president and Congress is shaped powerfully by the Constitution. The Framers were far more concerned with checking the potential abuses of power than with speedy or easy legislating. They wanted Congress and the president to be at odds, and they endowed Congress with the capacity to withstand executive pressure and to dictate policy if it so willed. Even if it is dominated by the president's party, Congress as an institution insists on playing its independent constitutional role according to its own needs and internal dynamics. No president seeking to succeed can forget those realities.

HISTORICAL DEVELOPMENT

"Whether legislator, opinion-maker, commander, or administrator," argued presidential scholar Clinton Rossiter, "the President molds lasting policy in every sector of American life."[61] Indeed, as political scientist Bertram Gross wrote in 1953, "Except in wartime, Presidents are now judged more by the quality of the legislation they propose or succeed in getting enacted than by their records as executive."[62] The presidency today is seen almost as another house of Congress, with presidents involved deeply in all aspects of the legislative process and judged by how well they can mobilize support for their programs.

The contrast between these contemporary analyses and the experiences of early presidents is staggering. Rather than expecting the president to formulate a legislative program and lobby for its enactment, Congress through the 1800s usually resisted presidential involvement in lawmaking as an unwarranted intrusion.[63] Textbook notions that Congress alone makes law, which the president then simply administers, were taken seriously. Presidents who forgot this constitutional nicety were quickly reminded of it by members of Congress always on guard against such presumptuousness.

Whether the Framers actually meant the president to play so passive a role is hotly debated. Certainly they viewed the presidency chiefly as a bulwark against congressional mischief or tyranny. Yet Alexander Hamilton argued in *Federalist* No. 70 that "energy in the executive is a leading character of good government."[64] The Framers rejected the more monarchical schemes for the executive proposed early on by Hamilton and others, but they also rejected making the president entirely subordinate to or separate from Congress. The legislature makes the law, but the Framers did give the president a limited number of instruments for influencing legislation. How effectively the president could bring those resources to bear, however, would be another question.

Early Presidents

George Washington discovered rather quickly how difficult it would be for a president to influence legislation. He was the first—and the last—president ever to sit with Congress during actual floor debate. On August 22, 1789, in line with his early view that oral communications were indispensable to fruitful relations between the branches, Washington personally presented to the Senate the particulars of an Indian treaty—the very first treaty to be considered under the procedures prescribed by the Constitution—and requested the Senate's immediate advice and consent. But the Senate did not automatically approve the treaty. Its main points were read aloud—twice, because some senators could not hear for the noise coming in off the street—after which only awkward silence ensued. Sen. William Maclay of Pennsylvania then called for a reading of the treaty itself, and of its accompanying papers, and supported a move to refer the entire matter to a committee for further study. Maclay, as he later wrote in his journal, "saw no chance of fair investigation of subjects if the President of the United States sat there, with his Secretary of War, to support his opinions and over-awe the timid and neutral part of the Senate." Washington, wrote Maclay, "started up in a violent fret" at the proposal to refer the matter to committee, exclaiming, "This defeats every purpose of my coming here." The president eventually calmed down and agreed to a two-day delay, but on his return he found many senators still uneasy about his presence. After completing the business at hand, Washington vowed that he would not repeat the experience.[65]

Washington nonetheless actively sought more indirect influence over legislation. He began the practice of relying on his cabinet members to lobby members of Congress, a task taken up with particular enthusiasm by Secretary of the Treasury Hamilton, whose ardent belief in an energetic presidency and tireless use of his department to initiate and lobby for legislation soon sparked a backlash—and not just in Congress. Secretary of State Thomas Jefferson, despite his overall support for Washington, objected strenuously in a letter to the president that Hamilton's "system flowed from principles adverse to liberty, and was calculated to undermine and demolish the republic, by creating an influence of his department over the members of the legislature."[66]

Jefferson, whose Democratic-Republican Party in principle glorified the concept of congressional supremacy, also eschewed personal lobbying when he became president. He also went so far as to suspend the fledgling tradition of personally delivering an annual State of the Union message. *(See "The State of the Union Address," p. 103.)* But Jefferson was no passive chief executive. He carefully maintained the forms of separation of powers and congressional supremacy but relied heavily on cabinet members and the strong congressional caucus of his party, which held the majority in Congress, to initiate and dominate legislative activity. Secretary of the Treasury Albert Gallatin acted as his primary liaison to the party caucus, but Jefferson personally picked the party's floor leaders, who then became known as the president's chief congressional representatives. The strength of the party caucus, held together in many ways by Jefferson's own political skills (and his widely acclaimed dinner parties), produced a style of governing that in many ways paralleled parliamentary systems.

After Jefferson, however, "King Caucus" gave way to congressional supremacy. Jefferson's model of party government decayed as splits within the Democratic-Republican Party eroded its usefulness as a mechanism for executive leverage. Power flowed back to Congress as an institution, and strong congressional leaders such as Henry Clay and John C. Calhoun actively set the agenda of government through the 1820s. House Speaker Clay in particular dominated tariff and public works matters and with his allies even forced a reluctant James Madison to confront the British in the War of 1812. Congress also began to develop its own institutional expertise in policy making, in particular through the standing committees, which during the mid-1800s evolved into power centers in their own right as presidents came and went.

Andrew Jackson in the 1830s momentarily reinvigorated the role of the (now) Democratic Party and its national convention as a means for setting the national agenda. More notably, the breadth and strength of his party organization allowed Jackson to become the first president to appeal directly to the public over the heads of Congress on such issues as the National Bank and the tariff.[67] However, Jackson's overall legislative strategy was largely reactive, and he relied heavily on his veto power to check hostile congressional initiatives. The idea that the president should actively propose and shepherd legislation through Congress was still controversial, and the increasing power of the standing committees limited Jackson's capacity to dominate Congress through the party.[68]

Aside from these few relatively active presidents, and not including Lincoln's emergency actions during the Civil War, nineteenth-century legislating generally was a congressional affair. The president's constitutional responsibilities over the armed forces and foreign policy mattered little, since the United States during most of this century kept resolutely out of international politics and maintained a minimal peacetime defense and foreign policy apparatus. On the domestic side, the federal government concerned itself largely with relatively parochial matters like post offices and other public works projects. Except in times of crisis, government through the 1800s did relatively little on a national scale. The presidency played a secondary role in policy formation. Congress never shied away from reminding presidents of their "proper" role, and even Abraham Lincoln toward the end of the Civil War was admonished by House leaders that the president "must confine himself to executive duties—to obey and execute, not make the laws. . . ."[69]

Shift Toward Presidential Leadership

The legislative role of the presidency began to change toward the end of the nineteenth century as powerful economic, technological, and social forces reshaped the American landscape, and as the United States began to play a greater role in international affairs. The industrial revolution brought about a transition from a self-sufficient farm economy to an urban manufacturing economy, from largely localized business concerns to huge national corporations, and, as a result, a shift from a minimalist view of federal government action to calls for it to do more. The issues of the day—such as interstate commerce, corporate monopoly, child labor, food and drug purity, monetary policy, agricultural research, and rail transportation—became more national in scope, often overlapping with the international trade and diplomacy issues that were growing in importance as the United States became more active in the world.

These trends altered prevailing views about the role of the national government and, by extension, of the presidency. Calls

President Theodore Roosevelt was an energetic legislative leader, but his cousin Franklin D. Roosevelt went still further. FDR redefined the role of the national government through his New Deal legislation and vastly expanded the size of the executive branch.

for more active executive leadership on legislation began to be heard as Congress increasingly found itself ill-equipped institutionally to handle broad national questions. The legislature by nature is better able to deal with issues that can be broken down by congressional districts or state lines, such as allocation of funds for post offices, than with issues having no clear constituency boundaries. Moreover, popular perceptions that Congress was not attentive to emerging national and international problems legitimized the notion of an energetic president. As the nation entered the new era, the constitutional forms of the two branches in most respects stayed the same, but their dynamics were to change subtly.

Theodore Roosevelt, who once said the president "can be as big a man as he can," was perhaps the first "modern" president.[70] Keenly aware that his was the only purely national voice, Roosevelt saw the presidency as a "bully pulpit" for shaping public opinion and pushing legislation through Congress. "In theory the Executive has nothing to do with legislation," Roosevelt wrote in his *Autobiography.*

> In practice, as things are now, the Executive is or ought to be peculiarly representative as a whole. As often as not the action of the Executive offers the only means by which the people can get the legislation they demand and ought to have. Therefore a good executive under the present conditions of American political life must take a very active interest in getting the right kind of legislation, in addition to performing his executive duties with an eye single to the public welfare.[71]

Roosevelt practiced what he preached. The Pure Food and Drug Act of 1906, a landmark consumer law that established the Food and Drug Administration, was pushed through a Congress dominated by agriculture and business interests largely on the strength of the president's advocacy, along with wide newspaper publicity. Roosevelt also established the national park system, attacked monopolies, and negotiated the end to a war between Japan and Russia—for which he won the Nobel Peace Prize. Even more instructive was Roosevelt's decision to send a U.S. naval squadron on a global tour in a show of military strength intended mainly to impress other naval powers. A Congress suffused with isolationism refused to appropriate money simply to "show the flag," but Roosevelt scraped together enough funds from other navy accounts to send the fleet, with a few newspaper reporters conveniently aboard, halfway around the world. He then openly challenged Congress to provide enough money to bring the ships home. Public opinion so strongly supported Roosevelt that Congress quickly surrendered.

Theodore Roosevelt was unique in many ways—boundless in energy, aggressively intellectual, eager for public acclaim—but his legacy did not disappear. The nation and Congress had been given a taste of energetic presidential leadership, and succeeding chief executives found both the public and Congress more receptive to their initiatives.

William Howard Taft, Roosevelt's immediate successor, advocated a far less grandiose view of the office. Nonetheless, as political scientist James Sundquist points out, Taft went against the tradition of official presidential noninterference in the legislative process by being the first president since Washington to formally present draft legislation to Congress.[72] Woodrow Wilson in 1913 became the first president since John Adams to deliver his State of the Union message personally before a joint session of Congress. He thereafter used the address as a statement of his legislative agenda and to put into practice his belief that the president should lead government more actively.[73] Wilson also boldly asserted his right to guide legislation, arguing in a special address to Congress, "I have come to you as the head of the government and the responsible leader of the party in power to urge action now, while there is time to serve the country deliberately, and as we should, in a clear air of common counsel."[74] The legislation that Wilson wanted Congress to pass, the Federal Reserve Act of 1913, was drafted largely in conferences at the White House, with Wilson personally in charge.

The Franklin Roosevelt Model

Despite these gradual changes in the presidency during the first third of the twentieth century, the office of the presidency remained a largely reactive force opposing Congress, not the source of initiative and leadership that Americans demand today. Although Theodore Roosevelt and Woodrow Wilson in selected instances had taken the lead with legislation, particularly when conditions for presidential initiative were most favorable, the office itself lacked institutional mechanisms for sustained legislative influence. In the 1930s, however, the office underwent major, permanent changes, and the presidency of Franklin Roosevelt became the model for the contemporary presidency.

Franklin Roosevelt stepped into the presidency in 1933 as the nation faced unprecedented economic and social pressures. The Great Depression had devastated the national economy, forcing millions into unemployment and crippling public faith in government. Roosevelt's predecessor, Herbert Hoover (1929–1933), relied largely on the market system to resolve the crisis, but voters thought Hoover's confidence was misplaced and blamed him for the country's hardships. As a result, Hoover suffered a humiliating defeat in the 1932 presidential election. The emergency worsened dramatically in early 1933, just prior to Roosevelt's inauguration, requiring major action and giving Roosevelt the opportunity to lead the country in ways no previous peacetime president ever had. Congress, which itself had proved unable to resolve the crisis, awaited strong direction. Conditions for redefining the very essence of the presidency were ripe.

Roosevelt's immediate attack on the depression was the beginning of a sweeping and sustained rearrangement of national domestic policies, a legacy that endures to some degree to this day. The famous and archetypal "First Hundred Days" of Roosevelt's first term saw Congress, convened in special session, give the new president a blank check to remold the federal government, introduce new programs, and do almost anything necessary to turn the economy around. Roosevelt and his battalions of energetic "New Dealers" took on the task with joyful gusto, pushing major legislation through a willing Congress with unprecedented speed. *(See box, The First Hundred Days of Franklin D. Roosevelt, right.)* As presidential scholar Clinton Rossiter said of Roosevelt, "In the first Hundred Days he gave Congress a kind of leadership it had not known before and still does not care to have repeated."[75]

Central to Roosevelt's success in 1933 was the link he established between the presidency and the American people, a connection achieved in great part because of his ability to communicate directly to citizens via radio. "This nation asks for action, and action now," he said simply in his first inaugural address, which sparked nearly half a million letters of support. "We must act, and act quickly."[76]

Roosevelt's speeches, radio "fireside chats," and frequent meetings with reporters all spoke directly to the American people and indirectly to Congress about his dreams and priorities. In the process, Roosevelt focused sustained public attention on the presidency.

THE FIRST HUNDRED DAYS OF FRANKLIN D. ROOSEVELT

Franklin D. Roosevelt, sworn into office on March 4, 1933, convened the Seventy-third Congress into special session on March 9 to consider the Emergency Banking Act, which it passed after eight hours of debate. Roosevelt at first considered sending Congress back home after passage of the act, but the window of opportunity for even more action presented by the crisis seemed too valuable to waste. As historian Arthur M. Schlesinger Jr. later wrote, "In the three months after Roosevelt's inauguration, Congress and the country were subjected to a presidential barrage of ideas and programs unlike anything known to American history."[1]

Below are the major accomplishments of the now legendary "First Hundred Days":

March 9	Emergency Banking Act: reformed the national banking system
March 20	Economy Act: authorized cuts in federal spending
March 22	Beer and Wine Revenue Act: legalized sale of beer and wine
March 31	Civilian Conservation Corps: created employment for youths in a wide range of conservation efforts
April 19	Abandonment of gold standard: detached value of currency from gold
May 12	Federal Emergency Relief Act: created a national relief system
May 12	Agricultural Adjustment Act: established a national agricultural policy
May 12	Emergency Farm Mortgage Act: refinanced farm mortgages
May 18	Tennessee Valley Authority Act: provided for the unified development of the Tennessee Valley
May 27	Truth in Securities Act: required full disclosure of a firm's financial shape when it issued new securities
June 13	Home Owners' Loan Act: refinanced home mortgages
June 16	National Industrial Recovery Act: created a system of federally supervised industrial self-regulation and a $3.3 billion public works program
June 16	Glass-Steagall Banking Act: separated commercial and investment banking; guaranteed bank deposits
June 16	Farm Credit Act: reorganized federal farm credit programs
June 16	Emergency Railroad Transportation Act: created greater coordination in national railroad system

1. Arthur M. Schlesinger Jr., *The Coming of the New Deal* (Boston: Houghton Mifflin, 1959), 20.

EL CAMINO COLLEGE LIBRARY

Roosevelt's actions during the New Deal era and World War II combined to redefine the role of national government and the presidency as an institution. By the time FDR died in 1945, the executive branch had exploded in size and in the scope of its responsibilities, and the presidency itself had gained a wider array of resources for influencing legislation, making budgets, and implementing programs. The presidency no longer was a single person but an institution, one growing in size and potency as Congress gave the president more staff and more resources to manage the federal bureaucracy, initiate public policy, and lead the nation. Congress delegated these responsibilities to the presidency because legislators realized that the president was better situated to lead during times of perceived crisis and, more important, because Americans demanded an energetic presidency.

When Harry Truman took up Roosevelt's mantle in 1945 he sat at the center of an office much transformed during the course of FDR's twelve years in office. Under Roosevelt the presidency had come to include many roles. The president had become the national cheerleader, a role that television would enhance by making it far easier to communicate ideas and symbols directly to the mass public. He had become legislative leader, required both to initiate and to shepherd new policies through a potentially recalcitrant Congress. He had become the chief executive officer of a large and active government organization, with the responsibility of managing and directing the federal bureaucracy toward the common good. He had become a world ambassador—no job for those ignorant of or unconcerned about international affairs. And, more important, he had become largely responsible for the nation's success or failure. Roosevelt had appropriated for the presidency a role traditionally and constitutionally held by Congress. No longer would the presidency remain a passive office, even if its occupant possessed neither Roosevelt's skills nor his vigor.

The FDR administration used this figure of Uncle Sam as one way of explaining to the public the extensive changes and reforms brought about by New Deal legislation.

The Roosevelt Legacy

Roosevelt's legacy has been a problematic one for contemporary presidents. The office has grown in power and prestige, but perhaps not proportionately with expectations about what presidents must deliver. Those in the Oval Office must present and implement broad national programs, but separation of powers ensures that presidents' futures are not in their own hands. The emergence of the United States as a world power after World War II has made it necessary for presidents to exercise their role as commander in chief more fully and consistently than when the nation played little part in international political and military affairs, but these foreign responsibilities frequently clash with public demands that domestic matters be given top priority. Television has brought the world more intimately into every home and the pace of events has quickened demonstrably; but coalitions of support also seem more fleeting, and governing seems all the harder. The world is smaller, and public expectations about government are greater, creating for the presidency a burden of leadership that may prove too much to bear.[77]

This is not to argue that presidents have no control over their own destinies, but the extent of their control seems at times to depend less on personal intellect or social skills than on the social, economic, and political contexts within which they govern. Their control also depends on the willingness of other governing institutions, particularly Congress, to cooperate, which is by no means guaranteed. Lyndon Johnson, for example, was a master of the legislative process, having had a long career in Congress as House member, senator, and Senate majority leader. Even so, Johnson's achievement in enacting the most sweeping social agenda since Roosevelt's Hundred Days depended at least as much on the trauma following John Kennedy's assassination, a national mood supporting broad social change, and an unusually cooperative congressional majority after his sweeping 1964 election victory, as on Johnson's own legislative skills. Johnson's successes in 1965, when Congress approved some 69 percent of his legislative requests, were tempered by the knowledge that times would soon change.[78] "I have watched the Congress from either the inside or the outside, man and boy, for more than 40 years," Johnson commented early in 1965, "and I've never seen a Congress that didn't eventually take the measure of the president it was dealing with."[79]

Jimmy Carter discovered that harsh reality very early in his administration when a Congress dominated by his party proved skeptical of his comprehensive energy plan. Carter's problems in 1977 and later stemmed not only from his relative lack of experience in and even distaste for Washington politics, but from the very changes that had taken place in Congress, and in American politics generally, during the preceding decade. Congress had become far more open, more fragmented, and more independent, forcing presidents to adapt to new ways of influencing the legislature. Johnson was able to push through his Great Society programs largely because of his ability to rally a few key committee chairs and other congressional leaders, but Carter found it necessary to lobby virtually every member, a decidedly more difficult and frustrating task.

Even Reagan, whose masterful rhetorical skills helped him translate his 1980 election victory into early legislative success, found his later efforts frustrated by his inability to induce Congress to follow his lead. His two immediate successors, George Bush and Bill Clinton, fared even worse in many ways, regardless of which party controlled Congress. Given the sustained reassertion of congressional power with the end of the cold war and the prospects for even greater social and institutional constraints on presidential power for the rest of the century, Lyndon Johnson's warning to other presidents is an apt one.

The question of context thus is essential to analyzing a president's ability to set the agenda of government and to persuade Congress to enact those priorities. According to presidential scholar Louis Koenig, Congress most consistently follows presidential leadership in three situations.[80] The first is during perceived crises, when Congress and the nation invariably turn to the president for leadership. Roosevelt and the first Hundred Days is the most-cited example, for it is almost impossible to conceive that the New Deal could have been passed under "normal" political conditions.

Second, matters of national security and foreign affairs, in which the Constitution gives the presidency primacy, find Congress generally more amenable to presidential initiatives. This was particularly true between World War II and the end of the Vietnam War, when a general view that partisan "politics ended at the water's edge" gave postwar presidents an unparalleled range of flexibility. The tendency for Congress to accede to presidential demands in defense and foreign policy issues led more than one president to cloak purely domestic programs in the mantle of national security to obtain easier passage. The interstate highway system, federal education programs, and the space program all were defined as essential to national security or pride—highways for easier movement of defense forces, greater education spending to "catch up" to the Soviets after the launch of *Sputnik,* and the Mercury, Gemini, and Apollo programs to win the "space race." These programs thus won far greater national support than they might have otherwise.

Third, presidents reap benefits from "abnormal" contexts—the combined effects of skilled political leaders, superior partisan dominance in Congress, changing societal values, and, especially, timing. Virtually every new president enjoys a postelection "honeymoon" with Congress, a period during which the new occupant of the White House can push priorities within an atmosphere of general cooperation. Presidents usually have their greatest legislative successes during their first six months in office. Their relative degree of success has varied, depending on the scope of the electoral victory, the dominant national mood, the strength of congressional majorities, and, of course, the president's personal abilities.

The ability of any president to dominate the agenda of government, to plan and propose new initiatives, and to lobby successfully for these initiatives depends on more than personal skills or intellect. The character of the U.S. political system, the nature of the times, and the types of issues under debate all affect the extent to which any president can influence the national agenda and the legislative process. Regardless of the powers and prestige of the office, presidents are not entirely in control of their own destinies.

THE STATE OF THE UNION ADDRESS

The annual State of the Union address has become an essential and potent instrument with which presidents seek to influence the national agenda. It is today the primary means by which presidents review their accomplishments and outline their goals, yet the constitutional requirement that presidents give Congress information on the state of the Union has not always played so central a role in presidential strategies. Although both George Washington and John Adams appeared personally before Congress to deliver their annual messages, Jefferson in 1801 submitted his report in writing because he felt a personal appearance aped the practice whereby the monarch personally opened each new session of the British Parliament. By eliminating a quasi-monarchical rite, notes historian Arthur M. Schlesinger Jr., Jefferson hoped to instill stronger values of republicanism (that is, representative government) in the young American system.[81]

Jefferson set a precedent that lasted more than a century. Not until Woodrow Wilson in 1913 did a president appear again before Congress to deliver the address. Wilson revived the earlier tradition set by Washington because he believed that presidents should make personal appeals to the nation and to Congress. Wilson expressed his view in his first personal appearance before Congress for a special message on finance:

I am very glad indeed to have the opportunity to address the two houses directly, and to verify for myself the impression that the president of the United States is a person, not a mere department of the government hailing Congress from some isolated island of jealous power, sending messages, and not speaking naturally and with his own voice, that he is a human being trying to cooperate with other human beings in a common service. After this experience I shall feel quite normal in all our dealings with one another.[82]

Wilson also changed the content of the annual message. Before his time the State of the Union message usually was a laborious recitation of department and agency activities. It seldom contained substantive legislative proposals; Congress made law, and suggestions made by presidents were to be given no greater weight than those offered by average citizens. The single nineteenth-century exception to this informal but ironclad rule only underscored prevailing views. Grover Cleveland deviated from tradition and devoted his entire 1887 message to ideas about tariff reform, but his temerity at openly suggesting ideas to Congress sparked a tremendous debate in the press, divided his Democratic Party, and apparently contributed to his defeat in 1888.[83]

Since Wilson the State of the Union address has become the major vehicle for expounding the president's legislative agenda and priorities, a tendency magnified by the onset of television. Today the president's annual appearance before a joint session of Congress is a major national event. Indeed, it is the kind of quasi-monarchical rite that Jefferson would have opposed. It is a moment of high ceremony, a pageant duly attended by the members of Congress, the cabinet, the joint chiefs of staff, justices of the Supreme Court, foreign dignitaries, and invited guests. Television cameras pan the House chamber as the president speaks, recording the reactions of particular members of the audience to specific presidential statements or proposals. Media commentators and other political experts routinely begin to judge the presidential "performance" before the president leaves the Capitol. The issues raised by the president get serious consideration in the press, if not always in Congress, and the opposition party usually feels compelled to ask for equal time to state its views. *(See Table 2-3.)*

Despite, or perhaps because of its sheer symbolism, the power of the annual address to shape public opinion and spur on Congress should not be underestimated. Kennedy, for example, used it to launch a national effort to put a person on the moon before the end of the 1960s. Johnson passionately promoted his civil rights and Great Society social programs, and Nixon used the opportunity to propose sweeping reorganization of the federal establishment and to defend U.S. actions in Vietnam. Reagan, a master of television, used the annual address to spark national and congressional debate on tax reform, on aid to the rebels in Nicaragua, and on his Strategic Defense Initiative weapons program. The nation discusses whatever presidents discuss, if only for a while. Often, the president's priorities become those of government.

TABLE 2-3 Presidential Appearances before Congress, 1789–1996

President	*Number of appearances*	*Occasions*
Washington	10	8 annual messages (1789–1796); 2 inaugural addresses (1789, 1793—second inaugural before Senate only)
J. Adams	6	4 annual messages (1797–1800); inaugural address (1797); relations with France (1797)
Wilson	26	6 annual messages (1913–1918); tariff reform, bank reform, relations with Mexico (1913); antitrust laws, Panama Canal tolls, relations with Mexico, new tax revenue (1914); impending rail strike (1916); "Peace without Victory" (Senate only), breaking relations with Germany, arming of merchant ships, request for war declaration against Germany (1917); federal takeover of railroads, "14 points" for peace, peace outlook, need for new revenue, request for ratification of women's suffrage amendment (Senate only), armistice (1918); request for approval of Versailles treaty (Senate only), high cost of living (1919)
Harding	7	2 annual messages (1921–1922); federal problems (1921); 2 on the Merchant Marine (1922); coal and railroads (1922); debt (1923)
Coolidge	2	1 annual message (1923); George Washington's birthday (1927)
Roosevelt	16	10 annual messages (1934–1943); 100th anniversary of Lafayette's death (1934); 150th anniversary of First Congress (1939); neutrality address (1939); national defense (1940); declaration of war (1941); Yalta conference report (1945)
Truman	17	6 State of the Union messages (1947–1952); prosecution of the war (1945); submission of UN charter (Senate only, 1945); Congressional Medal of Honor ceremony (1945); universal military training (1945); railroad strike (1946); Greek–Turkish aid policy (1947); aid to Europe (1947); national security and conditions in Europe (1948); 50th anniversary of the liberation of Cuba (1948); inflation, housing, and civil rights (1948); steel industry dispute (1952)
Eisenhower	7	6 State of the Union messages (1953–1954; 1957–1960); Middle East (1957)
Kennedy	3	3 State of the Union messages (1961–1963)
Johnson	8	6 State of the Union messages (1964–1969); assumption of office (1963); Voting Rights Act (1965)
Nixon	7	4 State of the Union messages (1970–1972, 1974); Vietnam policy (1969—separate addresses to House and Senate); economic policy (1971); Soviet Union trip (1972)
Ford[a]	6	3 State of the Union messages (1975–1977); assumption of office (1974); inflation (1974); state of the world (1975)
Carter	6	3 State of the Union messages (1978–1980); energy program (1977); Middle East talks at Camp David (1978); SALT II arms control treaty (1979)
Reagan	11	7 State of the Union messages (1982–1988); 2 budget addresses (1981); Central America (1983); U.S.-Soviet summit (1985)
Bush	5	3 State of the Union messages (1990–1992); budget address (1989); Persian Gulf crisis (1991)
Clinton[b]	5	3 State of the Union messages (1994–1996); budget address (1993); health policy reform (1993)

SOURCES: *Guide to Congress,* 4th ed. (Washington, D.C.: Congressional Quarterly, 1991), 542; *Congressional Quarterly Weekly Report,* various issues.

NOTES: a. On October 17, 1974, President Gerald R. Ford testified before the Subcommittee on Criminal Justice of the House Judiciary Committee on his pardon of former president Richard Nixon for crimes possibly committed during the Watergate affair. b. Through 1996. Note also that Presidents Reagan, Bush, and Clinton each gave a speech to Congress within weeks of their inauguration. This speech, while not technically a State of the Union address, served to outline the new president's broad legislative agenda.

The State of the Union address is an important part of the "conversation" between presidents and Congress, a constant dialogue that may be as formal as the address or as informal as the daily contact among presidents, presidential aides, members of Congress, and Capitol Hill staff.[84] This dialogue can be examined in part by listing the major themes expressed in State of the Union messages of Presidents Kennedy through Clinton. *(See Table 2-4.)*

During the 1970s, for example, the emphasis shifted from foreign to domestic policy concerns, particularly the economy. As political scientist Charles O. Jones notes, "Many of the domestic requests by Nixon, Ford, and Carter were reform measures seeking to reshape the structure and substance of programs enacted in the 1960s—a shift from issues requiring expansion of government to those demanding consolidation or even contraction of government."[85] The emphasis shifted back somewhat to foreign policy in the 1980s, reflecting the focus of the Reagan administration, and then returned to domestic concerns in the early 1990s.

The address also is a moment for presidents to proclaim successes, express their grand desires for the future, and engage in a little political theater. Reagan was adept at using his time to praise American "heroes" and to chastise Congress for the way it prepares budgets. *(See box, The State of the Union Address as Political Theater, p. 106.)* Using the address for such symbolic purposes has its dangers, however, particularly when events outstrip plans. In 1986 the Reagan administration intended to make full use of the launch of the space shuttle *Challenger* to praise "teacher in space" Christa McAuliffe as an example of the bright future of the nation. The *Challenger* was launched on the day the speech was scheduled, but its explosion and the deaths of the seven astronauts forced the postponement of the address. Reagan instead went on television that night to speak of the accident and to express his belief that the nation had to get past the tragedy.

The State of the Union message is required by the Constitution, but over time Congress through statute has required the president to make other annual reports. The Budget Act of 1921 requires the president to submit an annual budget message, and the Employment Act of 1946 mandates an annual report on the economy. Hundreds of other reports, messages, and legislative proposals are submitted to Congress annually, all bearing the president's imprint and expressing White House views on important policy matters. As such, each one has potential political influence.

PREPARING LEGISLATION

A president's priorities generally, but not always, require formal congressional approval. Setting the national agenda is but the initial stage in successful presidential leadership, if *leadership* is defined simply as getting proposals approved by Congress. In this process presidents throughout history have relied on a wide array of personnel and resources.

TABLE 2-4 Major Themes in State of the Union Addresses, 1961–1996

President	*Year*	*Major themes*
Kennedy	1961	Economy; social programs
	1962	Getting America moving; economy; military strength
	1963	Cuba; economy; tax reduction
Johnson	1964	JFK legacy; budget
	1965	Great Society domestic programs
	1966	Vietnam, foreign and defense policy
	1967	Maintaining previous momentum
	1968	Vietnam, foreign and defense policy
	1969	Review of achievements
Nixon	1970	Vietnam, foreign and defense policy
	1971	Vietnam; economic and social policy
	1972	Foreign and defense policy; plea for action on previous requests
	1973[a]	Natural resources; economy; social policy
	1974	Energy; economic issues
Ford	1975	Economy; taxes; energy
	1976	Economic and energy issues
	1977	Energy; achievements
Carter	1978	Economic and energy issues
	1979	Inflation; SALT II
	1980	Foreign and defense policy
	1981[a]	Record of progress; budget priorities
Reagan	1982	Economic and budget issues
	1983	Economic and budget issues
	1984	Federal deficit; foreign policy
	1985	Tax reform; government spending
	1986	Foreign policy; welfare reform
	1987	Foreign policy
	1988	Economic and budget issues
Bush	1990	Broad domestic and foreign policy issues
	1991	Support for Persian Gulf mission
	1992	Economic and budget issues
Clinton	1994	Domestic policy; jobs; crime; health reform
	1995	"Reinventing government"; domestic policy issues
	1996	Broad domestic policy issues

SOURCES: Charles O. Jones, "Presidential Negotiation with Congress," in *Both Ends of the Avenue: The Presidency, the Executive Branch, and Congress in the 1980s,* ed. Anthony King (Washington, D.C.: American Enterprise Institute, 1983), 103; *Congressional Quarterly Weekly Report,* various issues.

NOTE: a. Written message to Congress.

Drafting legislation is the first formal phase in the process. For the president to take an active part in drafting bills departs from strict interpretations of separation of powers, because only Congress has constitutional power to make law. But presidents always have done so. Early presidents were highly circumspect about their roles and usually tried to avoid any appearance of interposing their views in a realm zealously guarded by Congress. George Washington, for example, quietly discussed ideas for new measures with cabinet officials and members of Congress. He even secretly helped to compose the odd bill, but he studiously avoided open and direct roles in forming legislation. Instead he assigned cabinet members to consult formally with Congress, an activity deemed more legitimate because department heads appeared regularly before congressional committees on routine business. Congress itself validated this strategy by directing Secretary of the Treasury Hamilton to draft and submit recommendations for a new national bank, a resolution of state

THE STATE OF THE UNION ADDRESS AS POLITICAL THEATER

Woodrow Wilson in 1913 revived the earlier tradition of presidents personally delivering the State of the Union address to Congress, but it was not until the advent of radio and, later, television that the annual speech took on powerful symbolic meaning. Widespread public access to radio allowed Franklin D. Roosevelt, for example, to speak directly to the American people and rally the nation out of the depression of the 1930s. But television, with its particular capacity to present emotional visual images, has elevated the State of the Union address to true public theater, complete with an audience (members of Congress assembled) and critics (network commentators). Televised annual addresses have become less a litany of dry statistics than a panorama of past accomplishments, current endeavors, and future dreams. Increasingly, the State of the Union address has become the primary vehicle in setting the nation's annual agenda, with presidents judged on how *well* they delivered their messages. The medium and the message have indeed coalesced.

John F. Kennedy inaugurated the use of television to breathe vibrancy into the annual message, but it was Ronald Reagan, the acknowledged master of visual media, who used the address to its greatest effect thus far. Whether he used it to needle Congress, praise heroes, or express his dreams for America, the State of the Union address in Reagan's hands became an eagerly awaited and heavily analyzed event. Reagan may not have written his own words or dreamed up the various symbolic appeals used—such matters were left to professional speechwriters—but he was the deliverer of the message to the people. The following excerpt from President Reagan's 1988 State of the Union address shows how one president transformed this once banal annual accounting into the preeminent national political event.

. . . Now, it is also time for some plain talk about the most immediate obstacle to controlling federal deficits. The simple but frustrating problem of making expenses match revenues—something American families do and the federal government can't—has caused crisis after crisis in this city. . . . I will say to you tonight what I have said before—and will continue to say: The budget process has broken down; it needs a drastic overhaul. With each ensuing year, the spectacle before the American people is the same as it was this Christmas—budget deadlines delayed or missed completely, monstrous continuing resolutions that pack hundreds of billions of dollars' worth of spending into one bill—and a federal government on the brink of default.

I know I'm echoing what you here in the Congress have said because you suffered so directly—but let's recall that in seven years, of 91 appropriations bills scheduled to arrive on my desk by a certain date, only 10 made it on time. Last year, of the 13 appropriations bills due by October 1st, none of them made it. Instead, we had four continuing resolutions lasting 41 days, then 36 days, and two days, and three days, respectively. And then, along came these behemoths. This is the conference report—1,053-page report weighing 14 pounds. Then this—a reconciliation bill six months late, that was 1,186 pages long, weighing 15 pounds; and the long-term continuing resolution—this one was two months late and it's 1,057 pages long, weighing 14 pounds. That was a total of 43 pounds of paper and ink. You had three hours—yes, three hours, to consider each, and it took 300 people at my Office of Management just to read the bill so the government wouldn't shut down.

Congress shouldn't send another one of these. No—and if you do, I will not sign it. Let's change all this; instead of a presidential budget that gets discarded and a congressional budget resolution that is not enforced, why not a simple partnership, a joint agreement that sets out the spending priorities within the available revenues? And let's remember our deadline is October 1st, not Christmas; let's get the people's work done in time to avoid a footrace with Santa Claus. And yes, this year—to coin a phrase—a new beginning. Thirteen individual bills, on time and fully reviewed by Congress. . . .

SOURCE: *Congressional Quarterly Weekly Report*, January 3, 1988, 221.

debts, and the promotion of manufacturing—tasks Hamilton took on with such relish that he sparked severe criticism of his dominance over the legislative process.[86]

Hamilton's chief critic, Secretary of State Thomas Jefferson, proved no less energetic once he became president. Although his party publicly stressed congressional supremacy, Jefferson secretly composed bills, which he transmitted through his department secretaries to party loyalists in the legislature, and used his cabinet heavily for maximum influence on legislating. Jefferson's party caucus, which enjoyed a solid congressional majority, enabled him to maintain the fiction of his complete separateness from lawmaking even as he wielded a strong hand behind the scenes.

Other nineteenth-century presidents continued this pattern of using cabinet officials to lobby for legislation. They had few alternatives. Presidents had few personal staff members, and Congress did not appropriate funds for even clerical assistance until 1857. Nor did they have extensive networks of personal advisers and assistants.[87] Cabinet officials gave presidents valuable access to congressional committees, acted as the chief executive's political eyes and ears, and, as political scientist James Young has noted, "allowed Presidents to maintain, for what it was worth, the outward appearance of conformity to community norms which decreed social distance between the President and Congress."[88]

But this system had its disadvantages. Chief among them was the reality that department heads frequently were selected to pay off political favors or to accommodate rival factions within the president's party.

Presidents never were entirely sure of their own cabinet's primary loyalties and had to guard against the tendency of strong cabinet officials to cultivate their power bases in Congress. Lincoln, for example, was plagued constantly by the need to maneuver around such formidable political figures as Secretary of State William Seward and Secretary of the Treasury Salmon P. Chase, who led their factions within the Republican Party and regularly clashed with Lincoln over Civil War policies.

The Institutional Presidency

The picture of the nineteenth-century presidency is one of a lone figure with little reliable assistance. Contemporary presidents, by contrast, reside at the heart of an immense executive institution, aided in their tasks by about fifteen hundred special assistants, personal aides, policy experts, and clerical staff distributed among several specialized White House agencies. *(See Table 2-5.)* The Executive Office of the President (EOP) is the president's personal bureaucracy, designed expressly to help the chief executive oversee cabinet department and agency activities, formulate budgets and monitor spending, craft legislation, lobby Congress, and, above all, promote the president's priorities.

This support system began to take shape when Congress, recognizing that departments all too often bypassed the president in their pleas for new appropriations, passed the Budget and Accounting Act of 1921, which required the president to coordinate all executive branch spending proposals and present a unified annual budget. Congress created the Bureau of the Budget (BOB) to assist presidents in their tasks. Thus arose the notion of "central clearance," the use of BOB to monitor all executive branch spending, to judge new funding requests before they went to Capitol Hill, and, especially, to quash budget proposals not in line with the president's agenda. The president for the first time had a mechanism to coordinate and perhaps control executive branch activities.[89]

Franklin Roosevelt's New Deal spawned a staggering growth in executive branch responsibilities, which in turn strained the capacity of the presidency to coordinate and control government expenditures and actions. In 1939 the Bureau of the Budget was moved to the Executive Office of the President, which was newly created out of widespread recognition that presidents sorely needed sustained personal staff assistance. Roosevelt extended the BOB's central clearance functions to include screening bills passed by Congress and recommending to the president whether they should be approved.

TABLE 2-5 Size of Executive Office of the President, Various Offices, 1941–1995

Year	*White House Office*	*Office of Management and Budget*[a]	*National Security Council*
1941	53	305	—
1945	61	565	—
1950	295	520	17
1955	290	444	28
1960	446	434	65
1965	292	506	39
1970	491	636	82
1975	525	664	85
1980	426	631	74
1985	362	569	61
1990	391	568	60
1995[b]	400	553	57

SOURCES: Bureau of the Census, *Statistical Abstract of the United States* (Washington, D.C.: Government Printing Office, various editions); U.S. Office of Personnel Management, *Federal Manpower Statistics, Federal Civilian Workforce Statistics*, bimonthly.

NOTES: a. Known until 1970 as the Bureau of the Budget. b. Estimate.

These central clearance responsibilities were magnified even more in 1970 when Congress transformed the BOB into the Office of Management and Budget (OMB), which Richard Nixon then made into the president's chief instrument of domestic policy advocacy. Subsequent presidents have extended OMB's power and reach even further. Today no legislative proposal generated within the executive branch goes to Congress without prior OMB clearance; no new regulation goes into effect until OMB approves; and no bill passed by Congress hits the president's desk until OMB judges how well it meets the president's policy and budgetary goals. Once a relatively quiet and even neutral accounting department, OMB today is the powerful, partisan, and often controversial defender of the president's agenda.

Other parts of the Executive Office of the President complement OMB's activities. The Council of Economic Advisers, normally composed of three noted economists, advises the president on economic matters and how they affect national politics. The National Security Council acts as the president's foreign policy advisory mechanism, designed to transcend the institutional boundaries of the various foreign policy bureaucracies and to give the president a broad view of national security questions.

Individual presidents also create specialized offices within the EOP to emphasize a particular focus. President Bush, for example, created a Council on Competitiveness chaired by Vice President Dan Quayle to review all proposed bills or regulations specifically for their possible effects on business and "economic competitiveness" generally. The council proved highly controversial, particularly in its activities concerning social policy and environmental matters, and was disbanded in 1993 by the Clinton administration.

At the apex of the executive branch pyramid sits the White House Office, which is home to the president's closest personal aides and special assistants, and which is chiefly responsible for spearheading the president's agenda and coordinating the activities of the entire executive branch. The contemporary presidency thus is an *institution* with resources and powers that remain potent regardless of the personal traits of individual chief executives.

This White House bureaucracy exists solely because the presidency today is required to design and lobby for legislative proposals, monitor and coordinate government spending, and promote an overall national agenda. The late twentieth century is very different from the days when presidents crafted legislation in secret or found themselves unable to oversee spending within the various departments.

Ironically, the very institutional capacity to carry out all these tasks presents presidents with a new dilemma: how to ensure

HOW A BILL BECOMES A LAW

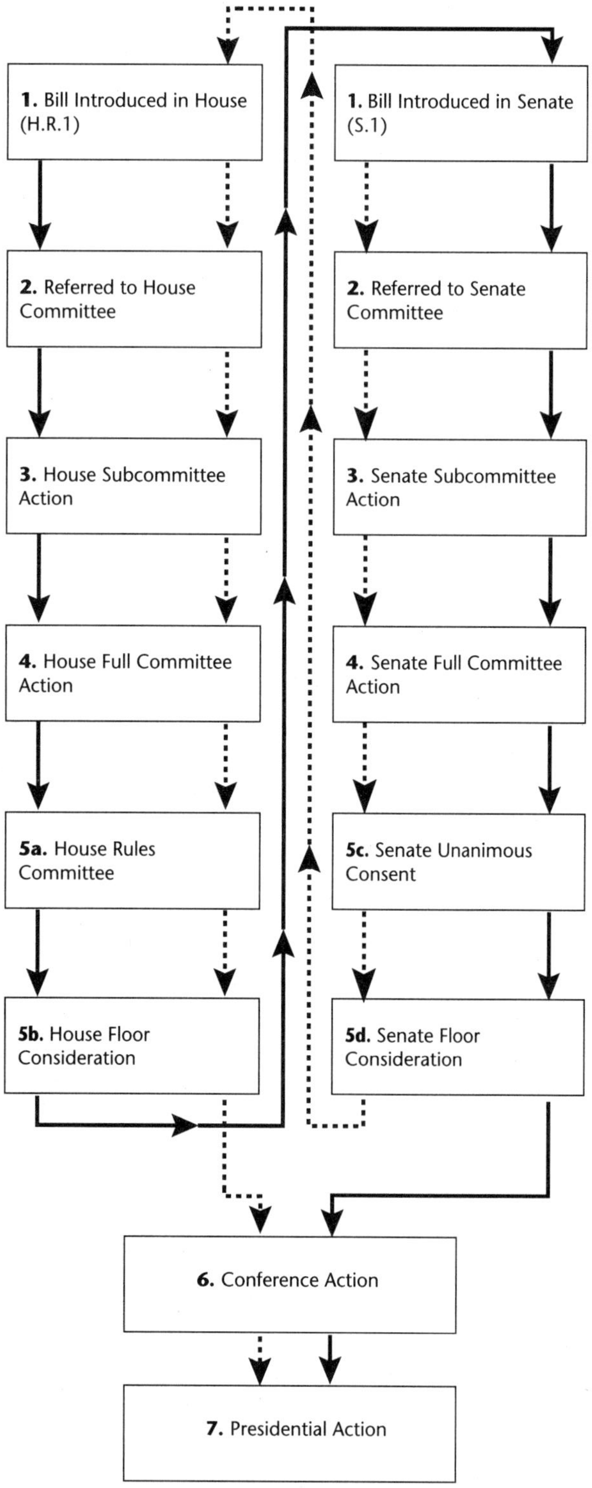

1. INTRODUCTION OF A BILL IN HOUSE OR SENATE

A proposal that will eventually become law must be introduced by a member of Congress. Often when a member introduces a bill, he or she will find someone in the other chamber to introduce a "companion bill." Each bill is given a number as it is introduced, and numbering is sequential. House bill numbers start with *HR,* Senate bill numbers start with *S.*

A bill written in the executive branch and proposed as an administration measure usually is introduced "by request" by the chair of the congressional committee that has jurisdiction.

2. REFERRAL TO COMMITTEE.

After a bill is introduced it is referred by the parliamentarian to a standing committee. The committee chair then decides which subcommittee will consider the measure.

3. SUBCOMMITTEE ACTION.

The subcommittee holds hearings on the bill. Testimony may be taken from invited witnesses only, or the committee may issue an open call and hear from anyone who wishes to speak. At this point administration representatives have a chance to urge support for a bill. Subcommittee hearings also provide an opportunity for them to oppose a bill they do not like.

When hearings are completed, the bill is "marked up," that is, rewritten to incorporate the subcommittee's changes. These changes may be designed to strengthen (or weaken) the provisions or they may be politically inspired to improve (or reduce) a bill's chance of passage. If the president has objections, it is at this point that friendly committee members and White House lobbyists attempt to amend the bill to meet presidential approval. When the subcommittee has finished its work, the bill is sent to the full committee.

4. FULL COMMITTEE ACTION.

The full committee may ratify the subcommittee's actions, or it may repeat the subcommittee's steps by holding more hearings and marking up the bill a second time. This second markup gives the administration another chance to alter the bill if its effort to make changes at the subcommittee level failed. Whether or not the subcommittee steps are repeated, only the full committee formally reports the bill back to the chamber for floor action; a subcommittee cannot report a measure directly.

5A. HOUSE RULES COMMITTEE.

After the full committee reports the bill, it is placed on a "calendar" and is ready for floor consideration. In the House, controversial or complicated bills are referred to the Rules Committee, which determines the framework for debate and amendment. A special rule written by the Rules Committee specifies how long debate will last, who will control the time, and how many and what type of amendments may be offered.

After the Rules Committee has recommended a rule, the full House votes on whether to accept it. If the rule does not allow amendments that the president favors, or if the legislation contains provisions the president would like to see deleted, the White House may lobby House members to defeat the rule. The White House is seldom successful in defeating a rule; but when it is, that success is a major victory for the president.

5B. HOUSE FLOOR CONSIDERATION.

If, as usually happens, the House accepts the rule, the next step is debate on the bill. Normal House rules limit each member to one hour during general debate, but often the rule imposes more rigid time limits. Roll call votes may be requested if a certain number of members agree to the request. Roll call votes are taken electronically in the House and usually last fifteen minutes.

If the bill originated in the House, it is referred to the Senate for action after passage (see solid line). If the House is completing consideration of a measure referred from the Senate and the bill has not been amended, it is cleared for presidential action. If the bill is a referral from the Senate and has been substantially amended, it may be referred to a conference committee *(see No. 6)*.

5C. SENATE UNANIMOUS CONSENT.

To expedite floor consideration, the Senate has developed a procedure, known as the "unanimous consent agreement," similar to the special rules written by the House Rules Committee. A unanimous consent agreement is worked out informally by the majority and minority leaders and by any senator with an interest in the bill under consideration. The agreement specifies how much time will be allotted for debate, what amendments will be considered, and how the time will be divided. Unlike a House rule, however, which needs a simple majority to pass, a unanimous consent agreement must be accepted by all senators on the floor at the time it is proposed. A single objection defeats the agreement.

5D. SENATE FLOOR CONSIDERATION.

Floor consideration under a unanimous consent agreement in the Senate is similar to action under a rule in the House. If a unanimous consent agreement cannot be worked out, however, the Senate operates under its normal rules, which are much less restrictive than House rules. There is no time limit on debate. Members opposed to a bill under consideration sometimes "filibuster"—that is, hold the floor by speaking for an extended period of time—to delay or kill a bill. A filibuster can be ended only if sixty senators agree to a "cloture" petition to limit debate. As a result, floor proceedings in the Senate usually take much longer than in the House. Voting in the Senate is not electronic. The roll is called by a clerk who records each senator's vote.

If the bill under consideration originated in the Senate, it is then referred to the House for action after passage (see broken line). If the Senate is completing consideration of a measure referred from the House and the bill has not been amended, it is cleared for presidential action. If the bill is a referral from the House and has been substantially amended, it may be referred to a conference committee *(see No. 6)*.

6. CONFERENCE ACTION.

A bill must be approved by both chambers in identical form before it can be sent to the president. If there are major differences between the versions passed by the House and the Senate, the bill may go to a conference committee, which works out a compromise. The committee usually consists of senior members of the committees that reported the bill. If the president has reservations or objections or prefers the bill passed by one chamber to the version passed by the other, it is in the conference that the White House attempts to influence members to adopt a final version that is acceptable to the administration.

When the conference is completed, the committee files a conference report to which both the House and the Senate must agree. If either rejects the conference agreement, the bill dies. If both agree to the conference report, the measure then goes to the president for final action.

A conference often can be avoided, however. Even if one chamber has amended a bill substantially, it can refer the measure back to the originating chamber, which may accept all the amendments (clearing the bill for the president), accept some and reject others, or even add some amendments of its own (in which case the bill then bounces back to the other chamber a second time). This back-and-forth process can continue until both chambers have agreed to the measure in identical form, thus clearing it for presidential action. In reality, most bills are cleared in this manner, avoiding an official conference.

7. PRESIDENTIAL ACTION.

The president has several options once a bill is received from Congress. If the president approves the bill, he signs it, dates it, and usually writes the word "approved" on the document. If the president disapproves, he vetoes the bill by refusing to sign it and returns it to Congress within ten legislative days of its presentation (Sundays excluded) with a message stating his reasons. The message is sent to the chamber that originated the bill. If no action is taken on the message, the bill dies.

Congress, however, may vote to overturn a veto. Debate can precede this vote, with motions permitted to lay the message on the table, postpone action on it, or refer it to committee. If both chambers vote by a two-thirds majority (of those present and voting) to "override" the veto, the bill becomes law. Otherwise the bill is dead.

Normally if the president does not sign the bill within the ten-day period and Congress is in session, the bill becomes law without his signature. However, should Congress adjourn before the ten days expire and the president has failed to sign the measure, it does not become law. This procedure is called the pocket veto.

When bills are passed finally and signed, or passed over a veto, they are given law numbers in numerical order as they become law. There are two series of numbers, one for public and one for private laws, starting at the number "1" for each two-year term of Congress. They are then identified by law number and by Congress—for example, Private Law 21, 104th Congress; Public Law 250, 104th Congress (or PL 104–250).

that the Executive Office of the President itself responds to the president's needs and wishes. Presidents cannot be involved personally with every action that occurs below them. They must rely on subordinates to monitor and guide the behavior of an institution that itself is designed to monitor and guide the behavior of the executive branch as a whole. Nineteenth-century presidents bemoaned their lack of staff resources; presidents today wonder how they can make their own vast organization run loyally and well.

The President's Agenda

Much of the legislation Congress ponders originates from within the executive branch. No longer do presidents maintain a fiction of separation from the legislative process. Indeed, contemporary presidents more often than not are judged by the quality and timing of their annual policy agendas. Congress and the public demand that presidents initiate legislation and criticize severely those who do not. Eisenhower, for example, did not propose a formal legislative agenda in his first year in office, only to receive sharp rebukes from both parties. "Don't expect us to start from scratch on what you people want," said one angry House member to an administration official. "That's not the way we do things here. You draft the bills and we work them over."[90]

A multiplicity of sources provides the ideas that form the intellectual foundation of the president's program. Before Franklin Roosevelt's administration, presidents could work out their agenda from their personal views and experiences, because the role of the executive branch was limited and the problems requiring presidential attention were relatively few. Theodore Roosevelt's aggressive national park and wildlife conservation policies stemmed at least in part from his background as a western rancher and big-game hunter. Hoover's experiences as secretary of commerce under Calvin Coolidge (1923–1929) guided his priorities, at least until the Great Depression overtook his presidency.

Recently, however, as the data compiled by presidential scholar Paul Light suggest, a surprising proportion of a chief executive's domestic program may come from "outside" sources—Congress, national and international events, the departments and agencies of the executive branch, and public opinion. *(See Table 2-6.)* Congress, with its hundreds of members and thousands of staff, is fertile ground for legislative ideas. Many of the formal legislative proposals that come officially from the White House actually stem from ideas and proposals that have bounced around Capitol Hill for years, waiting to be adopted as political circumstances permit.[91] One such example of policy adoption was Kennedy's domestic program, a large portion of which was based on ideas and options promoted to no avail by liberal congressional Democrats during the Eisenhower years. What Kennedy could not get through Congress, Lyndon Johnson later incorporated into his Great Society program. The same perspective applies to Reagan's vaunted tax reduction bill of 1981, which was the "offspring" of a Republican tax plan pushed by Rep. Jack Kemp (N.Y.) and Sen. William Roth (Del.) during the late 1970s. Hundreds of proposed policies float about at all times, each awaiting the power of a president to lift it out of the mass of proposals and give it life.[92]

TABLE 2-6 Sources of Ideas for the President's Domestic Agenda

Source	*Respondents mentioning source (percent)*
EXTERNAL SOURCES	
Congress	52
Events and crises	51
Executive branch	46
Public opinion	27
Party	11
Interest groups	7
Media	4
INTERNAL SOURCES	
Campaign and platform	20
President	17
Staff	16
Task forces	6

SOURCE: Paul C. Light, *The President's Agenda* (Baltimore: Johns Hopkins University Press, 1983), 118.

NOTE: Number of respondents: 118. Respondents were past and current White House aides who were asked, "Generally speaking, what would you say were the most important sources of ideas for the domestic agenda?"

Crises or other major events also structure the domestic agenda, probably more than presidents desire or care to admit. This is true particularly as Americans have come to expect government to respond forcefully to new or sudden problems. There is no question, for example, that Hoover's inability to rein in the depression led to his defeat in 1932 and that Franklin Roosevelt attained mythical status for his innovative ("try anything") attack on the economic crisis and for his overall leadership during World War II.[93] The 1957 Soviet launch of *Sputnik* startled Eisenhower into major spending for science education and the space program. The energy crisis of the 1970s, sparked largely by huge hikes in oil prices by producing nations, dominated the fiscal and budgetary agendas of both Ford and Carter. National concern about the AIDS (Acquired Immune Deficiency Syndrome) epidemic forced the Reagan administration to increase research funding to combat the disease, while the Bush administration sent American troops to Somalia undoubtedly in response to public sentiments in favor of alleviating the suffering there. Although presidents enjoy a tremendous institutional capacity to define the agenda of government, many times they are forced to respond to issues or events out of their control, a condition that probably will intensify in the future as the effects of global communications on domestic politics become all the more apparent.[94]

Executive branch bureaucrats provide another wellspring of policy ideas or options, despite the propensity of presidential candidates to attack the bureaucracy during their election campaigns. Career civil servants are deeply dedicated to particular

Presidents frequently place a trusted friend or political ally in the position of attorney general. John F. Kennedy appointed his brother Robert.

policy areas and possess the technical expertise and perspectives that come from long tenure. Their experiences can help new presidents initiate new policies or simply avoid repeating the errors of the past.

The degree to which any president adopts ideas generated from within the professional bureaucracy depends in large part on personal ideology and style. The White House staffs of Nixon and Reagan, for example, were highly suspicious of the motives and political leanings of career civil servants and tried whenever possible to draw policy making directly into the White House.[95] Democrats, however, usually seem to share civil servants' fundamental beliefs in the positive role of government and thus have shown a greater willingness to tap bureaucratic ideas.

Whatever the source of any agenda item, presidents must test its technical, economic, and, especially, political soundness before sending it off to Congress. Proposals that fail to take politics into account are ripe for disaster. The degree to which this is true is probably proportionate to the degree of change intended. Incremental changes do not as a rule generate massive political resistance, but plans that seek comprehensive change almost guarantee strong reactions from a wide array of affected interests.[96] Carter's massive effort to reform national energy policy, for example, was hammered out by a panel of experts but suffered embarrassing political defeats once it was sent to Congress. The same fate befell Clinton's plan for health care reform, despite the administration's efforts to include as many perspectives as possible before sending the plan to Congress. The sheer size of the intended reform may have created the seeds of its own opposition.

Presidents seek out a wide range of expertise in an effort to avoid such fates, but, as they find out, no source is perfect. Professionals within the EOP, for example, are valuable sources of technical expertise or economic analysis, but they may not be attuned to the political climate or understand well the vagaries of Capitol Hill. Personal aides and trusted friends are valued for their political acumen and their ability to say things to the president that others would not dare. Every president has such intimates, be they the Californians making up Reagan's "kitchen cabinet," Carter's "Georgia mafia," or Franklin Roosevelt's "brain trust." But such people may also be new to Washington or blinded to political reality by their loyalty to the president when controversial decisions must be made.

Cabinet secretaries, in contrast to the days when they were the president's primary advisers (and sometimes competitors), today play a secondary role in judging proposals unless they also enjoy close personal ties to the president or preside over a department particularly important to presidential priorities. Presidents frequently fill the position of attorney general, for example, with a close friend or political ally who then enjoys ready access to the Oval Office. Kennedy appointed his brother Robert; Nixon looked to his friend and former law partner, John Mitchell; and Reagan appointed his longtime aide, Edwin Meese. Each of these acted as more than a department head; they also were close friends.

By contrast, some cabinet members rarely see the president in private, even on issues central to their departments, and complain that their phone calls are routed to presidential aides whom they technically outrank. Samuel Pierce, for example, was secretary of housing and urban development throughout the Reagan presidency, yet he rarely played a central role in policy development because his department was peripheral to the president's agenda. (In fact, as one famous story goes, Reagan even failed to recognize Pierce at a reception for city mayors.) Some cabinet members also are regarded with deep suspicion because they tend to promote departmental interests over the president's agenda, particularly after they have been in office for some time. Cabinet secretaries who "go native" find their access cut off and advice ignored, even when it could prove valuable.

Members of Congress of either political party may be keenly attuned to the political feasibility of new proposals but, as elected officials in their own right, they may have their own particular agendas to promote. Given their distinct electoral and governing roles, they also may find that their perspectives differ dramatically from the president's. Carter, for one, deeply distrusted members of Congress, who he felt were too parochial. Indeed, he discovered to his dismay the tenacity of local interests in Congress once his proposals went to Capitol Hill. All presidents find this out eventually, and most realize that members of Congress must be heard, if only so that they can warn of the potential obstacles that lie ahead.

Career federal bureaucrats know what is feasible technically and economically, but they may have their own policy and institutional goals to consider. Loyalty to their agencies or programs may supersede any loyalty to a particular president. Besides, career bureaucrats will be in their positions long after any one president is gone from the White House. They generally can wait out an administration hostile to their views until the political winds change or new leaders come to office.

Outside experts such as academics can offer new ideas and perhaps can lend an aura of expertise and legitimacy to controversial issues but, like many experts, may not have enough understanding of what is feasible politically. Moreover, there is no guarantee that any recommendations made by panels of experts ever will amount to more than reams of paper sitting in a file cabinet. What experts propose often goes far beyond what politicians can reasonably use at any time.

There are, in sum, many possible sources for ideas and expertise available to any president, but only the individual in the White House can decide which sources are to be tapped. Activist presidents like Franklin Roosevelt and Lyndon Johnson were voracious consumers of advice from a great number of sources. Roosevelt was known to surround himself with assistants who disagreed violently on major issues just so that he could get a broad spectrum of opinion. Johnson was famous for his midnight telephone calls to sleepy senators demanding the latest scoop on a piece of legislation. Both had keen political instincts, and for them information was a resource to be used actively in political battles.

President Bill Clinton, early in his presidency, appeared to share this style, which above all requires tremendous personal energy and intellect. This approach can be overwhelming if the president does not find a way to reduce the deluge of information hitting the Oval Office daily. Presidents who do not adequately delegate tasks to subordinates risk overload.

Other presidents prefer to let information and policy options "bubble up" through the ranks of advisers and experts, using their closest aides to synthesize advice and present a short list of alternative courses of action. Eisenhower, Reagan, and Bush—all Republicans who focused heavily on foreign policy issues—operated in this manner. Reagan was notably content to let his aides parse out competing choices and to withhold his own views until presented with one or two options. The president's role in this approach is relatively passive, but it can work well when those who actually weigh the alternatives keep the president's values and priorities firmly in mind. Problems arise when a president's aides fail to do so, or when they keep the president in the dark about their activities.

Presidential styles hinge most on personal views and skills, overall goals, and perspectives on the job itself. Carter saw the president's job as one of problem solving, and insisted on being informed of or involved in virtually every decision—including, as one story goes, the schedule for the White House tennis courts. His problem, critics charged, was that he was too immersed in the minutiae of policy to discern or convey to the public the broader goals of public policy or of his office. Reagan, by contrast, apparently viewed himself as being like a chairman of the board. He was content to dictate broad goals and directions while allowing his aides to work out specific policy options. His tendency to remain aloof from the particulars of policy often made him appear uninformed in press conferences, but even Reagan's critics admitted that the passion of his ideals provided his subordinates with clear guidelines by which to judge and select policies.

LOBBYING CONGRESS

After legislation is drafted, presidents next must persuade Congress to go along. Presidential scholar Richard Neustadt argues that the primary power of the presidency is the power to persuade others to follow the presidential agenda, but the Constitution is silent about just how presidents are to do so.[97] That silence is convenient. Presidents seeking little in the way of change can claim that separation of powers gives them little capacity to influence Congress directly, although assertive presidents can use this constitutional silence to justify almost any means not expressly forbidden by law or accepted practice. Generally the way presidents organize their lobbying activities and the styles they employ to influence Congress reflect their particular ideology, their specific policy goals, their knowledge about how government works, and their overall personal skills. It also reflects whether—or how much—Congress is willing to be influenced, a state of receptiveness that always is in doubt.

Presidents through the early 1900s were careful to obey the forms of separation of powers. They had few instruments for influencing legislation, and their activities generally were constrained by prevailing beliefs in congressional supremacy. Party loyalty, favorable newspaper coverage, and politically connected cabinet members were a nineteenth-century president's primary resources, and presidential lobbying tended to be loosely organized and discreet. This picture had changed dramatically by the 1940s as both government and prevailing public attitudes about the nature of presidential leadership underwent fundamental reordering. But the evolution of presidential lobbying from the indirect and passive styles of earlier presidents to the open and well-organized practices of today took decades.

The Eisenhower administration established the first Office of Congressional Relations. Ike appointed Bryce Harlow, left, an experienced House committee staff member, but Kennedy was more aggressive in his choice of a longtime political ally, Lawrence F. O'Brien, right.

Theodore Roosevelt may have cut a more dramatic public figure, but Woodrow Wilson stands out among early twentieth-century presidents for pursuing a strongly personal approach to congressional relations. Although Wilson shied away from open and "direct" lobbying, he vigorously pulled party strings to ensure Democratic support for his agenda and went so far as to sit in on congressional committee deliberations on trade legislation. His chief congressional lobbyist, Postmaster General Albert Burleson, used postal positions as inducements for loyalty to the president's program. Wilson also relied on John Nance Garner, a House Democrat from Texas, as his confidential lobbyist within the House. Garner, who sat on the influential Ways and Means Committee, once a week would enter the White House through a side door and consult with Wilson privately on current congressional news and prospects for the president's legislation.

Less than two decades later, Franklin Roosevelt abandoned any pretense of regal noninvolvement and employed an open and direct lobbying strategy. Roosevelt is considered the father of contemporary presidential lobbying styles, beginning with his own sustained and overt role in policy formation. He effectively goaded Congress into action through radio appeals to the public and through a careful cultivation of friendly relations with the press. His personal assistants—James Rowe, Thomas Corcoran, and Benjamin Cohen—wrote bills and lobbied legislators openly. Like Wilson, Roosevelt relied heavily on patronage to reward loyalty and to punish deserters, using Postmaster General James Farley, who also served as chair of the national Democratic Party, as his chief enforcer. Inducements included preferential treatment on public works projects and other New Deal spending programs, funds critical to hard-pressed Democrats during election years, and promises for personal campaign appearances by the popular president.[98]

Formalizing the Process

Although Roosevelt's overall influence in Congress waxed and waned with changes in immediate political conditions, he constructed a more vigorous and central role for the presidency in the legislative process. Indeed, Roosevelt inaugurated or perfected many of the lobbying techniques employed by contemporary presidents, but he did not make lobbying a formal process. Roosevelt would assign a presidential aide to lobby for a program or bill only if it got into trouble. Legislative liaison—the practice of having aides constantly cultivate a receptive environment in Congress—remained an informal affair, in many ways reflecting Roosevelt's more personal approach to politics and his dislike of rigid organizations.[99]

Dwight Eisenhower, the former general, adopted the antithesis of Roosevelt's highly personal and avowedly disorganized approach. As political scientist Eric Davis has pointed out, Eisenhower was the first president to formalize the executive lobbying process by creating the Office of Congressional Relations (OCR), a specialized structure reflecting his own hierarchical orientation and general dislike of direct lobbying. Eisenhower, who was less comfortable than Roosevelt in the rambunctious world of politics, also wanted the OCR to act as a buffer between himself and members of Congress, even those from his party.[100] Heading the OCR was Bryce Harlow, a veteran House committee staff member who had no other responsibilities than to cultivate cordial relations with Congress and, especially, to keep House and Senate Republicans happy. But Harlow's office seldom took an active role in legislative development, largely because Eisenhower spent more time opposing congressional Democratic proposals than in pushing his agenda.

John Kennedy, by contrast, planned an aggressive legislative agenda and strengthened the liaison office by appointing longtime political ally Lawrence O'Brien as chief lobbyist. O'Brien wanted congressional liaison staff not only to generate support for specific proposals but also to "create a general climate in favor and receptivity toward the president and the administration among members of Congress, and . . . use these positive perceptions as a resource when attempting to obtain support for particular pieces of legislation."[101] O'Brien organized the OCR along lines paralleling the political makeup of Congress itself, assigning a staff member to interact with virtually every faction and bloc in the legislature. He constructed cooperative relationships with agency personnel, party leaders, and interest groups—whoever might be useful or necessary to the president's success. Many scholars consider O'Brien to be the architect of modern legislative liaison, and the specific system he established continued through the Carter administration.

Even with O'Brien's efforts, Kennedy generally was unable to push an expansive legislative agenda because conservative Democrats in Congress strongly opposed new social programs and civil rights legislation. Kennedy's narrow victory over Richard Nixon in 1960 did not give him enough personal political clout to pressure even fellow Democrats to go along with his agenda. Although Kennedy's liaison office was credited with a handful of notable victories on trade and tax matters, the political climate in Congress was such that no organized lobbying could readily control it. Later presidents would discover that a good liaison office could not overcome a weak political hand.

Lyndon Johnson fared quite differently. He was successful initially because Kennedy's assassination created in the nation and in Congress a desire to pass some of the slain president's legislation, and later because his own massive 1964 election victory over Barry M. Goldwater gave him the kind of public "mandate" that crafty politicians like Johnson can capitalize on with Congress. What is more, the 1964 election brought in many new liberal House Democrats, giving Johnson added congressional support for his domestic policy agenda. Johnson retained the liaison office built by Kennedy to augment his own considerable personal political skills, and he insisted that O'Brien and his liaison staff be consulted closely before initiatives were taken. So closely did Johnson work with Congress that political scientist Charles O. Jones characterizes Johnson's legislative style as akin to that of a majority leader—which Johnson had been in the Senate before becoming vice president under Kennedy.[102] Johnson, always a creature of Congress, believed that legislators should be consulted regularly on policy initiatives. He knew how to include members of Congress in decision making, was careful not to overload the system, and was sensitive about making loyal supporters look good. Above all, Johnson sought out compromise behind the scenes, going directly to the people only as a last resort, and his liaison staff worked hard to develop and maintain cooperative relationships all over Capitol Hill.[103]

Richard Nixon cared little for domestic political issues and perhaps even less for Congress. He preferred to focus on foreign policy, which required far less congressional involvement. He seldom got personally involved in lobbying and rebelled against the sort of bargaining that Johnson relished. Where Johnson integrated the liaison office into his overall congressional strategy, Nixon removed it from the process and instead relied heavily on a close circle of personal aides for legislative advice and strategy. Where Johnson was accessible to many views and members of Congress, Nixon shielded himself behind a wall of assistants. And where Johnson relied on compromise, Nixon tended to confront and to stick with his course regardless of political considerations.

Nixon's legislative style was not particularly conducive to moving an active legislative program, but in many ways it was well suited to forcing a hostile Congress to accede to his demands or risk a veto, particularly when the politically astute president knew he had public support. Nixon's early successes attest to the degree to which presidents can confront Congress and get their way when they enjoy a high degree of popularity. The opposite also was true: as Nixon's public support fell so did his capacity to stop Congress from overriding his opposition to major pieces of legislation, such as the 1973 War Powers Resolution.

Gerald Ford in many ways operated more like the Democrat Lyndon Johnson than like fellow Republican Nixon, probably because Ford and Johnson shared longer careers in Congress and believed in the institution more than did Nixon. Like Johnson, Ford believed in working with all members of Congress and deployed his legislative liaison team to cultivate friendly relations with both parties. Unlike Johnson, Ford was a minority president, with Democrats in control of both houses of Congress. Like Nixon, he had to rely on the veto as a central part of his overall legislative strategy, using his liaison staff to build coalitions to support his vetoes. In this sense, at least, Ford was highly effective, but an unelected president succeeding a president who was forced to resign had little political capital with which to craft and push through a broad domestic agenda.

Jimmy Carter was an outsider who had less interest in the process of consensus building than in the substance of policy, and he had a dim view of traditional Washington politics. "Legislative liaison for Carter," Eric Davis suggested, "simply was a matter of convincing members of Congress of the correctness of his positions on the issues."[104] His liaison team as a result was organized initially along issue lines, as opposed to the geographical and voting bloc patterns employed since O'Brien. No single staff assistant could discuss a wide array of issues—or make deals across issues—with any single member of Congress. Also, the Carter White House initially turned its back on the O'Brien method of courting members constantly and doling out favors to loyalists and party leaders. Carter's aides initially were so disdainful of or ignorant in the norms and mores of Washington that even House Speaker Thomas P. O'Neill, whom Carter would need desperately to push through his legislative agenda, could not get good seats for his guests at the inaugural gala—a slight that an old-school politician like O'Neill would never entirely forget or forgive.[105]

Carter's legislative strategy in many ways reflected his arguably accurate reading of the new political realities of the post-

Watergate, post-Vietnam era. Johnson's style of legislative liaison looked tawdry to a public increasingly wary of presidential machinations and insistent that presidents speak directly to them on major issues. Carter thus tended to present his case to the public first, believing that his primary task was to persuade citizens to his side of an issue and thereby create a political climate favorable to congressional action. But Carter may have erred too much on the side of first gaining the public's support. Congressional leaders often were not consulted in advance of Carter's statements, and legislative liaison tended toward the exchange of information rather than the still-critical building of legislative coalitions of support.[106] Carter in his first year also made the mistake of interpreting his election as a mandate for dramatic change, bombarding Congress with dozens of bills at once, overloading the legislative process and spreading his lobbying resources thin. After a somewhat disappointing first six months—in which Carter victories came only because of large Democratic majorities in Congress—the White House reorganized the liaison office in line with the old O'Brien model and worked harder to consult with congressional leaders.

Charles O. Jones characterized Carter as a political layman, a label that was true insofar as traditional styles of negotiation were concerned.[107] But Carter met a far more complex and frustrating political climate than had Johnson, especially in Johnson's first two years in office. Public faith in government and willingness to follow political leaders was at a nadir after Watergate and Vietnam, and Congress itself had changed dramatically in the interim. Johnson could rely heavily on congressional leaders to carry his banner, because the congressional hierarchy still was strong enough to keep party members in line. But that hierarchy had all but dissolved by the time Carter was elected in 1976, and Carter was faced with the need to construct temporary coalitions among as many members as possible in order to succeed. So fluid had American politics become by the late 1970s that one political scientist likened it to building coalitions out of sand—hard to work with and never quite permanent.[108] Given these realities, Carter's strategy of going directly to the public on important issues may have been the best possible approach.

Ronald Reagan used Carter's general strategy to better effect during his first year, although it was augmented by an experienced and well-organized legislative liaison staff. House Speaker O'Neill called Reagan's victory on the 1981 budget package "the greatest selling job I've ever seen." Reagan's success came about through a mixture of dramatic public appeals by the president, the work of administration officials sent to generate support in key Democratic constituencies, and a good deal of old-fashioned bargaining.[109] Jones has likened Reagan's lobbying style to that of Franklin Roosevelt, with emphasis placed on communicating views and ideals to the public and generating pressure on Congress to go along.[110]

Even for Reagan, however, the strategy had its limits. Appeals to the public can work only so often and only on particularly dramatic issues. Going public tends to have diminishing returns the longer and more frequently a president relies on that strategy, which Reagan discovered during his second term in office. Indeed, Reagan in his second term, particularly after the Democrats took control of both chambers of Congress in 1987, reflected the strategies used by Nixon and Ford.

Reagan's immediate successors, regardless of political party, were to discover the difficulty of relying on the public route without having Reagan's unique persona. Neither George Bush nor Bill Clinton—very different personalities facing different legislative terrain—could translate their personal appeals into significant legislative victories. For Bush, the stalemate with a Democratic-controlled Congress was both partisan and ideological, and even Bush's high public approval rating after the Persian Gulf War did not produce action from Congress.[111] For Clinton, the legislative victories of his first two years in office depended almost entirely on remarkably strong party support, with the occasional coalition with Republicans on crime and trade matters. But such an "inside" strategy failed Clinton miserably on health care, largely because his party was fragmented badly on the issue and because Republicans were united in their opposition to Clinton's agenda. For both Bush and Clinton—as for any president—the broad political forces at work at the time had more effect on their legislative records than any particular lobbying strategy.

Styles of Presidential Lobbying

There is no single best way for presidents to lobby Congress, but certain devices—such as favors, consultation, and personal phone calls—are always useful. Each president's particular style and way of organizing lobbying activities reflect personal skills, interests, and views about the relationship among the branches of government. Presidents who see themselves as partners with Congress, such as Johnson, operate far differently than those like Nixon, who see the presidency as independent of and generally in competition with the legislature.[112] Each style has its strengths, but neither guarantees success. After all, pushing a legislative agenda also means having to deal with a Congress that sees itself as the energetic center of U.S. government.

Still, even "failed" presidents enjoy a modicum of success in Congress, if success is measured by the percentage of bills supported by the president that Congress passes into law.[113] By some measures, Carter, despite his apparent weaknesses, enjoyed a great deal of overall success in Congress, while Reagan, for all his mass popularity and rhetorical skills, on average fared much worse. The reason for this disparity may be simply that Carter enjoyed generally supportive Democratic majorities in Congress, while Reagan constantly encountered at least one house dominated by his political foes. President Clinton, despite low public support during his first two years in office, received congressional support of 86.4 percent according to Congressional Quarterly vote studies. Yet the perception that Clinton was a more effective legislative leader only emerged after he challenged the Republican Congress, especially during the 1995-1996 budget battle. Clinton's support in the Republican Congress, which had fallen to 36.2 percent in 1995, jumped to 55.1 percent in 1996.

-oteworthy is the inverse relationship over time between the improvement in any administration's lobbying and organizational skills and the inevitable decline in congressional support for that same administration. This paradox perhaps is less mystifying when one compares presidential success in Congress with the president's popularity. Both scores drop over time, suggesting how broad presidential popularity affects legislative success. Members of Congress, George Edwards III points out, "respond to the president's current popularity among their supporters," and thus are reluctant to oppose a popular president.[114] They do not, however, hesitate to vote against a president whose public support has weakened, particularly if the president is from the opposing party.

Despite the tendency of the mass media to focus on personalities, whether a president succeeds or fails probably has less to do with personal attributes or styles than with the political conditions at the time. Presidents certainly can influence political conditions, but they cannot control them. Presidents must play the political cards dealt to them by the broader political system, and by the world at large. Successful presidents may be those whose particular strengths or values meshed well with the tenor of the times or with current congressional majorities. Or they may simply have been lucky.

PUBLIC APPEALS

As suggested above, every president has found it necessary on occasion to go directly to the people to exert pressure on a recalcitrant Congress. This tendency has increased with the decline in strong political party loyalties and with the emergence of television as a primary means for communication. Be it through speeches to the nation on television, leaks of information to favored newspaper reporters, or orchestrated public demonstrations of support, presidents find some way to recruit public opinion in their fights with Congress when they believe conditions and issues warrant it. *(See Table 2-7.)*

Going directly to the people has become easier, and thus more desirable, as modern telecommunications technology, particularly television, has enabled presidents since the 1940s to speak their minds with less worry that their messages will be garbled by intermediaries. The rise of television as the primary means by which most Americans receive their news is a primary factor in the emergence of the contemporary presidency and its power to influence the national agenda. Nonetheless, going directly to the people has its risks, for success hinges largely on the issue in question, a president's own rhetorical skills, and the mood of the public at the moment. None of these factors is predictable.

TABLE 2-7 Television Addresses by Presidents, 1961–1996

President	*Year*	*Topic*
Kennedy	1961	Urgent national needs; Berlin Wall
	1962	Racial unrest; quarantine of Cuba
	1963	Civil rights bill; test ban treaty
Johnson	1963	Kennedy assassination
	1965	Voting rights bill
	1968	Bombing halt/withdrawal from election
Nixon	1969	National unity in Vietnam; Vietnam peace proposals; Vietnam troop reductions
	1970	Vietnam; Cambodia incursion (2); peace in Indochina
	1971	Withdrawal of troops; economic policy
	1972	Report of trip to the People's Republic of China
	1973	Watergate; national energy policy
	1974	White House tapes; resignation
Ford	1974	Post-Nixon resignation speech; inflation
	1975	State of the world
Carter	1977	Energy crisis; energy policy
	1979	Energy crisis; national morale; Soviet troops in Cuba; military spending
	1980	Failure of Iran rescue mission; anti-inflation
	1981	Farewell speech
Reagan	1981	Economic policies and proposals (4)
	1982	Federal budget; Middle East; Lebanon; arms control
	1983	Strategic Defense Initiative and Central America; Grenada; Lebanon
	1985	Tax reform; U.S.-Soviet summit (Geneva)
	1986	Military spending; aid to contras (2); U.S.-Soviet summit (Iceland); Iran arms sales
	1987	Iran arms sales; economic summit; Iran-contra affair; Bork nomination; U.S.-Soviet summit (Washington)
	1988	Contra aid
	1989	Farewell address
Bush	1989	Drug war; invasion of Panama
	1990	Deployment of forces to the Persian Gulf; budget agreement
	1991	Commencement of attack on Iraq; cease-fire announcement
	1992	Deployment of relief forces to Somalia
Clinton	1993	Economic plan; air raid on Iraq
	1994	Situation in Somalia; "middle class bill of rights"
	1995	U.S. peacekeeping mission in Bosnia

SOURCES: *Congressional Quarterly Almanac,* various issues, and *Congressional Quarterly Weekly Report,* various issues.

NOTE: Table does not include State of the Union and inaugural addresses, which also are televised; it includes only those addresses that are not part of a ceremonial occasion.

Early Use of Public Appeals

Presidents before the twentieth century neither had the technologies to speak directly to the people nor did they generally conceive of their roles in exactly the same manner as do their contemporary counterparts. The Founders' fear of demagogues, and their consequent efforts to insulate selection of the president from the mass public, influenced the earliest presidents profoundly. Congress, not the president, was meant to represent the people, and Congress generally considered it illegitimate and intrusive for a president to try to pressure its members on legislation.

From the earliest days of the presidency, however, some presidents did attempt to influence public opinion through indirect, often subtle means. Thomas Jefferson relied heavily on his popular dinner parties to influence key legislators, newspaper reporters, and other important political figures. But it was Andrew Jackson among earlier presidents who began the practice of appealing to the common people for support. Jackson, after all, had come to office as an outsider—he was the first president not to come from one of the original thirteen colonies—and a foe of the established ways of doing business. Jackson used his popularity with the people to influence Congress where possible, in many ways presaging the contemporary presidency by artfully arranging for official documents to be leaked to supportive newspapers, using friendly journalists to convey his views and desires, and relying on his party organization to stir up public support and put pressure on Congress. "King Andrew," as his enemies came to call him, not surprisingly reaped a great deal of criticism for his unorthodox practices, and most pre–Civil War presidents did not follow his pattern. None had Jackson's popularity or his activist philosophy about the role of the presidency.

Abraham Lincoln was usually on the defensive with Congress over his war policies, but he overcame its opposition by winning public support through the newspapers. Lincoln wrote numerous letters and opinion columns, to which friendly publishers such as Horace Greeley gave favorable coverage. Lincoln generated other supportive stories through leaks to reporters. It also was said that Lincoln grew his beard after a supporter remarked that his bare face (and lack of chin) did not look "presidential" enough, and inexpensive lithographs (a new technology) of the newly bearded commander in chief soon graced many a Union household.

Theodore Roosevelt thrived on publicity and made himself easily available to favorite reporters. His love of the press was reciprocated, for the flamboyant and erudite Roosevelt made for good copy.[115] Roosevelt is credited with creating the official White House press release, which he often issued on Sundays—traditionally the slowest news day—to give newspapers something to print the next day. He also devised off-the-record or "background" press briefings, which he frequently used to float "trial balloons" as one way to assess public and congressional opinion on issues. Woodrow Wilson outdid Roosevelt in going directly to the public by resuming the practice of delivering the State of the Union address personally and by instituting regular and formal press conferences. He was most effective, however, in making direct appeals to the public usually through the newspapers or speeches before Congress. The notable exception was his grueling nationwide tour in 1919 to generate support for the Versailles treaty. The president was followed by a "truth squad" of senators who opposed the treaty, and the journey ruined his health. Wilson's efforts to go to the people went for naught, for the Senate failed to ratify the treaty.

Franklin Roosevelt and Radio

Although Theodore Roosevelt and Wilson were masters at generating favorable public opinion through the press, they lacked easy access to technology that could enable them to go directly into every citizen's home. But Franklin Roosevelt entered the White House just as radio entered its heyday, and the ebullient New Yorker made superb use of the medium. His public speeches, the twenty-seven "fireside" radio chats, hundreds of formal press conferences, countless informal background sessions with selected reporters, and shrewd use of the newsreels, all constructed a public persona that millions of Americans would recall fondly for decades. So great was the public response to Roosevelt's first inaugural address, in which he averred that "the only thing we have to fear is fear itself," that humorist Will Rogers wrote, "If he burned down the Capitol, we would cheer and say, 'Well, we at least got a fire started somehow.'"[116]

Roosevelt used radio directly to educate and persuade, and there was no greater example than his first "fireside chat" to the nation concerning the bank crisis that worsened on the eve of his inauguration. Roosevelt explained how the banking system worked and why it was important that people take their money out of their mattresses and put it back into their savings accounts. They did, and Roosevelt was credited with ending the crisis. As Arthur M. Schlesinger Jr. wrote, the fireside chats "conveyed Roosevelt's conception of himself as a man at ease in his own house talking frankly and intimately to neighbors as they sat in their living rooms."[117]

The radio speeches and chats were intended for more than soothing the public: they were meant to move Congress into action on Roosevelt's agenda. According to political scientist Wilfred Binkley, Roosevelt "had only to glance toward a microphone or suggest that he might go on the air again and a whole congressional delegation would surrender. They had no relish for the flood of mail and telegrams they knew would swamp them after another fireside chat to the nation."[118] Roosevelt, particularly after the first year, did not always win when he went to the airwaves, but those in opposition never took for granted his power to move the public.

The Television Presidency

Roosevelt proved successful with radio in no small part because the medium forces listeners to use their imaginations to visualize both the speaker and the topic under discussion. He had a powerful voice, which offered to the listener an image of strength and determination. The radio image of Roosevelt belied the physical reality: stricken with polio at the age of thirty-nine, Roosevelt could not walk. Americans may have known of Roosevelt's disability in the abstract—it certainly was no secret—but they were not reminded of it continually because, due to a tacit agreement with the press, he rarely was photographed below the waist. But if Roosevelt had run for the presidency in the age of television—foremost a visual medium—he would not have been able to control his public image so masterfully. Whether he could have been elected in the first place, since so many people equate physical strength with strong "leadership"—much less rally a nation through depression and war—is one of the tantalizing "what ifs" of history.

The contemporary presidency in many ways lives and sometimes dies by television. Eisenhower was the first president to permit press conferences to be filmed for television, but it was

Kennedy, arguably the first president of the television age, who was the first to allow live telecasts of his press conferences. The public for the first time watched the press question a president live, with no chance for the White House to edit the president's comments. Kennedy's ease with television, his intellect, and his humor made television a potent tool for communicating with the American people. His persuasive television appearance was not enough, however, to ensure congressional approval of his programs.

Lyndon Johnson, superb as he was in the art of personal lobbying, proved uneasy with television, although his live address urging the passage of the 1965 Voting Rights Act did move the nation and Congress. Johnson was probably the first president to discover television's double-edged sword as Americans absorbed televised images of urban riots and antiwar demonstrations, and for the first time witnessed the horrors of war by watching the evening news. These televised images frequently appeared to contradict Johnson's assertions about the pace of social progress at home and the successful waging of the war in Indochina, contradictions that shook the nation's confidence in its government. Johnson was particularly wounded by public reaction to the massive North Vietnamese Tet offensive in early 1968, a coordinated assault on South Vietnamese cities that undercut his statements that the war was winding down. For the North Vietnamese the attack, although a military disaster, was a psychological victory. Johnson's public support plummeted, and he decided not to run for reelection. Johnson's experience was but an early example of how television-magnified events can influence a president's agenda and popularity.

Richard Nixon, who felt that the official press had been hostile to his candidacy in 1960 and saw how Johnson had fared with the media, used television directly and extensively to retailor his image with the public. His distrust of the Washington press corps, which often proved unwilling to rally around the administration's Vietnam policy, led the president to speak directly to the American people far more often than had his predecessors. In his November 1969 address to the nation on Vietnam, for example, Nixon asserted that a "silent majority" of citizens supported his actions despite what members of the press wrote.[119] Nixon also held few Washington press conferences, which he felt only offered opportunities for his critics to attack him, and instead began to hold press conferences in parts of the country where journalists might be more deferential to his office.

Nixon used Vice President Spiro Agnew to make vigorous attacks on the news media, a tactic that produced one of the most memorable phrases in American political lore. In a September 1970 speech in San Diego, Agnew railed that the Washington press corps was filled with "nattering nabobs of negativism. They have formed their own 4-H Club—the 'hopeless, hysterical hypochondriacs of history.'"[120] The tactic was clear: discredit the news media and connect the president more directly to the American people.

Nixon also used television successfully to pressure Congress in selected instances, such as his televised veto of a 1970 appropriations bill. Thousands of supportive telegrams subsequently poured into both the White House and Capitol Hill, sending the impression of massive popular support for Nixon's position. Whether this reaction was spontaneous or orchestrated by Nixon's supporters was irrelevant to many members of the House, which upheld the veto.

As with Johnson, however, television played a major part in Nixon's downfall. The nation watched in fascination as the daily drama of the 1973 Senate Watergate hearings played out on television. Nixon's own performances during televised press conferences, and even in speeches to the nation, seemed to many viewers to be the picture of a president trying to deceive the public. Following the emergence of evidence of Nixon's possible complicity in the Watergate cover-up, the president resigned in disgrace on August 9, 1974.

His successor, Gerald Ford, worked to reverse the distrust between the White House and the media built up during the previous years. Where Nixon basked in the trappings of the office Ford worked to convey a simpler image; for example, he allowed himself to be photographed making his own breakfast. Where Nixon rarely held press conferences Ford held many—and earned high praise from the media for his openness and honesty. Ford did not escape unscathed, however: his every stumble or slip was grist for the humor mill—an irony, no doubt, for a former football all-American. In trying to humanize the office Ford risked being seen as "unpresidential," an image that all presidents try to avoid.

Jimmy Carter, given his populist background and belief that Americans had tired of the "imperial presidency," early on cultivated an image as an outsider by holding televised "town meetings" to which citizens called in questions. Carter also tried his version of Roosevelt's fireside chats, sitting before a fire wearing a cardigan sweater. But what had worked for Roosevelt in the days of the depression and radio did not work for Carter on television in the post-Watergate era. Too many Americans regarded Carter's approach as superficial symbolism, and his efforts to use television to stir the public generally failed. His talk to the nation on the energy crisis, which he called "the moral equivalent of war," evoked no widespread support and even spawned jokes that the acronym for "moral equivalent of war" was MEOW. Carter's supporters argued that such criticism was unfair, that the president's attempts to rally the American people seemed to come up short less because of Carter's faults than because the public was far less inclined to follow presidential directions than it may have been before Vietnam and Watergate. Public trust in government had waned measurably in the late 1970s, they noted, making Carter's task all the more difficult. Whatever the cause, Carter's attempts to communicate directly to the public and rally its support frequently fell on deaf ears, and Congress generally went its own way.

Carter's well-known difficulties should not mask his real successes, however. Most notable was the televised signing of the 1979 Camp David peace accords, a moment of high drama when

To reverse the mutual distrust between the White House and the media built up during the Nixon administration, Ford worked to convey a simpler image to the press. Here he allows photographers to take pictures as he makes his breakfast.

Egyptian president Anwar Sadat signed a peace treaty with Israeli prime minister Menachem Begin. Carter, who had been personally instrumental in bringing these longtime adversaries together, used the signing to rally congressional support for significant American aid to both Israel and Egypt.

Generally, however, Carter proved more a victim than a manipulator of television, particularly after Iranian revolutionaries seized and held fifty-three American hostages for more than a year. Americans each night witnessed on their television sets the humiliation of the hostage situation—a long "crisis" that actually spawned the popular nightly ABC news show, *Nightline.* Carter's inability to free the hostages contributed to his loss to Ronald Reagan in 1980.

Reagan, the former movie and television actor, quickly proved a powerful contrast to Carter in his ability to use the media to his political advantage. As radio had been to Franklin Roosevelt, television was to Reagan, and the president relied heavily on his rhetorical talents to whip up support for his dramatic budget and tax policy victories in 1981. Of particular potency was Reagan's May 1981 appeal to a joint session of Congress for support on his budget package, his first public appearance since he was wounded badly in a March 1981 assassination attempt. So powerful was the moment, and so massive was the outpouring of public support for the president, that the Democratic-dominated House passed his package a few days after the speech. Reagan like no other president used television to establish intimacy with the American people. Few could resist the emotional pull of his 1984 speech on the cliffs overlooking France's Omaha Beach on the fortieth anniversary of the Normandy invasion, or of his eulogy for the astronauts who died in the 1986 space shuttle disaster.[121]

But even for Reagan television had a double-edged effect. Public responsiveness to televised appeals almost inevitably wanes the more frequently a president relies on them, as Reagan discovered during his second term. Startling revelations about secret arms sales to the Iranian government and their possibly illegal use to fund the supply of arms to American-backed rebels fighting the government of Nicaragua eroded public confidence in Reagan's leadership. Televised congressional hearings on the affair raised broad public concern about the president's overall command of his office. By 1988, when the three major networks refused to carry another appeal for aid to Nicaraguan rebels because it "was not news," it was apparent that the skills so integral to Reagan's early successes no longer were potent enough to prevail.

Even with Reagan's later woes, his immediate successors would discover painfully that Reagan had a rare gift for using television to connect himself to the public. They also discovered, as did Reagan, that popular approval does not always translate into better prospects for legislative success. As Charles Jones argues, popularity is "sometimes a recognition or reward for an action deemed successful or an acknowledgment that things are going well."[122] While George Bush enjoyed a stunningly high level of popularity at the end of the Persian Gulf War, he nonetheless was a one-term president. Bush's inability to capitalize on his popularity in part grew out of his apparent discomfort with the demands of the television presidency, an institution that favors constant visibility, adeptness at verbal communication, and a nuanced understanding of the symbolic power of the office. The national economic recession and broad public perception that the nation was heading in the wrong direction also contributed to Bush's defeat in the 1992 election, but his presidential style certainly played a role. The same point might be made about Clinton's inability to turn broad but diffuse public support for health care reform into solid congressional support behind his reform plan. Like any lobbying tool, the effectiveness of television is limited and may depend on factors that lie well outside of any president's control.

Even with the problems experienced by Bush and Clinton, the president of the United States still has an unparalleled capacity to dominate the national debate because of the office's unique ability to command media attention. The president is but one person, while Congress is a vast and often messy institution. In a battle between the branches, the resident of the White House who possesses good rhetorical skills has a tremendous (though not foolproof) advantage over the branch of government given the constitutional mandate to make the law. Indeed, some observers worry that the president's capacity to dominate national debate may drown out many other voices demanding to be heard. Presidents can take credit for ideas that Congress developed, or, conversely, they can blame Congress for their failures. The danger, political scientist Bruce Miroff has concluded, is that presidents could "take over so much of the public space that citizens would perceive the political world chiefly through presidential actions."[123]

A big question for the 1990s and beyond is whether Miroff's concern will be borne out in a future of increasingly fragmented and diverse sources of information and entertainment—presidents today compete with everybody else for attention on hundreds of cable television stations, talk radio, and computer networks, among other media—or whether it reflected a particular and nonreproducible era in American history. John Kennedy could command almost universal public viewership because viewers had few alternatives to the major television networks, but Bill Clinton had to compete hard for the public's attention, with far less consistent success, particularly since other political actors—including members of Congress—enjoyed their own independent capacity to make direct overtures to key segments of the mass public. In such a fragmented media environment no one person, not even a president, may be able any longer to "monopolize" the public space, and presidents may be forced to work even harder to mobilize public support for legislative initiatives.

NOTES

1. See, for example, Charles O. Jones, *The Presidency in a Separated System* (Washington, D.C.: Brookings, 1994); and David Mayhew, *Divided We Govern: Party Control, Lawmaking, and Investigations, 1946–1990* (New Haven, Conn.: Yale University Press, 1991).

2. Louis Fisher, *The President and Congress* (New York: Free Press, 1972), 18–21. See also A. E. Howard, ed., *The United States Constitution: Roots, Rights, and Responsibilities* (Washington, D.C.: Smithsonian Institution Press, 1992).

3. Thomas Jefferson, "Notes on Virginia," in *The Life and Selected Writings of Thomas Jefferson,* ed. Adrienne Koch and William Peden (New York: Random House, Modern Library, 1944), 237.

4. *Guide to Congress,* 4th ed. (Washington, D.C.: Congressional Quarterly, 1991), 552. The power theoretically exists to this day, although no English sovereign has used the veto since 1707.

5. John Adams, "The State Constitutions as Analogy and Precedent," in Howard, ed., *The United States Constitution: Roots, Rights, and Responsibilities,* 3–22.

6. James Sundquist, *Constitutional Reform and Effective Government* (Washington, D.C.: Brookings, 1986), 30.

7. Ibid., 30–31.

8. The exemption of constitutional amendments from the veto was established by the Supreme Court in *Hollingsworth v. Virginia,* 3 Dall. 378 (1798).

9. Alexander Hamilton, James Madison, and John Jay, *The Federalist Papers,* ed. Clinton Rossiter (New York: New American Library, 1961), 443.

10. Ibid., 322.

11. Ibid., 444.

12. The Constitution gives presidents the authority to approve or veto legislation within ten days after a bill is *presented* to the White House, as opposed to after it is *passed* by Congress. Bills passed by Congress cannot be presented to the president until they have been signed by the Speaker of the House and the president of the Senate (that is, the vice president, although this function is performed normally by the president pro tempore). Thus, an indefinite gap can occur between passage and presentation. There have been times, in fact, when Congress has delayed presentation of bills because the president has been out of the country. Presidents also have maneuvered to delay presentation of bills to create opportunities for pocket vetoes. In 1970, for example, Richard Nixon had Vice President Spiro Agnew exercise his authority to sign legislation, which Agnew then delayed in carrying out so that several bills would not be presented to Nixon until just a few days before adjournment. For a discussion of this maneuver, see Eric Redman, *The Dance of Legislation* (New York: Touchstone Books, 1973).

13. As upheld by the Supreme Court in *Missouri Pacific Railway Co. v. United States,* 248 U.S. 277 (1919).

14. Clinton Rossiter, *The American Presidency,* 2d ed. (New York: Harcourt, Brace, 1960), 91.

15. See James Bryce, *The American Commonwealth,* vol. 1, 2d ed. (New York: Macmillan, 1911), 64. The Supreme Court in 1926 ruled that the power to remove political appointees resided with the president alone. See *Myers v. United States,* 272 U.S. 52 (1926).

16. Louis Fisher, *Presidential Spending Power* (Princeton, N.J.: Princeton University Press, 1975), 25.

17. Jones, *The Presidency in a Separated System,* 224–225.

18. See, for example, Neil MacNeil, *Forge of Democracy: The House of Representatives* (New York: David McKay, 1963), 244–245.

19. Jimmy Carter, *Keeping Faith: The Memoirs of a President* (New York: Bantam Books, 1982), 101.

20. *Guide to Congress,* 554.

21. Robert Pear, "Court Is Asked to Define Power of the Pocket Veto," *New York Times,* November 9, 1986, E1.

22. Bryce, *American Commonwealth,* 59.

23. See Richard E. Neustadt, *Presidential Power: The Politics of Leadership from FDR to Carter* (New York: Wiley, 1980).

24. Thomas E. Cronin, *The State of the Presidency,* 2d ed. (Boston: Little, Brown, 1980), 81.

25. George C. Edwards III, *Presidential Influence in Congress* (San Francisco: Freeman, 1980), 24.

26. *1992 CQ Almanac* (Washington, D.C.: Congressional Quarterly, 1993), 6.

27. Neustadt, *Presidential Power,* 63.

28. See, for example, Redman, *Dance of Legislation,* 243.

29. *Pocket Veto Case,* 279 U.S. 644 (1929).

30. Arthur M. Schlesinger Jr., *The Imperial Presidency* (New York: Popular Library, 1974), 237.

31. *Wright v. United States,* 302 U.S. 583 (1938).

32. See Redman, *Dance of Legislation,* 275–277.

33. *Kennedy v. Sampson,* 511 F.2d 430 (D.C. Cir. 1974).

34. *Kennedy v. Jones,* Civil Action no. 74–194 (D.D.C.).

35. Pear, "Power of the Pocket Veto," 4.

36. *Barnes v Carmen,* 582 F. Supp. 163 (D.D.C. 1984); *Barnes v. Kline,* 759 F.2d 21 (D.C. Cir. 1985). The lone dissenter was Judge Robert Bork, who argued that members of Congress had no right to sue the president in the first place and that the court had no jurisdiction over such issues. Lawyers for Congress argued that the courts have every right to adjudicate disputes between Congress and the executive.

37. *Burke v. Barnes,* 479 U.S. 361 (1987).

38. *1990 CQ Almanac* (Washington, D.C.: Congressional Quarterly, 1991), 21–22.

39. *1991 CQ Almanac* (Washington, D.C.: Congressional Quarterly, 1992), 235.

40. See Louis Fisher, *The Politics of Shared Power,* 3d ed. (Washington, D.C.: CQ Press, 1993), 199.

41. Ibid., 198.

42. Andrew Taylor, "Congress Hands President a Budgetary Scalpel," *Congressional Quarterly Weekly Report,* March 30, 1996, 864–867.

43. Edwards, *Presidential Influence in Congress,* 20.

44. Stuart Taylor Jr., "Court Rebuffs Reagan on Deferral of Spending Ordered by Congress," *New York Times,* January 21, 1987, A1.

45. Edwards, *Presidential Influence in Congress,* 21.

46. Fisher, *Politics of Shared Power,* 21.

47. *1990 CQ Almanac,* 16.

48. George Will, "Power to the President," *Newsweek,* October 12, 1981, 120.

49. Sundquist, *Constitutional Reform and Effective Government,* 209–215.

50. See Fisher, *Politics of Shared Power,* 198–202.

51. On problem definition and agenda setting, see Frank R. Baumgartner and Bryan D. Jones, *Agendas and Instability in American Politics* (Chicago: University of Chicago Press, 1993); and David A. Rochefort and Roger W. Cobb, eds., *The Politics of Problem Definition: Shaping the Policy Agenda* (Lawrence: University Press of Kansas, 1994).

52. E. E. Schattschneider, *The Semi-Sovereign People: A Realist's View of Democracy in America* (Hinsdale, Ill.: Dryden, 1960), 66.

53. See Arthur M. Schlesinger Jr., *The Age of Roosevelt: The Coming of the New Deal* (Boston: Houghton Mifflin, 1959).

54. Bruce Miroff, "Monopolizing the Public Space: The President as a Problem for Democratic Space," in *Rethinking the Presidency,* ed. Thomas E. Cronin (Boston: Little, Brown, 1982), 218–252.

55. For a cogent discussion of the constants of American governance and their effects on presidential leadership, see Bert A. Rockman, *The Leadership Question: The Presidency and the American System* (New York: Praeger, 1984), chap. 3. See also R. Kent Weaver and Bert A. Rockman, eds., *Do Institutions Matter? Government Capabilities in the United States and Abroad* (Washington, D.C.: Brookings, 1993); and Jones, *The Presidency in a Separated System.*

56. For an honest defense of this perspective, see Thomas P. O'Neill Jr., with William Novak, *Man of the House: The Life and Political Memoirs of Speaker Tip O'Neill* (New York: Random House, 1987).

57. Norman J. Ornstein, Thomas E. Mann, and Michael J. Malbin, *Vital Statistics on Congress, 1995–1996* (Washington, D.C.: CQ Press, 1995), 53.

58. Stories of battles for the president's ear are legion. See Hugh Heclo, *A Government of Strangers: Executive Politics in Washington* (Washington, D.C.: Brookings, 1977). Books on individual presidencies are many; a recent one is Bob Woodward, *The Agenda: Inside the Clinton White House* (New York: Simon and Schuster, 1994).

59. For a president's perspective, see Carter, *Keeping Faith,* 83–84.

60. Neustadt, *Presidential Power,* 33; for a critique of the American system, see Sundquist, *Constitutional Reform and Effective Government.*

61. Rossiter, *American Presidency,* 140.

62. Bertram Gross, *The Legislative Struggle: A Study of Social Combat* (New York: McGraw-Hill, 1953), 101.

63. See James Sundquist, *The Decline and Resurgence of Congress* (Washington, D.C.: Brookings, 1981).

64. Hamilton, Madison, and Jay, *Federalist Papers,* 423.

65. See George M. Haynes, *The Senate of the United States: Its History and Practice,* vol. 1 (Boston: Houghton Mifflin, 1938), 62–63.

66. Quoted in George B. Galloway, *History of the House of Representatives* (New York: Thomas Crowell, 1969), 12.

67. Edward S. Corwin, *The President: Office and Powers, 1789–1957,* 4th ed. (New York: New York University Press, 1957), 21.

68. Ibid., 23.

69. Quoted in Galloway, *History of the House,* 245–246.

70. Corwin, *President: Office and Powers,* 28.

71. Theodore Roosevelt, *Theodore Roosevelt: An Autobiography* (New York: Macmillan, 1913), 282.

72. Sundquist, *Decline and Resurgence of Congress,* 130.

73. Corwin, *President: Office and Powers,* 269.

74. Special address to a joint session of Congress, June 23, 1913; cited in Corwin, *President: Office and Powers,* 269.

75. Rossiter, *American Presidency,* 140.

76. Schlesinger, *The Age of Roosevelt,* 1.

77. See, for example, Rockman, *Leadership Question.*

78. *Guide to Congress,* 3d ed. (Washington, D.C.: Congressional Quarterly, 1982), 762.

79. Quoted in Roland Evans and Robert Novak, *Lyndon B. Johnson: The Exercise of Power* (New York: New American Library, 1966), 490.

80. Louis Koenig, *The Chief Executive,* 5th ed. (New York: Harcourt Brace Jovanovich, 1986), 145–146.

81. "Annual Messages of the Presidents: Major Themes of American History," in *The State of the Union Messages of the Presidents, 1790–1966,* ed. Fred L. Israel (New York: Chelsea House, 1966), xiv.

82. *Public Papers of Woodrow Wilson,* vol. 1, 32; cited in Corwin, *President: Office and Powers,* 269.

83. Fisher, *Shared Power,* 18; see also H. Wayne Morgan, *From Hayes to McKinley* (Syracuse, N.Y.: Syracuse University Press, 1969), 274–319.

84. Charles O. Jones, "Presidential Negotiation with Congress," in *Both Ends of the Avenue: The Presidency, the Executive Branch, and Congress in the 1980s,* ed. Anthony King (Washington, D.C.: American Enterprise Institute, 1983), 99.

85. Ibid., 102.

86. Fisher, *President and Congress,* 52–53.

87. Cronin, *State of the Presidency,* 118.

88. James S. Young, *The Washington Community* (New York: Columbia University Press, 1966), 167.

89. For a superb discussion of the evolution of "central clearance," see Fisher, *Presidential Spending Power.*

90. Richard E. Neustadt, "The Presidency and Legislation: Planning the President's Program," *American Political Science Review* 49 (December 1955): 1015; see also Stephen J. Wayne, *The Legislative Presidency* (New York: Harper and Row, 1978), 19.

91. Paul Light, "Presidents as Domestic Policymakers," in Cronin, *Rethinking the Presidency,* 360; and Mark A. Peterson, *Legislating Together: The White House and Capitol Hill from Eisenhower to Reagan* (Cambridge, Mass.: Harvard University Press, 1990).

92. See, for example, John W. Kingdon, *Agendas, Alternatives, and Public Policy* (Boston: Little, Brown, 1984). On the intellectual genesis of the 1986 tax reform act, see Jeffrey Birnbaum and Alan Murray, *Showdown at Gucci Gulch: Lawmakers, Lobbyists, and the Unlikely Triumph of Tax Reform* (New York: Random House, 1987).

93. See *History of America, 1932–1972* (Boston: Little, Brown, 1974), 95.

94. See Christopher J. Bosso, "Setting the Public Agenda: Mass Media and the Ethiopian Famine," in *Manipulating Public Opinion: Essays on Public Opinion as a Dependent Variable,* ed. Michael Margolis and Gary Mauser (Monterey, Calif.: Brooks-Cole, 1989), 153–174. On the interconnectedness of "foreign" and "domestic" issues, see James Rosenau, *Turbulence in World Politics: A Theory of Change and Continuity* (Princeton, N.J.: Princeton University Press, 1990).

95. See Joel D. Aberbach and Bert A. Rockman, "Clashing Beliefs within the Executive Branch: The Nixon Administration Bureaucracy," *American Political Science Review* 70 (June 1975): 456–468.

96. There is a substantial literature on the relative merits and pitfalls of incremental versus comprehensive policy change. For a good overview, see Charles O. Jones, *Introduction to the Study of Public Policy,* 3d ed. (Monterey, Calif.: Brooks-Cole, 1984), especially chaps. 2 and 6.

97. Neustadt, *Presidential Power.*

98. The election of Lyndon Johnson to the House of Representatives in 1937 offers a good case in point about Roosevelt's potency as a campaign re-

source. See Robert Caro, *The Years of Lyndon Johnson: The Path to Power* (New York: Random House, 1981).

99. Eric L. Davis, "Congressional Liaison: The People and the Institutions," in King, *Both Ends of the Avenue,* 60.

100. Ibid., 61.

101. Ibid., 62.

102. Jones, "Presidential Negotiation with Congress," 106.

103. See Davis, "Congressional Liaison," 78–79.

104. Ibid., 65.

105. O'Neill, *Man of the House,* 310–311.

106. Davis, "Congressional Liaison," 65.

107. Jones, "Presidential Negotiation," 118.

108. Anthony King, "The American Polity in the Late 1970s: Building Coalitions in the Sand," in *The New American Political System,* ed. Anthony King (Washington, D.C.: American Enterprise Institute, 1979), 371–395.

109. Roger H. Davidson and Walter J. Oleszek, *Congress and Its Members,* 5th ed. (Washington, D.C.: CQ Press, 1996), 308. For an insider's view of the 1981 tax and budget battles, see David Stockman, *The Triumph of Politics: The Inside Story of the Reagan Revolution* (New York: Harper and Row, 1986).

110. Jones, "Presidential Negotiation," 126.

111. See Richard Rose, *The Postmodern President: George Bush Meets the World,* 2d ed. (Chatham, N.J.: Chatham House, 1991).

112. Jones, "Presidential Negotiation," 123–125.

113. See Mayhew, *Divided We Govern*; and Jones, *The Presidency in a Separated System.*

114. Edwards, *Presidential Influence in Congress,* 110.

115. See Edmund Morris, *The Rise of Theodore Roosevelt* (New York: Ballantine, 1979).

116. Quoted in William Manchester, *The Glory and the Dream: A Narrative History of America, 1932–1972* (Boston: Little, Brown, 1974), 91.

117. Schlesinger, *The Age of Roosevelt,* 559.

118. Wilfred E. Binkley, *President and Congress* (New York: Vintage, 1962), 305.

119. Cited in William Safire, *Safire's Political Dictionary* (New York: Ballantine, 1978), 649.

120. Ibid., 444. The phrase "nattering nabobs . . ." was penned by speechwriter William Safire, who later became a popular newspaper columnist and, alternately, a writer on the English language. The term *nabob* is Hindi in origin and has come to mean in English a self-important person.

121. On Reagan's use of television, see, among others, Mark Hertsgaard, *On Bended Knee: The Press and the Reagan Presidency* (New York: Farrar, Straus, Giroux, 1988); and Sam Donaldson, *Hold on, Mr. President!* (New York: Random House, 1987).

122. Jones, *The Presidency in a Separated System,* 115.

123. Miroff, "Monopolizing the Public Space," 230.

SELECTED BIBLIOGRAPHY

Aberbach, Joel D. *Keeping a Watchful Eye: The Politics of Congressional Oversight.* Washington, D.C.: Brookings, 1990.

Bryce, James. *The American Commonwealth.* Vol. 1. 2d ed. New York: Macmillan, 1911.

Corwin, Edward S. *The President: Office and Powers, 1787–1984.* 5th rev. ed. New York: New York University Press, 1984.

Cronin, Thomas E., ed. *Rethinking the Presidency.* Boston: Little, Brown, 1982.

Dodd, Lawrence C., and Bruce I. Oppenheimer, eds. *Congress Reconsidered.* 5th ed. Washington, D.C.: CQ Press, 1993.

Edwards, George C. III. *At the Margins: Presidential Leadership of Congress.* New Haven, Conn.: Yale University Press, 1989.

Fenno, Richard F. *The President's Cabinet.* Cambridge, Mass.: Harvard University Press, 1963.

Fisher, Louis. *Presidential Spending Power.* Princeton, N.J.: Princeton University Press, 1975.

Greenstein, Fred. *Leadership in the Modern Presidency.* Cambridge, Mass.: Harvard University Press, 1988.

Hargrove, Erwin C., and Michael Nelson. *Presidents, Politics, and Policy.* Baltimore: Johns Hopkins University Press, 1984.

Hart, John. *The Presidential Branch: From Washington to Clinton.* 2d ed. Chatham, N.J.: Chatham House, 1995.

Heclo, Hugh. *A Government of Strangers: Executive Politics in Washington.* Washington, D.C.: Brookings, 1977.

Hess, Stephen. *Organizing the Presidency.* Rev. ed. Washington, D.C.: Brookings, 1988.

Jones, Charles O. *The Presidency in a Separated System.* Washington, D.C.: Brookings, 1994.

King, Anthony, ed. *Both Ends of the Avenue: The Presidency, the Executive Branch, and Congress in the 1980s.* Washington, D.C.: American Enterprise Institute, 1983.

Mansfield, Harvey C., Sr., ed. *Congress Against the President.* New York: Academy of Political Science, 1975.

Mayhew, David. *Divided We Govern: Party Control, Lawmaking, and Investigations, 1946–1990.* New Haven, Conn.: Yale University Press, 1991.

Nelson, Michael. *The Presidency and the Political System.* 4th ed. Washington, D.C.: CQ Press, 1994.

Neustadt, Richard. *Presidential Power: The Politics of Leadership from FDR to Carter.* New York: Wiley, 1980.

Peterson, Mark A. *Legislating Together: The White House and Capitol Hill from Eisenhower to Reagan.* Cambridge, Mass.: Harvard University Press, 1990.

Polsby, Nelson W. *Congress and the Presidency.* 4th ed. Englewood Cliffs, N.J.: Prentice-Hall, 1986.

Reedy, George E. *The Twilight of the Presidency: From Johnson to Reagan.* New York: New American Library, 1987.

Rockman, Bert A. *The Leadership Question: The Presidency and the American System.* New York: Praeger, 1984.

Rose, Richard. *The Postmodern President: The White House Meets the World.* Chatham, N.J.: Chatham House, 1988.

Rossiter, Clinton. *The American Presidency.* 2d ed. New York: Harcourt, Brace, 1960.

Schlesinger, Arthur M., Jr. *The Imperial Presidency.* New York: Popular Library, 1974.

Sundquist, James. *Constitutional Reform and Effective Government.* Rev. ed. Washington, D.C.: Brookings, 1992.

Thurber, James A., ed. *Divided Democracy: Cooperation and Conflict between the President and Congress.* Washington, D.C.: CQ Press, 1991.

Wayne, Stephen J. *The Legislative Presidency.* New York: Harper and Row, 1978.

Weaver, R. Kent, and Bert A. Rockman, eds. *Do Institutions Matter? Government Capabilities in the United States and Abroad.* Washington, D.C.: Brookings, 1993.

CHAPTER 3

Chief Diplomat

BY STEPHEN H. WIRLS AND DANIEL C. DILLER

IN THE NINETEENTH CENTURY, when U.S. foreign interests were limited primarily to trade and western expansion, presidents often could concentrate on domestic policy. Today the wide array of U.S. economic, political, and military commitments virtually ensures that presidents will spend at least half of their time on foreign affairs.

The Constitution makes the president the formal head of state. As the "sole organ of intercourse" with foreign nations, the president speaks for the nation as a whole and is often the focus of national hopes and fears, pride and shame.[1] As chief negotiator and national spokesperson, the president has great leverage in any competition with Congress for control of the nation's foreign policies, and important decisions on foreign affairs often have been made by the president after consultations with only a few trusted advisers. The desire of political friends and foes alike to present a united front has frequently produced initial support for and general deference to the president's lead.

Circumstances such as wars or threats of armed conflict enhance this advantage and have allowed presidents simply to dominate the formulation and implementation of foreign policy. During such times, John F. Kennedy noted, "The big difference [between domestic and foreign policy] is that between a bill being defeated and the country [being] wiped out."[2] Even during periods of relative international calm, foreign policy has remained an area of unique importance to the presidency. Foreign affairs issues usually have offered presidents the greatest freedom to exercise their power and the best opportunity to affect policy personally. In contrast, it is more common for domestic policy decisions to originate in the bureaucracy, involve many officials, require less secrecy, be affected by interest group politics, and be subject to strict congressional constraints. Consequently, presidents may choose to retreat to the refuge of foreign affairs where they can exercise their powers most freely and be the leader of the nation.

However, the Constitution does not give presidents sufficient authority to make foreign policy on their own. As in other areas, the branches of the federal government share foreign policy powers, and Congress has many means of influence over the substance and execution of general and specific policies. In addition, policy must be coordinated within a complex of often competing advisers, departments, and agencies. Consequently, even under the most favorable conditions, presidents frequently struggle to maintain control of policy formulation and implementation. In the current era, lacking the ideological clarity of the cold war and the unifying fears of nuclear confrontation between two superpowers, achieving presidential leadership and control of foreign policy has become more difficult and complicated.

Presidents regularly seek to lead in foreign affairs, which often afford the president the opportunity to gain an enduring place in history. Steadfast wartime leadership, the prevention or resolution of dangerous crises, bold policy and diplomatic initiatives, and historic summit meetings with important foreign leaders can create presidential legends: Thomas Jefferson's Louisiana Purchase, the Monroe Doctrine, James K. Polk's national expansion, Theodore Roosevelt's Panama Canal, Harry S. Truman's Marshall Plan, Richard Nixon's trip to China, Jimmy Carter's Camp David summit.

On the other hand, the foreign policy records of few administrations are completely successful. Although George Washington's administration was honored for a balanced policy of neutrality, the Jay Treaty with Great Britain provoked virulent partisan attack. Thomas Jefferson's purchase of the Louisiana territory must be paired with the miserable failure of his embargo against Great Britain. Woodrow Wilson, the victorious war leader, was humiliated by the defeat of the Treaty of Versailles and his internationalist foreign policy. Jimmy Carter's triumph in facilitating an Israeli-Egyptian peace accord at Camp David was followed by his inability to resolve the hostage crisis with Iran. As Ronald Reagan's hard-line anti-Communist policies were bearing some fruit, his administration was mired in the Iran-contra scandal.

Recent presidents who entered office possessing greater expertise and interest in domestic policy have been distracted, seduced, or overwhelmed by foreign affairs. Lyndon B. Johnson's plans for a "Great Society" were undercut by the resource demands of the Vietnam War and the divisions the war created in the American public. Carter, a former governor with little foreign policy experience, became personally absorbed with foreign policy issues such as recognition of the People's Republic of China, arms control, and the Camp David peace process between Egypt and Israel. Reagan's bold domestic agenda of cutting taxes and balancing the budget was complicated by the massive increases in defense spending necessary to implement his foreign policy agenda. Events in Somalia, North Korea, Haiti, and Bosnia taught Bill Clinton that no president can avoid the often perilous complications of foreign affairs.

Distribution of Foreign Policy Power

On balance, the Constitution gives the president fewer powers related to the making of foreign policy than Congress. Moreover, the powers of the presidency are checked in ways that seem designed to prevent the president from making unilateral commitments in foreign affairs. The only unshared power in this area is the president's responsibility to "receive Ambassadors and other Public ministers." Presidents may appoint ambassadors only with the "Advice and Consent of the Senate," and the Senate was meant to be involved throughout all treaty negotiations. The executive power is limited by the laws the president is to "faithfully" execute. The president's authority as commander in chief is constrained, as a policy-making power, by Congress's constitutional control over declarations of war and the raising and support of all armed forces.

Besides its influence over the use of force and the powers it shares with the president, Congress has broad foreign policy powers that are checked only by the president's veto. Congress controls the legal context of international affairs through its powers "to define and punish Piracies and Felonies committed on the high Seas and Offences against the Law of Nations; . . . and make Rules concerning Captures on Land and Water." Most significant is Congress's authority to "regulate Commerce with foreign Nations." These powers are broadened by the "elastic" power to "make all Laws which shall be necessary and proper for carrying into Execution the foregoing Powers. . . ."

Altogether, Congress's formal constitutional authority in foreign affairs is broader and less qualified than the president's. In addition, the legislative branch's general power to make laws, control appropriations, and "provide for the common Defence and general Welfare of the United States" gives it broad authority to become involved in any foreign policy decision or action not specifically reserved for the president by the Constitution.[3] Congress and, especially, the Senate were, it seems, to control general policy and any long-term foreign commitments.

Obviously this strict reading of the Constitution does not fully or accurately describe the actual distribution of foreign policy responsibilities and influence. A more complete account of the Framers' design must acknowledge that they anticipated and encouraged a presidential ambition that would clash with the other branches. The Framers also expected that this officer, "seated on the summit of his country's honors," would not be content as a mere executive and congressional agent. Rather, the design of the office encourages the president to "undertake extensive and arduous enterprises for the public benefit, requiring considerable time to mature and perfect."[4] This anticipation of a presidential inclination toward grand policy initiation justifies presidential scholar Edward S. Corwin's description of the Constitution as "an invitation to struggle for the privilege of directing American foreign policy."[5]

The affirmative grants of power in the Constitution do not begin to answer all the questions about how foreign policy decisions should be made and implemented, and the actual distribution of shared foreign policy powers between the president and Congress could be established only by events. The particular struggles have produced periods of interbranch stalemate and partnership, presidential subordination and domination.

> He shall have Power, by and with the Advice and Consent of the Senate, to make Treaties, provided two-thirds of the Senators present concur; and he shall nominate and, by and with the Advice and Consent of the Senate, shall appoint Ambassadors, other public Ministers and Consuls. . . . He shall receive Ambassadors and other public Ministers.
>
> —*from Article II, sections 2, 3*

Presidential Dominance of Foreign Policy

In 1948, addressing members of the Jewish War Veterans, President Truman stated, "I make foreign policy."[6] Most historians and political scientists would agree that Truman's assessment of presidential power exaggerates only slightly the influence of modern presidents over foreign policy. Between World War II and the end of the cold war with the Soviet Union, presidents won most of the interbranch struggles for primacy in foreign relations. Congress retained an important role in foreign affairs. On many occasions Congress was able to frustrate, delay, modify, or negate presidential foreign policy. The president, however, dominated the formulation and initiation of foreign policy, and Congress's actions were usually responses to presidential policies. Certainly, the American public and foreign governments expect the president to make decisions and to implement them. It is even common for members of Congress from both parties to criticize a president for failing to provide foreign policy leadership. Presidents perceived as indecisive or weak in foreign relations quickly lose popularity.

Because the constitutional division of power between the executive and legislative branches is relatively ambiguous in the area of foreign affairs, one cannot attribute the establishment of presidential control over foreign relations simply to the affirmative grants of power in the Constitution. The ambiguity of the document ensured that skills, circumstances, public opinion, customs, and precedents would order and reorder the distribution of influence over foreign affairs. The branch most capable of asserting its interests and demonstrating its ability to make effective foreign policy would likely emerge as the more powerful. This branch has proved to be the executive. However, the principle of "presidential control," as a general account of foreign policy making, describes only the cold war period. It is less accurate as a characterization of the current era, beginning with the disintegration of the Soviet Union and the Warsaw Pact. Conflicts between President Clinton and Congress from 1993 to

1995 over foreign aid, U.S. participation in UN missions, and many other foreign policy issues suggest a return to a sharper struggle for control of foreign policy.

PRESIDENTIAL ADVANTAGES

The history of foreign policy making and the eventual rise of presidential responsibility for leadership and control have been shaped by a mix of more or less mutable influences: presidential skills, public opinion, precedents, constitutional principles, and circumstances. The presidents' enduring advantages are their status as chief of state and the various constitutional powers that establish them as the principal communicator, the "sole organ of the nation in its external relations, and its sole representative with foreign nations."[7] Although presidents do not have the full authority to commit the nation and Congress to a foreign policy, their powers, at the very least, allow them to speak first in defining a policy and course of action for the nation. When coupled with the status as the only nationally elected officer (along with the vice president), these powers give an enterprising and determined president considerable leverage over policy. Insofar as any contradiction to their lead may reflect on the nation, presidents can saddle the congressional opposition with responsibility for embarrassing the nation and harming the general credibility of the presidency in future negotiations. These advantages are enhanced by the presidents' other positions. As commander in chief of the armed forces, head of the diplomatic corps, and head of the intelligence agencies, presidents should be in the best position to judge the capacity of the U.S. government to carry out a given foreign policy. Congress has regularly recognized the inherent advantages of the presidency's focused responsibility. Unlike Congress, with its many voices and centers of power, presidents are able to work with speed and secrecy—two capabilities that are indispensable in many diplomatic situations, and especially in crises that threaten the security of the nation. Finally, presidents are the most identifiable leaders and visible symbols of the nation and are, therefore, the most capable of rallying national support in a crisis.

Turning these advantages into enduring presidential dominance depends on a number of other factors. Presidents must establish plausible constitutional principles that support their policy-making ambitions, principles that place within their control the ambiguities and voids in the Constitution, such as the responsibility for policy proclamations, international agreements other than treaties, flexible employment of armed forces, and military actions short of war. A significant constitutional resource is the executive power. Because it is difficult to define precisely where policy making stops and execution begins, even a narrow understanding of the executive power affords presidents some policy influence. Moreover, presidents have claimed that the general executive power authorizes them to fill the constitutional voids and to dominate areas of ambiguity.

Congress retains a substantial arsenal of constitutional counterclaims and can at any time reassert itself. The persuasiveness of presidential assertions of authority depends in part on precedent: claims of authority that have received the approbation or acquiescence of Congress, the courts, and public opinion. Successful assertions, and especially those backed by actions with favorable results, tend to strengthen the president's constitutional position and reaffirm the practical advantages of presidential control over policy. Precedents can, however, cut the other way. The war in Vietnam was prosecuted under an expansive interpretation of presidential authority built up through many cold war precedents. However, the ultimate effects of the war were a weakened practical argument for presidential control of foreign policy; Congress's reassertion of its constitutional powers; and greater skepticism concerning the president's claims of broad constitutional authority.

Reaping the full potential of constitutional and practical precedents requires the cooperation of circumstances. Any crisis in foreign affairs that directly or indirectly threatens the security and well-being of U.S. citizens, the nation, or close allies will focus attention on the president, as the chief of state and as the officer most able to respond flexibly and decisively in diplomatic and military matters. Congress regularly recognizes its clumsy inability to compete with these presidential qualities. As Alexis de Tocqueville noted more than 150 years ago:

> If the Union's existence were constantly menaced, and if its great interests were continually interwoven with those of other powerful nations, one would see the prestige of the executive growing, because of what was expected from it and what it did.[8]

When de Tocqueville wrote this, and for some time after, the United States followed a policy of relative isolation. The enduring elements of foreign policy were westward expansion and commerce. The latter especially was dominated by Congress through its full authority over tariffs and trade. After World War II, the expansive global commitments and permanent national security crisis met de Tocqueville's conditions and led to a full and enduring realization of the president's constitutional and practical potential in foreign policy leadership and control. Presidential scholars do not, as yet, have enough experience to assess accurately the effects of the post–cold war era on presidential powers in this area, though the frequent conflicts between Congress and President Clinton about issues such as participation in United Nations missions indicate that securing presidential leadership in the future will be much more difficult.

JUDICIAL ENHANCEMENT OF PRESIDENTIAL POWER

The president's practical and constitutional advantages in competing with Congress for control of foreign policy are greatly enhanced by the fact that the judicial branch has, generally, either affirmed presidential assertions or refused to settle conflicts between the president and Congress, especially in this area. *(See box, Supreme Court Cases Related to the President's Foreign Policy Powers, p. 126.)*

SUPREME COURT CASES RELATED TO THE PRESIDENT'S FOREIGN POLICY POWERS

Ware v. Hylton, 3 Dall. 199 (1796). The Court ruled 4–0 that treaties made by the United States overrode any conflicting state laws. The 1783 Treaty of Paris with Britain, which ended the American Revolution, provided that neither Britain nor the United States would block the efforts of the other nation's citizens to secure repayment of debts in the other country. This provision rendered invalid a Virginia law allowing debts owed by Virginians to British creditors to be "paid off" through payments to the state.

Foster v. Neilson, 2 Pet. 253 (1829). By a 5–0 vote, the Court refused to rule on a boundary dispute involving territory east of the Mississippi River claimed by both the United States and Spain. Chief Justice John Marshall described the matter as a "political question," which it was not the business of the judiciary to resolve.

Holmes v. Jennison, 14 Pet. 540 (1840). A fugitive from Canada, detained in Vermont, sought release through a petition for a writ of *habeas corpus.* After the state supreme court denied his petition, he asked the Supreme Court to review that action. The Court dismissed the case for lack of jurisdiction, but Chief Justice Roger B. Taney declared in his own opinion that states were forbidden by the Constitution to take any independent role in foreign affairs, and thus state governors could not surrender a fugitive within their jurisdiction to a foreign country who sought the fugitive's return.

The Prize Cases, 2 Black 635 (1863). These cases involved the capture of four ships seized while trying to run the Union blockade of Confederate ports, which Lincoln instituted in April 1861 and Congress sanctioned in July. By a 5–4 vote, the Court sustained the president's power to proclaim the blockade without a congressional declaration of war. A state of war already existed, the majority said, and the president was obligated "to meet it in the shape it presented itself, without waiting for Congress to baptize it with a name. . . ."

Geofroy v. Riggs, 133 U.S. 258 (1890). The Court ruled 9–0 that it is within the scope of the treaty power of the United States to regulate the inheritance by aliens of land and other property in the United States. The Court declared that the treaty power was unlimited except by the Constitution.

Missouri v. Holland, 252 U.S. 416 (1920). After lower courts ruled an act of Congress protecting migratory birds an unconstitutional invasion of powers reserved to the states, the U.S. government negotiated a treaty with Canada for the protection of the birds. After the Senate approved it, Congress again enacted protective legislation to fulfill the terms of the treaty. The Court sustained this second act by a 7–2 vote. It ruled that in order to implement a treaty, Congress may enact legislation that without a treaty might be an unconstitutional invasion of state sovereignty.

United States v. Curtiss-Wright Export Corp., 299 U.S. 304 (1936). Although ambiguous, this is the leading case on the general foreign affairs powers. By a 7–1 vote the Court upheld an act of Congress authorizing the president, at his discretion, to embargo arms shipments to foreign belligerents in a South American war. The Court asserted that the national government has undefined, "inherent" powers in foreign affairs. Justice George Sutherland also argued that the president was "the sole organ of the federal government in . . . international relations." His powers as the "sole organ" were "plenary and exclusive."

United States v. Belmont, 310 U.S. 324 (1937). In the executive agreements that established diplomatic relations between the Soviet Union and the United States in 1933, the two nations had agreed that Soviet assets in the United States would be used to pay the claims of U.S. citizens for property seized in the Soviet Union at the time of the Russian revolution. When U.S. government officials tried to recover funds from the accounts of Russian nationals in New York banks, the state maintained that its laws prohibited the action. The Supreme Court, however, ruled that the executive agreements upon which the action was based constituted an international compact that, like a treaty, superseded conflicting state laws.

Goldwater v. Carter, 444 U.S. 996 (1980). In December 1978, President Jimmy Carter announced that the United States would terminate the 1945 Mutual Defense Treaty with the Republic of China (Taiwan) as part of the process of establishing diplomatic relations with the People's Republic of China. Sen. Barry Goldwater (R-Ariz.) brought a suit to stop the action, maintaining that treaty termination, like treaty ratification, required the prior approval of the Senate. The Court tacitly sided with the president by dismissing the case as a political question outside the realm of judicial review.

The courts have avoided resolving constitutional conflicts between Congress and the president in the area of foreign policy through the "political questions" doctrine. As Justice Robert Jackson argued in 1948:

> the very nature of executive decisions as to foreign policy is political, not judicial. Such decisions are wholly confided by our Constitution to the political departments of the government. . . . They are decisions of a kind for which the Judiciary has neither aptitude, facilities nor responsibility and which has long been held to belong in the domain of political power not subject to judicial intrusion or inquiry.[9]

The Supreme Court has also affirmed broad, inherent national powers in foreign affairs and war, though without settling the exact boundaries between the president and Congress. The most comprehensive of these rulings came in *U.S. v. Curtiss-Wright,* delivered in 1936.

In 1934 Congress passed a joint resolution granting the president full discretion in determining the government's policy toward private arms shipments to warring nations in South America. After President Franklin D. Roosevelt used this authority to impose an embargo on Bolivia, the Curtiss-Wright Export Corporation conspired to send arms to Bolivia. In court lawyers for Curtiss-Wright argued that the law was an unconstitutional delegation to the executive of Congress's legislative power.

The Court's decision is rather difficult to fathom. The Court clearly argued for a fundamental distinction between domestic and foreign affairs powers; although the national government's domestic powers are strictly limited by the Constitution, its foreign affairs authority comprises all the powers of a sovereign nation. In other words, the Constitution's specific grants do not define the scope of the government's "inherent" powers, and the government generally has access to an unspecified and undefined range of powers in war and foreign affairs.

Moreover, the Court argued that the president's specific powers establish him as the "sole organ of the federal government in the field of international relations." However, this seems to be limited to the exclusive authority to "speak or listen as a representative of the nation" and does not imply that the president has full policy-making authority. As Justice George Sutherland indicates in his summary, the president is not independent of Congress in broader questions of policy:

> It is important to bear in mind that we are here dealing not alone with an authority vested in the President by an exertion of legislative power, but with such an authority plus the very delicate, plenary, and exclusive power of the president as the sole organ of the federal government in the field of international relations—a power which does not require as a basis for its exercise an act of Congress, but which, of course, like every other governmental power, must be exercised in subordination to the applicable provisions of the Constitution. It is quite apparent that if, in the maintenance of our international relations, embarrassment—perhaps serious embarrassment—is to be avoided and success for our aims achieved, congressional legislation which is to be made effective through negotiation and inquiry in the international field must often accord to the President a degree of discretion and freedom from statutory restriction which would not be admissible were domestic affairs alone involved.[10]

U.S. v. Curtiss-Wright was a landmark decision. Although the ruling does not seem to support historian Arthur M. Schlesinger Jr.'s conclusion that the Court "affirmed the existence of an inherent, independent and superior presidential power, not derived from the Constitution and not requiring legislation as the basis for its exercise," the ruling did ground past practices in constitutional doctrine, and it provided the president and Congress with a wealth of possible claims to authority.[11]

CONFLICTS AND PRECEDENTS DURING THE WASHINGTON ADMINISTRATION

Although George Washington exercised his foreign affairs power with great restraint by today's standards, he and his closest adviser, Secretary of the Treasury Alexander Hamilton, believed the president had the constitutional authority and the practical duty to take the initiative in foreign policy. As a result Washington set several precedents that enlarged the foreign affairs powers of the young presidency beyond a literal reading of the enumerated powers in the Constitution. He established the president's authority to recognize foreign governments, to demand that foreign ambassadors be recalled, to negotiate treaties without the direction of the Senate, and to withhold from the House documents pertinent to treaty negotiations. Most important, Washington demonstrated that in foreign affairs the president could use the office's inherent executive power to take actions that were authorized neither by Congress nor by a specific presidential foreign policy power in the Constitution. In so doing, his administration initiated a debate that produced history's most complete and enduring constitutional arguments for and against broad presidential authority in foreign affairs.

Neutrality Proclamation of 1793

Washington set the precedent for unilateral presidential policy making by proclaiming the neutrality of the United States in the war between France and Great Britain in 1793. Although the treaty of alliance with France signed in 1778 was still in effect, and many Americans favored the French, Washington was anxious to avoid involving the United States in the conflict, fearing that it would disrupt the strengthening of the American economy and political institutions.

On April 22, 1793, he issued a proclamation which declared that the United States would be "friendly and impartial" toward the belligerents. Although the proclamation was unpopular with many Americans, Congress followed Washington's lead by passing the Neutrality Act of 1794, which endorsed the policy of neutrality already in effect. Washington had shown that the president's executive power could be used to make foreign policy rather than just execute congressional directives.

Hamilton-Madison Debate

Secretary of State Thomas Jefferson was not convinced that the president's action was constitutional. Washington had acted without explicit constitutional authority. Moreover, Jefferson reasoned, because only Congress could declare war, the president lacked the authority to decide unilaterally that the nation would *not* fight a war. However, his objections to Washington's policy were minor compared to the horror induced by Hamilton's "Pacificus" essays defending the proclamation. Hamilton's defense evolved into a more general argument for broad, inherent presidential powers in war and foreign affairs. At Jefferson's urging, Virginia representative James Madison, under the pseudonym of "Helvidius," wrote a series of responses.

Hamilton's argument took two tacks. First, he argued that Washington was acting within his ordinary authority as chief executive in interpreting the legal obligations of existing treaties and in informing the government and the citizens of their responsibilities under the law. The expansiveness of the other tack was breathtaking. Through a careful, and sometimes clever, analysis of the constitutional text, Hamilton argued that constellations of specific presidential powers implied that the treaty power and the general war power were executive in nature. Therefore, he concluded, Congress's powers in those areas ought to be interpreted narrowly, as strictly construed exceptions to executive power. The crucial argument was that the Constitution grants the president broad and undefined *inherent* powers through the vesting clause of Article II; whereas Congress is given the "legislative Powers *herein granted*," the executive power is "vested in a President" without a similar limitation. This broad power would not only authorize proclamations but also fill every relevant void in the Constitution. Hamilton acknowledged that the president's use of this power interfered with the free exercise of Congress's power to declare war, but this was an unavoidable consequence, he argued, of the president and Congress having "concurrent powers" in this area.[12]

Jefferson felt that it would be improper for him, as a member of Washington's cabinet, to attack Hamilton's argument in public. He urged Madison to respond to Hamilton: "Nobody answers him and his doctrines are taken for confessed. For God's sake, my dear Sir, take up your pen, select the most striking heresies and cut him to pieces in face of the public."[13]

Madison's argument rested less on the constitutional text than on a general principle of legislative sovereignty and strict rule of law: "the natural province of the executive magistrate is to execute laws, as that of the legislature is to make laws. All his acts, therefore, properly executive, must presuppose the existence of the laws to be executed."[14] This restrictive interpretation of the executive power then guided his very restrictive reading of all presidential powers in foreign affairs and war. Thus, according to Madison, the president's role in foreign affairs was confined to executing the laws, treaties, and declarations of war made by Congress and performing those duties, strictly construed, that are specifically enumerated in the Constitution. According to Madison, Congress was the branch of government properly entrusted to formulate foreign policy, including declarations of neutrality.

Although Hamilton's generous reading of the president's constitutional authority has never been fully accepted by the other branches, it has provided presidents with a coherent constitutional foundation for their more adventurous assertions of authority. Indeed, many presidents have spoken and behaved as if they had a general, comprehensive power to conduct foreign affairs, while Congress could only participate if it found an opportunity to use one of its specific powers.

Congressional Cooperation and Conflict

In spite of their constitutional and practical advantages in the conduct of foreign policy, presidents have regularly struggled, and periodically failed, to control U.S. foreign policy. Congress has significant authority that can be used to thwart and redirect presidential initiatives. At times Congress has refused to follow the president's leadership and has attempted to legislate its own policy course. Even in eras of presidential domination, Congress has demonstrated that no foreign policy program can be sustained for long without its support. Foreign policy has, therefore, often been shaped through cooperation and accommodation between the two branches.

EARLY COOPERATION AND CONFLICT

Congressional majorities often were willing to cooperate with early presidents on foreign affairs matters. For example, Congress passed the Neutrality Act of 1794 a year after President Washington had declared American neutrality in the war between Britain and France, even though many members of Congress had opposed the original proclamation. In 1803 the Senate followed Jefferson's lead by ratifying the treaty with France that transferred the Louisiana Territory into U.S. control. The full record of these two administrations is, however, more mixed. Although the Senate approved it in 1795, Washington's Jay Treaty with Great Britain ignited a partisan explosion that led to demands from the House for papers related to the negotiations. Against the strong wishes of Jefferson, Congress repealed his embargo policy just before the end of his term.

In 1816 a report by the Senate Foreign Relations Committee reflected Congress's recognition of the practical advantages of presidential leadership in foreign affairs and of the limited practical scope of the Senate's power of advice and consent:

> The President is the Constitutional representative of the United States with regard to foreign nations. He manages our concern with foreign nations and must necessarily be most competent to determine when, how, and upon what subject negotiations may be urged with the greatest prospect of success. For his conduct he is responsible to the Constitution. The committee considers this responsibility the surest pledge for the faithful discharge of his duties. They think the interference of the Senate in the direction of foreign negotiations [is] calculated to diminish that responsibility and thereby to impair the best security for the national safety. The nature of transactions with foreign nations, moreover, requires caution and unity of design, and their success frequently depends on secrecy and dispatch.[15]

NINETEENTH CENTURY

For a number of reasons, presidents during much of the last two-thirds of the nineteenth century exerted less foreign policy leadership than had earlier presidents. The resolution of the slavery question, the development of the American West, and the Reconstruction of the South following the Civil War were the most important political issues of the period. The primary foreign relations issues—foreign trade and the acquisition of territory from foreign governments—were two matters in which Congress had a large role. Nonetheless, Presidents Chester A. Arthur, Benjamin Harrison, and William McKinley exerted significant influence over trade policy during the last half of the nineteenth century.

Moreover, following the Civil War, congressional power was at its peak. The executive branch suffered a number of serious setbacks, including the impeachment and near removal of President Andrew Johnson from office and the passage of the Tenure of Office Act in 1867, which allowed the Senate to prevent a president from removing an appointee from office.[16] In general, the Senate controlled the executive branch. More to the point, from

1871 to 1895 every major treaty failed to gain the Senate's consent.[17]

The Spanish-American War in 1898 marked a major turn in foreign policy as the nation dropped its traditional policy of nonintervention. Although President McKinley originally sought a peaceful resolution of the conflict with Spain over its rule in Cuba, Congress and public opinion favored intervention. The nation went to war and emerged victorious with overseas territories as distant as the western Pacific. To the end of fostering of trade, McKinley extended the nation's international interests and engagements. In particular, the annexation of the Philippines involved the nation in a wide range of Far Eastern affairs, especially those affecting trade. This imperial policy helped merge the president's foreign affairs and war powers, giving the president greater leverage over Congress in making and implementing foreign policy.

THEODORE ROOSEVELT'S ADMINISTRATION

Following the Spanish-American War presidents expanded their control over foreign affairs. In 1901 McKinley was assassinated, and his vice president, Theodore Roosevelt, succeeded to the presidency. For the next seven and a half years, Roosevelt frequently ignored or circumvented Congress while boldly asserting a broad executive prerogative to pursue his perception of U.S. interests abroad. In 1903 he used U.S. naval power to back a small Panamanian revolt against Colombian rule; recognized the state of Panama, which emerged from the revolution; and quickly negotiated a treaty with the new Panamanian government giving the United States the right to dig the Panama Canal. In 1905, after the Senate refused to ratify a treaty giving the United States control of the Dominican Republic's customshouses, Roosevelt implemented his policy through an executive agreement. The same year, Roosevelt personally directed mediation efforts between Russia and Japan without consulting Congress. His efforts led to the Portsmouth Conference in New Hampshire, which ended the Russo-Japanese War and won him the Nobel Peace Prize. In 1907 Roosevelt decided to send the U.S. fleet on a world cruise, primarily to impress the Japanese with U.S. naval strength. Congress threatened to deny funding for the mission but relented when Roosevelt declared he had sufficient funds to send the navy to the Pacific—and Congress would be left to decide whether it wanted the ships back.[18]

Roosevelt freely admitted that he had avoided involving Congress in major foreign policy actions. In 1909, while still in office, he wrote: "The biggest matters, such as the Portsmouth peace, the acquisition of Panama, and sending the fleet around the world, I managed without consultation with anyone; for

In a bid to end the war between Russia and Japan, Theodore Roosevelt, middle, meets with delegates from the two countries at the 1905 Portsmouth Conference. Winning the Nobel Peace Prize for his successful effort, Roosevelt is the only U.S. president to date to win the award.

when a matter is of capital importance, it is well to have it handled by one man only."[19]

VERSAILLES TO WORLD WAR II

Presidential disregard for Congress's role in foreign policy reached new heights in 1919. Woodrow Wilson traveled to Versailles, France, to participate personally in the negotiation of a peace treaty to end World War I. Under strong pressure from Wilson, the conference agreed to include provisions in the treaty establishing a League of Nations. The president brought the treaty back to the United States and began a vigorous national campaign for Senate approval. During the war, Congress had cooperated with Wilson by granting him unprecedented war powers. Once the threat had passed, however, the Senate was ready to reassert legislative influence over foreign policy. Wilson, however, ignored the growing opposition within the Senate and refused to involve senators in the Versailles negotiations or even to inform them of U.S. negotiating positions. In 1919 and 1920, the Senate refused to approve the treaty, thus keeping the country out of the League of Nations.

The demise of the Versailles treaty signaled a new period of congressional activism in promoting a foreign policy of isolation. During the next two decades Congress limited U.S. involvement overseas, with little resistance from the executive branch. When war threatened in Asia and Europe in the late 1930s, Congress, reflecting the isolationism of the public, tried to legislate neutrality through an embargo on arms shipments and strict controls on the president.[20] But when war finally began, Franklin Roosevelt, like presidents before him in times of crisis, acquired enormous powers through his assertiveness and Congress's grants of authority, which were motivated by the need for national unity.

POSTWAR PRESIDENTIAL POWER

After World War II ended, presidential authority in foreign affairs continued to grow. The period brought many new responsibilities and dangers that required a chief executive capable of quick, decisive action and enhanced presidential stature as an international leader. The United States had emerged from the war as the most powerful nation on earth and the leader of the non-Communist world. The threat of Communist expansion brought the whole globe into the sphere of U.S. interest. The United States had swung from isolationism in the late 1930s to unprecedented international involvement in the late 1940s, aligning itself with virtually any willing country and sending billions of dollars in economic and military aid to foreign countries.

More immediate dangers to the security of the United States grew along with its commitments. Advances in missile technology and Soviet development of the atomic bomb in 1949 and the hydrogen bomb in 1953 made a devastating attack on the American homeland a possibility. The fall of China to Communist forces in 1949 reinforced the belief of many Americans that the United States had to be ready to use troops if necessary to stop Communist expansion.

The continual conjunction of military threats and foreign policy in this complex and hostile international environment contributed to a consensus for strong presidential leadership in foreign policy. Congress recognized that only the executive branch had the means to collect and analyze the huge amount of information on foreign policy issues and to act with the speed and flexibility that seemed necessary to manage U.S. global commitments. In addition, the presidential role of guardian of the nuclear switch magnified the commander in chief's stature as guardian of the free world, thereby enhancing presidential authority in other areas of defense and foreign policy.

On the one hand, some major initiatives, such as the Marshall Plan, were developed in close cooperation with congressional leaders. On the other hand, Congress repeatedly passed resolutions supporting presidential policy discretion and authorizing the president to use force if necessary to deal with particular international problems. In 1955 Congress authorized the president to use force to defend Formosa (Nationalist China) and the neighboring islands if they were attacked by Communist China. An even broader resolution was passed in 1957 that supported the "Eisenhower Doctrine," which announced the intention of the United States to defend Middle Eastern countries "against aggression from any country controlled by international communism." The House and Senate passed resolutions in 1962 declaring their support for any presidential action, including the use of force, that was necessary to defend the rights of the United States in Berlin. The same year Congress adopted similar resolutions pertaining to the Cuban Missile Crisis.

In August 1964 Congress passed the sweeping Tonkin Gulf resolution with only two senators out of 535 members of Congress in opposition. *(See box, "Tonkin Gulf Resolution," p. 176.)* The resolution had been proposed by the Johnson administration in response to cloudy evidence of North Vietnamese torpedo boat attacks on U.S. vessels off the coast of Vietnam.[21] The resolution acknowledged and supported the president's full authority to take "all necessary measures to repel any armed attacks against the forces of the United States and to prevent further aggression." At least two months before the incident, Johnson's National Security Council staff had prepared a draft of a similar resolution supporting presidential freedom to act in Vietnam.[22] Because Johnson never asked Congress for a declaration of war, he used the Tonkin Gulf resolution in subsequent years as evidence of congressional support for his expansion of U.S. involvement in the conflict in Vietnam.

CONGRESSIONAL REBELLION AND REASSERTION

Congress was partly responsible for the expansion of executive power between 1945 and 1969. In the interests of national unity and anti-Communism, the legislature had consented to and even encouraged presidential autonomy in foreign and defense matters. Congress tended to follow whatever policy direction the president chose and, implicitly or explicitly, accepted the enlarged presidential interpretations of executive power.[23] In the late 1960s, however, Congress began to rebel against what many members considered a dangerous monopoly in foreign policy powers. They objected to the growing capacity of presidents to exclude Congress from participation in foreign and defense policy decisions. Following the Tonkin Gulf resolution, for example, President Johnson sought appropriations necessary to the escalating military involvement in Southeast Asia and never sought congressional approval for any policy or strategy decision about the war. Members of Congress were also unhappy with the increasing number of international commitments made by executive agreement without congressional approval that, in particular, expanded the scope of the war.

In June 1969, by an overwhelming 70–16 vote, the Senate adopted a "national commitments" resolution, which declared the sense of the Senate that a national commitment by the United States results "only from affirmative action taken by the executive and legislative branches of the United States government by means of a treaty, statute, or concurrent resolution of both houses of Congress specifically providing for such a commitment." In 1969 and 1970, some members of Congress repeatedly attempted to terminate funds for U.S. military activities in Indochina. During that period, Congress also used its investigative powers to probe the extent of U.S. commitments abroad.

In the early 1970s the revelations of a secret Defense Department study of the decision-making process surrounding the Vietnam War, known as the *Pentagon Papers,* the unwillingness of Presidents Johnson and Nixon to include Congress in foreign policy decisions, and the Watergate scandal spurred movements in Congress to recapture the foreign affairs powers it had lost to the executive branch. In 1972 Congress passed the Case Act, which established more rigorous requirements for the reporting of international agreements to Congress by the executive branch. The following year Congress passed the War Powers Resolution over President Nixon's veto. The measure set a sixty-day limit on any unauthorized presidential introduction of U.S. troops into hostilities abroad.

In 1974 Congress passed a major trade reform bill only after approving the Jackson-Vanik amendment, which linked trade concessions for Communist countries to their easing restrictions on the emigration of Jews. The same year Congress imposed a ban on military aid and arms shipments to Turkey. In 1978 the Senate conducted a long and contentious debate on the Panama Canal treaties and approved them only after adding numerous amendments. During this period Congress also conducted investigations of the intelligence community and began to take a more active interest in the specifics of the Defense Department's budget.

Congressional activism in foreign affairs appears to have become a permanent feature of U.S. foreign policy. Congress has routinely submitted alternative plans for weapons acquisition, arms control, and policies on regional problems. In addition, it has passed nonbinding resolutions stating its concerns on a variety of foreign policy issues. Although Congress often supported President Reagan's actions, many of his foreign policies, such as arms sales to moderate Arab nations, were accompanied by tough and sometimes unsuccessful battles for congressional approval. Military assistance to the Nicaraguan rebels, as part of Reagan's general anti-Communist foreign policy, met stiff resistance in Congress, and the administration's attempts to circumvent congressional restrictions led to extensive congressional investigations and general damage to the Reagan administration. President George Bush began his administration in 1989 by forging a bipartisan accord with Congress to defuse the issue. In 1990, faced with mounting congressional criticism, Bush sought congressional approval for his decision to drive the Iraqi army out of Kuwait. In 1991, in the wake of the 1989 Tiananmen Square massacre of prodemocracy demonstrators by the Chinese government, only the failure to override Bush's veto prevented Congress from imposing a human rights condition on the extension of most-favored-nation status to China.[24]

Congress certainly has not usurped the president's role as formulator, initiator, and negotiator of U.S. foreign policy, and the president's influence in foreign affairs remains great. Yet as the post–cold war era matures, Congress's role in foreign policy will probably expand and compete more regularly with the president's, and the success of a president's foreign policies will depend more on congressional support.

Congress has significant foreign policy powers, and it influences many elements of foreign policy. Congress shares with the president the "plenary power" of the national government in foreign affairs; it has "vast powers to define the bounds within which a president may be left to work out a foreign policy."[25] Congress has not asserted these powers fully even during periods of presidential weakness such as the second Nixon administration. Yet the potential is there.

Congress can dominate any policy involving trade. For example, contrary to the wishes of presidents, it has imposed trade sanctions on the former Soviet Union, Uganda, and South Africa. It has used its power over trade to force the president into negotiations, or retaliation, concerning the unfair trade practices of other countries.

Control over spending is Congress's most powerful and comprehensive power. Congress has used this power to control foreign aid and, particularly, arms sales. Foreign aid money is a useful tool that presidents would rather have under their discretion. However, Congress now "earmarks" funds for most military and economic aid.[26] Congress has blocked and mandated spending contrary to the president's wishes. For example, it forbade Nixon to spend for military operations in Laos and Cambodia (1973) and blocked all military assistance to Angola (1975). In 1986 and 1987 Congress used its control over weapons procurement to prevent the Reagan administration from implementing its controversial interpretations of the ABM and SALT II treaties.

President Clinton faced numerous attempts by Congress to

dictate policy through the spending power. In 1995 congressional opposition led Clinton to withdraw his request for emergency funds to support Mexico's collapsing economy. Instead, he used existing executive branch funds to implement the policy. Congress then attempted to require congressional approval for the use of those funds. In October 1995 Congress passed a bill mandating the relocation of the U.S. embassy building in Israel from Tel Aviv to Jerusalem. Clinton opposed the measure as detrimental to the Mideast peace effort, yet he allowed it to become law without his signature. More generally, Congress in 1995 considered deep cuts in the foreign aid budget and extensive policy restrictions on the use of the remaining funds. The Clinton administration threatened to veto the bill as mandating an isolationist foreign policy and as hindering the president's ability to manage the nation's foreign policy.

In general, Congress can be a potent forum for investigations and public criticism of presidential policy. The effectiveness of this capacity depends on congressional willingness to criticize the president and the willingness of the media and the public to listen. The recent dramatic changes in international circumstances suggest that Congress will use these resources to greater effect. After the collapse of the Soviet Union, the Warsaw Pact, and European communism in general, Presidents Bush and Clinton lacked the great leverage gained from a continuous global military and political emergency. The growing independence of the European Union and the evident ebbing of American influence in NATO have lowered the president's stature as a world leader and weakened any argument that deference to his preferences is essential to the security of the nation and its allies. As issues such as international trade come to the fore, and as the conjunction of military might and foreign policy is more intermittent, the president is likely to face a more influential and assertive Congress.

The first four years of the Clinton administration seemed to confirm this expectation. President Clinton struggled, as did President Bush, to formulate general principles of foreign policy outside of the area of trade. Even in that area, President Clinton's successes with the North American Free Trade Agreement (1993) and the General Agreement on Tariffs and Trade (1994) were notable for the weak support he received from his party. Commitments of U.S. forces in Somalia, Haiti, and Bosnia raised extensive congressional protests as well as proposals and resolutions to limit the president's authority to commit forces.

Of particular concern was the participation of the United States in multilateral peacekeeping operations. Initially, the Clinton administration operated under a general principle, and enthusiastic endorsement, of international engagement through UN and other multilateral missions. Strong congressional reactions led to modifications in specific cases and to a more general retreat from this policy. For example, after the multilateral mission in Somalia was redefined from famine relief to a more aggressive policy of subduing the warring factions—resulting in eighteen American soldiers being killed—Congress forced Clinton to negotiate a deadline for withdrawing U.S. forces.

From the start, in 1993, Clinton's policy toward the bloody conflicts among Bosnian Serbs, Croats, and Muslims in the former Yugoslavia generated constant congressional criticism and numerous proposals to limit or change the nature of U.S. involvement in the joint UN/NATO relief and mediation efforts. One of the most important of these was the 1994 amendment forcing Clinton to end U.S. enforcement of the arms embargo of Bosnia. This was the first time the United States has withdrawn from a NATO-sponsored operation. *(See box, Bosnia and Alliance Politics, p. 133.)*

In an effort to ward off more general congressional intrusions, the Clinton administration in 1994 revised its policy concerning UN missions, restricting U.S. participation to those operations that were vital to either national or global security. Nonetheless, in 1995 and 1996 Congress enacted spending bills that cut U.S. payments to the United Nations for peacekeeping missions for fiscal years 1996–1997. In addition, these bills required the president either to cite a national security need or to gain congressional approval before U.S. troops could participate in a multilateral mission. Congressional efforts to place permanent restrictions on U.S. participation in UN operations failed in the Senate.

Power of Communication

The Constitution's separation of powers between independent branches left open the question of which branch had the power to receive communications from foreign countries and to speak for the nation. Under the Articles of Confederation, these responsibilities belonged to Congress. The Constitution assigns to the president the three main communication powers: negotiating treaties, sending ambassadors, and receiving ambassadors. The Framers recognized that communications is a function more suited to an office occupied by a single person than to a large deliberative body. Disputes have arisen over the extent to which communication powers entail a policy-making authority.

Washington was eager to establish the presidency as the only organ of government empowered to communicate officially with foreign governments. He recognized that if both the president and Congress presumed to speak for the nation, diplomacy would be impossible, and foreign governments might try to exploit the confusion. During the first year of his administration, Washington received a letter from King Louis XVI of France notifying "the President and Members of the General Congress of the United States" that Louis's son had died. Washington told Congress that he had received the letter and that he would send a reply to France. The president informed the king that "by the change which has taken place in the national government of the United States, the honor of receiving and answering your Majesty's letter of the 7th of June to 'the President and Members of Congress' has devolved upon me."[27]

In 1793 Washington's secretary of state, Thomas Jefferson, echoed this assertion when he explained to the French ambassador, Edmond Genêt, that the president "being the only chan-

BOSNIA AND ALLIANCE POLITICS

President Clinton's struggle to shape U.S. and alliance policy toward the civil war in the former Yugoslavia has illustrated the complexities, foreign and domestic, of alliance politics in the post–cold war era. After the end of communist rule, the former Yugoslavia descended into a terrible civil war between Serbs, Croats, and Bosnian Muslims. In 1993 President Clinton announced that U.S. involvement in the conflict would be limited strictly to multilateral operations, and the United States began participating in a UN and NATO mission to provide humanitarian relief.[1] This involved U.S. air forces enforcing no-fly zones over certain regions to restrict Serbian attacks and to protect relief operations.

Congressional attitudes toward U.S. involvement were mixed. On the one hand, Congress in 1992 passed, with strong bipartisan support, a nonbinding resolution calling on the president and the UN to act, even with force, to stop the fighting. On the other hand, there were congressional efforts, related also to the operations in Somalia and Haiti, to restrict the president's authority to commit forces to multilateral operations. In 1993 Congress passed a nonbinding resolution stating that no ground forces could be sent to the region without congressional authorization.

In 1994 President Clinton took a tougher stand, calling for airstrikes against the Bosnian Serbs for violating cease-fire agreements, interfering with the relief operation, and besieging various cities that NATO and the UN had, in 1993, designated as protected Muslim enclaves or "safe areas." In 1994 U.S. jets led strikes against Serb positions. However, these intermittent strikes failed to halt Serbian aggression. The European NATO nations resisted more aggressive response out of concern for their ground troops participating in the UN cease-fire and relief efforts. Clinton was unable to lead NATO toward a more consistently forceful response either through airstrikes or through lifting the arms embargo that was crippling the military efforts of the Bosnian Muslims.

However, Clinton was also unwilling to break his commitment to multilateral action, and his policy seemed to be shaped as much by a desire to maintain alliance cohesion as by the situation in Bosnia *per se.* In 1994 Congress attempted to dictate policy by pressing Clinton to seek an end to the UN embargo and, failing that, to end U.S. participation in enforcing it. In an extraordinary move, Congress voted to cut off funds for U.S. enforcement, leading the United States, for the first time, to withdraw from a NATO-approved operation. In trying to repair relations with NATO, the Clinton administration revised its position toward NATO's softer line of seeking a negotiated settlement. On the other side, prominent members of Congress, especially Senator Robert Dole, who became the Senate majority leader in 1995, criticized NATO for failing to punish and stop Serbian aggression. Calling NATO "helpless, hopeless" and "maybe irrelevant," Dole proposed withdrawing the peacekeepers, ending the embargo, and intensifying the airstrikes against the Bosnian Serbs. In a highly unusual move for a member of Congress, he made a well-publicized trip through European capitals to present his criticisms and alternatives.[2] In the summer of 1995 Congress passed the Bosnia and Herzegovina Self-Defense Act, which directed the president, under specific conditions, to terminate the U.S. arms embargo against Bosnia and to press for the termination of the UN arms embargo. Clinton vetoed the bill.

In June 1995, after Bosnian Serb forces took hundreds of UN peacekeepers hostage as protection against NATO airstrikes, President Clinton promised additional U.S. forces, including ground troops, to aid in the redeployment or withdrawal of the UN forces. Clinton defended this commitment to deeper involvement as necessary to support allies, particularly France and Great Britain, and maintain NATO cohesion. However, congressional criticism led him again to back away from committing ground forces. In August and September, after Bosnian Serb forces overran two of the UN "safe areas," U.S. forces led a series of massive airstrikes against Bosnian Serb positions. In the face of congressional criticism, Clinton then promised 20,000 U.S. troops to assist in NATO's oversight of a peace accord. Clinton deepened his commitments by having the United States host the peace talks.

Once the peace accord was signed in Paris in December 1995, Clinton began sending troops on his own authority and without effective congressional resistance. Some, such as Senator Dole, who were opposed to sending ground forces, nonetheless argued that contradicting the president's commitments would harm U.S. credibility as an ally and international leader. The House passed resolutions contradicting the president's authority to send troops, opposing the mission, and yet supporting the troops deployed. The Senate passed a resolution supporting the president's commitments while asserting a one-year limit on the deployment of U.S. forces. When Clinton in November 1996 extended the peacekeeping mission for another eighteen months, observers predicted that Congress would grumble but go along with the longer deployment.

1. Louis Fisher, *Presidential War Power* (Lawrence: University Press of Kansas, 1995), 158.
2. "Republicans Lay Siege to Clinton's Policy," *Congressional Quarterly Weekly Report,* December 3, 1994, 3452–3453.

nel of communication between this country and foreign nations, it is from him alone that foreign nations or their agents are to learn what is or has been the will of the nation; and whatever he communicates as such, they have the right, and are bound to consider, as the expression of the nation."[28]

Washington's conception of the president's role as national communicator was accepted without serious challenge. In 1799 John Marshall reaffirmed the president's position as the instrument of communication with foreign governments when as a member of the House of Representatives he declared, "The President is the sole organ of the nation in its external relations, and its sole representative with foreign nations."[29] The same year Congress passed the Logan Act, which prohibited any person other than presidents or their agents from communicating with another country with the intention of affecting its policy concerning an issue of contention with the United States.[30] Presum-

A large crowd gathers as John F. Kennedy delivers his famous "Ich bin ein Berliner" speech at the Berlin Wall in 1963.

ably the Logan Act could be invoked if a senator or representative attempted to usurp the president's power to communicate officially with foreign nations. Informal discussions with foreign leaders by members of Congress have become accepted practices. Speaker Jim Wright's 1987 attempt, secretly and independent of the Reagan administration, to negotiate a settlement between the Nicaraguan government and the contra rebels was widely criticized across both parties and branches.[31]

More frequently, members of Congress use publicity to affect negotiations. In 1986 Senator Richard Lugar's media campaign helped persuade President Reagan to withdraw his support for Philippine dictator Ferdinand Marcos in favor of the democratically elected Corazon Aquino. Similarly, in 1991 Senator Albert Gore Jr.'s use of the press helped turn the Bush administration toward cooperation in negotiating an international treaty on global warming.

FOREIGN POLICY DECLARATIONS

In practice the president's exclusive authority to communicate with other nations extends well beyond ceremonial functions as chief of state. From Washington to the present, presidents have found that they can make and influence foreign policy simply by making a statement. Presidents have used their communications power to make commitments, formalize decisions, and establish broad policy goals.

Coming from the chief of state and "the sole representative with foreign nations," presidential declarations are, de facto, national commitments. Consequently, Congress often is left with a choice between supporting a presidential commitment and undermining both the president as the national representative and the confidence of other nations in U.S. policy. How a president expresses U.S. interests and intentions, therefore, can shape U.S. foreign policy. Kennedy's famous speech at the Berlin Wall in 1963, for example, encouraged the people of Berlin to expect U.S. protection, thereby committing the United States to its defense.

Theodore Roosevelt explained the connection between communication and policy:

> The president carries on the correspondence through the State Department with all foreign countries. He is bound in such correspondence to discuss the proper construction of treaties. He must formulate the foreign policies of our government. He must state our attitude upon questions constantly arising. While strictly he may not bind our government as a treaty would bind it, to a definition of its rights, still in future discussions foreign secretaries of other countries are wont to look for support of their contentions to the declarations and admissions of our secretaries of state in other controversies as in a sense binding upon us. There is thus much practical framing of our foreign policies in the executive conduct of our foreign relations.[32]

PRESIDENTIAL DOCTRINES

Beyond specific international commitments, presidents have also outlined general tenets of foreign policy, which have come to be labeled "doctrines." The most famous and durable policy statement by a president has been the Monroe Doctrine. In 1823 President James Monroe announced during his annual message to Congress that the United States would resist any attempt by a European power to interfere in the affairs of a Western Hemisphere country that was not already a European colony. Monroe did not consult Congress before his announcement, and some of its members believed the president had overstepped his authority. House Speaker Henry Clay proposed a joint resolution supporting the president's policy, but it never was acted upon. Not until 1899 did the Monroe Doctrine receive a congressional endorsement.[33]

Theodore Roosevelt built upon the Monroe Doctrine in 1904 when he announced in his annual message to Congress what became known as the Roosevelt Corollary. Roosevelt claimed for the United States the right to act as the Western Hemisphere's policeman if "chronic wrongdoing or impotence" in a country required U.S. intervention.

Broad foreign policy "doctrines" are associated with the administrations of many contemporary presidents. The Truman Doctrine stated that "it must be the policy of the United States to support free peoples who are resisting attempted subjugation by armed minorities or outside pressures."[34] The Eisenhower Doctrine, which was supported by a joint resolution, claimed for the United States the right to intervene militarily in the Middle East to protect legitimate governments from attacks by Communist forces. The Nixon Doctrine (also known as the Guam Doctrine) proposed to continue giving allies military and economic aid while encouraging them to reduce their reliance on U.S. troops. The Carter Doctrine declared the Persian Gulf area to be a vital U.S. interest and warned that the United States would use force to prevent any attempt by an outside power to gain control of it. The Reagan Doctrine declared the Reagan administration's intention to support anti-Communist insurgencies around the world to further a policy of rolling back Communism. Only the president's policy declarations have a chance to become accepted as national policy, yet they are not always accepted by Congress and do not always last beyond the administration that announces them.

In the post–cold war era, it is likely that presidents will have difficulty formulating any sort of general commitments and principles of action. President Bush's vague "New World Order" and President Clinton's similarly ill-defined policy of international engagement through multilateral operations may have been the results of these new circumstances. In addition, presidents will have to be more cautious in making commitments as Congress has become less hesitant in contradicting presidential policy.

The Treaty Power

The authors of the Constitution used only one clause to explain how treaties were to be made. Article II, section 2, clause 2, declares that the president "shall have the Power, by and with the Advice and Consent of the Senate, to make Treaties, provided two-thirds of the Senators present concur. . . ." This concise statement blends responsibilities between the legislative and executive branches. Clearly the president is responsible for conducting the actual treaty negotiations. And clearly the president cannot conclude a treaty without first obtaining the consent of the Senate. The Constitution, therefore, ensures that no formal treaty can be concluded without a strong interbranch consensus, and that presidential negotiations will tend to be influenced by the disposition of the Senate.

The executive branch has established itself as the more influential branch in treaty making. As the sole organ of communication with foreign countries, commander in chief, and head of the foreign policy bureaucracy, presidents have been equipped with the means necessary to lead in most phases of the treaty-making process. The president dominates decisions concerning whether and when treaty negotiations will be pursued. The president chooses the negotiators, develops the negotiating strategy, and submits completed draft treaties to the Senate for approval.

Moreover, the president's power to "make" treaties is interpreted as including the final power of ratification. Once the Senate has approved a treaty, it does not become law until the president ratifies it. Thus, the president has significant leverage over any attempts by the Senate to amend a treaty. If the president decides to ratify a treaty the Senate has approved, an exchange of ratifications occurs between the signatories. Then the treaty is promulgated—that is, officially proclaimed to be law—by the president. At any time the president may stop the treaty-making process. Thus, the president has the power of initiative over a treaty from its conception to its ratification.[35]

CREATION OF THE TREATY POWER

In the eighteenth century, treaties were considered to be the primary tool of foreign policy, and the authors of the Constitution deliberated extensively on how treaties should be made. Under the Articles of Confederation, the treaty power was completely entrusted to the legislature. It selected negotiators, wrote and revised their orders, and made the final decision whether a treaty would be accepted or rejected. At the Constitutional Convention, delegates initially assumed that this legislative power would be given to the new Congress and specifically to the Senate, which was designed to be wiser and more stable than the House. Late in the convention's deliberations, and after the executive had been made fully independent of the legislature, the convention divided the treaty-making power between the executive and the Senate.[36]

The Framers recognized that the president, as a single national officer, would be "the most fit agent" for making "preparations and auxiliary measures," for managing delicate and often secret negotiations, and for adapting to often rapidly changing circumstances. John Jay noted other advantages of a single negotiator:

> It seldom happens in the negotiation of treaties, of whatever nature, but that perfect secrecy and immediate dispatch are sometimes requisite. There may be cases where the most useful intelligence may be obtained, if the persons possessing it can be relieved from apprehensions of discovery. . . . and there doubtless are many . . . who would rely on

the secrecy of the president, but who would not confide in that of the Senate, and still less in that of a large popular assembly.[37]

Similar considerations favored the exclusion of the House from treaty deliberations. Hamilton and Jay argued in *The Federalist Papers* that the Senate is favored by its smaller size, its wiser membership chosen by the "select assemblies" of the states, and the stability secured by longer and overlapping terms. These features would also encourage the Senate to focus on the long-term interests of the nation as a whole. The extraordinary majority required for treaty approval in the Senate would, it was argued, ensure that no treaty would become law without high levels of scrutiny and approval.[38]

By giving the president the power to "make" treaties "by and with the Advice and Consent of the Senate," the authors of the Constitution bolstered the prestige of the executive. They must have understood that the president's position as chief negotiator would afford him great influence over policy. However, they spoke of the Senate controlling the overall "system" of foreign policy. The Framers seemed to have expected that senatorial "Advice and Consent" would operate throughout the process and that the president would obtain "their sanction in the progressive stages of a treaty."[39]

The Constitution also strengthened the legal status of treaties. One weakness of the national government under the Articles of Confederation was its dependence on the states to implement treaties. Congress could not force the states to recognize treaty provisions as law. As a result, several states had violated certain articles of the Peace Treaty of 1783 with Great Britain.

The convention's answer to this problem was Article VI, clause 2, of the Constitution, which states, "All Treaties made, or which shall be made, under the Authority of the United States, shall be the supreme Law of the Land; and the Judges in every State shall be bound thereby, any Thing in the Constitution or Laws of any State to the Contrary notwithstanding."

Chief Justice John Marshall interpreted this clause in his opinion in *Foster v. Neilson* in 1829. He confirmed that any treaty or portion of a treaty that did not require legislation to fulfill its provisions was binding on the states and had equal force to federal law. Therefore, although Congress may have to enact legislation to carry out acts stipulated by a treaty, any self-executing treaty or part of a treaty automatically attains the status of a law, enforceable by the courts. Provisions of various treaties periodically have been the target of legal challenges, but the Supreme Court has never declared a treaty or provision of a treaty made by the United States to be unconstitutional.[40]

PRESIDENTIAL PRIMACY IN TREATY NEGOTIATIONS

The Constitution clearly states that both the president and the Senate have a role in treaty making, but the form of the Senate's advice on treaty matters and its influence over negotiations has changed over time.

President Washington's initial interpretation of the treaty-making clause was that "Advice" meant he was to seek Senate opinions in person before his representatives began negotiations. On August 21, 1789, Washington and his secretary of war, Henry Knox, questioned the Senate in its chambers about a treaty to be negotiated with the Creek Indians. After some debate, the Senate decided to postpone its response to Washington's questions until the following week so that it could discuss the negotiations further. Washington, who had expected an immediate reply, returned on Monday, August 24, and received answers to his questions, but he was angered by the Senate's indecisiveness and pessimistic that he could rely on that body for timely consultations on treaty matters. He never again attempted to use it as an executive council before treaty negotiations. Nonetheless, during the early years of his presidency, Washington conscientiously wrote to the Senate for advice on treaty matters before and during negotiations. He also routinely submitted the negotiators' instructions to the Senate and kept that body informed of the progress of talks.[41]

The Senate's role in treaty negotiations would likely have been enhanced had Washington established a precedent of consulting with that body in person. Subsequent presidents, however, agreed with Washington that the advice and consent of the Senate were best obtained from a distance. Several twentieth-century presidents, including Wilson and Truman, went to the Senate to propose or to lobby for treaties, but no president has ever returned to the Senate chamber to seek direct advice on treaty matters.

Washington's handling of the important Jay Treaty of 1794, which avoided war with Great Britain, demonstrated that he had abandoned his initial interpretation of the Constitution's treaty-making clause. In preparation for the Jay Treaty negotiations, Washington only submitted the appointment of his negotiator, Chief Justice John Jay, to the Senate for approval. He withheld from the Senate Jay's instructions about the sensitive negotiations, and the negotiations were held in London without Senate involvement.

Rather than challenging the president's power to make a treaty independently of the Senate, that body responded by amending the completed Jay Treaty in a manner similar to the method by which it amended legislation. Washington accepted the Senate's authority to do this, and after initial protests, the British ratified the amended treaty. The Jay Treaty established a process of treaty making that subsequent administrations and Senates would emulate. As Corwin observed, "The Senate's function as an executive council was from the very beginning put, and largely by its own election, on the way to absorption into its more usual function as a legislative chamber, and subsequent developments soon placed its decision in this respect beyond all possibility of recall."[42]

The often significant influence the Senate has over treaty negotiations comes more from its power to reject a treaty than from any constitutional provision that the president should consider the Senate's advice when making treaties. The Senate, or a minority thereof, can intrude into negotiations by making the conditions of its final approval quite clear. Presidents have, therefore, often cooperated closely with the Senate in the negotiation of a treaty because they recognize that Senate involvement would increase the chances for approval. Excluding the Senate from the negotiating process has often led to troubles and defeats for presidents.[43]

Moreover, Congress can use its control over other policies to influence a president's treaty negotiations. In 1983 a number of senators threatened to vote against funding the MX missile, a crucial piece of Reagan's defense modernization program, unless he modified his negotiating position at the Strategic Arms Reduction Talks in Geneva.[44]

THE TREATY-MAKING PROCESS

The first step in making a treaty is negotiating with a foreign power. This stage is controlled by the president and presidential advisers and representatives. During or before this phase members of Congress may offer advice to the president or express their views on the negotiations individually or collectively. A resolution communicating Congress's disapproval may cause the president to change negotiating strategies or abandon a treaty altogether.

A supportive resolution, however, may contribute to the executive branch's enthusiasm for a particular treaty. In 1948, for example, the Senate's Vandenberg Resolution, which preceded the development of NATO and other alliance systems, advised the president to negotiate regional security agreements.[45] Regardless of congressional protests or encouragement, the president and representatives of the president cannot be prevented from initiating and conducting treaty negotiations with another country.

Although the executive branch has the power to negotiate a treaty without Congress, many presidents have found that involving individual senators in the negotiating process can be a useful political tool. Such involvement can take several forms. During most treaty negotiations influential senators are at least asked for their opinions on the proceedings, but a president may also ask senators to help select the negotiating team, observe the negotiations, follow the progress of the talks through briefings, or even be negotiators.[46]

Until the end of Madison's administration in 1817, the names of treaty negotiators were referred to the Senate for confirmation. The Senate repeatedly protested subsequent presidents' neglect of that practice, but the Senate never was able to establish firmly its right to confirm negotiators.

The practice of sending the instructions of treaty negotiators to the Senate for review, which Washington had followed early in his presidency, proved to be even more temporary. After Washington's administration, no president asked the Senate to consider the terms of a treaty not yet agreed upon, until Polk submitted the skeleton of a treaty ending the war with Mexico in 1846. Preliminary drafts of treaties were sent to the Senate in a few instances by four other presidents—James Buchanan, Lincoln, Andrew Johnson, and Ulysses S. Grant. In 1919 the Senate requested a copy of the proposed Treaty of Versailles as presented to the representatives of Germany. The secretary of state replied: "The president feels it would not be in the public interest to communicate to the Senate a text that is provisional and not definite, and finds no precedent for such a procedure."[47]

Wilson generally excluded the Senate from the Versailles treaty negotiations, and the Senate rejected this important treaty. Most later presidents grasped the obvious lesson. While World War II was still being fought, Franklin Roosevelt established the Joint Advisory Committee on Postwar Foreign Policy to provide a forum where members of Congress and the executive branch could discuss the composition of an international peace organization. This committee, along with the administration's private consultations with Senate leaders, helped create bipartisan support for the United Nations.[48] When the negotiations on the United Nations Treaty began in 1945, Truman included senators from both parties in the U.S. delegation.

The Carter administration also tried to limit Senate objections to the SALT II (Strategic Arms Limitation Talks) treaty it hoped to negotiate with the Soviet Union by encouraging senatorial participation in the process. Selected senators were allowed to observe the negotiations, and the administration consulted closely with Senate leaders while the negotiations were in progress. During these consultations senators voiced suggestions and concerns that prompted Carter to instruct his negotiators to modify their position on several issues.[49] The Senate observers in those talks also persuaded the Soviet Union to provide crucial information on their nuclear forces by arguing that the Senate would never approve the treaty without it. In 1991 the Senate Intelligence Committee's concerns over verification procedures in the Intermediate Nuclear Forces Treaty led President Bush to renegotiate the relevant sections.[50]

Once U.S. negotiators have agreed on the terms of a treaty with a foreign government, the president must decide whether to submit the draft to the Senate for consideration. If it appears that Senate opposition to a treaty will make approval unlikely, the president may decide to withdraw the treaty to avoid a political defeat. Also, international events may change the president's mind about the desirability of ratifying a treaty. Carter withdrew the SALT II treaty from Senate consideration to protest the Soviet invasion and occupation of Afghanistan.

If the president decides to submit a treaty to the Senate for consideration, the Constitution requires that two-thirds of the Senate vote in favor of the treaty for it to be approved.

The Senate is not compelled by the Constitution either to approve or to reject a treaty as it has been negotiated by the executive branch. It may attach amendments to a treaty that require the president to renegotiate its terms with the other signatories before the Senate grants its approval. In 1978 the Senate added a number of conditions and reservations to the treaty that provided for the transfer of the Panama Canal to Panamanian control after the year 2000. The most notable of these amendments was written by Sen. Dennis DeConcini (D-Ariz.). It claimed for

On September 7, 1977, President Jimmy Carter and Panamanian leader Brig. Gen. Omar Torrijos Herrera signed the Panama Canal Treaty, which transferred control of the canal to Panama after the year 2000. The Senate ratified the treaty in 1978.

the United States the right to take whatever steps were necessary, including military force, to open the canal if its operations ceased.[51] The Panamanian government agreed to accept the Senate amendments without renegotiation. Such amendments, however, often make agreement between the United States and its negotiating partner impossible.

U.S. presidents have little choice but to accept the Senate's power to force renegotiation of parts of a treaty. In effect, when the Senate gives its consent on condition that its amendments are accepted by the negotiating partner of the United States, it is rejecting the treaty while outlining a revision of the treaty to which it grants its consent in advance.[52] Presidents in turn may decide not to renegotiate if they believe the senatorial amendments make the treaty undesirable.

The Senate also has the power to add nonbinding written reservations to a treaty before approving it. This option can be used when the Senate accepts the basic terms of a treaty but wishes to impose its interpretation on the document and its implementation. In 1991 the Senate attached a reservation to the Conventional Forces in Europe Treaty that stated that the United States would consider the Soviet Union's failure to fulfill its pledge to eliminate additional weapons as equivalent to a violation of the treaty.[53] In 1992 the disintegration of the Soviet Union complicated the ratification process for the first Strategic Arms Reduction Treaty. President Bush had to negotiate "protocols" with the newly independent states, committing them to abide by the terms of the treaty, and the Senate then attached a reservation to the treaty stating that these protocols and all other related agreements were fully part of the treaty's formal terms.

However, foreign governments may disagree with, or take offense at, such resolutions. Ratification of the 1976 Treaty of Friendship and Cooperation with Spain was delayed several months by Spanish objections to nonbinding Senate resolutions attached to the treaty. The issue was resolved by an agreement between Congress, the Ford administration, and the Spanish government to attach the resolutions to the U.S. instrument of ratification, the document outlining the U.S. understanding of the treaty, but to exclude them from the Spanish instrument of ratification and the treaty ratification document exchanged by the two countries.[54]

After the Senate approves and the president ratifies a treaty, the treaty may require legislation, such as the appropriation of funds or the enactment of criminal laws. Because these tasks can only be accomplished by Congress, such treaties are referred to as "non-self-executing."[55] Consequently, non-self-executing treaties give Congress another chance to pass judgment upon them after ratification. Although Congress rarely has chosen to undermine a treaty by refusing to appropriate funds or enact implementing legislation, its right to do so is well established.[56]

TREATY APPROVAL

The Senate has approved without changes about 90 percent of the treaties presidents have submitted to it. This success rate is a less striking testament to presidential leadership than it may appear. Presidents regularly anticipate senatorial objections in negotiating a treaty, and they must, as in other legislative matters, make deals to gain the votes of particular senators.[57] Moreover, to avoid a political defeat, presidents often have withdrawn treaties from consideration that were in jeopardy of Senate rejection. Other treaties were neither approved nor rejected by the Senate, but instead left in political limbo. For example, the Genocide Treaty, which instructed signers to prevent and punish the crime of genocide, was approved by the Senate in 1986, almost thirty-seven years after Truman submitted it to that body. Many more pacts that could have taken the form of treaties were concluded as less formal executive agreements between the president and a foreign government to avoid the possibility of Senate rejection.

Nevertheless, the success rate probably reflects the inclination of senators, as well as their counterparts in the House, to

TABLE 3-1 Major Treaties Killed by the Senate, 1789–1996

Date of vote	President	Country	Vote Yea	Vote Nay	Subject
March 9, 1825	J. Q. Adams	Colombia	0	40	Suppression of African slave trade
June 11, 1836	Jackson	Switzerland	14	23	Personal and property rights
June 8, 1844	Polk	Texas	16	35	Annexation
June 15, 1844	Polk	German Zollverein	26	18	Reciprocity
May 31, 1860	Buchanan	Mexico	18	27	Transit and commercial rights
June 27, 1860	Buchanan	Spain	26	17	Cuban Claims Commission
April 13, 1869	Grant	Great Britain	1	54	Arbitration of claims
June 1, 1870	Grant	Hawaii	20	19	Reciprocity
June 30, 1870	Grant	Dominican Republic	28	28	Annexation
January 29, 1885	Cleveland	Nicaragua	32	23	Interoceanic canal
April 20, 1886	Cleveland	Mexico	32	26	Mining claims
August 21, 1888	Cleveland	Great Britain	27	30	Fishing rights
February 1, 1889	B. Harrison	Great Britain	15	38	Extradition
May 5, 1897	McKinley	Great Britain	43	26	Arbitration
March 19, 1920	Wilson	Multilateral	49	35	Treaty of Versailles
January 18, 1927	Coolidge	Turkey	50	34	Commercial rights
March 14, 1934	F. Roosevelt	Canada	46	42	St. Lawrence Seaway
January 29, 1935	F. Roosevelt	Multilateral	52	36	World Court
May 26, 1960	Eisenhower	Multilateral	49	30	Law of the Sea Convention
March 8, 1983	Reagan	Multilateral	50	42	Montreal Aviation Protocol
June 11, 1991	Bush	Multilateral	—	—	Annex II, international convention on load lines[a]
June 11, 1991	Bush	Multilateral	—	—	Amendments to Annex II, international convention on load lines[a]

SOURCE: Lyn Ragsdale, *Vital Statistics on the Presidency: Washington to Clinton* (Washington, D.C.: Congressional Quarterly, 1996), 315.
NOTE: a. Not formally rejected by a roll call vote, but instead returned to the president.

follow the president's lead in foreign affairs in the interest of projecting a united front abroad. Members of Congress do not wish to be seen as saboteurs of presidential policy. Moreover, when a president concludes a draft treaty with another nation, in the eyes of the international community the United States has made a commitment. Even though the Senate has full constitutional power to reject a treaty, it must balance its reservations about a particular treaty against the damage rejection would inflict on international confidence in the United States and its chief of state. Finally, senators of the president's party often will side with the president on a particular treaty for the sake of the party's welfare and unity even if they have reservations about the agreement. If the president's party happens to be in control of the Senate, obtaining approval for a treaty may require the support of fewer than half of the senators from the opposition party. However, in order to win passage of implementing legislation for both NAFTA (1993) and GATT (1994), Clinton needed the support of majorities in the Republican Party to overcome weak support among Democratic legislators.

Although the Senate's approval record has been overwhelmingly positive, there have been significant exceptions. Between 1871 and 1898, no major treaty was approved. The most famous treaty rejected by the Senate was the Treaty of Versailles, which ended World War I and established the League of Nations. *(See Table 3-1.)*

The method by which Congress approves treaties has been the target of periodic criticism. John Hay, the secretary of state under McKinley and Theodore Roosevelt who fought several losing battles with the Senate over treaty approval, called the power of the Senate to veto treaties the "original mistake of the Constitution."[58] After the Senate refused to approve the Versailles treaty, proposals surfaced in both the executive and legislative branches to reduce the fraction of Senate members needed to approve a treaty from two-thirds to three-fifths or to a simple majority. Other proposals would eliminate the requirement of an extraordinary majority in the Senate and replace it with simple majority approval by both houses of Congress. Several resolutions to this effect were introduced in Congress during the 1920s and 1940s, yet none has come close to being implemented.

TERMINATION OF TREATIES

Although Article VI, clause 2, of the Constitution declares that treaties are the "supreme Law of the Land," the federal government is not legally constrained from terminating a treaty through agreement with the other party, in response to the other party's violations of the treaty, or for any other reason. However, the Constitution provides no guidelines as to which branch determines that a treaty should be revoked and what sort of approval is needed from another branch. Consequently, both the president and Congress at various times have successfully exercised the power to terminate treaties.[59]

In 1979 this issue was brought before the Supreme Court when the Carter administration sought to terminate the 1954 Mutual Defense Treaty with the Republic of China (Taiwan) as part of the process of establishing formal relations with the People's Republic of China (PRC). The treaty had a clause permitting withdrawal, but President Carter took the action without consulting the Senate in advance. Sen. Barry Goldwater (R-Ariz.) and twenty-three other members of Congress brought suit to prevent Carter's unilateral termination of the treaty.

U.S. District Court Judge Oliver Gasch ruled in October 1979 that Carter's action violated the principle of separation of powers and that both historical precedents and the text of the Constitution indicate that treaty termination requires the consent of two-thirds of the Senate or a majority of both houses of Congress. A U.S. Court of Appeals overturned Gasch's decision. However, the Supreme Court dismissed the complaint, with five justices arguing that either this case or the issue in general was not fit for judicial resolution.[60]

Executive Agreements

An executive agreement is a pact other than a treaty made by the president or representatives of the president with a foreign leader or government. The executive agreement is a particularly powerful foreign policy tool. Presidents have asserted that their power to execute the laws, command the armed forces, and function as the sole organ of foreign policy gives them the full legal authority to make these pacts without any congressional approval. Unlike treaties, they do not supersede U.S. laws with which they conflict, but in every other respect they are binding.

Although the vast majority of international pacts are executive agreements, the vast majority of executive agreements either are routine extensions of existing treaties or are based on broad legislative directives.[61] Agreements made by the president to carry out legislation or treaty obligations are often called "congressional-executive international agreements." Other executive agreements have been supported by joint resolutions. Presidents occasionally have chosen to seek the approval of a majority of both houses of Congress for executive agreements when they did not have the support of two-thirds of the Senate but did want, or need, some type of specific congressional consent. This practice has, at times, elicited strong objections from senators, but it is generally supported by partisan majorities and by the House, which is, through this procedure, given a much larger voice in foreign policy.[62] Congressional authorization and joint approval have been used frequently in areas, such as tariffs, where congressional, or House, authority is definitive.

The very small percentage of agreements (around 3 percent) that do not fall under these categories are the "pure" executive agreements, which are negotiated and implemented without any congressional approval. The president's authority to make such agreements has always not been disputed, and especially not in cases when the president is otherwise acting within his sphere of authority and when the practical advantages of a flexible power of agreement are great. For example, the commander in chief must frequently make and alter agreements with allies during the course of a war. However, the proper scope of the president's unilateral authority to commit the nation has often been disputed. As the scope of executive agreements has broadened, these have become the most important and the most controversial pacts.

The use of executive agreements has grown dramatically in the twentieth century. From 1789 to 1839, executive agreements made up only 31 percent of all international agreements, while more than 95 percent of international pacts made between 1980 and 1990 were executive agreements. As of 1992, the United States had entered into approximately 1,500 treaties and approximately 13,500 executive agreements.[63] Executive agreements also have come to be used to conduct business once reserved for treaties. Contemporary presidents can accomplish virtually anything through an executive agreement that can be accomplished through a treaty.

CONSTITUTIONAL DILEMMA

The Constitution does not prohibit executive agreements, and the Court in *U.S. v. Curtiss-Wright* explicitly affirmed the power of the national government to make international agreements other than treaties. However, the Founders' careful division of the treaty power in the Constitution must be interpreted as an attempt to ensure that Congress has a direct voice in making international commitments. The use of executive agreements by presidents and their representatives to avoid congressional interference has been widely regarded by constitutional scholars and members of Congress as a serious deterioration of constitutional checks and balances in the area of foreign policy.

The development of the United States into a world power with security commitments and economic interests in every corner of the world has made some degree of executive flexibility in making executive agreements desirable. Like Jefferson, who was confronted with the irresistible opportunity to buy the Louisiana Territory, contemporary presidents are sometimes faced with an international situation that calls for making commitments with speed and secrecy. Also, executive agreements often provide a simpler method of transacting less important international business that would overload the already tight legislative schedule if treaties were used.

The crux of the problem is that some important international agreements should receive some sort of congressional approval, yet there are no concrete guidelines to indicate which pacts need Senate consent, which need approval by both houses, and which can be handled simply by the president. Presidents may, therefore, use their discretion in deciding how to make a particular agreement. Numerous presidents, faced with the prospect of fighting for two-thirds approval in the Senate, have used executive agreements to skirt the treaty requirements imposed by the Constitution rather than abandon a diplomatic initiative. Treaties, therefore, have become an exception to the rule, which is presidential policy making.

Despite the use of executive agreements to avoid the treaty ratification process, the Supreme Court has repeatedly upheld the president's power to make international agreements without the consent of the Senate. The Court's ruling in *U.S. v. Belmont* in 1936 was particularly significant. At issue was the president's authority to conclude unilaterally several agreements connected with the 1933 recognition of the Soviet Union. In delivering the Court's opinion, Justice George Sutherland wrote:

> The recognition, establishment of diplomatic relations, the assignment, and agreement with respect thereto, were all parts of one transaction, resulting in an international compact between the two governments. That the negotiations, acceptance of the assignment and agreements and understandings in respect thereof were within the competence of the president may not be doubted. Governmental power over internal affairs is distributed between the national government and the several states. Governmental power over external affairs is not distributed, but is vested exclusively in the national government. And in respect of what was done here, the Executive had the authority to speak as the sole organ of that government.[64]

Justice Sutherland could have based his opinion that the president had the authority to make these agreements on the president's indisputable power to recognize foreign governments. Although he did mention the relevance of this presidential power, he seemed to find authority for the agreements in the president's broader power as the sole organ of foreign policy.[65]

LANDMARK EXECUTIVE AGREEMENTS

The first major executive agreement concluded between a president and a foreign power was the Rush-Bagot agreement with Great Britain.[66] The pact, which imposed limitations on naval forces on the Great Lakes, was concluded under the supervision of President Monroe in 1817. A year after the agreement was put into operation Monroe decided that he wanted congressional approval of his act of diplomacy. He sent the agreement to the House and Senate and asked if they thought it required the consent of the Senate. The Senate endorsed the "arrangement" with a two-thirds vote but did not consider its action to be an approval of a treaty, and instruments of ratification were never exchanged between the United States and Great Britain.[67]

Although Monroe's executive agreement was significant in establishing a precedent, President John Tyler's annexation of Texas by executive agreement in 1845 was even more important, because it was the first time a president had used an executive agreement to accomplish what would have been defeated in the treaty process.[68] Tyler wished to bring Texas into the Union to keep it out of foreign hands and to serve the southern slave interests, but he was not close to having the necessary two-thirds support in the Senate to conclude a treaty of annexation. With sufficient public support for annexation, he called for a joint resolution to bring Texas into the nation. The resolution passed the House by a 120–98 vote and the Senate by a spare two-vote margin. Armed with this resolution, Tyler invited Texas to become a state. In 1898 McKinley annexed Hawaii as a territory by the same method.[69]

Predictably, Theodore Roosevelt was not timid about using executive agreements to accomplish foreign policy objectives that would have been delayed or undermined by the treaty process. When Santo Domingo (now the Dominican Republic) fell into heavy debt to European creditors in 1905, Roosevelt oversaw negotiations of an agreement that extended U.S. protection to Santo Domingo and put the United States in control of collecting the country's customs. The United States would turn over part of the revenue to the Dominican government and pay the country's creditors gradually with the rest. Roosevelt hoped that the Senate would consent to the draft treaty, but when the Senate refused to approve the treaty, he continued the arrangement under an executive agreement.[70]

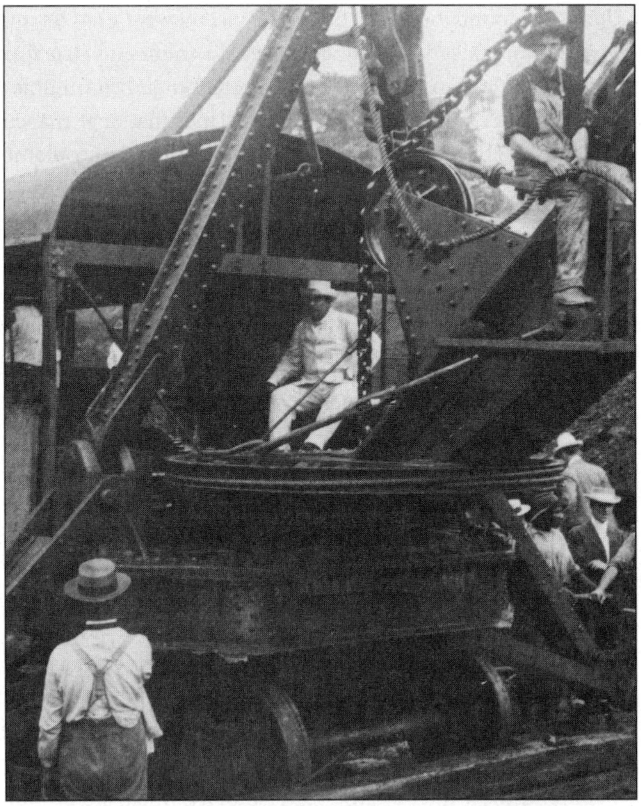

During the eighteenth and nineteenth centuries, no president while in office traveled outside the United States. Theodore Roosevelt broke this precedent when he visited Panama in 1906 to inspect the canal under construction.

Franklin Roosevelt also used an executive agreement to avoid the treaty process when he provided destroyers to the British in 1940. The United States was still officially neutral at that time, and a predominantly isolationist Senate would not have approved a treaty providing Britain with ships to defend against German submarines. Roosevelt therefore used an executive agreement to trade old U.S. destroyers for the right to lease several British naval bases in the Western Hemisphere. Because the deal was in violation of two neutrality statutes and altered the neutral status of the United States, it was clearly an agreement that should have been accompanied by some sort of congressional approval.[71]

The development of NATO illustrates another use of executive agreements. NATO was established by a short treaty containing only fourteen articles that pledged the signatories to maintain and improve their collective defense capabilities.

Upon this foundation, executive agreements were used to construct an organization with an integrated command structure, detailed battle plans, extensive transportation and communications facilities, and routinely scheduled multinational maneuvers. Although the senators who voted for ratification could not have foreseen the enormous development of NATO that would take place through executive agreements, the original treaty did provide the Senate with an opportunity to approve the concept of an alliance with Western European nations.[72]

A dramatic example of the dangers and limits of executive agreements was President Nixon's written assurance to President Nguyen Van Thieu of South Vietnam in 1973 that the United States would "respond with full force" if North Vietnam violated the Paris Peace Agreement, which ended the U.S. military presence in Vietnam. Thieu had consented to the Paris Agreement based on Nixon's personal promise. Nixon's promise, however, did not reflect the mood either of Congress or of the American people at the end of the Vietnam War. It was not honored when the North Vietnamese invaded South Vietnam in 1975. Nixon's agreement was little more than the optimistic personal promise of a president who almost certainly would not have had the means to keep it, even if he had remained in office. Thieu, however, regarded Nixon's pledge as a national commitment, and the United States lost credibility when the promise was not kept.[73]

In 1993 and 1994 two massive international agreements were approved by ordinary majorities in Congress. The North American Free Trade Agreement (NAFTA) and a new General Agreement on Tariffs and Trade (GATT) comprehensively revised the nation's trade policy. Yet both were validated only by authorizing legislation passed in the House and Senate. It has been standard practice for more than a century for Congress to authorize the president to make tariff adjustments through executive agreements, and the House would have had a well-founded complaint if such extensive changes in tariff laws had been submitted only to the Senate.[74] However, these agreements, involving many other countries, covered the full range of tariffs and settled general and specific policies on trade. Moreover, GATT went beyond the adjustment of tariffs and committed the nation's trade practices to a regime of oversight and sanction by an international body, the World Trade Organization. Even so, the loudest objections were to the agreement itself and not to the mode of approval.

ATTEMPTS TO LIMIT EXECUTIVE AGREEMENTS

Since the end of World War II, Congress has made two major attempts to control the president's power to make international agreements and secret commitments. The more intrusive one was a constitutional amendment proposed by Sen. John W. Bricker (R-Ohio) in 1953 that would have placed restraints on the president's power to make executive agreements and decreased the effect of the agreements on domestic law. The second occurred in the early 1970s and culminated in the Case Act of 1972, which was intended to compel the executive branch merely to report all executive agreements to Congress or to selected congressional committees. Except for a clarification of the Case Act passed in 1977, subsequent efforts by Congress to make the executive branch more accountable for its agreements with other nations have been unsuccessful.

Bricker Amendment

Senator Bricker, a conservative Republican, chaired the Foreign and Interstate Commerce Committee. In the postwar era, when the United States was expanding its defense commitments and its participation in international organizations, the Brickerites argued that the president's broad power to make international agreements that are supreme over the constitutions and laws of states (see *U.S. v. Belmont*, 1937) threatened the constitutionally guaranteed rights of the states and the American people.[75] Moreover, many senators were alarmed by the growing tendency to use executive agreements to implement military alliance pacts and UN programs. In January 1953 Bricker and sixty-three cosponsors introduced an amendment aimed at establishing congressional review of executive agreements and making treaties unenforceable as domestic law without accompanying legislation. The amendment stated:

> 1. A provision of a treaty which denies or abridges any right enumerated in this Constitution shall not be of any force or effect.
> 2. No treaty shall authorize or permit any foreign power or any international organization to supervise, control, or adjudicate rights of citizens of the United States within the United States enumerated in this Constitution or any other matter essentially within the domestic jurisdiction of the United States.
> 3. A treaty shall become effective as internal law in the United States only through the enactment of appropriate legislation by the Congress.
> 4. All executive or other agreements between the President and any international organization, foreign power, or official thereof shall be made only in the manner and to the extent to be prescribed by law. Such agreements shall be subject to the limitations imposed on treaties or the making of treaties in this article.
> 5. The Congress shall have power to enforce this article by appropriate legislation.

The third and fourth provisions would have radically altered the way the United States enters into agreements with foreign governments. Every treaty and executive agreement would have required implementing legislation to make them enforceable as domestic laws, and any executive agreement made by a president would have been subject to regulation by Congress. The ability of presidents to make foreign policy through executive agreements and to negotiate treaties without involving Congress would have been severely curtailed.

The amendment did not, however, come to a vote by the time Congress adjourned in August 1953. In 1954 a milder version of the Bricker amendment came within one vote of passing the Senate with a two-thirds majority. Thereafter, support for the amendment ebbed, in part because President Dwight D. Eisenhower strongly opposed it.

The Case Act

In the early 1970s a more modest movement surfaced in Congress to restrain the indiscriminate use of secret agreements. The impetus for this effort was a Senate subcommittee's discovery in 1969–1970 that the executive branch had made secret commitments and terms of agreements during the 1960s. The Security Agreements and Commitments Abroad Subcommittee of the Senate Foreign Relations Committee, chaired by Sen. Stuart Symington (D-Mo.), uncovered secret agreements with Ethiopia, Laos, Thailand, South Korea, Spain, the Philippines, and other countries.

The Nixon administration deepened congressional resentment by concluding important executive agreements with Portugal and Bahrain about military bases. The Senate passed a resolution asserting that the agreements should have been made in the form of treaties, which would have required Senate consent.

Congress responded more generally by passing the Case Act in 1972. The act obligates the executive branch to inform Congress of all executive agreements within sixty days after they have been concluded. It also requires the executive branch to inform Congress of all executive agreements in existence at the time the law was signed. Finally, it provides that the House and Senate committees with jurisdiction over foreign affairs be informed of any executive agreements that the president determines need to be kept secret to ensure national security. The Senate passed the bill by a unanimous 81–0 vote and the House by voice vote.[76] In the years following passage of the Case Act several bills were proposed that were intended to establish a congressional procedure for disapproving executive agreements. Such a bill, introduced by Sen. Sam J. Ervin Jr. (D-N.C.), passed the Senate in 1974, but the House did not act upon it. Hearings on two similar bills were held in 1975 by the Senate Judiciary Subcommittee on the Separation of Powers, but they did not lead to legislation.

After several years, Congress found that many executive agreements were not being reported under the provisions of the Case Act; executive branch officials had labeled them "understandings" rather than executive agreements. Congress reacted by passing legislation in 1977 that required Congress to be informed of any verbal or informal understanding made by any representative of the U.S. government that might constitute a commitment.

Although the Case Act and the legislation that followed it do not limit the president's power to make executive agreements, legislators are more likely to be able to check this executive branch power if they know what sort of agreements the president is making. Because Congress can conduct investigations, issue resolutions, pass legislation, and control appropriations, it does have tools with which it can challenge and refuse to honor executive agreements it believes are unwise or improper. This is especially true of the many executive agreements that depend on supporting legislation.

The Recognition Power

Although the Constitution does not explicitly grant presidents the power to recognize foreign governments, Congress has generally accepted that presidents have this power as a consequence of the authority to appoint (Article II, section 2) and receive (Article II, section 3) ambassadors. Because the acts of sending an ambassador to a country and receiving its ambassador imply recognition of the legitimacy of the foreign government involved in the exchange, presidents have successfully claimed the general authority to decide which foreign governments will be recognized by the United States. Also, because presidents decide which nations will be recognized, it follows that they have the power to terminate relations with another nation.

This interpretation of presidential power was not universally accepted at the beginning of the Republic. Madison, writing as Helvidius, argued that the duty to receive ambassadors did not give the president the power to rule on the legitimacy of foreign governments.[77] In *The Federalist Papers,* Hamilton did not acknowledge the connection between the ceremonial power to receive ambassadors and the recognition of nations, and he may have considered recognition a power shared with the Senate. Hamilton described the power to receive ambassadors as "more a matter of dignity than of authority. It is a circumstance which will be without consequence in the administration of the government."[78]

The first use of the president's power of recognition occurred in 1793 when Washington agreed to receive Edmond Genêt, the ambassador of the new French Republic. Because most of the members of Congress who were inclined to resist the growth of executive power into areas not specifically granted in the Constitution were also supporters of the new republican regime in France, this expansion of the president's power to receive ambassadors was not questioned.[79] All subsequent presidents have assumed the right to make recognition decisions.

Washington's decision to accept Genêt's credentials soon began to cause the president problems. Genêt attempted to exploit the American people's sympathy for revolutionary France by privately enlisting their support against his country's enemies, Great Britain and Spain. His activities undercut Washington's Proclamation of Neutrality and threatened to draw the United States into the European hostilities. Washington, therefore, demanded that the French government recall Genêt. The French ordered their ambassador to return home but retaliated by demanding that Washington recall the U.S. minister to France, Gouverneur Morris, on the grounds that he had supported plots to restore the French monarchy.[80] Washington thus established that the president could expel a foreign representative whose conduct was judged unacceptable.

A president also can recognize the rights or interests of national or political groups that do not hold political power. In 1978 Jimmy Carter announced a qualified recognition of the in-

At a White House ceremony on the South Lawn on September 13, 1993, President Bill Clinton witnesses the historic signing of the peace treaty between Israel and the Palestine Liberation Organization.

terests of the Palestinians living in Israeli occupied territories by saying that any Middle East peace settlement must recognize "the legitimate rights of the Palestinian people" and "enable the Palestinians to participate in the determination of their own future."[81] Following the agreement of mutual recognition between Israel and the Palestine Liberation Organization (PLO) in 1993, President Clinton and Congress moved to accept the PLO as the legitimate representative of the Palestinians by removing restrictions on, for example, its ability to establish offices in the United States.

Presidents may choose not to exercise the recognition power unilaterally. In 1836 Andrew Jackson realized that the act of recognizing the Republic of Texas could have the effect of a declaration of war against Mexico, which regarded Texas as a Mexican territory. Although Jackson did not repudiate his authority to recognize Texas or any other nation, he announced his willingness to allow Congress to decide if Texas should be recognized: "It will always be considered consistent with the spirit of the Constitution, and most safe, that it [the recognition power] should be exercised when probably leading to war, with a previous understanding with that body by whom war can alone be declared, and by whom all the provisions for sustaining its perils must be furnished."[82]

Congress has powers that it could use to influence recognition decisions. For example, it could implicitly recognize a nation by appropriating funds for the necessary diplomatic positions. On the other hand, it could eliminate such funding to force the president to withdraw recognition. Only rarely has Congress used its powers to influence presidential decisions. The resolution authorizing President McKinley to expel Spain from Cuba contained an explicit recognition of Cuba's independence as a nation.[83] In 1995 both houses of Congress considered bills that recognized the government in exile as the legitimate government of Tibet, which is occupied by the People's Republic of China, and recommended the appointment of a special envoy with the "personal rank" of ambassador. Clinton vetoed the final measure in 1996. Otherwise, Congress has no direct role in the recognition process beyond the Senate's approval of the president's nominee for the ambassadorship, which it can refuse to grant. As with treaties, Congress can pass nonbinding resolutions concerning particular questions of recognition. After France was conquered by the Nazis in World War II, for example, the Congress passed resolutions supporting the Roosevelt administration's agreement with other nations in the Western Hemisphere not to allow the transfer of the sovereignty of any European colony in the Americas to another European power.

RECOGNITION AS A POLICY STATEMENT

A decision to recognize or not to recognize a nation can be a major policy statement that expresses the attitudes and intentions of the United States toward an ideology, toward the character or behavior of a nation's government, and sometimes toward an entire region. Such policy statements can have profound consequences.

For example, in 1913 President Wilson refused to recognize the Mexican regime of Victoriano Huerta on the grounds that it was immoral and did not represent the will of its people.[84] Since Wilson made this decision, the ideology and morality of a foreign regime have become accepted factors in determining whether a government should be recognized. Successive presidents refused to recognize the revolutionary Communist regimes in Russia from 1917 to 1933, and China from 1949 to

U.S. LEGAL RELATIONSHIP WITH TAIWAN

The repercussions for U.S. relations with Taiwan from President Carter's recognition of the People's Republic of China (PRC) illustrated the effect a recognition decision can have on U.S. laws and relations with other nations. Successive presidents had refused to recognize the PRC since it was established in 1949. Instead, the United States recognized the Republic of China, the nationalist Chinese government that had fled to Taiwan after its defeat by the Communist Chinese armies. Growing cooperation and friendship between the United States and the PRC in the 1970s, however, made the establishment of diplomatic relations with Beijing a matter of practical importance. In December 1978, the Carter administration announced that it intended to recognize the PRC as the "sole legal government of China" on January 1, 1979.

This recognition could be accomplished only by withdrawing U.S. recognition of the Republic of China as China's legal government. Since many laws and agreements involving commercial, cultural, and security relations with other countries depend on a nation's diplomatic status, the legal framework of the U.S. relationship with Taiwan had to be rebuilt. Without new legislation establishing a special relationship with the Republic of China, the United States could not deal with Taiwan as another nation.

Consequently, Congress passed the Taiwan Relations Act in March 1979. The act was intended to ensure that normal relations would continue between Taiwan and the United States, even though the United States no longer recognized the Republic of China regime that governed the island. The legislation established the American Institute in Taiwan through which the United States would conduct relations with Taiwan. The institute was created as a private, nonprofit corporation that was authorized to enter into, execute, and enforce agreements and other transactions with Taiwan and perform consular functions for U.S. citizens. The act also authorized U.S. government employees, especially Foreign Service officers, to take temporary leaves of absence from their posts in order to work for the institute. While in Taiwan, they would not be considered U.S. government employees, but they would retain their seniority, pensions, and other benefits when they returned to work for the government. Thus, the Taiwan Relations Act created a nonprofit corporation that could do virtually anything done by an embassy.

Besides creating the American Institute in Taiwan, the act recognized the validity of Taiwan domestic law, contracts entered into under Taiwan law, and all U.S. agreements and treaties with Taiwan except the 1954 mutual defense treaty, which was terminated at the end of 1979. It also authorized the president to grant Taiwan's unofficial representatives in the United States diplomatic privileges and treat Taiwan as a nation with an immigration quota equal to that of the PRC. These and dozens of other provisions of the Taiwan Relations Act addressed the legal difficulties created by the withdrawal of U.S. recognition of the Republic of China. In 1995, under pressure from Congress, the State Department issued a visa to the president of Taiwan. The visa allowed him to travel in the United States but only as a private citizen. This was the first such visa issued since 1979. To protest this affront to its claim of sovereignty, the PRC recalled its ambassador, broke off arms control talks with the United States, and test-fired missiles within eighty-five miles of Taiwan.

1979. President Clinton's 1995 decision to recognize the Communist regime in Vietnam was controversial, and the House passed a measure barring the use of funds for an embassy in Hanoi. Clinton continued the policy, begun in 1959, of withholding recognition from Cuba. A president also may deny recognition of a government's legal authority over a part or all of the territory claimed by that government. For example, the United States refused to recognize the legitimacy of the Soviet Union's annexation of Latvia, Lithuania, and Estonia in 1940.

Theodore Roosevelt's recognition of Panama in 1903 following its U.S.-backed revolt from Colombia paved the way to a treaty that gave the United States the right to dig the Panama Canal. It also led to a treaty in 1921 between Colombia and the United States that provided for the United States to pay Colombia $25 million in reparations for the loss of its Panamanian territory.

Truman's recognition of Israel on May 15, 1948, was a very controversial change of policy. A few minutes after Jews in Palestine proclaimed the state of Israel, Truman rejected the advice of his State Department and made the United States the first nation to recognize the new country. The recognition indicated U.S. support for Israel and effectively blocked a United Nations plan to keep Palestine under a temporary trusteeship.[85]

The president's power to sever diplomatic relations has been used as an ultimate sanction to protest another country's behavior. Severance of relations is usually reserved for situations when the differences between the two nations are so great that there is no hope they may be resolved through normal diplomatic procedures. It is customary to break diplomatic ties with a country before declaring war against it, but many events short of war have prompted presidents to terminate relations. In 1979 President Carter ended diplomatic relations with Iran in response to the hostage crisis.

Even when relations have been broken with a particular country, communication usually continues. "Interests sections" may be established in each country's capital in the embassies of a third country. Foreign nations that lack diplomatic relations with the United States also have used their representatives to the United Nations to communicate with U.S. officials. Nevertheless, such measures do not accommodate communication between the two countries with the same efficiency as normal diplomatic exchanges. A less drastic method employed by presidents to communicate their displeasure with another nation is the temporary recalling of the U.S. ambassador in that country for "consultations." President Carter used this tactic after the Soviet invasion of Afghanistan, when he recalled Thomas J. Watson, the U.S. ambassador in Moscow, to Washington.

THE UNITED NATIONS AND U.S. FOREIGN POLICY

U.S. membership in the United Nations, and particularly in the UN Security Council, has raised some important problems concerning control of the nation's foreign policy. First, the UN Participation Act of 1945 decided which branch would direct

U.S. troops are interviewed by the press about their mission, begun by President George Bush in 1992, to stabilize the government in Somalia. The task proved too difficult and President Bill Clinton ordered the withdrawal of all troops in 1994.

U.S. participation in this international body. The U.S. representative is subject to Senate approval but otherwise serves "at the pleasure of the president." Thus the president retains control over day-to-day participation in UN affairs.

A second, more general problem is how participation in the UN affects and should affect national policy and commitments. Unlike other multilateral organizations, such as NATO, which have had specific aims, the UN charter covers peace and security around the globe, without regard to specific U.S. interests. Moreover, in the current era, the Security Council has been released from the stalemate imposed by the cold war between the United States and the Soviet Union. The UN's potential commitments in its humanitarian and peacekeeping roles have multiplied. In addition, in 1993 the UN Secretary General, Boutros Boutros-Ghali, proposed an expansion of UN resources so that it could move beyond passively monitoring peace accords and act with force in settling disputes. Therefore, the United States' potential obligations to provide aid, including armed forces, to the Security Council have also grown.

The general problems of how far and in what ways the United States should stay involved in international affairs have been changing. In the 1990s the United States began losing its cold war status as an essential military and economic ally, and its influence even in NATO began to wane. As fewer conflicts within and between countries have the clear global implications that once supported U.S. intervention and leadership, presidents will have to find different ways to maintain U.S. influence in international affairs. Moreover, on the domestic side, presidential leadership of broad U.S. international engagement during the cold war was facilitated by the fact that the conflict between the Communist and the free world united the nation's security interests with its moral purpose as a defender of democracy and liberty. In the post–cold war era, moral purpose and national interest will not coincide so clearly, and the probability of conflict over foreign policy will increase.

Consequently, a policy of international engagement through multilateral efforts will be complicated by conflicts between evident national interest and alliance policy. However, a president who limited the nation's participation in UN missions to matters directly affecting U.S. interests would frustrate the UN's global mission. On the other hand, broad participation in that general mission would risk the loss of control over foreign policy. The Clinton administration, from the start, struggled with this dilemma. President Clinton began his administration with an enthusiastic endorsement of expanded use of UN missions and of broad U.S. participation in them as a means of remaining engaged in international affairs in the post–cold war era. However, this general policy and specific missions suffered extensive congressional criticism and attempts to limit the president's authority to involve U.S. forces in UN missions.

Much of the criticism stemmed from the operation in Somalia to relieve the famine caused, in part, by a civil war. U.S. participation began under President Bush in 1992 with broad congressional and popular support. The operation was transformed in June 1993 after twenty-three UN peacekeepers were killed by one of the warring factions. U.S. warplanes and ground troops were then involved in a retaliatory strike. The UN, with President Clinton's approval, shifted to a more ambitious mission of subduing the armed factions and rebuilding the nation's political order. In October, eighteen U.S. Rangers were killed and eighty were wounded in an assault on one faction's headquarters. The new policy raised the possibility of extensive U.S. involvement and sacrifice in a country remote from U.S. interests.

This event also raised anew some general concerns about the effects of the UN on national policy and sovereignty. In the absence of the global threat of Communist expansion, the U.S. interests served by the expenditure of lives and tax dollars in remote parts of the world had become more difficult to define and explain. Unlike the Gulf War, in which the United States had a clear interest in protecting the flow of oil from the Persian Gulf states as well as a moral concern for the integrity of national borders, the United States had only indirect interests, beyond moral and humanitarian concerns, in Somalia. Therefore, the debates over the Somalia operation revolved around the degree to which the United States should involve itself in policing the world in the absence of national or global security interests. These concerns were reinforced by Clinton's commitments to other UN efforts in Haiti and Bosnia.

In 1993 Congress began drafting legislation that would have required withdrawal from Somalia. Eventually, Congress and the Clinton administration agreed on a deadline on use of funds for the operation. In addition, the legislation required that U.S. forces remain under U.S. operational command.[86] In response to these and other criticisms and proposals, the Clinton administration announced more restrictive policy guidelines for U.S. participation in UN missions and especially those that may involve combat. Specifically, such missions must involve national interests or "a real threat to international peace and security." The statement also proposed cutting the proportion of the UN peacekeeping budget for which the United States was responsible from 30 percent to 25 percent. The Clinton administration defended UN missions as effective and as an important part "of our national security policy" and argued that congressional proposals would be an imprudent and unconstitutional intrusion on the president's foreign policy and war powers.[87]

Nonetheless, in 1995 and 1996 Congress enacted bills that cut U.S. payments to the UN for peacekeeping missions for fiscal years 1996–1997. In addition, these bills restricted the authority of the president to place U.S. troops under the operational control of a foreign commander. Congressional efforts to place permanent restrictions on U.S. participation in UN peacekeeping operations died in the Senate.

MUTUAL SECURITY AGREEMENTS

Mutual security agreements raise issues similar to those raised by the UN charter. Following World War II, the U.S. policy of containing Communist expansion, backed by its military strength, led presidents to offer security commitments and alliance partnerships to countries concerned with their ability to defend themselves. In doing so presidents improved relations with many countries, extended U.S. global influence, and strengthened U.S. defenses. Entering an alliance has often been a contentious political issue because commitments to fight beside alliance partners under attack can draw a nation into a war.

Since World War II presidents often have entered alliances without formal action by Congress. On August 14, 1941, for example, President Roosevelt signed the Atlantic Charter, which laid the groundwork for an Anglo-American alliance once the United States had entered World War II. Roosevelt then signed the Declaration of United Nations on January 1, 1942, which pledged the United States and, by the end of the war, forty-five other nations to support the allied war effort and not make a separate peace with the enemy nations.[88] After the war, Presidents Truman and Eisenhower used executive agreements to expand NATO into a unified defense organization with a standing military structure. Although no formal alliance treaty exists between the United States and Israel, presidents since Truman have maintained the extensive U.S. commitment to Israeli security.

An important presidential responsibility is maintaining alliance cohesion for the sake of present and future needs. An alliance that is not unified will likely be ineffective and will contribute little to U.S. security. Alliance disputes may affect the probability and effectiveness of future cooperation. Therefore, the president is compelled to consider the effect of U.S. foreign and military policy on the cohesion of its alliances and on public opinion within the allied countries.

Even when a foreign policy action does not directly involve an alliance, a president must weigh its effect on allied countries. The concerns of Presidents Johnson and Nixon that other U.S. allies would see abandonment of South Vietnam as evidence of U.S. inability to fulfill its commitments contributed to the escalation of U.S. involvement and their refusal to withdraw American troops from Vietnam without attempting to ensure South Vietnamese security.

In every alliance the United States has joined since World War II, it has been the dominant military power, and this power was necessary to deter and resist the power of, in particular, the Soviet Union and the People's Republic of China. This status gave the president a considerable bargaining advantage over alliance partners. With the disintegration of the Soviet Union and the Warsaw Pact, U.S. influence in alliances has become weaker. Lacking an overriding interest in mutual defense, there have been more potential conflicts between national or regional interests and alliance cohesion.

More than ever, presidents will have to lobby allied leaders to support their initiatives just as they lobby members of Congress to support their legislative proposals. Insofar as a president can persuade allies to support U.S. foreign policies, alliances can still enhance the president's domestic power. However, failure to gain cooperation can be costly, and alliance responsibilities can harm rather than enhance presidential prestige and influence. Congress is less likely to challenge the foreign policy of a president who is perceived as an effective international leader. However, a president who has not been able either to deliver ally support for U.S. policies or to ensure that alliance policy serves U.S. interests will face greater congressional criticism and intrusion.

Power to Appoint Diplomatic Personnel

Article II, section 2, of the Constitution states that the president shall, "nominate, and by and with the Advice and Consent of the Senate, shall appoint Ambassadors, other public Ministers and Consuls." The power to appoint, and the power to remove, those individuals who would be communicating directly with foreign leaders is crucial in establishing the president as the sole organ of foreign communications. The success of a president's foreign policy program depends greatly on the personalities and abilities of the people who fill important diplomatic and advisory posts.

The difficulty of selecting ambassadors and high-level foreign policy officials has increased dramatically for presidents since the early years of the Republic. George Washington and his immediate successors had only a few posts to fill and were able to appoint men whom they knew personally. As the U.S. government grew and expanded its involvement in world affairs, presidents were increasingly forced to delegate responsibility to their advisers for selecting candidates for less important posts.

Although the president appoints officials, Congress has the constitutional power to create offices. Nevertheless, presidents have used executive orders to create government bodies that required them to make appointments. Kennedy established the Peace Corps in this manner, and Gerald Ford unilaterally created the Committee on Foreign Intelligence and the Intelligence Oversight Board.[89]

Senate confirmation of presidential nominees for diplomatic posts often has been routine, but there have been exceptions. For example, Eisenhower's appointment of Charles E. Bohlen as ambassador to the Soviet Union barely survived the confirmation vote, even though Eisenhower's party controlled the Senate.[90] In 1985 and 1986, Sen. Jesse Helms (R-N.C.) held up the confirmations of a number of nominees, including Richard Burt for ambassador to West Germany, to protest either the nominee or some related matter of policy. In 1990 Helms's opposition led to the withdrawal or rejection of two of President Bush's nominees. In 1989 President Bush faced wider congressional criticism for a slate of nominees that included many who were notable not for diplomatic experience but for having made large contributions to his campaign and the Republican Party.[91] In 1994 a GOP filibuster led by Sen. Robert C. Smith (R-Colo.) prevented President Clinton from appointing Sam Brown as U.S. ambassador to the Conference on Security and Cooperation in Europe.

POLITICAL APPOINTEES VERSUS THE FOREIGN SERVICE

A question that complicates the diplomatic appointments of contemporary presidents is how to divide ambassadorships and important State Department posts between political appointees and the State Department's own career foreign service officers. Senior foreign service officers can offer a president valuable diplomatic experience that can prevent foreign policy mistakes. Also, because they serve successive presidents, they can provide continuity in foreign policy between administrations.[92] Yet presidents often have been reluctant either to waste a source of political rewards or to entrust important ambassadorships and assistant secretary posts to foreign service officers, who are less likely than political appointees to be responsive to the president's directives. Because their careers do not depend on the president but on a self-run promotion system, and because many regard foreign policy as an endeavor that should not be subject to partisan politics, foreign service officers have a greater reputation for resisting presidential policies than do political appointees.

Political appointees can more easily be found who share the president's philosophy, are politically minded, and appreciate how their job fits into the president's comprehensive domestic and foreign policy goals. If an administration favors political appointees, however, the president may gain a measure of diplomatic control at the expense of greater diplomatic expertise at U.S. embassies, the goodwill of the State Department, and the morale of the Foreign Service. An option open to the president is to balance appointments by reserving many ambassadorships for foreign service officers while nominating political appointees to posts crucial to the execution of the president's particular foreign policy goals.[93]

SYMBOLISM AND POLITICS OF APPOINTMENTS

Presidents must take into account more than a candidate's abilities and qualifications when making an appointment. They must consider how the appointment will be perceived. The symbolism of presidential appointments can profoundly affect foreign policy, especially at the beginning of the president's term. Appointments provide the president with an opportunity to indicate to Congress, the American people, and foreign governments the foreign policy goals the new administration intends to pursue. Reagan's appointment of conservative Jeane Kirkpatrick as ambassador to the United Nations reaffirmed his intention to make anti-Communism a foreign policy theme of his administration, just as Carter had underscored his commitment to human rights and third world issues with his appointment of Andrew Young to the same post. In 1986 President Reagan indicated his administration's attitude toward South Africa's racial policies by appointing an African American diplomat, Edward Perkins, as U.S. ambassador to that country.

Diplomatic appointments also give presidents certain political opportunities. They may choose to broaden their base of support within their party by appointing to ambassadorships people who originally opposed their nomination. Presidents also can try to build up trust and cohesion within their new administration by giving department and agency heads broad discretion in selecting subordinates.

Presidents sometimes have used appointments to create an

Ronald Reagan's appointment of conservative Jeane Kirkpatrick, left, as ambassador to the United Nations reaffirmed his intention to make anti-Communism a foreign policy theme, just as President Jimmy Carter had underscored his commitment to human rights with the appointment of Andrew Young, right, to the same post.

atmosphere of bipartisanship. Kennedy believed that by appointing Republicans to senior foreign policy posts in his administration he could disarm potential congressional resistance to his policies. Treasury secretary Douglas Dillon, defense secretary Robert McNamara, national security adviser McGeorge Bundy, director of the Central Intelligence Agency (CIA) Allen Dulles, and disarmament chief John J. McCloy were all Republicans, as were John A. McCone and William C. Poster, who eventually replaced Dulles and McCloy, respectively. Other presidents have made appointments with bipartisanship in mind, though no modern president has appointed as many members of the opposing party to such important foreign policy jobs as Kennedy did.[94]

PRESIDENTIAL ENVOYS

Many presidents have used personal emissaries not subject to Senate confirmation to conduct foreign policy. Often such presidential representatives have been employed to carry out specific diplomatic missions. The use of personal envoys allows presidents to inject their own ideas and proposals directly into negotiations without having to go through the State Department or other official channels in which policy could be opposed or compromised. The presence of a personal envoy sent by the president sometimes can stimulate stalemated negotiations by lending greater prestige to the talks and demonstrating the president's interest in them. Presidential representatives also can provide the president with an additional source of information that is relatively free of institutional biases.

The use of presidential envoys is not specifically allowed or disallowed in the Constitution. Envoys fall somewhere between ambassadors, who are permanent representatives requiring Senate approval, and treaty negotiators, who are selected for more specific missions. As presidents gained full control over the latter, they have become free to appoint special envoys for all sorts of diplomatic missions. Personal envoys of presidents function outside of permanent government positions, do not have their duties enumerated in the Constitution, serve only as long as the president asks them, and often receive no compensation.[95]

Washington did not believe that the Constitution prohibited him from using private representatives to conduct diplomacy. In 1791 Gouverneur Morris, who held no public office at the time, carried out important negotiations with the British at Washington's direction. By using a personal representative Washington could explore the possibilities for a treaty without having to involve Congress or deal with the formalities of official treaty negotiations.

The first major controversy over the appointment of diplomats not confirmed by the Senate occurred during Madison's presidency. In 1813 Madison sent a delegation to the negotiations in Europe that produced the Treaty of Ghent, which ended the War of 1812 with Great Britain. The president had dispatched the negotiators without submitting their names for confirmation by the Senate, which was in recess. Madison's critics argued that he could not appoint ministers to offices that had not been authorized by Congress and that the appointments were illegal because the Senate did not have the chance to approve them. The president responded by claiming that it was unnecessary for Congress to create a diplomatic post if the president determined that a need had arisen for one, and that the president was free to fill any vacancy that happened to occur during a congressional recess.[96] Since Madison's time, however, Congress has enacted legislation that gives it control over the creation of new ambassadorships.

Many presidents have used special envoys or personal representatives instead of ambassadors for specific diplomatic tasks. In 1831 Jackson sent unconfirmed representatives to Turkey to conclude a trade and navigation treaty, and in 1893 Cleveland gave his own emissary, J. H. Blount, "paramount authority" over the Senate-approved resident minister in Honolulu at talks on the annexation of Hawaii.[97] Two twentieth-century presidents, Wilson and Franklin Roosevelt, established the use of personal representatives as a common diplomatic device of the president. Wilson made extensive use of his close friend Col. Edward House to perform diplomatic missions in Europe before and during World War I. Wilson also named House to the U.S. delegation to the peace talks in Paris at the end of the war and sent former secretary of state Elihu Root to Russia in 1917 during World War I to urge the Russian government not to make a separate peace with Germany. Franklin Roosevelt employed Harry Hopkins, a personal aide, as a negotiator in Great Britain and the Soviet Union during World War II. Among other accomplishments, Hopkins helped negotiate and direct the lend-lease agreements under which the United States supplied war materiel to Great Britain and other countries at war with Germany. Early in his first administration, President Reagan used Phillip C. Habib as a special envoy to the Middle East to negotiate settlements of the conflict in Lebanon between Israel, Syria, and the Palestine Liberation Organization.

A curious use of the special envoy was former president Jimmy Carter in his diplomatic missions during the Clinton administration to North Korea, concerning its nuclear weapons program, and to Haiti, concerning the return of its democratically elected government. In both cases, Carter had presented himself publicly as a willing mediator who could resolve the diplomatic deadlocks. In accepting Carter as an envoy, President Clinton seemed unwilling to take responsibility for missing a chance to resolve the disputes and avoid armed conflict, even though Carter had clearly demonstrated a willingness to publicize his criticisms of the president's policies and to negotiate settlements that contradicted those policies. It is also possible that Carter provided a means for Clinton to back away from earlier commitments.

Summit Meetings

Although presidents have always been responsible for the conduct of diplomacy, presidents themselves rarely met with foreign leaders until World War II. The difficulties of travel, the isolated location of the United States, and the traditional belief that presidents should stay close to their administrative and legislative responsibilities in the capital inhibited presidents from acting as their own negotiators. Today, if a president were to avoid meetings with leaders of foreign governments, the press and public alike would criticize the chief of state as being uninterested in international affairs, or even isolationist. Presidents have found that a highly publicized summit tends to raise their public approval rate. *(See "Presidential Popularity," p. 224, in Chapter 15.)*

Winston Churchill is credited with coining the term *summit.* In 1953 he used the word when he called for a conference between the leaders of the Soviet Union and the Western powers. The media picked up the term and used it to describe the Geneva conference between Soviet and Western leaders in 1955. After Geneva, meetings between national leaders increasingly were referred to as *summits.*[98] The term is used to distinguish meetings that are actually attended by the recognized leaders of states from meetings between foreign ministers or lower-level officials.

PRESIDENTIAL DIPLOMACY

Although presidential travel to foreign nations was impractical before the twentieth century, presidents throughout U.S. history have conducted personal diplomacy with foreign leaders through direct exchanges of letters. Personal letters between leaders could accomplish some of the goals of the modern summit meeting. They gave a president the chance to send and receive information, ideas, and proposals without using intermediaries and to establish trust through personal rapport with a foreign leader. Presidential letters were especially important to early presidents who did not have the benefit of an extensive diplomatic network with representatives in many foreign capitals. President Jefferson, whose years as secretary of state under Washington had provided him with extensive diplomatic experience, had an ongoing correspondence with Czar Alexander I of Russia during the Napoleonic wars.[99]

Early presidents also met with foreign emissaries who traveled to the United States. The first high-ranking official of a foreign government to visit the United States was a personal emissary of the ruler of Tunis who came to America in 1805 to discuss the passage of U.S. commercial ships in the Mediterranean. The marquis de Lafayette, who had led colonial troops against the British in the American Revolution, was the first official guest to be invited to the United States by the U.S. government. President Monroe received him in 1824 after he arrived on an American ship that Congress had dispatched to France.[100] During the rest of the nineteenth century, visits to the United States by foreign dignitaries were common. Visits by the heads of state of other nations, however, remained rare. Up to the end of World War I, presidents received only about thirty heads of state.[101]

Presidential Travel

During the eighteenth and nineteenth centuries a precedent developed against presidents traveling outside the country during their term. Theodore Roosevelt became the first president to break this precedent when he visited Panama in 1906 to inspect the canal under construction. Presidential travel abroad remained uncommon until World War II, when Franklin Roosevelt made a series of trips to Canada and overseas to confer with allied leaders about military strategy and the composition of the postwar world. Truman followed Roosevelt's example by attending the Potsdam Conference in 1945 with Joseph Stalin and Churchill (and, later, Clement R. Attlee).

President Eisenhower, however, institutionalized the role of the president as international diplomat with his foreign trips,

FDR made a series of trips overseas to confer with Allied leaders about military strategy and postwar issues. In February 1945, an ailing Roosevelt meets with Winston Churchill and Joseph Stalin at Yalta in the Crimea.

including his 22,000-mile "Quest for Peace" tour of eleven nations in 1959. He believed that establishing goodwill toward the United States in foreign nations was an important presidential function. Accordingly, many of his stops in foreign countries were devoted to ceremony and speech making. After Eisenhower, presidential visits abroad were an accepted part of the president's job and were highly coveted by the leaders of foreign nations.

Eisenhower's successors continued his practice of frequent overseas visits. President Kennedy met with Premier Nikita Khrushchev in Vienna in 1961 and toured Europe in 1963, at which time he delivered his famous "Ich bin ein Berliner" speech in Berlin. President Johnson initially declined taking trips abroad because he had no vice president, but after the election in 1964 he made several overseas trips, including visits to Australia, the Philippines, Vietnam, and Latin America. Nixon embarked on a major European tour in 1969 only a month after he became president. In 1972 he signed the SALT I treaty in Moscow and became the first U.S. president to visit the People's Republic of China, which was in itself a momentous change in policy. President Gerald R. Ford also went to the Soviet Union, meeting Leonid Brezhnev in Vladivostok in 1974. All the more recent presidents have met frequently with foreign leaders overseas, including meetings with Soviet and Russian leaders in Vienna (1979), Geneva (1985), Reykjavik (1986), Malta (1989), and Moscow (1991 and 1995).

In 1972 Richard Nixon became the first U.S. president to visit the People's Republic of China. Here he is greeted by Chinese Communist party chairman Mao Tse-tung.

Constitutional Questions

The Constitution clearly establishes the president's right to conduct diplomatic negotiations personally. A more controversial constitutional question about summit meetings was whether a president traveling abroad could properly fulfill the obligations of office.

No one questioned the constitutionality of Theodore Roosevelt's short trip to Panama in 1906 or of William Howard Taft's meeting with the Mexican president just across the border in 1909. When President Wilson announced in late 1918 that he planned to go to Europe to attend the peace conference in Versailles, however, numerous critics objected that Wilson's safety could not be ensured and that he would lose touch with the everyday business of running the country during the lengthy Atlantic crossing.[102]

Resolutions were introduced in both houses of Congress that would have declared the presidency vacant and required the vice president to assume the president's powers if Wilson left the country. Former president Taft defended Wilson's plans, however. He argued in an article in the *Washington Post* on December 5, 1918, that the president could properly fulfill the duties of his office while overseas. He wrote: "There is no constitutional inhibition, express or implied, to prevent the president's going abroad to discharge a function clearly given him by the Constitution. That instrument says that he shall make treaties. . . . It is a curious error to assume that the president himself may not attend a conference to which he can send a delegate."[103] The congressional resolutions against Wilson's trip never got out of committee. Wilson's critics continued to attack the wisdom of his policy, but he went to Europe without a major confrontation over the constitutionality of his trip.[104]

The jet airplane and modern means of communication have eliminated any such concerns. Modern presidents travel with large staffs and stay in constant touch with administration and congressional officials in Washington, D.C. Although presidents taking a lengthy foreign trip will spend less time on domestic affairs while out of the country, they have the means to carry out virtually any presidential function from any place in the world.

SUPERPOWER SUMMITRY

The most famous summit meetings have been those during and after World War II, and especially those between U.S. presidents and the leaders of the Soviet Union. *(See Table 3-2.)* Every president from Roosevelt to Bush met with a Soviet leader at least once. In some cases, such as the summits in Moscow in 1972, Vienna in 1979, Washington in 1987, and Moscow in 1991, the meeting was a culmination of the arms control process at which an agreement was signed. In other cases, like the 1985 Geneva Summit, the 1986 Reykjavik Summit, and the 1989 Malta Summit, the leaders hoped to stimulate arms control negotiations. The media and public attention that accompanied these meetings between the leaders of the superpowers was inspired by hopes that they could produce an agreement or understand-

TABLE 3-2 U.S.-Soviet Summit Meetings, 1945–1991

Date	*Location*	*Leaders*	*Topic*
July–August 1945	Potsdam	President Harry S. Truman, Soviet leader Josef Stalin, British prime ministers Winston Churchill and Clement R. Attlee	Partition and control of Germany
July 1955	Geneva	President Dwight D. Eisenhower, Soviet leader Nikolai A. Bulganin, British prime minister Anthony Eden, French premier Edgar Faure	Reunification of Germany, disarmament, European security
September 1959	Camp David, Md.	President Dwight D. Eisenhower, Soviet leader Nikita S. Khrushchev	Berlin problem
May 1960	Paris	President Dwight D. Eisenhower, Soviet leader Nikita S. Khrushchev, French president Charles de Gaulle, British prime minister Harold Macmillan	U-2 incident
June 1961	Vienna	President John F. Kennedy, Soviet leader Nikita S. Khrushchev	Berlin problem
June 1967	Glassboro, N.J.	President Lyndon B. Johnson, Soviet leader Aleksei N. Kosygin	Middle East
May 1972	Moscow	President Richard M. Nixon, Soviet leader Leonid I. Brezhnev	SALT I, anti-ballistic missile limitations
June 1973	Washington, D.C.	President Richard M. Nixon, Soviet leader Leonid I. Brezhnev	Détente
June–July 1974	Moscow and Yalta	President Richard M. Nixon, Soviet leader Leonid I. Brezhnev	Arms control
November 1974	Vladivostok	President Gerald R. Ford, Soviet leader Leonid I. Brezhnev	Arms control
June 1979	Vienna	President Jimmy Carter, Soviet leader Leonid I. Brezhnev	SALT II
November 1985	Geneva	President Ronald Reagan, Soviet leader Mikhail Gorbachev	Arms control, U.S.-Soviet relations
October 1986	Reykjavik	President Ronald Reagan, Soviet leader Mikhail Gorbachev	Arms control
December 1987	Washington, D.C.	President Ronald Reagan, Soviet leader Mikhail Gorbachev	Intermediate Nuclear Force (INF) Treaty, Afghanistan
May 1988	Moscow	President Ronald Reagan, Soviet leader Mikhail Gorbachev	Arms control, human rights
December 1988	New York	President Ronald Reagan, Soviet leader Mikhail Gorbachev	U.S.-Soviet relations
December 1989	Malta	President George Bush, Soviet leader Mikhail Gorbachev	Arms control, Eastern Europe
May–June 1990	Washington, D.C.	President George Bush, Soviet leader Mikhail Gorbachev	Arms control
September 1990	Helsinki	President George Bush, Soviet leader Mikhail Gorbachev	Middle East crisis
July 1991	Moscow	President George Bush, Soviet leader Mikhail Gorbachev	Arms control and Soviet economic and political future

ing that would reduce the chances of nuclear war and lead to a more cooperative coexistence.

The era of nuclear confrontation between the two superpowers, and their allies, made summits an unavoidable, if not always effective, mode of presidential diplomacy. As former president Nixon argued, developing mutual understandings between the superpowers of their respective interests and patterns of behavior was the primary purpose of a superpower summit. These understandings, which he called "rules of engagement," could not resolve differences between the two countries or end their adversarial relationship; rather, they would reduce the possibility that a crisis would lead to war.[105]

The 1989 Malta summit meeting between President Bush and Soviet leader Mikhail Gorbachev marked a dramatic change in the nature of U.S.-Soviet relations and summit meetings. Gorbachev had allowed, and even encouraged, the independence movements in Soviet bloc countries, and at this meeting the two leaders acknowledged the end of the cold war. Later summit meetings focused on advancing arms reduction treaties and normalizing relations. The 1994 meeting between President Clinton and Russian president Boris Yeltsin was like an ordinary bilateral meeting between the president and the head of an allied country.

EVALUATING SUMMIT DIPLOMACY

Although summit diplomacy in the current era has been used less and for less critical matters than during the cold war, presidents still will be tempted to use summits at the very least to focus attention on their world status and foreign policy leadership. As in the past, there are numerous disadvantages and risks of summit meetings compared with conventional diplomacy.

The media attention given summits may distort their substance or lead to popular disillusionment by raising public expectations of improved relations with another country beyond what is warranted. The spontaneity possible at summits may yield agreements that have not received proper scrutiny or that commit the president to a policy without allowing for the option to modify it after further review. Summits may also distract presidents from their other responsibilities. Because the success of a summit depends on the performance of the president, relations with other countries can be harmed if the president is inexperienced or inadequately prepared. Frequent summits may harm the morale of professional diplomats if they perceive that their talents are being ignored in favor of direct presidential negotiations.[106]

Despite these dangers, a summit meeting has the potential to be a valuable diplomatic tool, if the president and the president's advisers understand the risks and pursue prudent, realizable goals.

Diplomatic historian Elmer Plischke cites a number of advantages of summit meetings that can make them valuable additions to conventional diplomacy. By becoming personally acquainted, a president and a foreign leader may reduce tensions, clarify national interests, and establish mutual respect. Summits also allow presidents to focus national attention on specific issues and to improve public understanding of them. In addition, diplomatic impasses may be overcome at summits by shifts in policy that only the top leaders are empowered to make. Of course, successful summits can enhance the image of the president and of the United States.[107] However, after his 1995 meeting with Russian president Boris Yeltsin, President Clinton was criticized by members of Congress for failing to secure changes in Russian policies that opposed the inclusion of eastern European nations in NATO and favored aiding Iran's nuclear development program.

The advantages and disadvantages of summit meetings are products of the same diplomatic conditions. For example, the potential for a summit to produce a quick breakthrough in stalemated negotiations and the risk that a summit can lead to a hasty, poorly conceived agreement both arise from the president's authority to modify bargaining positions and conclude an agreement on the spot. A summit, therefore, is a special diplomatic environment with opportunities and pitfalls. This environment can be used profitably by skilled, prepared presidents with a firm conception of what they are trying to accomplish and what they are willing to risk; or it can produce a diplomatic disaster if presidents are inexperienced, unprepared, or overly influenced by domestic political pressure and media attention.

Manager of the Foreign Policy Bureaucracy

The president's management of the foreign policy bureaucracy is less visible than the president's performance as a diplomat, but it is as important to the success of U.S. foreign policy. The "foreign policy bureaucracy" loosely refers to all executive branch personnel whose primary duties pertain to foreign affairs. Almost every department and agency has employees engaged in activities that affect foreign relations, but the State Department, the Defense Department, the Joint Chiefs of Staff, the intelligence agencies, the National Security Council, and the National Security Council staff dominate the foreign policy-making process. Other agencies, such as the Arms Control and Disarmament Agency (ACDA), the U.S. Information Agency (USIA), and the Agency for International Development (AID), deal with specific aspects of foreign policy.

In 1995 the Republican 104th Congress considered a significant restructuring of the foreign policy bureaucracy. One proposal was to fold the ACDA, USIA, and AID into a "super" State Department under the unified control of the secretary of state. When that bill did not advance, Congress passed a bill that would have abolished one or more of these agencies. President Clinton vetoed the bill in 1996 with Congress failing to override the veto.[108]

Although the president is responsible for the conduct of foreign affairs, modern foreign policy cannot be made by one person. Policy results from a process of consultation and compromise among the president and the president's top foreign affairs advisers. Moreover, the lower levels of the administration perform functions that are essential to the success of foreign policy. Presidents Kennedy and Nixon preferred to base their decisions on the advice of a small, close-knit group of advisers, but even presidents such as these need an administrative apparatus to collect information and intelligence, research policy problems, plan for long-range contingencies, represent the United States abroad, and implement presidential directives. A president can attend to only a few of the most pressing matters at one time, and so others must oversee the vast array of daily functions.

It is not only the complexity of this administrative and policy network that makes foreign policy management a massive and continuous presidential headache. Different departments, such as State and Defense, have competing concerns and different modes of operation. As well, more permanent civil servants, such as foreign service officers, tend to resist the president's policy initiatives and to ignore his momentary political needs. The welter of management problems leads each new president to reorganize the policy and administrative structure in the often vain hope of achieving tight control and coherence.

EXPANSION OF THE FOREIGN POLICY BUREAUCRACY

During Washington's administration, the foreign policy bureaucracy consisted of the secretary of state, a small group of clerks, and a few carefully chosen ambassadors to key European states. Although U.S. contacts with other nations expanded during the next hundred years, the foreign policy apparatus of the executive branch remained small. In addition, the low salaries of diplomats and the practice of appointing wealthy campaign contributors and party functionaries to diplomatic posts hindered the development of a professional diplomatic corps.[109] At the end of the nineteenth century the United States began to upgrade the quality and status of its diplomats to correspond with the nation's growing involvement in international trade and politics. Presidents increasingly relied on the State Department for information, analysis, and staff support.

With the coming of World War II and the emergence of the United States as a superpower with broad international responsibilities, presidents needed greater bureaucratic resources to support their foreign policy decision making. The United States was an international leader and the protector of the free world. In the postwar years, it entered into numerous alliances and mutual defense agreements, distributed massive amounts of military and economic aid, hosted the United Nations, and actively participated in most international organizations. The nation's and the president's foreign policy responsibilities proliferated. An expanded bureaucracy was required to administer the growing number of U.S. programs and activities overseas and to provide the president with the information and analysis necessary for constructing effective foreign policies.

As a result, not only did the State Department increase in size, but other departments and agencies were created or expanded to provide military, economic, scientific, and intelligence-gathering expertise that the State Department was not equipped to provide. The State Department thus lost its preeminent role and became one player among many in the field of foreign policy. Nevertheless, it has remained the president's primary instrument of negotiation with foreign countries and an important source of information, analysis, and advice on foreign relations.

In 1949 Congress created the Defense Department by unifying the individual armed services. Although the United States rapidly demobilized after World War II, the North Korean invasion of South Korea in 1950 and the growing Soviet threat convinced U.S. leaders that, for the first time in American history, the country needed a large standing military.[110] The size of the unified military budget and the number of people in the armed services ensured that the civilian and military leaders of the new Defense Department would have considerable bureaucratic clout.

Moreover, the most important foreign policy issues had become intertwined with defense and national security issues. Containing Soviet expansionism, forming and maintaining anti-Communist alliances, and remaining ahead in the nuclear arms race were among the most important international goals of the United States. Defense officials consequently became important players in foreign policy decision making. *(See "Department of Defense," p. 193, in Chapter 4.)*

The National Security Act of 1947 created the Central Intelligence Agency (CIA) to gather and analyze information from every corner of the globe and to provide the president with a covert operations capability. The CIA along with other intelligence-gathering agencies constitute the intelligence community. The community's members include the Defense Intelligence Agency, the intelligence offices of the individual armed services, the State Department's Bureau of Intelligence and Research, the Federal Bureau of Investigation, and the massive National Security Agency, which intercepts and analyzes communication signals. The director of central intelligence was given preeminent status in the intelligence community, with primary responsibility for coordinating intelligence activities and advising the president on intelligence matters. *(See box, Oversight of Intelligence Activities, p. 155.)*

The CIA inherited many of the functions and personnel of the Office of Strategic Services, which had carried out covert operations during World War II. The Japanese sneak attack on Pearl Harbor had impressed the U.S. leadership with the need to have sources of information beyond those provided by U.S. embassies. In addition, Moscow's aggressive use of its intelligence apparatus and the difficulty of extracting information from the closed Soviet society by conventional means seemed to demand a similar intelligence effort by the United States.

NATIONAL SECURITY COUNCIL

Along with creating the CIA, the 1947 National Security Act established the National Security Council (NSC). The NSC is a

OVERSIGHT OF INTELLIGENCE ACTIVITIES

Because of the requirements of secrecy, the National Security Act of 1947 gave the president nearly exclusive responsibility for oversight of covert intelligence activities. Before the mid-1970s, Congress rarely showed an interest in covert operations, and the president and the intelligence agencies did not willingly offer information about them. Congress routinely approved billions of dollars in funds for the intelligence community with only a few members of its appropriations committees knowing how the money was being spent.

In the mid-1970s, however, numerous revelations of unethical, unauthorized, and illegal activities by the CIA and other intelligence units were uncovered by congressional investigations. Among other abuses, the CIA had helped overthrow the democratically elected government of Socialist president Salvador Allende in Chile. In addition, the FBI and other intelligence agencies were found to have conducted illegal surveillance operations and engaged in other activities that violated the civil liberties of individual Americans.

In response, Congress passed a series of laws that created House and Senate intelligence committees and strengthened congressional oversight of intelligence activities. The Hughes-Ryan Amendment to the 1974 foreign aid bill and the 1980 Intelligence Oversight Act required that the president report all U.S. covert intelligence operations to designated congressional committees in a timely fashion. To complement Congress's actions, President Gerald Ford established the Intelligence Oversight Board, a White House three-member panel to oversee intelligence activities and report any questions of illegality to the president through the attorney general. The failure of these measures to control the misuse of covert operations was clear in the Iran-contra affair.

In 1994 Aldrich H. Ames, a high-level CIA officer, was arrested on charges of selling classified information to the Soviet Union and, later, Russia. Over the course of nine years, Ames had passed on thousands of documents, compromising more than one hundred intelligence operations. This information probably led to the assassinations of a number of double agents working for the United States. The Ames case exposed the inadequacies in the CIA's internal security procedures. Over the years the CIA had promoted Ames even though his evident drinking problem had regularly interfered with his work. His lavish lifestyle, funded by the sales of state secrets, was either not noticed or not investigated. In addition, the CIA did not conduct an internal investigation after a number of double agents were assassinated. When the CIA director, R. James Woolsey, failed to dismiss any of the negligent officers, Congress intervened.

Citing the CIA's "gross negligence," Congress in 1994 began investigating CIA operations with an eye toward restructuring the intelligence bureaucracy, and it began considering legislation to remedy the more immediate problems. The White House argued that intelligence matters ought to be handled within the executive branch, and President Bill Clinton issued a directive that incorporated many of the reform proposals being considered by Congress. Nonetheless, in September 1994, Congress passed, and Clinton signed into law, a bill (PL 103–359) overhauling the process of internal investigations. It gave government investigators greater access to the financial and travel records of CIA personnel and turned investigations of all security breaches over to the FBI.

This law also established the blue-ribbon Commission on the Roles and Capability of the United States Intelligence Community, which was charged with reviewing the missions, procedures, and structure of the intelligence services. Its 1996 report proposed no major reforms.

presidential advisory body consisting of the president, vice president, and secretaries of defense and state. In addition to these statutory members, the director of central intelligence and the chairman of the Joint Chiefs of Staff are designated as statutory advisers to the NSC.

The National Security Act stated that the NSC's responsibility was "to advise the President with respect to the integration of domestic, foreign, and military policies relating to the national security so as to enable the military services and other departments and agencies of the government to cooperate more effectively in matters involving the national security." Ideally, the NSC would be a smaller and more focused forum than the cabinet, drawing together the president's top defense, diplomatic, economic, and intelligence advisers to consider broad issues of national security.

However, Congress created the NSC not exactly to assist presidents but to force upon them a more collegial decision-making process.[111] In Congress's eyes, decisions in national security matters had become excessively centralized in the White House. Presidents could not be obliged, however, to convene meetings of the NSC or to regard the meetings that were held as decision-making forums. Some have used the NSC as a forum for generating and discussing policy options. Many presidents have chosen to de-emphasize NSC meetings, preferring to rely on small groups of trusted advisers to make decisions, using the council only to approve them. Others have used the NSC as the formal centerpiece of an extensive web of committees and interagency groups considering foreign policy. The NSC occasionally has been used as a decision-making forum during crises, including the North Korean invasion of South Korea in 1950, the Soviet invasion of Czechoslovakia in 1968, and the *Mayaguez* incident in 1975. At various times the NSC also has been used for less dramatic functions such as policy planning and budget review.[112]

In addition to creating the National Security Council, the National Security Act established an NSC staff to serve the president and the NSC members. The staff has become a major player in foreign policy making. The most important presidential adaptation of the NSC apparatus has been the use of the NSC staff, through which, and contrary to Congress's intention, presidents have been able to centralize decision making and implementation in the White House.

Crucial to the staff's influence has been the evolution of the assistant to the president for national security affairs, a post established by Eisenhower and commonly referred to as the "national security adviser." Originally, the national security adviser was to facilitate foreign policy making by coordinating NSC meetings and overseeing the staff that served the NSC. However, under Eisenhower's successors the national security adviser was often as or more influential than cabinet members. As a presidential aide, the national security adviser is not confirmed by the Senate and is not burdened by responsibilities for managing an agency or department. The power of the national security adviser within the administration depends entirely on the president.

Because the national security adviser and most NSC staffers owe their position and status to the president, they have few competing loyalties. Some NSC staffers who are drawn from other departments and agencies may retain institutional loyalty to their parent organization, but during their tenure on the NSC staff they are responsible only to the president. In addition, the NSC staff is virtually beyond the reach of the legislative branch since it has no statutory responsibility to report to Congress. Presidents therefore can use the national security adviser and the NSC staff as a research and advisory arm independent of other agencies and departments. National security advisers such as Henry Kissinger and Zbigniew Brzezinski have served as dominant policy advisers and as negotiators in the most important matters, using the NSC staff to support this work. In the extraordinarily broad and intensive diplomatic efforts of the Nixon administration, Secretary of State William P. Rogers was eclipsed by Kissinger and had no important advisory role.

The accomplishments of Kissinger and Brzezinski built a strong case for the virtues of centralizing foreign policy operations in the White House. However, investigations of the Iran-contra affair in 1986 and 1987 revealed that the NSC staff could be used to implement not only covert operations but also operations that circumvented the law and were, otherwise, of questionable wisdom. This scandal led to calls for a more collegial decision-making structure, whether oriented around the secretary of state or a reorganized NSC.[113]

President Bush made the position of national security adviser stronger than it had been in the Reagan administration. His national security adviser, Brent Scowcroft, played a major role during the Gulf War, and he was generally a voice for more conservative positions on relations with the Soviet Union and Middle East peace prospects. However, foreign policy making during the Bush administration was dominated by Secretary of State James A. Baker III, with whom President Bush had extensive professional and personal ties. Baker shaped policy in the various arms reductions talks with the Soviet Union and was directly involved in all phases of the transition to post–cold war relations with the Soviet Union. His close relationship with Soviet foreign minister Eduard Shevardnadze facilitated agreements on arms control, dismantling the Berlin Wall, and reunification of East and West Germany. He also assembled and helped to maintain the international coalition opposing Iraq's invasion of Kuwait.[114]

In 1989 the dismantling of the Berlin Wall and the reunification of West and East Germany exemplified collapsing Communist control of Eastern Europe and heralded the end of the cold war.

Similarly, Clinton's national security adviser, Anthony Lake, was far less prominent in foreign policy decisions and activity than Secretary of State Warren Christopher.

FOREIGN POLICY-MAKING PROCESS

Although the National Security Council and the executive departments and agencies that deal with foreign affairs are established by law, it is up to the president to create and maintain a responsive and effective foreign policy-making process. Because numerous executive branch units are working on foreign policy, their work must be coordinated to minimize the duplication of their efforts, to minimize institutional conflict, and to ensure that each unit has access to the president. Therefore, as managers of the foreign policy bureaucracy, presidents must establish procedures that determine how policy options and information should be presented to them, who should have access to intelligence, how the efforts of various departments and agencies should be coordinated, how the agendas of foreign policy meetings should be set, who should regularly attend these meetings, who should chair these meetings, and who should be responsible for overseeing policy implementation.

Managing the Foreign Policy-making Process

Since World War II, the central problem concerning the process of producing foreign policy has been deciding who should manage that process. The president must ultimately be the referee of the inevitable bureaucratic struggle within the administration for influence, resources, and prestige, but the responsibility of determining the substance of policy leaves the president little time for matters of management. Therefore, some executive branch unit must serve as the facilitator of the foreign policy-making system. The main rivals for this responsibility have been the State Department under the secretary of state and the NSC staff under the national security adviser. From the Kennedy to the Ford administration, presidents tended to look to their national security advisers to manage their foreign policy-making system. Critics of this trend have maintained that the oversight, coordination, and leadership of the foreign policy-making system properly belong to the State Department.[115] They argue that the State Department was intended to be preeminent in foreign affairs, and that its foreign policy expertise, accountability to Congress, and network of embassies in foreign capitals make it the best choice to run the president's foreign policy-making system. The presidents from Ford to Clinton have tried various combinations, emphasizing initially the importance of the secretary of state.

The State Department, however, has institutional interests like any department that inhibit its ability to be an arbiter between competing departments and agencies. Just as the military mission of the Defense Department or the intelligence mission of the CIA disposes those units to approach foreign affairs from a unique perspective, State's diplomatic mission disposes it to prefer its own foreign policy strategies. Even if State Department officials were able to mediate disputes between other bureaucratic units impartially, those units would never regard State as a neutral department.

The perpetual problem in foreign policy management is finding structures and procedures that can accomplish a number of demanding and often incompatible goals: oversight and coordination of the many and varied departments and agencies administering foreign policy; full information and debate in policy formulation; institutional experience and memory; responsiveness to circumstances; and responsiveness to presidential policy decisions and changes of course. Presidents tend to begin their terms with elaborate structures for collegial deliberation and complementary systems of administrative coordination. Over time, presidents often find these structures to be indecisive, unresponsive, rife with departmental infighting and parochialism, and generally lacking in coherence. Presidents tend to turn to a small group or a single adviser, whether the secretary of state, the national security adviser, or the chief of staff.

When decisions are made by a small group, however, wise and successful policy depends on the skills, knowledge, and integrity of the president and his few advisers. Nixon's successes depended on his intense focus on foreign affairs and on the extraordinary qualities and Herculean diplomatic efforts of Henry Kissinger. The same organization but with third-rate national security advisers and a less focused president helped produce the Iran-contra fiasco.

Even when a more intimate circle of advisers functions well in making policy, a gulf may develop between the policy makers centered in the White House and the administrative arms in the departments and agencies. Then departments and agencies can pursue their distinct and permanent interests by frustrating implementation and by seeking support in the congressional committees with which they are associated.

Foreign Policy Decision-making Systems

Harry Truman's well-founded suspicion that Congress had created the NSC to check his authority and his strained relationships with his first two secretaries of defense, James Forrestal and Louis Johnson, initially led him to ignore the NSC. He attended only twelve of the first fifty-seven NSC meetings.[116] During the Korean War the NSC developed a more important policy-making role. Truman attended most meetings and he used the group to forge presidential foreign policies. Nevertheless, Truman still emphasized its advisory nature and frequently consulted its individual members or ad hoc groups rather than relying on the entire NSC for policy advice.

Dwight Eisenhower's foreign policy decision-making system reflected his military background. He presided over highly structured weekly meetings of the NSC and created NSC subcommittees to consider specific policy issues. He also established the "Planning Board," a staff body charged with foreign policy planning, and the "Operations Coordinating Board," an interagency committee charged with overseeing implementation of executive decisions.[117] Although Eisenhower's system had the advantages of ensuring that all parties would participate in decision making and that the president would not become bogged down in details better left to subordinates, it often has been criticized as being too rigid and formalistic. Meetings were sometimes held because they were routinely scheduled rather than because they were necessary. Eisenhower also insisted that his top advisers reach a consensus on issues. His demand for unanimity led to policy papers that were too general and vague to provide direction to lower-level personnel charged with implementing policy.

John Kennedy replaced Eisenhower's formal committees with a less structured collegial decision-making system. Kennedy's reliance on the advice of departmental experts who had advocated the disastrous U.S.-supported Bay of Pigs invasion of

Cuba by Cuban nationals in April 1961 had convinced him that he needed independent sources of national security advice in the White House. As a result, the NSC staff under the direction of the national security adviser, McGeorge Bundy, not only facilitated the decision-making process, it generated and evaluated policy options for the president. Formal NSC meetings were de-emphasized. During the Cuban Missile Crisis Kennedy relied on an assembly of his closest advisers known as the "Executive Committee." Unlike the NSC, membership in this ad hoc group depended not on statutory requirements, but on the trust and confidence of the president.[118]

Lyndon Johnson made few changes in either Kennedy's national security decision-making system or the personnel who ran it. The number of advisers involved in ad hoc policy-making sessions declined, however, especially when the Vietnam War was the topic. Johnson developed the practice of discussing the war at Tuesday lunch meetings attended by five or six close advisers. The president used NSC meetings primarily to announce and discuss decisions that had already been made. In 1966 Johnson created formal interdepartmental groups to develop and coordinate policy proposals that would flow up to the NSC, but the work of these groups was largely confined to peripheral issues unrelated to the war.[119]

Richard Nixon tried to create a foreign policy-making system that incorporated the best aspects of the Eisenhower and Kennedy-Johnson systems. He created a formal interagency committee structure similar to Eisenhower's to ensure that all departments and agencies would be heard. Unlike Eisenhower's committee system, however, Nixon's was intended to produce several policy options for the president's consideration rather than an interdepartmental consensus. The committees also were designed to make less important decisions, thereby allowing the president and his top advisers to concentrate on the most important issues. Nixon established a strong NSC staff that enabled the president and his national security adviser, Henry Kissinger, to monitor the activities of the committees.

Although most scholars consider Nixon's NSC system to be a well-conceived blueprint for national security decision making, that blueprint was not always followed. His strong interest in national security affairs and the delicate nature of the negotiations to end the Vietnam War and improve relations with the Soviet Union and the People's Republic of China led to a centralization of decision making in the hands of Nixon, Kissinger, and the NSC staff that excluded other top advisers and departments. Late in Nixon's presidency, the Watergate scandal dominated the president's time, causing him to rely even more on Henry Kissinger and a small circle of trusted advisers.[120]

Nixon's successor, Gerald Ford, was able to restore balance to the foreign policy decision-making system. Ford used the NSC staff and national security adviser Brent Scowcroft primarily as coordinators of national security decision making rather than as policy advisers. The president still relied heavily on Kissinger, who had become secretary of state in 1973, but the views of other departments and agencies were integrated more often into national security decisions than they had been during the latter years of Nixon's presidency.

Henry Kissinger served as Nixon's principal foreign policy spokesperson and negotiator. In 1973 he became secretary of state.

Jimmy Carter simplified the NSC committee system and established a decentralized advisory system of "shops" that would filter proposals up to his office. To ensure that he would not be insulated from a diversity of opinion, he had department and agency leaders report directly to him rather than through the chief of staff or the national security adviser. Initially, his principal adviser was the secretary of state, Cyrus Vance, who took the lead in general policy formulation. Over time Carter leaned more heavily on the NSC staff and his national security adviser, Zbigniew Brzezinski. Carter's system suffered from a lack of coherence and from frequent disagreements between Brzezinski and Vance, who resigned his post in May 1980 after opposing the failed U.S. attempt to rescue American hostages in Iran.

Ronald Reagan initially announced his intention to give dominant roles in national security policy making to his secretaries of defense and state. Nevertheless, Reagan rejected a plan submitted by Secretary of State Alexander Haig Jr. to designate the State Department as the manager of foreign policy. The president took a whole year before setting up a formal foreign policy-making system that stressed cabinet predominance.[121] From the beginning of the administration, however, the NSC staff was given a smaller role than under Presidents Nixon, Ford, and Carter. Reagan's first national security adviser, Richard Allen, did not even have direct access to the president. Although subsequent national security advisers William Clark, Robert McFarlane, John Poindexter, Frank Carlucci, and Colin Powell did have daily access to the president, none dominated the policy-making process as Henry Kissinger and Zbigniew Brzezinski.

The most distinguishing feature of the Reagan foreign policy-making system was the president's hands-off administration. Ronald Reagan allowed his cabinet secretaries and other subordinates vast discretion in responding to the day-to-day issues affecting their area of foreign policy. He limited his participation primarily to the articulation of broad themes. Some observers during Reagan's presidency praised this style of leadership as an example of how presidents should delegate responsibilities to save their energies for the most important decisions and avoid being overwhelmed by the details of foreign policy. However, the Iran-contra scandal, which was uncovered in 1986, demonstrated the dangers of Reagan's detachment from administration. NSC staff member Lt. Col. Oliver North, along with national security adviser Vice Adm. John Poindexter and other administration officials, arranged secret arms sales to Iran, a terrorist state, as barter for U.S. hostages. This contradicted the administration's stated policy and the advice of senior administration officials. In addition, North and Poindexter used the profits from the arms sales to circumvent Congress's prohibition of U.S. government military aid to the contras in Nicaragua. The Tower Commission, appointed by the president to review his NSC system in the wake of the affair, commented on Reagan's management style in its 1987 report:

> The President's management style is to put the principal responsibility for policy review and implementation on the shoulders of his advisers. Nevertheless, with such a complex, high-risk operation and so much at stake, the President should have ensured that the NSC system did not fail him. He did not force his policy to undergo the most critical review of which the NSC participants and the process were capable. Never did he insist upon accountability and performance review. Had the President chosen to drive the NSC system, the outcome could well have been different.

The scandal forced the resignation and indictment of several White House officials and led the president to project a more visible role in foreign policy making.

President Bush was directly involved in the foreign policy deliberation and decisions of his administration. He worked very closely with his secretary of state, James A Baker III, on major initiatives. Otherwise, two subgroups within the NSC, the Principals Committee and the Deputies Committee, handled most of the policy decisions and implementation. Bush called few formal NSC meetings, and was criticized for the informality of his approach to national security decision making.[122]

THE BUREAUCRACY AS A SOURCE OF PRESIDENTIAL POWER

The foreign policy bureaucracy can be a great asset to presidents in their struggle with Congress for control of foreign policy and their efforts to provide effective foreign policy leadership. The bureaucracy's most obvious benefit is that it enables presidents and their closest advisers to concentrate on the decisions and initiatives they deem most important while the bureaucracy deals with the many small foreign policy matters the executive branch must handle daily. President Nixon and his national security adviser, Kissinger, spent the vast majority of their foreign policy time during Nixon's first term on three problems: ending the Vietnam War, opening up China, and improving relations with the Soviet Union. Most other foreign policy matters were left to the bureaucracy. Although Nixon and Kissinger certainly neglected other important matters as a result, the extraordinary attention they were able to give these principal issues made progress possible.

The bureaucracy's capacity to supply the president with information and advice is another asset. No institution, including Congress, has information sources on foreign affairs that can compare with the array of channels supplying the president with current intelligence and professional opinions. Most modern presidents have been briefed daily on foreign policy issues by their secretary of state, national security adviser, or other top aides. These officials receive information and proposals that have been distilled and funneled up to them from their respective departments. This information and advice make it possible for a president to address foreign policy issues intelligently without being an expert.

Besides the information available from normal advisory and diplomatic resources, the nation's vast intelligence-gathering capabilities are at the president's service. The director of central intelligence coordinates intelligence activities and relays important intelligence directly to the president. Many foreign policy decisions, particularly those that involve the use of force, cannot be made without access to intelligence information. For example, President Kennedy decided to blockade Cuba during the Cuban Missile Crisis after he and his advisers had carefully analyzed all intelligence information.[123] The president's access to sensitive intelligence has provided a rationale for presidential autonomy in foreign policy. Congress's recognition of this presidential advantage contributed to its frequent willingness to accept presidential leadership in foreign affairs after World War II. Since the Vietnam War, however, Congress has more actively sought access to intelligence and has been more reluctant to accept presidential evaluations of international issues.

The professional foreign policy bureaucracy also provides continuity in the policies of successive administrations. When a new president takes office the general policy directives that provide guidance to the bureaucracy change and the political appointees who head the various departments and agencies are new, but the bureaucrats continue to collect intelligence, write reports, make recommendations, and maintain diplomatic relations with other nations. Useful initiatives begun by the previous president have a chance to find a place in the new administration, and foreign governments that are frustrated by the frequent changes in presidential leadership can take comfort in the continuing presence of career officials with whom they have dealt in the past.

THE BUREAUCRACY AS AN IMPEDIMENT TO PRESIDENTIAL POWER

Although presidents have formal authority over the foreign policy bureaucracy, it is too vast to command and does not always serve their purposes. Indeed, since the end of World War II, executive branch departments and agencies often have been a greater obstacle to presidential will in foreign affairs than has Congress. Executive branch obstruction occurs, in large part, because the goals and interests of the bureaucracy often have conflicted with those of the president. Political scientist Richard Neustadt has explained why presidents have found it difficult to control the bureaucracy:

> Everything somehow involves the President. But operating agencies owe their existence least of all to one another—and only in some part to him. Each has a separate statutory base; each has its statutes to administer; each deals with a different set of subcommittees at the Capitol. Each has its own peculiar set of clients, friends, and enemies outside the formal government. Each has a different set of specialized careerists inside its own bailiwick. Our Constitution gives the President the 'take-care' clause and the appointive power. Our statutes give him central budgeting and a degree of personnel control. All agency administrators are responsible to him. But they also are responsible to Congress, to their clients, to their staffs, and to themselves. In short, they have five masters.[124]

The president cannot, therefore, expect his commands to move bureaucrats, well down the line, exactly as he desires. As Neustadt said, the president must "convince such men that what the White House wants of them is what they ought to do for their sake and on their authority."[125]

The sheer number of people involved in even minor matters makes this task daunting. Moreover, foreign service officers, military personnel, members of the intelligence community, and other career executive branch employees involved in foreign affairs are neither dependent on the president for their jobs nor necessarily in agreement with presidential goals and policies. Career bureaucrats naturally are concerned with the long-term welfare of their particular department or agency. They usually will fight against policies that could diminish their responsibilities or resources, and they often will resent decisions that show an obvious disregard for their institutional point of view. In addition, foreign policy bureaucrats may regard presidents and their political appointees as temporary invaders of the foreign policy realm whose political goals harm the permanent interests of the United States.

Members of the foreign policy bureaucracy have several means by which they can resist presidential will in foreign affairs. They can delay or undermine the execution of presidential directives, provide the president only with information and options that do not conflict with their interpretation of an issue, leak details of a controversial or covert policy to Congress or the media, publicly oppose a policy, or resign in protest. The president may have the constitutional power to order an agency to carry out a particular task, but if that agency drags its feet or otherwise undermines implementation of the order, the president's power can be diluted or even neutralized.

The most important means available to presidents of controlling the bureaucracy and communicating to it their foreign policy vision is the power to appoint the officials who will head the departments and agencies. These officials serve as department managers as well as members of the inner circle of presidential advisers. In choosing these appointees the president must reconcile, on the one hand, the need to find qualified persons with administrative talent who will be respected by the departments they head, with, on the other hand, the president's desire to maintain control over the bureaucracy. Even the most loyal presidential appointee, however, usually will develop a competing loyalty to the department or agency, which may at times conflict with the goals of the president.[126]

NOTES

1. *U.S. v. Curtiss-Wright Export Corp.*, 299 U.S. 304 (1936).
2. Quoted in Theodore C. Sorensen, *Kennedy* (New York: Bantam, 1966), 573.
3. Louis Henkin, *Foreign Affairs and the Constitution* (New York: Norton, 1972), 76–77.
4. James Madison, "No. 51," and Alexander Hamilton, "No. 72" in *The Federalist Papers*, Alexander Hamilton, James Madison, and John Jay (New York: New American Library, 1961), 321–322, 437.
5. Edward S. Corwin, *The President: Office and Powers, 1787–1984*, 5th ed. (New York: New York University Press, 1984), 201.
6. Quoted in Clinton Rossiter, *The American Presidency*, 2d ed. (New York: Harcourt Brace and World, 1960), 15.
7. John Marshall, quoted in *U.S. v. Curtiss-Wright Export Corp.*, 299 U.S. 304 (1936).
8. Alexis de Tocqueville, *Democracy in America*, ed. J. P. Mayer (Garden City, N.Y.: Anchor, 1969), 126.
9. *Chicago & S. Airlines v. Waterman SS. Corp.*, 333 U.S. 103 (1948), 111.
10. Quoted in Christopher H. Pyle and Richard M. Pious, eds., *The President, Congress, and the Constitution* (New York: Free Press, 1984), 238.
11. Arthur M. Schlesinger Jr., *The Imperial Presidency* (Boston: Houghton Mifflin, 1973), 102–103. See also Henkin, *Foreign Affairs and the Constitution*, 27 n. 19.
12. *The Letters of Pacificus and Helvidius* (Delmar, N.Y.: Scholars' Facsimiles & Reprints, 1976), 5–15.
13. Ibid., ix.
14. Ibid., 57.
15. Quoted in Arthur Bernon Tourtellot, *The Presidents on the Presidency* (Garden City, N.Y.: Doubleday, 1964), 272.
16. Pyle and Pious, eds., *The President, Congress, and the Constitution*, 204–205.
17. James M. Lindsay, *Congress and the Politics of U.S. Foreign Policy* (Baltimore: Johns Hopkins University Press, 1994), 15.
18. Richard Harmond, "Theodore Roosevelt and the Making of the Modern Presidency," in *Power and the Presidency*, ed. Philip C. Dolce and George H. Skau (New York: Scribner's, 1976), 72–73.
19. Theodore Roosevelt to H. C. Lodge, January 28, 1909, quoted in Schlesinger, *The Imperial Presidency*, 89.
20. Richard M. Pious, *The American Presidency: the Politics of Power from FDR to Carter* (New York: Basic Books, 1979), 53.
21. For a discussion of the Tonkin Gulf incident, see Leslie H. Gelb and Richard K. Betts, *The Irony of Vietnam: The System Worked* (Washington, D.C.: Brookings, 1979), 100–104; and Eugene Windchy, *Tonkin Gulf* (New York: Doubleday, 1971).
22. Gelb and Betts, *The Irony of Vietnam*, 103–104.
23. Robert E. DiClerico, *The American President*, 4th ed. (Englewood Cliffs, N.J.: Prentice-Hall, 1995), 58.
24. Lindsay, *Congress and the Politics of U.S. Foreign Policy*, 89–90.
25. Corwin, *The President*, 222.
26. Lindsay, *Congress and the Politics of U.S. Foreign Policy*, 86.
27. Quoted in Tourtellot, *The Presidents on the Presidency*, 274.
28. Quoted in Pious, *The American Presidency*, 334.
29. Quoted in Corwin, *The President*, 207–208.
30. Henkin, *Foreign Affairs and the Constitution*, 301.
31. Lindsay, *Congress and the Politics of U.S. Foreign Policy*, 120–121, 126.
32. Quoted in Tourtellot, *The Presidents on the Presidency*, 298.
33. Schlesinger, *The Imperial Presidency*, 27.

34. Quoted in Schlesinger, 128.

35. Cecil V. Crabb Jr. and Pat M. Holt, *Invitation to Struggle: Congress, the President and Foreign Policy,* 4th ed. (Washington, D.C.: CQ Press, 1992), 15.

36. Jack N. Rakove, "Solving a Constitutional Puzzle: The Treaty Making Clause as a Case Study," *Perspectives in American History,* New Series, I:1984, 233–281.

37. John Jay, "No. 64," in *The Federalist Papers,* 392–393.

38. George H. Haynes, *The Senate of the United States* (Boston: Houghton Mifflin, 1938), 575.

39. Alexander Hamilton, "No. 75," in *The Federalist Papers,* 452–453.

40. Buel W. Patch, "Treaties and Domestic Law," *Editorial Research Reports,* March 28, 1952, 241.

41. Abraham D. Sofaer, *War, Foreign Affairs and Constitutional Power: The Origins* (Cambridge, Mass.: Ballinger, 1976), 95–96.

42. Corwin, *The President,* 240.

43. Louis Fisher, *Constitutional Conflicts Between Congress and the President,* 3d rev. ed. (Lawrence: University Press of Kansas, 1991), 219.

44. Lindsay, *Congress and the Politics of U.S. Foreign Policy,* 95.

45. Joseph E. Kallenbach, *The American Chief Executive: The Presidency and the Governorship* (New York: Harper and Row, 1966), 505.

46. Pious, *The American Presidency,* 336.

47. F. M. Brewer, "Advice and Consent of the Senate," *Editorial Research Reports,* June 1, 1943, 352.

48. Louis W. Koenig, *The Chief Executive,* 5th ed. (New York: Harcourt Brace and World, 1986), 206.

49. DiClerico, *The American President,* 46.

50. Lindsay, *Congress and the Politics of U.S. Foreign Policy,* 65, 123.

51. Theodor Meron, "The Treaty Power: The International Legal Effect of Changes in Obligations Initiated by the Congress," in *The Tethered Presidency: Congressional Restraints on Executive Power,* ed. Thomas M. Franck (New York: New York University Press, 1981), 116–117.

52. Henkin, *Foreign Affairs and the Constitution,* 134.

53. Lindsay, *Congress and the Politics of U.S. Foreign Policy,* 80.

54. Meron, in "The Treaty Power," 105–108.

55. Kallenbach, *The American Chief Executive,* 507.

56. Corwin, *The President,* 205–206.

57. Pious, *The American Presidency,* 338–340.

58. Quoted in Henkin, *Foreign Affairs and the Constitution,* 377.

59. Henkin, *Foreign Affairs and the Constitution,* 168–170.

60. Pyle and Pious, eds., *The President, Congress, and the Constitution,* 258–265.

61. Loch K. Johnson, *The Making of International Agreements: Congress Confronts the Executive* (New York: New York University Press, 1984), 12.

62. Lindsay, *Congress and the Politics of U.S. Foreign Policy,* 83.

63. Ibid., 82.

64. Quoted in Henkin, *Foreign Affairs and the Constitution,* 177–178.

65. Ibid., 178–179.

66. Schlesinger, *The Imperial Presidency,* 86.

67. Ibid., 86–87.

68. Lawrence Margolis, *Executive Agreements and Presidential Power in Foreign Policy* (New York: Praeger, 1986), 7–9.

69. Ibid., 9.

70. Tourtellot, *The Presidents on the Presidency,* 277.

71. DiClerico, *The American President,* 47–48.

72. Francis O. Wilcox, *Congress, the Executive, and Foreign Policy* (New York: Harper and Row, 1972), 160–161.

73. DiClerico, *The American President,* 48.

74. Corwin, *The President,* 245–246.

75. Johnson, *The Making of International Agreements,* 86–87.

76. *Congressional Quarterly Almanac, 1972* (Washington, D.C.: Congressional Quarterly, 1972), 619.

77. Corwin, *The President,* 212.

78. Alexander Hamilton, "No. 69," in *The Federalist Papers,* 420.

79. Schlesinger, *The Imperial Presidency,* 14.

80. Kallenbach, *The American Chief Executive,* 493.

81. Seth P. Tillman, *The United States in the Middle East* (Bloomington: Indiana University Press, 1982), 221.

82. Quoted in Tourtellot, *The Presidents on the Presidency,* 291.

83. Corwin, *The President,* 216–219, 486 n. 105.

84. Crabb and Holt, *Invitation to Struggle,* 18.

85. Pious, *The American Presidency,* 335.

86. Louis Fisher, *Presidential War Power* (Lawrence: University Press of Kansas, 1995), 153–154.

87. U.S. Department of State Dispatch, vol. 5, #20 (May 16, 1994); Fisher, *Presidential War Power,* 160–161.

88. R. Gordon Hoxie, *Command Decision and the Presidency* (New York: Reader's Digest Press, 1977), 40.

89. Arthur S. Miller, *Presidential Power in a Nutshell* (St. Paul, Minn.: West, 1977), 37.

90. Koenig, *The Chief Executive,* 206–207.

91. *Congressional Quarterly Almanac, 1989* (Washington, D.C.: Congressional Quarterly, 1990), 537–541.

92. Robert E. Hunter, *Presidential Control of Foreign Policy: Management or Mishap* (New York: Praeger, 1982), 79–80.

93. Ibid., 84.

94. Koenig, *The Chief Executive,* 217.

95. Henkin, *Foreign Affairs and the Constitution,* 46.

96. Corwin, *The President,* 235.

97. Ibid., 236.

98. Elmer Plischke, *Diplomat in Chief: The President at the Summit* (New York: Praeger, 1986), 13.

99. Kallenbach, *The American Chief Executive,* 498–499.

100. Plischke, *Diplomat in Chief,* 121.

101. Kallenbach, *The American Chief Executive,* 499.

102. Dorothy Buckton James, *The Contemporary Presidency,* 2d ed. (Indianapolis: Pegasus, 1974), 127–128.

103. Quoted in Plischke, *Diplomat in Chief,* 202.

104. Ibid., 200–202.

105. Richard Nixon, "Superpower Summitry," *Foreign Affairs* 64, no. 1 (fall 1985): 1.

106. Plischke, *Diplomat in Chief,* 460–473.

107. Ibid., 456–460.

108. *Congressional Quarterly Weekly Report,* May 20, 1995, 1437–1439; *Congressional Quarterly Weekly Report,* May 4, 1996, 1235.

109. Marcus Cunliffe, *American Presidents and the Presidency* (New York: American Heritage, 1972), 286.

110. Amos A. Jordan, William J. Taylor, and Lawrence J. Korb, *American National Security: Policy and Process,* 4th ed. (Baltimore: Johns Hopkins University Press, 1984), 167–168.

111. Pious, *The American Presidency,* 362.

112. John E. Endicott, "The National Security Council," in *American Defense Policy,* 5th ed., ed. John F. Reichart and Steven R. Sturm (Baltimore: Johns Hopkins University Press, 1982), 521–522.

113. See, for example, Carnes Lord, *The Presidency and the Management of National Security* (New York: Free Press, 1988), chap. 4.

114. Christopher Madison, "Scrambling Vicar," *National Journal,* April 20, 1991, 924–928.

115. For an outline of a state-centered foreign policy-making system, see I. M. Destler, *Presidents, Bureaucrats, and Foreign Policy* (Princeton, N.J.: Princeton University Press, 1974), 254–294.

116. Endicott, "The National Security Council," 522.

117. Zbigniew Brzezinski, "The NSC's Midlife Crisis," *Foreign Policy* 69 (winter, 1987–1988): 84–85.

118. Jordan, Taylor, and Korb, *American National Security,* 98.

119. Ibid., 91–92.

120. Charles W. Kegley Jr. and Eugene R. Wittkopf, *American Foreign Policy: Pattern and Process* (New York: St. Martin's Press, 1979), 258–259.

121. Brzezinski, "The NSC's Midlife Crisis," 90.

122. Jordan, Taylor, and Korb, *American National Security*, 100, 215–216.

123. Graham T. Allison, *Essence of Decision* (Boston: Little, Brown, 1971), 46–62.

124. Richard E. Neustadt, *Presidential Power and the Modern Presidents* (New York: Free Press, 1990), 34.

125. Ibid., 30.

126. Hunter, *Presidential Control of Foreign Policy*, 18.

SELECTED BIBLIOGRAPHY

Corwin, Edward S. *The President: Office and Powers, 1787–1984*. 5th ed. New York: New York University Press, 1984.

Crabb, Cecil V., and Pat M. Holt. *Invitation to Struggle: Congress, the President and Foreign Policy*. 4th ed. Washington, D.C.: CQ Press, 1992.

Destler, I. M. *Presidents, Bureaucrats, and Foreign Policy*. Princeton, N.J.: Princeton University Press, 1974.

Fisher, Louis. *Constitutional Conflicts Between Congress and the President*. 3d rev. ed. Lawrence: University Press of Kansas, 1991.

Henkin, Louis. *Foreign Affairs and the Constitution*. New York: Norton, 1975.

Hunter, Robert E. *Presidential Control of Foreign Policy: Management or Mishap*. New York: Praeger, 1982.

Johnson, Loch. *The Making of International Agreements: Congress Confronts the Executive*. New York: New York University Press, 1984.

Kallenbach, Joseph E. *The American Chief Executive: The Presidency and the Governorship*. New York: Harper and Row, 1966.

Koh, Harold Hongju. *The National Security Constitution: Sharing Power After the Iran-Contra Affair*. New Haven: Yale University Press, 1990.

Lindsay, James M. *Congress and the Politics of U.S. Foreign Policy*. Baltimore: Johns Hopkins University Press, 1994.

Margolis, Lawrence. *Executive Agreements and Presidential Power in Foreign Policy*. New York: Praeger, 1986.

Neustadt, Richard E. *Presidential Power and the Modern Presidents*. New York: Free Press, 1990.

Pious, Richard M. *The American Presidency: The Politics of Power from FDR to Carter*. New York: Basic Books, 1979.

Plischke, Elmer. *Diplomat in Chief: The President at the Summit*. New York: Praeger, 1986.

Pyle, Christopher H., and Richard M. Pious, eds. *The President, Congress, and the Constitution*. New York: Free Press, 1984.

Schlesinger, Arthur M., Jr. *The Imperial Presidency*. 2d ed. Boston: Houghton Mifflin, 1989.

Wilcox, Francis O. *Congress, the Executive, and Foreign Policy*. New York: Harper and Row, 1971.

CHAPTER 4

Commander in Chief

BY DANIEL C. DILLER AND STEPHEN H. WIRLS

THE FRAMERS of the Constitution distrusted both executive and military power and believed the potential for tyranny was great when the two were combined. Among the colonial grievances cited in the Declaration of Independence were the charges that the British monarch had "kept among us, in times of peace, Standing Armies without the Consent of our legislatures" and "affected to render the Military independent of and superior to the Civil Power." The document also denounced the quartering of troops in American homes, the impressment of American sailors for British warships, and the unjust war being waged against the colonies. The delegates to the Constitutional Convention were determined to restrain military power to prevent the new government from committing the types of offenses that they believed the British had perpetrated on the colonies. Their main instruments for accomplishing this constitutional goal were the checks and balances between separated powers. They therefore rejected a proposal to grant the president the authority to declare war and divided the war-making power between the executive and Congress.

Nevertheless, the Framers were practical and recognized that they must not cripple their nation's ability to defend itself, especially against sudden attack. Although many war powers, including the decision to go to war, could be given to Congress, command of U.S. forces during a conflict necessitated the unified and flexible leadership that only a single person could provide. As Alexander Hamilton noted: "Of all the cares or concerns of government, the direction of war most peculiarly demands those qualities which distinguish the exercise of power by a single hand."[1] The Framers therefore assigned the commander-in-chief power to the presidency, taking comfort in the certainty that George Washington would be the first person to hold that office.

Few presidents, however, have been as well suited, in skills and integrity, for the role of commander in chief as Washington. Some presidents have mismanaged military affairs, and a few have misused their military power. The dramatic expansion of presidential authority in national security affairs during the decades following World War II led eventually to confrontations between the executive and legislative branches over the scope and use of the war powers, including charges of usurpation or abuse of power by the president. But contrary to the experiences of many other nations, no president has used the forces at his command to interfere with the ordinary course of electoral accountability or the powers and functions of the other branches. The historical record of the United States could not have been improved had the Framers separated the role of commander in chief from the presidency. As political scientist Clinton Rossiter wrote: "We have placed a shocking amount of military power in the President's keeping, but where else, we may ask, could it possibly have been placed?"[2] The relatively minor abuses and misuses of presidential power should be weighed against the use of that power in the Civil War, World War I, and World War II, which demonstrated that a strong president willing to interpret the commander-in-chief power broadly is in the best position to lead the military, unite the American people, and focus the efforts of the nation on victory when war threatens its security.

Distribution of War-making Power

There was general agreement at the Constitutional Convention that the person who occupied the highest civilian office should also be the commander in chief of the nation's military forces. Article II, section 2, of the Constitution states: "The President shall be Commander in Chief of the Army and Navy of the United States, and of the Militia of the several States, when called into the actual Service of the United States." This statement is all the Constitution says about the president's war-making power.

The Framers did not regard war making as an inherently executive function. Indeed, they originally gave the legislature the comprehensive power to "make war." Fearing that a legislature, cumbersome in itself and frequently out of session, might inhibit action in an emergency, the delegates separated the power to declare war from the power to command or direct the military forces. The latter was given to presidents, leaving them free to repel invasions.[3] Nonetheless, the Framers sought to prevent the president from making war alone, and Congress was given the bulk of the war-related powers. The clauses outlining Congress's powers (Article I, section 8) are detailed and specific:

> To declare War, grant Letters of Marque and Reprisal, and make Rules concerning Captures on Land and Water; To raise and support Armies . . . ; To provide and maintain a Navy; To make Rules for the Government and Regulation of the land and naval forces; To provide for calling forth the Militia to execute the Laws of the Union, suppress Insurrections and repel Invasions; To provide for organizing, arming, and disciplining, the Militia, and for governing such Part of them as may be employed in the Service of the United States, reserving to the States respectively, the Appointment of the Officers, and the Authority of training the Militia according to the discipline prescribed by Congress.

The President shall be Commander in Chief of the Army and Navy of the United States, and of the Militia of the several States, when called into the actual Service of the United States.

—*from Article II, section 2*

As Congress's enumerated war powers indicate, the Framers intended Congress to have authority over the raising, equipping, and organizing of the armed forces, while the president would direct the military in times of war. The two branches would share power over the military, an instrument of government often abused when controlled by a single master. A president seeking to become a military dictator would be hindered by Congress's exclusive authority to raise, equip, and organize the armed forces. This includes the authority to eliminate all standing forces. Presidents might wish to act, but without Congress's support they would lack the necessary tools to do so.

The exact authority of the commander in chief was left undefined. Nothing is said directly about his authority to initiate military actions short of war in the absence of an invasion or attack. Similarly, the Constitution says nothing directly about the power of Congress to control the scope of conflict once it has declared war.

In the minds of most of the Framers, and in the clear implications of the Constitution, these questions were settled in favor of congressional control and limited presidential power. If the Framers intended to "chain the dog of war" by tying it to the representative and deliberative branch, they also tried to account for the necessity of decisive action in emergencies by giving the commander-in-chief power to a single officer. The resulting textual ambiguities have allowed presidents to argue that they possess any power or duty traditionally associated with the office of supreme military commander, rather than just the single function of commanding the armed forces. Consequently, a broad range of actions and powers has been justified under a generous interpretation of the commander-in-chief clause. In addition, foreign policy and chief executive powers give presidents responsibilities in the area of national security that are used in conjunction with the commander-in-chief power to expand the president's war powers.

In practice, controlling the war power has depended less on precise constitutional provisions and more on the checking capacity of well-balanced institutions.

POWER TO DECLARE WAR

Although Congress's power to raise armies and fund wars and the president's command of the military in times of war are unquestioned, the authority to decide when and where to employ military force has been the subject of conflict between the executive and legislative branches. The Framers' suspicions of executive power ruled out granting the president the exclusive authority to declare war. Yet their decision to give Congress alone the power to declare war is significant. They could have given the president the power to declare war with the "advice and consent of the Senate" as they had with the treaty power. Instead, the authors of the Constitution deliberately delegated to Congress the sole authority to declare war. Moreover, it is clear from the writings of the Framers that they regarded the act of declaring war as more than a formality. By giving Congress the power to declare war they sought to contain executive ambition and to ensure that these momentous decisions would be made by the deliberative branch and especially by representatives closest to the people who would be called upon to shoulder the cost in lives and treasure. James Madison wrote:

> Those who are to conduct a war cannot in the nature of things be proper or safe judges whether a war ought to be commenced, continued, or concluded. They are barred from the latter functions by a great principle in free government, analogous to that which separates the sword from the purse, or the power of executing from the power of enacting laws.[4]

By separating the power to declare war from the power to conduct it, the Framers kept the power to initiate armed conflict in the hands of Congress while leaving the power to repel sudden attacks in the hands of the president. The Framers recognized that speed and secrecy, which only a single decision maker could provide, were essential to the safety of the nation if it came under attack. Beyond this adjustment the Framers believed they had sufficiently checked the president's war-making authority, and the general distribution of constitutional authority seems clear: Congress decides when to go to war unless the United States is attacked. In *The Federalist Papers,* Hamilton, one of the foremost advocates of a strong chief executive at the Constitutional Convention, narrowly interpreted the commander-in-chief power:

> The president is to be commander-in-chief of the army and navy of the United States. In this respect his authority would be nominally the same with that of the King of Great Britain, but in substance much inferior to it. It would amount to nothing more than the supreme command and direction of the military and naval forces, as first general and admiral of the Confederacy; while that of the British king extends to the *declaring* of war and to the raising and *regulating* of fleets and armies—all of which, by the Constitution under consideration, would appertain to the legislature.[5]

Hamilton's simple formula is, however, full of ambiguities. How is war to be defined? Does the power to declare war extend to a power to authorize any or all uses of force short of war? Are there military missions short of war that the president can order without congressional authorization? Can the president order an attack to preempt an attack from a potential enemy? Can the president order U.S. forces to invade the territory of a neutral nation in pursuit of enemy forces?

The Framers seemed to have agreed that Congress was to control the initiation of all significant military actions. The Constitution gives Congress not only the power to declare war but also the power to "grant Letters of Marque and Reprisal." This now antiquated instrument allows Congress to authorize, for example, privateers to operate against enemy boats in U.S. waters. More generally, the Constitution seems to give Congress power over actions, such as retaliations and reprisals, that are hostile in nature but fall short of war.

In *Bas v. Tingy* (1800), the Supreme Court affirmed the authority of the United States to engage in limited or "imperfect" wars, and it affirmed Congress's full authority in all decisions to take the United States from a state of peace into a state of limited hostility or war. Not only could Congress authorize an "imperfect" war by statute, as opposed to a declaration, but it also had full authority to limit the conflict in relation to places, objects, and time. In other words, congressional authority in limited wars extended beyond initiation and deeply into the strategic and tactical questions that are often understood as the prerogative of a commander in chief.[6]

In sum, the consensus of the founding generation was, as President Washington argued, that the Constitution "vests the power of declaring war with Congress; therefore no offensive expedition of importance can be undertaken until they have deliberated upon the subject, and authorized such a measure."[7] Although some ambiguity remains about what an expedition "of importance" would be, the general thrust toward congressional control is clear. The historical record is, however, far more complicated. Congress has declared war only five times—the War of 1812, the Mexican War, the Spanish-American War, World War I, and World War II—and the United States has been involved in more than one hundred violent military conflicts and incidents. Some of these have been explicitly authorized by Congress, and many have not. Some of the unauthorized actions were insignificant and arose out of the obvious ambiguities of the Constitution. Others, however, were quite large in scale and arose from radically expansive interpretations of the commander-in-chief power.

This historical record suggests that presidents, having direct command of military forces and being responsible for defending the nation, have been in a better position than Congress to exploit the constitutional ambiguity. Consequently, when presidents have believed that a war or military action was necessary, they usually have found ways to maneuver the nation into a conflict.

POWER TO DECLARE NEUTRALITY AND END DECLARED WARS

Because only Congress has the authority to declare war, some students of the Constitution have reasoned that only Congress has the power to declare that the nation will not become involved in a war. Secretary of State Thomas Jefferson made this argument in 1793 when President Washington proclaimed that the United States would remain "friendly and impartial" in the war between the British and the French.[8] Many Americans favored France, their ally in the American Revolution, but Washington believed the treaty of alliance with France did not require U.S. involvement in the conflict and that any involvement would disrupt the nation's political and economic development. Jefferson supported Washington despite his reservations about the constitutionality of the president declaring neutrality. As a concession to Jefferson, Washington left the word "neutrality" out of his proclamation.

Washington's proclamation of neutrality set off a famous debate in the *Gazette of the United States* between Hamilton, who justified Washington's action, and Madison, who opposed Hamilton's expansive reading of the executive power. Hamilton conceded that the legislature had the exclusive right to declare war but asserted that until war is declared, the executive has both the responsibility to maintain peace and broad discretion in the choice of means. Madison saw the proclamation of neutrality as a usurpation of Congress's power to declare war. Hamilton and Madison were less concerned with neutrality than with the larger issue of whether a president could declare unilaterally what U.S. foreign policy would be. Over time, Hamilton's view that the president can make U.S. foreign policy has prevailed over Madison's strict interpretation of presidential power. *(See "Hamilton-Madison Debate," p. 127, in Chapter 3.)*

Washington asked Congress to pass judgment on the proclamation, and Congress eventually ratified the president's action by passing the Neutrality Act of 1794.

Subsequently, the custom also developed that Congress would not declare war without a presidential request. Yet on two occasions Congress demonstrated that it could move a president to accept a war even if the president had reservations about the wisdom of doing so. In 1812 a majority of members of Congress convinced President James Madison that war against the British was necessary. In 1898, with public opinion on its side, Congress pressured a reluctant William McKinley to ask for a declaration of war against Spain.

Congress and the president share the authority to end a war. The commander in chief has the power to order the military to stop fighting or to withdraw from an area of conflict. However, if Congress has declared war, the president cannot unilaterally end the legal state of war that exists. Congress must take some action that supersedes its declaration of war. Out of concern over executive abuse, the Framers considered, but rejected, a clause allowing the Senate to conclude a peace treaty on its own authority. As it stands, wars are usually concluded through Senate ratification of a treaty negotiated by the president ending the war and establishing peaceful relations with the enemy nation. The Mexican War, the Spanish-American War, and hostilities in the Pacific theater of World War II were officially terminated in this manner. Congress also may formally end a state of war by repealing its declaration of war. This method was used in 1921 after Congress had refused to ratify the Versailles treaty at the end of World War I and in 1951 formally to end war with Nazi Germany.[9]

The constitutional dilemmas in initiating and concluding armed conflicts have been complicated by the development and expansion of the president's powers, which have given him greater latitude to engage the United States in major conflicts without congressional authorization.

Development of Presidential War Powers

The Constitution's assignment of the office of commander in chief to the president created the basis for presidential war powers, but a more precise outline of these powers had to evolve through events. Most early presidents held a narrow interpretation of their commander-in-chief role that was similar to Hamilton's description of the president as the nation's "first general or admiral."

Even within this narrow interpretation, however, the practical scope of this and related powers in the context of a major conflict or declared war was not defined. Presidential war powers expanded dramatically to meet the general crises of the Civil War and the two world wars. The flexibility, secrecy, speed, and unity of command associated with the president were seen as crucial to the preservation and defense of the United States. In the circumstances of these wars, presidential power expanded from purely military issues into ancillary questions of the national budget, the domestic economy, and domestic security. According to political scientist Edward S. Corwin, "The principal canons of constitutional interpretation are in wartime set aside so far as concerns both the scope of national power and the capacity of the President to gather unto himself all constitutionally available powers in order the more effectively to focus them upon the task of the hour."[10] Presidential actions that would have raised a great deal of protest in peacetime were accepted in the name of necessity when the security of the nation was at stake.

Extensions of presidential power in wartime have established precedents which future presidents could use to justify broad interpretations of their authority. Woodrow Wilson's expansion of presidential war power paved the way for Franklin D. Roosevelt's extraordinary wartime authority, just as Wilson had referred to Lincoln's exercise of power when justifying his own. Until World War II, however, presidents could not continue to wield exceptional power as if an emergency continued beyond the end of armed conflict. After World War II, circumstances changed. President Truman retained his emergency powers, many of which were delegated by congressional action, by refusing to declare that the emergency had passed. Moreover, the rise of the cold war with the Soviet Union fostered the development of more permanent and extensive presidential war and emergency powers.

The cold war and especially the development of nuclear weapons created a more or less permanent state of national security emergency. These circumstances fostered and sustained a high level of discretion in the commander in chief's authority to use force until the late 1960s and early 1970s when Congress reacted to executive branch abuses of power by attempting to reassert its role in national security affairs. Although the executive branch still dominates national security policy and has retained the ability to initiate armed conflicts, Congress has scrutinized national security affairs more closely and has been able to restrict presidential policies on a variety of issues, including funding for selected weapons systems and military aid to allied nations and guerrilla organizations. In 1995 both houses of Congress passed bills that would restrict the president's authority to commit forces to UN missions and to place them under foreign command as part of a multilateral operation.

Until the latter stages of the Vietnam War the expansion of the president's war powers usually had been accomplished with Congress's approval and often with its active support. Congress validated many of Lincoln's actions, passed legislation delegating sweeping wartime powers to both Woodrow Wilson and Franklin Roosevelt, and acquiesced to the accumulation of power by presidents after World War II.

But Congress also had successfully reasserted its authority following each war. The Supreme Court has occasionally ruled against exercises of presidential war power, but it seldom has done so when a war was in progress and often has let stand presidential actions on the grounds that they are political matters that should be resolved between the executive and legislative branches.

A major exception was *Youngstown Sheet & Tube Co. v. Sawyer* (1952), in which the Court ruled against Truman's extension of his emergency and commander-in-chief powers into domestic economic affairs when he ordered a government takeover of a steel mill that was threatened by a labor strike. However, as the Court's approval of the internment of Americans of Japanese descent during World War II demonstrates, the Court has recognized the authority of the president acting in concert with Congress to take virtually any action in response to a grave national emergency.[11]

EARLY PRESIDENTS

Early presidents generally adhered to the principle that Congress was responsible for committing the United States to war. John Adams consulted with Congress in 1798 before allowing U.S. naval forces to attack French vessels that were preying on U.S. commercial shipping. Congress refrained from the drastic step of declaring war, but it passed legislation authorizing the president to order U.S. military forces to battle the French.[12] This action set the precedent, affirmed by the Supreme Court, that the United States could engage in armed conflicts short of war, but only if "authorized" by Congress. Jefferson and Madison also believed presidents should respect Congress's power to authorize war, yet the events of their administrations demonstrated the desirability of more flexible commander-in-chief power.

Jefferson and the Barbary Pirates

In 1801 American ships in the Mediterranean were being attacked by pirates from Tripoli and the other Barbary Coast states of Algeria, Morocco, and Tunisia. Jefferson wanted to take quick action to resolve the problem. He dispatched a squadron of ships to the Mediterranean with instructions to offer the rulers of the Barbary Coast states payments to leave U.S. shipping alone. Jefferson anticipated trouble, however, and informed the commodore of the squadron:

> But if you find on your arrival in Gibralter that all the Barbary Powers have declared war against the United States, you will then distribute your forces in such a manner, as your judgment shall direct, so as best to protect our commerce and chastise their insolence—by sinking, burning, or destroying their ships and vessels wherever you shall find them.[13]

Jefferson did not disclose these orders to Congress when he went before that body December 8, 1801, to request approval to take the offensive in the naval war that was already being fought. Rather, he emphasized the constitutional restraints under which the squadron operated:

> I sent a small squadron of frigates into the Mediterranean, with assurance to that power Tripoli of our desire to remain in peace, but with orders to protect our commerce against the threatened attack. . . . One of the Tripolitan cruisers . . . was captured, after a heavy slaughter of her men, without the loss of a single one on our part. . . . Unauthorized by the Constitution, without the sanction of Congress, to go beyond the line of defense, the vessel, being disabled from committing further hostilities, was liberated with its crew.[14]

Congress passed legislation early in 1802 authorizing the naval war that eventually led to a treaty with the Barbary powers. Jefferson had used deception and a *fait accompli* to secure the Mediterranean for U.S. commercial shipping while publicly asserting Congress's authority to determine when military force would be used.[15]

Hamilton, however, found Jefferson's consultations with Congress needless. He asserted that the president did not have to ask Congress's permission to turn loose the navy because "when a foreign nation declares or openly and avowedly makes war upon the United States, they are then by the very fact already at war and any declaration on the part of Congress is nugatory; it is at least unnecessary."[16]

Despite Jefferson's willingness to violate his principles in pursuit of objectives he considered important, he generally abided by the principle of congressional authorization. In 1805 when Spanish subjects in Florida made incursions into the newly acquired Louisiana Territory, Jefferson told Congress: "Considering that Congress alone is constitutionally invested with the power of changing our condition from peace to war, I have thought it my duty to await their authority for using force. . . . The course to be pursued will require the command of means which it belongs to Congress exclusively to yield or to deny." When Congress chose not to grant Jefferson the authority to attack the Spanish in Florida, he accepted its decision.[17]

The War of 1812

The War of 1812 was the first declared war in U.S. history. Sentiment for the war had been aroused by British captures of American commercial ships and their crews, allegations that the British were supplying hostile Indians on the frontier with arms, and a desire to acquire foreign territory in Canada and Florida. The initial advocates of the war were not President Madison and his close advisers, but members of Congress from the South and the West. These "War Hawks" represented areas that were troubled by Indian attacks and falling agricultural prices. In contrast, the Federalist merchants of the Northeast, who were making large profits on export shipments that avoided capture, were against the war. They feared that war would interfere with their commerce much more than sporadic British seizures of their ships.

Especially because Congress, although bent on war, had not provided for an adequate army and navy, Madison tried sincerely to resolve disputes with the British through diplomacy. He was eventually persuaded that the nation must go to war to protect its rights. On June 1, 1812, the president asked Congress for a declaration of war. In his address to lawmakers asking for a declaration of war Madison called war making a "solemn question which the Constitution wisely confides to the legislative department of the Government."[18] The declaration was passed 79–49 by the House and 19–13 by the Senate. Members of Congress from the South and the West prevailed over their colleagues from the Northeast.

Not only was the nation divided over the war, it was also unprepared to fight. The small American navy was hopelessly overmatched, and despite the war's popularity in the South and West the army had difficulty recruiting volunteers. U.S. forces suffered a string of humiliating defeats including the capture and burning of Washington, D.C., by the British in August 1814.

After the British forces withdrew from the capital, Congress assembled to consider the war effort. Yet, with the army still at only about half its authorized strength and enlistments falling off, Congress failed to agree on a conscription bill proposed by James Monroe, Madison's secretary of war and state. Fortunately, the British withdrew from the capital, and the Treaty of Ghent ending the war was signed on December 24, 1814.

Outside of declared wars, presidents retained some flexibility in the unilateral use of force to further their policies. President Monroe's secret and ambivalent orders allowed General Andrew Jackson to pursue the Seminole Indian raiders into Spanish Florida and to attack Spanish forts suspected of sheltering and aiding the raiders. This action, apparently by design, helped convince the Spanish of the vulnerability of the Florida defenses and move them toward a negotiated sale of the much desired territory.[19]

THE ANNEXATION OF TEXAS AND THE MEXICAN WAR

Texas declared its independence from Mexico in 1836 and indicated that it was interested in becoming part of the United States. Although most Americans supported the principle of expansion, the slavery issue made annexation of a new state a tricky political problem for any president. Presidents Andrew Jackson and Martin Van Buren avoided actions on the Texas issue that would anger voters in the North who were opposed to an extension of slavery. However, John Tyler, who succeeded to the presidency following the death of William Henry Harrison

U.S. and Mexican forces clash at the Battle of Buena Vista in 1847. In hopes of securing territory occupied by Mexico but claimed by Texas, President James K. Polk maneuvered the country into a "defensive" war after U.S. soldiers were attacked by Mexican forces.

in 1841, was a proslavery Virginian who wished to strengthen the slave states and limit English influence over Texas.[20] He began secret negotiations on annexation with Texas and initiated a pro-annexation campaign. The Texans, however, were concerned that if they agreed to annexation they would be invaded by Mexico. They informed Tyler that they would be reluctant to agree to annexation without guarantees that he would protect them with U.S. forces. This created a dilemma for Tyler, whose narrow interpretation of the Constitution had led him to reject presidential authority to use military force without congressional approval except in defense of the nation. In early 1844 Tyler showed that he valued the acquisition of Texas more than his own strict constructionist principles when he ordered the deployment of U.S. forces in Texas and the Gulf of Mexico while the secret negotiations proceeded. When the needed two-thirds of the Senate refused to approve the annexation treaty produced by the negotiations, Tyler asked Congress to validate the agreement with a majority vote of both Houses. The joint resolution was passed.[21]

President Polk had greater ambitions for expanding the United States, and he used his commander-in-chief power to maneuver the nation into war with Mexico. Polk had decided to ask Congress for a declaration of war, yet he provoked an attack when, in 1846, he ordered Gen. Zachary Taylor to deploy his army in a strip of disputed territory near the Rio Grande that was claimed by Texas but occupied exclusively by Mexicans. The Mexican forces attacked Taylor's army, killing a number of American soldiers. The clash ensured the passage of a declaration of war since Polk could claim that Mexico was the aggressor. He told Congress: "Now, after reiterated menaces Mexico has invaded our territory and shed American blood on American soil."[22] On May 13, 1846, Congress recognized "a state of war as existing by act of the Republic of Mexico." Polk's successful maneuvering demonstrated the capacity of the commander in chief to weaken congressional control over the initiation of armed conflict.

LINCOLN AND THE CIVIL WAR

President Lincoln's extraordinary exercise of power during the Civil War demonstrated how far the authority of the presidency could be expanded in wartime. Lincoln believed he faced a choice between preserving the Union and adhering to a strict interpretation of the Constitution. He feared that if he carefully observed the law he would sacrifice the flexibility necessary to prevent the destruction of the nation. In April 1864 he explained his reasoning in a letter to Albert Hodges:

> I did understand, however, that my oath to preserve the Constitution to the best of my ability impressed upon me the duty of preserving by every indispensable means, that government—that nation, of which that Constitution was the organic law. Was it possible to lose the nation and yet preserve the Constitution? By general law, life and limb must be protected, yet often a limb must be amputated to save a life; but a life is never wisely given to save a limb. I felt that measures otherwise unconstitutional might become lawful by becoming indispensable to the preservation of the nation. Right or wrong, I assumed this ground and now avow it.[23]

Lincoln did not come to this conclusion lightly. As a member of the House of Representatives, he had questioned the legality and propriety of President Polk's actions that led to the Mexican War. *(See box, Lincoln's Attack on Presidential War Powers, p. 170.)* Lincoln's expansion of his own war-making powers as president, therefore, did not result from a cavalier attitude toward the Constitution but from his recognition of an unprecedented emergency.

Lincoln's Expanded Powers

The Civil War began on April 12, 1861, when Confederate forces attacked Fort Sumter in Charleston, South Carolina. Recognizing that strict constructionists in Congress might object to emergency measures he thought necessary to deal with the crisis, Lincoln delayed the convocation of Congress until July 4. He used this three-month period to order a series of executive actions to meet the military emergency.[24]

On May 3, 1861, Lincoln called for the mobilization of seventy-five thousand state militia under a 1795 act that authorized the president to issue such a call. Although this action was considered within the powers of the president, most of Lincoln's actions during the early months of the war, from spending without congressional authorization to suspending *habeas corpus* (the constitutional guarantee against arbitrary detention and imprisonment), had no explicit constitutional or congressional sanction. In the same proclamation used to mobilize the militia, Lincoln unilaterally increased the size of the regular army by twenty-three thousand troops and the navy by eighteen thousand. In addition he ordered nineteen vessels added to the navy and directed the secretary of the Treasury to advance $2 million to authorized persons to pay for military requisitions. Lincoln also ordered a blockade of Southern ports, suspended the writ of *habeas corpus* in the vicinity of routes used by Union forces between Washington, D.C., and Philadelphia, ordered foreign visitors to observe new passport regulations, restricted "treasonable correspondence" from being carried by the Post Office, and directed the military to arrest and detain persons "who were represented to him" as contemplating or participating in "treasonable practices."[25]

When Congress finally convened on July 4, Lincoln asked the members to ratify the actions he had taken in their absence. He maintained that some of his emergency measures "whether strictly legal or not, were ventured upon under what appeared to be a popular demand and a public necessity, trusting then, as now, Congress would readily ratify them." In justifying his suspension of *habeas corpus* Lincoln made the constitutional argument that in spite of the placement of the provision on *habeas corpus* suspension in Article I, the Framers must have intended the president to share with Congress the suspension authority because emergencies requiring such action would not always occur when Congress was in session. Yet Lincoln defended his action on practical grounds as well, asking Congress, "Are all the laws but one to go unexecuted, and the Government itself go to pieces lest that one be violated?" In asking this question Lincoln implied that an emergency threatening the existence of the nation may empower the president to ignore parts of the Constitution to defend the whole.[26]

During the summer, Congress debated a joint resolution that sanctioned Lincoln's acts. Nagging doubts about the legality of his suspension of *habeas corpus* and blockade of Southern ports prevented a vote on the resolution. Near the end of the session, however, a rider attached to a pay bill for army privates that approved Lincoln's actions was rushed through Congress. On August 6, 1861, Congress passed the bill and its rider, which declared the president's acts pertaining to the militia, the army, the navy, and the volunteers "in all respects legalized and made valid . . . as if they had been issued and done under the previous express authority and direction of Congress."[27]

In expanding his war-making powers during the Civil War, Lincoln was acutely aware of placing the preservation of the Union above strict adherence to the Constitution. "Was it possible to lose the nation and yet preserve the Constitution?" he wrote. "By general law, life and limb must be protected, yet often a limb must be amputated to save a life."

Throughout the war, Lincoln continued to extend his commander-in-chief power beyond its constitutional limits. In 1862, when voluntary recruitments were not adequately supplying the army's need for additional troops, Lincoln ordered a draft. The same year he extended his suspension of the writ of *habeas corpus* to persons throughout the entire nation who were "guilty of any disloyal practice." He also declared that these persons could be tried by military courts. On January 1, 1863, Lincoln issued the Emancipation Proclamation freeing "all persons held as slaves within any State or designated part of a State, the people whereof shall then be in rebellion against the United States," a sweeping confiscation, or destruction, of private property without due process or compensation. Lincoln maintained that his commander-in-chief power gave him the authority to issue the

LINCOLN'S ATTACK ON PRESIDENTIAL WAR POWERS

As president, Abraham Lincoln stretched presidential power until it approached dictatorship. He carefully justified his extraordinary emergency powers under the commander-in-chief clause and his duties to protect the Constitution and "to take Care that the Laws be faithfully executed." As a young member of the House of Representatives, Lincoln had criticized President Polk's maneuvers to provoke a war with Mexico and argued for a restrictive interpretation of the president's authority to initiate war. In a letter to William H. Herndon, his law partner in Illinois, Lincoln explained his view of that power:

Washington, Feb. 15, 1848

Dear William:

. . . Let me first state what I understand to be your position. It is, that if it shall become *necessary, to repel invasion,* the President may, without violation of the Constitution, cross the line, and *invade* the territory of another country; and that whether such *necessity* exists in any given case, the President is to be the *sole* judge.

. . . Allow the President to invade a neighboring nation, whenever *he* shall deem it necessary to repel an invasion, and you allow him to do so, *whenever he may choose to say* he deems it necessary for such purpose—and you allow him to make war at pleasure. Study to see if you can fix *any limit* to his power in this respect, after you have given him so much as you propose. If, today, he should choose to say he thinks it necessary to invade Canada, to prevent the British from invading us, how could you stop him? You may say to him, "I see no probability of the British invading us" but he will say to you "be silent; I see it, if you dont."

The provision of the Constitution giving the war-making power to Congress, was dictated, as I understand it, by the following reasons. Kings had always been involving and impoverishing their people in wars, pretending generally, if not always, that the good of the people was the object. This, our Convention understood to be the most oppressive of all Kingly oppressions; and they resolved to so frame the Constitution that *no one man* should hold the power of bringing this oppression upon us. But your view destroys the whole matter, and places our President where kings have always stood. Write soon again.

Yours truly,
A. Lincoln[1]

1. *The Collected Works of Abraham Lincoln,* ed. Roy P. Basler (New Brunswick, N.J.: Rutgers University Press, 1953), 451–452.

proclamation, since the liberation of slaves reduced the labor force of the South, thus hindering its ability to carry on the war. It also provided a new group of army recruits.[28]

The Prize Cases

Although the Supreme Court eventually objected to Lincoln's order that civilians could be tried in military courts, it did sanction his prosecution of a total war against the South. When hostilities began, the president had ordered a blockade of Confederate ports to prevent the South from selling cotton to England and importing supplies. The owners of four vessels seized by the blockade sued for redress on the grounds that the seizures were illegal since Congress had not declared war against the South. They argued that Lincoln's duty to suppress the insurrection was not equivalent to the power to wage war. Therefore, an act of war such as a blockade could not legally be ordered by the president in the absence of a declaration of war.

In 1863 the Supreme Court rejected these arguments in its 5–4 decision on the *Prize Cases.* Writing for the majority, Justice Robert C. Grier explained:

> It is not necessary to constitute war, that both parties should be acknowledged as independent nations or sovereign states. A war may exist where one of the belligerents claims sovereign rights as against the other. . . . A civil war is never solemnly declared; it becomes such by its accidents—the number, power, and organization of the persons who originate and carry it on. When the party in rebellion occupy and hold in a hostile manner a certain portion of territory; have declared their independence; have cast off their allegiance; have organized armies; have commenced hostilities against their former sovereign, the world acknowledges them as belligerents, and the contest a war.[29]

The decision supported Lincoln's interpretation that the insurrectionist South was without sovereign rights, while the North possessed all rights of a belligerent in wartime. Moreover, the decision gave Lincoln confidence that the Court would not restrict his expansive interpretation of his commander-in-chief powers in the future. Although this case dealt specifically with the president's power to respond to a general insurrection, advocates of a strong presidency have often cited it when arguing in favor of a broad interpretation of presidential war power.[30]

THE SPANISH-AMERICAN WAR

The 1895 Cuban rebellion against Spanish rule occurred when the United States was ready to seek a wider role in global affairs. For some Americans the Cuban crisis offered an opportunity to flex American muscle against a European power and extend U.S. influence. Others, aroused by slanted reports in the press of Spanish atrocities in Cuba, wished to rescue the island's inhabitants from Spanish tyranny. This combination of forces resulted in a popular crusade in the United States to aid Cuban independence.

President Grover Cleveland resisted the temptation to satisfy the nation's appetite for war with Spain during the last two years of his term. In a curious reversal of roles, he even warned members of Congress that, as commander in chief, he would refuse to prosecute any declaration of war.[31] William McKinley entered office in 1897 similarly determined to avoid war. After the mysterious sinking of the U.S. battleship *Maine* in Havana harbor in February 1898, however, McKinley could no longer stand up to congressional belligerence and public opinion. He asked Congress on April 11, 1898, to approve American armed intervention in Cuba. Spain already had acceded to many American demands for a settlement of the Cuban crisis, but on April 25, Congress passed a declaration of war authorizing the president to use military force to expel Spain from the island. It was adopted by the Senate 42–35 and by the House 310–6.

The brevity of the war, the ease with which victory was won, and the popularity of the conflict made McKinley's job as commander in chief easier. Although he had resisted war, McKinley nonetheless extended the conflict from Cuba to Spanish holdings in the Pacific: the Philippines and Guam. The issue of what to do with the Philippines was quite controversial. McKinley decided to take possession of the islands as part of a broader policy of expanding U.S. trade in the Far East.[32]

On December 10, 1898, Spain signed a treaty relinquishing its control over Cuba and ceding the Philippines along with Puerto Rico and Guam to the United States. The Senate approved the treaty after a month of debate by a vote of 57–27, only one vote more than the necessary two-thirds majority, and for the first time a president and Congress acquired territory outside the North American continent through war.

THE WORLD WARS

The first involvement of the United States in an overseas war of massive scale provided the occasion for the most dramatic expansion of presidential wartime powers since the Civil War. The basis for Woodrow Wilson's power differed from Lincoln's, however, in that Lincoln had taken emergency actions independently of Congress, whereas Wilson was handed most of his expanded war-making authority by statute.[33] Congress gave Wilson not only expanded control of the military and discretion to fight subversion and espionage but also unprecedented control over industries and the allocation of scarce resources. For example, the Lever Food and Fuel Act of 1917 gave the president "full authority to undertake any steps necessary" for the conservation of food resources. In addition, the 1918 Overman Act gave the president complete authority to reorganize the executive branch. Congress was willing to make these broad delegations of power to Wilson because most members believed that the scope and urgency of the war required unified control and direction of all operations and resources related to the war effort.

In essence, Congress did not just give Wilson broad discretion in implementing its statutes, it abdicated legislative power to him for the duration of the war. Many delegations of authority to the president simply stated their objectives and left Wilson to decide how to achieve them. He commandeered plants and mines, requisitioned supplies, fixed prices, seized and operated the nation's transportation and communications networks, and managed the production and distribution of foodstuffs. The Council of National Defense, an umbrella agency created by Wilson, administered the economy during the war. Wilson created the War Industries Board using his authority as commander in chief. Wall Street broker Bernard Baruch, who had been appointed by Wilson to head the board, became a virtual dictator over American industry. The president also established by executive order the Committee of Public Information, under whose direction a system of voluntary news censorship was instituted and various government publicity services were organized. On April 28, 1917, Wilson imposed strict censorship of cable messages, which later was extended to other forms of communication with foreign countries under authority of the Trading with the Enemy Act of October 6, 1917.

PRESIDENTIAL CLAIMS TO POLICE ACTION

Periodically, presidents have advanced and acted on doctrines that expand the scope of the president's authority to initiate armed conflict. One such doctrine derives from the executive power and asserts that the president is responsible for protecting the lives and property of U.S. citizens and may deploy armed forces anywhere to fulfill this duty. For example, in 1900 McKinley sent troops into China, ostensibly to protect American lives threatened by a domestic insurrection called the Boxer Rebellion. This doctrine authorizes the president to initiate conflicts that could lead to war, and it affords the president a pretext for intervening in a wide variety of circumstances and places in pursuit of other aims. This doctrine muddled the well-established constitutional principle, designed to control the executive, that Congress has sole authority to take the nation from a state of peace to a state of war.

Similarly, President Theodore Roosevelt's 1904 "corollary" to the Monroe Doctrine asserted that the United States would not only resist foreign intervention in the Western Hemisphere, but it would also "police" the hemisphere by intervening in the domestic affairs of other countries if misbehavior or political turmoil threatened to invite foreign intervention. Presidents from Roosevelt to Calvin Coolidge, as well as Lyndon B. Johnson, Ronald Reagan, George Bush, and Bill Clinton, have assumed that the president alone has the authority to initiate such actions, and they have acted on this basis in Colombia, the Dominican Republic, Nicaragua, Honduras, Cuba, Mexico, and Haiti. This doctrine weakens congressional control of the war power. Moreover, Roosevelt's assertion of authority suggests that a presidential foreign policy proclamation or doctrine can become the basis for extending the president's power to project armed forces and enter into hostile action, the Constitution notwithstanding.[1] President Polk may have embraced the "manifest destiny" of the nation to expand to the Pacific, but he did not act as if his preferences were sufficient authority for going to war with Mexico. Specifically and generally, Roosevelt's bold assertion helped alter the basis of presidential claims to a broad commander-in-chief power. *(See also "Police Actions and Rescue Missions," p. 204.)*

1. Louis Fisher, *Presidential War Power* (Lawrence: University Press of Kansas, 1995), 35–36, 45–54.

Presidential war power reached its apex during World War II. Constitutional scholar Edward S. Corwin wrote, "The relation . . . of the First World War to the Second as regards constitutional interpretation is that of prologue and rehearsal."[34] Like Wilson during World War I, Franklin Roosevelt was delegated wide powers by Congress to manage the economy and direct the war effort, but Roosevelt went beyond Wilson in asserting his power as commander in chief to take any action he deemed necessary to the war effort.

Overcoming Neutrality

The president's war powers were tightly restrained during the 1930s by the prevailing mood of isolationism in Congress and among the American people. Congress enacted and Roosevelt signed a series of laws designed to keep the United States out of the conflicts brewing in Europe and Asia. These laws included the Neutrality Acts of 1935 and 1937, which prohibited shipments of arms, ammunition, or implements of war to any belligerent nation, including those that had been the victims of aggression. After Hitler's invasion of Poland in September 1939, which brought Great Britain and France into the war against Nazi Germany, Roosevelt began maneuvering the country toward active support of Britain and the other allies, whose survival he believed was crucial to U.S. security.

On September 3, 1940, Roosevelt announced that he had concluded an agreement with Great Britain under which that country would receive fifty "overage" destroyers in return for the right to lease certain British territory in the western Atlantic for U.S. naval and air bases. Roosevelt's destroyer deal was accomplished through an executive agreement—a legally binding pact between the president and the British government—rather than a Senate-ratified treaty. The trade violated at least two congressional statutes, but Roosevelt's attorney general, Robert Jackson, asserted that the president acted legally under his commander-in-chief authority to "dispose" of the armed forces. It was also argued that the commander in chief was responsible for securing adequate bases for national defense.

On March 11, 1941, Congress passed the Lend-Lease Act, described by Corwin as the most "sweeping delegation of legislative power" ever given to a president.[35] It authorized the president to manufacture any defense article and to "sell, transfer title to, exchange, lease, lend or otherwise dispose of" the defense articles to the "government of any country whose defense the President deems vital to the defense of the United States." The act gave President Roosevelt the power to aid the Allied cause as he saw fit by virtually any means short of using the armed forces.

Yet Roosevelt did use the armed forces to aid the Allied cause despite the absence of any congressional sanction for acts of war. After Germany occupied Denmark in April 1941, Roosevelt ordered U.S. troops to be stationed in Greenland. Three months later, American forces occupied Iceland. Both moves were made without consulting Congress, which had forbidden the deployment of U.S. reserves and draftees outside the Western Hemisphere in the Reserves Act of 1940 and the Selective Service Act of 1941.[36] Moreover, by the summer of 1941, U.S. naval vessels under presidential orders were escorting Allied convoys across the Atlantic. After the U.S.S. *Greer* exchanged shots with a German submarine on September 4, the president declared that henceforth U.S. warships providing protection to supply convoys bound for Britain would be under orders to attack Axis vessels on sight. Three months before Congress declared war, therefore, Roosevelt had already maneuvered the nation into an undeclared naval war in the Atlantic.[37]

Roosevelt's "Dictatorship"

The U.S. entry into World War II was accompanied by the concentration of virtually all war powers in the president's hands. Congress delegated vast authority to the president to prosecute the war as it had during World War I, but it also acquiesced to Roosevelt's many unsanctioned appropriations of power and his broad interpretations of congressional statutes. Although Roosevelt saw the wisdom of obtaining Congress's approval for controversial actions, he was far more assertive than Wilson in using his commander-in-chief power to establish complete control over the war effort.

Roosevelt created dozens of executive regulatory agencies that were not based on a specific statute, such as the Office of Emergency Management, Board of Economic Warfare, National War Labor Board, Office of Defense Transportation, and War Production Board. Anything remotely connected to the nation's war effort, including managing national resources and economic activity, was regulated by these war management agencies, which were responsible to the president rather than to existing departments or independent regulatory agencies. Roosevelt justified their creation by citing general delegations of power from Congress, the powers available to him under his emergency proclamations of 1939 and 1941, and his own powers as commander in chief.[38]

On September 7, 1942, the president demonstrated how far he believed his war powers extended. In a speech to Congress, Roosevelt issued an ultimatum to lawmakers to repeal certain provisions contained in the Emergency Price Control Act of 1942:

> I ask the Congress to take this action by the first of October. Inaction on your part by that date will leave me with an inescapable responsibility to the people of this country to see to it that the war effort is no longer imperiled by threat of economic chaos.
>
> In the event that the Congress should fail to act, and act adequately, I shall accept the responsibility and I will act.
>
> At the same time farm prices are stabilized, wages can and will be stabilized also. This I will do.
>
> The President has the power, under the Constitution and under Congressional acts, to take measures necessary to avert a disaster which would interfere with the winning of the war. . . .
>
> I have given the most thoughtful consideration to meeting this issue without further reference to the Congress. I have determined, however, on this vital matter to consult with Congress. . . .
>
> The American people can be sure that I will use my powers with a

> full sense of my responsibility to the Constitution and to the country. The American people can also be sure that I shall not hesitate to use every power vested in me to accomplish the defeat of our enemies in any part of the world where our own safety demands such defeat.
>
> When the war is won, the powers under which I act automatically revert to the people—to whom they belong.[39]

With this declaration, Roosevelt claimed, according to Corwin, "the right and power to disregard a statutory provision which he does not deny, and indeed could not possibly deny, that Congress had full constitutional authority to enact, and which, therefore, he was under obligation by the Constitution to 'take care' should be 'faithfully executed.'"[40] Roosevelt was threatening to suspend the Constitution in the interest of national security if Congress did not act. Not even Abraham Lincoln during the Civil War had claimed the power to repeal a specific congressional statute.

Many members of Congress were shaken by Roosevelt's ultimatum, and a few denounced it. Republican senator Robert A. Taft of Ohio called the speech "revolutionary and dangerous to the American form of government . . . an assertion that the laws of this country can be made by executive order."[41] The American public, however, supported Roosevelt's position; and with the war raging, there was little desire in Congress to engage the president in a constitutional showdown. Congress therefore amended the law to meet Roosevelt's objections.

POSTWAR CONGRESSIONAL ACQUIESCENCE

After World War II differences between the United States and the Soviet Union brought on the cold war, a state of continuous international tension that contributed to increased presidential control over national security policy. The specter of an aggressive Soviet Union pushing out wherever the West failed to resist made Congress reluctant to impose restrictions on executive action. A consensus developed that because presidents possessed both the capacity to act immediately and the access to the most detailed and reliable information, they alone were suited to direct foreign and military policy. Their status as leaders of the free world and caretakers of the U.S. nuclear arsenal, the most devastating military force ever created, contributed to their unchallenged authority.

The Korean War

When the North Korean army swept into South Korea on June 24, 1950, Harry S. Truman believed he had to act to save South Korea and discourage further Communist aggression. The next day the United States called an emergency session of the United Nations (UN) Security Council, which passed a resolution condemning the invasion and asking UN members to "render every assistance" to South Korea. By coincidence the Soviets were boycotting the Security Council to protest the exclusion of the new Communist government of China from the UN. Consequently, their representative was not present to veto the resolution. That evening Truman made up his mind to use air and naval forces to defend South Korea. He authorized Gen. Douglas MacArthur to evacuate Americans from South Korea, transport supplies to the South Koreans, and bomb military targets below the thirty-eighth parallel. After Truman announced his intention to defend South Korea and initiated U.S. involvement, the UN Security Council passed a second resolution explicitly calling on members to give military assistance to South Korea. By June 30 Truman had authorized MacArthur to use U.S. ground forces and to bomb targets in North Korea, thereby completing the U.S. commitment to defend South Korea.[42]

The Korean War involved a massive qualitative change in presidential assertion of war powers. President Truman claimed and exercised an authority to engage the United States in a war without any congressional declaration or authorization. Truman could easily have secured a congressional resolution approving his use of military forces in Korea, but the president wished to avoid an appearance of dependence on Congress. Truman had been advised by Secretary of State Dean Acheson and chair of the Senate Foreign Relations Committee Tom Connally (D-Texas) that his commander-in-chief power and the UN Security Council resolution gave him ample authority to use the armed forces. According to Secretary of State Acheson, Truman considered the presidency "a sacred and temporary trust, which he was determined to pass on unimpaired by the slightest loss of power or prestige."[43] Past presidents had ordered U.S. forces to rescue Americans overseas, police the hemisphere, or undertake some other type of limited military mission. The Truman administration cited these precedents in justifying its interpretation of the commander-in-chief power.[44]

However, the Korean War was quite without precedent in American history. Although the president's power to use the armed forces for very limited missions was well established, presidential authority to commit the nation to a large-scale, bloody war of indefinite length involving hundreds of thousands of military personnel was not. By every definition the United States was waging war in Korea, regardless of the Truman administration's restrictions on the use of military force against Chinese territory and its assertions throughout the war that U.S. involvement amounted to participation in a UN "police action."[45]

In addition, Truman's use of a United Nations Security Council resolution as a basis for unilateral presidential action contradicts the language and history of the UN Charter. As constitutional scholar Louis Fisher argues, no treaty could alter the Constitution by delegating the war power to the UN or to the president. Both the Charter and the UN Participation Act specify that any Security Council agreement involving the use of troops will be subject to ratification in accordance with each country's "constitutional processes." The congressional debate concerning the effect of the UN Charter on the war powers revolved around whether the relevant constitutional process was senatorial approval or a two-house resolution. The Charter was approved with the understanding that both houses of

Congress would have to authorize the use of armed forces in hostilities, and the UN Participation Act clearly affirmed this.[46]

A few Republicans protested Truman's failure to involve Congress in the decision. Influential Republican senator Robert Taft announced on June 28 that although he agreed that U.S. forces should be used in Korea, the president had "no legal authority" to send them without the approval of Congress. In general, members of Congress overwhelmingly supported Truman's decision to commit U.S. forces and, initially, did not challenge Truman's sweeping claims of authority. During the fall of 1950, the war remained popular as UN forces were successful in driving the North Koreans up the peninsula. In November General MacArthur's forces had occupied most of North Korea and appeared close to reunifying North and South.[47] In November and December, however, Communist Chinese forces entered the war and drove UN forces back across the thirty-eighth parallel into South Korea.

With Congress already alarmed by reversals in the military campaign, Truman announced on December 19 that he planned to send four more divisions to Europe to bolster Allied defenses under NATO. This time the president's intention to send so many troops abroad without congressional approval triggered a congressional reevaluation of U.S. defense and foreign policy that was known at the time as the "great debate." The debate, which lasted from January to April of 1951, was concerned not only with Truman's deployment of troops to Europe, but also with the president's authority to involve the nation in the Korean War.

The fear, expressed most fully by Senator Taft, was that the president could use treaties and executive agreements as authority to place U.S. armed forces in situations that would nullify Congress's control over the initiation of war. In the end the Senate passed two resolutions approving the dispatch of four divisions to Europe. One of the resolutions declared that it was the sense of the Senate that Congress should approve any future deployment of ground troops to Europe.

Truman hailed the resolutions as an endorsement of his policies. They were not. But the Senate and the House failed to pass any binding resolutions that would have put teeth into their assertions of constitutional prerogative in controlling the commitment of the nation's forces. Similar debates leading to similarly weak legislative responses were repeated during the next twenty years.

Truman's actions set the stage for a period of broad presidential control of foreign and national security policy. Truman did suffer a setback in 1952 when the Supreme Court ruled in *Youngstown Sheet and Tube Co. v. Sawyer* that he did not have the authority to take over steel mills to prevent a strike that would damage the Korean War effort. Otherwise, as historian Arthur M. Schlesinger Jr., wrote: "By bringing the nation into war without congressional authorization and by then successfully defending his exercise of independent presidential initiative, Truman enormously expanded assumptions of presidential prerogative."[48]

Joint Resolutions

The period following the Korean War was characterized by the passage of congressional resolutions granting or acknowledging the authority to use such force as presidents deemed necessary to repel armed attacks or threats against designated nations or regions. The purpose behind a number of these resolutions was to deter potential aggressors by making it clear that the U.S. government was united in a commitment to respond. Between 1955 and 1962 four joint resolutions of this type were passed. The Formosa Resolution, signed into law on January 29, 1955, authorized presidents to use U.S. forces to protect Formosa and the Pescadores Islands against attack from the People's Republic of China. The Middle East Resolution, signed into law on March 9, 1957, proclaimed U.S. intentions to defend Middle East countries "against any country controlled by international communism." The Cuban Resolution, signed into law on October 3, 1962, authorized presidents to take whatever steps they believed necessary to defend Latin America against Cuban aggression or subversion and to oppose the deployment in Cuba of Soviet weapons capable of threatening U.S. security. The 1962 Berlin Resolution did not have the force of law but expressed the sense of Congress that the United States was determined to defend West Berlin and the access rights of the Western powers to that city.

These resolutions received wide support in Congress, although they did have critics who charged that the resolutions gave too much discretionary power to the president and absolved Congress from any responsibility for national security. Schlesinger describes the extent of congressional abdication during this period:

> In the decade after Korea Congress receded not alone from the effort to control the war-making power but almost from the effort to participate in it, except on occasions when national-security zealots on the Hill condemned the executive branch for inadequate bellicosity. Mesmerized by the supposed need for instant response to constant crisis, overawed by what the Senate Foreign Relations Committee later called "the cult of executive expertise," confused in its own mind as to what wise policy should be, delighted to relinquish responsibility, Congress readily capitulated to what Corwin at the start of the fifties had called "high-flying" theses of presidential prerogative.[49]

The Vietnam War

No single president was entirely responsible for U.S. participation in the war in Vietnam. A succession of presidents gradually increased U.S. military involvement in Southeast Asia. In 1954 Vietnamese revolutionary forces defeated the French, who had controlled the region as a colonial power. President Dwight D. Eisenhower had continued the Truman administration's policy of sending aid to the French, but Eisenhower refused to intervene militarily to prevent a French defeat. After the French departed, Vietnam was temporarily partitioned with the Com-

Soldiers of the U.S. 9th Division patrol through an abandoned rice paddy past a flooded shell crater during the Vietnam War. Throughout history presidential ability to wage war had continually expanded until Congress passed the War Powers Resolution in 1973. The resolution reasserted congressional authority to approve military activities begun by the president.

munist government of Ho Chi Minh ruling the North and anti-Communists in Saigon controlling the South. President Eisenhower undercut reunification efforts, which he feared would result in Communist control over the entire country, by ignoring the scheduled reunification elections in 1956 and supporting the non-Communist regime in the South. The North Vietnamese and their supporters in the South launched a guerrilla war in an effort to achieve reunification through force. Although Eisenhower stepped up economic and military aid to the Saigon government, which included a small number of U.S. military advisers, he avoided more extensive U.S. military involvement.

President John F. Kennedy, however, fearing the collapse of the Saigon government, responded to South Vietnamese requests for greater assistance by sending additional military advisers and counterinsurgency units to South Vietnam. Before he was assassinated, Kennedy had deployed 16,500 U.S. military personnel in Vietnam.

President Lyndon B. Johnson continued the gradual escalation of the involvement of U.S. armed forces in the widening war. The Gulf of Tonkin incident in August 1964 resulted in a resolution supporting any presidential effort to combat North Vietnamese aggression *(See box, Tonkin Gulf Resolution, p. 176).* Armed with this congressional sanction and fearing an imminent Communist takeover, Johnson ordered the first regular combat troops to Vietnam in 1965. Their mission was to defend the U.S. airbase at Danang, but soon they were conducting patrols and actively engaging the enemy in combat. Although Johnson believed his commander-in-chief powers and the Tonkin Gulf resolution gave him the authority to send the troops to Vietnam, he nevertheless wanted Congress on record as approving the move. He therefore requested a specific appropriation of $700 million for U.S. military operations in Vietnam. Within two days, both houses had passed the bill with little dissent.[50] By 1968 Johnson had increased U.S. troop strength in Vietnam to more than 500,000. The Communists' Tet offensive early that year, although militarily unsuccessful, caused Americans including Johnson to begin to lose confidence that the war could be won.

President Richard Nixon began slowly withdrawing U.S. forces from Vietnam in 1969. Nixon's goal was to extricate the United States from the Vietnam quagmire while achieving "peace with honor." In January 1973, the United States and North Vietnam signed a peace accord. The North Vietnamese returned U.S. prisoners of war and allowed the regime of South Vietnamese president Thieu to remain in power. In return the United States withdrew its forces from Vietnam and allowed North Vietnamese army units already in South Vietnam to remain there. Without U.S. military support, however, South Vietnam was unable to defend itself against a 1975 North Vietnamese offensive that resulted in the fall of Saigon. Although President Nixon had promised Thieu that the United States would intervene if Communist forces threatened to conquer the South, Nixon had resigned the presidency in 1974, and Congress refused to fund any further military involvement in Southeast Asia.

Although less so than the Korean War, the Vietnam War was a presidential war. Decision making about goals and strategy in Vietnam was dominated by the executive branch with little congressional influence. Neither Johnson nor Nixon sought congressional approval for their prosecution of the war after 1965. Nevertheless, the picture of these presidents carrying on mili-

TONKIN GULF RESOLUTION

Each of the joint resolutions sanctioning presidential use of force passed by Congress between 1955 and 1962 represented a declaration of national policy upon which there was broad agreement. The supporters of these resolutions considered them to be effective means with which Congress could create a united front behind presidential action. This was the intention of members of Congress when they voted almost unanimously in favor of the Tonkin Gulf resolution in 1964.

On August 2, 1964, the U.S. destroyer *Maddox,* which the navy contended was on a routine mission in the Tonkin Gulf off the coast of North Vietnam, was attacked by North Vietnamese patrol boats. Two nights later the *Maddox,* which had been joined by another destroyer, the *C. Turner Joy,* reported a second patrol boat attack. Neither ship was damaged. President Lyndon B. Johnson responded to the incidents by ordering U.S. warplanes to bomb North Vietnamese torpedo boat bases.

Johnson informed Congress that U.S. ships had been attacked and asked both houses to pass a resolution empowering him to respond to further North Vietnamese aggression. The administration depicted the incidents as unprovoked acts of belligerence. On August 7, Congress passed the Gulf of Tonkin Resolution by votes of 88–2 in the Senate and 416–0 in the House. The resolution stated that "Congress approves and supports the determination of the President, as Commander-in-Chief, to take all necessary measures to repel any armed attack against the forces of the United States and to prevent further aggression." It declared that the United States was "prepared, as the President determines, to take all necessary steps, including the use of armed force, to assist any member or protocol state of the Southeast Asia Collective Defense Treaty requesting assistance in defense of its freedom."[1]

In the debate on the resolution, Sen. John Sherman Cooper (R-Ky.) questioned the chairman of the Foreign Relations Committee, J. William Fulbright (D-Ark.), on the implications of the resolution:

Cooper: In other words, we are now giving the President advance authority to take whatever action he may deem necessary? . . .

Fulbright: I think that is correct.

Cooper: Then, looking ahead, if the President decided that it was necessary to use such force as could lead into war, we will give that authority by this resolution?

Fulbright: That is the way I would interpret it.[2]

By overwhelmingly passing the resolution, Congress was following the practice set during the previous decade of deferring to the president's judgment in national security matters in the name of expediency and unity.

The Tonkin Gulf resolution has often been described as a "blank check." Members of the Johnson administration and the president himself frequently cited the resolution as evidence of congressional authorization of their policies in Vietnam. Although the resolution in combination with U.S. membership in the Southeast Asia Treaty Organization may not have been the "functional equivalent" of a declaration of war, as Under Secretary of State Nicholas Katzenbach claimed in 1967 during testimony before the Senate Foreign Relations Committee, it did provide a justification for almost any presidential military decision in Vietnam.

Investigations by the Senate Foreign Relations Committee in 1968 revealed that the *Maddox* was actually gathering sensitive intelligence within the territorial waters claimed by the North Vietnamese and that a South Vietnamese naval attack against North Vietnam was taking place near the place of the *Maddox* patrol. Furthermore, the investigations showed that the administration anticipated the North Vietnamese attacks. U.S. intelligence had warned that the North Vietnamese navy was under orders to respond to U.S. vessels in the vicinity of the South Vietnamese operation as if they were part of that operation, and U.S. ships had been moved to reinforce the *Maddox* before it was attacked.[3]

The Johnson administration had deceived Congress. Not only had the president permitted the ships to be sent into a situation where they were likely to be attacked, but when the attack did occur, he maintained that it was a completely unprovoked act against an American ship on a routine mission in international waters. In addition, although the crews of the *Maddox* and *C. Turner Joy* did fire at what they believed were enemy vessels, evidence suggested that the second attack may have been the product of nervousness and poor visibility. In 1965, Johnson remarked on the second attack, "For all I know, our Navy was shooting at whales out there."[4] Nevertheless, the second attack was presented to Congress as completely factual.

The 1968 revelations about the Tonkin Gulf incidents and growing congressional discontent with the war led to the repeal of the Tonkin Gulf resolution on December 31, 1970. The repeal provision was added to a foreign military sales bill, which was signed by President Richard Nixon on January 12, 1971. However, the Nixon administration claimed that the president's commander-in-chief power gave him sufficient authority to carry on the war.

1. Quoted in Christopher H. Pyle and Richard M. Pious, *The President, Congress and the Constitution* (New York: Free Press, 1984), 339–340.
2. Quoted in Leslie H. Gelb with Richard K. Betts, *The Irony of Vietnam: The System Worked* (Washington, D.C.: Brookings, 1979), 103.
3. Richard M. Pious, *The American Presidency* (New York: Basic Books, 1979), 387.
4. Quoted in Gelb, *The Irony of Vietnam,* 104.

tary activities in Indochina without congressional consent often was overdrawn by critics of the war. Congress continually voted in favor of military appropriations and the draft, without which Johnson and Nixon could not have carried on the war for long. Once troops and materiel had been committed to battle, most members of Congress believed that denying U.S. forces the money and reinforcements they needed to wage the war would be perceived as unpatriotic.

RESURGENCE OF CONGRESS

Not until 1969, when Congress recognized that the growing number of U.S. casualties in Vietnam, the fading prospects that the war could be won, and doubts about the morality of U.S. involvement had begun to turn the American public against the war, did Congress begin to assert its war powers. In that year the Senate passed the National Commitments Resolution, which stated that a national commitment "results only from affirmative action taken by the legislative and executive branches . . . by means of a treaty, statute, or concurrent resolution of both houses of Congress specifically providing for such commitment." Although the resolution only expressed the sense of the Senate and had no force of law, it represented Congress's growing dissatisfaction with its exclusion from national security and foreign policy decisions. Later in the year Congress adopted an amendment supported by President Nixon prohibiting the use of U.S. ground forces in Laos and Thailand. For the first time in three decades, Congress had exercised its authority to limit military activities overseas.[51]

In 1970, even as U.S. forces were being withdrawn from Southeast Asia, President Nixon secretly ordered U.S. forces into Cambodia to attack Communist sanctuaries. When Nixon announced the operation on April 30, 1970, many college campuses erupted in protest against the expansion of the war, and four student demonstrators were killed by National Guard troops at Kent State University in Ohio. An estimated 100,000 protesters marched on Washington. After months of debate, a lame-duck Congress passed an amendment in December 1970 barring the use of U.S. ground forces in Cambodia. This amendment had little effect because Nixon had withdrawn U.S. ground troops from Cambodia months before and lawmakers had backed away from prohibiting the use of U.S. aircraft over Cambodia. Later in December, Congress repealed the Tonkin Gulf resolution.

During the early 1970s momentum for legislation that would restore Congress's role in the foreign policy process continued to build in Congress. President Nixon undertook a series of controversial military actions without consulting Congress. He provided air support for South Vietnam's 1971 invasion of Laos, ordered North Vietnam's Haiphong harbor mined in May 1972, and launched massive bombing raids against North Vietnam in December 1972. Furthermore, Nixon's "secret" war in Cambodia in 1970, the publication of the *Pentagon Papers* in 1971 (which disclosed the deception of the executive branch during the 1960s), and the revelations about secret national security commitments uncovered by a Senate Foreign Relations subcommittee chaired by Stuart Symington (D-Mo.) contributed to the growing perception of lawmakers that executive branch secrecy was out of control. After three years of work and debate, Congress's attempts to construct a bill that would reestablish its foreign policy and national security powers culminated in the passage of the War Powers Resolution in 1973.

War Powers Resolution

Implicit in the War Powers Resolution (HJ Res. 542, PL 93-148), which was enacted in November 1973 over President Nixon's veto, was an admission by Congress that it had contributed to the debacle in Vietnam by abdicating its war-making responsibilities to the executive branch. The results of the Vietnam War had cast grave doubts on the assumption that the executive branch, with its superior intelligence resources, its unity of command, and its ability to act quickly, should be largely responsible for determining when and how the nation should go to war. With the passage of the War Powers Resolution Congress attempted to reassert its constitutional prerogative to authorize all significant military engagements. The bill's preamble stated that its purpose was

> to fulfill the intent of the framers of the Constitution of the United States and insure that the collective judgment of both the Congress and the President will apply to the introduction of U.S. armed forces into hostilities, or into situations where imminent involvement in hostilities is clearly indicated by the circumstances, and the continued use of such forces in hostilities or in such situations.

The most important and controversial provisions of the legislation outlined the situations under which presidents could commit troops; permitted Congress at any time by concurrent resolution to order the president to disengage forces involved in an unauthorized military engagement; and required presidents to withdraw armed forces from a conflict within sixty days—ninety if the president certified that more time was necessary to disengage U.S. military personnel from a conflict safely—unless Congress specifically authorized the continued use of U.S. forces. *(See box, War Powers Provisions, p. 178.)* Other provisions in the act obligated presidents to report to Congress within forty-eight hours on large troop movements abroad and urged them to consult with Congress "in every possible instance" before ordering U.S. forces into hostilities or a situation where hostilities might be imminent.

These provisions are not internally consistent. On the one hand, the "Purpose and Policy" section seems to confine presidential authority within strict constitutional limits; a president may introduce armed forces into a hostile situation only if Congress has formally authorized the action or if there is a national emergency created by an attack on the United States, its territories, or its armed forces. On the other, the procedural sections on reporting, consultation, and time limits imply that the president has the authority to introduce troops on his own for sixty days.

To strengthen the resolution's clear purpose that all long-

WAR POWERS PROVISIONS

The 1973 War Powers Resolution:

- Stated that the president could commit U.S. armed forces to hostilities or situations where hostilities might be imminent only pursuant to a declaration of war, specific statutory authorization, or a national emergency created by an attack upon the United States, its territories or possessions, or its armed forces
- Urged the president "in every possible instance" to consult with Congress before committing U.S. forces to hostilities or to situations where hostilities might be imminent, and to consult Congress regularly after such a commitment
- Required the president to report in writing within forty-eight hours to the Speaker of the House and president pro tempore of the Senate on any commitment or substantial enlargement of U.S. combat forces abroad, except for deployments related solely to supply, replacement, repair or training; required supplementary reports at least every six months while such forces were being engaged
- Authorized the Speaker of the House and the president pro tempore of the Senate to reconvene Congress if it were not in session to consider the president's report
- Required the termination of a troop commitment within sixty days after the president's initial report was submitted, unless Congress declared war, specifically authorized continuation of the commitment, or was physically unable to convene as a result of an armed attack upon the United States; allowed the sixty-day period to be extended for up to thirty days if the president determined and certified to Congress that unavoidable military necessity respecting the safety of U.S. forces required their continued use in bringing about a prompt disengagement
- Allowed Congress, at any time U.S. forces were engaged in hostilities without a declaration of war or specific congressional authorization, by concurrent resolution to direct the president to disengage such troops
- Set up congressional procedures for consideration of any resolution or bill introduced pursuant to the provisions of the resolution
- Provided that if any provision of the resolution was declared invalid, the remainder of the resolution would not be affected

term military engagements must have explicit congressional authorization, Congress included a provision in the resolution denying that a president could infer congressional authorization for the introduction of troops into hostilities or potentially hostile situations "from any provision of law . . . including any provision contained in any appropriation Act, unless such provision specifically authorizes the introduction of United States Armed Forces into hostilities or into such situations and states that it is intended to constitute specific statutory authorization within the meaning of this resolution." The provision also denied the president the authority to infer congressional authorization for presidential war making from a ratified treaty. Thus Congress attempted to restrict the means through which it could be said to have approved presidential war making to explicit authorizations of military action.

Passage of the War Powers Resolution was heralded by its supporters as a major step in reasserting Congress's war-making powers. Republican senator Jacob K. Javits of New York, a chief architect of the Senate's version of the legislation, declared:

> With the war powers resolution's passage, after 200 years, at least something will have been done about codifying the implementation of the most awesome power in the possession of any sovereignty and giving the broad representation of the people in Congress a voice in it. This is critically important, for we have just learned the hard lesson that wars cannot be successfully fought except with the consent of the people and with their support.[52]

The resolution was opposed by some conservatives in both houses and a small group of liberals who agreed that the measure was unconstitutional, but for different reasons. The leading liberal opponent of the resolution, Democratic senator Thomas F. Eagleton of Missouri, called the act "the most dangerous piece of legislation" he had seen in his five years in the Senate.[53] Eagleton and other liberal critics of the War Powers Resolution charged that although it may force the president to deal with Congress within ninety days after troops are committed, it sanctions virtually any use of the military by the president during those ninety days, thereby enhancing rather than restricting presidential war-making power. He warned: "By failing to define the president's powers in legally binding language, the bill provided a legal basis for the president's broad claims of inherent power to initiate a war. Under the formula, Congress would not participate in the warmaking decision until *after* forces had been committed to battle."[54] Although the resolution gave Congress the power to withdraw troops from a conflict, Eagleton believed Congress would rarely have the political will to do so, because such action would be seen by many constituents as unpatriotic or lacking in resolve.

In President Nixon's October 24, 1973, veto message of the war powers bill, he stated that the resolution would impose restrictions on the authority of the president that would be "both unconstitutional and dangerous to the best interests of the nation."[55] On November 7, the House overrode the president's veto by a vote of 284–135—only four votes more than the required two-thirds majority. Later in the day the Senate followed with a 75–8 override vote. The congressional override was made possible, in part, by the Watergate scandal, which had weakened Nixon's support among legislators of his party.

LEGAL QUESTIONS

Many of the War Powers Resolution's critics and even a few of its supporters have expressed doubts that all of its provisions will stand up to judicial review. President Nixon denounced the war powers bill as unconstitutional when he vetoed it in 1973. The major provisions of the bill, he contended, would "purport to take away, by a mere legislative act, authorities which the president has properly exercised under the Constitution for almost 200 years." These provisions were unconstitutional, he asserted, because "the only way in which the constitutional powers of a branch of the government can be altered is by amending the Constitution—and any attempt to make such alterations by legislation alone is clearly without force."[56]

Neither the executive branch nor a majority of members of Congress has appeared eager to let the Supreme Court decide if the War Powers Resolution is an unconstitutional legislative intrusion into the powers of the president. It may be that both branches have believed they have more to lose than to win from such a confrontation. On the one hand, because presidents have been able to ignore the most potent provisions of the War Powers Resolution, they have had little incentive to seek a decision on the issue in court that might force them to comply more strictly with its provisions. On the other hand, Congress may have been dissuaded from mounting a legal challenge to presidential war making by the Supreme Court's historic tendency to favor the presidency on matters of foreign policy and national security. A Supreme Court ruling striking down the resolution would deprive lawmakers of any leverage provided by their threats to invoke the resolution and would symbolically weaken Congress's claim to a place in the national security decision-making process.

The Chadha *Decision*

In 1983 the Supreme Court's decision in an unrelated case called into question at least one crucial provision of the War Powers Resolution. The Court ruled 7–2 in *Immigration and Naturalization Service v. Chadha* that legislative vetoes of presidential actions are unconstitutional. Legislative vetoes are provisions of laws that give Congress the power to review and rescind executive actions otherwise authorized by law. They had been used by Congress for more than fifty years, primarily to maintain some control over executive implementation of congressional policies. The Court in *Chadha* ruled that legislative vetoes circumvent the president's constitutionally granted executive and veto powers. Writing for the majority, Chief Justice Warren Burger emphasized, "The hydraulic pressure inherent within each of the separate branches to exceed the outer limits of its power, even to accomplish desirable objectives, must be resisted."[57]

The *Chadha* ruling raised questions about the sections of the War Powers Resolution empowering Congress to compel the president to withdraw U.S. forces engaged in hostilities by passing a concurrent resolution, which does not require presidential approval. Such a concurrent resolution may constitute a legislative veto over executive action.[58] However, the War Powers Resolution does not delegate any power to the president, and it denies that introducing armed forces into hostilities is within the president's constitutional authority. The resolution may, therefore, fall outside the reach of the *Chadha* decision. As Louis Fisher argues, the Constitution itself gives Congress a veto insofar as it must authorize military action. Giving the president a veto over any resolution restricting military action would require a two-thirds majority in both houses to control his war-making power.[59]

The *Chadha* ruling did not affect the reporting and consultation provisions of the War Powers Resolution or the provision delineating the types of situations under which the president could use the armed forces. Presidents have not, however, considered themselves bound by the latter provision. Independent of *Chadha,* they have questioned its constitutionality on the grounds that it places unreasonable restrictions on the president's freedom to defend the nation.[60]

USES OF FORCE UNDER THE WAR POWERS RESOLUTION

Every president has denied the constitutionality of the War Powers Resolution, and every president has used military force, frequently on a large scale, without complying with its terms. Presidents seldom consulted Congress before using the military. They have dissembled about the nature of the hostilities, and efforts by Congress to force these presidents to start the sixty-day war powers clock usually have been ignored. When presidents have reported to Congress, they have generally claimed full constitutional authority for their actions. The resolution may have had the effect of encouraging presidents to avoid a confrontation with Congress by confining missions to the resolution's sixty-day window. Presidents have otherwise been relatively unrestrained in their use of military force during the initial sixty-day period. These operations have underscored the resolution's inability to control tightly presidential war making in the absence of Congress's firm determination to assert its authority.

Mayaguez *Incident*

The first major test of the War Powers Resolution occurred on May 12, 1975, when Cambodian Communist gunboats seized the U.S. merchant ship *Mayaguez* and its crew of thirty-nine off the disputed island of Poulo Wai in the Gulf of Siam. President Ford unilaterally ordered U.S. forces to free the sailors and their ship and to bomb Cambodian targets in retaliation. The rescue attempt succeeded in freeing the *Mayaguez* and its crew but resulted in the deaths of forty-one marines.

In this case, there was general agreement that the president had the authority to commit U.S. troops without receiving congressional authorization. Ford complied with the war powers provision that required him to report to Congress within forty-eight hours, but he consulted with only selected members of Congress and only after the order to attack had been issued.

Ford, however, defended his approach: "When a crisis breaks out, it is impossible to draw the Congress in with the decision-making process in an effective way." Ford also criticized the resolution itself as "a very serious intrusion on the responsibilities of the President as Commander-in-Chief and the person who formulates and ought to execute foreign policy."[61]

Iranian Hostage Rescue Attempt

In April 1980, President Carter sent a small contingent of U.S. forces into Iran in an attempt to rescue forty-nine American embassy personnel held hostage in Tehran. Equipment failure forced the mission to be aborted after eight commandos died in a helicopter crash. Carter justified his decision not to consult with Congress by citing the mission's dependence on secrecy. Many members of Congress agreed with Carter's decision. Sen. John Glenn (D-Ohio) remarked, "If I were on that raid, I wouldn't want it all over Capitol Hill."[62] Carter also maintained that the mission was a "humanitarian" rescue attempt rather than a military action against an enemy nation and therefore fell outside the scope of the War Powers Resolution.[63]

Lebanon

In 1982 President Reagan sent U.S. troops to Lebanon as part of a multinational peacekeeping force. Marines initially were introduced into that country on August 24, 1982, with the specific mission of observing the evacuation of Palestine Liberation Organization (PLO) forces from Beirut under an agreement mediated by the United States. The marines left Beirut on September 10, after the PLO withdrawal had been completed. Before this operation, the president held constructive consultations with the foreign relations committees of both houses.[64] Reagan had reported to Congress on the deployment of marines the day before it took place. He nevertheless would not concede the validity of the War Powers Resolution and stated only that he was reporting to Congress "consistent" with the resolution rather than "under" it.[65]

After the assassination of President Bashir Gemayel of Lebanon on September 14, 1982, and the massacre of Palestinians at the Sabra and Shatila refugee camps by Lebanese Christian militia on September 16, President Reagan ordered twelve hundred U.S. marines to return to Lebanon. The mission of the peacekeeping force, which arrived on September 29, was to join with Italian, French, and British forces in providing a buffer between warring factions, thereby improving stability in Lebanon and the Middle East.

Congress debated whether the marines were in a situation where hostilities were "imminent," but it did not demand that the War Powers Resolution's sixty-day clock be started. On August 29, 1983, U.S. forces sustained their first casualties. President Reagan authorized the marines to defend themselves from their positions and ordered warships in the Mediterranean to shell positions in the hills outside Beirut from which the marines had been receiving hostile fire.

Congressional pressure forced the president to negotiate with Congress on terms for keeping the marines there. On October 12, President Reagan signed a joint resolution that started the War Powers Resolution clock but also authorized him to keep the marines in Lebanon for eighteen months. The compromise resolution stated that the marines had been in a situation of imminent hostilities since August 29, 1983, and that this legislation was "the necessary specific statutory authorization under the War Powers Resolution for continued participation by United States Armed Forces in the Multinational Force in Lebanon." On the one hand, despite this congressional involvement, the compromise favored the president and demonstrated Congress's reluctance to apply the War Powers Resolution's strict terms to presidential use of the military.[66] On the other hand, the resolution was the basis for the congressional criticism and threats that brought the president to the bargaining table.

President Reagan stated his reservations about the constitutionality of the War Powers Resolution in 1983 when he signed the joint resolution:

> I do not and cannot cede any of the authority vested in me under the Constitution as President and as Commander-in-Chief of the United States Armed Forces. Nor should my signing be viewed as any acknowledgment that the President's constitutional authority can be impermissibly infringed by statute, that congressional authorization would be required if and when the period specified in . . . the War Powers Resolution might be deemed to have been triggered and the period had expired, or that the 18-month authorization may be interpreted to revise the President's constitutional authority to deploy United States Armed Forces.[67]

On October 23, 1983, the suicide terrorist bombing of the marine headquarters in Lebanon killed 241 Americans. During the winter the chaotic situation in Lebanon failed to stabilize, and the president ordered the marines to withdraw on February 7, 1984.

Grenada

On October 25, 1983, two days after the killing of 241 marines in Lebanon, President Reagan ordered nineteen hundred U.S. troops to invade the small Caribbean island of Grenada. The action, which Reagan referred to as a "rescue mission," was undertaken to overthrow Grenada's pro-Cuban, Marxist government, to restore order to the island, and to ensure the safety of approximately one thousand American citizens living there, most of whom were medical students. U.S. forces were joined by troops from six Caribbean nations belonging to the Organization of East Caribbean States, which had officially asked the United States to intervene.

Reagan reported to Congress but claimed that he was acting under his own authority. The House overwhelmingly voted that the sixty-day clock of the War Powers Resolution had begun when U.S. troops invaded Grenada, and the Senate prepared to pass similar legislation. The president declared an end to the fighting on November 2, and he announced plans to withdraw all combat troops by December 23, the end of the sixty-day period.[68]

Because U.S. troops had quickly achieved their objectives while sustaining few casualties, and because the invasion was very popular among the U.S. public, Congress generally supported the Grenada action. The president, however, was sharply criticized by many members of Congress for failing to consult with them meaningfully before the invasion. Reagan had briefed selected congressional leaders about the mission on the evening of October 24, but this briefing was called merely to inform them that troops had already begun their voyage to Grenada. Sen. Charles McC. Mathias (R-Md.) observed after the invasion that the British prime minister was informed of the invasion before congressional leaders.[69]

Libyan Bombing Raids

On April 14, 1986, President Reagan ordered U.S. warplanes to bomb targets in the Libyan cities of Tripoli and Benghazi in response to the alleged involvement of Libyan leader Col. Muammar Qaddafi in recent terrorist acts. The operation received broad support from members of Congress of both parties.

Many prominent lawmakers, however, again criticized President Reagan's method of consulting with Congress. Reagan informed twelve congressional leaders of the attack on April 14 when the planes were halfway to their targets. Senate Minority Leader Robert Byrd complained that the meeting amounted to "notification" rather than consultation. Senate Foreign Relations Committee chair Richard G. Lugar (R-Ind.) disputed Byrd's interpretation, saying the president indicated he would call off the mission if it met with strong congressional objections.[70]

Persian Gulf Naval Escorts

In 1987, during the war between Iran and Iraq, Iranian attacks on Kuwaiti neutral ships threatened to slow the flow of Arab oil through the Persian Gulf. In response to Kuwaiti pleas for assistance, President Reagan offered on March 10, 1987, to place tankers owned by Kuwait under the U.S. flag so they could be escorted through the gulf by U.S. warships. The escort of the Kuwaiti tankers was intended to ensure the flow of oil through the gulf and to prevent the Soviet Union, which Kuwait also had asked for help, from increasing its influence among moderate Arab nations and its naval presence in the gulf.[71]

On May 17, before the escort operation had begun, the U.S.S. *Stark* was mistakenly attacked by an Iraqi warplane. The ship was struck by a missile that killed thirty-seven crew members. The attack prompted Congress to ask the Reagan administration for a report detailing the risks and objectives of its Persian Gulf policy. Many members of Congress pressed the administration to delay the reflagging operation, but no binding legislation was passed.

On July 24, two days after the escort missions began, a reflagged Kuwaiti tanker was damaged by an Iranian mine. Critics of the administration's Persian Gulf strategy pointed to the incident as evidence that the naval escorts could involve the United States in the gulf war, and many lawmakers called on the president to invoke the War Powers Resolution. The Reagan administration refused, however, to acknowledge that the escort missions placed U.S. forces into hostilities or an area of imminent hostilities even though military personnel were receiving danger pay.[72]

Panama

In December 1989, President George Bush sent U.S. forces into Panama. "Operation Just Cause" was a major intervention in a sovereign nation at peace with the United States undertaken without congressional authorization. President Bush justified the invasion as necessary to protect American lives and property, to arrest Panamanian leader Manuel Noriega as a drug trafficker, to ensure the integrity of the Panama Canal Treaty, and to restore democracy to Panama. Factually, and as justifications for an invasion, all of these reasons were highly debatable, especially as bases for presidential authority to invade another nation.[73]

Leading up to the invasion, President Bush had kept congressional leaders informed about developments in Panama and the canal zone, and he informed them by phone hours before the invasion was launched. After the operation began, his formal notice to Congress was accompanied by an assertion that the War Powers Resolution was "unconstitutional."[74] Nonetheless, Bush seemed careful to confine the operation to the resolution's sixty- to ninety-day limit.

The Persian Gulf War

In August of 1990, Iraqi leader Saddam Hussein invaded Kuwait. Citing both the gross violation of national sovereignty and the vital national interest in protecting the flow of critical oil supplies from the Middle East, President Bush responded swiftly with a massive U.S. military buildup in the neighboring nation of Saudi Arabia. These forces were sent without congressional consultation. President Bush notified Congress but denied that the 100,000 troops were in any situation of likely hostilities.[75] Members of Congress, some from the Republican ranks, criticized Bush's unilateral action, in part because of the size of the commitment. Bush denied any need for congressional authorization even after he sent an additional 150,000 military personnel. Although he claimed that the policy was to establish a defensive "shield," clearly the forces had been increased to offensive capability. Consequently, members of Congress called on Bush to seek authorization for any offensive action.

President Bush sought instead to build an international coalition and to secure a UN Security Council resolution authorizing offensive action. In late November 1990, the Security Council authorized UN members to use all necessary means to restore the sovereignty of Kuwait. Bush claimed that this resolution and his constitutional authority as commander in chief gave him sufficient authority to act. However, ruling on a suit filed by 54 members of Congress seeking an injunction against any offensive action, Judge Harold Greene argued that, although he could not issue an injunction at that time, congressional authorization was required by the Constitution.[76]

In January 1991, Bush asked for congressional support for "Operation Desert Storm," which would drive the Iraqis out of Kuwait. After a lengthy debate in both houses, Congress explicitly "authorized" offensive action under the War Powers Resolution while limiting that action to the terms of the Security Council resolution.[77] Bush, however, denied the validity of the

In November 1990 President George Bush and Gen. H. Norman Schwarzkopf review U.S. troops stationed in the Persian Gulf region. Three months later the United States led a coalition of twenty-eight nations to a crushing victory over Iraq in liberating Kuwait.

War Powers Resolution and denied that congressional authorization was constitutionally required. The only historical precedent to Bush's extraordinary claim of authority to engage in a foreign war without congressional authorization is Truman's sending troops to Korea.

Bombing Baghdad

In June 1993, President Clinton ordered a missile attack against Iraq in response to an Iraqi plot to assassinate former president George Bush while he was visiting Kuwait. Although the plot had been thwarted two months earlier, Clinton justified his actions as "self-defense" against an attack on the United States. He did not consult with Congress and relied on the UN Charter as well as his authority "with respect to the conduct of foreign relations and as Commander in Chief."[78]

Somalia

Late in his term, and under pressure from Congress, President Bush ordered troops to Somalia, which was suffering from a civil war. The aims of the mission were strictly limited to assisting in the international effort to relieve the famine-wracked population and preparing for a more permanent UN force to continue the operation.

The operation was redefined in June 1993 after 23 UN peacekeepers were killed by one of the warring factions. U.S. warplanes and ground troops then joined in a retaliatory strike. The UN, with President Clinton's approval, shifted to a more ambitious mission of subduing the armed factions and rebuilding the nation's political order. In October, eighteen U.S. Rangers were killed and eighty wounded in an assault on one faction's headquarters.

Although U.S. forces were under fire, being killed, and receiving combat pay for an offensive operation, Clinton did not consult with, or formally report to, Congress on the change in policy. With the death of American soldiers, the operation had become unpopular, and Congress began drafting legislation that would require withdrawal. Unlike Bush in the Gulf War, Clinton lacked any compelling national interest to justify the Somalia mission. In addition, critics charged that U.S. policy was being driven by UN policy. Eventually, Congress and the Clinton administration agreed on a deadline on use of funds for the operation. The agreement also required that U.S. forces remain under U.S. operational command. The Somalia mission began a long debate over U.S. foreign policy after the cold war and in particular over U.S. participation in multilateral missions as part of the nation's foreign policy.[79]

Haiti

The problems with defining the principles and interests underlying U.S. foreign policy and participation in multilateral operations were evident again in the Clinton policy toward Haiti. This policy was also met with broad congressional criticism and numerous attempts to restrict the president's capacity to commit forces in multilateral operations.

In 1991 a military coup overthrew the democratically elected government of Jean-Bertrand Aristide. President Bush declared that the coup "would not stand" and initiated an economic boycott as well as other nonmilitary measures to pressure the military rulers of Haiti. President Clinton continued the Bush policies until the military rulers openly reneged on their July 1993 agreement to cede power and U.S. forces sent to assist the transition were prevented from landing in October 1993. Then Clinton committed his administration to more forceful action to restore the democratically elected government. Congress debated a number of measures to restrict the president's capacity to send armed forces but passed, in May 1994, only a nonbinding resolution that asserted the need for congressional authorization.[80]

In July 1994, the UN Security Council passed a resolution inviting member nations to use "all necessary means" to restore the democratic government. The Senate passed another nonbinding resolution stating that the Security Council action was not sufficient authority, but Clinton denied that he needed congressional authorization. As the invasion was being put into motion, a delegation led by former president Jimmy Carter reached an accord with the military leaders, who agreed to allow the return of Aristide and his government. U.S. troops occupied Haiti to provide support and stability, and in October 1994, Aristide returned.

Bosnia

In 1993 the United States began participating in a joint UN/NATO effort to relieve the famine caused by the civil war between Serbs, Croats, and Muslims in the former Yugoslavia. U.S. forces were dispatched to help enforce a ban on unauthorized military flights over Bosnia-Herzegovina. President Clinton did not seek congressional authorization either for deployment or for engagement in combat. In 1994 U.S. jets took part in NATO attacks upon Bosnian Serb forces. Clinton used his commander-in-chief power as well as the UN and NATO resolutions to claim the full authority to order these missions.

Congress made several attempts to legislate restrictions on the use of U.S. forces in Bosnia. In 1993 Congress and Clinton agreed on a nonbinding resolution outlining conditions for the placement of U.S. forces under foreign command and stating that funds should not be used to deploy ground forces to oversee a peace agreement.[81] In August 1995 U.S. forces led extensive NATO airstrikes against Bosnian Serb positions, and in September Clinton promised 20,000 U.S. troops to assist in NATO's oversight of a peace accord. Clinton deepened this commitment by having the U.S. host the peace talks in Dayton, Ohio. Once the peace accord was signed in Paris on December 14, 1995, Clinton began sending troops on his own authority and with a promise to limit the mission to one year. The House passed resolutions contradicting that authority, opposing the mission, and yet supporting the troops deployed. The Senate passed a resolution supporting the president's commitments while asserting the one-year limit on the mission. In November 1996 President Clinton extended the mission for another eighteen months. Observers predicted that Congress would complain but go along with the longer deployment.

EFFECTS OF THE WAR POWERS RESOLUTION

Contrary to the warnings of some conservative critics, the War Powers Resolution has not proven to be an unreasonable hindrance on the president's ability to protect the United States and its allies. Since the passage of the resolution in 1973, neither a congressional resolution nor the automatic sixty-day time limit has forced a president to disengage troops from a conflict. Moreover, presidents have appeared undaunted by the resolution's potential to restrict the introduction of U.S. armed forces into hostile situations. Although the War Powers Resolution has not been effective as law, it has had political effects. During Reagan's deployment of marines in Lebanon in 1982 and 1983, the prospect of the invocation of the War Powers Resolution resulted in a formal compromise between the White House and Congress on the limits of a military operation. Similarly, President Clinton was forced by an assertive Congress to agree to an even stricter time limit on forces in Somalia.

As these cases demonstrate, the War Powers Resolution alone has not and will not reestablish Congress as the branch that decides when the United States will go to war. The effectiveness of the resolution depends on the collective will of Congress to challenge presidential actions. If this collective will exists, Congress has ample means to check the president's war-making power and to expand its role in deciding when and how military force should be used. Moreover, the resolution could be strengthened as law. As it stands, the resolution is based on an interpretation of the president's commander-in-chief power and, therefore, has been weakened by the historical precedents that back a president's claims of broad authority to commit armed forces. The resolution could be strengthened by basing it instead on Congress's clear authority over expenditures. The president's authority to commit troops could be tied more closely to explicit authorization of funding.[82] In 1995 Congress considered measures that would repeal the War Powers Resolution and place permanent restrictions on U.S. participation in multilateral operations, including UN peacekeeping missions. Both measures stalled in the Senate.

International Agreements and the War Powers

As events beginning with the Korean War demonstrate, controlling presidential use of force has been complicated by U.S. participation in the United Nations and numerous mutual security agreements with other nations. Presidents have used the UN Charter, Security Council resolutions, and other multilateral agreements as authority to commit U.S. forces without additional congressional authorization. They have claimed that Congress granted the authority to act by approving these agreements. They also have used these agreements to invoke their broad foreign policy powers as additional authority for the unilateral use of force.

UNITED NATIONS PEACEKEEPING

Presidents often have promoted UN peacekeeping missions and, when appropriate, have offered the services of the U.S. military to those missions. Some advantages that UN peacekeeping missions have over unilateral U.S. action in many regions are that UN peacekeepers are less threatening to the nations where they are deployed, the economic costs to the United States are reduced, and a UN peacekeeping force can promote a spirit of

The UN Security Council consists of fifteen members: five permanent seats (United States, Russia, Great Britain, France, and the People's Republic of China), and ten seats assigned on an elected basis every two years. Decisions by the council to use military force must be unanimous.

international accountability and cooperation in solving a particular regional problem. President Clinton was, early in his administration, an enthusiastic supporter of an expanded use of UN missions and of broad U.S. participation in them as a way to remain engaged in international affairs in the post–cold war era. Especially since U.S. soldiers were killed in Somalia in 1993, Clinton's policy has generated broad controversy as well as legislative attempts to restrict U.S. participation in UN missions.

The primary responsibility for the peace and security function of the United Nations resides with the Security Council. The council assesses threats to peace and attempts to use peaceful measures to prevent aggression. If nonmilitary actions fail or are inappropriate, the Security Council may vote to use military force.[83] A Security Council decision to use military force or to create a detachment of military observers cannot be adopted without the unanimous approval of the council's permanent members. The United States, Russia, Great Britain, France, and the People's Republic of China are permanent members of the Security Council. UN peacekeeping forces have been used to separate combatants, monitor cease-fire agreements, and protect civilians in places such as the Congo, Cyprus, Cambodia, Indonesia, West New Guinea, and the border between India and Pakistan. UN forces in the last three places included U.S. personnel.

During the cold war, UN missions were limited by the veto power of the United States and the Soviet Union. For example, the most dramatic use of the UN security function, the Security Council's resolution to resist the North Korean invasion of South Korea in 1950, was possible only because the Soviets were protesting the exclusion of the People's Republic of China from the council and were not present to exercise their veto. When the Soviet Union threatened to exercise its Security Council veto to block the creation of any UN peacekeeping force for the Sinai, as part of the 1979 Camp David peace accords between Egypt and Israel, the United States was compelled to organize a multinational force, which included U.S. troops.

During the late 1980s the status of UN-sponsored peacekeeping forces grew as UN peacekeepers were awarded the 1988 Nobel Peace Prize and the Soviet Union and United States both advocated the use of UN peacekeeping troops to monitor negotiated settlements of several regional conflicts. The United Nations created new peacekeeping forces to oversee peace accords in Afghanistan, Angola, and Cambodia, as well as to prevent the spread of war from Bosnia and Serbia into the Former Yugoslav Republic of Macedonia. Moreover, a qualitative change in the type of missions undertaken was proposed by UN Secretary General Boutros Boutros-Ghali in 1992. He suggested the possibility of a permanent UN force not simply to oversee peace accords but to intervene forcefully to settle disputes.

This expanded use of UN peacekeepers and the potential for more aggressive use of UN forces has led to criticisms in Congress and attempts to restrict U.S. participation in peacekeeping missions. The primary issue has been the president's authority, under the UN Charter and Security Council resolutions, to commit armed forces without congressional authorization. Although presidents have argued that their powers in conjunction with UN resolutions provide sufficient authority, such claims are not supported by the text and legislative history of the UN Charter and the United Nations Participation Act. Indeed, those debates focused on whether approval of the UN Charter by the president and the Senate could alter constitutional authority over war making.

The UN Charter speaks of member nations supplying armed forces in accord with Security Council "special agreements" that are to be subject to ratification through each member nation's "constitutional processes." The most contentious issue in the

1945 Senate debate on U.S. membership in the UN was the nature of those "processes": who had the power to commit U.S. forces to Security Council peacekeeping operations? The Senate did not want to hand the executive exclusive authority to provide the United Nations with troops, and the House refused to allow the Senate and the president to usurp its constitutional role. The clear understanding that emerged from the debate was that majorities in both houses of Congress would be needed to authorize the commitment of armed forces to UN missions.[84]

This understanding was affirmed in the United Nations Participation Act of 1945:

> The President is authorized to negotiate a special agreement or agreements with the Security Council which shall be subject to the approval of the Congress by appropriate Act or joint resolution, providing for the numbers and types of armed forces, their degree of readiness and general location, and the nature of facilities and assistance, including rights of passage, to be made available to the Security Council on its call for the purpose of maintaining international peace and security. . . .

Thus presidents are expressly prohibited by the Participation Act from unilaterally concluding an agreement with the Security Council under their powers to negotiate treaties, execute the laws, or defend the United States. The president cannot legally aid or commit U.S. forces to UN military missions without an approving congressional resolution.[85] Nonetheless, Presidents Truman (Korea), Bush (Kuwait), and Clinton (Haiti) have used UN resolutions as authorization to commit armed forces without congressional approval.

Events during the Clinton administration led to rising criticism of U.S. participation in UN missions. Early in his administration, President Clinton enthusiastically embraced broad U.S. engagement in world affairs through the UN and other multilateral organizations. However, in the absence of the global threat of communist expansion, the U.S. interests served by the expenditure of lives and tax dollars in remote parts of the world are more difficult to define and explain. Unlike the Gulf War, in which the United States had a clear interest in protecting the flow of oil from the Persian Gulf states, the United States had only indirect interests, beyond humanitarian concerns, in Somalia, Haiti, and Bosnia. Therefore, the debates over U.S. participation revolved around the degree to which the United States should involve itself in policing the world in the absence of national or global security interests.

U.S. participation in UN missions can be measured in a number of ways. On the one hand, the United States supplies only a small number of troops to official UN peacekeeping forces. In 1994, only about 800 of 63,000 UN military personnel were Americans. On the other hand, the United States is more extensively involved in conjunction with UN activities and resolutions. For example, the 1994 Haiti operation was under the aegis of a UN resolution, but U.S. troops were not sent as part of a UN command. In early 1995, more than 60,000 U.S. troops were involved in such "contingency" operations with more than half of those stationed in South Korea.[86]

In 1993 Congress passed a nonbinding resolution specifying the conditions under which the president should place U.S. forces under foreign command and placing conditions on participation in UN missions.[87] In 1995 both houses of Congress considered similar measures to restrict U.S. participation in UN missions. One provision would subtract the cost of unreimbursed spending on "contingency" operations from U.S. payments to the UN for peacekeeping missions. Because the unreimbursed expenses exceed U.S. peacekeeping payments to the UN by as much as five hundred million dollars a year, the measure would, as intended by its proponents, hinder UN peacekeeping generally by eliminating all U.S. monetary support.

Congress also has considered particular restrictions on the president's authority to commit troops to UN operations as a way to limit U.S. participation. One measure would cut off all funds for any unit placed under the operational control of a foreign commander unless the president affirms that such an arrangement was necessary to U.S. national security interests. U.S. forces have been under foreign operational command during World War II and the Gulf War, as well as in NATO and South Korean operations.

In response to these criticisms and proposals, the Clinton administration announced more restrictive policy guidelines for U.S. participation in UN missions, especially those that may involve combat. Specifically, such missions must involve national interests or "a real threat to international peace and security." The statement also proposed cutting the proportion of the UN peacekeeping budget for which the United States is responsible from 30 to 25 percent. Nonetheless, the Clinton administration defended UN missions as effective and as an important part "of our national security policy."

Moreover, the guidelines reiterated that all U.S. forces were ultimately under the direction of the commander in chief. While suggesting various procedures for consultation with Congress, these guidelines still asserted that the president had, under the UN and other alliances, the full authority to commit armed forces. President Clinton maintained that the congressional proposals would be an imprudent and unconstitutional intrusion on the president's foreign policy and war powers.[88]

ALLIANCES AND MUTUAL SECURITY AGREEMENTS

The United States shunned alliances throughout most of its history. During most of the nineteenth and early twentieth centuries the military establishments of the great powers of Europe were primarily concerned with defending against threats from their neighbors. Because the security of the United States did not depend on having allies, the American people generally preferred to remain isolationist. Except for the Franco-American Alliance of 1778, which was effectively voided by George Washington's 1793 neutrality proclamation toward Britain and France, the United States had never participated in a formal peacetime alliance until after World War II.[89] Even when the United States entered World War I against Germany in 1917, U.S. leaders demonstrated the national aversion to alliances by claiming to be only an "associated power" of Britain and France.

World War II shattered the isolationist policies of the United States. The nation emerged from the war not just as a member of the international community, but as a world leader. The growth of Soviet military power and the establishment of Soviet control over Eastern Europe after World War II led many nations to seek the security of an alliance or friendly relationship with the United States. Under Truman and Eisenhower the United States enthusiastically erected a global network of multilateral and bilateral alliances intended to contain Soviet expansionism. The Rio Pact, signed in 1947, reaffirmed the longstanding U.S. commitment to defend the Western Hemisphere. The 1949 North Atlantic Treaty created the North Atlantic Treaty Organization (NATO), an alliance between the United States, Canada, and most Western European democracies that developed into the cornerstone of U.S. containment strategy. The ANZUS alliance was formed between Australia, New Zealand, and the United States in 1951. The United States also joined the Southeast Asia Treaty Organization (SEATO) in 1954 and established ties with, although not membership in, a Middle Eastern alliance known as the Central Treaty Organization (CENTO) in 1956. These multilateral alliances were complemented by bilateral alliances with Japan and the Philippines in 1951, Korea in 1953, Taiwan in 1954, and Iran, Pakistan, and Turkey in 1959.[90]

The purpose of, and motivation to maintain, these alliances have been in a state of flux in the post–cold war era. Many of them, including SEATO and CENTO, no longer exist. Without an overriding single interest in mutual defense or a dependence on U.S. economic, military, and especially nuclear power, there are more potential conflicts between national interests and alliance policy. The movement of European NATO nations toward the more Europe-centered defense structure of the Western European Union (WEU) has been encouraged by the withdrawal of the United States from the NATO-sponsored naval blockade of the former Yugoslavia.[91] Indeed, the weakening of U.S. influence in NATO is manifest in the many conflicts between the United States and the other NATO nations over alliance policy and actions in that region. President Clinton has been committed to working through NATO and the UN, and his policy toward Bosnia has been shaped by a desire to avoid ruptures between the United States and its NATO allies. In 1995 Clinton vetoed a bill directing him to depart from UN and NATO policy by terminating the U.S. arms embargo against Bosnia, and he committed the United States to providing 20,000 troops to support NATO's oversight of a Bosnian peace accord. *(See box, Bosnia and Alliance Politics, p. 133.)*

ALLIANCES AND THE WAR POWERS

U.S. membership in an alliance creates additional presidential responsibilities and claims to war-making authority. The most important of these is the president's obligation, as commander in chief and the person who executes the laws, to fulfill the terms of a treaty. This obligation depends on the terms of the alliance agreement and the declared policy of the United States. The NATO treaty states that "an attack on one or more [of the parties] shall be considered as an attack against all of the parties." Advocates of presidential power could argue that by ratifying a treaty with such language Congress has given presidents the same authority to repel an invasion of a NATO country as they have to repel an attack on the United States.[92] Those on the other side argue that a treaty, involving only the Senate and the president, cannot alter the Constitution, which gives the House of Representatives a controlling voice in the commitment of armed forces. Indeed, Article II of the North Atlantic Treaty specifies that its provisions shall be "carried out by the Parties in accordance with their respective constitutional processes."[93]

Beyond the language of a treaty, the declared policy of the United States has had significant effects on the president's authority and ability to act in defense of an alliance partner. During the cold war, the president would have been expected to direct U.S. troops to repel an attack on NATO. Similarly, presidents would have assumed they had full authorization to respond to attacks on South Korea and Japan, not only because of treaties with those nations, but because many U.S. troops have been based there and numerous acts of Congress have recognized and supported U.S. defense commitments in East Asia. As the dire general threats recede in the post–cold war era, the effects of such commitments on subsequent policy and presidential latitude in use of force will be weaker.

President as Military Commander

The commander-in-chief clause gives presidents clear authority to command the military as the nation's first general and admiral. They possess all decision-making powers accorded to any supreme military commander under international law. Presidents not only order troops into battle, they are expected to approve major strategic decisions and keep a watchful eye on the progress of any military campaign. Most presidents since World War II have even regarded specific tactical decisions related to certain military operations to be among their commander-in-chief responsibilities.

In making the president the commander in chief the Framers attempted to ensure that civilian authority would always direct the armed forces. Military leaders who might use their authority over the army and navy to accumulate political power or enhance their personal reputation would be subordinate to the president who was elected by the entire country and was responsible for the welfare and security of all the people. Designating the president as commander in chief also aided effective military leadership by establishing a single leader at the top of the military hierarchy who was recognized by all as the legitimate and indisputable supreme military commander.

Military experience has been common among presidents. Al-

Dwight D. Eisenhower was one of twelve generals who later served as president. On D-Day—June 6, 1944—he personally encouraged American paratroopers of the 101st Airborne Division before their drop into France as the vanguard of the invasion.

though some presidents who have led the nation during wartime, such as James Madison and Woodrow Wilson, had no military experience, as of 1995 twenty-six of forty-one chief executives had served in the military. A remarkably high number of these were high-ranking officers. Twelve served as generals, and six of these twelve—George Washington, Andrew Jackson, William Harrison, Zachary Taylor, Ulysses S. Grant, and Dwight Eisenhower—attained at least the rank of major general.[94] Three presidents—Grant, Eisenhower, and Carter—graduated from a military academy. Franklin Roosevelt, another wartime president who never entered the military, gained defense-related experience as assistant secretary of the navy. Although few presidents could be classified as military experts, as a group they possessed more knowledge of military affairs than they did of many other policy areas.

PRESIDENTIAL DIRECTION OF MILITARY OPERATIONS

The degree to which presidents have become involved in the direction of military operations has varied according to their own military expertise and the circumstances of the military situation. Once troops have been committed to battle, presidents have usually delegated authority for battlefield strategy to their generals and admirals. The Constitution, however, does not prohibit a president from taking direct command of troops in the field. Several delegates to the Constitutional Convention suggested that the president should be prohibited from taking personal command of troops, but the convention rejected these proposals.[95]

George Washington was regarded as his nation's greatest general, and neither Congress nor the American public would have thought it wrong for him to have led U.S. troops into battle while he was president. In 1794 Washington came close to doing just that when he personally supervised the organization of the militia charged with putting down the Whiskey Rebellion.[96] In 1799 when an undeclared naval war with France threatened to spread to the North American continent, John Adams delegated his authority as commander in chief to George Washington. Adams, who recognized his own lack of military experience and the advantages of enabling the country to rally around a national legend if war came, asked Washington to accept the post of "Lieutenant General and Commander-in-Chief of all the armies raised or to be raised in the United States." Washington agreed on the condition that he would not have to take command of the army unless "it became indispensable by the urgency of circumstances." The hostile engagements with France remained confined to the high seas, and Washington never had to leave his retirement at Mount Vernon to assume active command of U.S. forces.[97]

The poor performance of Union generals during the early stages of the Civil War and the proximity of the fighting to Washington, D.C., compelled Abraham Lincoln to become deeply involved in battlefield strategy. He occasionally issued direct orders to his generals regarding their troop movements and frequently conferred with them at the front. Although Lincoln's interference in purely military matters has been criticized by some historians and applauded by others, he did allow his generals broad discretion in their implementation of his orders. After Lincoln had given command of the army to General Grant, in whom he had confidence, the president ceased to involve himself in tactical decisions.[98]

President Woodrow Wilson, like John Adams, recognized his lack of military experience and delegated responsibility for strategy and tactics to military leaders. Moreover, the distance between the president and the fighting made personal leadership impractical. He confined his commander-in-chief role during World War I to the domestic war effort and broad military decisions, such as his rejection of a French and British proposal in 1918 that the United States open a major front in Russia in order to prevent the Germans from transferring troops to the West after the Russians had negotiated a separate peace with Germany.[99]

World War II created conditions that necessitated the involvement of the president in strategic decisions. Because the war effort against Germany and Japan depended on the concert-

During the early stages of the Civil War, Abraham Lincoln became deeply involved in battlefield strategy. He occasionally issued direct orders to his generals regarding their troop movements and frequently conferred with them at the front.

ed action of the United States, Great Britain, the Soviet Union, and other nations, Allied strategy had to be determined through negotiations among the leaders of these countries. As a result, Presidents Roosevelt and Truman made decisions, such as when to launch the invasion of Europe and where to concentrate U.S. forces, not just because they were the commander in chief, but also because they were the nation's chief diplomat.

The tendency of presidents to become involved in planning the details of military actions increased with the advent of the nuclear age. Nuclear weapons created an environment of constant danger in which any use of U.S. armed forces could escalate into a nuclear confrontation. Consequently, modern presidents have seldom been willing to order a military operation without personally overseeing its execution. Perhaps the most extreme example of presidential involvement in planning military operations in the nuclear era was Lyndon Johnson's participation in the selection of specific bombing targets in North Vietnam.[100]

Sophisticated communication technologies also have contributed to presidential involvement in military operations by making contact between the president and local military commanders possible. For example, in April 1988, the pilot of a navy aircraft patrolling the Persian Gulf observed Iranian gunboats attacking a set of oil rigs. Because U.S. forces in the Persian Gulf were authorized to respond only to attacks on American aircraft, ships, and facilities, the pilot radioed his aircraft carrier for permission to attack the Iranian vessels. The pilot's request was transmitted up the chain of command from the aircraft carrier commander to the admiral in charge of the naval task force. Then the request was relayed via satellite through the chief of the U.S. Central Command in Florida to the chairman of the Joint Chiefs of Staff and the secretary of defense at the Pentagon, who called President Reagan. The president authorized U.S. planes to attack the Iranian gunboats, and the order was relayed back through the chain of command to navy pilots who moved to attack only three minutes after permission had been requested.[101]

COMMAND OF NUCLEAR WEAPONS

Despite the absurdity of a modern president ever leading U.S. troops into battle, the realities of nuclear warfare have made the president the nation's "first soldier." The decision to use nuclear weapons or to delegate the authority to use them to local military commanders is entirely the president's. Presidential authority over the nation's nuclear arsenal is derived from the commander-in-chief power and the need to make the decision to use nuclear weapons with speed and secrecy. For example, in the event of a submarine-launched nuclear attack, the president would have no more than ten to twelve minutes to receive positive verification of the attack, decide how to respond, and transmit orders to the military commanders in charge of U.S. nuclear forces. Even if the attack were launched from missile silos in Russia, the president would have little more than twenty to thirty minutes before the weapons detonated.[102] A decision that has to be made this quickly must be assigned to a single individual with indisputable authority.

Although presidents alone have the authority to order the use of nuclear weapons, they do not possess perfect control over them. The U.S. nuclear arsenal consists of thousands of nuclear warheads, delivery vehicles for all types of nuclear missions, and a vast network of personnel, computers, communications equipment, and information and intelligence gathering and processing systems necessary to manage the weapons.[103] Because of the size and complexity of the U.S. nuclear weapons arsenal and the requirements of deterrence, presidents cannot depend on controlling every weapon by simply pushing a button or making a phone call. Their control could be undermined by the failure or destruction of U.S. early warning and communications systems, of personnel who manage the nuclear weapons, or of the weapons themselves.

Presidential control of nuclear weapons has been aided by permissive action links (PALs), which are electronic locks that prevent nuclear weapons from being fired without prior presidential authorization. Intercontinental ballistic missiles (ICBMs) based in missile silos and nuclear warheads carried by U.S. strategic bombers are equipped with PALs. The military commanders of certain other types of nuclear weapons, however, have the physical capability, although not the authority, to launch them without receiving a presidential order. Nuclear missiles deployed in submarines, for example, are not equipped with PALs and therefore could be fired by the officers of a submarine who mistakenly believed that the president had issued a launch order. The navy continually seeks to minimize the danger of an unauthorized nuclear launch through intensive psychological screening of submarine personnel and elaborate launch procedures that require the coordination of several officers aboard any one vessel.

EVOLUTION OF PRESIDENTIAL NUCLEAR DECISION MAKING AND STRATEGIES

Since Franklin Roosevelt directed U.S. scientists to build the atomic bomb, presidents have dominated nuclear weapons policy and the formulation of nuclear strategy. Nuclear age presidents during the cold war counted nuclear decision making as among their most important and burdensome responsibilities. Dwight Eisenhower once said in a speech:

> When the push of a button may mean obliteration of countless humans, the President of the United States must be forever on guard against any inclination on his part to impetuosity; to arrogance; to headlong action; to expedience; to facile maneuvers; even to the popularity of an action as opposed to the righteousness of an action. . . . He must worry only about the good—the long-term, abiding, permanent good—of all Americans.[104]

U.S. Nuclear Monopoly

Harry Truman asserted that the welfare of Americans had motivated him to use the atomic bomb against Japan. In the summer of 1945, after the war against Nazi Germany had been won, President Truman decided to drop newly manufactured atomic bombs on the Japanese cities of Hiroshima and Nagasaki to bring an end to World War II. Truman officially maintained that using the atomic bombs was the only way to end the war without an invasion of Japan. In a radio address to the American public on August 9, 1945, after both atomic bombs had been dropped, Truman explained that he had ordered the attacks "to shorten the agony of war, in order to save the lives of thousands and thousands of young Americans."[105]

Historical evidence suggests, however, that the decision was not a simple choice between dropping the bomb and sacrificing tens of thousands of U.S. soldiers in an island assault. Certainly

A dark mushroom cloud rises 20,000 feet above Nagasaki, Japan, after the dropping of the atomic bomb on August 9, 1945. President Harry S. Truman ordered the bombing—here and three days earlier on Hiroshima—the only wartime use of nuclear weapons to date.

Truman wanted to end the war abruptly to prevent the Soviet Union, which was about to enter the war against the Japanese, from having a role in the occupation of Japan. He also may have regarded the bomb as an impressive demonstration of American power that would cause the Soviets to be more conciliatory toward the West.[106]

From the bombing of Hiroshima to the early 1950s, the United States enjoyed a nuclear monopoly. The Soviet Union tested its first atomic bomb in 1949, but it did not have an operational capability for several more years. The U.S. ability to destroy Soviet population centers with atomic weapons served as an effective deterrent against the threat to Western Europe from superior numbers of Soviet conventional forces.[107] Although the U.S. nuclear advantage prevented war with the Soviet Union through the 1940s and 1950s, the Korean War demonstrated the difficulty of using nuclear weapons in limited wars. Truman rejected their use in Korea because allied opinion was squarely against the move, and he believed the limited U.S. nuclear arsenal needed to be conserved to defend against a Soviet attack on Western Europe. A moral prohibition against the use of nuclear weapons also had developed, especially against the citizens of an underdeveloped nation like North Korea who were victims of communist expansion.

U.S. Nuclear Superiority

The small Soviet nuclear arsenal developed in the 1950s was much inferior in number and quality to the U.S. nuclear force. President Dwight Eisenhower attempted to use U.S. nuclear superiority to deter Soviet aggression. He believed that maintaining a conventional military force capable of countering the Soviets and their clients anywhere in the world would be disastrous for the federal budget and would not be supported by the American public. In addition, a threat to use nuclear weapons against China had helped end the Korean War. The administration therefore declared in 1954 that the United States would use nuclear weapons not only in response to a Soviet attack on Western Europe, but also in response to unspecified lesser provocations.[108]

This strategy, which was known as "massive retaliation," lacked credibility as a response to limited acts of Communist aggression such as Soviet-supported guerrilla movements or political subversion. Furthermore, as the Soviet nuclear capability grew during the 1950s, the possibility that the United States could launch a nuclear attack against the Soviet Union without itself and its allies receiving a nuclear counterblow became remote. The successful Soviet launch of the *Sputnik* satellite in 1957 even engendered false speculation that the gap in military technology that Americans assumed to be in their favor actually favored the Soviets.

President Kennedy sought to bring declared nuclear policy in line with current realities. Upon taking office, he announced a new strategy of "flexible response." Kennedy and his advisers saw that improvements in the Soviet nuclear arsenal had diminished the capacity of U.S. nuclear forces to deter anything but a Soviet nuclear attack or massive invasion of Western Europe. Kennedy also recognized that the United States was faced with many forms of Communist aggression that called for limited responses. Kennedy, therefore, ordered wide-ranging improvements in U.S. military capabilities. Nuclear deterrence remained the centerpiece of U.S. defense, but conventional and counterinsurgency forces also were built up to be able to wage limited wars.[109]

Soviet placement of medium-range nuclear missiles in Cuba in 1962 precipitated a crisis that pushed the United States to the brink of nuclear war with the Soviet Union. Kennedy refused to accept this alteration of the balance of forces. He ordered a blockade of Cuba to prevent further construction of the Soviet missile sites and demanded that the Soviets withdraw the missiles. After two tense weeks, during which Kennedy estimated the chances of nuclear war at "between one out of three and even," the Soviets agreed to remove their missiles.[110] The Cuban Missile Crisis highlighted the threat to U.S. security from the growing Soviet nuclear arsenal and stimulated a further modernization of nuclear weaponry.

Like the Korean War, the Vietnam War demonstrated the doubtful utility of nuclear weapons in limited conflicts. Although the Johnson administration had staked its reputation and the honor of the country on a bloody war, it refused to use nuclear weapons against North Vietnam because of the moral prohibition against their use and the risk of a wider war with the Soviet Union or China.

The Era of Parity

Presidents Nixon and Ford subscribed to the basic nuclear strategy established by Kennedy and Johnson. The concept of strategic defense—building defensive weapons systems capable of destroying attacking enemy missiles and bombers—had been widely debated during Johnson's presidency. President Nixon, however, concluded a treaty in 1972 with the Soviet Union that placed strict limitations on antiballistic missile systems. This formalized the doctrine of "mutual assured destruction" (MAD) that had characterized the nuclear relationship between the superpowers since the Soviets achieved strategic nuclear parity in the late 1960s. The MAD doctrine asserted that neither superpower could attack the other with nuclear weapons without its rival launching a devastating counterstrike. Each, therefore, would achieve security by holding the population of the other hostage.

During the Carter administration, U.S. nuclear war strategy was reevaluated. Presidential Directive 59 (PD-59), which was signed by President Carter in July 1980, stressed that the United States had to be prepared to fight a protracted nuclear war lasting up to sixty days. The directive ordered nuclear planners to develop a wider range of limited nuclear war options and assigned a higher priority to destroying the Soviets' leadership, military capabilities, and economic base if nuclear war occurred. It also called for an improvement of U.S. command, control, and communications to ensure that the president and other top leaders could direct a protracted nuclear war effectively.[111] Critics of PD-59 charged that U.S. officials had made nuclear war more likely by promoting the perceptions that a nuclear war could be fought like any other war and that nuclear destruction could be limited to an acceptable degree. On the other hand, the Carter administration argued that preparing to fight a nuclear war was the best way to deter one.

Ronald Reagan assumed the presidency in 1981 vowing to rebuild U.S. defenses, including nuclear forces. He contended that during the 1970s while the United States observed the letter and spirit of nuclear arms control agreements, the Soviets had continued to build nuclear weapons that would give them a first strike advantage in a nuclear war. Reagan argued that this "window of vulnerability" in the U.S. deterrent could be closed either by building new U.S. weapons or by getting the Soviets to reduce and reconfigure their arsenals. This policy led to a new phase in arms control.

Nuclear Arms Control

Since the development of atomic weapons, presidents have tried to enhance U.S. and world security by controlling the development and deployment of nuclear arms. Arms control agreements have been an important measure of a president's diplomatic success, and every president from Eisenhower to Bush concluded some agreement with the Soviet Union/Russia or the international community that contributed to the control or reduction of nuclear weapons.

As commander in chief and possessor of the treaty negotiation power, presidents have dominated arms control policy. Congress has tried to goad the president into action, for example, by creating the Arms Control and Disarmament Agency in 1961.[112] The Senate also can exercise negative control over arms control agreements by blocking ratification of a treaty. However, the president has general control over the initiation and overseeing of arms control negotiations. Because arms control agreements are perceived to be among the most important agreements made by the president, they generally have been concluded as treaties. The Senate usually has chosen to approve arms control treaties, but ratification has not been automatic. Three nuclear arms control treaties have remained unratified: the 1974 Threshold Nuclear Test Ban Treaty, the 1976 Peaceful Nuclear Explosions Treaty, and the 1979 Strategic Arms Limitation Treaty (SALT II).

Presidents may choose to avoid the Senate treaty ratification process, however, by concluding arms control accords in the form of executive agreements. In 1972 President Richard Nixon signed the SALT I Interim Offensive Arms Agreement, which imposed limitations on the strategic nuclear arsenals of both superpowers, but he did not submit the agreement to the Senate as a treaty. Presidents may also choose to abide by an arms control treaty that the Senate has refused to ratify. President Jimmy Carter announced in 1980 that the United States would not violate the provisions of the unratified SALT II treaty if the Soviet Union also did not violate it. President Ronald Reagan continued Carter's policy of observing SALT II until late 1986 when the administration announced that because of Soviet violations the United States would no longer consider itself bound by the treaty. However, Congress continued to abide by its limits through its appropriations control over weapons development and deployment.

A major shift in arms control policy was initiated by the Reagan administration in 1982. Critics of earlier arms control had argued that past agreements, in limiting the growth of arsenals, generally favored the Soviet Union, which was building massive, multiple warhead rockets. These rockets could deliver a devastating first strike. In conjunction with a weapons modernization program, the Reagan administration announced a new negotiating goal of arms *reductions* to eliminate the Soviet advantage. Because the Soviets would resist any such measure, many dismissed this as a ploy by Reagan to avoid all arms negotiations while also shifting the responsibility for stalemate onto the Soviets. Indeed, arms talks on this principle stalled during Reagan's first term. However, the end result, driven in part by the political revolutions in the Soviet Union and the Warsaw Pact countries, were four treaties, concluded between 1987 and 1993, that reduced nuclear and conventional arms. Each required the Soviet Union, and later Russia, to make disproportionately large arms cuts. *(See Table 4-1, p. 192.)*

President Richard Nixon and Soviet general secretary Leonid Brezhnev shake hands after the signing of the SALT I Agreement.

The first arms reduction agreement was the Intermediate Nuclear Forces (INF) Treaty, signed in 1987, which mandated the removal and destruction of most medium-range missiles in the European theater. This paved the way for progress on the first Strategic Arms Reduction Treaty (START I), which covered long-range missiles. Before that treaty was completed, President Bush signed the Conventional Forces in Europe Treaty in 1990. This treaty addressed the large Soviet/Warsaw Pact advantage in conventional arms, which had to be reduced before any reductions in the U.S./NATO nuclear deterrent could be settled. START I was signed in 1991. However, Senate ratification was delayed by the collapse of the Soviet Union. Protocols of agreement to abide by the treaty's terms had to be negotiated between the United States and the newly independent nuclear nations of the former Soviet Union such as Ukraine.[113] Before START I was ratified, President Bush initiated new force cuts and negotiations toward another reduction treaty (START II), which was signed by Bush and Russian president Boris Yeltsin in January 1993. Both treaties have been ratified.

In recent years, the focus of arms control has shifted to controlling the development and deployment of nuclear weapons by additional nations and the threat of regional nuclear con-

TABLE 4–1 Major Arms Control Agreements

President	*Year signed*	*Agreement*	*Senate action*	*Provisions*	*Parties*
Kennedy	1963	Partial Nuclear Test Ban Treaty	Ratified	Prohibits nuclear tests under water, in the atmosphere, and in outer space	Multilateral
Johnson	1967	Outer Space Treaty	Ratified	Prohibits all military activity, including deployment of nuclear weapons, in outer space	Multilateral
Johnson	1968	Nuclear Nonproliferation Treaty	Ratified	Prohibits acquisition of nuclear weapons by nations not already possessing them and establishes international safeguards to prevent the spread of nuclear weapons capability	Multilateral
Nixon	1971	Sea Bed Treaty	Ratified	Prohibits deployment of nuclear weapons on the ocean floor	Multilateral
Nixon	1972	SALT I ABM Treaty	Ratified	Limits size and number (two) of anti-ballistic missile systems in U.S. and Soviet Union. A 1974 executive agreement reduced number of sites permitted to one.	U.S.–Soviet Union
Nixon	1972	SALT I Interim Offensive Arms Agreement	Executive agreement; no action	Established a five-year freeze on number of intercontinental ballistic missiles and submarine-launched ballistic missiles deployed by U.S. and Soviet Union	U.S.–Soviet Union
Nixon	1974	Threshold Nuclear Test Ban Treaty	Unratified	Prohibits underground nuclear test explosions greater than 150 kilotons	U.S.–Soviet Union
Ford	1976	Peaceful Nuclear Explosions Treaty	Unratified	Prohibits nuclear explosions greater than 150 kilotons for excavation and other peaceful purposes	U.S.–Soviet Union
Carter	1979	SALT II Offensive Arms Treaty	Unratified	Limits numbers and types of strategic nuclear weapons	U.S.–Soviet Union
Reagan	1987	Intermediate Nuclear Forces Treaty	Ratified	Mandates the removal and destruction of all land-based nuclear missiles with ranges between 300 and 3,400 miles	U.S.–Soviet Union
Bush	1991	Conventional Forces in Europe Treaty	Ratified	Reduced conventional weapons and troop strength of NATO and the former Warsaw Pact nations	Multilateral
Bush	1991	Strategic Arms Reduction Treaty (START I)	Ratified	Mandates a one-third reduction in long-range nuclear warheads and restrictions on delivery systems	U.S.–former Soviet Union nations
Bush	1993	Strategic Arms Reduction Treaty (START II)	Ratified	Sets a ceiling of 6,500 warheads per nation, requiring a two-thirds reduction in warheads and elimination of multiple warheads (MIRV's)	U.S.–Russia

flicts. Presidents Bush and Clinton worked independently and with the United Nations in trying to enforce the Nuclear Nonproliferation Treaty against Iraq, Iran, North Korea, and Pakistan.

Antiballistic Missile Defense Policy

On March 23, 1983, a proposal by Reagan sparked a significant change in U.S. nuclear strategy. In a nationally televised address he urged the scientific community to develop the technology for a space-based antiballistic missile defense that would some day make nuclear weapons "impotent and obsolete."[114] Implicit in the plan was a rejection of the status quo doctrine of mutual assured destruction. Reagan proposed to achieve security in the future not solely by deterring a Soviet nuclear attack, but also by being able to destroy most incoming Soviet missiles. The Reagan administration also was hoping that the cost of trying to match U.S. development of strategic defenses would weaken the Soviets and move them toward arms reductions.

Although Reagan's optimistic vision led to an extensive research and development program (called the Strategic Defense Initiative by its supporters and "Star Wars" by its opponents), many scientists admitted that even if insulating the United States from a Soviet missile attack were possible, it would take decades of research and hundreds of billions of dollars to accomplish. By 1987 budget constraints and growing scientific skepticism that Reagan's "Peace Shield" could be built led to a reorientation of the plan toward the more attainable goal of using defensive weapons to enhance deterrence.[115] In 1991, with the success of the arms reduction talks (START) and with the collapse of the Warsaw Pact and the Soviet Union, President Bush and Congress again reoriented the development of strategic defenses, including ground-based systems, toward defending against a limited nuclear attack or an accidental launching.[116] In 1993, President Clinton pursued this aim with the intention of remaining within the terms of the 1972 Antiballistic Missile Treaty (ABM), which limits the development and deployment of strategic missile defenses. His "Ballistic Missile Defense" program focused on the development of ground-based systems to be used as "theater" defenses for troops in the field. These systems would also be available to defend the home front. In 1995 Congress considered measures promoting a more rapid development and deployment of a national defense system. Clinton opposed and vetoed measures mandating deployment of a national defense system. He said that the measures violated the ABM treaty and interfered with progress on arms reductions.

President as Defense Manager

Before World War II the United States maintained a small peacetime defense establishment. The isolation and size of the nation rendered it nearly immune to serious invasions by the armies of Europe. This geographic advantage as well as antimilitaristic principles and policy worked against the maintenance of large standing armies. When the United States found itself in a war, it mobilized troops and resources until the war was won, after which the armed forces demobilized and the country returned to a state of peace and nonalignment.

After World War II a national consensus developed that the United States should adopt an internationalist defense policy designed to contain the expansion of Communism and limit the coercive potential of Soviet military strength. In pursuit of these regional objectives presidents signed a number of regional mutual security treaties, the most important of which was the North Atlantic Treaty, which committed the United States to the defense of Western Europe. The expanded defense commitments of the United States and its adversarial relationship with the Soviet Union caused the United States to maintain a large peacetime military establishment for the first time in its history.

Although the Constitution gives Congress the authority to raise and equip an army and navy, much of the task of administering the defense bureaucracy and maintaining the nation's defenses in the post–World War II era has been delegated to or assumed by the president and the executive branch. The growth in the size and activities of the military and the perception that nuclear weapons and the cold war had created a condition of constant emergency combined to legitimize the president's role as defense manager. The president functioned not just as the commander in chief in wartime but also as the manager of the routine operations and preparations of the military in peacetime.

THE DEFENSE ESTABLISHMENT

The president is positioned at the top of a large and complex defense establishment. The Defense Department is made up of three military services and numerous agencies, offices, and unified multiservice commands, all under the leadership of the secretary of defense. Between the mid-1980s and the mid-1990s, the number of active duty military personnel was cut by about 25 percent, from two million to around one and one-half million. The Defense Department employs more than one million civilians, about one-third of all federal civilian employees. In addition to the Defense Department, other executive departments and agencies have national security roles. The Central Intelligence Agency (CIA) and State Department provide intelligence about foreign governments and groups; the Federal Bureau of Investigation is responsible for combating domestic espionage; the Energy Department develops, tests, and produces nuclear warheads; and the Federal Emergency Management Agency oversees civil defense programs. The Defense Department, however, is the president's principal means of executing national security policy.

Department of Defense

Before 1947 the War and Navy Departments functioned independently of each other. Each had its own cabinet-level secretary, military command structure, and procurement operations. The National Security Act of 1947 created the post of secretary

Robert S. McNamara, defense secretary from 1961 to 1968, greatly expanded the role of the Office of the Secretary of Defense. In his controversial 1995 book on Vietnam, McNamara admitted that as defense secretary he knew that U.S. prosecution of the war was flawed.

of defense, but its occupant was not given a staff or significant power over the individual services. The defense secretary functioned as the coordinator of the loose confederation of the Departments of the Army (the old War Department) and Navy, and the new Department of the Air Force. A 1949 amendment to the National Security Act created the Defense Department and recognized the primacy of the defense secretary, but in practice the individual services retained authority over their budgets and were administered autonomously by the service secretaries. The three services were not unified into one military organization because reformers believed such an organization could more easily threaten civilian control of the military.

The Department of Defense Reorganization Act of 1958 placed the secretary of defense at the top of the military command structure, second only to the president. The act gave the secretary the means to centralize authority over defense operations and planning within the Office of the Secretary of Defense (OSD). In 1961 Robert S. McNamara became defense secretary with a mandate from President Kennedy to take control of the Defense Department. McNamara greatly expanded the role of OSD and demanded unequivocal support from the military for the administration's programs.[117] McNamara remained defense secretary until 1968. He established the four major roles of the modern defense secretary: principal adviser to the president on defense issues, deputy commander in chief behind the president, director of the Defense Department and its huge military budget, and representative of the Defense Department before Congress and within the executive branch. This enlargement of the role of the secretary of defense gave presidents greater control over the defense establishment and assisted in the integration of defense and foreign policy.

Joint Chiefs of Staff

The Joint Chiefs of Staff (JCS) is the body of military officers responsible for formulating unified military strategy and providing the president with advice on military matters. The JCS consists of a chairman appointed from any of the services, the chiefs of staff of the army and the air force, the chief of naval operations, and the commandant of the Marine Corps.

All five of the chiefs are appointed by the president with the advice and consent of the Senate. Since 1967, the chairman has been appointed for a two-year term, which can be renewed once by the president. The four service chiefs serve one nonrenewable four-year term.

A president can appoint several types of officers to the Joint Chiefs of Staff, depending on the president's conception of its advisory role. Most chiefs have been officers nominated by their services and accepted by presidents with little consideration of their political compatibility with the administration. The president may receive the goodwill of the services for endorsing their choices, but the president will have little political control over these nominees. Presidents also have looked beyond the service's candidates and chosen officers whose professional reputation has come to their attention. These appointments may displease the services, but they allow a president to choose an officer with experience and a temperament compatible with the administration.

Finally, a few presidents have appointed close associates to the JCS. For example, John Kennedy appointed Gen. Maxwell Taylor chairman of the JCS in 1962. Taylor had earlier been offered the post of director of the CIA in 1961 but had chosen instead to become a special military representative to the White House. When the general was appointed chairman of the JCS, he quickly became a member of Kennedy's inner circle of advisers. The military usually dislikes such nominees because their first priority is promoting the policies of the president rather than protecting their service's interests.[118]

Since 1947, when the JCS was created, it has been criticized by many observers, including influential service chiefs and blue-ribbon panels commissioned to study its organization. These critics identified several problems with the JCS. First, the joint chiefs were given the conflicting tasks of being service chiefs responsible for the welfare of their services and members of the JCS responsible for developing unbiased policy plans and proposals for the president. The chiefs have seldom been able to do both and have usually put service interests first. Second, because the entire JCS was considered to be the president's military adviser, the chiefs have been compelled to develop consensus positions. As a result, their advice has consisted of uncontroversial compromise recommendations of little value to the president. Third, although the JCS was supposed to develop military plans, it was outside the military's chain of command. Consequently, JCS budgetary, procurement, and strategy proposals often have been unrelated to the needs of the commanders in chief (CINCs) of the multiservice operational commands in specified geographic areas.[119]

In 1986 President Reagan signed a bill reorganizing the JCS. The intent of the legislation was to improve interservice coordination and to create an organizational framework that would streamline the chain of command and minimize the influence of service parochialism on the military advice given to the president by the JCS.

The reorganization bill sought to accomplish these goals by increasing the authority of the chairman of the JCS. By making the chairman of the JCS the president's supreme military adviser, the bill's advocates theorized that the chairman would be free to develop advice and options independent of service interests. The bill created the post of vice chairman and placed the JCS staff under the direct control of the chairman to bolster the chairman's bureaucratic resources. To ensure that the service chiefs would continue to have an advisory role, the chairman was required to forward their dissenting views to the president and secretary of defense upon the chiefs' request. The bill also enhanced the authority of the CINCs, giving them greater control over the training, supply, organization, and operations of their command.[120]

Presidential Control of the Military

Despite the enhanced authority of the civilian leadership of the Defense Department since 1947, presidents have not dominated the military. Like any government organization, the military has its own organizational objectives and is capable of resisting policies it believes are against its interests. Military leaders have been particularly successful in cultivating friends in Congress who pressure the administration to accept the military's perspective on given issues.

In addition to the military's political clout, presidential control of the armed forces is limited by the president's dependence on the military for evaluations of the nation's military capabilities. Civilian advisers can offer opinions on many military problems, but their assessments must depend on the factual information supplied by the military. Moreover, estimates of the force requirements and prospects for success of a given combat operation can only be supplied by the military.[121] The president may be confident that a particular military operation is justified on moral and political grounds, but the president rarely will order the operation if the military is pessimistic about its chances for success. Presidents also depend on the military to implement their military orders. Whereas presidential initiatives in areas such as diplomacy can be accomplished through several channels, only the military can carry out a combat operation.

The political leverage of the armed services and their monopoly on military information and resources, therefore, has forced the White House to bargain with the services for cooperation in implementing its programs. Presidents, however, are not always willing and able to compromise with the military. Presidents seeking to reduce their dependence on military sources of defense information and to overcome military opposition to their orders and plans can take several steps. They can support defense reorganizations, bring a military officer into the White House as an adviser, rely on the secretary of defense and other civilian advisers for military advice, give the Office of Management and Budget (OMB) greater authority over defense spending, and appoint presidential commissions to study defense problems.[122]

Presidents also can exercise control of the military through their appointments of military officers. Congress establishes the ranks to which officers can be promoted, and the Senate confirms presidential appointees, but the power to assign military officers to posts including the Joint Chiefs of Staff gives presidents the opportunity to shape the leadership of the military. Moreover, one of the most important instruments of presidential control is the commander in chief's prerogative in wartime to dismiss members of the military who are incompetent or insubordinate.

DEFENSE BUDGET

A frustrating and complicated aspect of presidential defense management is the defense budget. Every year the executive branch must submit to Congress a defense budget, which proposes both the general defense spending level and the specific military programs on which funds will be spent. The general spending level is a highly visible political issue on which many Americans have an opinion—even presidential candidates feel compelled to announce their intentions. The specifics, however, must be determined through a complex process of conflict and compromise among the president, Congress, the Defense Department's civilian leadership, and the individual armed services, all under the lobbying pressure of defense contractors and public interest groups.

The amount of money devoted to the defense budget and the manner in which it is spent affect the defense policy and capabilities of the United States by determining what services and weapons systems will be funded and at what level. In addition, the defense budget profoundly affects diplomacy. The size and composition of the defense budget create a backdrop for U.S. international relations. Adversaries and allies alike scrutinize the defense budget for clues about U.S. global intentions. For example, increases in defense spending, particularly for items such as naval vessels and aircraft, may signal to foreign governments an administration's intention to pursue a more activist foreign policy. Cuts in defense spending may indicate an effort to redirect or scale back U.S. defense commitments. Particularly in the late 1980s and 1990s, in the face of massive budget deficits, all parties

TRUMAN AND GENERAL MACARTHUR

The most famous clash between a president and a member of the armed forces was Harry S. Truman's dispute with Gen. Douglas MacArthur during the Korean War. The conflict led to Truman's dramatic firing of MacArthur and tested the principle of presidential control of the military.

Few military leaders in the history of the United States were as respected and revered by the American public as General MacArthur was in the early stages of the Korean War. He had been a decorated hero of World War I, the triumphant commander of U.S. forces in the Pacific in World War II, and the successful military governor of Japan, overseeing that nation's transformation into a modern democratic state. When the Korean War broke out he was made supreme commander of the UN forces in Korea. His landing at Inchon behind North Korean lines in September 1950 reversed the tide of the war and reinforced his reputation as a tactical genius. Many Americans and members of Congress saw MacArthur as indispensable to the success of the Korean War effort. Republican leaders regarded the well-known, eloquent, and handsome general as a potential candidate in a future presidential election.

The conflict between Truman and MacArthur arose over their differing opinions of the goals to be pursued in the Korean War. The United States had sent forces to Korea under the authority of the United Nations in June 1950 after the North Koreans had invaded South Korea. Truman's original intention had been to drive the North Korean forces out of South Korea and reestablish a secure border at the thirty-eighth parallel. By October 1950, U.S. troops had accomplished this goal, but the successful military campaign led Truman and his advisers to order MacArthur to cross into North Korea and attempt to unify the nation.[1] Nevertheless, Truman was concerned about provoking Communist China and prohibited MacArthur from attacking North Korean bases in China.

MacArthur, however, envisioned an Asian strategy in which the United States would seek to overthrow the government of Communist China by encouraging guerrilla war inside the country, bombing Chinese targets, and supporting an invasion of China by hundreds of thousands of Nationalist Chinese troops from Formosa. At the least, MacArthur wanted the latitude to bomb North Korean sanctuaries and supply lines inside China. During the fall of 1950 he openly criticized Truman's policies and encouraged his supporters in Congress to press the administration to give him discretion to widen the war.

In November 1950, with U.S. forces close to crushing the North Korean army, Communist China entered the war and pushed U.S. forces back across the thirty-eighth parallel. MacArthur blamed his retreat on Truman's constraints. Truman responded with a presidential directive on December 5 that instructed overseas military commanders and diplomats to clear all public statements with Washington, but MacArthur continued to make inflammatory comments. Unable to accept either Truman's strategy or Gen. Matthew Ridgeway's remarkable progress on the battlefield, MacArthur in a March 7 press statement blamed Truman for the "savage slaughter of Americans."[2]

On March 24, MacArthur tried to undercut Truman's efforts to arrange cease-fire negotiations with the Chinese by issuing a proclamation that insulted the Communist Chinese government and suggested that the United States might "depart from its tolerant efforts to contain the war to the area of Korea. . . ." MacArthur failed to explain or apologize for the communiqué. On April 5, House Minority Leader Joseph Martin (R-Mass.), a MacArthur ally, read a letter from the general on the floor of the House. "If we lose the war to Communism in Asia, the fall of Europe is inevitable . . . ," MacArthur wrote, concluding, "There is no substitute for victory." Truman could no longer tolerate MacArthur's insubordination. After a week of meetings with his top advisers, it was announced at a news conference at one o'clock in the morning on April 11 that the president was relieving MacArthur of his command.[3]

Truman's public approval ratings, as measured by the Gallup organization, slipped from an abysmal 28 percent in late March to just 24 percent after he fired MacArthur. Sixty-one percent of Americans disapproved of the way he was doing his job. Impeachment became a common topic of discussion as members of Congress accused the president and his top advisers of appeasing Communism or even being under the influence of Communist agents.[4] MacArthur's welcome home as a war hero intensified the pressure on the Truman administration. The general delivered an emotional farewell address before Congress on April 19 and received a New York City parade attended by an estimated seven million people.

The Truman administration, however, was able to focus attention away from MacArthur's patriotic appeals and denunciations of Truman's policies to the general's insubordination and the constitutional principle of civilian control of the armed forces. At the joint Senate Foreign Relations and Armed Services Committees' hearings on MacArthur's firing and Korean War strategy, administration officials united behind the president in denouncing MacArthur's actions and endorsing military restraint in Korea. Most important, Truman received the support of the military. Chairman of the Joint Chiefs of Staff Gen. Omar Bradley told the committees that MacArthur's Korean strategy "would involve us in the wrong war, at the wrong place, at the wrong time, and with the wrong enemy."[5] Talk of impeachment subsided, and Congress took no action against the president. Truman had successfully defended his commander-in-chief authority and reaffirmed the principle of civilian control over the military.

1. John Spanier, *American Foreign Policy Since World War II*, 11th ed. (Washington, D.C.: CQ Press, 1988), 76.
2. David M. McCullough, *Truman* (New York: Simon and Schuster, 1992), 834–835.
3. Ibid., 836–843.
4. James A. Nathan and James K. Oliver, *United States Foreign Policy and World Order*, 2d ed. (Boston: Little, Brown, 1981), 149.
5. McCullough, *Truman*, 853–854.

President Truman pins a medal on Gen. Douglas MacArthur at their October 15, 1950, meeting on Wake Island. Truman called the meeting to discuss MacArthur's strategy in Korea. Six months later, Truman would fire MacArthur for insubordination.

in the budget process have fought over the redistribution of scarce resources and the redefinition of strategic needs. In the past few years, that debate has focused on the relative importance of spending on force readiness (training, supply, and logistics) and weapon systems, the production of which may profoundly affect the economic well-being of particular congressional districts and states.

The defense budget has enormous consequences for the U.S. economy. Even after the deep cuts since 1991, the approximately 250 billion dollar defense budget is the largest part of the discretionary budget—the part of the national budget that can be cut or shifted from year to year. *(See "The Uncontrollable Budget," p. 260, in Chapter 6.)* Defense spending affects the economy in particular ways as well. Although most economists believe that tax cuts stimulate the economy to a greater extent than increased military expenditures do, boosting defense spending can increase the demand for goods and services, which, in turn, can reduce unemployment and lift the country out of a depression or recession. Defense spending can spur technological development with various commercial applications and is essential to the economies of particular regions.

Defense Budget Process

The annual defense budget is a large and complex document that is prepared with the participation of numerous bureaucratic entities including the National Security Council, Office of Management and Budget, and many Defense Department agencies. About a year and a half before a fiscal year begins, the defense secretary issues a study assessing military threats and defines departmental goals and spending priorities. Using this outline the military services develop budget requests. These requests are reviewed and amended by the defense secretary and OMB, who reevaluate them in the context of defense and nondefense spending priorities. The resulting comprehensive defense budget is then submitted to Congress.[123]

Presidential participation in the defense budget process is limited by the size and complexity of the budget. Even if a president has had executive branch experience with the defense budget, the many demands of the presidency would not allow its occupant to become immersed in the details. The president therefore must rely heavily on career military officers and Defense Department bureaucrats familiar with the process.

Nevertheless, presidents influence the general outlines of the defense budget more than any other individuals or groups because their assessments of U.S. military capabilities and the threats to U.S. national security carry great weight in any debate. Presidents cannot be expected to review every item in the defense budget, but they do determine the approximate level of defense spending, and their general defense policy affects which types of programs will be emphasized. Although a president rarely will participate in discussions of how much to pay privates, a presidential policy of improving the quality of recruits will guide those discussions.

Besides establishing a general national security policy, presidents function as the final arbiter of disputes between executive departments and agencies about specific defense budget decisions. OMB and the Defense Department often disagree on budget issues because OMB's mission of overseeing spending often clashes with Defense's mission of enhancing national security. Early in his term, Reagan had to choose between the conflicting defense budget recommendations of Defense Secretary Caspar Weinberger, who had been charged with building up the nation's defenses, and OMB Director David Stockman, who had been given the task of reducing federal spending. Reagan sided with Weinberger, thus subordinating budget reduction to the defense buildup.[124]

Following World War II, Congress usually gave presidents most of the funds they requested for defense. Especially since the end of the cold war, Congress has scrutinized the defense budget more carefully, though always with an eye toward protecting local interests. For example, in 1976 Congress made closing military bases almost impossible to shield bases from budget cuts. In 1988, under the weight of massive budget deficits, Congress and the president initiated a complex base closure process that removed Congress from specific choices. Under the new procedure, an independent commission submits a list of recommended closings. Congress is allowed to accept or reject only the list as a whole, and its decision is subject to a presidential veto. Since the procedure was initiated, Congress has decisively defeated all attempts to reject the commission's recommendations.

The executive branch has retained the initiative in the de-

A Minuteman missile is launched from Vandenberg Air Force Base, California. Land-based missiles are one leg of the U.S. nuclear triad. Nuclear weapons are also deployed from aircraft and naval vessels.

fense budget process, but Congress has challenged the president on funding for individual weapons systems and defense programs such as the MX missile. In addition, the creation of the Congressional Budget Office in 1974 and the expansion of congressional committee staffs that deal with the defense budget have enhanced Congress's ability to detect waste and fraud in the spending programs that are approved.[125]

Weapons Development and Procurement

Presidents and their scientific and military advisers must choose which weapons systems to develop and build from a wide variety of options. Numerous agencies and offices within the Pentagon engage in weapons research, development, and acquisition, including the Defense Advanced Research Projects Agency, the Defense Logistics Agency, and the offices of Research and Advanced Technology, Research and Engineering, Operational Test and Evaluation, and Spares Program Management. In 1986 Congress enacted laws creating the office of under secretary of defense for acquisition and designating the under secretary as the Pentagon's third-ranking official in an attempt to centralize oversight and direction of the huge procurement bureaucracy.

Weapons procurement decisions seldom are based solely on rational calculations of how a particular weapons system may contribute to national security. The individual services press presidents and top defense officials to adopt various procurement strategies. The development of the U.S. nuclear triad—the policy of deploying some nuclear weapons on land-based missiles, others on bombers, and the rest on submarines and surface ships—resulted in part from the individual services' demands for a nuclear mission. Even groups within the services will maneuver to protect their share of their service's procurement funds.

Technological advances also drive weapons procurement. Since the end of World War II the defense establishment has operated under the premise that the quality of weapons is more important than their quantity. Presidents must serve as a mediator between competing factions in the procurement process and attempt to develop a mix of weapons that best meets the needs of national security at an affordable cost.

Presidents seldom become personally involved in minor procurement matters, but they must approve major decisions about purchases of highly visible and expensive items such as ships, missiles, and large numbers of aircraft. Such purchases often result from the presidents' appraisal of the balance of forces. For example, in the early 1980s, Reagan's determination that U.S. strategic nuclear forces were threatened by a window of vulnerability led to the deployment of the MX missile and a revival of the B-1 bomber project, which had been scrapped under Carter.

Weapons systems often take more than a decade to move from conception to deployment and may be conceived under one president, tested under another, and mass produced under a third. Presidents have been reluctant to cancel weapons systems that have reached the production stage because of the time and money that have already been spent on their development. In addition, the longer a weapons program has been in existence, the more likely it will be to have developed constituencies in the defense bureaucracy and Congress who will resist its cancellation. President Carter's decision not to build the B-1 bomber in 1977 and Secretary of Defense Cheney's 1991 decision to cancel the A-12 attack plane are rare examples of executive branch cuts after a weapon was ready for production.

Ultimately, presidents must secure congressional approval for appropriations to pay for the projects they favor. Not only must presidents contend with members of Congress who do not share their views of procurement priorities, presidents must deal with lawmakers who defend weapons because they happen to be built in their home states and districts.

Budget and Procurement Inefficiency

General and long-standing perceptions that the defense budget was filled with fraud and waste were heightened during the Reagan administration. Numerous anecdotes suggested that there were serious problems with defense procurement and budgeting procedures. For example, it was reported that military services were purchasing a twelve-cent Allen wrench for $9,606 and toilet seats for $640. Many such horror stories are based on a misunderstanding. To simplify accounting, contractors will distribute their total cost of production for an entire system equally across every item within that system. Thus the larger cost of developing and producing, for example, a self-contained toilet for a transport plane would be distributed equally, for purposes of accounting, across all parts, including the relatively inexpensive toilet seat. So the "price" of the seat only seems to be high.[126] The problems of procurement lie elsewhere.

Although waste occurs in every government department and agency, several characteristics of the Defense Department have made its problem particularly acute. The enormous size of the defense budget not only creates more opportunities for waste, it makes central control of its details nearly impossible.[127] Neither the president, the secretary of defense, OMB, nor Congress can judge the worthiness of every one of the thousands of line items that make up the defense budget.

In addition, the amounts and complexity involved in development and procurement increase the opportunities for outright fraud. In the late 1980s, several major defense contractors were found guilty of price gouging, bribery, and tax fraud. In June 1988 the Justice Department disclosed evidence of a procurement scandal, involving dozens of defense contracts costing tens of billions of dollars, that threatened to dwarf all previous defense budget scandals.

A crucial problem is the Defense Department's methods of making and tracking payments. To begin with, the flow of money is staggering. The Defense Department pays out $35 million an hour in payroll alone. Each year hundreds of billions of dollars flow through the department and out to private contractors. In 1995 investigations by the General Accounting Office and the Defense Department's comptroller, John J. Hamre, revealed that the department's antiquated accounting systems could not keep track of who had paid whom and for what. At least $15 billion spent during the preceding decade could not be accounted for. One official estimated that each year the department overpays contractors by at least $500 million. An overhaul of the system was under way in 1995. Because the procurement system cannot be shut down for repairs, the department's comptroller compared any attempt at reform to "changing a tire on a car while driving 60 miles an hour."[128]

The Pentagon's unique buyer-customer relationship with the contractors that supply it with weapons and equipment has also led to waste. The Defense Department has not applied the same standards to defense contractors that an average consumer would apply to a manufacturer of consumer goods. The Pentagon often has paid contractors for unexpected expenses incurred in the production of a weapons system rather than letting the company assume the risk of cost overruns. Arms manufacturers also have been given primary responsibility for testing their own products and have not been required to provide warranties for the equipment they sell to the Pentagon.

Moreover, interservice rivalries still adversely affect the coherence of defense budget planning. Each service and defense agency initially develops its own budget requests. Each service tends to promote its interests at the expense of the others. The services often have failed to consult with one another when developing budget and procurement proposals. They have sought weapons and funding that will enable them independently to perform missions they perceive as traditional and glamorous regardless of the needs of the other services.

In response to procurement waste and scandals, a study of procurement reform was commissioned in 1990. The 1993 commission report was incorporated into Vice President Gore's general study of government efficiency, the National Performance Review. The major recommendations for streamlining military procurement were part of legislation passed in 1994. Among other changes, the legislation reduced the regulatory requirements for smaller contracts and allowed many contracts with specific providers to be replaced by off-the-shelf purchases from the best available sources.

MILITARY PERSONNEL POLICY

Although the Constitution charges Congress with the responsibility to "make rules for the government and regulation" of the army and navy, the executive branch has substantial authority in military personnel policy. Much of this authority has been delegated to the executive branch by Congress, but authority also has been claimed by presidents under the commander-in-chief power to make regulations that do not conflict with congressional statutes. As a result, the laws passed by Congress governing the armed forces have been supplemented by a body of executive rules and regulations.[129]

Presidents have usually taken the initiative in proposing changes in the size of the armed forces, the methods by which the ranks are filled, and where U.S. forces will be stationed. Ultimate authority for raising an army resides in Congress, but legislators often have accepted presidential actions and recommendations on these issues.

Recruitment and the Draft

Conscription was not used in the United States until the Civil War. The 1863 Enrollment Act set up a draft system run by the War Department and administered by military officers. During World War I Congress again authorized conscription to fulfill troop goals. The 1917 Selective Service Act was challenged in the courts, but the Supreme Court upheld Congress's authority to draft Americans in a series of cases known as the *Selective Draft Law Cases.* Moreover, the Court held that military service was one of a citizen's duties in a "just government."

Not until 1940, however, did Congress pass a draft bill while the nation was at peace. Although the United States had not yet become involved in World War II, President Franklin Roosevelt urged Congress to adopt the measure. In the summer of 1941, with the threat of war looming larger, Roosevelt had a difficult fight before winning enactment of amendments that widened

HOMOSEXUALITY AND MILITARY SERVICE

Attempting to fulfill a campaign pledge, President Clinton stirred up a political typhoon in 1993 by announcing his determination to end the ban on homosexuals in the armed services. The military's policy was to discharge anyone who engaged in homosexual activities or even disclosed his or her homosexual orientation. The military had made it a practice actively to investigate and ferret out homosexuals. During the decade leading up to 1993, the armed services had discharged more than 14,000 individuals under this policy.[1]

Clinton had the authority to change this policy. The president, as commander in chief, has the constitutional power to "make Rules for the Government and Regulation of the land and naval Forces" as long as these rules do not conflict with congressional decisions. Nonetheless, the president's announcement was greeted with strong resistance especially from prominent members of the defense establishment, including the Joint Chiefs of Staff and Sen. Sam Nunn, a leading congressional authority on defense and a member of the president's party. The criticism may have been amplified by President Clinton's lack of credibility in military matters; it was generally known that he had actively avoided military service during the Vietnam War.

Under a threat from Congress to override the president by writing a ban on homosexual orientation into law, President Clinton settled on a compromise policy known as "don't ask, don't tell." A ban on homosexual conduct was retained, but recruits would no longer be asked about their sexual orientation, and individuals were to keep their orientation to themselves. Investigations would be initiated only by senior officers with reasonable cause to suspect a violation of the ban on homosexual conduct. Congress wrote the ban on homosexual conduct into law. These modest changes fell far short of President Clinton's original intentions. A federal district court in 1995 struck down the compromise policy as an unconstitutional infringement of free speech. The Justice Department announced it would appeal the ruling, and there was general agreement in Congress that the compromise policy would eventually stand.

Both his original policy and his handling of the criticisms damaged Clinton's reputation and political influence.

1. *Congressional Quarterly Almanac 1992* (Washington, D.C.: Congressional Quarterly, 1993), 454.

the draft. The measure was passed in the House by just one vote. Although earlier drafts had been administered by the War Department, the Selective Training and Service Act of 1940 established an independent Selective Service System, headed by a presidential appointee, to oversee the draft.

In 1947 Congress followed President Truman's recommendation to allow the 1940 draft act to expire. A year later when enlistments failed to meet troop needs, Truman proposed a renewal of the draft and universal military training. Truman's plan would have required all physically and mentally able men to receive one year of military training and serve six months in the reserves. Congress rejected universal military training but passed the Selective Service Act of 1948, which renewed the peacetime draft.

Congress extended the draft several times during the next two and a half decades with the support of a series of presidents. After the 1973 signing of the Paris peace accords, ending U.S. involvement in the Vietnam War, Congress followed the recommendation of President Nixon and allowed the draft to expire that year. The draft's expiration was the first step in establishing an all-volunteer armed forces, an idea that had been under study since 1969. Military pay was raised dramatically to attract volunteers. Since 1973 the armed services have succeeded in meeting their personnel requirements.

In his State of the Union address on January 23, 1980, Jimmy Carter asked Congress to reinstitute draft registration. Carter was motivated to make the proposal by the international tension created in late 1979 by the takeover of the U.S. embassy in Tehran and the invasion of Afghanistan by the Soviet Union. Draft registration was intended to reduce the time required to bring draftees into the armed services after a mobilization. Congress approved the plan, although it rejected Carter's request to register women. The measure provided only for registration and did not empower the president to draft young men without a further authorization from Congress.[130] Although Reagan opposed draft registration during the 1980 presidential campaign, he ordered its continuation in January 1982.

Peacetime Military Deployments

Although the commander-in-chief power provides presidents with a justification to determine unilaterally where troops should be deployed even in peacetime, they have generally respected laws limiting their freedom to deploy troops.[131] In 1940 Congress attached a proviso to the Selective Training and Service Act that prohibited troops drafted under the act from being used outside the Western Hemisphere. Franklin Roosevelt accepted this limitation, although he maintained that Iceland was part of the Western Hemisphere and sent troops there in 1941.

A more recent example of a congressional limit on troop deployments occurred in 1982. In that year, Congress attached to a defense appropriations bill an amendment limiting the number of active-duty U.S. military personnel stationed in Europe to 315,000. The Reagan administration opposed the limit, arguing that increases in U.S. troop strength in Europe might be required by changes in the military balance between NATO and the Soviet Union and its allies. Despite the administration's objections, Defense Secretary Caspar Weinberger assured Congress that the troop ceiling would be observed. The amendment included a provision that allowed the president to waive the troop limit if the president certified that "overriding national security requirements" made such action necessary. This provision was a recognition by Congress that the purpose of peacetime military deployments is to deter war and that the president as commander in chief should have wide authority to redeploy troops for that purpose.

If a president did refuse to observe limitations Congress placed on peacetime troop deployments, Congress still would have the option of cutting off funds for the base where the troops were stationed or for the supplies needed to sustain the troops. Since 1993, Congress has considered a number of proposals that would limit the president's capacity to deploy U.S. forces in Bosnia, Haiti, and in any UN peacekeeping mission without specific congressional authorization.

Presidential Wartime Emergency Powers

In 1810, after Thomas Jefferson had left the presidency, he wrote:

> A strict observation of the written laws is doubtless *one* of the high duties of a good citizen, but it is not the *highest.* The law of necessity, of self-preservation, of saving our country when in danger, are of higher obligation. To lose our country by a scrupulous adherence to written law would be to lose the law itself, with life, liberty, property . . . thus absurdly sacrificing the end to the means.[132]

Jefferson maintained that such acts of self-preservation, although justified, were strictly illegal and in no way authorized by the Constitution. Later presidents have derived their emergency powers from a broad reading of constitutional authority and have claimed the authority to violate parts of the Constitution to ensure the security of the nation.

When it is evident that conditions of national peril exist, Congress and the American public turn to the president for leadership. Under such conditions Lincoln and Franklin Roosevelt stretched, reinterpreted, and in some cases brazenly violated the Constitution in the name of national security. Their claims to an inherent executive power to safeguard the nation were accepted because the American people generally agreed with their assessment of the gravity of the emergency at hand.[133] Presidential assertions of an inherent executive power based on a doubtful claim of national emergency, however, will likely fail the test of public and judicial scrutiny. President Nixon was not able to convince the American people or the courts that his administration's use of wiretaps and break-ins was in the interest of national security.

Nowhere does the Constitution mention presidential emergency powers, but the courts often have been sympathetic to exercises of emergency power by presidents in wartime, especially when action is taken with the cooperation of Congress. Yet this approval has not been automatic, especially when the rights and property of U.S. citizens are involved. Total war in any age requires sacrifices from civilians and security measures at home, but a wartime emergency does not give the president unrestrained freedom to violate the rights of Americans.

GOVERNING CONQUERED TERRITORY

On many occasions U.S. military forces have occupied enemy territory during hostilities. Presidential authority to administer a recently occupied territory through the armed forces is nearly absolute. Neither the Constitution of the United States nor the former laws of a conquered nation constrain the president. Several hundred Supreme Court cases have upheld the president's authority to function as a dictator over occupied territory subject only to the "laws of war."[1] Presidents and their appointed military representatives may set up new government institutions, make laws by decree, establish a court system, collect taxes, or do anything else they believe necessary to administer the conquered area. Presidential rule over occupied territory lasts until it is annexed to the United States or a treaty is concluded that transfers power back to a local government. The president may not, however, unilaterally annex acquired territory. Article IV of the Constitution grants Congress the power to "dispose of and make all needful Rules and Regulations respecting the Territory or other Property belonging to the United States." Therefore, Congress must approve a treaty of cession or pass legislation annexing the territory before it can become part of the United States.[2]

1. Clinton Rossiter, *The Supreme Court and the Commander in Chief* (Ithaca, N.Y.: Cornell University Press, 1976), 122–123.
2. Joseph E. Kallenbach, *The American Chief Executive: The Presidency and the Governorship* (New York: Harper and Row, 1966), 541.

MARTIAL LAW AND CIVIL RIGHTS

The most extreme wartime emergency measure a president may take is a declaration of martial law. Under such a declaration, ordinary law and judicial process are temporarily replaced by military rule. Substitution of military for civilian authority may be general or confined to a region. In addition, it may be absolute, or it may apply only to a specific civil function by the military. Even cases of limited martial law, however, invariably result in the curbing of individual rights.

The Constitution does not provide for a power to declare martial law, although it does mention the suspension of *habeas corpus* under Article I, which outlines Congress's powers. The declaration of martial law, however, is usually presumed to be a presidential function flowing from the president's powers to command the armed forces and execute the laws. Because there is no specific constitutional basis for martial law, presidents must justify their decision to proclaim it on the grounds that protecting the welfare and security of the nation requires them to govern through military force rather than established laws.

No president has ever declared a condition of absolute martial law that applied to the entire country. Moreover, not since President Lincoln placed several areas of the nation under martial law during the Civil War has any president directly proclaimed martial law on behalf of the national government. Martial law has been declared, however, by presidential agents or military officers, often with the explicit or implied approval of the president. For example, Gen. Andrew Jackson declared martial law in New Orleans before his battle with the British there in 1814; the commander of federal troops sent to Idaho in 1899 to quell labor unrest declared martial law with President McKinley's approval; and after the Japanese attack on Pearl Harbor on December 7, 1941, the territorial governor of Hawaii declared martial law on the islands with the support of Franklin Roosevelt.[134]

Although the courts may reject the president's assessment of the necessity of martial law, historically they have done so only after the emergency has passed. In 1866 the Supreme Court ruled in *Ex parte Milligan* that Lincoln's suspension of the civil court system in Indiana during the Civil War was illegal.[135] Similarly, in 1946 the Court declared in *Duncan v. Kahanamoku* that the establishment of martial law during World War II in Hawaii by the governor with President Roosevelt's approval had been unlawful.[136] Yet neither decision had any effect on either president's ability to abrogate civil liberties during the wars.

Suspension of Habeas Corpus

The only emergency power mentioned in the Constitution is the crucial provision for the suspension of the writ of *habeas corpus*—the right of prisoners to have the legality of their detention reviewed by the courts and to be released upon the court's orders. The Constitution states: "The Privilege of the Writ of Habeas Corpus shall not be suspended, unless when in Cases of Rebellion or Invasion the public Safety may require it." The Framers did not, however, specify who had this power, although their placement of it in Article I has led many legal scholars, judges, and legislators to argue that it was intended as a congressional power.

The issue of presidential suspension of *habeas corpus* arose most dramatically during the Civil War. In response to sabotage by Confederate sympathizers, President Lincoln ordered in the spring of 1861 that *habeas corpus* be suspended along the route between Washington and Philadelphia. Lincoln believed this and other emergency measures were essential to the survival of the Union.

On May 25, John Merryman, a prominent Maryland citizen who had been involved in secessionist activities in that state, was arrested by military authorities. Merryman immediately appealed to Chief Justice Roger Taney for a writ of *habeas corpus.* Taney reviewed the case and ordered the army to release Merryman, but Lincoln defiantly refused to permit his release. Taney denounced Lincoln's action and wrote an opinion asserting that the Constitution had conferred authority to suspend the writ on Congress, not the president. Lincoln maintained that since the suspension of *habeas corpus* was an emergency measure and emergencies could occur when Congress was out of session—as it had been in this case—presidents must have authority to suspend the writ unilaterally.

The conflict between the president and the chief justice showed that a president willing to defy legal procedures during a genuine crisis that was widely recognized as such could suspend *habeas corpus* regardless of whether the president has the constitutional authority to do so. Presidential scholar Clinton Rossiter remarked,

> The one great precedent is what Lincoln did, not what Taney said. Future Presidents will know where to look for historical support. So long as public opinion sustains the President, as a sufficient amount of it sustained Lincoln in his shadowy tilt with Taney and throughout the rest of the war, he has nothing to fear from the displeasure of the courts. . . . The law of the Constitution, as it actually exists, must be considered to read that in a condition of martial necessity the President has the power to suspend the privilege of the writ of habeas corpus.[137]

Trial of Civilians by Military Courts

In addition to suspending *habeas corpus,* President Lincoln also declared that for some crimes civilians could be tried by military courts. On September 24, 1862, he announced that as long as the Civil War continued,

> all rebels and insurgents, their aiders and abettors, within the United States, and all persons discouraging volunteer enlistments, resisting militia drafts, or guilty of any disloyal practice affording aid and comfort to rebels against the authority of the United States, shall be subject to martial law and liable to trial and punishment of courts-martial or military commissions.

Lincoln went on to suspend *habeas corpus* for such persons and declared that they could be imprisoned in military facilities. Although Congress had passed legislation approving many of Lincoln's emergency measures, it never approved his subjection of civilians to military courts.[138]

Lambdin P. Milligan, a citizen of Indiana, was arrested in 1864 by military authorities who charged him with aiding a Confederate raid into Indiana from across the Ohio River. On May 9, 1865, Milligan was found guilty and sentenced to death. Milligan's case eventually came before the Supreme Court.

The Court held 9–0 in *Ex parte Milligan* that the president did not have the authority to subject civilians to military tribunals in an area where civilian courts were functioning.[139] The Court also ruled 5–4 that even the president and Congress together lacked power to authorize trials of civilians by military courts outside of a war zone. The majority opinion, written by Justice David Davis, admitted that in regions "where war actually prevails" and makes it "impossible to administer criminal justice according to the law," military government is justified. However, the Court rejected the idea that such conditions existed in Indiana—hundreds of miles from the war front—where civilian courts were functioning normally.

Beyond their verdict, the justices used this case to defend the inviolability of the Constitution. Davis wrote:

> The Constitution of the United States is a law for rulers and people, equally in war and in peace, and covers with the shield of its protection all classes of men, at all times, and under all circumstances. No doctrine involving more pernicious consequences was ever invented by the

wit of man than that any of its provisions can be suspended during any of the great exigencies of government.

Ex parte Milligan is regarded as significant by legal scholars for demonstrating that even during the most dire military emergency there are constitutional limits to presidential power. However, the logic in Lincoln's defense of his policy is also compelling:

To state the question more directly, are all the laws, *but one*, to go unexecuted, and the government itself go to pieces, lest that one [law] be violated? Even in such a case, would not the official oath to faithfully execute the laws be broken, if the government should be overthrown, when it is believed that disregarding the single law, would tend to preserve it?[140]

When the Supreme Court ruled on *Milligan* in 1866, the war was over and President Lincoln was dead. Consequently, the Court was able to strike down a presidential emergency action without confronting an incumbent president during a wartime crisis.

Korematsu v. United States

Three-quarters of a century after *Milligan,* however, a case involving the violation of individual rights by an exercise of wartime emergency power came before the Court while the emergency still existed.

Following the Japanese attack on Pearl Harbor on December 7, 1941, President Roosevelt ordered several controversial measures to enhance security on the West Coast. These included the imposition of a curfew on persons of Japanese descent and the relocation of 120,000 Japanese-Americans to internment camps in the U.S. interior. Both the curfew and the relocation applied to persons of Japanese ancestry regardless of their citizenship or loyalty. Congress subsequently passed legislation validating the president's directives.

This wholesale suspension of the rights of American citizens led to several Supreme Court cases. The Court ruled unanimously in *Hirabayashi v. United States* that together the president and Congress had the power to impose the curfew and that the extreme emergency created by Japan's threat to the Pacific Coast made the curfew justifiable.[141] The Court did not reach a consensus, however, on the more severe violation of rights involved in the relocation of Japanese-Americans. In *Korematsu v. United States* it ruled 6–3 that the threat to national security justified the joint action of Congress and the president.[142] Writing for the majority, Justice Hugo Black explained, "Compulsory exclusion of large groups of citizens from their homes, except under circumstances of direct emergency and peril, is inconsistent with our basic governmental institutions. But when under conditions of modern warfare our shores are threatened by hostile forces, the power to protect must be commensurable with the threatened danger." In a bitter dissenting opinion, Justice Francis Murphy rejected the premise of the Court's decision that the emergency on the West Coast warranted the exclusion from the West Coast of all persons of Japanese ancestry. "Such exclusion," he wrote, "goes over 'the very brink of Constitutional power' and falls into the abyss of racism."

Justice Robert Jackson's dissenting opinion got closer to the heart of the dilemma. On the one hand, he admits that there are military emergencies that warrant extraordinary measures. Moreover, Jackson argued, against the opinion of both the Court and the dissenters, that judges are not qualified to assess the circumstances. On the other hand, he argues that the Court ought not to corrupt the law by ruling that momentarily necessary violations of civil rights are also constitutionally permissible.

But if we cannot confine military expedients by the Constitution, neither would I distort the Constitution to approve all that the military may deem expedient. That is what the Court appears to be doing.... [A] judicial construction of the due process clause that will sustain this order is a far more subtle blow to liberty than the promulgation of the order itself.... The principle then lies about like a loaded weapon ready for the hand of any authority that can bring forward a plausible claim of an urgent need.... I should hold that a civil court cannot be made to enforce an order which violates constitutional limitations even if it is a reasonable exercise of military authority.[143]

SEIZURE OF PROPERTY

During wartime it sometimes is necessary for a government to seize property of its citizens that is vital to the war effort. Congress has traditionally passed legislation governing the seizure of property belonging to U.S. citizens. Before and during World War I, Congress empowered the president to seize transportation and communications systems if such actions became necessary. President Wilson used these statutes to take over railroad, telephone, and telegraph operations, which were returned to civilian control after the war. Similarly, Franklin Roosevelt was authorized by the War Labor Disputes Act of 1943 to seize control of industries important to the war effort that were in danger of being shut down by labor disputes.[144]

Presidents have not always waited, however, for Congress to grant them the authority to seize property before they took action. Lincoln personally authorized military units to take possession of telegraph lines during the Civil War, and Wilson in 1914 ordered the seizure of a wireless station that refused to comply with naval censorship rules. Franklin Roosevelt took control of several strike-threatened industries before Congress authorized such action with the War Labor Disputes Act of 1943. Yet unilateral seizures of property by presidents have been exceptions to accepted practice, and the courts generally have rejected the proposition that presidents possess inherent emergency powers that authorize them to seize private property.

The most famous court case dealing with the president's power to seize private property in wartime was *Youngstown Sheet and Tube Co. v. Sawyer,* also known as the *Steel Seizure Case.* In it the Supreme Court ruled that President Truman did not have the authority to seize steel mills about to be closed by strikes despite the ongoing Korean War. United Steel workers threatened to strike on April 9, 1952. Truman believed that the strike would damage the Korean War effort by causing steel shortages. On April 8, he directed Secretary of Commerce Charles Sawyer to seize and operate the steel mills. He justified his seizure of the mills solely on the basis of his power as commander in chief and his responsibility to execute the laws. Truman conceded in his report to Congress that it had the authority to countermand his directive, but Congress failed to approve or reject the president's action.

The steel companies brought suit against the government, seeking an injunction to stop the president's action. The case quickly reached the Supreme Court, where, by a vote of 6–3, Truman's action was held unconstitutional. The Court claimed that the president had usurped Congress's law-making power. It cited several acts in which Congress had provided procedures for responding to strikes that Truman had ignored. In the debate on one of these laws, the Taft-Hartley Act of 1947, Congress had considered empowering the government to seize an industry to prevent strikes but had refused to include such a provision in the law. Truman, therefore, had not just taken action without congressional authorization; he had taken an action that Congress had rejected.[145]

Although it is unclear whether the Court would have ruled differently had the emergency been more grave or had Congress not rejected the inclusion of property seizure provisions in the Taft-Hartley Act, the decision was a blow to the president's commander-in-chief authority. In a concurring opinion Justice William O. Douglas explained:

> There can be no doubt that the emergency which caused the president to seize these steel plants was one that bore heavily on the country. But the emergency did not create power; it merely marked an occasion when power should be exercised. And the fact that it was necessary that measures be taken to keep steel in production does not mean that the President, rather than the Congress, had the constitutional authority to act.[146]

In an era of rapidly expanding presidential power, the *Steel Seizure Case,* as Clinton Rossiter observed, "revived, for the moment, the notion that Presidents were subject to congressional limitations in foreign affairs."[147]

Armed Forces as a Tool of Presidential Foreign Policy

The armed forces of the United States have assisted presidents in achieving foreign policy goals. A president confronted with an international problem often has the option to use the military to address that problem. Military strength has enabled presidents to intimidate potential aggressors, impress trading partners, reassure friends, strengthen alliances, and mediate international disputes. Presidents have been reluctant to deploy armed forces in a crisis, but nearly every twentieth-century president has done so, sometimes with negative results. Beyond the military's potential to use or threaten force in a specific international hot spot, the strength of U.S. armed forces since World War II has allowed presidents to improve relations with other countries by offering them security guarantees and memberships in multinational alliances—although such inducements will prove less potent in the absence of a hostile superpower. President Clinton has tried to adapt to these new circumstances by stressing participation in multilateral operations.

From the time the Constitution was ratified until the present, presidents have used the military to accomplish limited missions in peacetime. Presidents have ordered the armed forces to protect settlers from Indians, repel bands of foreign outlaws, punish nations and groups for belligerent or criminal behavior, rescue U.S. citizens abroad, support friendly governments and train their armies, fight pirates and terrorists, warn potential enemies against taking aggressive action, deliver humanitarian aid, and secure disputed lands. The Constitution does not specifically sanction these peacetime military operations, but presidents have justified them under their power to command the military, defend the United States and its citizens, enforce the laws, and conduct foreign policy.

POLICE ACTIONS AND RESCUE MISSIONS

Of all peacetime military operations, the most consequential have been police actions and rescue missions ordered by presidents to protect U.S. citizens and interests abroad. The vast majority of these operations have been minor incidents. Indeed, many of them were so brief that Congress would not have had time to deliberate on an authorizing resolution if the president had asked for one. Presidents have argued that these limited missions require no congressional authorization because they fall under the executive power and have limited goals. As long as military operations did not threaten to involve the United States in a wider war and casualties remained low, presidential popularity usually has been bolstered by limited uses of force. Operations more remote from immediate national interests, however, such as the relief operation in Somalia, may harm a president's public standing.

Congress and the courts generally have refrained from challenging the president's authority to protect U.S. citizens and property overseas even when military actions taken under presidential orders have been unjust. For example, in 1854 a naval commander acting on the vague but belligerent orders of President Franklin Pierce completely destroyed the Nicaraguan city of Greytown when it refused to pay inflated damage claims filed by a U.S. company. Congress investigated the incident but did not condemn the Greytown bombardment or make Pierce account for his actions. A U.S. district court dismissed a suit filed by a Greytown property owner against the naval commander on the grounds that the bombardment was a political matter.[148]

Not all presidents have believed the commander-in-chief clause gave them the power to order limited military missions in the absence of congressional approval. For example, Pierce's successor, James Buchanan, claimed that without the consent of Congress he could not "fire a hostile gun in any case except to repel the attacks of an enemy."[149] Most twentieth-century presidents, however, have interpreted the commander-in-chief power broadly to fit the needs and goals of the moment.

No president did more to expand presidential authority to order limited military missions, in principle and in practice, than Theodore Roosevelt. In what became known as the Roosevelt Corollary to the Monroe Doctrine, he asserted the president's right to exercise an "international police power" in Latin America to protect U.S. and hemispheric interests and peace. He argued that if Latin American governments were unable to rule justly, maintain civil order, or meet their international obligations then they were jeopardizing the security of the hemisphere.

After Roosevelt presidents exercised the "police power" in the Western Hemisphere with little hesitation or consultation with Congress. William Taft, Woodrow Wilson, Calvin Coolidge, John Kennedy, Lyndon Johnson, Ronald Reagan, George Bush, and Bill Clinton all used U.S. forces—or foreign troops trained and supplied by the United States—to intervene in the affairs of Latin American nations.[150] Most recently in 1994, President Clinton threatened an invasion of Haiti to restore the democratic government to power. A negotiated settlement with Haiti's military rulers made the invasion unnecessary but still involved U.S. troops in overseeing the transition to democracy.

Even if the president's power to order limited military missions is conceded, there is still the problem of defining which missions fall under the president's police and rescue powers and which should be authorized by a congressional sanction if not a declaration of war. Like the power to repel invasions, the police and rescue powers can be manipulated by presidents to justify military actions that Congress might not sanction. For example, President Reagan ordered nineteen hundred troops to the tiny Caribbean island of Grenada in 1983 on what he called a "rescue mission." The administration maintained that the pro-Cuban military coup had placed U.S. citizens on the island in danger and threatened to turn Grenada into a Cuban-supported Communist military base. U.S. troops evacuated about one thousand Americans from the island and proceeded to depose Grenada's new leadership.[151]

The invasion of Grenada was clearly more than a rescue mission. The president used armed force to accomplish geopolitical goals without the consent of Congress. Nevertheless, the historical precedent supporting the authority of presidents to order military missions and the perceived urgency of the situation at hand have influenced presidents and the U.S. public more often than strict interpretations of the Constitution and of international law.

MILITARY EXERCISES AND SHOWS OF FORCE

Throughout U.S. history presidents have ordered conspicuous deployments of U.S. military power to dissuade potential aggressors, support allies, and reinforce U.S. diplomatic bargaining positions. Shows of force were initially limited by the

MILITARY RESPONSES TO TERRORISM

Throughout U.S. history, presidents have called on the military to battle not just other nations but also extragovernmental groups that have threatened Americans and their interests. For example, the navy often fought pirates in the eighteenth and nineteenth centuries, and in 1916 President Woodrow Wilson sent Gen. John J. (Blackjack) Pershing and six thousand troops into Mexico in pursuit of the Mexican bandit Pancho Villa after he had raided Columbus, New Mexico.

Since the 1970s international terrorist groups have threatened the safety of U.S. citizens much as international pirates and bandits did in earlier centuries. Terrorist groups have used violence to gain media attention and strike back at powerful nations they perceive as contributing to their particular plight. Often these terrorist acts have involved attacks on or captures of innocent civilians. Since the mid-1970s the U.S. military has placed greater emphasis on antiterrorist preparations. Intelligence agencies have expanded their efforts to identify terrorists, and elite counterterrorist units have been formed to provide presidents with a more credible military option should they decide to use force against terrorists.

Although terrorist groups cannot match the military power of the United States or other industrialized nations, military operations against them have seldom been a practical option. Terrorists have been difficult to identify, and they often have blended into the populace of foreign nations or surrounded themselves with hostages. Presidents who use force indiscriminately risk harming innocent civilians, endangering the lives of hostages, lending credibility to terrorist claims of U.S. injustice, and creating a cavalier image of the United States within the international community. Presidents therefore generally have refrained from using military force against terrorists except when those responsible for a terrorist act could be positively identified and attacked with precision. Rather, antiterrorist policy has focused on sanctioning the nations supporting terrorist organizations, such as Syria and Iran.

The Reagan administration's military operations against terrorists and their sponsors, however, showed that military force could be used to strike back at the roots of terrorism. In October 1985, the president ordered navy fighters to intercept an Egyptian airliner carrying terrorists who had seized a passenger ship and killed a U.S. citizen in the Mediterranean. On April 14, 1986, Reagan directed U.S. warplanes to bomb targets in Libya after U.S. intelligence obtained evidence that Libyan leader Col. Muammar Qaddafi sponsored a terrorist bombing of a Berlin nightclub. The attack set a precedent for U.S. military retaliation against any state proven to sponsor terrorist attacks against U.S. citizens. However, a similar strike against a larger and more politically important nation is very unlikely.

After a truck bombing killed nineteen Americans at a U.S. army base in Saudi Arabi in June 1996, President Clinton indicated that the United States was committed in finding the terrorists responsible: "We will pursue this. . . . Those who did it must not go unpunished." No evidence of a foreign nation's involvement in this terrorist act surfaced by the end of 1996.

weakness of the U.S. military. The demonstrations of force that presidents did order before World War II almost always involved the navy.

Millard Fillmore sent a squadron of ships under Commodore Matthew Perry to Japan in 1853. The Japanese had kept their ports closed to westerners and had abused U.S. seamen shipwrecked off their shores. Perry was instructed to show the Japanese U.S. naval power, demand that U.S. sailors be treated with respect, and propose a commercial relationship between the two countries. Perry's expedition resulted in the Treaty of Kanagawa, which declared friendship between the United States and Japan, opened several Japanese ports to U.S. commercial vessels, and established provisions for the treatment of U.S. citizens shipwrecked off Japan.

Perhaps the most famous show of force by a president was Theodore Roosevelt's dispatch of the U.S. fleet in 1907 on a cruise around the world. The cruise was primarily intended to impress Japan with U.S. naval power. Roosevelt was concerned by indications of Tokyo's belligerence and wished to demonstrate his own resolve to oppose any act of aggression by the Japanese. He believed the "Great White Fleet's" cruise also would be a valuable exercise and would promote respect and goodwill for the United States throughout the world. The trip went smoothly, with the navy observing protocol at each port of call. Roosevelt later asserted, "The most important service that I rendered to peace was the voyage of the battle fleet around the world."[152]

Shows of force may be used to reassure a friendly government as well as to warn a belligerent one. On March 17, 1988, President Reagan sent 3,150 additional U.S. troops to Honduras in response to the incursion there of Nicaraguan government troops. The Nicaraguan forces reportedly crossed the Honduras border to destroy a supply depot of the antigovernment Nicaraguan contra rebels, who were supported by the Reagan administration. Secretary of State George Shultz said of the troops: "They're not near where the fighting is taking place, but they're designed to say to the Government of Honduras that, 'we are your friend and we stand with you, and if you are invaded you can count on the United States.'"[153] The contingent of troops conducted maneuvers in Honduras and withdrew from the country after ten days without engaging in combat.

In October 1994, President Clinton rushed U.S. forces to Kuwait in response to Iraqi troop movements toward the Kuwaiti border. Clinton's aim was to demonstrate to the Iraqis that the United States was again prepared and willing to resist any aggression in that region.

TRAINING AND ADVISING FOREIGN TROOPS

During the cold war, military advisers became an established part of the superpowers' struggle for influence. Both the United States and the Communist bloc sent military personnel into third world countries to instruct the local armed forces in organization, tactics, and the use of weapons. Often these military advisers were sent specifically to teach local troops how to use military equipment that the superpower had given or sold to that nation.

Because U.S. military advisers usually are instructed not to participate in combat, their deployment traditionally has not required congressional approval. Sending military advisers to a foreign country, however, can be controversial. The introduction of U.S. military advisers into a foreign country can be the first step toward greater involvement in that country's problems. This certainly was true of the U.S. experience in Vietnam, which began with the deployment of fewer than one thousand military advisers in that country by Dwight Eisenhower. John Kennedy and Lyndon Johnson dramatically increased the number of U.S. military personnel in Vietnam to meet the growing military threat to the Saigon government. Beginning with the Kennedy administration, although U.S. forces were still called "advisers," they had active combat roles. By the end of 1963 more than 16,000 advisers were in Vietnam. A year later this number had swelled to 23,210.[154]

When President Reagan introduced military advisers into El Salvador in 1981, critics of Reagan's policy charged that the U.S. military involvement in Central America could escalate as it had in Vietnam. Reagan promised to limit the number of U.S. military advisers in El Salvador to fifty-five, but the House Foreign Affairs Committee was concerned enough to outline in a report what it considered to be unacceptable activities for U.S. military advisers in all countries. These included accompanying local units into combat, arming or fueling combat aircraft, and delivering weapons and supplies to local troops in combat areas. Although these guidelines did not have the force of law, they did set a standard for the conduct of U.S. military advisers.

NOTES

1. Alexander Hamilton, *Federalist* No. 74, in *The Federalist Papers* (New York: New American Library, 1961), 447.
2. Clinton Rossiter, *The American Presidency,* 2d ed. (New York: Time, 1960), 13.
3. Max Farrand, *The Records of the Federal Convention of 1787* (New Haven: Yale University Press, 1966), I:318–319.
4. James Madison, *The Gazette of the United States,* August 24, 1793, quoted in *The Power of the Presidency,* ed. Robert S. Hirschenfield (New York: Atherton, 1968), 59.
5. Hamilton, *Federalist* No. 69, 417–418.
6. 4 U.S. 37 (1800); Louis Fisher, *Presidential War Power* (Lawrence: University Press of Kansas, 1995), 2–3, 18–19, 23–24.
7. Quoted in Fisher, *Presidential War Power,* 15.
8. Michael P. Riccards, *A Republic, If You Can Keep It: The Foundation of the American Presidency, 1700–1800* (New York: Greenwood Press, 1987), 152–153.
9. Joseph E. Kallenbach, *The American Chief Executive: The Presidency and the Governorship* (New York: Harper and Row, 1966), 535–536.
10. Edward S. Corwin, *The President: Office and Powers, 1787–1984,* 5th rev. ed. (New York: New York University Press, 1984), 297.
11. Clinton Rossiter, *The Supreme Court and the Commander in Chief* (Ithaca, N.Y.: Cornell University Press, 1976), 48–52.
12. Robert E. DiClerico, *The American President,* 4th ed. (Englewood Cliffs, N.J.: Prentice-Hall, 1995), 31.

13. Quoted in Richard M. Pious, *The American Presidency* (New York: Basic Books, 1979), 392.
14. James D. Richardson, *A Compilation of the Messages and Papers of the Presidents, 1789–1910* (New York: Bureau of National Literature, 1917), 1:314–315.
15. Pious, *The American Presidency,* 392.
16. Quoted in Corwin, *The President,* 229.
17. Quoted in Arthur M. Schlesinger Jr., *The Imperial Presidency* (Boston: Houghton Mifflin, 1989), 23.
18. Quoted in Thomas Eagleton, *War and Presidential Power* (New York: Liveright, 1974), 23.
19. Christopher H. Pyle and Richard M. Pious, eds., *The President, Congress, and the Constitution* (New York: Free Press, 1984), 293–295.
20. Lawrence Margolis, *Executive Agreements and Presidential Power in Foreign Policy* (New York: Praeger, 1986), 9.
21. Schlesinger, *The Imperial Presidency,* 39–41.
22. Quoted in Wilfred E. Binkley, *The Man in the White House* (Baltimore: Johns Hopkins University Press, 1964), 192.
23. John Nicolay and John Hay, eds., *The Complete Works of Abraham Lincoln* (New York: Francis Tandy, 1891), 10:66.
24. Schlesinger, *The Imperial Presidency,* 58.
25. Corwin, *The President,* 264.
26. Ibid., 265.
27. Phillip Shaw Paludan, *The Presidency of Abraham Lincoln* (Lawrence: University Press of Kansas, 1994), 81–82.
28. Binkley, *The Man in the White House,* 194.
29. *Prize Cases,* 67 U.S. (2 Black) 635 (1863).
30. Rossiter, *Supreme Court,* 71–75.
31. Fisher, *Presidential War Power,* 42.
32. Louis L. Gould, *The Presidency of William McKinley* (Lawrence: University Press of Kansas, 1980), 96–98.
33. Corwin, *The President,* 271–272.
34. Ibid., 272.
35. Ibid.
36. Eagleton, *War and Presidential Power,* 64.
37. Jacob K. Javits, *Who Makes War* (New York: Morrow, 1973), 225–226.
38. Schlesinger, *The Imperial Presidency,* 115.
39. Quoted in Corwin, *The President,* 285–286.
40. Edward S. Corwin, *Presidential Power and the Constitution* (Ithaca, N.Y.: Cornell University Press, 1976), 114.
41. Quoted in Javits, *Who Makes War,* 230.
42. Cecil V. Crabb Jr. and Pat M. Holt, *Invitation to Struggle: Congress, the President and Foreign Policy,* 4th ed. (Washington, D.C.: CQ Press, 1992), 134–136.
43. Dean Acheson, *Present at the Creation: My Years in the State Department* (New York: Norton, 1969), 415.
44. Schlesinger, *The Imperial Presidency,* 133.
45. James L. Sundquist, *Decline and Resurgence of Congress* (Washington, D.C.: Brookings, 1981), 109.
46. Fisher, *Presidential War Power,* 70, 77–81.
47. R. Gordon Hoxie, *Command Decision and the Presidency* (New York: Reader's Digest Press, 1977), 178.
48. Schlesinger, *The Imperial Presidency,* 141.
49. Ibid., 169.
50. Sundquist, *Decline and Resurgence of Congress,* 124–125.
51. Ibid., 249.
52. Quoted in *Congressional Quarterly Almanac 1973* (Washington, D.C.: Congressional Quarterly, 1974), 906.
53. Ibid., 906–907.
54. Eagleton, *War and Presidential Power,* 203.
55. Quoted in *Congressional Quarterly Almanac 1973,* 907.
56. Ibid., 907.
57. *Immigration and Naturalization Service v. Chadha,* 462 U.S. 919 (1983).
58. *Congressional Quarterly Almanac 1983* (Washington, D.C.: Congressional Quarterly, 1984), 568–569.
59. Fisher, *Presidential War Power,* 194–197.
60. Pious, *The American Presidency,* 404–405.
61. Quoted in Larry Berman, *The New American Presidency* (Boston: Little, Brown, 1987), 75.
62. Ibid., 76.
63. DiClerico, *The American President,* 41.
64. Jacob Javits, "War Powers Reconsidered," *Foreign Affairs* (fall 1985): 135.
65. Robert J. Spitzer, *President and Congress* (New York: McGraw-Hill, 1993), 176.
66. Javits, "War Powers Reconsidered," 136.
67. Quoted in Crabb and Holt, *Invitation to Struggle,* 148.
68. Fisher, *Presidential War Power,* 141–142.
69. Javits, "War Powers Reconsidered," 137.
70. Pat Towell, "After Raid on Libya, New Questions on Hill," *Congressional Quarterly Weekly Report,* April 19, 1986, 839.
71. Mary H. Cooper, "Persian Gulf Oil," *Editorial Research Reports,* October 30, 1987, 567.
72. Pat Towell, "New Gulf Incident Rekindles an Old Debate," *Congressional Quarterly Weekly Report,* April 23, 1988, 1051–1058.
73. Fisher, *Presidential War Power,* 145–148.
74. Spitzer, *President and Congress,* 180.
75. Ibid., 182.
76. *Dellums v. Bush,* 752 F. Supp. 1141 (D.D.C. 1990).
77. Fisher, *Presidential War Power,* 150–151.
78. Ibid., 152.
79. Ibid., 153–154.
80. Ibid., 155–156.
81. Ibid., 157–161.
82. Ibid., 192.
83. Corwin, *The President,* 249.
84. Sundquist, *Decline and Resurgence of Congress,* 105–106; Fisher, *Presidential War Power,* 77–79.
85. Corwin, *The President,* 251; Fisher, *Presidential War Power,* 80–81.
86. Dick Kirschten, "A Contract's Out on U.N. Policing," *National Journal,* January 1, 1995, 231–232.
87. 107 Stat. 1478–80, sec. 9001 (1993).
88. U.S. Department of State Dispatch, vol. 5, #20 (May 16, 1994); Fisher, *Presidential War Power,* 160–161.
89. Hoxie, *Command Decision and the Presidency,* 130.
90. Amos A. Jordan and William J. Taylor Jr., *American National Security: Policy and Process* (Baltimore: Johns Hopkins University Press, 1984), 473.
91. "Wooing the WEU," *The Economist,* March 4, 1995, 56–57.
92. Pious, *The American Presidency,* 395–396.
93. Fisher, *Presidential War Power,* 93–97.
94. Kallenbach, *The American Chief Executive,* 531.
95. Charles A. Beard, *The Republic* (New York: Viking, 1944), 101.
96. Riccards, *A Republic, If You Can Keep It,* 164–166.
97. Jacob E. Cook, "George Washington," in *The Presidents: A Reference History,* ed. Henry F. Graff (New York: Scribner's, 1984), 24.
98. Corwin, *The President,* 294.
99. Kallenbach, *The American Chief Executive,* 530.
100. Jordan and Taylor, *American National Security,* 85.
101. Molly Moore, "Stricken Frigate's Crew Stitched Ship Together," *Washington Post,* April 22, 1988, A1.
102. Jordan and Taylor, *American National Security,* 231.
103. For a detailed description of the U.S. nuclear infrastructure, see William Arkin and Richard W. Fieldhouse, *Nuclear Battlefields* (Cambridge, Mass.: Ballinger, 1984).
104. *Public Papers of the Presidents of the United States, Dwight D. Eisenhower, 1960–1961* (Washington, D.C.: Government Printing Office, 1963), 851.
105. *Public Papers of the Presidents of the United States, Harry S Truman, 1945* (Washington, D.C.: Government Printing Office, 1961), 212.
106. James A. Nathan and James K. Oliver, *United States Foreign Policy*

and World Order, 2d ed. (Boston: Little, Brown, 1981), 41–42.

107. Hoxie, *Command Decision and the Presidency,* 13–14.

108. Miroslav Nincic, *United States Foreign Policy: Choices and Tradeoffs* (Washington, D.C.: CQ Press, 1988), 292.

109. Arthur M. Schlesinger Jr., *A Thousand Days* (Greenwich, Conn.: Fawcett, 1965), 778–783.

110. Theodore Sorensen, *Kennedy* (New York: Harper and Row, 1965), 705.

111. Arkin and Fieldhouse, *Nuclear Battlefields,* 87.

112. James M. Lindsay, *Congress and the Politics of Foreign Policy* (Baltimore: Johns Hopkins University Press, 1994), 102.

113. *Congressional Quarterly Almanac 1992* (Washington, D.C.: Congressional Quarterly, 1993), 513–514.

114. For text of speech and further commentary, see *Historic Documents of 1983* (Washington, D.C.: Congressional Quarterly, 1984), 305–316.

115. R. Jeffrey Smith, "Pentagon Scales Back SDI Goals," *Washington Post,* March 27, 1988, A1.

116. *Congressional Quarterly Almanac 1991* (Washington, D.C.: Congressional Quarterly, 1992), 407–408.

117. Lawrence J. Korb, "The Evolving Relationship between the White House and the Department of Defense in the Post-Imperial Presidency," in *The Post-Imperial Presidency,* ed. Vincent Davis (New Brunswick, N.J.: Transaction, 1980), 103.

118. Richard K. Betts, *Soldiers, Statesmen, and Cold War Crises* (Cambridge, Mass.: Harvard University Press, 1977), 52–68.

119. For discussions of the problems that led to the reform of the JCS, see James Buck, "The Establishment: An Overview," in *Presidential Leadership and National Security: Style, Institutions, and Politics,* ed. Sam C. Sarkesian (Boulder, Colo.: Westview, 1984), 59–64; and John G. Kestor, "The Role of the Joint Chiefs of Staff," in *American Defense Policy,* ed. John F. Reichart and Steven R. Sturm (Baltimore: Johns Hopkins University Press, 1982), 527–545.

120. Pat Towell, "Major Pentagon Reorganization Bill Is Cleared," *Congressional Quarterly Weekly Report,* September 20, 1986, 2207–2208.

121. Morton Halperin, "The President and the Military," in *The Presidency in Contemporary Context,* ed. Norman C. Thomas (New York: Dodd, Mead, 1975), 277.

122. Ibid., 280–284.

123. Alice Maroni, "The Defense Budget," in *Presidential Leadership and National Security,* 194–196.

124. Ibid., 196.

125. Richard Haass, "The Role of the Congress in American Security Policy," in *American Defense Policy,* 558–560.

126. James Fairhall, "The Case for the $435 Hammer," *Washington Monthly,* January 1987, 47–52.

127. George F. Brown Jr. and Lawrence Korb, "The Economic and Political Restraints on Force Planning," in *American Defense Policy,* 583.

128. Quoted in Dana Priest, "Billions Gone AWOL," *Washington Post Weekly Edition,* May 22–28, 1995, 6–7.

129. Kallenbach, *The American Chief Executive,* 543.

130. Marc Leepson, "Draft Registration," *Editorial Research Reports,* June 13, 1980, 427–430.

131. Kallenbach, *The American Chief Executive,* 537.

132. Quoted in Pyle and Pious, eds., *The President, Congress, and the Constitution,* 62.

133. Robert S. Hirschfield, "The Scope and Limits of Presidential Power," in *Power and the Presidency,* ed. Philip C. Dolce and George H. Skau (New York: Scribner's, 1976), 301–302.

134. Kallenbach, *The American Chief Executive,* 553–554.

135. *Ex parte Milligan,* 4 Wallace 2 (1866).

136. *Duncan v. Kahanamoku,* 327 U.S. 304 (1946).

137. Rossiter, *Supreme Court,* 25.

138. Ibid., 27.

139. *Ex parte Milligan,* 4 Wallace 2 (1866).

140. Quoted in Pyle and Pious, eds., *The President, Congress, and the Constitution,* 67.

141. *Hirabayashi v. United States,* 320 U.S. 81 (1943).

142. *Korematsu v. United States,* 323 U.S. 214 (1944).

143. Quoted in Pyle and Pious, eds., *The President, Congress, and the Constitution,* 118–119.

144. Kallenbach, *The American Chief Executive,* 557.

145. Corwin, *Presidential Power and the Constitution,* 124–125.

146. *Youngstown Sheet and Tube Co. v. Sawyer,* 343 U.S. 579 (1952).

147. Rossiter, *Supreme Court,* xxi.

148. Javits, *Who Makes War,* 104–115.

149. Quoted in Arthur Bernon Tourtellot, *The Presidents on the Presidency* (Garden City, N.Y.: Doubleday, 1964), 326.

150. Donald L. Robinson, *To the Best of My Ability* (New York: Norton, 1987), 224; Fisher, *Presidential War Power,* 145–148, 154–157.

151. Nincic, *United States Foreign Policy,* 231–233.

152. Theodore Roosevelt, *An Autobiography* (New York: Scribner's, 1920), 548.

153. Quoted in Steven V. Roberts, "3,000 G.I.'s and Questions," *New York Times,* March 18, 1988, A1.

154. Timothy J. Lomperis, *The War Everyone Lost and Won* (Washington, D.C.: CQ Press, 1984), 60.

SELECTED BIBLIOGRAPHY

Corwin, Edward S. *The President: Office and Powers, 1787–1984.* 5th rev. ed. New York: New York University Press, 1984.

Crabb, Cecil V., Jr., and Pat M. Holt. *Invitation to Struggle: Congress, the President and Foreign Policy.* 4th ed. Washington, D.C.: CQ Press, 1992.

Ely, John Hart. *War and Responsibility: Constitutional Lessons of Vietnam and Its Aftermath.* Princeton, N.J.: Princeton University Press, 1993.

Fisher, Louis. *Presidential War Power.* Lawrence: University Press of Kansas, 1995.

Javits, Jacob K. *Who Makes War.* New York: Morrow, 1973.

Jordan, Amos A., and William J. Taylor Jr. *American National Security: Policy and Process.* Baltimore: Johns Hopkins University Press, 1984.

Kallenbach, Joseph E. *The American Chief Executive: The Presidency and the Governorship.* New York: Harper and Row, 1966.

Koh, Harold Hongju. *The National Security Constitution: Sharing Power After the Iran-Contra Affair.* New Haven, Conn.: Yale University Press, 1990.

Nincic, Miroslav. *United States Foreign Policy: Choices and Tradeoffs.* Washington, D.C.: CQ Press, 1988.

Pious, Richard M. *The American Presidency.* New York: Basic Books, 1979.

Rossiter, Clinton. *The Supreme Court and the Commander in Chief.* Ithaca, N.Y.: Cornell University Press, 1976.

Sarkesian, Sam C., ed. *Presidential Leadership and National Security: Style, Institutions, and Politics.* Boulder, Colo.: Westview, 1984.

Schlesinger, Arthur M., Jr. *The Imperial Presidency.* Boston: Houghton Mifflin, 1989.

CHAPTER 5

Chief of State

BY DANIEL C. DILLER

EVERY GOVERNMENT must have a chief of state who symbolizes the nation and presides over ceremonial functions. In many countries this responsibility is fulfilled by a monarch with little governmental authority or an official whose post was created to shelter the chief executive from ceremonial drudgery. In the United States, however, this task has fallen to the chief executive.

The ceremonial activities for which presidents are responsible are as diverse as those that monarchs must perform, but presidents also must perform their duties as chief executive, commander in chief, chief diplomat, chief legislator, and head of their party. Presidents, therefore, can devote only a fraction of their time to ceremonial activities.

The chief of state role, however, involves more than presiding over ceremonial functions for which the president must put on a smile and put the business of the nation on hold. Like a monarch, a U.S. president is the embodiment of the American people and a focal point for national unity. Presidents symbolize the country's history, liberty, and strength. They can delegate ceremonial functions to their representatives, but while they are in office they cannot escape their chief of state role. At every moment they represent the United States to the international community and to the American people.

Ceremonial Duties and Functions

As chief of state, presidents preside over an endless series of ceremonies that range in tone from the solemnity of the inauguration to the informality of a White House barbecue. They greet foreign ambassadors, dedicate monuments, pin medals on war heroes, buy Easter seals and Girl Scout cookies, visit schools, throw out the first ball on opening day of the baseball season, and hold state dinners for foreign chiefs of state. National ceremonies have much the same purpose for the country as religious rituals have for a church. Ceremonies create shared symbols and sentiments that comfort, motivate, and unify the American congregation.

Although presidents may occasionally find ceremonial events tiresome, they provide opportunities to dramatize and personalize their presidencies. At ceremonial occasions presidents campaign for their reelection, make policy proposals, articulate their political philosophies, underscore the need for unity, create an atmosphere of confidence, and promote patriotism and national pride. Presidents who neglect ceremonial duties may have more time to develop policy and run the government, but they are sacrificing a tool of leadership that can be used not only to inspire the nation to greater accomplishments, but also to improve their own popularity.

CONSTITUTIONAL CEREMONIAL DUTIES

The Constitution designated several ceremonial duties that presidents are obliged to perform. They are required to take an oath of office, periodically inform Congress of the state of the Union, and receive "Ambassadors and other public Ministers." These constitutional ceremonial duties support the assumption of the chief of state role by George Washington and his successors because they make the president appear as the leader of the whole nation. Both the oath of office ceremony and State of the Union address physically place the president out in front of other government officials and focus the nation's attention on the president's opinions and recommendations. In addition, the president's duty to receive ambassadors implies that foreign governments are to regard the president as the official representative of the United States. Because the international community sees the president as chief of state, domestic chief of state responsibilities could not be assumed gracefully by anyone but the president.

Oath of Office and Inauguration

Article II, section 1, clause 8, of the Constitution requires the president-elect to recite the following thirty-five-word oath before assuming the presidency: "I do solemnly swear (or affirm) that I will faithfully execute the Office of President of the United States, and will to the best of my Ability preserve, protect, and defend the Constitution of the United States." The occasion for this oath taking is not described in the Constitution, but the inaugural ceremony at which it is administered has become one of the U.S. government's most important traditions and the president's first chief of state function.

Like a coronation, the inaugural ceremony symbolically invests presidents with the power of their office. At the inauguration the president appears before the people not as the manager of one of the three coequal branches of government but as the paternal leader of the nation who swears to "preserve, protect, and defend" the Constitution.

Benjamin Harrison commented on the significance of the oath of office in his 1888 inaugural address:

> . . . [F]rom the beginning of the government the people, to whose service the official oath consecrates the officer, have been called to witness

CONSTITUTIONAL BASIS OF PRESIDENTIAL CHIEF OF STATE ROLE

The Framers of the Constitution did not specifically designate the president as the nation's chief of state, but they created no other office that reasonably could claim the chief of state power. Presidents are the logical possessors of the title of chief of state under the Constitution because they are chosen by a national electorate, are never out of session, and are recognized as the voice of U.S. foreign policy. Consequently, the president can be said to represent the entire nation, is always available to provide ceremonial leadership, and is positioned to perform both international and domestic ceremonial functions.

The Framers never considered establishing a chief of state office separate from the presidency. The creation of a single office that would be filled by one person serving as both the ceremonial and executive leader of the nation, however, was not their only option. The continuing transfer of executive power from the monarch to the prime minister in Great Britain provided the Framers with a model of a political system in which the ceremonial and executive functions were separated.[1] Given the objections of many members of the convention to any pretense of royalty in the presidency and the unanimous concern that no president would have the means to become a despot, it is somewhat surprising that the Framers accepted the fusion of the two roles without debate.

One can imagine the convention designating a member of Congress such as the Speaker of the House or president pro tempore of the Senate as chief of state, especially because most of the delegates considered the legislature to be the most important branch of government. Such an arrangement would have augmented Congress's power by making it the ceremonial focus of the government, while diminishing the symbolic resources available to any president who sought dictatorial power.

The Framers also could have created an executive council composed of several persons instead of a unitary presidency. The Framers seriously considered this option, but the focus of their debate was on the safety of lodging enormous executive powers in the hands of one person, not on dividing presidential functions between executive officials. The original proposal for a single executive, made by James Wilson of Virginia, was strongly opposed by Benjamin Franklin, Edmund Randolph, George Mason, Roger Sherman, and other prominent members of the convention who feared that having a single executive would lead to despotism or the subordination of the country's interests to the interests of the executive's home region. After several days of debate, however, the Framers decided to reject proposals for a plural executive or an executive advisory committee attached to the presidency in favor of a single executive.[2] Presumably, had the convention opted for an executive committee instead of a single president, the chief of state power would have resided in the entire committee, rather than with one specified member.

According to political scientist Rexford G. Tugwell, an executive committee would not have captured the imagination of the American people the way individual presidents have:

> Since he [the president] would not have been alone in the White House in semi-royal state, with relatives and associates of consuming interest to all his fellow citizens, it would not have been a matter of such consequence whether or not he had an invalid wife and irresponsible children, . . . or whether he possessed social graces as well as wisdom and political talent. He would not, in other words, have been the focus of interest and the symbol of Union for the whole American people, watched with avid curiosity and criticized inevitably by those with standards of conduct differing from his own.[3]

By creating a single executive, the Framers guaranteed that public attention and therefore symbolic power would flow to the president.

1. Erwin C. Hargrove and Michael Nelson, *Presidents, Politics, and Policy* (Baltimore: Johns Hopkins University Press, 1984), 20.
2. Donald L. Robinson, *To the Best of My Ability* (New York: Norton, 1987), 69–76.
3. Rexford G. Tugwell, *The Enlargement of the Presidency* (Garden City, N.Y.: Doubleday, 1960), 481.

---

the solemn ceremony. The oath taken in the presence of the people becomes a mutual covenant. The officer covenants to serve the whole body of the people by a faithful execution of the laws, so that they may be the unfailing defense and security of those who observe them.

The oath of office also conjures up heroic images of the nation's heritage. The new president's recitation of the same oath that George Washington, Thomas Jefferson, Abraham Lincoln, Woodrow Wilson, Franklin Roosevelt, and every other president has repeated conveys a sense of historic continuity and links the incumbent to the glories of past presidencies.

George Washington established the tradition that presidents should deliver an inaugural address after taking the oath of office. Most presidents have used this speech not to outline specific policy proposals or score partisan points but to restate their political and moral philosophies, invoke the traditions of the Founders, establish a mood of optimism, challenge the nation to pursue ambitious goals, and appeal for unity.

Unity is an important and common theme of inaugural addresses because presidential elections tend to divide the nation along party lines.[1] After the bitterly divisive election of 1800, which led outgoing president John Adams to snub Thomas Jefferson's inauguration, Jefferson declared, "We have called by different names brethren of the same principles. We are all Republicans. We are all Federalists." John F. Kennedy called for unity in 1961 after his close election victory over Richard Nixon: "We observe today not a victory of party, but a celebration of freedom." Jimmy Carter opened his inaugural address by praising his 1976 election opponent, President Gerald Ford: "For myself and for our nation, I want to thank my predecessor for all he has done to heal our land." Similarly, Bill Clinton included a word of praise in his inaugural for his defeated opponent George Bush: "I salute my predecessor, President Bush, for his half century of service to America."

The inauguration and the parades and parties that have usually followed it also provide the first glimpse of the new chief of state's ceremonial style. After the stiff formality and royal pomp observed during the Washington and Adams administrations, Jefferson wanted his inaugural to symbolize the democratic spirit he intended to bring to the presidency. He therefore eschewed a carriage in favor of walking unceremoniously from his boardinghouse to the Capitol to take the oath of office.

Andrew Jackson's election was regarded as a triumph for common people. To symbolize his link with the average person he opened the doors of the White House to anyone who wished to attend his postinaugural party. Thousands of enthusiastic supporters descended on the White House, destroying furniture, china, glassware, and other household items.

Kennedy's inaugural was a formal affair that reflected the intellectual and cultural sophistication he would bring to his presidency. Kennedy sent 155 special inaugural invitations to noted writers, artists, and scholars, had Robert Frost read a poem at the inaugural ceremony, and decreed that male participants in the ceremony should wear top hats.

Jimmy Carter, like Jefferson, used his inaugural to project a simpler presidential image. He wore a business suit instead of formal dress and chose to walk in his inaugural parade rather than ride in a limousine.

Pomp came back into style with the election of Ronald Reagan. His 1981 inaugural festivities—the most expensive in history up to that time—included a parade with eight thousand marchers, eight $100-a-ticket balls, and a nationally televised inaugural "gala" that featured many Hollywood celebrities. The cost of the festivities was estimated at $16 million, compared with just $3.5 million spent for the Carter inaugural in 1977. Reagan's 1985 inaugural cost $20 million despite the cancellation of some events because of severely cold weather.

Presidents Bush and Clinton followed Reagan's lead, holding elaborate inaugural celebrations. Bush's 1989 inaugural cost $30 million and featured a parade with 214 marching bands and 12,000 participants. Clinton's 1993 inaugural cost about $25 million and featured eleven inaugural balls.

State of the Union Address

The Constitution also states that the president "shall from time to time give to the Congress information of the State of the Union, and recommend to their Consideration such Measures as he shall judge necessary and expedient." From this clause developed the ritual of the president's annual message, or "State of the Union address," as it has been known since 1945. *(See "The State of the Union Address," p. 103, in Chapter 2.)*

George Washington delivered the first annual message to Congress on January 8, 1790. John Adams, who enjoyed royal formalities, followed Washington's precedent, but Thomas Jefferson objected to having presidents deliver their annual messages in person. Like many of his Democratic-Republican colleagues, he thought the custom, which had derived from the British monarch's speech from the throne at the opening of Parliament, had royal pretensions. As part of his effort to "put the ship of state back on its republican tack," he submitted his report to Congress in writing.[2]

Rutherford B. Hayes was the first president to use an eagle as the official presidential seal. In 1903 Theodore Roosevelt added a circular seal around it, bearing the words, and in 1945 Harry Truman changed the eagle's head from one side to the other. The ring of fifty stars represents the fifty states.

Subsequent presidents followed Jefferson's example until 1913 when Woodrow Wilson took the suggestion of journalist Oliver Newman and went before Congress to read his annual message. Wilson saw the change as a way to make the address more personal and dramatic. He explained in the address that he wanted to verify "that the President of the United States is a person, not a mere department of the Government hailing Congress from some isolated island of jealous power, sending messages, not speaking naturally and with his own voice—that he is a human being trying to cooperate with other human beings in a common service." Some members of Congress echoed Jefferson's objections to the practice, but the response to Wilson's speech was generally favorable. It became acceptable once again for presidents to deliver the annual message in person, and every president since Franklin Roosevelt has chosen to do so.[3]

As with the inauguration, the symbolism of the contemporary State of the Union address reinforces the image of the president as the preeminent leader of the nation, rather than the leader of one of its coequal branches. The Congress, cabinet, and Supreme Court assemble in the House chamber and wait for the president to arrive, like courtiers awaiting a king. After being announced, the president is greeted by a standing ovation. Moreover, the event itself implies presidential preeminence, because the president's opinion of the state of the Union is the reason for the assemblage. Neither Congress nor the judiciary has a similar opportunity to address the top representatives of the entire government in a formal, ritualistic setting.

The invention of radio and television changed the primary audience of the address from Congress to the American people. Presidents still address Congress, but their remarks are intended primarily for public consumption. Presidents have used this opportunity to put pressure on Congress to vote for their legislative agenda by appealing to the American public for support. Beginning in 1966, the major networks provided air time to the opposition party after the State of the Union address. That year Senate Minority Leader Everett M. Dirksen (Ill.) and House Minority Leader Gerald R. Ford (Mich.) delivered the Republican response to President Johnson's address.

Reception of Ambassadors

The Constitution gives the president the responsibility to "receive Ambassadors and other public Ministers." The authors of the Constitution regarded the reception of foreign visitors as a purely ceremonial responsibility. It was to be given to the president, according to Alexander Hamilton, because Congress could not conveniently perform this function. He wrote in the *Federalist* No. 69 that presidential reception of ambassadors "is more a matter of dignity than of authority. It is a circumstance which will be without consequence in the administration of the government; and it was far more convenient that it should be arranged in this manner than that there should be a necessity of convening the legislature, or one of its branches, upon every arrival of a foreign minister."[4] Subsequently, however, the presidential responsibility to receive ambassadors was used by presidents as a constitutional justification of their authority to recognize or deny recognition to foreign governments. *(See "The Recognition Power," p. 143, in Chapter 3.)*

In the spirit of this constitutional provision, presidents have customarily received the official ambassador of every recognized foreign government. Unfortunately, the growth of the Washington diplomatic corps during the twentieth century and the overcrowded presidential schedule have forced presidents to receive most ambassadors, especially those from smaller countries, in groups at the White House to save time.

CUSTOMARY CEREMONIAL FUNCTIONS

Presidents and their representatives perform numerous chief of state functions that do not have their origins in the Constitution and are not based on a specific legal sanction. Some of these activities have been established as annual events by a succession of presidents. Others are seized upon by individual presidents for their public relations value. Presidents can choose to de-emphasize their chief of state role by delegating ceremonial functions to the vice president and others, but they cannot escape many events and practices that the American people have come to regard as part of the president's job. A president who claimed to be too busy to light the national Christmas tree or congratulate the World Series champions would waste valuable opportunities to score political points and would risk being per-

ROBERT FROST'S INAUGURAL POEM

Presidents have sometimes attempted to use the celebrity and visibility of their office to promote changes in the lifestyle of the nation. John Kennedy intended to use his position to encourage interest in the fine arts and U.S. culture. He and his wife, Jacqueline, set an example for the nation by frequently patronizing the work of artists, musicians, and writers.

Kennedy began his patronage of the fine arts the day he became president. He asked the venerable poet Robert Frost to recite a poem at his inauguration ceremony on January 20, 1961. The eighty-six-year-old Frost planned to read a short introductory verse he had composed for the occasion followed by his poem "The Gift Outright." After Boston's Cardinal Cushing delivered a long invocation, the chair of the Inaugural Committee, Sen. John Sparkman, introduced Frost. The poet began reading his introductory verse, but the bright sunlight magnified by the glare from the snow that had fallen the day before blinded him. Frost read only three lines before stopping:

Summoning artists to participate
In the august occasions of the state
Seems something artists ought to celebrate.

He said, "I'm not having a good light here at all. I can't see in this light." He tried to continue with the help of Vice President-elect Lyndon B. Johnson, who shaded the poet's manuscript with a top hat, but Frost still could not see. He gave up on the introductory verse, saying, "This was to have been a preface to a poem which I do not have to read." He then recited "The Gift Outright" from memory in a clear voice, changing the last phrase at Kennedy's request from "such as she *would* become" to "such as she *will* become."

The Gift Outright

The land was ours before we were the land's.
She was our land more than a hundred years
Before we were her people. She was ours
In Massachusetts, in Virginia,
But we were England's, still colonials,
Possessing what we still were unpossessed by,
Possessed by what we now no more possessed.
Something we were withholding made us weak
Until we found out that it was ourselves
We were withholding from our land of living,
And forthwith found salvation in surrender.
Such as we were we gave ourselves outright
(The deed of gift was many deeds of war)
To the land vaguely realizing westward,
But still unstoried, artless, unenhanced,
Such as she was, such as she would become.

John F. Kennedy's inaugural was a formal affair that reflected the intellectual and cultural sophistication he would bring to the presidency. Robert Frost reads a poem while Vice President-elect Lyndon Johnson uses his top hat to block out the sun.

ceived as indifferent to American life. Like the three ceremonial functions based on the Constitution, these informal chief of state activities emphasize the president's role as the leader of the nation, but, in addition, many of them serve to humanize the president and symbolically bridge the gap between the president and the people.

National Voice

The president serves as a ceremonial spokesperson for the nation. A presidential proclamation or dedication is a national stamp of approval for cultural events, national monuments, public works projects, charity drives, and special weeks and days. Such proclamations promote national concern and awareness of worthy organizations and causes by indicating that the president thinks the object of the proclamation is important enough to recognize. Often presidents highlight their recognition of a charity, organization, or movement by inviting its leaders to the White House. Such an invitation is a further measure of the group's importance, because the president's schedule must be interrupted to accommodate the visit.

Presidential recognition gives an event, cause, group, or monument a place in the national consciousness. It also emphasizes the unity of the United States and can inspire patriotic sentiments. A new hydroelectric dam is said to be not just a source of power for a particular region, but an engineering feat and a symbol of American industrial might and technological ingenuity. The work of a charitable organization such as the American Red Cross is praised as an example of the nation's caring spirit.

Presidential endorsements are constantly in demand by organizations and charities, and the president's staff must choose which will receive presidential time. Many of the causes presidents endorse from year to year are determined by precedent. The United Way, Easter Seals, American Cancer Society, and many others receive annual presidential endorsements. Yet the type of causes that receive presidential recognition may also reflect the incumbent's political interests or philosophy. For example, Ronald Reagan's frequent endorsement of charities was consistent with his goal of promoting an increase in the nation's charitable giving as a partial alternative to increased government spending on social services. George Bush carried on this theme with his "Thousand Points of Light" commendations, which highlighted voluntary initiatives undertaken in society's behalf by particular individuals or groups.

Conveyor of Awards and Congratulations

In accordance with their role as national spokesperson, presidents are expected to be the conveyors of national awards and congratulations. Presidents routinely invite citizens to the White House, where they congratulate them on their accomplishments and present them with an award or memento of their visit. Presidents also bestow a variety of official awards, the most prominent of which is the Presidential Medal of Freedom, the highest civilian honor bestowed by the government. *(See box, Presidential Medal of Freedom, p. 214.)*

Presidents have used this role as a tool of moral and patriotic leadership. In congratulating popular American heroes, presidents make a moral statement by holding up those individuals to the nation as examples to emulate. Presidential congratulations encourage citizens to be as dedicated as a spelling bee champion, as brave as a war hero, as creative as a great artist, or as resilient as a person celebrating a hundredth birthday. For example, on June 12, 1995, President Clinton joined the national accolades for Air Force Captain Scott F. O'Grady by inviting him to a well-publicized White House lunch. O'Grady had become a

PRESIDENTIAL MEDAL OF FREEDOM

The cultural equivalent of the Congressional Medal of Honor, which is the top honor for battlefield heroism, the Presidential Medal of Freedom is the nation's highest award for civilian achievement. Only the president can award the lustrous red, white, and blue enameled medal, which recognizes significant contributions to American life, the country's national security, or even to world peace.

Created by President John F. Kennedy in 1963, the Presidential Medal of Freedom remains a rare and highly coveted honor today. Only about three hundred people have received the medal to date. But the winners themselves come from nearly every imaginable background—scientists, writers, government officials, artists, movie stars, and even sports legends. Among past winners are astronaut Neil Armstrong, world famous comedienne Lucille Ball, Civil War historian Bruce Catton, labor leader Cesar Chavez, former first lady Betty Ford, longtime senator William Fulbright, industrialist Edgar Kaiser, and baseball great Jackie Robinson.[1]

President Kennedy decided to create an award for civilian achievement soon after he took office in 1961. The idea fit in well with his larger strategy, which sought to infuse the country with a new sense of energy and idealism. Highly publicized award ceremonies for public service and cultural excellence would only serve to underscore the message.

After considerable study, the White House decided to revamp a little used, existing medal—the Medal of Freedom—which had been created by President Harry S. Truman in 1945 to recognize contributions to America's national security. Early in 1963 President Kennedy issued the executive order renaming the Medal of Freedom and establishing new, broad-based criteria for awarding the Presidential Medal of Freedom to individuals "who had made especially meritorious contributions to (1) the security or national interests of the United States, or (2) world peace, or (3) cultural or other significant public or private endeavors." The White House then set about creating the new medal, and both President Kennedy and First Lady Jacqueline Kennedy played an active role in its design.

Following unexpected delays, the first award ceremony for the Presidential Medal of Freedom was finally set for December 6, 1963. Then, tragically, President Kennedy was assassinated that November in Dallas. While the nation mourned Kennedy's death, President Lyndon Johnson and former first lady Jacqueline Kennedy decided that going ahead with the award ceremony as scheduled would help begin the process of healing. So it happened that President Johnson presented the first medals to those recipients chosen by President Kennedy.

President Johnson and every president who followed him have awarded additional medals during their terms of office. It is entirely up to the president to decide who gets the award, or even whether it is to be given at all. Some presidents, like President Ronald Reagan, have thoroughly enjoyed giving the medal and have held fairly regular award ceremonies, usually at the White House. On the other hand Reagan's predecessor, President Jimmy Carter, sought to downplay the medal and except for his last year in office, awarded it only sparingly.

All presidents generally have tried to select medal winners who have had long and distinguished careers and who represent various endeavors, such as art, business, or civil rights activism. Sometimes specific, highly publicized accomplishments have garnered awards. President Richard Nixon, for example, gave president's medals to the astronauts of the history-making *Apollo 11* moon mission in 1969 (and to the astronauts and Mission Operations Team of the near-tragic *Apollo 13* mission in 1970).

Government service is a persistent theme among the recipients. President Lyndon Johnson made a point of rewarding key figures in his administration with the president's medal, and other presidents followed suit. For example, President Ford named his secretary of state, Henry Kissinger, and President Carter his national security assistant, Zbigniew Brzezinski. Three former presidents, John Kennedy (from Johnson), Lyndon Johnson (from Carter), and Ronald Reagan (from Bush), and two former vice presidents, Hubert Humphrey (from Carter) and Nelson Rockefeller (from Ford), also have won the award. In all about a third of the president's medals have gone to government officials.

President Nixon introduced an interesting innovation, that of selecting several recipients from the same discipline and presenting their awards at a group ceremony. The April 1970 ceremony ultimately produced an unanticipated irony though: President Nixon awarded the medals to eight leading journalists. He could not have known then that the news media would in a few years become his scourge as it relentlessly investigated the Watergate scandal. Over two decades later President Bill Clinton revived the idea of selecting recipients from the same field of endeavor when he presented medals to five noted reformers at a ceremony November 30, 1993. Clinton also used the award to foster bipartisan healing after the 1996 presidential election, when he awarded the medal to Bob Dole, his vanquished opponent in the 1996 race. Dole was honored for his years of congressional service and military heroism in World War II.

While Presidential Medal of Freedom winners are usually Americans, presidents also have selected a few foreign dignitaries over the years. President Kennedy, for example, included the internationally renowned cellist Pablo Casals in his list, President Reagan gave a posthumous medal to slain Egyptian president Anwar el-Sadat, and President George Bush gave one to Lech Walesa, hero of Poland's Solidarity movement.

1. Bruce Wetterau, *The Presidential Medal of Freedom: Winners and Their Achievements* (Washington, D.C.: Congressional Quarterly, 1996).

heroic figure by evading capture by Serbian military units after his jet was downed over Bosnia-Herzegovina. He was rescued June 8, by a helicopter commando mission ordered by the president.

President Reagan developed presidential congratulations into a political art. He made a practice of weaving the introduction of carefully selected heroic Americans into his upbeat State of the Union addresses. His heroes included an infantry medic who rescued wounded soldiers in Grenada, a twelve-year-old prodigy of gospel music, a woman about to graduate from West Point despite having escaped to the United States from Vietnam only ten years before with no possessions or knowledge of English, and a seventy-nine-year-old Harlem woman who cared for infants born of mothers addicted to heroin.

Congratulating a famous hero brings obvious political benefits to presidents. For example, members of championship sports teams are now routinely invited to the White House where they will joke with the president and present the chief executive with a jersey, game ball, or other memento of their victory. The president can become identified with their sport, demonstrate good humor, and be photographed with America's current sports idols. Presidents gain similar public relations benefits from congratulating artists, scientists, heroic members of the armed forces, and others who have performed feats of skill, intelligence, or courage.

First Average American

Alexis de Tocqueville, a French aristocrat and author who traveled widely in the United States during the first half of the nineteenth century, observed that "public officers themselves are well aware that the superiority over their fellow citizens which they derive from their authority they enjoy only on condition of putting themselves on a level with the whole community by their manners."[5] Most presidents have understood that although Americans want their president to be an exceptional person who is intelligent, decisive, and inspiring, they also want a leader with common tastes and experiences. Americans want to believe that their president, like the log cabin presidents of the nineteenth century, rose to the top through hard work, moral integrity, and a little ambition.

The public values common sense as much as an Ivy League education. The ability to understand the needs and desires of the average American is as important as understanding the most complicated foreign policy or economic problems. In short, people want their president to be an exceptional example of an average American.

Presidents have realized that while the regal trappings of the presidency fortify their power and prestige, they must also project a populist image to satisfy the democratic ideals of the American people. Presidents who appear too urbane or who flaunt the privileges of their office risk alienating many citizens who are attracted to politicians with folksy images. Presidents John Quincy Adams and Martin Van Buren lost their reelection bids to Andrew Jackson and William Henry Harrison, respectively. The challengers in these two elections successfully contrasted their self-made, populist personae with the stiff and educated styles of the incumbents. Similarly, in the 1952 and 1956 presidential elections, Adlai Stevenson's sophisticated image was not much of an asset against Dwight D. Eisenhower, an unpretentious war hero with an engaging smile.

Presidents seek out opportunities to display their common touch. Often this is done simply by publicizing a president's hobbies, habits, and family life. The American public was told that Ronald Reagan chopped his own firewood and snacked on jellybeans, Jimmy Carter played softball and liked Willie Nelson's music, Gerald Ford took a daily swim and cooked his own breakfast. The day after Lyndon B. Johnson's reelection in 1964, he was photographed roping steers on his Texas ranch like any hard-working cowboy. Jimmy Carter made a media event out of his construction of a tree house on the White House grounds for his daughter, Amy.[6]

Both George Bush and Bill Clinton projected inconsistent portraits of a first average American. Bush possessed a personable and accessible manner, demonstrated in his penchant for writing personal thank you notes. He talked frequently of his all-American experiences including his college baseball career, his service during World War II, and his raising a family in Texas. He relished such common diversions as horseshoe pitching and fishing. Yet Bush also was a Yale-educated millionaire and the son of a Connecticut senator. During his long vacations at his summer home in Maine, he made little effort to disguise his wealthy lifestyle, playing multiple rounds of golf and piloting a twenty-eight-foot powerboat in the ocean. One embarrassing moment occurred during a 1992 campaign visit to a supermarket in Maryland where Bush was visibly amazed by price-scanning equipment that had been a feature of grocery stores for many years. Bush's patrician background and apparent isolation from American life contributed to the impression that he was out of touch.

Bill Clinton's biography as a self-made man who rose from a difficult childhood in tiny Hope, Arkansas, provided a solid base on which to build an image as the first average American. Clinton skillfully used his small town origins to his advantage during the 1992 campaign. But after becoming president his early failure to project a common image contributed to his sharp drop in popularity. The initial impression many Americans developed of their new president was of a cerebral, but unfocused, Ivy League "policy wonk" with Hollywood pretensions. Perhaps the most damaging incident occurred on May 18, 1993, when *Air Force One* was delayed at the Los Angeles airport, keeping two runways closed because of standard security procedures, so that the president could get a $200 haircut from a Beverly Hills hairdresser noted for his work on movie stars.

Political scientist Fred Greenstein wrote of Clinton's first months in office: ". . . [H]is tendency was to confine himself to impersonal and distinctly noninspirational messages on such

Throwing out the first baseball of the 1910 major league season, President William Howard Taft began a tradition that most succeeding presidents have followed.

themes as the need to 'grow the economy.' He and his associates did little to humanize his presidency: Hillary Clinton became the all-business Hillary Rodham Clinton; daughter Chelsea dropped from sight; and the campaign bus was garaged."[7]

Clinton responded to his sliding poll numbers by bringing David Gergen, a Republican media strategist, into his administration. Among other adjustments, Clinton improved in projecting a common man image. For example, he was frequently seen at sporting events. For example, during the 1993–1994 championship season for the basketball team at the University of Arkansas (where Clinton taught law in the 1970s), he was an enthusiastic booster. By 1995 Hillary Clinton had largely given up her high-profile public policy role in favor of a more traditional first lady agenda. But Clinton's embrace of a populist image was not complete. During the summers of 1993 and 1994, he and his family vacationed on Martha's Vineyard surrounded by celebrities and the wealthy. The Clinton's, however, chose the more remote and rustic Jackson Hole, Wyoming, and neighboring Yellowstone Grand Teton National Parks for their summer vacations in 1995 and 1996. Clinton remained an enigmatic first average American.

Presidential appearances at cultural events can reinforce the image of a president as an average person. Presidents attend historical and artistic exhibits, ethnic festivals, and other events where they can display their interest in American life. And, like Bill Clinton, presidents have been especially fond of attending sporting contests. Since William Howard Taft threw out the first baseball of the 1910 major league season on April 14 in Washington, most presidents have observed the tradition. Kennedy wanted to make such a good appearance at the yearly event that he secretly practiced his throwing on the White House grounds.[8] Since the Washington Senators franchise moved to Texas in 1971, presidents who have wished to throw out the first ball have had to travel to nearby Baltimore or other cities.

Observer of Holidays

National holidays reduce societal divisions by emphasizing universal patriotic themes and common traditions. Hundreds of millions of Americans of all races, religions, and regions share the common experience of watching fireworks on the Fourth of July or preparing a banquet on Thanksgiving. On Veterans Day virtually every American citizen will recall someone who served in the military, and on Memorial Day most will remember someone who died in a war. Holidays, therefore, draw a nation together and enhance citizens' sense of belonging to a single national culture.

As chief of state, presidents usually lead the nation's observation of a holiday. They light the national Christmas tree, deliver a patriotic address on the Fourth of July, and lay a wreath at the Tomb of the Unknown Soldier on Memorial Day. Details of the traditional holiday activities observed by the first family, such as what they ate on Thanksgiving and what gifts they exchanged at Christmas, usually are reported to the nation.

Presidents traditionally have issued statements celebrating official holidays such as Memorial Day and Thanksgiving and unofficial holidays like St. Patrick's Day. Presidents, however, cannot proclaim an official federal holiday without an act of Congress. George Washington was the first president to proclaim a national holiday. In response to a congressional recommendation, he declared that a national day of thanksgiving should be observed on Thursday, November 26, 1789.[9] This proclamation contributed to the development of the Thanksgiving holiday now observed in the United States. The most recent holiday established by the government was Martin Luther King Day. After initial opposition, Ronald Reagan signed legislation November 2, 1983, declaring the third Monday in January beginning in 1986 to be a legal federal holiday honoring the civil rights leader.

Standing in front of the coffin containing the body of Richard Nixon, President Clinton led the eulogizers for the former president in April 1994.

Mourner and Eulogizer

When a prominent American dies, the president is expected to lead the nation in mourning. The president routinely issues statements eulogizing Americans who have died. During the first five months of 1983, for example, President Reagan signed statements mourning the deaths of such diverse Americans as Alabama University football coach Paul "Bear" Bryant, entertainer Arthur Godfrey, presidential aide Joseph R. Holmes, three Secret Service agents who were killed in an auto accident, and sixteen Americans who died when the U.S. embassy in Beirut, Lebanon, was bombed by terrorists. Presidential attendance at funerals, however, generally is reserved for former presidents, high government officials, or people who had a close personal or political relationship with the president.

When presidents do attend funerals in the United States in their role as chief of state, they usually address the mourners. President Nixon delivered the eulogy at Eisenhower's state funeral at the U.S. Capitol on March 30, 1969. President Clinton delivered a eulogy at Nixon's funeral in California on April 27, 1994.

Presidents also must respond to the deaths of Americans who died while serving their country. Perhaps the most famous

President Ronald Reagan and staff grimly watch television reports on the *Challenger* disaster that killed seven astronauts. Americans often look to the president to lead them in dealing with national tragedy.

of all presidential speeches, Lincoln's Gettysburg Address, was delivered during Lincoln's visit to the site of the great battle where thousands of Union and Confederate troops lost their lives. During a war when many soldiers are dying, presidents rarely have time to memorialize individual members of the armed services. In peacetime, however, presidents usually honor any American hero whose death captures the attention of the nation. For example, President Reagan addressed the nation on January 31, 1986, at the memorial service for the seven astronauts killed in the *Challenger* space shuttle disaster, and President Clinton spoke at the April 23, 1995, memorial service for the victims of the Oklahoma City bombing.

As head of state, presidents receive invitations to the funerals of foreign leaders. President Johnson attended Konrad Adenauer's funeral in Cologne in April 1967, and President Nixon traveled to Paris to attend Charles de Gaulle's funeral in November 1970. Presidents rarely go to funerals overseas because of the difficulty of postponing other business and arranging security measures on short notice.

If the president does not go to the funeral, a representative is sent in the president's place. The decision of whom to send to a foreign funeral depends on the importance of the country to the United States, the current state of diplomatic relations between the two nations, and the deceased leader's political relationship with the United States. The vice president or secretary of state usually represents the president and the nation at the funerals of prominent world leaders. Former presidents who worked closely with a fallen leader also sometimes attend. President Reagan and Vice President Bush did not attend Egyptian president Anwar Sadat's funeral in October 1981 for security reasons, but Reagan asked former presidents Nixon, Ford, and Carter to represent the United States. At the funerals of leaders of countries that have a strained or minimal relationship with the United States, the U.S. ambassador to that country often will represent the president.

American Tourist

George Washington firmly established the precedent that presidents should travel among the American people. He made two regional tours as president: New England in 1789 and the South in 1791. Washington thought the purpose of these tours of the states was "to become better acquainted with their principle Characters and internal Circumstances, as well as to be more accessible to numbers of well-informed persons."[10] Since then, presidents have been expected to leave the capital occasionally to reacquaint themselves with the nation's problems and listen to the public's needs and complaints. Franklin Roosevelt explained his own need for such travels: "I have always thought it was part of the duty of the Presidency to keep in touch, personal touch, with the Nation . . . now I am going to the Coast . . . to have a 'look-see,' to try to tie together in my own mind the problems of the Nation, in order that I may, at first hand, know as much about the questions that affect all the forty-eight states as possible."[11]

Citizens may become apathetic toward politics and government if they perceive that it is a game played in the capital by leaders who do not care what happens in the rest of the country. By traveling out to the people in the "provinces," presidents can show their interest in the culture of particular regions. They can reawaken public interest in their administration's programs and in government in general.

The concerns of citizens that presidents remain in touch with the needs of the whole country were demonstrated by the successful presidential campaigns of Jimmy Carter in 1976, Ronald Reagan in 1980, and Bill Clinton in 1992. All three men campaigned against the "Washington establishment," which they said had lost touch with the desires of the people. To emphasize his accessibility and interest in local problems, President Carter during his presidency journeyed to several small towns where he answered the questions of citizens at town meetings and stayed overnight with local families.

Chief of State Role and Presidential Power

The president's chief of state role has received less scholarly attention than other presidential roles. The ceremonial and symbolic aspects of the presidency appear less important than the responsibilities that come with the president's other powers. When presidents veto bills, sign treaties, nominate Supreme Court justices, issue pardons, or order military actions, it is obvious that they have exercised presidential power. As chief of state, however, the president acts neither as a commander nor as an administrator. The effects of ceremonial leadership are less observable and impossible to quantify. Consequently, the chief of state duties are seldom described as a "power" and are sometimes denounced as a waste of the president's time.

Although the president's right to dedicate a monument or congratulate an astronaut may mean little, the symbolism of the chief of state role constitutes a real power because it enhances presidential authority and legitimizes and magnifies other presidential powers. As political scientist Clinton Rossiter explained, "No President can fail to realize that all his powers are invigorated, indeed are given a new dimension of authority, because he is the symbol of our sovereignty, continuity, and grandeur."[12]

The presidency, therefore, is elevated above other offices and institutions not just by its legal authority, but by its symbolic mystique. This mystique has been built up by two centuries of veneration for an office that has been occupied by many of our greatest national heroes. Rossiter wrote:

> Lincoln is the supreme myth, the richest symbol in the American experience. He is, as someone has remarked neither irreverently nor sacrilegiously, the martyred Christ of democracy's passion play. And who, then, can measure the strength that is given to the President because he holds Lincoln's office, lives in Lincoln's house, and walks in Lincoln's way? The final greatness of the Presidency lies in the truth that it is not just an office of incredible power but a breeding ground of indestructible myth.[13]

SYMBOLIC LEADERSHIP

Effective government requires more than rational deliberations and actions. Hearts are stirred and ranks are closed more easily by symbols than by reasoned arguments. Consequently, every government that hopes to provide effective leadership must provide symbols that unify, inspire, and reassure the people. The most powerful symbols are human symbols. Journalist Michael Novak, who worked for the Edmund Muskie and George McGovern campaigns in 1972, wrote of the necessity of human symbols: "Causes, institutions, and administrative processes must be personified before humans can passionately engage them. Humans are flesh and blood, and they understand best what is flesh and blood. . . . Thus the general law of politics: political movements depend for their general acceptance on the greatness of their leaders."[14] In the United States, the president, as chief of state, is the dominant political symbol for most Americans.

This symbolic stature enables presidents to exercise inspirational leadership from the stage of the White House. Americans want more from a leader than efficiency and honesty. They want a dramatic leader who can articulate their goals, motivate them, and even amuse them. Skillful presidents can use their symbolic assets to build the nation's morale and confidence and call on patriotic sentiments in a crisis. Political scientist Harold J. Laski explained the importance of a symbolic and inspiring leader to the people:

> They must see someone who can say in the grand way what they half-articulately feel. They must have the sense that they are a part of significant events. Dull government can only endure when government is unimportant; a long period of extraordinary prosperity will, as in the Coolidge regime, persuade men that dullness is the same as soundness. But where any significant part of the population is hard pressed, it looks to the president for relief; and it is then urgent that he give the appearance of active intervention on their behalf. A dull president will not last long in a period of crisis. His temptation, just because he is dull, is to throw the burden of responsibility upon the leaders in Congress. He thus ceases to be the symbol of action, and the nation feels deprived of that leadership to which it feels itself entitled.[15]

The chief of state role equips presidents with several symbolic assets through which they can reinforce their executive leadership. Presidents are seen as the symbol of national unity, the symbol of national continuity, and the symbol of the federal government. Although presidents may have varying success at using these assets to further their policies, all presidents possess them by virtue of holding office and exercising presidential powers.

Symbol of National Unity

The Constitution provided for three independent branches of government, but the president, rather than Congress or the courts, has become the symbol of national unity. The presidency's emergence as a unifying symbol was predictable. George Washington, who was a national symbol even before he became president, saw his presidential role primarily as that of a national unifier who would draw together the citizens of the thirteen states and the followers of various political philosophies into one nation. Although no president since has been able to remain as nonpartisan as Washington, few presidents have been slaves to their parties, and most have worked in some way to reduce national divisions. In addition, presidents are the most identifiable national leaders and the only elected officials (with the exception of vice presidents) who have a national constituency. As such they are seen as the guardian of the interests of the whole nation against the narrow demands of partisan and sectional groups.

The president's status as a symbol of national unity is an especially valuable political asset because much of what the president does as chief executive and party leader divides the nation. Political scientist Thomas E. Cronin has observed that presidents

> necessarily divide when they act as the leaders of their political parties, when they set priorities that advantage certain goals and groups at the expense of others, when they forge and lead political coalitions, when they move out ahead of public opinion and assume the role of national educators, and when they choose one set of advisers over another. A President, as a creative executive leader, cannot help but offend certain interests.[16]

Being a symbol of national unity allows presidents to heal some of the wounds they open while acting in their other roles and to maintain the public's confidence in them as leader of the entire nation. Eisenhower was particularly adept at projecting an image of an amiable unifier while hiding his political side, thereby maximizing the unifying potential of his chief of state role.[17]

The power of the presidency as a unifying symbol is demonstrated by the public's reaction to international crisis. Even when Americans disagree with the president's policies, they have tended to rally around their president when the nation's interests are threatened by a foreign power. Public opinion polls have shown that presidential approval ratings usually improve when the nation becomes involved in a war or other international crisis. For example, President Kennedy's public approval rating jumped 13 percent in 1962 after the Cuban Missile Crisis. In 1975 Ford's public approval rating shot up eleven points after he ordered marines to rescue the crew of the merchant ship *Mayaguez,* which had been seized by Cambodian forces. Bush's approval rating reached an astounding 89 percent after the swift defeat of Iraq by a U.S.-led coalition in the Persian Gulf War.

Although presidential approval ratings will improve the most when the public perceives that the president has acted skillfully or boldly to meet an international crisis, even clear foreign policy failures can add to a president's popularity. In May 1960, the Soviets shot down an American U-2 spy plane over Soviet territory. Eisenhower denied the United States was conducting intelligence overflights of the Soviet Union, but when Moscow produced the captured pilot, he took responsibility for the missions. Eisenhower's approval rating jumped 6 percent following the incident, despite heightened East-West tensions

GEORGE WASHINGTON AS THE FIRST CHIEF OF STATE

When George Washington became president, it was inevitable that the chief of state role would become a prominent aspect of the presidency. His status as a military hero and the leader most identified with the Revolution both in the United States and abroad made him a national symbol even before he became president. Because he had embodied the higher purposes of the Revolution, his acceptance of the presidency brought legitimacy to the Constitution. Presidents since Washington have derived respect and authority from their presidential office and powers. With Washington, however, the flow of benefits was reversed. It was he who brought legitimacy and prominence to an office that had no tradition or established operating procedures and would have been distrusted by the people had he not held it.[1]

Washington believed his primary task as president was to unify the country and establish strong political institutions. In no other presidency were ceremony and symbolism more important to the fulfillment of the president's goals. John Adams saw George Washington as a master of dramatic, symbolic leadership. Many years after Washington's death he commented, "We may say of him, if he was not the greatest President he was the best Actor of the Presidency we have ever had. His address to The States when he left the Army: His solemn Leave taken of Congress when he resigned his Commission: his Farewell Address to the People when he resigned his Presidency. These were all in a strain of Shakespearean and Garrickal excellence in Dramatic Exhibitions."[2]

Washington understood that everything he did as president would set a precedent for future presidents and that even small matters of ceremony could affect the reputation and success of the new government and his office. He wrote:

> Many things which appear of little importance in themselves and at the beginning, may have great and durable consequences from their having been established at the commencement of a new and general government. It will be much easier to commence the administration, upon a well adjusted system, built on tenable grounds, than to correct errors or alter inconveniences after they shall have been confirmed by habit.[3]

Washington, therefore, carefully performed ceremonial functions so as to strike a balance between the dignity and accessibility of the presidency. He traveled to his New York inauguration in a carriage, acknowledging the cheers of crowds, but gave a highly formal speech at his inauguration and did not participate in the public revelry surrounding the occasion. Early in his presidency he established a system of formal receptions known as "levees," which allowed him to frequently receive members of government and the public but also to maintain a solemnity that preserved his aura of authority. He also accepted the formal title of "President of the United States" granted by Congress but did not endorse or participate in Vice President John Adams's campaign to have Congress establish the ostentatious presidential title "His Highness the President of the United States and Protector of the Rights of the Same."[4]

Washington's attention to the details of his chief of state role had significance beyond establishing the proprieties of his office. Washington was also determined to strengthen the common identity of Americans and the primacy of the federal government over the states. The weakness of the federal government and its dependence on the states under the Articles of Confederation had greatly disturbed Washington and had been the motivation behind the establishment of the new government.

Convincing the nation of the primacy of the federal government and inspiring in the American people a sense of common identity were difficult tasks. The Constitution clearly gave the federal government legal preeminence over the states. Nevertheless, most Americans felt a greater allegiance to their state than to the Union, and state officials naturally tended to resist federal authority as an intrusion into their jurisdictions. The fledgling government lacked tools to implement government policy. In particular, the federal government had no army or navy and only a few federal marshals who could gather information and enforce federal laws. Consequently, Washington had to rely on state governors to provide militia and law enforcement officers to deal with violations of federal statutes.

Washington used his chief of state role to counter impressions that the federal government lacked authority and did not deserve the primary loyalties of the people. He traveled to every state to underscore national unity, taking trips to the northern states in 1789 and to the southern states in 1791. He also insisted that foreign governments deal with him, the representative of all the people, rather than with Congress, which was chosen by local constituencies. When Congress voted for a day of thanksgiving in November 1789, Washington issued the proclamation rather than having Congress ask the states to issue it, as had been done with similar declarations under the Articles of Confederation.[5]

Even when seemingly trivial matters of protocol were concerned, Washington was careful to assert the primacy of the presidency and the federal government. During his tour of New England in 1789 he asked to dine with John Hancock, the governor of Massachusetts, but indicated that Hancock should call on him first. When Hancock claimed to be too ill to visit the president, Washington canceled dinner and wrote a stiff note to the governor: "The president of the United States presents his best respects to the Governor, and has the honor to inform him that he shall be at home 'till 2 o'clock. The President of the United States need not express the pleasure it will give him to see the Governor; but at the same time, he most earnestly begs that the Governor will not hazard his health on the occasion."[6] Washington scored an important symbolic victory for the presidency and the Constitution when Hancock relented after a two-day standoff. The governor, who continued to profess an illness, was carried to the president's lodgings by several servants.[7]

1. Glenn Phelps, "George Washington and the Founding of the Presidency," *Presidential Studies Quarterly* 17 (spring 1987): 352.
2. Quoted in Clinton Rossiter, *The American Presidency,* 2d ed. (New York: Harcourt, Brace and World, 1960), 92.
3. Quoted in James Hart, *The American Presidency in Action, 1789* (New York: Macmillan, 1948), 12.
4. Joseph E. Kallenbach, *The American Chief Executive: the Presidency and the Governorship* (New York: Harper and Row, 1966), 274.
5. Phelps, "George Washington and the Founding of the Presidency," 351.
6. Quoted in ibid., 351–352.
7. Hart, *The American Presidency in Action, 1789,* 20.

and the collapse of a summit meeting in Paris later in the month.

Similarly, after the U.S.-sponsored Bay of Pigs invasion of Cuba by exiled Cuban nationals in 1961, Kennedy's approval rating improved eleven points to 83 percent, even though the invasion was universally considered a disaster.[18] The public rallied around Eisenhower and Kennedy in these situations not because they achieved anything, but because they were the symbols of the United States during a time of international confrontation.

Symbol of Continuity

Presidents also benefit from occupying an office that is identified with the continuity of the United States and the stability of its political institutions. The American people see the president not only as the current national leader but also as the latest in a long line of presidents who have guarded the freedom and laws of the United States.

Lincoln, perhaps the most celebrated U.S. president, is remembered primarily for preserving the Union. When political rivals challenge the president, they are in the position of confronting the defender of the Constitution and the heir of Washington, Jefferson, Lincoln, and the Roosevelts.

Presidents who are linked to past administrations or eras through their prepresidential service may be able to fortify their symbolic power by emphasizing these past associations. Political scientist Stephen Skowronek writes of James Monroe:

> His most precious leadership resources were his standing as the last of the fading line of revolutionary notables and as the undisputed heir to the legacy of Jefferson and Madison. Making the case for continuity in politics was his special province; cloaking change with the appearance of consistency, his most distinctive skill. Monroe may have been a bit obsessed with matters of personal countenance and proper comportment, but then he had little else to offer by way of influence and control. . . . All those who saw him were reminded in this way of his past service to the nation, and his whole personal history was brought to bear on the new projects of his administration.[19]

Yet special links to the past need not be present for a president to take advantage of the inherent continuity symbolized by the office. When Bill Clinton went to Normandy in June 1994 to commemorate the fiftieth anniversary of D-Day, he could not claim to have a personal link to the heroics that he would honor. He was the first president born after World War II, and he had avoided service in the military during the Vietnam War. As chief of state, however, he was inherently linked to American history, the survival of the nation, and the succession of generations. His speeches on the occasion emphasized the victory of the World War II generation and the obligation of his own generation to build on their sacrifice.

The history of the presidency itself demonstrates the stability of the nation's political institutions. Power has always been transferred peacefully from one president to the next. The unbroken chain of presidents has survived assassinations, civil war, impeachment proceedings, election fraud, and a presidential resignation. Even before the presidency faced any of these trials its continuity impressed Martin Van Buren who wrote, "The President under our system, like the king in a monarchy, never dies."[20]

When presidents leave office they continue to symbolize the United States of a past era and the continuity of the nation's democratic institutions. Although there have been exceptions, retiring presidents customarily attend the inaugural ceremonies of their successors, thereby symbolically demonstrating the strength of the Constitution, which provides for the peaceful and orderly transfer of presidential power.[21] Former presidents also can contribute to an image of stability during crises. At John Kennedy's funeral, Herbert Hoover, Harry Truman, and Dwight Eisenhower sat with Lyndon Johnson in a show of nonpartisan support. Together they constituted a powerful symbol of continuity that reassured a nation not yet recovered from the shock of Kennedy's assassination.[22]

Symbol of Government

As chief of state the president symbolizes not only the nation but also its government. Because the presidency is occupied by a single familiar individual who has broad executive powers, including the prerogative to initiate policy, it is the most dynamic and understandable element of the federal government.

For many Americans what the president is doing becomes synonymous with what the government is doing. For example, a president unveiling a tax reform proposal to a national television audience is more easily understood than the bargaining and consultations within the executive branch that produced the proposal or the complex political and procedural battles that will be fought over the tax reform issue in Congress. The proposal is seen as emanating not from the Treasury Department or the executive branch, but rather from the president. Historians and journalists frequently organize American history according to presidential administrations. Policy programs, military conflicts, and economic conditions all become identified with the president who was serving at the time they occurred, even if that president was not primarily responsible for them. The presidency, therefore, is used by many Americans as a "cognitive handle," which personalizes and simplifies the detailed processes of governing the nation.[23]

Being the most visible symbol of government can work against presidents as well as for them. Public expectations of the president tend to be very high and often unreasonable. Because it is easier to blame an individual for society's problems than to understand all the complicated factors contributing to them, presidents receive much unjust criticism. Public dissatisfaction with federal government policies or local conditions over which the president has little control may be translated into disapproval of the president.

The precipitous drop in George Bush's approval ratings during the year and a half that preceded the 1992 election was due in part to his abdication of the symbolic power he had accrued as the victor of the Persian Gulf War. Bush failed to seize upon the opportunity provided by his 89 percent approval rating to put forward a bold domestic program or explain his economic policies, especially his assent to a tax increase in 1990.[24] He was able to unite the country against a foreign enemy, but he failed to offer a vision of how to respond to domestic troubles. As a result, Bush became identified with a stagnant economy and gridlocked government, regardless of his personal responsibility for domestic conditions.

Yet being a symbol of the entire government upon which the media and public focus attention gives presidents the power to dominate issues. When any significant event occurs, Americans look to the president for an assessment and a response. Michael Novak wrote of the power presidents have because they command the attention of the nation:

> If on television the president says our ships were attacked in the Gulf of Tonkin, then that attack (even if it did not occur) occupies our attention and demands that we refute it or accept it or dismiss it. Whatever we do, there stands the president's assertion, solid until painstakingly disproved. This power over our attention, over our power to structure issues, is so enormous that it dwarfs all others.[25]

TOOL OF FOREIGN POLICY

As chief of state, the president is the ceremonial representative of the United States to the international community. Presidents make ceremonial visits to foreign countries and greet foreign dignitaries who visit the United States. Whether presidents are receiving visitors in the White House or touring the world, they are expected to fulfill both their diplomatic and ceremonial responsibilities. When U.S. presidents visit Great Britain, for example, they usually have a ceremonial meeting with the reigning monarch and a policy meeting with the prime minister.

The international chief of state role, however, cannot be neatly separated from the president's activities as the architect of U.S. foreign relations. State visits and other international ceremonies and spectacles that the president undertakes as chief of state are tools of foreign policy. They are a means of communicating the intentions and attitudes of the administration and improving the relationships of the United States with foreign governments.

Presidents and their representatives also use international ceremonial appearances and events to lobby for the support of foreign peoples and leaders. The foreign public observes U.S. presidents most often in their chief of state role. When presidents admire landmarks, make speeches, and attend state dinners on their foreign trips, they are trying to increase their popularity overseas and establish a reservoir of goodwill to benefit U.S. interests. International respect for a president will enhance the image of the United States, the confidence of the U.S. public, and the president's ability to exert leadership in the international arena. President Eisenhower, who made the image of the United States a high priority, wrote near the end of his presidency that he had tried to maintain "a respectable image of American life before the world. Among the qualities American government must exhibit is dignity. In turn the principal governmental spokesman must strive to display it."[26]

The president's international chief of state role also creates unscheduled diplomatic opportunities. Between November 1982 and February 1985, three Soviet general secretaries died—Leonid Brezhnev, Yuri Andropov, and Konstantin Chernenko. As chief of state of an important nation, President Reagan received invitations to their funerals in accordance with international protocol. These occasions provided Reagan with opportunities to meet face to face with Soviet leaders during a period when poor U.S.-Soviet relations would have made a planned meeting difficult, if not impossible, to arrange. President Reagan's decisions to send Vice President Bush as the U.S. representative to each funeral rather than attend himself underscored the hard line he was taking toward the Soviet Union at the time. Nevertheless, the funerals allowed the vice president to meet the succeeding Soviet general secretaries and speak to them about U.S. interests.

Greeting Foreign Leaders

Presidents must entertain many visiting chiefs of state, prime ministers, and other foreign dignitaries every year. These visits often include a photo session and a state dinner attended by selected members of Congress, administration officials, and national celebrities.

The manner in which presidents receive a foreign chief of state sends a signal to that leader and other nations about U.S. policy. President Carter's friendly greeting of Chinese vice premier Deng Xiaoping in January 1979 was a ceremonial act with profound diplomatic implications. Before, during, and after Deng's visit to the United States, the vice premier had pointedly

In May 1860 President James Buchanan greets Japan's first envoys to the United States.

attacked the leaders of the Soviet Union for pursuing an aggressive foreign policy. The Carter administration's warm reception of Deng and its refusal to condemn his belligerent rhetoric signaled tolerance for the vice premier's views and a clear tilt toward the Chinese in the trilateral relationship.

Presidents also can make a statement about their foreign policy priorities through their invitations to visit the United States. In 1977, for example, Carter wished to emphasize the importance of U.S. relations with its North American neighbors. Consequently, the first two foreign leaders he invited to the White House were President José López Portillo of Mexico and Prime Minister Pierre Trudeau of Canada.

Making International Tours

International tours by presidents and their delegated representatives often consist more of ceremonial activities than of policy discussions with foreign leaders. Because U.S. presidents have limited time and because ensuring their security is such a difficult and expensive task, a ceremonial visit to a foreign country is a sign of the value the United States attaches to its relations with that country. To be worthwhile, presidential visits do not have to produce a diplomatic breakthrough or even progress in ongoing negotiations. A president may visit a foreign nation solely to reaffirm U.S. interest in that nation or to focus global attention on a particular region or problem.

Before the 1950s, presidential travel to foreign countries was uncommon. When presidents did go abroad, they almost always did so to hold negotiations with foreign leaders. Woodrow Wilson went to Europe in 1918 to negotiate the Treaty of Versailles, which ended World War I. Franklin Roosevelt and Harry Truman traveled abroad to confer with Winston Churchill, Joseph Stalin, and other Allied leaders during World War II.

President Eisenhower's "Quest for Peace" tour of eleven Asian, European, and Middle Eastern nations in 1959 established the precedent that presidents could go abroad on goodwill missions designed primarily to increase foreign support of U.S. policies. Eisenhower traveled twenty-two thousand miles in nineteen days and was met in many cities by enthusiastic crowds numbering in the hundreds of thousands. His trip was almost entirely devoted to ceremonial activities. On December 3, in a televised speech to the nation before his departure, Eisenhower declared he was about to "set forth as your agent to extend once again to millions of people across the seas assurances of America's sincere friendship."[27] Eisenhower conceived of his trip as so purely symbolic that he refused Pakistani president Ayub Khan's request to discuss the contentious issue of the Pakistani-Indian border with Indian prime minister Jawaharlal Nehru unless Nehru raised the issue first.

Host nations expect a president who is visiting their country to sample their culture and make a pilgrimage to their most cherished landmarks. In 1972, when Nixon made the first trip to the People's Republic of China by a U.S. president, he traveled to the Great Wall and toured the Forbidden City, the ancient home of Chinese emperors. This sightseeing expressed U.S. respect for Chinese culture and symbolized the desire of the administration to widen contacts between the people of the two nations. Given the vast cultural differences and recent animosity between the United States and the People's Republic of China, this symbolism was an important element in establishing a lasting friendship. Similarly, President Nixon attended the Bolshoi Ballet and several state dinners during his historic visit to Moscow the same year.

Kennedy's trip to West Berlin in June 1963 demonstrated how the chief of state role could be used to buttress a foreign policy commitment. For several years the Soviet Union had made veiled threats against the city, which existed as a democratic enclave deep within Communist East Germany. In 1961 the Soviet and East German Communist leaders ordered a wall to be built to prevent East Germans from emigrating to West Berlin. The U.S. commitment to defend West Berlin was not new, but the vulnerability of the city to Soviet attack and the great consequences of nuclear war inevitably caused Berliners, as well as other Western Europeans, to question the U.S. commitment to the city. No matter how adamantly U.S. officials insisted that the United States would defend Berlin, establishing the credibility of the commitment was difficult.

While traveling in Europe in 1963, Kennedy delivered a speech at the Berlin Wall in which he declared "Ich bin ein Berliner" (I am a Berliner). The spectacle of the U.S. chief of state standing before the symbol of Communist oppression and declaring to 400,000 Berliners in their own language that he was one of them added new force to the U.S. commitment. As the commander in chief and manager of U.S. foreign policy, Kennedy had made the decision to reaffirm the standing U.S. policy to defend West Berlin. It was Kennedy's role as chief of state, however, that gave him the opportunity to infuse the U.S. commitment with a dramatic promise that linked the prestige of the United States and his own presidency to the defense of Berlin and Europe.

In 1985 President Reagan planned to make another dramatic presidential trip to West Germany to commemorate the fortieth anniversary of the end of World War II in Europe. To symbolize U.S.-West German reconciliation and friendship since the war, the president agreed to visit the German military cemetery at Bitburg and lay a wreath at a tomb for German casualties of the war. After the president had made a commitment to visit the cemetery, however, reports revealed that among its dead were members of the infamous Nazi SS, the group that oversaw the execution of millions of Jews in concentration camps before and during the war. Jewish and veterans groups immediately protested Reagan's itinerary. In an attempt to placate the president's domestic critics, the White House added a stop at the site of the Bergen-Belsen concentration camp to his trip. Nevertheless, the protests continued, and Reagan was confronted with the choice of offending significant numbers of American voters or offending his West German hosts. Reagan chose to absorb the

FOREIGN CHIEFS OF STATE

The division of the head of state and head of government roles between two or more individuals in most European governments demonstrates that a nation's chief executive does not also need to be its figurehead, as is the case in the United States. In many nations, including Great Britain, Belgium, The Netherlands, Sweden, Denmark, and Norway, a king or queen serves as chief of state even though the monarchy has lost executive powers. In these countries the monarchs have become integrative figures who embody the history and ideals of their nations.

In other countries, such as France, Israel, Italy, and Germany, the chief of state role is assigned to an elected official who serves alongside the head of the government.[1] Many democracies in Latin America have followed the model of the United States, lodging both the chief of state and chief executive powers in a single president.

Significantly, no democratic nation has both a monarch and a president, perhaps because the symbol of a nation cannot be divisible.[2] Yet no chief executive can be entirely insulated from ceremonial duties. Even when a chief of state's office is a cherished part of the national culture grounded in centuries of tradition, like the British monarchy, the person who actually wields power will be expected to preside at some symbolic functions. In particular, chief executives must greet important foreign visitors who want to meet with the most powerful person in the country, not just the reigning figurehead.

1. Merlin Gustafson, "Our Part-Time Chief of State," *Presidential Studies Quarterly* 9 (spring 1979): 164.
2. David F. Prindle, "Head of State and Head of Government in Comparative Perspective," *Presidential Studies Quarterly* 21 (winter 1991): 57.

domestic criticism of the cemetery visit to avoid embarrassing West German chancellor Helmut Kohl and undercutting his symbolic message of reconciliation to the German people.

PARTISAN POLITICS

When a political system separates the chief of state role from that of the chief executive, the chief of state can transcend partisanship. The British monarch takes no official position in the political struggles between British political parties. Such nonpartisanship is impossible for the U.S. president, who must function as the leader of a political party as well as chief of state.

Virtually everything the president does in public as chief of state has political significance. Political scientist David Prindle observed that skillful presidents can take advantage of the ambiguity of their office for partisan purposes: "A dominant president, that is, one that both functions as a symbol and has preeminent policy-making authority, is an ambiguous sort of figure. Ordinary citizens are liable to confuse the two roles, seeing the partisan utterances of the politician as the disinterested pronouncements of the symbol. The Head of State role can thus be used by clever presidents to overawe opposition to the programs they advocate as Head of Government."[28] The dignity and status conferred on presidents as the nation's ceremonial and symbolic leader increase their popularity with the American public and their bargaining advantages over other government officials. The chief of state role also provides presidents with a justification to preside over events with obvious public relations appeal. Chief of state activities can be staged to make presidents look patriotic, amiable, concerned, skilled, and noble. Because chief of state activities are built into the president's job description, the role allows presidents to campaign subtly throughout their term without having to appear overly political or self-serving.

Presidential Popularity

One of the most important factors affecting presidents' domestic political power is the public support they receive. When a solid majority of Americans backs the president on a particular issue, other political institutions, including Congress, rarely will challenge the president. The chief of state role is a political asset primarily because it fortifies the president's popularity.

Many Americans will support the office of the presidency because it symbolizes the nation and the government even when they disagree with the incumbent's policies. The popularity of the presidency is demonstrated by the high public approval ratings enjoyed by new presidents. Political scientists Erwin C. Hargrove and Michael Nelson have written that the "honeymoon" period between the American people and new presidents

> is, in a sense, an affirmation of faith in the office. . . . New presidents invariably receive the initial approval of millions of citizens who voted against them; vice presidents who succeed to the office, for whom no one voted, actually fare better. Even after experiencing two highly unpopular presidencies in a row, the second culminating in the near-impeachment and resignation of President Nixon, citizens rallied to the support of President Ford by a margin of 71 percent to 3 percent.[29]

Even the outcome of the Watergate scandal can be viewed as evidence of the presidency's popularity and strength rather than its fragility, since Nixon was not forced to resign until long after the depth of the scandal became known.[30]

Given that the presidency is more consistently popular than any incumbent can hope to be, presidents benefit from chief of state activities because they make them appear "presidential." Formal ceremonies such as the State of the Union address and a state dinner for a foreign head of state appeal to public patriotism and allow the president to look like the nation's leader and guardian. They also underscore the president's links with history and lead people to associate the incumbent with the past glories of the office. Nixon attempted to exploit the history of the presidency by placing a bust of Lincoln on his desk and wearing an American flag pin when he appeared on television during the Watergate scandal to assure the American public that he was innocent of any wrongdoing.[31]

The chief of state role also contributes to presidential popularity by personalizing the president. Less formal ceremonies such as a trip to a sporting event or a White House reception for a civic group make the president appear as an average, friendly

JIMMY CARTER'S ATTEMPT TO "DEPOMP" THE PRESIDENCY

During Jimmy Carter's presidential campaign leading up to his 1976 election, he perceived correctly that the American people were still disturbed by the Watergate scandal and wanted the next president to restore their trust in government. Carter's emphasis on establishing an honest and unpretentious administration helped propel him to the White House past several better known Democratic candidates and the Republican incumbent, Gerald Ford. As president, Carter was determined to eliminate barriers between the presidency and the people.

Carter began his campaign to "depomp" the presidency on his first day as president. Following his inauguration ceremony, he and his family got out of their limousine and walked up Pennsylvania Avenue to the White House. This gesture symbolized his intention to cut back on the privileges surrounding his office. After Carter's term was over, he wrote about his decision to walk back to the White House:

> I began to realize that the symbolism of our leaving the armored car would be much more far-reaching than simply to promote exercise. I remembered the angry demonstrators who had habitually confronted recent Presidents and Vice Presidents, furious over the Vietnam war and later the revelations of Watergate. I wanted to provide a vivid demonstration of my confidence in the people as far as security was concerned, and I felt a simple walk would be a tangible indication of some reduction in the imperial status of the President and his family.[1]

Thereafter Carter continued his efforts to simplify the imperial presidency. He sold the presidential yacht, carried his own garment bag, donated blood, and ordered the White House thermostat to be set at sixty-five degrees in the winter.[2] In addition, he stopped the practice of having "Hail to the Chief" played when he entered the scene of an official event, delivered an FDR-style fireside chat, and was often photographed in informal clothing.

Carter also attempted to dispel the imperial atmosphere surrounding the presidency by emphasizing his accessibility. During the first several months of his presidency, he held frequent press conferences and question-and-answer sessions with federal employees. He also attended town meetings in rural communities, conducted a phone-in talk show in which members of the public could ask him direct questions, and, when traveling within the country, lodged in the homes of American families.[3] Carter even invited John B. Shanklin, a Washington, D.C., hotel worker, to the White House as he had promised during a 1974 encounter with Shanklin at the outset of Carter's campaign for the Democratic nomination.

During his first months in office, Carter's openness appealed to the American people, and he enjoyed high public approval ratings. As time passed, however, Carter and his aides suspected that they had gone too far in eliminating pomp from the presidency. As the president's popularity dropped throughout most of his first year and a half in office, it appeared that Carter's accessibility and populist style had made him seem less presidential than past chief executives and had muted the patriotic message contained in presidential symbols. For some people, Carter's actions also seemed to be weakening the office of the president.[4] Carter recalled: "I overreacted at first. We began to receive many complaints that I had gone too far in cutting back the pomp and ceremony, so after a few months I authorized the band to play 'Hail to the Chief' on special occasions. I found it to be impressive and enjoyed it."[5] As his term progressed Carter tried to establish a balance between the regal symbols that contributed to an image of himself as a powerful, decisive president and the populist symbols that had helped him get elected.

Carter had initially misinterpreted what the public wanted following the Watergate scandal. Undoubtedly, they longed for honesty and openness in the White House, but not at the expense of the symbolism that contributed to the presidency's historic and paternal image. Indeed, the "imperial" presidency of Richard Nixon did not end in disgrace because he enjoyed the ceremonial display of his office, but rather because he had broken the law, cut himself off from everyone but a handful of advisers, and cynically betrayed the trust of the American people. Carter learned that the symbols of the presidency contribute to presidential power, and no president can reject them without risking an erosion of popular support.

1. Jimmy Carter, *Keeping Faith* (New York: Bantam Books, 1982), 17–18.
2. Larry Berman, *The New American Presidency* (Boston: Little, Brown, 1987), 314.
3. Harold M. Barger, *The Impossible Presidency* (Glenview, Ill.: Scott, Foresman, 1984), 378.
4. Thomas E. Cronin, *The State of the Presidency*, 2d ed. (Boston: Little, Brown, 1980), 159.
5. Carter, *Keeping Faith*, 27.

person who shares the everyday interests and concerns of Americans. Ceremonial activities, therefore, can be used to build the fondness, as well as the respect, the public has for a president.

Finally, many Americans will support an incumbent's foreign policies because the president is seen as the representative and symbol of the United States before the world. Few events make a president look more like a world leader than a summit meeting with a prominent head of state or a reception in a foreign country by hundreds of thousands of cheering foreign citizens hoping to catch a glimpse of the U.S. chief of state. Presidents attempt to maximize the public relations benefits of their chief of state role by dramatizing their foreign tours and staging them for television. President Nixon timed his historic arrival in Beijing in 1972 to coincide with Sunday night prime-time television viewing hours. The president's return to Washington was also timed to coincide with prime time, even though this required a nine-hour "refueling stop" in Alaska.[32]

Intragovernmental Relations

Although the public often thinks of presidents as leaders who "run the country," they are far from omnipotent. Congress can block most presidential initiatives, and the courts can declare a presidential action unconstitutional. Even cabinet officers and other members of the executive branch can check presidential power by withholding information, slowing down implementation of presidential directives, leaking details of controversial policies to the media, publicly announcing their opposition to a policy, or resigning to protest a presidential decision. Consequently, presidential power depends not only on the authority of presidents to issue orders and make proposals, but also on their ability to persuade others that those orders and proposals are correct.

The president's status as chief of state strengthens the president's ability to influence other members of the government. Political scientist Richard Neustadt observed:

> Presidential "powers" may be inconclusive when a President commands, but always remain relevant as he persuades. The status and authority inherent in his office reinforce his logic and his charm. . . . [F]ew men—and exceedingly few Cabinet officers—are immune to the impulse to say "yes" to the President of the United States. It grows harder to say "no" when they are seated in his oval office at the White House, or in his office on the second floor, where almost tangibly he partakes of the aura of his physical surroundings.[33]

Such presidential lobbying is hard to resist, especially for members of the president's own party who risk political isolation if they do not have a good record of supporting the president. Presidents, therefore, can exploit the symbolic power of their office to pressure an official or member of Congress for support.

Presidents can also use the glamour and social prestige of the White House to influence members of Congress and other public leaders by granting or denying them access to White House meetings and social functions. Officials want to be close to the president not just because they benefit from having access to the chief executive's authority, but also because they wish to bask in the glow of presidential celebrity. An invitation to a White House dinner or reception can be one of the most sought after "tickets" in Washington. It allows an individual to rub elbows with the most powerful and famous people in the country, and it is a confirmation of the recipient's importance to the nation and the president. Although presidents and their staffs will invite members of the other party to White House events in the name of bipartisanship, political allies of the president obviously will receive more invitations than political enemies. Politicians who engage the president in a particularly bitter political battle or become enmeshed in a scandal may be cut off from the president's presence entirely.[34]

Furthermore, when presidents are faced with a stubborn Congress, their status as chief of state contributes to their ability to appeal to the people over the head of the legislative branch. Presidents have done this by presenting their case to the people on an issue and hoping that favorable popular opinion and active public pressure on individual legislators will force Congress to back presidential policy. Franklin Roosevelt had great success with this tactic. His popularity with the American people weakened resistance in Congress to his New Deal programs. Reagan also used this strategy successfully. During his first year in office, he asked the public to pressure Congress to support his efforts to change dramatically the federal government's taxing and spending policies. Despite a solid Democratic majority in the House of Representatives, he was able to pass a large tax cut and bolster spending on defense.

Other presidents have been less successful at using public opinion. In September 1919 President Wilson undertook a cross-country crusade to promote U.S. entry into the League of Nations. After making dozens of speeches in twenty-nine cities across the Midwest and West, he became ill and returned to Washington, D.C., where he suffered a stroke on October 2. Despite Wilson's efforts, the public remained skeptical of an activist foreign policy, and the Republican-controlled Senate refused to ratify the Treaty of Versailles, which established the League.

President Carter saw himself as a Washington outsider who enjoyed a direct relationship with the people that would help him to deal with Congress on contentious issues. Carter discovered, however, that his election victory and initial personal popularity—which exceeded 70 percent during his first months in office—did not translate into public enthusiasm for his programs. His expectation of being able to confront Congress with strong public backing led him to neglect executive-legislative relations and made passage of his programs more difficult.[35]

President Clinton hoped that public pressure would push a skeptical Congress to adopt his comprehensive health care reform bill in 1994. On August 3, he held a news conference to demand action by Republicans in Congress on the bill. He also spoke to pro-health care reform rallies and endorsed a bus caravan touring the nation to drum up support. But opponents of the Clinton plan countered with their own campaign that portrayed Clinton's complex approach as an expensive, overly bureaucratic one that would limit choice of doctors and erode the quality of care. Despite the president's efforts, public support for his plan sank during August and September. The bill died without coming to a final vote in either house of Congress.

EXTRAGOVERNMENTAL POWER

The president is indisputably the nation's first celebrity. One 1969–1970 survey found that 98 percent of adult Americans knew who was president, a much higher percentage of recognition than for any other public figure except the vice president, who was known by 87 percent. In contrast, only 57 percent knew the name of one senator from their state, and only 39 percent could identify their representative in the House of Representatives. A 1995 national survey found even less recognition of public figures other than the president: only 60 percent could identify the vice president, 46 percent could name one senator from their state, and 33 percent could name their representative.[36]

The president, the first lady, and former occupants of the White House frequently head the list in "most admired person" polls. Most national radio and television news broadcasts will discuss the president's major activity of the day, and few adult

Americans would not be able to recite some basic details about the president's personal and political background. Each year almost two million people, many of whom stand in line for more than an hour, visit the White House. More than nine million people tried to call the White House during President Carter's call-in radio press conference in 1977. In just the first five months of the Clinton administration, the first family received 3.5 million pieces of mail. This constant attention not only contributes to the president's political power, it also gives presidents and their families great influence over national culture and attitudes.

Spiritual Leadership

Although one of the most cherished and accepted principles embodied in the Constitution is the separation between church and state, many Americans look upon presidents as moral and spiritual leaders. Presidents attend church services and national prayer breakfasts, address religious groups, discuss issues with religious leaders, and frequently invoke God in their speeches. Religious influence flows to presidents because they are the nation's foremost celebrities and the symbols of traditional American values. The moral and religious example they set affects the religious climate of the nation during their term.

The president's role as an unofficial spiritual leader was first exercised by George Washington, who said in his first inaugural address that

> it would be improper to omit in this first official act, my fervent supplications to that Almighty Being who rules over the Universe. . . . No people can be bound to acknowledge and adore the invisible hand, which conducts the Affairs of men, more than the People of the United States. Every step, by which they have advanced to the character of an independent nation, seems to have been distinguished by some token of providential agency.

Since then all presidents have mentioned God in their inaugural addresses.[37] Washington also added the words "so help me God" after the oath of office. Every president has followed Washington's example, thereby making an acknowledgment of God part of the president's first official act.

During the modern era the tendency of presidents to make religious and moral references has been more prevalent. Political scientist Barbara Hinckley found that religious and moral references in inaugural addresses occurred with greater frequency during the post–World War II period than before. The inaugural addresses of Presidents Truman through Reagan contained fourteen times as many religious and moral references as partisan political references. Even in the economic addresses of these presidents, moral and religious references were twice as common as partisan political references.[38]

Although Americans expect their president to profess a belief in God and occasionally participate in religious ceremonies and rituals, they are ambivalent about the president's religious role. The majority of Americans want their president to be a religious person, affirm religious values, and set a moral example, but they do not want the president to govern the country according to a private conception of God's will or to use the presidency to promote a specific religious faith. Carter, who considered himself a "born again" Christian, understood this ambivalence. He openly professed a deep faith in God but denied that he considered himself to be a religious leader.[39]

Rather than promoting a particular faith, presidents have generally promoted the concept of religion and the basic values common to most religions. Above all, presidents are expected to take an ecumenical approach to religion that does not offend any faith with significant numbers of adherents. As the first Roman Catholic to become president, Kennedy made a point of scheduling meetings with Protestant and Jewish groups during the first months of his presidency. Eisenhower often professed his faith in God and spoke of the importance of religion in American society, but he was careful not to define God narrowly. In a 1959 speech to the National Council of Churches, he stated that the spiritual unity of the West included not only Judeo-Christian traditions but also "the Mohammedans, the Buddhists and the rest; because they too, strongly believe that they achieve a right to human dignity because of their relationship to the Supreme Being."[40]

Cultural Leadership

People want to know the details of the lives of presidents and their families. Just as the British scan their newspapers and magazines for information about the royal family, the American public avidly follows the private lives of the first family, the closest American equivalent to royalty.

The national spotlight gives presidents and their families influence to affect the lifestyles, habits, and cultural activities of Americans. Presidents will often spark new trends in clothing, foods, hobbies, or athletics even if they do not try to do so. Franklin Roosevelt increased the popularity of cigarette holders and scotty dogs. John Kennedy's preference for rocking chairs, which he favored because of his chronic back ailment, led many Americans to get them for their own homes. Lyndon Johnson's taste for Mexican food convinced many Americans to try Mexican cuisine for the first time and stimulated the growth of fast food chains selling Mexican dishes. The company that manufactured Ronald Reagan's favorite kind of jellybean reported that its sales tripled after the media reported Reagan's fondness for their product in 1981.

First ladies can have an equally dramatic effect on national trends. Uncounted women, fascinated by the glamorous Jacqueline Kennedy, adopted her hairstyle and clothing tastes. Many Americans disapproved of Nancy Reagan's consultations with an astrologer, but popular interest in astrology increased after knowledge of her hobby was made public.

Some presidents have deliberately tried to influence the lifestyle of the nation. Theodore Roosevelt not only urged Americans to live an active life full of outdoor pursuits, he also set an example for his fellow citizens to emulate. He climbed trees on the White House grounds, swam in the Potomac, played marathon tennis matches, and went for "obstacle walks"

PUBLIC REACTION TO THE DEATH OF A PRESIDENT

The reaction of Americans to the death of a president provides dramatic evidence of the American public's emotional attachment to the presidency. The deaths of presidents have produced periods of simultaneous public grief more intense than those caused by any other type of national event. Americans regard the death of an incumbent president not just as the death of their elected leader, but as the death of the symbol of the government, the guarantor of the nation's security and stability, and a person almost as familiar as a family member.

Although no systematic studies were done of public reactions to the deaths of incumbent presidents before John F. Kennedy, anecdotal evidence suggests that Americans have often experienced a traumatizing grief when an incumbent president has died. Hundreds of thousands of people lined the railways to view the train carrying Abraham Lincoln's body from Washington, D.C., to Albany, New York, and west to its grave site in Springfield, Illinois. The massive outpouring of grief for Franklin Roosevelt, who had led the nation through the Great Depression and World War II, demonstrated that not only an assassination but also an incumbent's death by natural causes could produce a national spasm of emotion.

Nor was it necessary for the president to have been perceived as a great historical figure. After the shooting of James Garfield in 1881, large crowds took to the streets of major cities seeking news of the president's condition. The attack was the main topic of church sermons the following Sunday, and Garfield, who had entered office only four months before as a dark-horse candidate from Ohio, was lionized in the press as a great statesman.[1] Similarly, William McKinley and Warren Harding were mourned deeply by the public despite their relative lack of historical prominence.

Following the assassination of President Kennedy on November 22, 1963, social scientists at the National Opinion Research Center at the University of Chicago hastily constructed a survey designed to probe the American people's feelings in the aftermath of the tragedy. The interviewers asked 1,384 persons a series of questions about their reactions to the assassination. The responses indicated that the president's death had a much stronger effect on people than news of other kinds of disasters such as earthquakes or airline crashes.[2]

Only 19 percent of the respondents said they were able to continue their day "pretty much as usual" after hearing of the assassination. Sixty-eight percent of the respondents reported that at some time during the four-day period between the assassination and the president's funeral they "felt very nervous and tense." Fifty-seven percent said they "felt sort of dazed and numb." Fifty-three percent said they had cried.

The survey showed that the death of President Kennedy produced feelings in the American people usually associated with the death of a relative or close friend. Seventy-nine percent said when they first heard about the assassination, they "felt deeply the loss of someone very close and dear." Seventy-three percent felt anger, and 92 percent felt sorry for Kennedy's wife and children.

Paul B. Sheatsley and Jacob J. Feldman of the National Opinion Research Center observed:

> The presidential assassination seems clearly to have engaged the "gut feelings" of virtually every American. Events of this order are extremely rare. Survey after survey has consistently shown that most people are normally preoccupied with their own health, their own families, their own problems, and those of their friends and neighbors. . . . The election of an Eisenhower, the defeat of a Stevenson, a revolution in Cuba, the death of a Stalin—the surprise drop of an atomic bomb or the launching of a sputnik—such infrequent events, in contrast to the ordinary run-of-the-mill news, arouse the interest of almost everyone, but even they do not produce the cessation of ordinary activities, the almost complete preoccupation with the event, and the actual physical symptoms we have here described.[3]

1. Charles E. Rosenberg, *The Trial of the Assassin Guiteau* (Chicago: University of Chicago Press, 1968), 7.
2. Paul B. Sheatsley and Jacob J. Feldman, "The Assassination of President Kennedy: A Preliminary Report on Public Reactions and Behavior," *Public Opinion Quarterly* (summer 1964): 189–215.
3. Ibid., 206.

in which he would go over or through any obstacle that stood in his way. Roosevelt also promoted vigorous activity by inviting athletes, explorers, cowboys, and other citizens who led strenuous lives to the White House. In addition, Roosevelt waged a campaign to make simplified phonetic spelling acceptable but found that such a controversial cultural reform was beyond even his powers.[41]

John and Jacqueline Kennedy promoted artistic and intellectual pursuits during their years at the White House. Their patronage of cultural events and recognition of the achievements of writers, artists, and performers awakened American interest in the fine arts. The Kennedys invited famous entertainers and musicians to the White House for "command performances." The president and first lady also promoted interest in science and history. At one famous dinner in 1962 honoring American Nobel Prize winners, the president declared: "This is the most extraordinary collection of talent . . . that has ever been gathered together at the White House—with the possible exception of when Thomas Jefferson dined alone."[42] Mrs. Kennedy, dismayed by the meager White House library, stocked it with 1,780 great works of literature selected by James T. Babb, Yale University's librarian. She also recovered many historical pieces from museums, private collections, and White House storage areas and had the executive mansion redecorated in authentic early nineteenth-century style.

Presidential attempts to appeal to a broad array of American cultural interests have expanded during the post–World War II period. One study found that Truman and Eisenhower spoke to religious audiences, fraternal groups, journalists, educators, and youth groups during their first three years in office (with Tru-

This candid photo of JFK in the Oval Office has come to signify the heavy burden of the presidency.

man also speaking to a scientific group). Presidents Carter and Reagan also addressed all of these types of groups during their first three years, but added audiences concerned with medicine, the arts, sports, physical fitness, entertainment, mental health, community service, and the family.[43]

Chief of State Burdens

One of the justifications of the British monarchy offered by its contemporary proponents is that it shelters the prime minister from many ceremonial duties. Prime ministers can devote their time and energies to formulating policy and dealing with Parliament and foreign governments while the royal family presides at ceremonial functions and absorbs media and public attention. Presidents have no shield against ceremonial activities equivalent to the British monarchy. Although family members, vice presidents, cabinet secretaries, and other presidential associates can lighten the president's ceremonial burden, the president is responsible for innumerable ceremonial functions and never ceases to be chief of state. Between lobbying a member of Congress to support a bill and meeting with the National Security Council to discuss an international hot spot, the president may have to greet Olympic athletes or Miss America. The president's chief of state duties, therefore, may interrupt or even interfere with the president's duties as chief executive.

Calvin Coolidge, who as president refused to overcrowd his schedule, warned:

> The duties of the Presidency are exceedingly heavy. The responsibilities are overwhelming. But it is my opinion that a man of ordinary strength can carry them if he will confine himself very strictly to a performance of the duties that are imposed upon him by the Constitution and the law. If he permits himself to be engaged in all kinds of outside enterprises, in furnishing entertainment and amusement to great numbers of public gatherings, undertaking to be the source of inspiration for every worthy public movement, for all of which he will be earnestly besought with the inference that unless he responds civilization will break down and the sole responsibility will be on him, he will last in office about 90 days.[44]

Few presidents, however, have been able or have wanted to limit their activities the way Coolidge said he did, and several have driven themselves to exhaustion. Because the chief of state duties increase the presidential workload, one can argue that they are an onerous burden. In addition to the drain on a president's time and energy, the chief of state role can make the president more vulnerable to assassination attempts, reinforce unreasonable public expectations of the president, and contribute to an atmosphere of deference that may warp the president's judgment. In response to these problems, some observers of the presidency have suggested that the office be reformed so that the president, like the British prime minister, is free of ceremonial responsibilities.

DEMANDS ON TIME

Presidential time is a scarce resource. Presidents are ultimately responsible for everything that the executive branch does. They must have time to preside over policy meetings, review the work of their staff and cabinet, establish working relationships with members of Congress, read intelligence reports, study new policy proposals, hold press conferences, make decisions, and perform numerous other functions necessary to the operation of the government and their administration. In addition, they must find time for political campaigning, personal relaxation, and ceremonial functions.

No chief executive can begin to satisfy all the requests for presidential attention. Woodrow Wilson and Franklin Roosevelt, two presidents with a hands-on managerial style, complained of the burdens of their office. Wilson called the presidential workload "preposterous," and Roosevelt claimed to work fifteen-hour days.[45] Lyndon Johnson related in his memoirs: "Of all the 1,886 nights I was President, there were not many when I got to sleep before 1 or 2 a.m., and there were few mornings when I didn't wake up by 6 or 6:30."[46] Even presidents such as Eisenhower and Reagan, who were noted for their willingness to delegate responsibility and authority to their subordinates, faced daily decisions about which activities would have to be sacrificed to the pressures of time.

Although presidential responsibilities have expanded greatly in the twentieth century, eighteenth- and nineteenth-century presidents also had more work than time in which to do it. George Washington found himself overwhelmed by the number of visitors he had to receive and civic functions he had to attend. He complained: "From the time I had done breakfast and thence till dinner and afterwards till bedtime I could not get relieved from ceremony of one visit before I had to attend to another."[47] Washington approached the problem in his typical manner—by asking the advice of colleagues he trusted. He solicited the opinions of Alexander Hamilton, John Jay, James Madison, and John Adams. After hearing their recommendations, Washington decided to limit his public entertaining to a dinner every Thursday at four o'clock for government officials and their families, a public levee on Tuesday afternoons for men, and a public tea party on Friday evenings for men and women.[48]

The enormousness of presidential responsibilities received a judicial validation in 1807. Chief Justice John Marshall subpoenaed President Jefferson to appear before the grand jury in Richmond considering former vice president Aaron Burr's indictment for treason. Jefferson refused to appear. He justified his decision in part by explaining that a president's duties as chief executive should not be set aside for an appearance at a trial: "The Constitution enjoins his constant agency in the concerns of six millions of people. Is the law paramount to this, which calls on him on behalf of a single one?"[49] The court accepted Jefferson's refusal to appear and withdrew its request for his testimony. The president cooperated fully with the investigation and offered to give a deposition, but the court never asked him for one.

Numerous other nineteenth-century presidents bewailed the burdens of their office. President Monroe wrote to Congress just before his second term expired that the higher duties of the presidency, consisting primarily of legislative and administrative tasks, were "sufficient to employ the whole mind, and unceasing labors of any individual."[50] James Polk, who died less than four months after he left office, complained in his diary that his presidential duties left him "almost prostrated by fatigue."[51]

Of all presidential activities, ceremonial functions are usually regarded as the most expendable and are frequently delegated to other individuals. Each year the White House turns down hundreds of requests for the president's time from groups and organizations seeking to publicize their causes through an appointment with the president. When a crisis erupts, ceremonial functions that have been scheduled are sometimes cut to accommodate time constraints. Despite the White House's ability to trim the president's ceremonial schedule, chief of state functions still occupy blocks of the president's time. Many ceremonies over which presidents preside are trivial when compared with the weighty affairs of state. For example, in spite of tradition, appearing at the annual White House Easter egg outing is a questionable use of the president's time, considering the unending procession of problems that require the president's attention.

There is evidence, however, that although international ceremonial functions occupy much presidential time, the demands of the domestic chief of state role are less than one might expect. A study of the years 1952 and 1960 from the presidencies of Truman and Eisenhower, respectively, revealed that they spent only about one hundred hours per year, or about two hours per week, on domestic ceremonial functions. Sample surveys of the appointment calendars of Hoover, Franklin Roosevelt, Lyndon Johnson, Ford, and Carter indicated that these presidents spent about the same amount of time as Truman and Eisenhower in their domestic chief of state role.[52]

International chief of state duties, however, took up a much greater percentage of presidential time. For example, Eisenhower spent 376 hours in 1960—the equivalent of 47 eight-hour days—on foreign trips or in meetings in Washington with other heads of state.[53] Taken together, therefore, the international and domestic chief of state responsibilities constitute a significant drain on the president's time and may cause unwanted interruptions in the president's workday.

RISKS TO THE PRESIDENT'S HEALTH

Scholars and presidents generally have agreed that the presidency is a tremendous physical burden.[54] The pressures of the presidency can weaken the health of even the strongest person. Presidents usually work long hours, must occasionally take extended trips that require physical and mental stamina, and must endure enormous emotional stress arising out of the responsibilities of their job. Presidents seldom look as vigorous when they leave office as when they entered it.

One study of presidential longevity has shown that most

presidents have failed to reach the age to which they were expected to live at the time of their election. Excluding the four presidents who were assassinated (and Richard Nixon, who died in 1994 after the study was completed), twenty-one of the thirty-one presidents who died of natural causes failed to reach their individual life expectancy. As the nation and presidential responsibilities have expanded, so has the tendency of presidents to die prematurely. From 1841 to 1991 only four of twenty-seven deceased chief executives reached their individual life expectancies.[55] This occurred despite advances in medicine and the excellent medical care available to presidents.

Illnesses can and have inhibited the execution of presidential duties. Four presidents—William Henry Harrison, Zachary Taylor, Warren Harding, and Franklin Roosevelt—died of natural causes before their terms expired. Several other presidents, including Wilson and Eisenhower, were incapacitated by illness during their incumbency.[56]

Given the consequences of presidents becoming ill, reducing their workload without diminishing their effectiveness is a worthwhile goal of reform. Because common practice has demonstrated that many of the president's ceremonial duties can be delegated, these duties seem to be the logical starting place of efforts to trim the president's schedule.

George Reedy, who served as press secretary under Lyndon Johnson, has argued that even if ceremonial functions do take up valuable presidential time, the primary source of strain on presidents is not long workdays but the knowledge of the consequences of their actions.[57] From war to welfare reform, presidential policies can have life and death consequences. For presidents who have served during the atomic age, the knowledge of their responsibility as the person who must decide to use nuclear weapons can be particularly stressful. Lyndon Johnson wrote that he felt relief after hearing Richard Nixon complete the oath of office in part because "I would not have to face the decision any more of taking any step, in the Middle East or elsewhere, that might lead to world conflagration—the nightmare of my having to be the man who pressed the button to start World War III was passing."[58]

Reedy maintains, as others have, that chief of state duties can provide presidents with a psychological release from the overwhelming responsibilities of their office.[59] These ceremonial events allow presidents to get away from the strains of decision making, and because ceremonies are an accepted presidential responsibility, presidents are unlikely to feel as if they are neglecting their duties.

The effect of the chief of state role on a president's mental and physical health may depend on that individual's personality. For those presidents who revel in the spotlight of national attention, or are stimulated by an affirmation of public affection, such as Theodore Roosevelt, Franklin Roosevelt, Ronald Reagan, and Bill Clinton, chief of state duties can be the most enjoyable and rejuvenating aspect of the presidency. Those presidents, however, who are uncomfortable with the public attention showered upon them, such as William Howard Taft and Herbert Hoover, or who feel like they are wasting time when they divert their attention from policy matters, such as James Polk, will likely regard chief of state duties as a burden rather than a release.

RISKS TO THE PRESIDENT'S SAFETY

The assassination of a president is an even greater national disaster than the death of a president by natural causes. There may be time to prepare for the transfer of power to the vice president when a president dies from an illness, but an assassination usually does not allow for a period of administrative or emotional preparation. An assassination not only can cause governmental confusion; it can send the country into shock because people perceive an attack upon the president, the symbol of the United States, as an attack upon the nation itself.

Assassination attempts against presidents have not been uncommon. Lincoln, Garfield, McKinley, and Kennedy were killed by their assailants. Jackson, Truman, Ford (twice), and Reagan (who was wounded) survived attempts on their lives. In addition, President-elect Franklin Roosevelt was attacked three weeks before his first inauguration; and three presidential candidates, Theodore Roosevelt, Robert F. Kennedy, and George Wallace, all were shot—with Kennedy being killed. In all, presidents, presidents-elect, and presidential candidates have been attacked thirteen times. All but three of these attacks have occurred in the twentieth century.

Moreover, threats against the president's life and attempts by individuals to enter the White House grounds illegally have become increasingly frequent.[60] In the fall of 1994 three incidents underscored the constant threat to the president's safety. In September the pilot of a small plane crashed his craft on the White House grounds just short of the front of the residence. In October a gunman standing outside the White House fence randomly sprayed the back of the mansion with semiautomatic rifle fire before being subdued by onlookers. Late one night in December, in what might have been a drive-by shooting, gunshots fired from the direction of the Ellipse struck the White House grounds.

The most dangerous presidential activities are those that require the president to appear before a large crowd.[61] Because the chief of state role often involves such appearances, it contributes to the danger of assassination. The symbolic goal of many chief of state events is to bridge the gap between the government and the people. This goal is difficult to accomplish from inside a bullet-proof limousine or behind a wall of Secret Service agents. Consequently, presidents, especially those running for reelection, still occasionally seek personal contact with unscreened gatherings of voters while nervous Secret Service agents scan the crowd for possible danger. Yet the benefits of a ceremonial event or symbolic gesture in a location where the president's safety cannot be absolutely guaranteed must always be weighed against the risk of an assassination attempt.

The threat of assassination and the cumbersome security measures necessary to ensure the president's safety have forced

In a democratic gesture reminiscent of Andrew Jackson, Jimmy Carter walks with his wife and family down Pennsylvania Avenue from the U.S. Capitol to the White House in his inaugural parade, January 20, 1977.

changes in the way presidents perform their chief of state role. The days when presidents were expected to wade unprotected into a crowd of citizens to shake hands are gone. Just before leaving office Ronald Reagan commented that he would have liked to have gone to see a college football game between Army and Navy as many other presidents had done, but he did not because "nobody wants to run 75,000 people through a magnetometer." Reagan even justified his lack of church attendance, a traditional ceremonial activity of the president, on the grounds that security measures necessary to ensure his safety would disrupt the congregation.

In 1995 concerns about the security of the White House stemming primarily from the devastating truck bombing of an Oklahoma City federal building led to the closure of Pennsylvania Avenue in front of the White House. The closing of "America's main street" symbolized the difficulty of reconciling the necessity of protecting presidents with the tradition that they should have direct contact with the American people.

Orchestrated events in front of carefully screened groups and televised speeches and press conferences have become the usual methods by which presidents communicate with the American people. This development has contributed to the isolation of presidents. Now, when they spontaneously place themselves before a crowd, as the Carters and Clintons did when they left their limousines and walked up Pennsylvania Avenue after their inaugurations in 1977 and 1993, respectively, it is considered a brave and confident gesture.

EXCESSIVE PUBLIC EXPECTATIONS

For better or worse, the presidency is an idealized and romanticized office of which the American people have high expectations. With each election the public hopes for a president who will combine the best qualities of past presidents. They want a president with the confidence of Franklin Roosevelt, the international popularity of Dwight Eisenhower, the charisma of John Kennedy, and the legislative skill of Lyndon Johnson. Few individuals can ever live up to such expectations.

Moreover, the American people do not want just a president who will combine the skills and insight of past presidents; they want a leader who will satisfy requirements that are often contradictory. Political scientist Thomas Cronin has identified several paradoxes of the presidency that make the president's job nearly impossible. For example, the president must be gentle and decent but also forceful and decisive; a crusader with an agenda and a pragmatic compromiser; a leader able to inspire the nation but one who does not make unrealistic promises; and a common person who understands the American people but is also a leader of exceptional intellect and sophistication.[62]

Godfrey Hodgson has agreed that the expectations of the American people are not easily reconciled:

> The things "the people" want are mutually inconsistent. They want lower taxes and higher benefits. They want to be sure of the supply of gasoline, *and* they do not want to pay higher prices for it. They want national security and disarmament. They do not want American boys to be sent abroad to be killed, and they want the United States to be respected and feared. . . .[63]

The disillusionment created when presidents fail to meet the public's contradictory demands can lead to declining public approval over the course of a president's term. Public opinion polls have shown that presidential popularity usually peaks shortly after the president takes office. It then tends to fall steadily before reaching its nadir late in the second half of the four-year term. After hitting bottom the president's popularity may rise somewhat, but it never reaches the levels enjoyed during the president's first months in office. Although the exact causes of this pattern are uncertain, the public's unrealistic expectations work against presidential popularity.[64]

The chief of state role contributes to high public expectations of the presidency by causing the public to believe presidents have more power than they actually do. As chief of state and the official who represents the entire country, the president is the personification of the nation and the closest American equivalent to royalty. The president's familiarity and symbolic status cause the media and the public to focus their hopes and expectations upon the president. Political scientist Merlin Gustafson wrote, "When one person exercises both symbolic and political authority his public image tends to become distorted. A substantial portion of the public may be led to identify the presidential person with the governmental process, and assume that he alone determines national policy or 'runs the country.'"[65]

The public tends to blame and praise presidents for virtually everything that occurs during their terms regardless of their actual level of responsibility for conditions. For example, the public holds presidents responsible for economic prosperity even though the natural swings of the business cycle, foreign economic conditions, and economic shocks such as droughts and oil embargoes guarantee that even the best presidential economic policies will not yield economic growth all the time.

When judging presidents, the public often ignores the fact that the Constitution was designed to prevent any one person from completely dominating the government. Presidents must work with a Congress that may be controlled by the opposing party and is always composed of members primarily concerned with serving their home states and districts. Presidents also must avoid unconstitutional actions and must motivate executive branch subordinates who are capable of undermining presidential policies and initiatives. Presidents who cannot get their bills passed or their programs implemented often are accused of being weak leaders or poor compromisers. In short, even though presidents are constrained by the Constitution, they are often expected to be as effective as if they were absolute monarchs.

The danger of high public expectations and their negative effect on presidential approval ratings is that presidents may become obsessed with maintaining their popularity. This can cause presidents to take actions that are popular but that are not in the public interest. In the worst case, presidents may be tempted to skirt legal constraints in pursuit of effective leadership. Cronin has commented: "Our expectations of, and demands on, the office are frequently so paradoxical as to invite two-faced behavior by our presidents. We seem to want so much so fast that a president, whose powers are often simply not as great as many of us believe, gets condemned as ineffectual. Or a president often will overreach or resort to unfair play while trying to live up to our demands."[66] Even if a president is willing to sacrifice public approval to do what is right, the decline in popularity will make the president's task of leading the nation more difficult.

DANGERS OF DEFERENCE

Because presidents are partisan political leaders they are routinely attacked by their political opponents and scrutinized by a combative press. Yet because they are the chief of state, the symbol of the unity and majesty of the United States, they are also treated with deference.

Presidents are provided with a mansion, guards, aircraft, and custom-made automobiles and are waited upon by a host of servants. They are addressed as "Mr. President" even by close friends they have known for many years. The strains of "Hail to the Chief" greet them when they enter the scene of an important occasion. An omnipresent contingent of reporters seeks their thoughts on any subject, no matter how mundane or irrelevant to national policy. Despite the democratic origins of the presidency, the president enjoys the luxury and veneration usually reserved for monarchs.

The intoxicating effects of the deference given to presidents are reinforced by the historic significance of the presidency and the White House. Newly elected presidents become members of an elite and celebrated club. No matter how ordinary their political careers might have been before their succession or election, as soon as they take the oath of office they become major historical figures. They know historians will rate them on lists with Lincoln, Washington, and other immortal presidents. Election to the presidency ensures that many books will be written about their lives. When they have left office, politicians and journalists will continue to seek their opinions as elder statesmen. Presidential libraries will be constructed to hold their official papers, and when they die their graves will become national landmarks. Presidents are daily reminded of their place in history as they live in a house that is one of the nation's most cherished monuments and that was occupied by every president except George Washington. In the White House they are surrounded by the artifacts of past administrations. They can view the portrait of George Washington that was rescued by First Lady Dolley Madison in 1814 when the British burned the capital, or they can write at the desk given to President Rutherford B. Hayes by Queen Victoria in 1880 and used by many presidents since.

Outside the White House presidents can take a walk through the gardens past the magnolia tree planted by Andrew Jackson in memory of his wife, Rachel, or the Rose Garden originally planted by Ellen Wilson and redesigned under John Kennedy. George Reedy, who served as Lyndon Johnson's press secretary, has observed that an "aura of history" can envelop a president:

> He lives in a museum, a structure dedicated to preserving the greatness of the American past. He walks the same halls paced by Lincoln waiting feverishly for news from Gettysburg or Richmond. He dines with silver used by Woodrow Wilson as he pondered the proper response to the German declaration of unrestricted submarine warfare. He has staring at him constantly portraits of the heroic men who faced the same excruciating problems in the past that he is facing in the present. It is only a matter of time until he feels himself a member of an exclusive community whose inhabitants never finally leave the mansion.[67]

The deference shown presidents because they are chief of state and the mythic atmosphere created by presidential privileges and the regal White House environment may ennoble some presidents by giving them a sense of destiny or historic duty, but the royal trappings of the office also can have damaging effects. During the Nixon administration, the well-being of the president and the presidency became more important than the law. The respect given to Nixon as chief of state and the privileges of the presidency, which he relished, undoubtedly enabled Nixon and his staff to justify more easily to themselves violations of the law and unethical political tactics.

In addition, if the deference shown presidents causes them to believe they are always right and above criticism, meaningful debate on presidential policies may be squelched. Presidents who become overconfident of their own judgment may feel resentment toward staff members who disagree with their opinions. Such an attitude will likely cause subordinates to avoid expressing negative opinions to preserve their own influence with the president. Political scientist Robert DiClerico has written:

> Presidents have a tendency to become intoxicated by the deference and veneration shown to the Office they hold. They begin to see themselves as deserving of praise and come to view challenge and disagreement as an affront. . . . The isolation of presidents from the disquieting advice of staff members was especially pronounced in the Johnson and Nixon administrations. Both men were lacking in a sense of security, and consequently they were especially susceptible to the arrogance generated by the intoxicating atmosphere of the Presidency.[68]

Presidents accustomed to being treated like monarchs inside the White House grounds may also develop a deep resentment of criticism coming from outside the White House. This may cause a president to rely exclusively on a small group of loyal advisers. Even if the president permits disagreement and frank discussion within this group, an isolated decision-making process will deprive the president of valuable sources of insight and information.

PROPOSALS FOR CHANGE

Given the problems inherent in having a president who is both the nation's chief executive and chief of state, observers of the presidency have occasionally put forward proposals to reform the chief of state role. Change could be accomplished in two ways: through executive orders or practices that formalize the delegation of most chief of state duties away from the president, or through a constitutional amendment that assigns ceremonial duties to some other official or creates a new office of chief of state separate from the presidency. More sweeping reforms of the presidency, such as the creation of a plural executive or the incorporation of parliamentary elements into the American political system, also would affect the chief of state role.

Altering the president's chief of state role has not been a major concern of presidents and their advisers. The most prominent executive branch study of the issue was done by Eisenhower's Advisory Committee on Government Organization, also known as the Rockefeller Committee. The committee, which functioned throughout Eisenhower's tenure in office and studied the organization of the entire executive branch, recommended merely that the vice president perform many ceremonial duties to lighten the president's chief of state burden.[69] Presidents have commonly delegated ceremonial duties to the vice president and other individuals, but no president has set up formal rules concerning which officials would preside at which events. Even if such rules were implemented, the succeeding president might overturn whatever precedent had been set.

Most proposals for changing the president's chief of state power by amending the Constitution have come from scholars and public officials who have speculated on ways to make the presidency more efficient while acknowledging the difficulty of convincing the American people that such reforms are desirable.

One such proposal was a constitutional amendment introduced by Rep. Henry S. Reuss (D-Wis.) in 1975. It would have created an office of "Chief of State of the United States" separate from the presidency. The office as conceived by Reuss would be a purely ceremonial position. The president would nominate a candidate for chief of state who would be confirmed by a majority vote of both houses of Congress. To promote the office's nonpartisanship, the chief of state's four-year term would begin two years into the president's term and last two years into the next administration. There would be no limit on the number of terms a chief of state could serve. The amendment designated the chief of state as "the ceremonial head of the United States" and "the sole officer of the United States to receive ambassadors and other public ministers." In addition, the chief of state would carry out ceremonial duties "as recommended by the president." The chief of state was to be paid a salary identical to that of the president and to be subject to the same impeachment provisions.

When introducing the amendment, Reuss acknowledged that tinkering with the Constitution was controversial. He maintained, however, that the demands of the chief of state role on the president's time and the dangers of the "symbolic deification of the president" warranted amending the Constitution.[70]

Neither Congress nor the American people showed much interest in Reuss's amendment. Most Americans are not eager to alter an institution to which they are accustomed and with which they associate many of the nation's foremost heroes. Since Abraham Lincoln, Franklin Roosevelt, and other great presidents were able to use the power of the presidency to meet the nation's great crises, they reason, the solution to the nation's problems will not be found by changing the presidency but by electing leaders who can make it work.

Delegation of Chief of State Functions

Starting with George Washington, presidents have sought ways to control the number of ceremonial events over which they must preside. There are always more worthy causes to recognize and important events that deserve presidential attention than the president can attend. Presidents have managed to bridge part of this gap by delegating ceremonial tasks to family members, vice presidents, cabinet officers, close associates, and staff members. Like representatives sent to negotiate with foreign governments, these substitute chiefs of state have authority because they either occupy an important office within the administration or have a personal relationship with the president. Because they do not possess the power of the presidency, their presence does not have the symbolic force of a presidential appearance, but they are substitutes that most groups readily accept.

FIRST LADY AND FAMILY

Presidents have often delegated ceremonial functions to their wives. First ladies are fitting presidential representatives because they are nearly as well known as the president and are themselves recognized symbols of American history and culture. When a first lady addresses an organization or presides over a ceremonial event, the audience understands that the president is being represented by an intimate confidante and adviser.

Eleanor Roosevelt's ceremonial activism set the standard for modern first ladies. Franklin Roosevelt, who was crippled by polio, frequently sent his wife to the scene of strikes, disasters, and centers of poverty as his personal representative. She also traveled to England, South America, and the South Pacific during World War II to encourage U.S. troops and allies. Most succeeding first ladies also performed chief of state duties. Pat Nixon traveled widely with her husband and on her own. In 1972 she toured West Africa after representing the United States at the inauguration of the president of Liberia. Rosalynn Carter made an ambitious goodwill tour of Latin America in 1977 in which she carried out diplomatic as well as ceremonial missions. Nancy Reagan visited several foreign countries as her husband's representative, including Great Britain in 1981 for the wedding of Prince Charles and Lady Diana, Monaco in 1982 for the funeral of Princess Grace, and Mexico in 1985 to express concern for the victims of an earthquake. In the summer of 1995 Hillary Clinton and her daughter, Chelsea, made a five-nation tour of South Asia that focused on issues related to women and children. Mrs. Clinton also attended a United Nations conference on women's issues in China in September 1995 as chair of the U.S. delegation.

In 1995 First Lady Hillary Rodham Clinton and daughter Chelsea embarked on a twelve-day goodwill tour through Asia. Here, with the help of two guides, they ride an elephant in Nepal's Chitwan National Park.

First ladies not only have served as substitute chiefs of state for their husbands, they also have performed their own traditional ceremonial roles. First ladies are expected to serve as hostesses at state dinners and other White House social functions. In addition, during international trips, while presidents have met with foreign leaders, their wives have often taken part in ceremonies or visited local sights where the international press can photograph them admiring an example of the host country's scenic beauty or culture. For example, Pat Nixon visited the Moscow circus and the GUM department store while her husband met with Soviet leaders in 1972. First ladies often entertain the wives of foreign leaders who have visited the United States.

Other first family members also have been used as ceremonial representatives by presidents. Julie Nixon Eisenhower and Maureen Reagan both occasionally represented their fathers before civic groups. Jimmy Carter employed his son Chip as his personal roving emissary. The president explained Chip's role in response to a question asked on his famous nationally broadcast radio talk show in 1977: "When we have a special problem anywhere in the nation, and I want the people there to know how deeply concerned I am about it, I would like to have the opportunity to use members of my family to go and represent me personally, along with professionals who serve in the government."[71] Chip's travels included trips to Buffalo to express concern over a severe winter storm, to China as the president's representative in a congressional delegation, to Great Britain to participate in a ceremonial event with the royal family, and to the Middle East as part of a delegation seeking Arab approval for the Camp David peace accords. President Carter's mother, Lillian, also represented him at ceremonial occasions, including the funeral of the president of India in February 1977.

VICE PRESIDENT

During John Adams's tenure as the first U.S. vice president he remarked, "My country has in its wisdom contrived for me the most insignificant office that ever the invention of man contrived or his imagination conceived." Many of the vice presidents who followed Adams agreed with his appraisal of the office. The Constitution had given the vice president no formal policy-making or administrative powers other than to preside over the Senate and break tie votes in that body. Vice-presidential involvement in governing the country depended on the president's inclination to include the vice president in the policy-making process. Few vice presidents of the nineteenth and early twentieth centuries had a significant role within their administrations. Although post–World War II vice presidents have become more involved in policy making, they continue to perform many ceremonial functions.

Vice presidents are well positioned to act as substitute chiefs of state not only because they have the time to do it, but also because their office is associated with the presidency. Vice presidents run on the same ticket as their presidential running mates and are the only officials besides presidents who are elected by the entire nation.

In addition, although their office may at times seem trivial, vice presidents are first in line for the presidency. Fourteen vice presidents have become president, including eight who succeeded to the presidency when the incumbent died in office and one when the incumbent resigned. The political and historic link between the two offices makes the vice president an appropriate stand-in for the president at ceremonial functions.

Since the advent of the jet airplane, presidents have frequently sent their vice presidents on ceremonial missions overseas. Occasionally these missions have included serious negotiations with leaders of important nations, but often their purposes have been more symbolic than substantive. Hubert Humphrey explained the vice president's diplomatic role: "He can perform assignments that the President feels would be unwise for him to take on himself, but for which an official lower than Vice President would be unsuitable."[72]

These assignments have included representing the United States and the president at inaugurations, coronations, and funerals of foreign leaders and major world figures. George Bush, who traveled more than one million miles and visited more than seventy countries as vice president, frequently took President Reagan's place at ceremonial functions overseas. Bush's attendance at the funerals of foreign dignitaries became so common that he joked that his motto should be: "I'm George Bush. You die, I fly."[73] Vice presidents generally welcome any overseas trip regardless of its importance because foreign travel makes them appear busy and brings them more press attention than their usually undramatic domestic policy role.[74]

Presidents can enhance the symbolic effect of a vice-presidential trip by demonstrating their interest in it and designating the vice president as their personal envoy. John Kennedy would usually hold a publicized meeting with Lyndon Johnson before the vice president left on a foreign mission. Immediately after entering office, Jimmy Carter sent Walter Mondale on a tour of Europe and Japan to demonstrate the importance of close allied cooperation to the Carter administration. In a South Lawn ceremony, President Carter bolstered his vice president's status by declaring: "Vice President Mondale has my complete confidence. He is a personal representative of mine, and I'm sure that his consultation with the leaders of these nations will make it much easier for our country to deal directly with them on substantive matters in the future."[75] In November 1995, President Clinton faced a dilemma over whether to attend a long-scheduled meeting of the Asia-Pacific Economic Cooperation group in Osaka, Japan. The administration feared that if Clinton left the country during the ongoing budget stalemate (which had resulted in a partial government shutdown), he would face a storm of political criticism from Republican opponents in Congress. Clinton decided to send Vice President Gore to this meeting as his substitute.

The practice of sending vice presidents on foreign tours not only relieves presidents of their international ceremonial burdens, it also gives the president's "understudy" foreign policy experience. Vice presidents whose previous work in Congress or as governor of a state may not have given them extensive foreign policy experience can become better acquainted with world leaders and the process of international diplomacy in case they should have to assume the presidency. Most foreign leaders welcome a vice-presidential visit and recognize that the vice president one day could become president.

CABINET MEMBERS AND PERSONAL ADVISERS

Cabinet members often operate as assistant chiefs of state within the area of their department's concern. For example, the education secretary makes ceremonial visits to public schools; the housing and urban development secretary tours inner-city housing projects; the commerce secretary speaks to business groups; the interior secretary addresses environmentalist groups; and the defense secretary inspects military installations and presides at ceremonies honoring war heroes and veterans. These events symbolize the administration's concern with a particular issue or group. In addition, cabinet members often use ceremonial occasions or symbolic settings to make speeches that unveil a new program or announce a policy decision affecting their department.

The secretary of state has a special ceremonial role. After the president and vice president, the secretary of state is the nation's highest diplomatic and ceremonial representative. The secretary receives foreign ministers who visit the United States and often heads U.S. delegations at funerals, inaugurations, and other special ceremonies overseas that are not attended by the president or vice president. In matters of protocol the secretary of state also is considered to be the highest-ranking cabinet officer. This unofficial rank is reinforced by the Succession Act of 1947, which designates the secretary of state as the first cabinet officer in line for the presidency and the fourth government official after the vice president, Speaker of the House, and president pro tempore of the Senate.

Presidents occasionally have used close friends and White House advisers to perform chief of state duties. Unlike cabinet members, these chief of state stand-ins derive their legitimacy not from an office, but from their close political or personal relationship with the president. Woodrow Wilson sent his friend and confidant Col. Edward House, who held no government office, on five diplomatic missions to Europe. Franklin Roosevelt used Harry Hopkins, who carried the title "special assistant to the president," as his personal emissary to Allied leaders during World War II. Although both of these men functioned

Henry Kissinger became the most recognized symbol of President Richard Nixon's foreign policy. Originally national security adviser, he became secretary of state in 1973.

primarily as diplomatic operatives rather than as presidential representatives at ceremonial functions, they became so closely identified with Wilson and Roosevelt, respectively, that they not only spoke for their presidents when they met foreign leaders, they symbolized the presidency.

During the Nixon administration, National Security Adviser Henry Kissinger transformed his post from that of a behind-the-scenes presidential aide into a rival of the secretary of state for the diplomatic spotlight. The force of Kissinger's personality, his close relationship to President Nixon, and his celebrated diplomatic missions to the People's Republic of China and the Soviet Union made him the most recognized symbol of Nixon's foreign policy. During Kissinger's second trip to the People's Republic in October 1971, he performed ceremonial activities including visits to the Great Wall of China and other Chinese landmarks. Kissinger also was constantly at the president's side during the historic 1972 summit meetings in Beijing and Moscow. Kissinger's activities resembled those of the secretary of state so much that he was criticized by some defenders of the State Department for having usurped the role of the secretary. After Secretary of State William Rogers resigned, Kissinger assumed the post in September 1973.

NOTES

1. Karlyn Kohrs Campbell and Kathleen Hall Jamieson, "Inaugurating the President," *Presidential Studies Quarterly* 15 (spring 1985): 396–397.
2. Arthur M. Schlesinger Jr., "Annual Messages of the Presidents: Major Themes of American History," in *The State of the Union Messages of the Presidents 1790–1966*, vol. 1 (New York: Chelsea House, 1966), xiv.
3. Ibid., xvi.
4. Alexander Hamilton, *Federalist* No. 69, in *The Federalist Papers*, Alexander Hamilton, James Madison, and John Jay (New York: New American Library, 1961), 420.
5. Cited in Richard Pious, *The American Presidency* (New York: Basic Books, 1979), 5.
6. Harold M. Barger, *The Impossible Presidency: Illusions and Realities of Executive Power* (Glenview, Ill.: Scott, Foresman, 1984), 382.
7. Fred I. Greenstein, "The Presidential Leadership Style of Bill Clinton: An Early Appraisal," *Political Science Quarterly* 108 (No. 4, 1993–1994): 598.
8. Theodore C. Sorensen, *Kennedy* (New York: Harper and Row, 1965), 368.
9. James Hart, *The American Presidency in Action, 1789* (New York: Macmillan, 1948), 24–25.
10. Ibid., 17.
11. *Public Papers of the Presidents of the United States, Franklin Roosevelt, Containing the Public Messages, Speeches, and Statements of the President, 1937* (Washington, D.C.: Government Printing Office, 1938), 379.
12. Clinton Rossiter, *The American Presidency*, 2d ed. (New York: Harcourt, Brace and World, 1960), 18.
13. Ibid., 102–103. See also David K. Nichols, *The Myth of the Modern Presidency* (University Park: Pennsylvania State University Press, 1994), 22–23.
14. Michael Novak, *Choosing Our King* (New York: Macmillan, 1974), 8.
15. Harold J. Laski, *The American Presidency, an Interpretation* (New York: Harper and Brothers, 1940), 38.
16. Thomas E. Cronin, "The Presidency and Its Paradoxes," in *The Presidency Reappraised*, 2d ed., ed. Thomas E. Cronin and Rexford G. Tugwell (New York: Praeger, 1977), 79; David F. Prindle, "Head of State and Head of Government in Comparative Perspective," *Presidential Studies Quarterly* 21 (winter 1991): 56–57.
17. Fred I. Greenstein, *The Hidden-Hand Presidency: Eisenhower as Leader* (New York: Basic Books, 1982), 5.
18. Erwin C. Hargrove and Michael Nelson, *Presidents, Politics, and Policy* (Baltimore: Johns Hopkins University Press, 1984), 23.
19. Stephen Skowronek, *The Politics Presidents Make: Leadership from John Adams to George Bush* (Cambridge, Mass.: Harvard University Press, 1993), 89.
20. Quoted in Arthur Bernon Tourtellot, *The Presidents on the Presidency* (Garden City, N.Y.: Doubleday, 1964), 36.
21. Four presidents who finished their terms chose not to attend the inaugural ceremonies of their successors: John Adams, John Quincy Adams, Martin Van Buren, and Andrew Johnson.
22. Pious, *The American Presidency*, 7.
23. Dale Vinyard, *The Presidency* (New York: Scribner's, 1971), 5.
24. Craig Allen Smith and Kathy B. Smith, *The White House Speaks: Presidential Leadership as Persuasion* (Westport, Conn.: Praeger, 1994), 236–238.
25. Novak, *Choosing Our King*, 5.
26. Cited in Greenstein, *The Hidden-Hand Presidency*, 240.
27. *Public Papers of the Presidents of the United States, Dwight Eisenhower, Containing the Public Messages, Speeches and Statements of the President, 1959* (Washington, D.C.: Government Printing Office, 1960), 799.
28. Prindle, "Head of State and Head of Government in Comparative Perspective," 58–59.
29. Hargrove and Nelson, *Presidents, Politics, and Policy*, 21.
30. Pious, *The American Presidency*, 8–9.
31. Barger, *The Impossible Presidency*, 377.

32. Robert E. DiClerico, *The American President,* 3d ed. (Englewood Cliffs, N.J.: Prentice-Hall, 1979), 136.

33. Richard E. Neustadt, *Presidential Power: The Politics of Leadership From FDR to Carter,* 2d ed. (New York: Wiley, 1980), 27.

34. Herman Finer, *The Presidency: Crisis and Regeneration, an Essay in Possibilities* (Chicago: University of Chicago Press, 1960), 103.

35. Larry Berman, *The New American Presidency* (Boston: Little, Brown, 1987), 314–317.

36. Fred Greenstein, "What the President Means to Americans," in *Choosing the President,* ed. James David Barber (Englewood Cliffs, N.J.: Prentice-Hall, 1974), 125; Richard Morin, "Who's in Control? Many Don't Know or Care," *Washington Post,* January 29, 1996, A6.

37. James David Fairbanks, "The Priestly Functions of the Presidency: A Discussion of the Literature on Civil Religion and Its Implications for the Study of Presidential Leadership," *Presidential Studies Quarterly* 11 (spring 1981): 225.

38. Barbara Hinckley, *The Symbolic Presidency: How Presidents Portray Themselves* (New York: Routledge, 1990), 73–79.

39. Arthur J. Hughes, " 'Amazin' Jimmy' and 'A Mighty Fortress Was Our Teddy': Theodore Roosevelt and Jimmy Carter, the Religious Link," *Presidential Studies Quarterly* 9 (winter 1979): 80–81.

40. Quoted in James David Fairbanks, "Religious Dimensions of Presidential Leadership: The Case of Dwight Eisenhower," *Presidential Studies Quarterly* 12 (spring 1982): 264.

41. Joseph E. Kallenbach, *The American Chief Executive: The Presidency and the Governorship* (New York: Harper and Row, 1966), 280.

42. Sorensen, *Kennedy,* 384.

43. Hinckley, *The Symbolic Presidency,* 96.

44. Quoted in Tourtellot, *The Presidents on the Presidency,* 366.

45. Ibid., 365 and 369.

46. Lyndon Johnson, *The Vantage Point* (New York: Holt, Rinehart and Winston, 1971), 425.

47. Michael P. Riccards, *A Republic, If You Can Keep It: The Foundation of the American Presidency, 1700–1800* (New York: Greenwood Press, 1987), 87.

48. Ibid., 88.

49. Hart, *The American Presidency in Action, 1789,* 46.

50. U.S. Congress, House, *Congressional Record,* daily ed., 94th Cong., 1st sess., July 21, 1975, 23717.

51. Emmet John Hughes, *The Living Presidency* (Baltimore: Penguin, 1972), 86.

52. Merlin Gustafson, "Our Part-Time Chief of State," *Presidential Studies Quarterly* 9 (spring 1979): 166–167.

53. Ibid., 167.

54. Robert E. Gilbert, *The Mortal Presidency: Illness and Anguish in the White House* (New York: Basic Books, 1992), 1–18.

55. Ibid., 2–5.

56. Louis W. Koenig, *The Chief Executive,* 4th ed. (New York: Harcourt Brace Jovanovich, 1981), 81–84.

57. George E. Reedy, *The Twilight of the Presidency: From Johnson to Reagan,* rev. ed. (New York: New American Library, 1987), 45.

58. Johnson, *The Vantage Point,* 566.

59. Reedy, *The Twilight of the Presidency,* 46. See also Gustafson, "Our Part-Time Chief of State," 167; Thomas E. Cronin, *The State of the Presidency,* 2d ed. (Boston: Little, Brown, 1980), 158.

60. Frederick M. Kaiser, "Presidential Assassinations and Assaults: Characteristics and Impact on Protective Procedures," *Presidential Studies Quarterly* 11 (fall 1981): 545–548.

61. In seven of the nine attacks on incumbent presidents, the assailants assaulted the president with a handgun while the president was near a crowd. The exceptions were the attack in 1950 by two men with automatic weapons on Blair House in Washington, D.C., where Harry S. Truman was staying while the White House was being renovated, and the fatal shooting of John F. Kennedy by Lee Harvey Oswald, who used a high-powered rifle to kill the president as Kennedy traveled through Dallas in a motorcade in 1963.

62. Cronin, "The Presidency and Its Paradoxes."

63. Godfrey Hodgson, *All Things to All Men, The False Promise of the Modern American Presidency* (New York: Simon and Schuster, 1980), 241.

64. Cronin, "The Presidency and Its Paradoxes," 81.

65. Gustafson, "Our Part-Time Chief of State," 169.

66. Cronin, "The Presidency and Its Paradoxes," 69.

67. Reedy, *The Twilight of the Presidency,* 21.

68. DiClerico, *The American President,* 222.

69. Gustafson, "Our Part-Time Chief of State," 164.

70. *Congressional Record,* July 21, 1975, 23716–23719.

71. *Public Papers of the Presidents of the United States, Jimmy Carter, Containing the Public Messages, Speeches, and Statements of the President, 1977,* Book 1 (Washington, D.C.: Government Printing Office, 1977), 295.

72. Cited in Joel K. Goldstein, *The Modern American Vice Presidency* (Princeton, N.J.: Princeton University Press, 1982), 160.

73. David S. Cloud, "Loyal Lieutenant Bush Seeks Job at the Top," *Congressional Quarterly Weekly Report,* August 6, 1988, 2176.

74. Goldstein, *The Modern American Vice Presidency,* 160.

75. *Public Papers of the Presidents of the United States, Jimmy Carter, 1977,* Book 1, 11.

SELECTED BIBLIOGRAPHY

Barger, Harold M. *The Impossible Presidency: Illusions and Realities of Executive Power.* Glenview, Ill.: Scott, Foresman, 1984.

Campbell, Karlyn Kohrs, and Kathleen Hall Jamieson. "Inaugurating the President." *Presidential Studies Quarterly* 15 (spring 1985): 395–411.

Cronin, Thomas E., and Rexford G. Tugwell, eds. *The Presidency Reappraised.* 2d ed. New York: Praeger, 1977.

Gilbert, Robert E. *The Mortal Presidency: Illness and Anguish in the White House.* New York: Basic Books, 1992.

Greenstein, Fred I. *The Hidden-Hand Presidency: Eisenhower as Leader.* New York: Basic Books, 1982.

Gustafson, Merlin. "Our Part-Time Chief of State." *Presidential Studies Quarterly* 9 (spring 1979): 163–171.

Hargrove, Erwin C., and Michael Nelson. *Presidents, Politics, and Policy.* Baltimore: Johns Hopkins University Press, 1984.

Hart, James. *The American Presidency in Action, 1789.* New York: Macmillan, 1948.

Hinckley, Barbara. *The Symbolic Presidency: How Presidents Portray Themselves.* New York: Routledge, 1990.

Kallenbach, Joseph E. *The American Chief Executive: The Presidency and the Governorship.* New York: Harper and Row, 1966.

Nichols, David K. *The Myth of the Modern Presidency.* University Park: Pennsylvania State University Press, 1994.

Novak, Michael. *Choosing Our King.* New York: Macmillan, 1974.

Phelps, Glenn. "George Washington and the Founding of the Presidency." *Presidential Studies Quarterly* 17 (spring 1987): 345–363.

Pious, Richard. *The American Presidency.* New York: Basic Books, 1979.

Prindle, David F. "Head of State and Head of Government in Comparative Perspective." *Presidential Studies Quarterly* 21 (winter 1991): 55–71.

Reedy, George E. *The Twilight of the Presidency: From Johnson to Reagan.* New York: New American Library, 1987.

Riccards, Michael P. *A Republic, If You Can Keep It: The Foundation of the American Presidency, 1700–1800.* New York: Greenwood Press, 1987.

Rossiter, Clinton. *The American Presidency.* 2d ed. New York: Harcourt, Brace and World, 1960.

CHAPTER 6

Chief Economist

BY DANIEL C. DILLER AND DEAN J. PETERSON

THE AUTHORS of the Constitution clearly intended Congress to be the branch of government most concerned with the economic affairs of the nation. Article I, section 8, of the Constitution grants Congress numerous economic powers, including the authority to

> lay and collect taxes, duties, imposts and excises, to pay the debts and provide for the common defense and general welfare of the United States . . . ; borrow money on the credit of the United States . . . ; regulate commerce with foreign nations, and among the several states . . . ; and coin money, regulate the value thereof, and of foreign coin. . . .

In contrast, the Constitution grants the president no specific economic powers. Nevertheless, the Framers expected presidents to have significant influence over the economy. They would, after all, oversee the implementation of Congress's spending and taxing decisions, suggest economic legislation in their State of the Union address and other communications to Congress, negotiate commercial treaties with foreign nations, and have the power to veto legislation on economic matters.

Presidential economic power, however, has developed beyond these constitutional powers. Presidents have effectively used their visibility and their prerogatives in the execution of policy to promote their own economic programs. In addition, as management of the economy has grown more complex during the twentieth century, Congress has given presidents greater economic power through statutes.

Because the American people associate the presidency—the nation's most powerful and identifiable political office—with the performance of the federal government, they have come to expect presidents to produce economic prosperity for the United States just as presidents are expected to enforce its laws and ensure its security. As political scientist Clinton Rossiter observed near the end of the Eisenhower administration:

> The people of this country are no longer content to let disaster fall upon them unopposed. They now expect their government, under the direct leadership of the President, to prevent a depression or panic and not simply wait until one has developed before putting it to rout. Thus the President has a new function which is still taking shape, that of Manager of Prosperity.[1]

Limitations on Presidential Power over the Economy

Despite the expectations of the American people and the president's pivotal role in economic policy making, the president's ability to influence economic conditions does not measure up to presidential responsibility for them. All presidents would like to be able to adjust the economy from a central switch in the White House, but no absolutely reliable controls exist.

When unemployment, inflation, and budget deficits rise, presidents receive most of the blame. Herbert C. Hoover, Gerald R. Ford, Jimmy Carter, and George Bush lost their reelection bids in part because of the poor economic conditions that prevailed during their presidencies. The president's party also may suffer in midterm congressional elections if the economy is in a recession.

Presidents themselves are partially responsible for high public expectations of their economic management. As candidates, future presidents usually overestimate their ability to improve the economy.[2] To get elected, presidential candidates must promise to produce economic growth with low inflation, and balanced budgets, even if their predecessors have left them with serious economic problems that cannot be corrected quickly or easily.

This relationship between presidential popularity and the economy, however, may also work to a president's advantage. Presidents are quick to take credit for economic growth, price stability, and low unemployment. Presidential candidate Ronald Reagan capitalized on poor economic conditions in 1980 by asking voters, "Are you better off now than you were four years ago?" Voters responded "no" and elected Reagan to succeed Jimmy Carter. Four years later, when the economy was in the midst of a strong expansion after the recession of 1981–1982, Reagan repeated the question, and the American people reelected him in a landslide.

Four factors combine to limit the president's control over the U.S. economy. First, the chief executive must share power with other individuals and governmental bodies. As the enumeration of congressional economic powers shows, Congress has the constitutional authority to frustrate virtually any presidential economic initiative. Most important, the president cannot levy taxes or appropriate money without the approval of Congress.

Executive branch organizations also cut into presidential economic power. The independent Federal Reserve Board, which sets monetary policy, is not obliged to cooperate with the president. *(See "Monetary Policy," p. 266.)* Spending and taxing policies adopted by presidents to achieve one economic result may be undercut by monetary policies of the Federal Reserve Board that are designed to achieve a conflicting result. The president's own economic advisers also can check presidential pow-

ECONOMIC TERMS

Classical economic theory: a body of theory developed during the late-eighteenth and early-nineteenth centuries maintaining that economies naturally tend to achieve full employment and that government intervention in economic matters should be limited.

Contractionary policy: restrictive fiscal or monetary policy designed to decrease demand, thereby reducing inflation.

Deficit: The amount by which government expenditures exceed government receipts during a fiscal year.

Expansionary policy: stimulative fiscal or monetary policy designed to increase demand, thereby decreasing unemployment and promoting economic growth.

Federal Reserve System: the central bank of the United States; oversees the nation's banking system and controls monetary policy.

Fiscal policy: the manipulation of government spending and tax rates for the purpose of altering the levels of unemployment, inflation, and economic growth.

Gross national product: the value of goods and services produced by an economy in a given year; the principal measure of economic growth.

Inflation: a sustained increase in prices.

Keynesian theory: the body of economic theory developed by British economist John Maynard Keynes that advocates government intervention in the economy to stimulate or dampen demand as a way to deal with high unemployment or inflation.

Laissez faire: an approach to economic policy that advocates a limited government role in the economy in favor of a reliance upon free-market forces.

Monetarism: an approach to economic policy making that emphasizes the role of the money supply in determining inflation, unemployment, and economic growth.

Monetary policy: the manipulation of the money supply for the purpose of altering the levels of unemployment, inflation, and economic growth.

National debt: The amount of money owed by the federal government to all its foreign and domestic creditors at a given point in time.

Price stability: the absence of inflation.

Protectionism: an attempt by a government to protect the domestic markets of its industries from foreign competition by erecting trade barriers.

Recession: a prolonged downturn in the economy during which investment, incomes, and employment all decline.

Stabilization policy: monetary and fiscal policies designed to smooth undesirable fluctuations in inflation, unemployment, and the rate of economic growth.

Stagflation: simultaneous high inflation and unemployment.

Supply-side theory: an economic theory that focuses on the role played by incentives in achieving economic growth; supply-siders generally favor lower tax rates and government efforts to stimulate investments.

Tariff: a tax on imports or exports.

Trade barriers: protectionist devices such as tariffs or import quotas that make it more difficult for foreign companies to sell their goods and services in a given country.

Trade deficit: condition when a nation's imports exceed its exports.

er by implementing the chief executive's directives unenthusiastically or by refusing to join a policy consensus.

Each economic advisory organization has a different mission that disposes it to concentrate on a particular economic problem. The Office of Management and Budget (OMB) looks to trim the budget; the president's Council of Economic Advisers (CEA) focuses on lowering unemployment and inflation and promoting economic expansion; the Treasury Department oversees the national debt and develops international monetary policy; and the heads of other departments and agencies seek to protect funding for projects within their jurisdictions. *(See box, Economic Advisers to the President, p. 268.)* These missions often conflict, making agreement on policy goals difficult and creating rivalries within an administration.

A second factor limiting presidential control of the economy is the highly complex and theoretical nature of the science of economics. Presidents with little formal training in economics may feel overwhelmed, as did Warren G. Harding, who once confided to an associate:

> I don't know what to do or where to turn on this taxation matter. Somewhere there must be a book that tells all about it, where I could go to straighten it out in my mind. But I don't know where the book is, and maybe I couldn't read it if I found it. There must be a man in the country somewhere who could weigh both sides and know the truth. Probably he is in some college or other. But I don't know where to find him, I don't know who he is and I don't know how to get him.[3]

Even if presidents do trust the judgment of their economic advisers, there has been little consensus among economists since the early 1970s about which economic theory or theories should guide economic policy.[4]

A third factor limiting presidential economic control is the imprecision of economic data. When presidents attempt to adjust the economy, they assume that they have accurate and timely information about how the economy is performing. But economic statistics provide, at best, a rough approximation of economic reality. The size and complexity of an evolving economy of 250 million people necessitates that economic statistics be developed from "a slag heap of samples, surveys, estimates, interpolations, seasonal adjustments, and plain guesses."[5]

During the 1990s, economists and public policy makers increasingly questioned the accuracy of economic statistics. In particular, a consensus developed that the Consumer Price Index (the primary measure of inflation) was inexact.[6] In December 1996 the Senate's Advisory Commission to Study the Consumer Price Index concluded that the CPI was overstating the annual rate of inflation by 1.1 percent. An overstatement of this magnitude has severe implications for policy making and budgeting. Federal spending swells because increases for entitlements such as Social Security are indexed to the CPI. At the same time, tax collections fall because tax brackets and deductions are also tied to the CPI making less income taxable.

In addition, economic statistics and indicators do not measure the immediate conditions of the economy, but rather the conditions that prevailed between one and four months ago, depending on the particular economic measure. Consequently, presidents who take action on the basis of the latest economic information may be reacting to a problem that no longer exists or that is much worse than believed. In such cases presidential economic policies may destabilize the economy. A president's attempts to manage the economy, therefore, are only as good as the information upon which they are based.

When government figures indicate that unemployment is rising and consumer demand is falling, the president may wish to enact spending increases or a tax cut. If, however, the unemployment figures or the estimate of consumer demand is outdated, such antirecession measures could cause an inflationary spiral.

President Bill Clinton's 1993 stimulus package provides an illustration. Upon entering office, Clinton proposed a $16 billion spending bill to stimulate the economy, which was not performing well according to the available economic indicators. The proposal was defeated by a Republican filibuster in the Senate. A year after the package's defeat some economists felt that, regardless of the plan's other merits or faults, it could have adversely affected the economy. Clinton and his advisers did not know in early 1993 that the economy was already growing. A fiscal stimulus delivered during the second half of 1993, as the plan envisioned, could have increased inflationary pressures, just as the Federal Reserve Board was working to dampen inflation.

Similarly, an anti-inflation strategy based on inaccurate information can deepen a recession. At the beginning of 1980 the inflation rate reached 18 percent. Although many economists had predicted that a recession would occur during the first half of that year, mixed economic indicators suggested that the economy was still expanding. In March Carter and his advisers decided to impose credit controls designed to lower inflation. Later in the year, however, as more complete economic statistics about the first quarter became available, it was apparent that the recession predicted by economists was already under way when Carter initiated his anti-inflationary policies. The second quarter saw the sharpest decline in gross national product (GNP) in a single three-month period since World War II. Unemployment rose from 6.3 percent in March to 7.5 percent in June. Economic statistics had provided Carter with an incomplete economic picture that induced him to take measures that exacerbated the economy's troubles.[7]

The fourth factor limiting presidential control over the economy is forces outside the reach of the federal government. The economic policies of state and local governments may undercut those of the federal government; international events such as wars, oil price increases, or recessions in foreign countries may exacerbate U.S. economic problems; bad weather may limit agricultural production; public expectations may make certain economic options such as large cuts in Social Security politically impossible; and corporations may make business decisions that aggravate unemployment, inflation, the trade deficit, and other economic problems. A president making all the right decisions will not, therefore, necessarily produce a thriving economy, nor will an economically inexperienced or inept president inevitably bring on a national economic disaster or even a recession.

In spite of these limitations, no person has more influence over the U.S. economy than the president. As chief executive the president oversees the government's economic and regulatory functions and appoints cabinet and Federal Reserve Board members who make many economic decisions; as chief legislator the president proposes spending, tax, and other economy-related legislation and can use the veto—or the threat of the veto—to influence what legislation becomes law; as commander in chief the president oversees the multibillion-dollar purchases of the Defense Department; as chief diplomat the president negotiates with foreign governments about trade and currency issues; and as chief of state the president affects the morale, attitudes, and expectations of the American people.

Early Presidential Economic Management

From the beginning of the Republic presidents understood that promoting the nation's prosperity was as much a part of their job as ensuring its security and enforcing its laws. Presidents did not, however, attempt to affect the performance of the economy through spending and taxing decisions until the Great Depression of the 1930s. Before then, the classical theory of economics, associated with the writings of Adam Smith, the eighteenth-century British economist, generally prevailed. This theory held that a laissez-faire approach to economic activity—one that allowed farmers, merchants, and manufacturers to operate unencumbered by government intervention and regulation—would result in the most prosperous economic conditions. Consequently, if the economy was running smoothly, the president's economic responsibilities were primarily to execute the spending and revenue measures passed by Congress, promote a balanced budget, and work with business leaders and foreign governments to expand industrial development and trade.

The U.S. economy did not always run smoothly, however. As it became increasingly industrialized in the late nineteenth and early twentieth centuries, fluctuations in employment became

British economist Adam Smith promoted a laissez-faire approach to government economic activity. American presidents adhered to his theories until the 1930s, when the Great Depression called for a more activist presidential role in managing the economy.

more frequent and severe. Industry growth also created new demands on the nation's financial system and forced the government to protect consumers and workers from the power of monopolies. Americans came to believe that government should work to prevent crises and create a stable and fair business environment. Consequently, presidents in the late nineteenth and early twentieth centuries occasionally abandoned their laissez-faire stance and proposed or supported solutions to pressing economic problems. The public increasingly looked to the president, the symbol of government and the leader of the ruling party, for economic innovation and direction. By the time the Great Depression struck, laissez-faire attitudes toward the executive's economic role had already begun to give way to more activist conceptions of governmental and presidential power.

FINANCIAL FOUNDATIONS OF THE NEW NATION

George Washington ensured that economic affairs would have a central place in his administration when he appointed Alexander Hamilton as secretary of the Treasury. Hamilton often worked independently of Washington, who seldom intervened in his Treasury secretary's projects. Hamilton recognized that the international reputation of the United States and its ability to command respect among its citizens—many of whom felt stronger loyalties to their home state than to the new federal government—depended on the government's financial stability and the vibrancy of the American economy. Hamilton, therefore, aggressively promoted the interests of merchants and manufacturers and tried to create an atmosphere of confidence through measures that included the assumption of state debts by the national government and the establishment of a national bank.

Debt Assumption

Both the federal government and the states had gone heavily into debt to finance the Revolutionary War. Congress and the states had borrowed money from virtually anyone who would lend it. The United States owed money to the French government, Dutch bankers, state treasuries, and individual holders of bonds and promissory notes. A comprehensive plan was needed that would allow the government to pay back the debts without imposing burdensome taxes on its citizens, establish good international credit, and reconcile the competing interests of its domestic creditors.

Ten days after Hamilton assumed the office of secretary of the Treasury, the House of Representatives asked him to draft a plan for the "adequate support of the public credit." Hamilton used this simple mandate to construct an ambitious plan to resolve the debt situation and bring fiscal stability to the federal government.[8]

The scope and intricacy of Hamilton's plan surprised Congress when he presented it to that body on January 14, 1790. It called for federal assumption of the $25 million in debts incurred by the states during the Revolutionary War and re-funding of the national debt through various bonds and securities. Existing tariffs, which Congress eventually continued at Hamilton's urging, would provide the primary source of revenues to retire the debt gradually.

The most politically divisive aspect of the debt question was how and to what degree the federal government would assume the debts of states. Predictably, the states that had paid their wartime debts, including Virginia, Maryland, North Carolina, and Georgia, were against having the federal government take over the financial burdens of the states with large debts, while the latter, including Massachusetts, Connecticut, and South Carolina, pressed for full assumption.

Division over the assumption question initially led to rejection of Hamilton's plan by a slim margin in both houses of Congress. With Secretary of State Thomas Jefferson's help, however, a compromise was reached whereby the debt assumption bill was linked to a measure moving the capital from New York to Philadelphia for ten years and then to what would become Washington, D.C. This act placated a few southern members of Congress, who changed their votes. The bill was passed, and President Washington signed it on August 4, 1790.[9]

Establishment of the National Bank

The assumption of debts by the federal government was one component of Hamilton's plan to bring financial credibility and stability to the new nation; the other component was the establishment of a national bank. Hamilton outlined his bank proposal to Congress in December 1790. He asked Congress to charter a national bank to assist in the financial operations of the United States. It was to be run primarily by private directors and funded by private capital. Of the bank's original $10 million capitalization, only $2 million was to come from the Treasury, while the rest would be provided by individual investors.

Opponents and supporters of the bank saw that it would provide the president with added power over the economy and would serve as a symbol of the preeminence of the federal government. Many of the bank's detractors opposed it because they feared granting more influence to the federal government. Others, including Jefferson, argued that the bank was unconstitutional since the Constitution did not explicitly give the government the power to charter a bank.[10] Legislators in favor of the bill prevailed, however, and the legislation passed both houses by February 1791.

George Washington solicited the opinions of his cabinet on whether to sign the bill. Attorney General Edmund Randolph concurred with Jefferson that no authority existed in the Constitution for the bank's establishment. Washington, who conceived of the president's veto as a tool to prevent the passage of unconstitutional legislation, was concerned about this charge against the bank. Although he favored establishing the bank as a practical step toward a stronger U.S. economy, he was prepared to veto the bill if he became convinced of its unconstitutionality. On February 16, 1791, he asked Hamilton for an assessment of the objections of Jefferson and Randolph. Hamilton responded with his "Defense of the Constitutionality of an Act to Establish a Bank." The paper artfully refuted the Virginians' claim that the bank would be unconstitutional by emphasizing the necessity of a broad interpretation of the government's economic powers. On February 25, Washington signed the bill chartering the bank.[11]

The First Bank of the United States functioned well for twenty years, but Congress refused by one vote to recharter it in 1811. Because the bank was the brainchild of Federalist Hamilton, many members of the Democratic-Republican Party, which dominated U.S. politics in the early nineteenth century, opposed renewing its charter. Some party members agreed with Democratic-Republican Party leaders Thomas Jefferson and James Madison that the bank was unconstitutional. This strong political opposition to the bank, combined with the lobbying efforts of commercial banks that competed for business with the national bank, led to its demise.[12]

DEVELOPMENT OF PRESIDENTIAL INVOLVEMENT IN THE ECONOMY

The election of Thomas Jefferson as president in 1800 ushered in an economic era in the United States that was dominated by agrarian interests. Jefferson and his successors, most notably Andrew Jackson, rejected the Hamiltonian approach of concentrating the federal government's economic activities on the promotion and protection of industry and business.[13] Most economic regulatory activity and most responsibility for internal improvements that benefited commerce, such as the construction of roads, bridges, and railroads, were left to the states. Even central banking came to be considered outside the government's proper domain. Although it had refused to recharter the national bank in 1811, Congress chartered the Second Bank of the United States in 1816 after experiencing difficulties with national finance during the War of 1812. In 1832, however, Andrew Jackson vetoed the bill that would have rechartered the Second Bank of the United States—its charter later expired in 1836. The United States went without a central bank until 1914, when the Federal Reserve System was established.[14]

Nevertheless, the federal government did not entirely abandon business promotion. It maintained tariffs to protect industries from foreign competition, provided systems of money and patents, and in 1817 gave U.S. ships a monopoly on East Coast trade. Yet until the Civil War, the United States remained essentially an agrarian society with the proponents of agriculture dominating national politics.[15]

The Civil War brought both greater industrialization and the political division of northern and southern agrarian interests. The Republican presidents of the second half of the nineteenth century were generally conservatives who favored federal promotion of business affairs, but not federal regulation. These presidents, in cooperation with Congress, aided manufacturing and commercial interests by raising protective tariffs to new highs, giving land to railroads, and continuing to rely on regressive taxes.[16]

As the American business community grew, however, the need for regulation became more apparent. By the 1880s the power of major corporations had begun to alarm many members of the public. State governments no longer were adequate to control companies that operated in many states and functioned as monopolies. The federal government gradually responded to growing demands for regulation. In 1887 Congress passed the landmark Interstate Commerce Act, which created the first independent regulatory agency, the Interstate Commerce Commission, to regulate the nation's railroads.

In the 1890s Congress passed the Sherman Antitrust Act and other laws that gave the president and the executive branch the power to break up monopolies and otherwise regulate business activity. Presidents Theodore Roosevelt and William Howard Taft increased government prosecutions of antitrust cases and expanded other regulatory activities, setting the stage for further economic reforms under President Woodrow Wilson that would widen presidential authority over the economy.

During his first term, Wilson guided through Congress legislation establishing the Federal Reserve System, the Federal Trade Commission, and federal aid for agriculture. He also expanded the government's antitrust powers and labor regulations. When the United States entered World War I during his second term, Wilson responded with highly interventionist economic policies, such as the Lever Act of 1917, which included government management of the production, supply, and price of many commodities and government takeovers of the railroad, telephone, and telegraph industries. Although these policies ended shortly after the war, they set a precedent for government intrusion in the economy during times of crisis.[17]

Establishment of Income Tax

During the eighteenth and nineteenth centuries the federal government had financed its activities through excise taxes, sales of the vast national lands that stretched to the Pacific, and most important, tariffs. Tariffs were simple to administer but were not always an adequate source of income. In wartime, when the government required increased revenue, tariff receipts would fall as trade with other countries was disrupted.[18]

During the Civil War, Congress levied a tax on incomes to help make up the gap between peacetime revenues and wartime expenses. The tax expired in 1872, and there was no attempt to revive it until 1894 when Congress levied a 2 percent tax on personal incomes over $3,000. In 1895, however, the Supreme Court declared the income tax unconstitutional in *Pollock v. Farmers' Loan & Trust Co.* The Court held that an income tax was a direct tax that violated Article I, section 9, clause 4, of the Constitution, which prohibited direct taxes unless each state paid a share in proportion to its population.

With the support of President Taft, this obstacle was overcome on February 23, 1913, when the Sixteenth Amendment was ratified. It stated: "The Congress shall have power to lay and collect taxes on incomes from whatever source derived, without apportionment among the several states, and without regard to any census or enumeration." Congress passed a 1 percent income tax in 1913 with President Wilson's backing. But the power of the income tax as a source of revenue was not demonstrated until World War I, when an expanded income tax generated the revenues necessary for U.S. participation in the war.

Thereafter income taxes grew in importance. In 1915 customs duties and excise taxes provided 85 percent of federal revenues. By 1930 income taxes were providing over half of the funds coming into the Treasury, while the share from customs and excises had fallen below 30 percent.[19]

Although the Sixteenth Amendment had given Congress the power to levy income taxes, the amendment greatly expanded presidential power by providing a source of revenue that could finance presidential foreign policy and domestic initiatives. As political scientist Emmet J. Hughes noted, the income tax was "ready for lavish use by future Presidents to meet future needs or crises. And without such a reservoir of funds, there hardly could have followed any grand dreams of Presidential programs in the realms of welfare, education, health, housing, and transport."[20] The tax also enhanced the president's ability to make fiscal policy. Increasing and decreasing income taxes would become one of the methods most commonly used by presidents and Congress to combat inflation and recession.

Budget and Accounting Act of 1921

During the eighteenth and nineteenth centuries presidents had no formal responsibility to submit a budget to Congress or even conduct a comprehensive review of executive branch spending proposals. Executive departments and agencies submitted budget requests directly to Congress in a "Book of Estimates." A number of presidents, such as John Quincy Adams, Martin Van Buren, John Tyler, James K. Polk, James Buchanan, Ulysses S. Grant, and Grover Cleveland, did insist on revising budget estimates, but the budgeting process continued to be dominated by Congress and individual executive departments and agencies.[21]

During the budget process, there was no means by which Congress could balance expenditures with revenues or evaluate alternative spending programs. As a result, the overlapping or extravagant spending proposals submitted by executive departments and agencies could not be weeded out of the budget. Moreover, the lack of central coordination made the use of the budget as an instrument of fiscal policy impossible.[22]

Before and during World War I, the nation had incurred a series of budget deficits that created a debt problem and led Congress to seek to reform the financial machinery of the executive branch. With the 1921 Budget and Accounting Act, Congress set up new procedures and organizations to provide more central coordination of the budget process.[23] The act established two important offices—the Bureau of the Budget (which became the Office of Management and Budget in 1970) and the General Accounting Office. The former was created to centralize fiscal management of the executive branch under the president; the latter was designed to strengthen congressional oversight of spending.

The act also ended the practice of allowing executive departments and agencies to address their annual budget proposals directly to Congress. The Budget Bureau, originally a subdivision of the Treasury Department but later placed under the direct control of the president, became a central clearinghouse for all budget requests. The Budget Bureau evaluated these requests, adjusted them to fit the president's goals, and consolidated them into a single executive branch budget for Congress's consideration. Consequently, the Budget Act of 1921 transformed budget making from a random and fragmented process over which presidents had little control into a tool with which presidents could advance their social, economic, and defense priorities.

Presidential Economic Stabilization Policy

Every president has been concerned with the U.S. economy, but close presidential supervision of its performance is a relatively recent historical development. Before the Great Depression of the 1930s, Americans generally believed that extensive government intervention in the economy was counter-

A common sight during the Great Depression was a line of unemployed workers, such as here in 1939, waiting for daily jobs.

productive. The human suffering of the depression, however, convinced the American public and its leaders that the government should intervene to relieve and prevent periods of economic trauma. By the time World War II ended, a national consensus had developed that the government, and especially the president, should use every means available to produce the best economic conditions possible even if the economy was not depressed. The president had become not just a guardian against economic disaster, but an economic manager whose popularity usually depended on a strong and stable economy.

Postdepression presidents have attempted to create the best economic conditions possible through their *stabilization policies.* The U.S. economy, like all capitalist economies, experiences cyclical patterns of expansion and contraction in which the levels of inflation, unemployment, and economic growth vary. *(See Table 6-1.)* During contractionary periods businesses lose sales, investment decreases, unemployment grows, and prices tend to increase at a slow rate or even fall. During expansionary periods

TABLE 6-1 Inflation and Unemployment, 1929–1996 *(percent)*

Year	*Inflation, all items* [a]	*Unemployment*	*Year*	*Inflation, all items* [a]	*Unemployment*	*Year*	*Inflation, all items* [a]	*Unemployment*
1929	0.0	3.2	1957	3.3	4.3	1977	6.5	7.1
1933	-5.1	24.9	1958	2.8	6.8	1978	7.6	6.1
1939	-1.4	17.2	1959	0.7	5.5	1979	11.3	5.8
1940	0.7	14.6	1960	1.7	5.5	1980	13.5	7.1
1941	5.0	9.9	1961	1.0	6.7	1981	10.3	7.6
1942	10.9	4.7	1962	1.0	5.5	1982	6.2	9.7
1943	6.1	1.9	1963	1.3	5.7	1983	3.2	9.6
1944	1.7	1.2	1964	1.3	5.2	1984	4.3	7.5
1945	2.3	1.9	1965	1.6	4.5	1985	3.6	7.2
1946	8.3	3.9	1966	2.9	3.8	1986	1.9	7.0
1947	14.4	3.9	1967	3.1	3.8	1987	3.6	6.2
1948	8.1	3.8	1968	4.2	3.6	1988	4.1	5.5
1949	-1.2	5.9	1969	5.5	3.5	1989	4.8	5.3
1950	1.3	5.3	1970	5.7	4.9	1990	5.4	5.5
1951	7.9	3.3	1971	4.4	5.9	1991	4.2	6.7
1952	1.9	3.0	1972	3.2	5.6	1992	3.0	7.4
1953	0.8	2.9	1973	6.2	4.9	1993	3.0	6.8
1954	0.7	5.5	1974	11.0	5.6	1994	2.6	6.1
1955	-0.4	4.4	1975	9.1	8.5	1995	2.5	5.6
1956	1.5	4.1	1976	5.8	7.7	1996[b]	2.6	5.4

SOURCES: Labor Department, Bureau of Labor Statistics.
NOTE: a. Percentage change in consumer price index year to year. b. Estimate.

consumers spend more, investment increases, unemployment declines, and prices tend to increase at a faster rate. The objective of stabilization policy is to smooth out the natural swings in the economy so that unemployment does not become too severe during contractionary periods and inflation does not get out of control during expansionary periods. Ideally, an administration should achieve these goals while maintaining a steady rate of economic growth and balancing the federal budget, or at least running manageable deficits that can be corrected during periods of prosperity.

The tools presidents use to stabilize the economy are *fiscal policy* and *monetary policy.* Fiscal policy refers to the government's taxing and spending decisions. Presidents make fiscal policy in cooperation with Congress, which passes spending and tax bills. The government can choose to combat unemployment and stagnant economic growth by stimulating the economy through tax cuts or increased spending. It can choose to fight inflation by contracting the economy through tax increases or reduced spending. Monetary policy refers to decisions about the supply of money. Although presidents do not have legal control over monetary policy, which is determined by the independent Federal Reserve Board, they do exercise much informal influence over it.

THE NEW DEAL AND THE EMERGENCE OF KEYNESIAN THEORY

Before the Great Depression most economists believed that the president could best contribute to the health of the economy by working for a balanced federal budget and not overregulating business activity. Deficit spending by the federal government was regarded as an imprudent and irresponsible practice that eroded business confidence in the monetary system and produced inflation.

This conservative economic orthodoxy handcuffed President Herbert Hoover when the stock market crashed and the depression began in 1929. All of Hoover's efforts to turn the economy around proved ineffectual, and by 1933 unemployment had reached a staggering 25 percent. Like presidents before him, Hoover believed in the conventional wisdom that public debt could undermine the economic health of the nation just as private debt could undermine a person's financial well-being. He therefore was suspicious of deficit spending programs that would have reduced the severity of the depression. Nevertheless, in his search for an answer to the country's economic troubles Hoover did try a variety of measures, including a tax reduction, intended to put more money into the hands of the public. He quickly gave up on this approach, however, when it appeared not to be working and returned to a conservative strategy of cutting expenditures in an effort to balance the budget.[24] This policy, combined with the Federal Reserve Board's failure to expand the money supply, deepened the depression.[25] In fact, many modern economists believe the depression would have been limited to a severe recession had the president and the Federal Reserve Board not exacerbated the problem.

While campaigning for the presidency in 1932 Franklin D. Roosevelt did not advocate revolutionary fiscal policies. Like Hoover before him, he promised to cut expenditures and balance the budget. Indeed, during the campaign Roosevelt attacked Hoover for failing to achieve a balanced budget.

Roosevelt, however, was a pragmatic leader who believed that the government should take emergency measures to fight the depression. Once in office he initiated "New Deal" policies, government construction and relief programs that threw the federal budget into deficit. The deficit spending, however, was not a fiscal strategy designed to stimulate the economy but a byproduct of the president's decision to spend the money necessary to reduce the suffering of the poor, the elderly, and the unemployed and to begin putting Americans back to work.[26] Most New Deal initiatives were to be phased out as economic conditions improved, and indeed some were terminated within a few years. Other programs, however, including Social Security and federal credit assistance to home buyers, small businesses, and farmers, became permanent government activities.

While the United States and the world struggled through the depression, the theories of the British economist John Maynard Keynes became widely known. Keynes outlined his theories in *The General Theory of Employment, Interest and Money,* published in 1936. Keynes's thought focused on unemployment. He argued that recessions occurred when industrial, consumer, or government demand for goods and services fell. This caused unsold inventories to mount, industries to scale back their operations, and unemployment to rise.

Keynes posited that the government could counteract a recession by cutting taxes or increasing its expenditures. Lower taxes would put more money into the hands of consumers, thereby stimulating demand for goods and services. Tax cuts given to industry would create new jobs by boosting firms' investment in their productive facilities. Greater government expenditures would create jobs and prime the economy through a "multiplier effect." According to Keynes, each dollar spent by the government could stimulate private economic transactions equaling much more than the original dollar.

In May 1937, after the U.S. economy had achieved a partial recovery, a new recession confronted Roosevelt. This recession was caused in part by the Federal Reserve Board, which had again contracted the money supply in its concern to prevent inflation.[27] The president initially ignored the advice of newly converted Keynesians in his administration and attempted to cut spending in an effort to balance the budget. Roosevelt's strategy deepened the recession and solidified a consensus among his advisers in favor of government spending designed to stimulate demand. By April 1938 the president himself was convinced that greater government expenditures were needed to combat the depression. Roosevelt continued to pay lip service to a balanced budget, but he worked to increase expenditures and accepted growing budget deficits as a necessary evil in a difficult economic period.[28] Unemployment gradually declined from its 1933 high of 25 percent to less than 15 percent in 1940.

World War II ultimately brought massive government expenditures financed by borrowing that woke the U.S. economy from the nightmare of the 1930s. The war effort required a total mobilization of U.S. productive resources, which ended unemployment.[29] In 1944 unemployment stood at just 1.2 percent. Most economists saw the economic results of New Deal and wartime expenditures as a validation of Keynesian theory.

KEYNESIANISM AS ORTHODOX THEORY

By Franklin Roosevelt's last term in office Keynesianism had become the dominant economic theory in both policy making and academic circles. Many members of Congress believed that since Keynesian theory had provided the federal government with a tool with which it seemingly could hold down the level of joblessness, the government should be obliged to use that tool to promote full employment. In 1945 the Full Employment Act was introduced into the Senate. It mandated that full employment should be a national goal and that the government should run budget deficits when necessary to provide the investment and expenditures required to achieve it.

The bill alarmed many business leaders and economic conservatives, however, who saw the law as a first step toward budget deficits, inflation, and excessive regulation of the economy. Despite President Harry S. Truman's support for the Full Employment Act, the House promoted a more modest version, which eventually was passed by both chambers.[30]

The final version of the act was called the Employment Act of 1946. It stated that the government should work for "maximum employment, production and purchasing power" rather than "full" employment, and references to budget deficits as the tool that would be used to achieve high employment were deleted. A statement also was added that measures taken to implement the act must be consistent with the free enterprise system. Economist Herbert Stein wrote of the revision of the bill:

> Given the experience of the 1930s, it was inconceivable that the government would fail to commit itself to maintaining high employment.... But the form that commitment took in the United States, as embodied in the Employment Act of 1946, could hardly have been more satisfactory to conservatives. That is, after a major national discussion the Congress rejected an overly ambitious, inflationary definition of the goal, rejected exclusive reliance on deficit financing as the means, and reaffirmed its devotion to the free enterprise system.[31]

Although the proposed Full Employment Act had been watered down, the Employment Act of 1946 nevertheless demonstrated the new national consensus that government leaders should involve themselves deeply in the management of the economy. Beyond stating the government's responsibility to work for low unemployment, the act reinforced the president's role as the public official primarily responsible for managing the economy. Although the legislation did not provide presidents with new economic powers, it did require them to report annually to Congress on the state of the economy, and it created the Council of Economic Advisers, which gave presidents an economic advisory body answerable only to them.[32] These measures encouraged Congress, the business community, and the American public to continue to look to presidents for economic leadership as they had done during the depression.

Truman Administration

When Harry Truman succeeded to the presidency following Franklin Roosevelt's death in April 1945, the U.S. economy was booming. Annual federal expenditures had grown from just $8.8 billion in 1939 to $92.7 billion in 1945, and unemployment was virtually nonexistent. Many Americans feared that the economic sluggishness of the 1930s would return when the war ended, but the years following the war saw continued expansion and a relatively smooth transition from a wartime to a peacetime footing. Many women and elderly workers who had entered the workforce during the war because labor was in short supply retired when the war ended, thus making room in the workforce for returning soldiers. The influx of GIs also created greater demand for housing and consumer goods that partially offset the decrease in demand caused by reduced government spending for defense.

Inflation was a more serious problem. Although Truman had enthusiastically supported the original version of the Employment Act, which mandated measures to achieve full employment, as president he followed a pragmatic course that often made fighting inflation the highest economic priority. After the war, inflation was fueled by consumers who demanded goods that had been in short supply during the conflict. Moreover, wartime controls had held the prices of many goods below their true value. As these price controls were lifted in 1946 and 1947, prices rose dramatically to correct the artificial imbalance. Inflation, which had been just 2.3 percent in 1945, rose to 8.5 percent in 1946 and 14.4 percent in 1947. Truman, who had vetoed one price control removal bill but reluctantly signed a second in July 1946, urged labor groups to resist price and wage hikes and sent an anti-inflation program to Congress in October 1947 that included consumer credit controls, rent controls, price ceilings on selected products, and controls over the allocation of some scarce commodities. The Republican Congress put off most of the program until the following year and then enacted only part of it.[33] Inflation, however, peaked in 1947, falling to 7.8 percent in 1948 and then disappearing entirely in 1949 while the economy endured a recession.

In 1947 and 1948 Congress tried to force a tax cut on the president, which, it maintained, would reverse the tax and spend policies of Truman and of Roosevelt before him. Truman vetoed three such bills on the grounds that they would lead to budget deficits and greater inflation. Congress, however, overrode the last of Truman's vetoes in April 1948. The tax cut was timely, since the economy fell into a mild recession later in the year. The extra money in the hands of consumers stimulated demand, thereby reducing the recession's severity.

The Korean War, which began on June 24, 1950, when North Korea invaded South Korea, rekindled inflationary pressures that had eased after the post–World War II price acceleration.

Growing military expenditures on the war effort stimulated industrial activity. Demand for consumer goods also increased as consumers bought many items in anticipation of wartime shortages. In 1951 inflation shot back up to 7.8 percent. Congress reluctantly granted part of Truman's tax increase request and agreed to wage, price, and credit controls, which succeeded in holding inflation below 1 percent during 1952 and 1953.

Eisenhower Administration

In spite of the prominence of Keynesian thought among economists, President Dwight D. Eisenhower entered office skeptical of its utility. He emphasized the traditional conservative economic priorities of balancing the federal budget, limiting government interference in the economy, and, most important, fighting inflation.[34] During Eisenhower's eight years in office, he produced three budget surpluses—a significant achievement given that after 1960, the twentieth century would see only one budget surplus (1969).

Throughout his presidency, Eisenhower was willing to accept higher rates of unemployment than his Keynesian critics thought necessary. In response to a recession in 1953 and early 1954, the administration did accept some minor tax increases and sped up government expenditures. Although the administration took credit for helping the recovery with "speedy and massive actions," the modest antirecession measures of 1954 were an exception to Eisenhower's rule of nonintervention.[35]

During his second term Eisenhower pursued an anti-inflationary strategy in defiance not only of his critics but also of several of his own advisers, who urged him to support a tax cut. Unemployment averaged a postdepression high of 6.8 percent during the 1958 recession, but Eisenhower remained true to his noninterventionist principles. Moreover, he vetoed a number of spending bills during his last two years in office in pursuit of a balanced budget and low inflation.[36]

When signs of a recession appeared in the spring of 1960, Eisenhower's vice president, Richard Nixon, who was running for president that year, advocated following CEA chairman Arthur Burns's advice to increase defense expenditures and loosen credit. Eisenhower, however, sided with other administration economic advisers who rejected the proposal because they did not believe the recession, if there was one, would be of sufficient magnitude to warrant government intervention.[37] Nixon undoubtedly lost votes because of the economic slump.

Although Eisenhower's stiff resistance to antirecession measures appears old-fashioned, he was successful in holding down consumer prices, which never climbed more than 4 percent in any year of his presidency.

Kennedy Administration

With the election of John F. Kennedy to the presidency in 1960, Democrats believed they could change the economic goals of the nation. Kennedy and his advisers were determined to achieve full employment and sustained economic expansion through fiscal stimulation. They hoped to be able not just to correct the swings of the business cycle but to stimulate the economy to greater growth and productivity. They were motivated by their desire to alleviate poverty and to improve medical care, education, and other social services and by their concern over the apparent rapid growth of the Soviet economy and its military expenditures.

Kennedy believed the economy never would create jobs for everyone without government stimulation. He and his advisers were confident they could direct the economy to greater prosperity. For the first time the Keynesian views of professional economists were fully applied to the political situation.[38]

In the opening months of Kennedy's term, the economy was pulling itself out of the recession that had begun in 1960. Since the budget was in deficit and inflation was a concern, Kennedy hoped that he would not have to use fiscal stimulation to achieve his employment and expansion goals. By early 1962, however, the economy had begun to slow. Kennedy agreed with his advisers that the economy should be stimulated through increased government spending. They believed such a policy would help low-income people and be less controversial than a tax cut at a time when budget deficits persisted. Congress, however, resisted Kennedy's spending plans. Kennedy responded in late 1962 by proposing a tax cut.

The president and his economic advisers attempted to sell the tax cut by promoting the concept of the "full employment budget." The administration argued that although the government was currently running budget deficits, the greater tax revenues produced by an economy operating at full employment would result in budget surpluses. Therefore, if a tax cut could produce full employment and sustained economic expansion, it would increase government revenues rather than decrease them.[39] Kennedy lobbied Congress to pass the tax cut in 1963, but before he could persuade lawmakers to pass it, he was assassinated.

Johnson Administration

Following Kennedy's death, President Lyndon B. Johnson delivered an emotional speech to Congress on November 27, 1963. He asked lawmakers to honor Kennedy by passing his civil rights bill and asserted: "No act of ours could more fittingly continue the work of President Kennedy than the early passage of the tax bill for which he fought all this long year." Johnson also used his legendary lobbying skills and Congress's feelings for the slain president to push the tax cut through Congress quickly. Johnson signed the Revenue Act of 1964 on February 26. It was the largest tax cut in U.S. history up to that time. The act reduced personal income taxes for 1964 and 1965 by about 20 percent and corporate taxes by 4 percent.[40]

The 1964 tax cut was a milestone in the history of U.S. stabilization policy. It was the first time the president and Congress had intentionally stimulated the economy through a tax cut while the economy was expanding. Unemployment fell from 5.7 percent in 1963 to 4.5 percent in 1965. The impressive results of the tax cut generated enthusiasm and confidence among Presi-

On February 26, 1964, President Lyndon Johnson signs the Revenue Act of 1964 in the presence of congressional leaders. At the time, it was the largest tax cut in history.

dent Johnson's economic advisers. They believed they could "fine tune" the economy through Keynesian stabilization policies.

The Vietnam War, however, forced Johnson to reconsider his economic priorities. By 1966 expenditures on the war and "Great Society" social programs had caused a growing budget deficit and rising inflation. Johnson's advisers urged him to correct the overstimulation of the economy caused by the deficit spending through an excise tax or an increase in income taxes. Congress, however, showed no enthusiasm for a tax hike, and Johnson feared that higher taxes would erode public support for the Vietnam War.[41] Consequently, Johnson did not push for an income tax increase, and the task of fighting inflation was left to the Federal Reserve Board's monetary policy.

The following year, however, Johnson recognized that he had to slow inflation and reduce the deficit. He proposed new taxes, but Congress did not react to Johnson's 1967 tax hike proposal until the summer of 1968. By that year inflation had risen to 4.2 percent from just 1.7 percent in 1965, and the deficit had expanded to $25.2 billion from only $1.6 billion in 1965. This deficit disappeared in 1969, when Johnson's 10 percent tax increase, combined with the efforts of Johnson's successor, Richard Nixon, to cut government spending, led to the first budget surplus since 1960. This belated fiscal restraint failed, however, to eliminate the long-term inflationary pressures that had been built into the economy or the rising unemployment that was left for Nixon to combat.

THE EMERGENCE OF MONETARISM

Walter Heller, who served as chairman of the Council of Economic Advisers under Kennedy, declared in 1967 that "Economics has come of age in the 1960s."[42] Heller and many of his colleagues believed that the combination of Keynesian economic theory, computer technology, and enlightened leaders had made it possible for the government successfully to promote prosperity through stabilization policy. The low unemployment and inflation of the mid-1960s suggested that Heller's optimism was not unfounded.[43] Yet his remark contrasts sharply with the loss of confidence by economists during the 1970s that the economy could be fine-tuned.

The main problem with applying Keynesian theory to the management of the economy was that the political process made the Keynesian solution to inflation—cutting spending and raising taxes—difficult to enact. Politicians were predictably unwilling to adopt measures to control inflation because high taxes and cuts in government programs were unpopular with their constituents. Even if an administration were willing to propose a tax increase to combat inflation, it would seldom be able to persuade Congress to risk a recession, especially in election years.[44] Keynesian theory, therefore, offered presidents a politically practicable fiscal response only to recession.

The theory to which many national leaders turned was *monetarism.* The monetarists, led by economist Milton Friedman, argued that inflation occurs when the money supply is allowed to grow faster than the economy, because a greater number of dollars is available to chase the goods and services produced. The best way to control inflation, the monetarists believed, was to reduce the amount of money in circulation.

Economists had acknowledged since the late 1950s that monetary policy had a role in stabilizing the economy. The political problems involved in reducing inflation through fiscal policy during the late 1960s, however, gave monetarism a new attractiveness. The appointed members of the Federal Reserve Board who were responsible for regulating the money supply could cool down the economy without having to worry, as members of Congress and the president did, that their actions would cost them the next election. The solution to inflation would, therefore, be removed from the political atmosphere that made the Keynesian response unusable. When inflation was under control, the Federal Reserve Board could carefully relax its tight monetary policy to allow for greater economic growth.

The inflation dilemma became particularly acute in the 1970s when rising prices seemed beyond the control of presidents and Congress. Not only did national leaders find it difficult to muster the political will to fight inflation, but when they did cut government spending and raise taxes, inflation did not fall as expected. The inverse relationship between inflation and unemployment (increases in one had been accompanied by decreases in the other) implicit in Keynesian policies appeared to have disintegrated. Presidents could no longer be confident that a period of higher unemployment would result in lower inflation. Nor could higher inflation be relied upon to bring decreased unemployment. The prevailing conditions of high inflation and unemployment, which came to be known as *stagflation,* defied Keynesian logic and caused presidents to lean heavily on monetary policy.

Nixon Administration

Richard Nixon entered office intending to fight inflation through small spending cuts coordinated with a tight monetary policy. He hoped his incremental strategy would reduce inflation while holding unemployment near 4 percent.[45] Nixon submitted a budget to Congress for fiscal 1970 that would have yielded a small budget surplus. Congress did trim some spending but refused to go along with Nixon's cuts, many of which targeted social programs. The relationship between Nixon and the Democratic Congress became increasingly confrontational as the president vetoed a number of appropriations bills and resorted to impounding appropriated funds.[46] *(See "Impoundment Powers," p. 39, in Chapter 1.)*

Despite Nixon's budget cutting efforts and the Federal Reserve Board's tight monetary policy, inflation continued to rise. By 1970 inflation had reached 6 percent. Moreover, the increase in inflation was not accompanied by a corresponding decrease in unemployment, which had risen from 3.6 percent in 1968 to 4.9 percent in 1970. The worsening unemployment situation was exacerbated by the de-escalation of the Vietnam War, which brought hundreds of thousands of troops back into the civilian workforce.

Congress responded to the bleak economic conditions by passing the Economic Stabilization Act of 1970. Under this act, Congress gave the president the authority to combat inflation through wage and price controls. Nixon signed the act but renounced the use of such controls, saying on June 17, 1970: "I will not take this nation down the road of wage and price controls, however politically expedient they may seem." Nixon objected to wage and price controls because he believed they were an incursion on the rights of Americans and would only postpone a burst of inflation.

In 1971, with his reelection bid less than two years away, Nixon was unwilling to fight inflation by allowing a recession as Eisenhower might have done. Early that year he had abandoned his attempts to achieve a balanced budget and had initiated stimulative fiscal policies to combat rising unemployment, which averaged 5.9 percent for the year. Nixon, like John Kennedy, justified deficit spending by arguing that the budget would be balanced if the economy were operating at full employment and output. Nixon admitted to an interviewer in January 1971, "I am now a Keynesian in economics."[47]

Inflation, however, was the more troubling economic problem. The president was being pressured by Congress, the public, and even prominent leaders of his party to take dramatic action against inflation. On August 15, 1971, President Nixon announced that, owing to the economic crisis, he was using the authority granted to him by Congress the previous year to impose a wage and price control policy.

His "New Economic Policy" had several phases. Phase I froze wages, prices, and rents for ninety days. Phase II created a pay board and price commission that acted to limit inflation to 3 percent and wage increases to 5.5 percent per year. In January 1973 Phase III relaxed the controls, and in July of that year Phase IV replaced controls with commitments from businesses to limit price increases for a year. In April 1974 all wage and price control activity ended when Congress refused to extend President Nixon's wage and price control authority.

Initially the controls were successful and popular. Consumer prices rose 4.3 percent in 1971 but just 3.3 percent in 1972. Unemployment fell from 5.9 percent in 1971 to 5.6 percent in 1972 and 4.9 percent in 1973. The brightening economic picture helped Nixon easily win a second term as president in the November 1972 elections.

As Nixon had feared, however, the problems with wage and price controls began to surface during his second term. Shortages of some goods occurred when many manufacturers began exporting a greater share of their products overseas, where prices were higher. In addition, the numerous exemptions from the controls program that had been granted to various industries caused economic distortions. For example, grain prices had been exempted from controls while meat prices remained fixed. Consequently, high feed costs forced many meat producers to slaughter their stock, causing immediate meat shortages and meat price increases later in the decade.

More important, the wage and price controls proved to be only a temporary remedy for inflation. In 1972 the growing number of exemptions weakened the controls, and the consumer price index began rising again in the second half of the year. Then in October 1973 the economy received a severe shock when the Arab oil-producing states imposed an embargo on the United States in retaliation for its support of Israel during the Yom Kippur War of 1973. The price of a barrel of oil rose from

In February 1974, cars line up at gas stations, causing traffic jams in New Jersey, right, and across the country. In October 1973, the Arab oil-producing states had imposed an embargo on the United States for its support of Israel during the Yom Kippur War.

less than $3 in early 1973 to between $10 and $14 in 1974. Rising oil prices, a poor 1973 harvest, and the phasing out of price controls—begun in 1973 and completed in 1974—led to a dramatic jump in inflation. Prices increased 6.2 percent in 1973 and a painful 11.0 percent in 1974. That year the Nixon administration attempted to fight inflation with more restrictive fiscal and monetary policies, but the Watergate scandal made cooperation with Congress difficult. On August 9, Nixon resigned to avoid impeachment for his part in the Watergate affair.

Ford Administration

Like Nixon, Gerald Ford assumed the presidency intending to fight inflation through moderate fiscal restraint supported by a tight monetary policy. The inflationary effects of the 1973 Arab oil embargo and the removal of the wage and price freeze remained strong after Ford took office. He asked Congress for a 5 percent tax surcharge on corporations and the upper class and for selected spending cuts and deferrals.

A minor part of Ford's economic program, however, received the most attention. He encouraged Americans to fight inflation voluntarily by saving more, conserving energy, increasing charitable contributions, and resisting price and wage increases. The voluntary measures were to be symbolized by "WIN" buttons, which stood for "Whip Inflation Now." The buttons were ridiculed as a symbol of the ineffectuality of the administration's policies.[48]

Ford was forced to abandon his anti-inflationary strategy in early 1975. Data showed that the economy had fallen into a deep recession in 1974 before he took office, partly as a result of the sharp rise in oil prices, which forced businesses to cut back their operations. Unemployment reached 9 percent late in the year.

Ford responded in January 1975 by asking Congress for a $16 billion tax cut and new investment tax credits for business to stimulate the economy. Congress and the president compromised with a $23 billion tax cut bill that favored the lower class. The tax cut, however, was enacted in March 1975 when the recession began to ease. Consequently, by the time the benefits of the cut reached Americans, the economy was already growing.[49]

Despite the persistently high rates of inflation, many Democrats in Congress pressed the president to make low unemployment the nation's first economic priority. During the rest of 1975 and early 1976 Ford battled Congress over economic policy, repeatedly vetoing spending measures he considered inflationary. Nevertheless, Ford compromised on several appropriations bills, which, coupled with large unemployment compensation and welfare payments caused by the recession, increased the federal deficit to new highs of $53 billion in 1975 and $74 billion in 1976.

In early 1976 inflation leveled off, and the economy appeared to be improving just in time for Ford's reelection bid. Inflation had fallen from 11 percent in 1974 to 9 percent in 1975 and just 5.8 percent in 1976. Meanwhile, unemployment averaged 7.7 percent in 1976, which was an encouraging improvement after 8.5 percent in 1975. The country, however, voted for Jimmy Carter to replace Ford in the White House because the incumbent could not overcome the recent tough economic times and the legacy of Richard Nixon.

Carter Administration

Jimmy Carter took over an economy that had improved slightly during the last year of the Ford administration. The Federal Reserve Board's tight monetary policies had brought inflation down to 5.8 percent for 1976, and Carter entered office intending to lower unemployment.

Despite these hopes, the era would be dominated by forces outside Carter's control. During the late 1960s and 1970s, several factors had combined to produce an increasingly difficult economic environment in which astute stabilization policy could not be relied upon to produce prosperity. The inflationary pressures built up during the Vietnam War had not yet dissipated. In addition, the Organization of Petroleum Exporting Countries (OPEC) engineered the second major oil price hike of the decade in 1979. Oil prices increased from less than $15 a barrel in 1979 to almost $40 a barrel in 1981. Also, the growth of federal regulation during the 1970s in areas such as environmental protection, job safety, and consumer protection increased the cost of producing goods and contributed to inflation. Simultaneous with these inflationary pressures, the economy was declining in productivity relative to foreign competitors—a trend that had begun in the 1960s. Finally, the growth of federal benefit programs, especially Social Security and Medicare, had decreased the controllable portion of the budget that could be cut from year to year, nearly ensuring budget deficits in the absence of a tax increase or substantial spending cuts.[50] Although Carter was not responsible for the underlying economic conditions he faced as president, his policies did little to help the situation.

Upon entering office Carter proposed a stimulative program that included a $50 tax rebate per person. He withdrew the rebate proposal when economic statistics showed that unexpectedly strong economic growth threatened to spark a renewed surge of inflation, but much of the rest of his plan, including increased spending for jobs programs and public works, was enacted. Until late 1979, Carter gave priority to reducing unemployment. From 1977 to 1979 he encouraged the Federal Reserve Board to pursue a stimulative monetary policy that brought the biggest expansion of the money supply of any three-year period since World War II.[51] As a result, the economy continued the expansion that had begun in late 1975.

During this period, however, the public became increasingly concerned about inflation. Consumer prices had risen 7.7 percent in 1978, up from 5.8 percent in 1976. The OPEC price hike of 1979 triggered a further jump in inflation, which rose 11.5 percent for the year. On the eve of the 1980 election, Carter recognized that inflation had become the nation's foremost economic problem.

One of Carter's most fateful economic decisions was the appointment of Paul Volcker as chairman of the Federal Reserve Board in 1979. On October 6, 1979, Volcker indicated that he would use monetary policy vigorously to fight inflation. Although in the long run Volcker's contractions of the money supply were effective in bringing down inflation, the consumer price index did not respond to the tight monetary policy in 1979 and 1980. Consequently, interest rates soared without an accompanying drop in inflation. In 1979 prices increased 13.5 percent, real per capita income declined 0.7 percent, and the prime lending rate of banks stood at a whopping 15.25 percent. Carter complemented Volcker's tough stand with fiscal restraint designed to combat inflation and lower the budget deficit. Just as the demands of economic management had induced a conservative Nixon to adopt the very liberal tool of wage and price controls, so they led Carter to abandon his liberal goal of achieving low levels of unemployment and to adopt the traditionally conservative strategy of fighting inflation with monetary and fiscal policies while pursuing smaller budget deficits.[52]

For the first time since presidents began submitting an annual economic report thirty years before, Carter's 1980 report forecasted a recession. In the second quarter of that year the recession came as predicted, while double-digit inflation remained. During that year, Republican presidential nominee Ronald Reagan attacked Carter for producing a "misery index" (the sum of the inflation and unemployment rates) over 20. In August 1980 a CBS News/*New York Times* poll found that only 19 percent of those polled approved of Carter's "handling of the economy."[53] Although the economy's performance during the first three years of the Carter administration had not been as dismal as the public perceived, the sharp downturn in 1980 solidified the popular perception that Carter's policies had undermined the economy.[54] With voters convinced of the president's inability to manage economic affairs, Reagan defeated Carter in a landslide.

SUPPLY-SIDE EXPERIMENT

During the late 1970s, *supply-side economic theory* began to gain influential supporters. It was based on the premise that economic growth and low unemployment could best be achieved by promoting investment and productivity. Supply-side theorists advocated using tax policy to encourage individuals and businesses to invest more and be more productive. The supply-siders asserted that income tax rates affect people's choice between work and leisure and between saving and consumption. The more individuals are taxed, the less incentive they have to work and save. Similarly, the more businesses are taxed, the less money they have to invest in new plant and equipment that can raise their productivity.

By cutting taxes, the theorists believed, the government could increase personal and corporate productivity and investment, thereby increasing the amount of goods and services produced. Thus, whereas Keynesian economic strategists sought to promote economic growth by stimulating demand for goods and services, a strategy that often led to inflation, supply-siders focused on increasing the supply of goods and services. Since supply-siders claimed to be able to stimulate the economy without increasing inflation, their theory seemed to provide a promising approach to the economic condition that plagued the 1970s—simultaneous high inflation and high unemployment.

Many supply-side advocates also predicted that the expansion of the economy brought on by a supply-side strategy would generate enough revenue to decrease deficits even though tax rates were lower. This principle was illustrated by the Laffer Curve, developed by Arthur B. Laffer of the University of Southern California. Laffer posited that government revenues rise as tax rates rise until they reach a point at which the increases in revenue brought by higher rates are less than the loss of revenue caused by the public's reduced incentive to work. Laffer and his adherents challenged the assumptions of most professional economists by arguing that the tax rates in force under the Carter administration were above this optimal level. Therefore, they believed, tax revenues could be increased not by raising rates, which would intensify the disincentives to produce, but by lowering the rates so that they would be closer to the optimal rate of taxation.[55]

Ironically, in 1963 President Kennedy also had argued that his proposed tax cut would result in greater revenue. Although Kennedy's reasoning was based on Keynesian theory rather than supply-side theory, and his tax cut was enacted when economic conditions were very different from those of the late 1970s, some supply-siders pointed to the increase in tax revenue following Kennedy's tax cut as evidence of the validity of the Laffer Curve.[56]

With the nomination in 1980 of Ronald Reagan as the Republican presidential candidate, supply-side theory was thrust into the political limelight. Reagan had become a believer in supply-side theory during the late 1970s as he prepared to run for the Republican presidential nomination. Reagan had been defeated for the nomination in 1976 by incumbent Gerald Ford in part because Reagan had advocated an austere policy of budget cuts and the conditioning of tax relief on the success of deficit reduction.[57] Supply-side theory gave Reagan a justification for moving away from painful economic prescriptions without abandoning his conservative philosophies about balancing the budget.

Reagan campaigned on his plan to cut taxes and to balance the budget through increases in revenue that he hoped the tax cut would produce and through domestic budget cuts. Reagan's plan held out the promise of prosperity without increased budget deficits and inflation. During Reagan's campaign for the 1980 nomination, his Republican opponent and eventual vice president, George Bush, reflected the skepticism of many economists and politicians when he labeled Reagan's supply-side strategy "voodoo economics." The American public, however, elected Reagan in a landslide over incumbent Jimmy Carter.

Reagan Tax Cut

Ronald Reagan's first economic policy priority was passing the largest spending and tax cuts in U.S. history. His landslide victory enabled him to claim a mandate for his plan to cut personal income taxes by 30 percent, introduce new tax incentives for businesses, and cut nondefense expenditures sharply.

Some Democrats in Congress attacked the plan as a disguised attempt to lighten the tax burden of the wealthy while cutting back on government aid to the poor. Reagan and his advisers acknowledged that their tax cut would benefit upper-income individuals but argued that these were precisely the people who would be best able to invest their tax break, thus fueling the economic expansion for everyone. Reagan's critics called this reasoning a return to a predepression Republican "trickle down" strategy in which benefits for the rich were justified on the grounds that the poor would eventually benefit from a stronger economy.

Although many Americans perceived Reagan's taxing and spending strategy as inequitable, a strong majority of Americans supported it, and his congressional allies were able to push most of the plan through Congress despite the solid Democratic majority in the House. The president signed the Economic Recovery Tax Act of 1981 in August. It reduced individual tax rates 25 percent—five percentage points less than Reagan had wanted—over thirty-three months. In addition, the bill indexed the tax system for the first time ever to keep inflation from forcing taxpayers into higher brackets as their incomes kept pace with prices. Reagan also was successful in pushing $35 billion in 1982 nondefense spending cuts through Congress, along with $26.5 billion in defense spending increases.

Reagan had hoped that his tax cut would create an economic boom that would bring increases in tax revenues. These increased revenues along with lower domestic spending would reduce the federal budget deficit until the budget was balanced. In 1980, while running for the presidency, Reagan had attacked Carter and the Democratic-controlled Congress for their deficit spending and promised to balance the budget by 1983. By late 1981, however, economic statistics showed that the country was entering a recession. This recession, the deepest since the Great Depression, lasted through 1982. It widened the budget deficit because tax revenues were depressed by declining industrial output and personal income, while government spending on unemployment insurance and welfare increased.

In addition, after the initial wave of spending cuts, Reagan's budget cutting lost momentum as the administration and Congress refused to make major concessions to each other's priorities. In November 1981, after less than a year in office, Reagan conceded that he probably could not balance the budget in one term. In 1982, despite his position against taxes, Reagan agreed to a tax increase that reduced the 1981 tax cut by about a quarter, with most of the restored revenue coming out of corporate taxes.[58]

Economic Recovery

In 1982 the recession pushed unemployment to its highest annual rate—9.7 percent—since the Great Depression. But in 1983, the economy began a sustained period of economic growth that would last through the decade. By 1988, the last year of Reagan's term, unemployment had dropped to just 5.5 percent.

This period of growth, however, was not a remedy for the growing budget deficit. In 1983 the deficit reached $195 billion. Against the recommendation of several advisers, including CEA chairman Martin Feldstein and budget director David Stockman, Reagan refused to consider a further tax increase. He maintained that higher taxes would threaten economic growth and would not substantially reduce the budget deficit because Congress would find a way to spend most of the additional revenue.

In addition, the president fought against cuts in defense spending. Reagan had charged that Carter had allowed the nation's defenses to deteriorate while the Soviet Union continued to pursue a massive military buildup. According to Reagan, the growing Soviet advantage in military capability threatened the security of the United States and its allies. During the early 1980s public support for a military buildup and tensions between the United States and the Soviet Union led Congress to accept many of Reagan's defense spending proposals. Military expenditures rose from 5.0 percent of GNP in 1980 to 6.2 percent in 1987.

By bringing an end to the 1970s stagflation, the Reagan recovery had improved living standards for most Americans. But many economists believed that Reagan's policies were only partially responsible for the expansion. The collapse of the oil cartel of OPEC in the early 1980s produced falling oil prices, which helped reduce inflation and spur economic growth. In addition, the restrictive monetary policies of Federal Reserve Board chairman Paul Volcker, a Carter appointee, had wrung inflation out of the economy by 1982, setting up a period in which the president could concentrate on stimulating the economy with little worry that significant inflation would return. Ironically, Reagan, who had repudiated Keynesian economics, had presided over a period in which prosperity was achieved in part through tax cuts and massive deficit spending by the government, the classic Keynesian prescription for combating a recession.[59]

PRESIDENTIAL ECONOMIC MANAGEMENT IN THE ERA OF DEBT

Unprecedented budget deficits loomed over the otherwise prosperous economy of the mid-1980s. The budget deficit widened sharply from $79.0 billion in 1981 to $221.4 billion in 1986. Annual interest payments to finance the national debt had risen from $68.8 billion to $136.0 billion during the same period. By 1985 the enormous budget deficit led legislators to pass the Gramm-Rudman-Hollings Deficit Reduction Act with the support of President Reagan. *(See "Balanced Budget Amendment," p. 261.)* It was intended to force spending cuts aimed at balancing the budget by 1991. Despite cuts in defense spending and other deficit reduction measures, however, the budget deficit was still $152.5 billion in 1989. During the Reagan administration the national debt had nearly tripled from $994.8 billion in 1981 to $2.868 trillion in 1989.

The budget deficits that emerged from the Reagan era limited the flexibility of future presidents to conduct economic stabilization policy. George Bush and Bill Clinton could not contemplate a fiscal response to recession without first considering what such a response might do to the deficit and to interest rates. The two presidents depended almost entirely on the Federal Reserve Board to stabilize the economy in the short run. In addition, any long-term economic plan had to contain a strategy to lower the deficit. As a result, presidential economic policy making during the post-Reagan era was largely confined to budget struggles with Congress over the composition of deficit reduction packages.

The role of economic theory in presidential policy making also was diminished by the constraints of the budget deficit. Although the science of economics continued to produce new ideas and theories, few influenced economic policy making. In contrast to the Keynesianism of the Kennedy administration, the monetarism of the Nixon administration, or the supply-side theory of the Reagan administration, the economic policies of Bush and Clinton were not closely tied to any single economic school of thought. Clinton was much more activist than Bush, but neither proposed theory-based macroeconomic programs, like the Reagan tax cut. The budget situation forced Bush and Clinton, instead, to perform pragmatic balancing acts designed to check recession, inflation, and further debt.

Bush Administration

George Bush's political dilemma in handling the economy was more acute than that of most new presidents because he could not repudiate the policies of his predecessor. Republican President Reagan, for example, could explain the 1982 recession by blaming conditions that he had inherited from Carter, a Democrat. But Bush had served as Reagan's vice president and had promised to extend the Reagan peacetime economic expansion.

This would not be an easy task. The Reagan expansion had begun in 1983 and had been fueled in part by large tax cuts and defense expenditures. After such a long period of sustained expansion, the business cycle could be expected soon to produce a recession. Moreover, persistently high budget deficits and the collapse of the Soviet Union would create pressure to cut government spending, especially for defense. If recession did come, Bush would have little room to combat it with an expansionary fiscal policy.

Bush complicated his political position by pledging not to raise taxes. At the 1988 Republican convention he threw out a memorable challenge to Congress that was repeatedly quoted back to him during his presidency: "Read my lips—no new taxes!" The pledge made Bush appear decisive, and it sharply distinguished his economic platform from that of his Democratic opponent, Michael Dukakis. But with Congress firmly in the control of the Democrats and the budget deficit projected to grow, Bush's pledge reduced his capacity to govern. Only by compromising with Congress could President Bush hope to achieve a significant reduction in the deficit. But the Democratic Congress's budget priorities were targeted to benefit its constituencies, which were very different from Bush's. Moreover, Democratic leaders were aware that they could wound the president politically either by forcing him to break his "no new taxes" pledge or by allowing the deficit to rise. Congress would never let Bush off the hook by approving a deficit reduction package without a tax increase, especially when the "no new taxes" pledge had been used as a cudgel against Democrats in the 1988 election.[60]

In 1989 the Bush administration deferred serious budget discussions by releasing highly optimistic estimates of the size of near-term budget deficits. But by May 1990 it was clear to the Bush administration that the deficit would accelerate rapidly in the absence of a significant deficit reduction package. Bush indicated that month that he might accept a tax increase as part of a larger deficit reduction package. This set in motion highly partisan budget negotiations between the president and Congress.

On June 26, Bush agreed to include tax increases in a deficit reduction package. Negotiations made little progress, however, until September. By then Congress had the upper hand. The final budget deal passed Congress on October 28 and was signed by Bush on November 5. The five-year package contained discretionary spending cuts of $182.4 billion, most coming from defense. Tax increases, including the elevation of the top marginal income tax rate from 28 percent to 31 percent, totaled $146.3 billion during the period. Minor changes in entitlements, primarily Medicare and farm subsidies, and higher user fees for ports, airports, railroads, Coast Guard inspections, patent processing, and other government services added $99 billion. Lower interest payments resulting from the deficit reduction were projected as saving $68.4 billion.[61]

Bush attempted to put the best face on the budget deal by praising the deficit reduction it contained. He remarked, "I think the spending cuts, when you look at them, are good. The entitlement reform is good. The tough enforcement provisions are tougher than I ever thought we could ever get in any way out of this Congress." The Bush administration attempted to pin responsibility for the higher taxes on congressional Democrats, saying that it had been forced to pay a "ransom" of tax increases in order to secure congressional approval for spending cuts. But the president was the clear loser in the budget negotiations. Political scientist Stephen Skowronek wrote:

> . . . Bush had made the tax pledge the linchpin of his and his party's credibility, and when he pulled it out, the reaction was swift and predictable. The reversal put Republicans in far more difficult straits than Democrats, and Bush's fellow partisans rose up in revolt, charging their leader with the "big lie."[62]

The public fallout over Bush's broken pledge was less acute than it would have been had not the United States been engaged in the crisis arising from the Iraqi invasion of Kuwait. From August 2, 1990, when Iraq invaded, until February 1991, when the American-led coalition won a smashing victory, public attention was focused on the Middle East. The overwhelming success of the military operation sent President Bush's approval ratings as high as 89 percent. However, Bush could not translate this positive public sentiment into sustained support for his domestic policies.

After the war, Bush's close attention to foreign policy was perceived to come at the expense of economic policy. These perceptions, combined with a shallow but persistent recession that had begun in the summer of 1990, steadily eroded Bush's high level of support. In June 1992, fifteen months after the decisive victory in the Gulf War, a CBS News/*New York Times* poll showed that only 34 percent of the respondents approved of Bush's performance. Only 16 percent approved of his handling of the economy, a rating lower than President Carter's worst rating.[63]

During late 1991 and 1992, the decline of the economy focused voters' minds on Bush's broken pledge on taxes. Real economic growth averaged only about 1 percent per year, and real per capita income fell. Unemployment peaked at 7.4 percent, and the country endured more business failures than during any presidency since the Great Depression.[64]

Bush was criticized in the media for doing nothing to pull the country out of recession. Given the budget problem, however, there was not much that he could do. In the 1990 budget negotiations, he had campaigned for a cut in the capital gains tax as a tool to stimulate economic growth, but Democrats in Congress opposed it as a tax cut for the rich. Having negotiated hard in favor of spending cuts, Bush also could not turn around and offer a stimulus package of government spending.

Bush could not even point to deficit reduction to defend his 1990 budget deal. The 1990 agreement had undoubtedly held the deficit below where it otherwise would have climbed, but its budgetary impact was far below what was needed to solve the budget deficit problem or even reduce the deficit.[65] The cost of the Persian Gulf War, the ongoing government bailout of failed savings and loan institutions, inflation in government health care programs, and increased entitlement costs arising from the recession pushed the deficit from $221.4 billion in 1990 to an all-time high of $290.4 billion in 1992. To the public, Bush's tax increases had yielded nothing.

During the last two years of Bush's presidency, Congress criticized or ignored his economic initiatives. Economic data would later reveal that the nation had pulled out of recession and had begun a strong comeback in the fourth quarter of 1992. But by that time, the voting public had made up its mind. Bush was defeated by Democrat Clinton, who had promised to focus "like a laser beam" on the economy.

Clinton Administration

Bill Clinton entered office under circumstances similar to those of Reagan twelve years earlier. Like Reagan, he had defeated an incumbent in an election that was dominated by economic issues. Reagan had seized on a strong electoral mandate to propose sweeping economic changes. But Clinton had won only 43 percent of the popular vote in his victory. More important, Clinton faced a budget deficit close to $300 billion and a national debt exceeding $4 trillion. Clinton's economic program, like President Bush's, would be constrained by the necessity to address the debt problem.

During the campaign and immediately after his election, Clinton capitalized on the public perceptions of Bush as detached from economic policy by emphasizing that he would devote himself fully to economic matters. On December 15, 1992, at the conclusion of a two-day economic policy conference in Little Rock, President-elect Clinton described his commitment to make economic policy his priority:

> I'm not going to stop working and our team is not going to stop working until the economic challenges have been faced and tackled, until

we have given it our best shot and our best response. As long as people are out of work and children are left behind, as long as families struggle, as long as the potential of this country is not being fulfilled, we will not rest. We will explore every idea and challenge every prejudice; we won't stop looking or pushing or trying until our job is done.

Clinton's claim to economic leadership was not based on economic theory or ideology; it was based rather on a promise to put economic management at the core of his agenda and transcend the conflicting economic goals pushed by the left and right. Clinton attempted to distance himself from both the "tax-and-spend" policies of liberals and the "trickle-down" policies of conservatives.[66]

Clinton's budget proposal in early 1993 revealed three major economic priorities: reducing the deficit, shifting some of the tax burden from poor Americans to wealthy Americans, and expanding public investment—especially in infrastructure, education, environmental protection, and scientific research. He had postponed a campaign promise for a middle-class tax cut out of concern for the deficit. Considering that Republican presidents had been in power for twelve years, this was a relatively modest budgetary agenda.

But even with his party in control of both houses of Congress, Clinton found enactment of his budget priorities difficult. A Senate Republican filibuster killed a stimulus bill that would have spent $16 billion to give the economy an immediate boost. The filibuster was based primarily on budget concerns, but in hindsight a stimulus in the spring of 1993 could have overheated the economy, which had been growing strongly since the fourth quarter of 1992. Opposition by Republicans and conservative Democrats also forced the president to increase the ratio of spending cuts to tax increases in the budget, drop a controversial energy tax, and limit cuts in defense spending. His budget was attacked by congressional Republicans as a typical "tax and spend" budget that shortchanged deficit reduction. Even after substantial changes aimed at appeasing conservative Democrats, not a single Republican in either house voted for Clinton's budget. He was able to pass the budget by a 218–216 vote in the House and with Vice President Albert Gore Jr. breaking a 50–50 tie in the Senate.[67]

The budget contained little new investment, but it did shift some tax burden from the poor to the wealthiest taxpayers. The bill was estimated to achieve about $500 billion in budget savings over five years. Roughly half of the savings came from tax increases and half from spending cuts. The budget repudiated the policies of the Reagan era, though with its spending cuts and attention to the deficit, it was not a traditionally liberal economic plan. It was instead a pragmatic, deficit-driven compromise for which there was little enthusiasm, even within the Democratic Party. Like the 1990 budget bill, Clinton's budget demonstrated the constraints on presidential authority in budget matters and the central role of accommodation with Congress.[68]

The economy under President Clinton benefited during the first two years of his term from lowered interest rates and the upturn in the business cycle following the Bush recession. The improving economy and Clinton's deficit reduction measures also began to lower the federal deficit, which dropped from $290 billion in 1992 to $203 billion in 1994. But despite unemployment below 6 percent and inflation below 3 percent in 1994, voters continued to feel economic anxiety. Real wages remained stagnant even though unemployment had declined significantly. Some of this anxiety was reflected in growing protectionist sentiments. Clinton had achieved some of his most notable legislative successes in free trade, as he led successful bipartisan campaigns to push the North American Free Trade Agreement (NAFTA) and the General Agreement on Tariffs and Trade (GATT) through Congress. Yet large segments of the public, especially labor unions and the followers of presidential candidate H. Ross Perot, distrusted these agreements. *(See "Trade Policy," p. 271.)*

This undercurrent of economic anxiety contributed to the stunning Republican landslide in the 1994 congressional elections. The Republican victory defied the conventional wisdom that incumbent parties do well when the economy is growing.

At the beginning of 1995 the Clinton administration faced what no Democratic administration had faced since Truman: a Republican-controlled Congress. Republicans, led by Speaker Newt Gingrich, proposed revolutionary changes, including the achievement of a balanced budget in seven years, the enactment of a significant tax cut, and the passage of a balanced budget amendment and a line-item veto.

President Clinton's fiscal year 1996 budget was immediately denounced as irrelevant by Republican leaders in Congress. Under Clinton's plan, deficits were projected to remain near $200 billion for the foreseeable future. Many commentators speculated that the budget was designed to avoid offending constituent groups with budget cut proposals so that congressional Republican budget cutters would have to take the initial, politically risky step of making the deep cuts necessary to balance the budget. Clinton appeared ready to wage a rejectionist fight against the GOP plan, which sharply reduced the growth of Medicare and Medicaid spending.

But during the summer of 1995, Clinton surprised many of his Democratic allies by repudiating his initial budget and embracing a plan to balance the budget in ten years. By the fall, Clinton had indicated he might accept a seven-year balanced budget bill. He rejected, however, the Republicans' choice of spending cuts and the inclusion of tax cuts in the budget.

These differences led to one of the severest budget standoffs in American history. On November 20, 1995, Congress passed the fiscal 1996 budget reconciliation bill that was estimated to balance the budget in seven years. It would have cut $894 billion over that period by slowing the growth of entitlements and mandating cuts in future appropriations for discretionary programs. It also included a $245 billion tax cut. As expected, President Clinton vetoed this bill on December 6, claiming that it cut programs for the needy too deeply; made unsound programmatic reforms in Medicare, Medicaid, welfare, farm subsidies, and environmental programs; and contained an overly generous tax cut.

Two extended government shutdowns within the period of November 1995 to January 1996 brought Washington to a halt, as President Bill Clinton and Congress battled over how to balance the federal budget. Here a U.S. Park Service employee places a closed sign on the Washington Monument.

Even before Clinton's veto, Congress and the president were maneuvering for the public relations advantage in the budget dispute. Throughout much of November and December, Congress and the president held intermittent negotiations on the budget. Because almost half of the fiscal 1996 appropriations bills had not been passed, funding for many government agencies had expired on October 1. In the absence of a budget deal, keeping these agencies open required the passage of stopgap funding bills known as "continuing resolutions." Republicans sought to use this situation to gain negotiating leverage. Their price for passing the stopgap measures to keep the budget open was movement by Clinton toward their budget position.

Two partial government shutdowns—the two longest in history to date—resulted from this gamesmanship. Although Clinton agreed in principle to balancing the budget in seven years using conservative Congressional Budget Office figures, he refused to yield on his budget priorities. Polls showed that the majority of Americans supported Clinton's budget position and blamed the Republican Congress for both the government shutdowns and the budget stalemate. Clinton stated on November 19: "We must balance the budget, but we must do it in a way that is good for our economy and that maintains our values. That means we have to do it without devastating cuts in Medicare and Medicaid, in education and the environment."[69]

In January 1996, Republican leaders moved away from the shutdown strategy. By the end of April—seven months into the fiscal year—President Clinton and Congress finally agreed to a compromise on the final 1996 appropriations bill. The bill which cut $22 billion in domestic spending, fell short of the ambitious cuts the Republicans originally sought while it protected Clinton's priorities in education, job training, and environmental protection. Boosted by his budget stand against the Republican Congress and buoyed by continued good economic news, such as low unemployment and the budget deficit declining to $107 billion in 1996, Clinton won a convincing reelection in November. Immediately after the election Clinton said his top priority for his second term would be balancing the budget.

Presidents and the Budget

The budget is the most revealing annual document produced by an administration. Not only does it spell out the funding decisions of the White House, but it also is an important fiscal policy tool that can influence the levels of inflation, unemployment, and economic growth. As Gerald Ford has said, "The budget reflects the President's sense of priorities. It reflects his best judgment of how we must choose among competing interests."[71] It is therefore a document that affects presidential political and social programs as much as it affects fiscal policy.

As previously noted, the president had little effect on the budget-making process until Congress enacted the 1921 Budget and Accounting Act, which required the chief executive to submit a comprehensive executive branch budget to Congress. This act greatly enhanced presidential power and responsibility over the budget that was sent to Congress. The political, social, and economic priorities of presidents provide guidelines to OMB officials and others involved in constructing the budget. Presidents also must arbitrate disputes between agencies and hear last-minute appeals from agency heads who believe that a cherished program has been shortchanged.[72]

Although presidents acquired control over executive branch budget proposals, Congress often has resisted presidential attempts at budgetary leadership. Legislators are not required to accept the president's recommendations or even to use them as

FISCAL POLICY AND THE ELECTION CYCLE

The performance of the economy during a president's term affects the incumbent's chances for reelection as much as any other issue. In times of peace many Americans will "vote their pocketbooks," basing their votes on whether the American economy has given them the opportunity to meet their economic expectations. Moreover, an economy that improves during the year before an election can erase voters' memories of a longer period of economic stagnation or inflation.

Even second-term or newly elected presidents who are not immediately concerned with their own reelection chances understand that economic conditions will affect the outcome of midterm elections, which will determine the strength of their party in Congress. Since the entire House and one-third of the Senate face an election every other year, significant turnover in congressional membership is possible. If an administration loses too many congressional allies, its programs may be threatened and the president's reelection chances in two years may be weakened. Fiscal policy, therefore, is never completely free from the influence of electoral politics and in an election year may be dominated by it.

The connection between economic conditions and the political success of presidents is a powerful incentive for an incumbent administration to try to create short-term improvements in the economy before an election. Economist Edward R. Tufte identified several economic trends that correspond to the U.S. election cycle. His studies of the economy from 1948 to 1976 showed that the unemployment rate on presidential election days tends to be significantly lower than twelve to eighteen months before and after an election.[1]

The elections that occurred during Eisenhower's presidency were notable exceptions to this trend. Eisenhower believed that Americans were more concerned with achieving a balanced budget and low inflation than with low unemployment and economic growth. He therefore opposed short-term stimulations of the economy for political purposes. The Republican losses in Congress in 1954 and 1958 and John Kennedy's victory over Richard Nixon in 1960, all of which occurred during economic slumps, provide evidence that Eisenhower may have been wrong.[2] After his 1960 defeat, Nixon wrote:

> The bottom of the 1960 dip did come in October and the economy started to move up in November—after it was too late to affect the election returns. In October, usually a month of rising employment, the jobless rolls increased by 452,000. All the speeches, television broadcasts, and precinct work in the world could not counteract that one hard fact.[3]

Tufte also found that increases in Social Security payments—the most direct way to put more money into the hands of voters—usually were enacted with the president's approval in even-numbered years during the ten months preceding an election. Since the increases in payroll taxes required to pay for the higher Social Security payments start at the beginning of a year for administrative reasons, the price of Social Security increases was not felt by taxpayers until after the election.[4] In 1975, however, Social Security benefits were indexed so that recipients automatically receive annual cost-of-living increases to offset inflation, thereby weakening the justification for politically motivated benefit increases.

In addition to stimulative fiscal policies and increased transfer payments, other presidential economic policies have been affected by electoral politics. Lyndon Johnson did not press Congress for a tax hike in 1966 partly because he did not wish to focus attention on the growing costs of the Vietnam War before the midterm congressional elections.[5] Despite Nixon's personal distaste for severe government economic intervention, he imposed wage and price controls on the nation in August 1971 because the deteriorating economic situation threatened his upcoming 1972 reelection bid.[6]

Presidential efforts to manipulate the economy for political purposes are seldom in the best interests of the nation's long-term economic health. Although some politicians may argue that election year economic stimulations are attentive political responses to the desires of voters, the public pays a price for these short-term boosts. Presidents and Congresses do not always have the political will to take away preelection benefits and tax cuts after the election. Consequently, electoral pressures on economic policy contribute to budget deficits and inflation. Even when the president and lawmakers do agree on measures to offset their election year generosity, there is evidence that short-term decreases in unemployment brought about by election year tax cuts and spending hikes may be more transitory than the increases in inflation that usually accompany them.[7]

Beyond the inflationary and budgetary costs of pandering to voters' short-term economic desires, this practice makes coherent economic policy making difficult. Tufte concluded:

> The electoral-economic cycle breeds a lurching, stop-and-go economy the world over. Governments fool around with transfer payments, making an election-year prank out of the social security system and the payroll tax. There is a bias toward policies with immediate, highly visible benefits and deferred, hidden costs—myopic policies for myopic voters.[8]

1. Edward R. Tufte, *Political Control of the Economy* (Princeton, N.J.: Princeton University Press, 1978), 19–21.
2. Ibid., 7–9.
3. Richard M. Nixon, *Six Crises* (New York: Doubleday, 1962), 310–311.
4. Tufte, *Political Control of the Economy*, 29–33.
5. Norman C. Thomas and Joseph A. Pika, *The Politics of the Presidency*, 4th ed. (Washington, D.C.: CQ Press, 1996), 371.
6. Dorothy Buckton James, *The Contemporary Presidency*, 2d ed. (Indianapolis: Bobbs-Merrill, 1974), 106.
7. William R. Keech, "Elections and Macroeconomic Policy Optimization," *American Journal of Political Science* 24 (1980): 345–367.
8. Tufte, *Political Control of the Economy*, 143.

a starting point. The power of presidents to affect budget legislation has depended on their ability to forge congressional coalitions and generate public pressure on Congress to favor their initiatives and priorities.

In 1974, Congress passed the Congressional Budget and Impoundment Control Act, an attempt to revitalize the entire budget process and to link congressional deliberations on spending and revenue legislation. The act created a timetable designed to force action on the budget, moved the start of the fiscal year from July 1 to the following October 1 to give Congress more time to consider budgetary details, and established measures intended to aid Congress in evaluating the budget as a whole rather than as a group of unconnected spending bills. The act created the House and Senate Budget Committees to centralize congressional budget making and the Congressional Budget Office to provide Congress with an expert staff to analyze the budget.[73]

Although many members of Congress lauded the new process, it did not achieve its two primary goals: bringing more order to the budget process and reducing the federal deficit. Deficits continued to grow after 1974, and Congress struggled, often unsuccessfully, to meet the budgetary deadlines set down in the act.[74]

The potential of the 1974 Budget Act as an executive tool was realized in 1981. At that time Reagan used the process to push his dramatic fiscal program of increased defense spending, decreased domestic spending, and a large tax cut through Congress. The new centralized budget-making process in Congress allowed him to negotiate with congressional leaders on the substance of his entire budget plan rather than being forced to bargain on a dozen or more appropriations bills, each of which might have been opposed by a different congressional bloc. To get his budget approved, Reagan used his public popularity to build a conservative coalition in the House of Representatives despite the Democratic majority.

Political scientist Louis Fisher explained why the new process improved the position of the president:

> Whereas the politics of incrementalism under the old process had operated as a brake on radical changes, the Budget Act of 1974 strengthened Reagan's hand by requiring Congress to vote on an overall budget policy. . . . Although the administration did not get everything it wanted, the omnibus measure was more of an advantage to the executive branch than to Congress. By packaging all the cuts in a single bill, the White House was able to build a majority for final passage. Members could announce that they objected to specific cuts but supported the bill "on balance."[75]

Although the 1974 Budget Act made it easier for presidents to influence the congressional budget process, presidential budget initiatives were usually stymied when the opposing party controlled Congress. Between 1981 and 1996, both houses of Congress and the White House were controlled by the same party in only two years—1993 and 1994. Under conditions of divided government, the president's proposed budget rarely received much attention. After Reagan's stunning 1981 budget victory, his subsequent annual budgets were routinely termed "dead on arrival" by members of Congress. Similarly, in early 1995 Bill Clinton's fiscal 1996 budget, which projected deficits near $200 billion for the rest of the century, was immediately rejected by the new Republican-run Congress, which was seeking to balance the budget in seven years.

During a time of divided government, the president's power to present a budget to Congress remains relevant as a statement of administration priorities. But a far more important budgetary power is the veto. The prospect that the president will veto a budget bill or individual appropriations bills forces Congress to take account of presidential goals. Often this threat of a presidential veto will require direct negotiations between members of Congress and the president on the final form of a budget bill.

FEDERAL BUDGET DEFICITS

Since the late 1970s, the budget-making process has been a struggle to limit budget deficits despite erratic economic growth and dramatic increases in spending for entitlements, social programs, and defense. The American people consistently indicate in surveys that they believe government spending should be reduced. Yet this desire for less government spending is accompanied by a reluctance to sacrifice funding for specific programs that have developed constituencies. The public traditionally has believed the government spends too much in only a few policy areas such as foreign aid, welfare, and space exploration.[76] Thus the budget is one of the most persistent political dilemmas facing presidents. They must try to reduce overall spending while funding the programs that Americans have come to expect.

Budget deficits are not a phenomenon unique to the 1970s, 1980s, and 1990s. The federal government often has been forced to run deficits during wars and other national emergencies, including the depression. Yet not until the 1970s did budget deficits become a persistent peacetime economic problem. Between 1792 and 1946, the federal government produced ninety-three budget surpluses and sixty-one budget deficits. From 1947 to 1969, a period during which two wars were fought, the government produced eight surpluses and fifteen deficits; but since 1970 the budget has been in deficit every year.[77] *(See Table 6-2.)*

The size of deficits since the Vietnam War has been especially troubling. In the past, periods of deficit spending were followed by years of surplus or at least balanced budgets. From 1975 to 1996, however, budget deficits exceeded $45 billion every year except 1979. Moreover, the deficit widened dramatically under Reagan, surpassing $200 billion in 1983, 1985, and 1986. After a modest improvement from 1987 to 1989, the budget deficit once again jumped over $200 billion in 1990 and reached a high of $290.4 billion in 1992. Although the deficit was cut by more than 60 percent to $107 by 1996, economists and citizens continued to call on the president and Congress to control deficits and end the buildup of debt.

Large budget deficits have several negative effects on the

TABLE 6-2 U.S. Federal Debt, Budget Deficits, and Interest Payments, 1975–1996 *(billions of dollars)*

Fiscal year	*Total federal debt*	*Budget deficit*	*Deficit as percentage of GDP*[a]	*Interest payments*
1975	541.9	–53.2	3.5	23.2
1976	629.0	–73.7	4.4	26.7
1977	706.4	–53.7	2.8	29.9
1978	776.6	–59.2	2.7	35.5
1979	829.5	–40.7	1.7	42.6
1980	909.1	–73.8	2.8	52.5
1981	994.8	–79.0	2.7	68.8
1982	1,137.3	–128.0	4.1	85.0
1983	1,371.7	–207.8	6.3	89.8
1984	1,564.7	–185.4	5.0	111.1
1985	1,817.5	–212.3	5.4	129.5
1986	2,120.6	–221.2	5.2	136.0
1987	2,346.1	–149.8	3.4	138.7
1988	2,601.3	–155.2	3.2	151.8
1989	2,868.0	–152.5	2.9	169.3
1990	3,206.6	–221.2	4.0	184.2
1991	3,598.5	–269.4	4.7	194.5
1992	4,002.1	–290.4	4.9	199.4
1993	4,351.4	–255.1	4.1	198.8
1994	4,643.7	–203.1	3.1	203.0
1995	4,961.0	–163.9	2.3	232.2
1996[b]	5,224.8	–107.0	1.5	241.1

SOURCES: Treasury Department; Office of Management and Budget.
NOTE: a. Gross domestic product. b. Estimate.

economy. First, they can threaten the economy by "crowding out" corporate and private borrowers from the credit market. Because the government must borrow heavily to finance its deficit, it competes with businesses and individuals also seeking to borrow funds. This increased competition forces interest rates higher, causing loans to become more expensive. As a result, fewer businesses can afford to expand and modernize their operations, and fewer consumers can afford to finance purchases of expensive items such as houses and cars. The resulting reduction in demand may threaten economic growth.

Second, large deficits reduce the amount of funds available for achieving the nation's social and defense goals because interest must be paid on the national debt. As larger budget deficits have pushed the national debt toward $5 trillion, interest payments have taken up an increasing share of the federal budget. In 1994 interest payments on the federal debt totaled $203 billion, or almost 14 percent of federal government spending. This was more money than the government spent on any other budget category except defense and Social Security. The mounting debt represents a transfer of the burden of paying for government to future generations.

Third, budget deficits limit the government's flexibility to fight a recession through tax cuts and deficit spending because the president and Congress must be concerned about exacerbating the debt problem. Since tax revenues fall during a recession and unemployment insurance and welfare payments rise, the budget would be under further strain precisely when deficit spending would be needed to pull the economy out of recession.

Fourth, budget deficits of the 1980s and 1990s have become so large that domestic savings no longer can provide enough capital to service the debt. Consequently, the government must borrow from foreign sources to make up the difference. This makes the United States dependent on foreign investors and raises the small possibility of a "stabilization crisis," which can occur if foreign investors lose confidence in the dollar and liquidate their U.S. investments. Such a crisis could cause the dollar to plummet and interest rates and inflation to accelerate rapidly.[78]

The Uncontrollable Budget

Presidents hoping to limit budget deficits must face the fiscal difficulties brought by the spending items that are required from year to year by existing law. These are known as uncontrollable or mandatory budgetary items. Although the term "uncontrollable" is somewhat misleading since these programs can be changed by an act of Congress, it does accurately describe the lack of power presidents have over these items in any given year.

Before the depression, most of the federal budget was devoted to the costs of running the government and, in times of war, the costs of defense. With the establishment of Social Security in the 1930s, however, the government began making large-scale payments directly to people who qualified for them. These entitlements now include Medicare, Medicaid, welfare, job training assistance, student loan guarantees, food stamps, school lunches, farm subsidies, unemployment compensation, and federal retirement benefits. They are intended to alleviate suffering and poverty, promote the health and advancement of individuals, and provide a safety net for those members of society who cannot provide for themselves because of economic recession, poverty, old age, or physical infirmity. Some of these entitlement programs, such as welfare and unemployment insurance, also act as automatic economic stabilizers, because they increase the amount of money in the hands of the public when the economy goes into recession.[79]

These payments have consciously been expanded by Congress and several presidents, most notably Franklin Roosevelt and Lyndon Johnson, in an effort to use the wealth generated by the U.S. economy to promote social welfare and care for the less fortunate. Many federal entitlement programs were established or substantially enlarged during the 1960s, when the strong American economy seemed capable of providing funds for virtually any worthy purpose.

Entitlements pose a special problem for presidents because the payments are not based on a yearly congressional appropriation or the government's ability to pay for them. They continue from year to year unless a law is passed that supersedes or alters the measure that created them. Moreover, in 1974 Congress established cost-of-living increases for Social Security payments, thereby ensuring that these benefits would not be reduced by the eroding effects of inflation.[80]

Predictably, presidents and Congress have been hesitant to assume the political risk of significantly reducing entitlement programs as the capacity of the government to pay for them has fallen. The growth of entitlements has been accompanied by an increase in the activities of interest groups that attempt to protect these payments from cutbacks. Lobbyist organizations representing senior citizens, veterans, farmers, and other groups can pressure the president or members of Congress to protect benefits to their constituents by offering or withholding campaign contributions, threatening them with negative publicity, and mobilizing blocs of voters that can make or break their candidacies. The activities of these lobbyists and the negative public reaction to cuts in entitlements received by tens of millions of Americans have made large sections of the budget politically dangerous to touch.[81]

The ability of presidents to propose significant cuts in the budget from year to year has been reduced as federal entitlements have claimed a greater portion of the budget. In 1963 entitlement spending accounted for 22.6 percent of the budget. By fiscal year 1983 it had risen to 45.2 percent of the budget. Ten years later it represented 47.3 percent of the budget. Added to this percentage was the growing cost of interest on the national debt, which is determined by the size of the debt and prevailing interest rates and must be subtracted from the incoming revenue. In 1993, 14.1 percent of the budget was consumed by interest payments, compared with just 6.9 percent in 1963. Thus 61.4 percent of the budget in 1993 was mandatory spending that could not be cut without a change in the laws that authorized the entitlement programs.

Even within the shrinking discretionary spending category, the president's ability to propose budget cuts was limited because the federal government is obligated to pay for items that it has ordered in previous years. For example, large weapon systems such as a new fighter plane or nuclear missile must be paid for over a span of years. Consequently, funds committed to such items cannot be cut from a current budget without breaking contracts and wasting the funds spent on the items in past years. Expenditures for many other items in the budget, such as defense and the costs of operating the government, can be trimmed but not eliminated entirely.

Presidents seeking to reduce government spending in a particular year, therefore, can search for cuts in only a fraction of the budget. According to political scientists Kim Hill and John Plumlee, this trend has diminished presidential budgetary power: "Presidential budgetary discretion has been significantly eroded. . . . The President in fact must propose and defend a budget much of which is determined elsewhere and in prior years."[82]

Balanced Budget Amendment

The sharp growth of federal budget deficits during the 1970s and 1980s convinced many elected officials that the only way to control deficit spending was through a balanced budget amendment. Polls consistently demonstrated that at least three-fourths of the American public supported the concept of a balanced budget amendment to the Constitution. Such an amendment was seen by its supporters as the most effective means to ensure that the president and Congress would spend only the revenues that the government took in, since they would be required to do so by the highest law of the land. Under the pressure provided by the amendment, Congress and the president would be more capable of making the politically difficult budget decisions necessary to balance the budget.

Critics of a balanced budget amendment argued that such an amendment would be hard to enforce. Would the president and Congress be penalized for failing to balance the budget? If so, critics asked, who would be responsible for enforcing such penalties? In addition, since the precise amount of spending and revenues for the following year is affected by the size of transfer payments (such as those for Social Security, Medicare, and welfare), tax revenues, and other variables unknown to budget makers, a balanced budget amendment would depend on highly imprecise forecasts of spending and revenues that would be subject to dispute.[83]

A balanced budget amendment also would limit the usefulness of fiscal policy as a stabilization tool. If the government did live up to budget-balancing requirements, it would no longer be able to use fiscal policy to stabilize the economy. Since tax receipts fall and transfer payments rise during a recession, balancing the budget would require additional spending cuts or higher taxes that would likely deepen the recession. During expansionary periods budget balancing would risk spurring inflation because tax revenues would rise, requiring the government to spend more or cut taxes to dispose of the surplus.[84]

The balanced budget amendment found a strong proponent in Ronald Reagan. He advocated its passage during his campaign in 1980 and during the early days of his presidency. Some observers believed the amendment had a chance to be passed and ratified since it was supported by a popular president. When Reagan entered office in 1981, thirty-two states already had voted in favor of a constitutional convention to consider a balanced budget amendment. In 1982 the Senate voted 69–31, two votes more than the necessary two-thirds majority, for a constitutional amendment that would have required a balanced budget. In the same year, the House voted 236–187 for a similar amendment, falling 46 votes short of the necessary two-thirds. By 1983 growing skepticism that current budget deficits could be quickly reduced weakened the balanced budget amendment movement. Even the president's highly optimistic budget projections did not envision achieving a balanced budget within five years.[85]

For a time, congressional efforts to reform the budget process shifted away from the balanced budget amendment toward a statutory approach mandating that specified deficit reduction targets be reached in specified years. In 1985 Congress passed the Gramm-Rudman-Hollings Deficit Reduction Act with President Reagan's support. The bill was an acknowledgment that Congress and the president needed to be forced to make the tough budget-cutting decisions necessary to reduce the deficit. The legislation required annual $36 billion decreases

Sponsors of the landmark deficit reductions act, from left, Senators Warren Rudman, Phil Gramm, and Ernest Hollings, celebrate passage of the law in 1985 that required "across the board" cuts if deficit reduction targets were not met.

in the deficit for five years. To ensure that these budget cuts were made, the law mandated "across the board" cuts known as "sequesters" to meet the deficit reduction targets if the projected deficit for a fiscal year exceeded the targeted amount by more than $10 billion. The authors of the bill reasoned that since nobody would want these indiscriminate cuts—half of which were to come from defense and half from domestic spending—to occur, Congress and the president would meet the deficit reduction targets through normal budget procedures.

Critics of Gramm-Rudman-Hollings charged that it reduced the government's flexibility and encouraged the use of accounting techniques that would disguise rather than lower the budget deficit. Some critics also claimed that the bill was unconstitutional because the president and Congress would be abdicating their budget-making responsibilities if the automatic cuts were used. The Supreme Court objected to a more limited and technical aspect of the law. The Court ruled on July 7, 1986, that because the law assigned to the comptroller general the final responsibility for determining the size of the budget cuts and for executing the automatic cuts, the bill was unconstitutional; only the president and the executive branch are empowered to execute the laws. The comptroller general heads the General Accounting Office, which is considered part of the legislative branch.

Congress responded to the Court's ruling in September 1987 by passing an amendment that gave the Office of Management and Budget—an executive branch agency—the final authority to determine the magnitude of cuts necessary to meet the deficit reduction goals.[86]

The Gramm-Rudman-Hollings approach failed, however, because its statutory targets could be overturned by subsequent laws. In 1987 and 1990 Congress scaled back the deficit reduction targets when they became unrealistic. In addition, Congress and the president met the scaled-back deficit reduction targets for future budgetary years by depending on overly optimistic forecasts of economic growth.[87] The experience of Gramm-Rudman-Hollings demonstrated that if a budget process reform mandating a balanced budget was to be successful, it would have to be in the form of a constitutional amendment.

The November 1994 midterm election, which brought Republican control over both chambers of Congress, gave new hope to proponents of the balanced budget amendment. Passage of such an amendment had been one of the planks in the "Contract with America," a document publicized by the House Republican leadership that promised action on ten Republican priorities if the voters elected a Republican majority.

Unlike Presidents Reagan and Bush, President Clinton opposed the balanced budget amendment and lobbied against its passage. The House passed the amendment on January 26, 1995, by a vote of 300–132. In the Senate, however, proponents fell one vote short of the two-thirds majority necessary on March 2, when six Democratic members who had voted for a similar amendment in 1994 changed their votes. Republican leaders promised to continue their efforts to pass the amendment and send it to the states for ratification.

The version of the balanced budget amendment that nearly passed in 1995 would have had profound effects on the budget process and presidential power. It would have required that the federal budget be balanced every year starting in 2002—a requirement that could have been waived by a three-fifths vote of both houses of Congress. Such a vote might be achievable during wartime or severe national emergency, but it represented a high standard. In most years, passing the waiver would not be possible without strong presidential support.

If such an amendment were ratified by the states, the flexibility of presidents to propose new spending initiatives or pet programs would be curtailed sharply. For example, had such an amendment been in place during the 1980s, Ronald Reagan's initiative to boost defense spending substantially would probably have been impossible. On a smaller scale, President Clinton's national service program, established in 1993, would likely have been seen as an unnecessary luxury if a balanced budget had been required. Presidents and legislators faced with an ironclad requirement of balancing the budget would be much more skeptical of any new spending programs, large or small.

Budget Brinkmanship

After the 1995 failure of the balanced budget amendment in the Senate, Republican congressional leaders vowed to carry forward with their plans to balance the budget through the normal budget process. They were able to pass a budget resolution that was scored by the CBO as establishing a balanced budget by 2002. However, passage of a budget resolution is an early step in the budget process and does not require the president's signature. For a multiyear balanced budget plan to become law, it must be incorporated into a budget reconciliation bill and signed by the president. The veto power, therefore, gave President Clinton influence over the outcome of the budget struggle. *(See "Clinton Administration," p. 255.)* Either the president or Congress would have to give in to the other, or they would have to reach a compromise acceptable to both.

On most bills, a presidential veto that cannot be overridden by a two-thirds vote of both chambers puts an end to the initiative until the next Congress. But a vetoed budget inevitably results in a congressional counterproposal and negotiations with the president. The threat of a presidential veto had led in 1990 to extensive budget negotiations between the Democratic Congress and President Bush. Although Bush secured additional spending cuts, he also gave in to Congress's demands for tax increases. By signing the resulting budget bill, Bush violated his "no new taxes" pledge and contributed to his electoral defeat in 1992.

Presidential power in these budget negotiations will often depend on how stubborn the president is willing to be in the face of prolonged stalemate, a government shutdown, or even a government default. The veto (or threat of using it) allows presidents to precipitate a budget showdown with Congress, but they enter negotiations with inherent disadvantages. Since presidents exercise vetoes after a bill is passed, Congress retains the initiative throughout the process. The president cannot make Congress pass a bill, but Congress can make a president use the veto, repeatedly if necessary. In the long run, presidents are more likely to be blamed by the public for hardships that result from a budget stalemate than is an individual member of Congress. This is because presidents are most closely identified with the performance of the national economy and because a member of Congress is only one of many actors in the legislative branch.

The 1995–1996 budget stalemate, however, dem Congress as a whole may receive more public blame crisis than the president. Virtually every opinion showed that the public held Congress primarily respon ior the budget stalemate. Media stories focused heavily on the two government shutdowns precipitated by Congress, instead of the underlying budget questions. Congress's attempts to use the shutdowns to gain an agreement appeared counterproductive and petty to many Americans. The public response provided no pressure for President Clinton to compromise with his Republican congressional opponents. The outcome indicated that public opinion likely would determine the results of budget brinkmanship in the future.

PRESIDENTIAL CONTROL OVER APPROPRIATIONS

The Constitution did not spell out whether presidents were required to promptly spend funds appropriated by Congress or whether they could make independent judgments about the timing and even the necessity of putting appropriated funds to use. Many presidents during the nineteenth century took advantage of this constitutional ambiguity to impound appropriated funds they believed unnecessary or wasteful. In effect, the impoundment "power" gave presidents a second veto over appropriations since they could withhold funds Congress intended to spend.

After World War II presidents increasingly used impoundments as a fiscal policy tool. Presidents Truman, Eisenhower, and Kennedy all clashed with Congress over their withholding of appropriations for defense projects. In 1966 Lyndon Johnson impounded $5.3 billion in domestic appropriations to slow inflationary trends brought on by the Vietnam War.

Presidential impoundments reached their zenith under Richard Nixon, who impounded billions of dollars of appropriations during the first five years of his presidency. He argued that he was withholding funds only as a financial management technique designed to slow inflation. Democratic leaders in Congress, however, charged that Nixon used impoundments to overturn Congress's spending decisions and further his own social goals. For example, after Congress overrode a presidential veto to pass the 1972 Clean Water Act, Nixon impounded $9 billion that was intended to implement the act. The conflict between Nixon and Congress over impoundments led to the passage of a law that restricted presidential use of impoundments.[88]

Impoundment Control Act of 1974

The Impoundment Control Act of 1974 (which was one title of the Congressional Budget and Impoundment Control Act) created new procedures designed to prevent a president from impounding appropriations against the will of Congress. Under the act presidents were required to notify Congress when they decided to impound (rescind) appropriated funds permanently. Congress had forty-five days in which to signal its approval of this permanent impoundment, known as a rescission, by a majority vote of both houses. After forty-five days, if Congress had not approved, presidents were required to spend the money. The law also allowed presidents to defer spending appropriated funds by notifying Congress that they were doing so. The funds could be held until one of the houses of Congress overturned the deferral. In 1983, however, the Supreme Court overturned one-house legislative vetoes in *Immigration and Naturalization Service v. Chadha.* Subsequently, both houses of Congress had to pass legislation directing the president to spend the funds. But in 1987 the Supreme Court ruled that because the deferral authority was contingent on the unconstitutional one-house veto, the president could no longer exercise it.[89]

After presidential impoundment powers were scaled back in 1974, Congress adopted some presidential rescissions, but more often it ignored the president's proposed cuts or substituted cuts of its own. As a result many members of Congress argued that the 1974 restrictions on presidential impoundment authority had been a mistake. They wanted a strengthened presidential impoundment power that could help combat wasteful or unnecessary spending by Congress. These sentiments were focused during the 1980s and 1990s on the enactment of a "line-item veto."

Line-Item Veto

The *line-item veto* or *item veto* refers generically to a number of proposals intended to strengthen the president's authority to rescind specific spending items within an appropriations bill. The two most prominent forms of the line-item veto are the "enhanced rescission" and the "expedited rescission." *(See "Line-item Veto," p. 94, in Chapter 2.)*

Enhanced rescission authority would allow presidents to propose rescissions in appropriations bills as they can under the Impoundment Control Act. These rescissions would go into effect automatically, unless both chambers of Congress voted to reject them. The president could then veto the legislation disapproving of the rescissions, forcing both houses to muster a two-thirds vote to override the veto. The enhanced rescission represents a vast expansion of the presidential impoundment power because the president's rescission choices would prevail unless Congress could muster enough votes to clear the high hurdle of a veto override.

Expedited rescission authority is a more modest expansion of presidential power. Under this procedure presidents also would propose a set of rescissions. As under the Impoundment Control Act, these rescissions would not go into effect unless both houses of Congress approved them. But under an expedited rescission, Congress would be *required* to vote on the rescission proposals within a set time period. Thus, Congress could not overrule the president's rescission proposal merely through inaction.

Although many presidents have supported an item veto, Ronald Reagan was a particularly vocal advocate of the device. He repeatedly called on Congress to enact legislation giving him and future presidents this power. In his last State of the Union address in 1988, Reagan asked Congress to

> help ensure our future of prosperity by giving the President a tool that—though I will not get to use it—is one I know future presidents of either party must have. Give the president the same authority that forty-three governors use in their states, the right to reach into massive appropriations bills, pare away the waste, and enforce budget discipline. Let's approve the line-item veto.

As described by President Reagan, the line-item veto appeared to be a simple and effective way to control government spending. In reality, although it might help presidents to make some cuts in the budget, it is a highly controversial budgetary device. If the president were armed with the line-item veto, members of Congress would be tempted to pass many pork barrel spending items to satisfy their constituents while relying on the president to make the politically difficult choices about which items to cut. Even if the president were to veto a substantial number of these items, the budget might still contain more fat than if Congress had not been given a way out of its legislative responsibilities. The line-item veto also might make budgetary restraint more difficult because a president would be able to threaten a member of Congress with a line-item veto of a program that would benefit that member's state or district unless that member agreed to vote for a bill supported by the administration. Even if the line-item veto did result in less budget waste, it could cause a dramatic shift of legislative power to the president that would violate traditional American principles of separated powers.[90]

Some opponents of the line-item veto also have argued that its usefulness in limiting spending has been overestimated. A line-item veto would have no effect on entitlements, interest payments on the national debt, and other parts of the budget that cannot be controlled from year to year. Moreover, contrary to popular perceptions, few spending bills contain significant line items that could be cut with a line-item veto. Spending details are often found in the reports of congressional committees and agency budget justification documents, while the legislation funding the activities of a particular unit of an agency or department only mentions the lump sum allocated to it.[91] Given these limitations, the line-item veto is unlikely to be a solution to huge deficits. At best it would allow the president to make selected cuts in the discretionary budget.

The 1994 election brought to power in Congress Republicans who were committed to enacting a line-item veto. Such legislation was part of the House Republican "Contract with America." President Clinton was a longtime supporter of the line-item veto. He emphasized his backing in a March 20, 1995, statement urging Congress to ". . . pass the strongest possible line-item veto, and to make it effective immediately. If the Members of Congress from both parties are serious about cutting the deficit, give me this line-item veto, and I will get started right away."

Expectations in Congress were high that some form of the line-item veto could be passed and signed by the president. The

House and the Senate passed different versions of the line-item veto in 1995. Congressional Republicans, who were in no hurry to hand President Clinton line-item veto power over their fiscal 1996 budget, moved slowly to reconcile the two versions. Finally on March 27, 1996, after several months of bipartisan negotiations, the joint Senate-House conference report passed by a vote of 69–31 in the Senate. The next day the House passed it by a vote of 232–177. The historic measure, signed by Clinton in early 1996, went into effect on January 1, 1997, and will expire after eight years. The measure grants the president enhanced rescission authority and also limited authority to cancel targeted tax benefits, as well as new or increased entitlement programs. Opponents of the bill, however, promised to mount a court challenge against it, saying that it represented an unconstitutional delegation of legislative power to the executive. Indeed, six members of Congress filed a suit on this basis on January 2, 1997.

Tax Policy

Traditionally, presidents have exerted less influence over tax policy than over spending matters. Whereas presidents are required to submit an executive budget to Congress outlining their spending proposals each year, tax laws do not require the executive to make major annual revisions. In addition, legislators, especially members of the powerful House Ways and Means and Senate Finance Committees, have historically regarded tax policy as a special province of Congress.

Nevertheless, presidential influence over tax policy has grown significantly since World War II. This increase in influence has been furthered by the growth in presidential responsibility for economic policy.[92] As Congress and the nation have become accustomed to looking to the president for economic initiatives, the chief executive has taken over much of the burden of proposing and campaigning for changes in the tax code.

Within the executive branch, the Treasury Department has primary responsibility for tax policy. Its Office of the Tax Legislative Counsel drafts tax legislation and reviews tax regulations. The Office of Tax Analysis estimates the effect tax changes have on revenues. In addition, the Treasury Department's Internal Revenue Service (IRS) is responsible for collecting taxes and enforcing the tax laws passed by Congress. Other officials in the administration, particularly the OMB director, also are involved in formulating tax strategies.

In addition to proposing tax legislation, presidents influence tax policy by standing ready to veto tax bills passed by Congress that they believe are unfair, excessive, or harmful to the economy. Presidents after World War II rarely have had to veto tax bills, since the threat to veto them usually has been enough to stop congressional tax initiatives opposed by the president. Ronald Reagan's success at preventing tax increases during his second term despite huge budget deficits demonstrates the president's power over tax policy. Presidents may not be able to get their tax measures passed by Congress, but they will usually be able to stop or at least force the modification of any tax bill they do not like. Even George Bush, who paid a high political price for breaking his "no new taxes" pledge, did so only after months of negotiations on the composition of those tax increases and accompanying spending cuts.

Congress, however, has similar power to negate the president's tax proposals. Political scientist John Witte has written:

> "Although the earlier notion that presidents should set only general revenue targets has been replaced by more detailed, almost annual tax proposals, the majority of the tax agenda is still set by Congress. Furthermore, there is no doubt that when presidential requests run counter to legislative momentum or the short-term mood of Congress, they can and are summarily dismissed by congressional actions."[93]

The strategy of using tax policy as a tool of fiscal policy is complicated by the government's need for revenue. Although some tax cuts have generated greater revenues, most notably the Kennedy tax cut of 1964, tax cuts usually result in less revenue and higher deficits than would have ensued had they not been enacted. The supply-side economic theory that cutting tax rates would result in higher revenues became popular in the early 1980s, but the budget deficits that followed Reagan's 1981 tax cut diminished enthusiasm for this concept. *(See "Supply-side Experiment," p. 252.)* Tax cuts meant to stimulate the economy may succeed, but higher budget deficits may result. Conversely, raising taxes may increase revenues in the short term but also contract the economy, resulting in higher unemployment.

Tax cuts are a popular fiscal policy tool because they directly increase net personal income. Tax cuts have often been used successfully to stimulate the economy. The unpopularity of tax increases, however, has made them difficult to enact with the speed that is necessary if they are to be an effective fiscal policy tool. Godfrey Hodgson has written of Lyndon Johnson's experience with this problem:

> Even a timely shift in the direction of tax policy for macroeconomic reasons is generally beyond the capacity of . . . congressional procedures. Lyndon Johnson found this to his cost in 1965–68, when he tried to raise tax revenues to pay for the Vietnam War. His inability to do so may have cost him the presidency. Certainly it spelled the end for his great society programs and gave a sharp new impetus to the inflation combined with economic stagnation that has troubled the economy ever since.[94]

The wave of antitax sentiment that hit the United States during the late 1970s and 1980s further diminished the relevancy of anti-inflationary tax measures. Presidential candidates during this period who did advocate a tax increase, such as 1984 Democratic nominee Walter Mondale and 1988 Democratic contender Bruce Babbitt, were praised by many observers for their realism but fared poorly with voters. Mondale won only thirteen electoral votes in his election battle with Reagan, and Babbitt bowed out of the race for the 1988 Democratic nomination race after receiving meager support in the early primaries.

During the 1980s and 1990s, reforming the method of taxation became a major issue. In 1986, with Reagan's strong support, Congress passed the bipartisan Tax Reform Act. It was a sweeping attempt to simplify the tax code and eliminate loopholes without increasing or decreasing tax revenues. The initial impetus for the bill came from Reagan, who in January 1984 directed the Treasury Department to develop a plan to simplify the tax code.[95]

The resulting bill cut the number of tax brackets from fourteen to just two. It cut the top individual tax rate from 50 to 28 percent and taxed 85 percent of taxpayers at the bottom rate of 15 percent. Reagan hailed the law as "the best anti-poverty bill, the best pro-family measure, and the best job-creation program ever to come out of the Congress of the United States."

Few Americans, however, believed that the bill had made paying their federal income taxes much easier. By 1993 the number of income tax rates had grown from two back up to five. The income tax's complexity and the intrusiveness of IRS audits stirred a populist movement aimed at finding alternatives to the income tax system. Critics pointed out that the IRS estimated that it failed to collect about $127 billion per year in income taxes. Simultaneously, many economists and policy makers wanted to restructure the tax system so that it would target consumption, thereby raising the low U.S. savings rate that was weakening productivity gains and causing wages to stagnate.

Virtually all Republican candidates for president in 1996 announced their support for radical tax reform—either a flat tax that would target consumption or a national sales tax. The GOP's eventual nominee, Bob Dole, ran on a platform that called for a 15 percent tax cut for everyone. Dole lost the election to Clinton, who called for more modest tax reform—such as tuition credits. The success of tax reform in Clinton's second term will largely depend on strong presidential support of the issue. Few matters of public policy are more subject to partisan and parochial politics than tax reform, which readjusts the tax bills of businesses and individuals.

Monetary Policy

Monetary policy, like fiscal policy, is a tool with which the government attempts to stabilize the economy. It is based on the relationship of the supply of money in circulation to the performance of the economy. Since changes in the rate of growth of the money supply profoundly affect unemployment, inflation, and interest rates, the government can regulate economic activity by controlling the supply of money. Increasing the rate of growth of the money supply will stimulate the economy; decreasing it will contract the economy and combat inflation.

THE MECHANICS OF MONETARY POLICY

In contrast to fiscal policy, which is made through a slow public process of conflict and compromise among the president, Congress, and executive departments, monetary policy is determined within the Federal Reserve System, known as the "Fed." The Fed consists of twelve regional banks, several advisory bodies, and a Board of Governors. The members of the Board of Governors, who are appointed by the president, are responsible for setting monetary policy and overseeing the operations of the Federal Reserve System. The chair of the Federal Reserve Board dominates policy making at the Fed, and has often been described as the "second most powerful person" in Washington.

After 1836, when the charter of the Second Bank of the United States was allowed to expire, the United States did not have a central bank for the rest of the century. In 1907, however, a severe banking crisis prompted policy makers to reexamine the American banking system. In 1912 a commission appointed by Congress recommended that the country establish a central bank to regulate credit conditions and provide stability to the U.S. banking system. With these goals in mind, Congress in 1913 passed with President Wilson's support the Federal Reserve Act, which created the Fed.[96]

Congress gave the Federal Reserve System a permanent charter to avoid the type of political fight that prevented the First and Second Banks of the United States from being rechartered. The Federal Reserve Act does not mention a stabilization policy role for the Federal Reserve System. This role evolved gradually after the Great Depression, until stabilization of the economy through monetary policy became one of the Fed's primary functions.

The Fed studies the economy and constructs economic forecasts that it uses to determine its monetary policy. As with fiscal policy, the goals of monetary policy include low inflation, low unemployment, and strong economic growth. Fighting inflation, however, has traditionally been the Fed's first priority.

Managing the Money Supply

The Fed has several means through which it can change the rate of growth of the money supply. First, it can require commercial banks to keep a greater or smaller proportion of deposits on reserve. If this reserve requirement is lowered, banks have more money to lend, and the money supply grows faster. If the reserve requirement is raised, banks have fewer funds to lend, and the growth of the money supply slows. Second, the Fed can slow or accelerate the growth of the money supply by decreasing or increasing the interest rate at which banks may borrow funds from the Federal Reserve System. When this rate, known as the *discount rate,* increases, banks can afford to borrow less from the Fed and therefore will have less money to lend. A lower discount rate will put more money in the hands of banks by making it cheaper for them to borrow from the Fed. Finally, the Fed can alter the growth of the money supply by buying and selling U.S. securities. This process, known as *open market operations,* is by far the most commonly used method for affecting the money supply. When the Fed buys securities, it pumps money into the banking system. Selling securities to banks brings money into the Fed that banks could have loaned, thereby slowing the growth of the money supply.[97]

The Fed's manipulations of the money supply affect the performance of the economy through their influence on interest rates. If the Fed increases the money supply, interest rates fall because banks have more funds available to lend. The lower interest rates induce firms to borrow more money to invest in the expansion and modernization of their operations. This increase in investment causes the economy to expand. Consumers also find borrowing cheaper, so they are able to finance the purchase of expensive items such as homes and cars more easily. If the Fed slows the growth of the money supply, banks have fewer funds to lend, and the competition for these limited funds forces interest rates up. Firms and consumers respond to more expensive rates of interest by borrowing less money for investment and purchases, so the economy contracts.

Monetary Policy as a Stabilization Tool

As noted previously, persistently high federal budget deficits in the 1980s and early 1990s have reduced the utility of fiscal policy as an economic stabilization tool. This has meant that the Fed has had to shoulder the burden of responding to signs of inflation and recession.

Yet even before the era of high budget deficits, monetary policy was an attractive policy tool because it is less constrained by politics than is fiscal policy, which is produced through an unwieldy process of negotiation and compromise between the legislative and executive branches. Since the monetary policy-making structure created by Congress was intended to be nonpolitical, politicians usually have tried to avoid the appearance of interfering in the Fed's business. In addition, the complexity of monetary policy discourages many potential critics from looking over the Fed's shoulder.

Monetary policy's primary role in stabilization has been to fight inflation. Monetary policy has always had two advantages over fiscal policy as an inflation-fighting tool. First, the time required to decide on and execute a strategy is much shorter for monetary policy than for fiscal policy. After an economic problem has been recognized, the Fed can reach a monetary policy decision within days. In contrast, the president may not be able to develop a fiscal policy program and secure congressional approval for many months, if at all. Although monetary policy, once implemented, takes longer to affect the economy than fiscal policy, this delay is usually shorter than the delay caused by the fiscal policy process.[98] Second, the Fed's relative insulation from politics makes its fight against inflation simpler than the president's. Fiscal policy remedies for inflation—tax increases and cuts in federal spending—are seldom popular with voters. Since the members of the Fed are not elected, they cannot be turned out of office by voters who are unhappy with an anti-inflationary monetary policy.[99]

Despite these advantages, monetary policy, like fiscal policy, has its limitations. Although a tight monetary policy can be used to control inflation when the economy is growing too fast, during a period of stagflation when both unemployment and inflation are rising, restrictive monetary policies are likely to deepen the recession. The restrictive monetary policies of Fed chairman Paul Volcker during the late 1970s and early 1980s succeeded in lowering inflation dramatically, but they also contributed to the severe recession of 1981–1982. Although Volcker deserves much credit for making the tough policy choices necessary to relieve the high inflation that had plagued the U.S. economy since the Vietnam War, the Fed can become too concerned with inflation. The Fed's relative political independence and banking orientation can dispose it to emphasize low inflation at the expense of other economic goals. Specifically, the Fed may at times tolerate unacceptably high unemployment in its pursuit of low inflation.[100]

PRESIDENTIAL INFLUENCE OVER MONETARY POLICY

The Federal Reserve System is relatively free of formal congressional or executive control. Although there are other independent agencies, none serves such an important and politically sensitive function as formulating monetary policy.

The Fed ultimately is answerable to Congress, but the only formal powers Congress has over the Fed are Senate confirmation of appointees to the Board and the passage of legislation restricting or revising the Fed's powers. Congress can neither pass judgment on nor veto Fed policies. Since the Fed is self-financing (it is funded by the interest it receives from government securities and the fees it charges to banks), Congress also cannot gain leverage by threatening to withhold appropriations. The Fed's independent control of monetary policy is a potent restriction on presidential control of the economy. Except for their power to appoint Federal Reserve Board officials, presidents have no formal means through which they can influence monetary policy. Yet presidents will receive most of the blame or the praise for changes in the economy brought about by monetary policy. Given this situation, presidents naturally try to exert as much informal influence over Fed decisions as possible.

Often this influence is exercised through public statements by presidents or their subordinates suggesting changes in Fed policy. These statements usually are crafted to avoid overt criticisms of the Fed or threats against its independence. For example, on June 1, 1992, with President Bush's reelection chances jeopardized by a weak economy, Treasury Secretary Nicholas Brady commented: "I think it is clear that if the Fed pulls down the lever of money supply in 1992, as was the case in 1991 when the first appearance of growth started in midsummer, then we are taking a chance with this economic recovery that I don't think is wise for this country."[101] Such statements mark presidential monetary policy positions and distance the president from ensuing Fed policies that conflict with those positions.

Board members recognize a practical need to coordinate fiscal and monetary policy and, despite some prominent exceptions, have usually cooperated with presidential efforts to do so. The Fed also has been mindful that the president is the elected representative of the people who, theoretically, embodies the policy directions preferred by the American electorate.

Although the independence of the Fed is a restraint on presidential control of the economy, it does enable presidents to rely on the Board of Governors to make politically unpopular eco-

ECONOMIC ADVISERS TO THE PRESIDENT

As presidential economic responsibilities increased during the twentieth century, the fulfillment of those responsibilities became increasingly institutionalized. Congress created new organizations, and presidents expanded existing organizations to increase the executive branch's capacity to analyze, coordinate, and manage the American economy and economic relations with other countries. Although White House political advisers and virtually all cabinet secretaries have some influence on economic policy, three executive branch units dominate presidential economic policy making. These are the Treasury Department, the Council of Economic Advisers (CEA), and the Office of Management and Budget (OMB). The leaders of these three units function as the president's chief economic advisers and meet frequently with one another to coordinate economic policy.

Recent presidents also have established working groups beneath the three leaders with representatives from various departments to develop and analyze economic policies. President Clinton's Trade Policy Review Group, for example, comprised representatives from the State Department, the Office of the U.S. Trade Representative, the CEA, and the OMB. To coordinate the administration's overall economic policy, Clinton established the National Economic Council (NEC) under Robert E. Rubin, who would later become Treasury secretary. The NEC staff gathered the views of cabinet members and other administration officials and presented those views to the president for policy decisions.

DEPARTMENT OF THE TREASURY

The Treasury Department, one of the original cabinet departments created in 1789 by an act of Congress, was the first executive branch unit to be responsible for advising the president on economic policy and has remained an important participant in economic policy making throughout U.S. history. The department has a variety of economic responsibilities, including collecting taxes and customs, managing the nation's currency and debt, developing tax legislation, and working with foreign governments and the Federal Reserve to adjust the value of the dollar relative to other currencies. Because the Treasury oversees the financing of the debt, the department traditionally has advocated taxes that will bring balanced budgets and monetary policies that yield low interest rates.

The Treasury secretary's position as head of a large cabinet department lends status to the post relative to other top presidential economic advisers. The Treasury secretary's influence on presidential economic decision making, however, may be constrained in some administrations by the amount of time the secretary spends overseeing the many operational responsibilities of the department. As the world's economies have become more interdependent, the Treasury secretary's international economic policy activities have become increasingly important. James A. Baker III, Treasury secretary during Ronald Reagan's second term, spent much of his time formulating exchange rate policies and developing a plan to reschedule Latin American debt payments to the United States. In early 1995, immediately upon assuming the post of Treasury secretary, Robert Rubin orchestrated the commitment to Mexico of $20 billion in U.S. loans and loan guarantees and an additional $30 billion in international loans to avert severe international repercussions from Mexico's currency crisis.

COUNCIL OF ECONOMIC ADVISERS

The Council of Economic Advisers (CEA) is a three-member body appointed by the president and subject to Senate confirmation. It is headed by a chair who oversees the operations of the council's small staff, reports to the president, and represents the CEA before the rest of the executive branch and Congress.

The primary function of the CEA is to provide the president with expert economic advice and analysis. The Employment Act of 1946, which established the CEA as a unit in the Executive Office of the President, states that each member of the council "shall be a person who, as a result of his training, experience and attainments is exceptionally qualified to analyze and interpret economic developments, to appraise programs and activities of the government . . . and to formulate and recommend national economic policy." Because the council does not represent a large bureaucratic body and has no responsibilities in operating the government other than preparing the president's annual economic report, Congress hoped that the CEA would have the time and independence to provide presidents with long-term, nonpartisan advice on economic policy and professional analysis of economic conditions. Traditionally, the CEA was primarily concerned with promoting growth and managing the trade-off between inflation and unemployment. In recent years, however, it has addressed a wider range of economic issues, including trade, productivity, pollution, and health care.

The CEA's influence depends almost entirely on the president. If the president values its advice and involves it in decision making, the CEA can have considerable power because its three members and small staff of professional economists usually possess the greatest amount of economic expertise within an administration. Because of this expertise, however, CEA members can be vulnerable to charges from other economic advisers that they approach the realities of economic policy making from a perspective that is too theoretical. CEA members must, therefore, be careful to pay adequate attention to the president's political needs if they wish to retain their influence.

OFFICE OF MANAGEMENT AND BUDGET

In 1921 Congress created the Bureau of the Budget to coordinate and modify the budget estimates of the executive departments. It was originally located within the Treasury Department but was placed under the newly created Executive Office of the President in 1939. In 1970 Richard Nixon expanded its staff and duties and renamed it the Office of Management and Budget (OMB).

OMB's primary function is to formulate an executive branch budget for the president that considers how much revenue the government is likely to raise through taxes and how much each federal agency and program should receive. OMB, therefore, continually analyzes the merits of budget requests and makes recommendations to the president on what funding should be cut, maintained, or expanded. The office is also responsible for budget forecasts that estimate the size of the budget deficit or surplus. The institutional bias of OMB has been to limit spending. Since department and agency heads tend to request as much funding as is politically possible for their units, OMB has become the central budgetary control within the administration to pare down the budget requests.

The post of budget director has become highly politicized since the Nixon administration. Budget directors frequently testify before Congress and are involved in shaping and promoting the president's social agenda through their budget recommendations. David Stockman, budget director under Ronald Reagan from 1981 to 1985, epitomized the budget director's new role. President Reagan gave him a broad mandate to cut items from the budget in pursuit of smaller budget deficits. In the first six months of the Reagan administration, he became not only the dominant presidential adviser on the budget, but also a symbol of Reagan's domestic budget cuts and social agenda, which emphasized a more limited role for the federal government.

The forecasting role of OMB also has pushed it into the political spotlight. Because budgets depend on long-term forecasts of economic growth, tax receipts, and entitlement spending, the assumptions of OMB and its legislative branch counterpart, the Congressional Budget Office (CBO), are critical to plans aimed at reducing the deficit. In 1995 Congress insisted that President Clinton agree to base efforts to balance the budget on forecasts from the traditionally independent CBO. Most observers agree that direct presidential control of OMB has led to the politicization of its budget forecasts under recent presidents. Clinton agreed in November 1995 to use CBO budget estimates that were developed after consultations with OMB.

nomic decisions, thus taking some public pressure off the White House. For example, in 1965 Johnson's advisers urged him to propose a tax increase to cool down the economy, which was beginning to produce inflation. Johnson, however, refused to propose higher taxes, thus forcing the Fed to bear the responsibility for fighting inflation. When the Fed raised the discount rate, Johnson told reporters, "The Federal Reserve Board is an independent agency. Its decision was an independent action. I regret, as do most Americans, any action that raises the cost of credit, particularly for homes, schools, hospitals, and factories." Political scientist Richard Pious noted, "Had Johnson fought for the politically unpopular but necessary tax increase, there would have been no need to blame the board for its action."[102]

Presidential Appointment of Board Members

The most obvious source of influence presidents have over monetary policy is their power to appoint the members of the Fed's Board of Governors. The Federal Reserve Board of Governors consists of a chair appointed by the president to a four-year term with the approval of the Senate and six members appointed to fourteen-year terms, also subject to Senate confirmation. The members' terms are staggered so that one of their terms expires at the end of January in each even-numbered year. Barring deaths or resignations by board members, a president will appoint two members and a chair during each four-year term. In practice, however, presidents often make additional appointments to the Board of Governors. Perhaps because salaries paid to board members are generally far below what they can earn in the private sector, board members frequently resign before completing a full fourteen-year term.[103]

The chair's term, which is renewable, does not coincide with the president's term. Consequently, during the first part of their time in office first-term presidents must work with a chair appointed by their predecessor.

Given the influence of Fed chairs and their potential effect on a president's reelection chances, one would expect presidents to choose Fed chairs from among their closest economic allies. Yet the expectations of the financial and scholarly communities that presidents will appoint board members with high academic credentials and relatively nonpartisan backgrounds serve as a check against overly political appointments. Presidents are mindful that an appointment that appears to conflict with the Fed's traditional goals may cause financial markets to react in a way that hurts the economy (and therefore their own reelection chances). In addition, a president who nominates a close ally to be chair will be unable to disavow Fed policies that are perceived to be damaging to the economy.

Consequently, presidents often have reappointed Fed chairs who originally were appointed by their predecessors. In several cases, presidents have even reappointed a chair who was appointed by a president of a different party. William McChesney Martin was appointed Fed chair by President Truman in 1951. He was reappointed by Eisenhower, Kennedy, and Nixon, serving continuously until he retired in 1970. Paul Volcker, a Jimmy Carter appointee, was reappointed by Ronald Reagan. Alan Greenspan, a Reagan appointee, was reappointed by Presidents Bush and Clinton.

The chances that the Fed will cooperate with the president, however, are increased greatly if the Fed chair is appointed by the incumbent president and shares the president's basic economic philosophy. In 1977 President Carter's expansionary fiscal policy was countered by the anti-inflationary monetary policy of Fed chairman Arthur Burns, the conservative appointee of Richard Nixon. When Burns's term expired in 1978, Carter replaced him with G. William Miller, a Carter associate who worked closely with the president's economic team.[104]

Coordination of Fiscal and Monetary Policy

Although the organization of the Fed is designed to insulate it from outside influence, monetary policy is most effective when it is coordinated with the administration's fiscal policy. Coordination is accomplished through informal meetings between the Fed chair and the president's top economic advisers.

The Fed chair, the Treasury secretary, the budget director, and the chair of the CEA—a group known as the "quadriad"—usually will meet at least once a month to discuss coordination of fiscal and monetary policy. Any agreements forged out of these discussions, however, are nonbinding, and the Fed may pursue a monetary policy at odds with the administration's goals.

The intent of both fiscal and monetary policy is to promote economic stability and prosperity, but the effects of one may cancel, blunt, or distort the intended effects of the other if the president and the Fed do not cooperate. For example, the president may ask Congress to stimulate the economy by spending more than the government receives in revenues. This requires the government to borrow funds, which increases competition for loans, thereby driving up interest rates. The higher interest rates, however, may offset the stimulative effects of the government's spending increases unless the Fed accommodates the president's fiscal policy by increasing the money supply.

The Fed has sometimes "leaned against the wind" to counter administration policies it considered wrong. In 1957 the Fed kept a tight rein on the money supply while the Eisenhower administration was pursuing a moderately expansionary fiscal policy. Similarly, the Fed fought inflation during the late 1960s while spending on the Vietnam War and Lyndon Johnson's Great Society social programs stimulated the economy.

The Fed may even use public pressure to attempt to change administration policies. In 1977 Fed chairman Burns testified against Jimmy Carter's tax cut proposals, raising the possibility that if the tax cuts were passed, the Fed would use monetary policy to offset their stimulative effect.[105] Fed chairman Greenspan warned the incoming Bush administration through testimony before Congress on January 24, 1989, that the Fed would not tolerate an acceleration of inflation. George Bush and his economic advisers had placed a high priority on continued strong economic growth, but Greenspan indicated the Fed might slow growth in the near future to combat inflation, saying, "The Federal Reserve policy at this juncture might be well advised to err more on the side of restrictiveness than stimulus."[106]

Presidents, therefore, generally try to coordinate their fiscal policies with the Fed to produce the best economic results and limit political friction between economic policy makers. In 1993 President Clinton went out of his way to establish a good relationship with Greenspan, who had been appointed chair of the Fed in 1987 by President Reagan and reappointed in 1992 by Bush. In a show of their mutual desire for bipartisan coordination of economic policy, Greenspan sat with First Lady Hillary Rodham Clinton at the 1993 State of the Union address. Later that year, Clinton wrote to House Banking Committee chair Henry Gonzalez defending Fed policies. Gonzalez had introduced legislation aimed at restricting the Fed's independence. Clinton expressed his opposition to Gonzalez's efforts, saying: "There is a general feeling that the system is functioning well and does not need an overhaul just now." In early 1996, Clinton reappointed Greenspan to his third term.

Yet even as Clinton and Greenspan sought to establish a good working relationship, both demonstrated their independence. Clinton nominated Alan Blinder and Janet Yellen to fill two Federal Reserve Board seats that came open in 1994 and nominated Alice Rivlin and Laurence Meyer to Board seats in 1996. The appointment of these individuals, who were considered to be more tolerant of inflation than Greenspan, was perceived as signaling Clinton's desire for the Fed to be more growth oriented. For his part, Greenspan backed up the efforts of congressional Republicans to balance the budget by testifying that if their planned budget cuts deflated the economy, he would lower interest rates. The testimony came in February 1995, as President Clinton led the Democratic opposition to the Republican budget-cutting strategy. Later that year, Greenspan also began lobbying Congress and the president to consider a reduction in the Consumer Price Index (CPI) as a means of limiting the budget's growth. Tax brackets and most entitlements are adjusted upward each year by a percentage that is based on the CPI. This procedure was established so that inflation would not gradually increase taxes or erode the buying power of entitlement benefits. However, many economists believe that the CPI significantly overstates inflation, thereby providing an annual windfall to taxpayers and benefit recipients. In the fall of 1995 congressional Republicans supported the idea of reducing the CPI because it would have reduced the number of politically unpopular budget cuts the Republican leadership had to make in their 1995 proposal to balance the budget in seven years.

Proponents of greater executive control over monetary policy have proposed several reforms. The most radical would be to place the Federal Reserve under executive control and allow presidents and their advisers to set monetary policy in addition to performing their other economic functions. This reform would result in the greatest degree of coordination possible between fiscal and monetary policy, since the incumbent administration would be making both. It would, however, allow presidents to use monetary policy for political purposes. Presidents could quietly stimulate the economy through monetary policy in an election year to improve their chances of being reelected.

A more modest reform that has been considered by Congress but never passed is to make the term of the Fed chair coincide with the president's term of office. This would improve coordination since the president would presumably enter office with a like-minded Fed chair. The chair, however, would retain independent control over monetary policy.[107]

International Economic Policy

The president's international economic powers have become increasingly important as nations have become more economically interdependent. Because of high volumes of trade, integrated financial markets, multinational corporations, and other factors that bind the world's economies, prosperity in the United States cannot be sustained if other large economies, especially those of Western Europe and Japan, are ailing. Specific economic problems in other countries can be transferred to and

In June 1988 in Toronto, President Ronald Reagan attended his eighth economic summit. Next to him, clockwise, are Canadian prime minister Mulroney; French president Mitterrand; West German chancellor Kohl; Italian premier de Mita; ECC president Delors; Japanese premier Takeshita; and British prime minister Thatcher.

from the U.S. economy. For example, inflation caused by one economic power's expansionary conditions can contribute to inflation in other countries because consumers faced with domestic inflation may increase their purchases of less expensive imports. This increased demand for foreign goods puts pressure on prices outside the inflationary country and thus contributes to worldwide inflation. Similarly, a recession in one country can contribute to slower economic growth in other countries because consumers in the country experiencing a recession will have to cut back on their purchases of imports.

Because of this shared economic destiny among industrial nations, presidents must function not just as national economic managers, but also as international economic coordinators. They dispatch the U.S. trade representative to international negotiations aimed at reducing trade barriers, oversee the Treasury Department's negotiations with other finance ministries about the value of major currencies, and announce U.S. economic policies to the international community.

Since 1975 presidents also have attended annual economic summits where the leaders of the major industrial nations have met to confer on broad issues of economic policy. These meetings, which are attended by the leaders of the United States, Japan, Germany, France, Great Britain, Italy, and Canada (known collectively as the Group of Seven or G-7), have greatly increased international economic coordination. The summits have focused attention on the international component of economic policy, forced politicians to develop a better understanding of international economic issues, created a justification for frequent meetings between finance ministers and other economic officials, and provided a forum where economic matters can be discussed in the broader context of allied relations. Because the annual meetings compel the G-7 leaders to face one another, they have had a positive influence on free trade. The leader of a country that has erected protectionist trade barriers or taken other measures contrary to the interests of the group must justify those measures to the other leaders and face their collective pressure to reverse the action.

TRADE POLICY

Because the Constitution gives Congress the power "to regulate Commerce with foreign Nations," the rules governing foreign trade are set by legislation. Since the depression, however, trade legislation has contained broad grants of power to the president to implement the laws through international negotiations and through tariffs and other trade barriers designed to force other countries to open up their markets to American products.

Congress has granted the executive broad trade powers because only the president has the authority to negotiate with foreign governments. Therefore, when Congress adopted the strategy of pursuing mutual reductions in tariffs through international negotiations in 1934, it had to turn to the president to carry out those negotiations. In addition, Congress wanted to isolate U.S. trade policy from pressures for protectionism from specific industries. Since individual members of Congress have to be concerned with the economic conditions in their states and districts, protectionist sentiments have tended to be stronger in Congress than in the executive branch. If a single industry such as agriculture or steel predominates in a congressional district, that district's representative often will be disposed to support protectionist measures for that industry. According to political scientist Erwin Hargrove, by delegating power to the president Congress is able to respond to the local interests of its constituents without undermining the free trade position of the nation:

> Congress would rather not have responsibility for setting specific tariff levels because the flood of demands for individual industrial areas would be far too intense. Therefore, it has allowed the Executive to set such levels within parameters set by Congress. This permits members of Congress to make their requests in behalf of constituency interests

and still permit the President to do what is needed for a national position on international trade.[108]

Protectionism Versus Free Trade

The primary question that trade policy must decide is whether to pursue free trade or whether to erect barriers that protect U.S. industries but ultimately risk reducing the overall flow of trade. Few economists or politicians would argue against the proposition that the ideal trade environment for enhancing international prosperity is one in which nations can trade goods and services without trade barriers such as tariffs, import quotas, embargoes, and strict licensing procedures for importing goods. Yet even the most ardent free trade advocates recognize that the threat of protectionism is the most effective negotiating tool the government has to convince other nations to end their unfair trading practices. Appeals for protection from specific industries often have diverted national policy from the ideal of free trade. Nevertheless, since 1934, even when Congress has enacted bills to protect specific industries or to pry open foreign markets, policy makers in the executive branch have maintained the posture that the U.S. economy will benefit from free trade.

Throughout U.S. history, tariffs have been a contentious political issue. The nation's first Treasury secretary, Alexander Hamilton, supported high tariffs, which he hoped would nurture the infant industries of the Northeast. Although the tariffs enacted during the Federalist era were not swept away when Thomas Jefferson took power in 1800, the pro-agrarian Democratic-Republicans favored trade policies that enhanced the ability of farmers to sell their products overseas.

During most of the nineteenth century, the industrial and commercial interests of the North contended with the agricultural interests of the South over national tariff policy. Because the South depended on foreign markets for its agricultural products, it opposed tariffs that could trigger a retaliatory response from its foreign customers. In addition, tariffs raised the price of many goods the South needed to buy from foreign countries. The intersectional tensions over trade policy led to the nullification crisis in South Carolina in 1832. After Congress passed a high-tariff bill in 1832, the South Carolina state legislature passed an ordinance declaring the tariff void in that state. President Andrew Jackson, determined to assert federal authority, threatened to enforce the law in South Carolina with federal troops. Hostilities were averted when Jackson and South Carolina leaders accepted a compromise tariff. Tensions caused by the tariff issue remained, however, and eventually contributed to the secession of Southern states in 1861 that brought on the Civil War.

For the rest of the nineteenth century, tariffs remained high as American industries desirous of protection grew and the protariff Republican Party dominated national politics. Average U.S. tariff rates generally ranged from 35 to 50 percent of the cost of imports subject to tariffs. With the election of President Wilson in 1913, tariff policy was reversed. That year, with President Wilson's strong support, Congress enacted the Underwood-Simmons Tariff Act, which cut tariffs sharply. Wilson saw tariff reduction as a way to help American consumers, limit the influence of powerful probusiness lobbyists, and stimulate competition.

America's participation in World War I rekindled the "America first" sentiments in the United States that led to a return of high tariffs. The Tariff Act of 1921 and the Fordney-McCumber Act of 1922, both supported by Republican president Warren Harding, returned tariffs roughly to their pre-1913 levels.

When the depression struck in 1929, the governments of the major industrialized nations reacted by erecting trade barriers to protect their domestic industries. In 1930 Congress passed the Smoot-Hawley Act, which established the highest tariffs the United States had ever erected. The trade war of the early 1930s strangled trade between nations until it was a small fraction of what it had been. Protectionist measures left the world to dig out of the depression without the benefits of international trade.

The counterproductive results of Smoot-Hawley created a consensus among several generations of executive branch policy makers that a U.S. free trade posture was essential to American prosperity and international security. Political scientist I. M. Destler described the role of Smoot-Hawley in solidifying free trade as a goal:

> In this consensus, the Smoot-Hawley Act of 1930 played the same role for economic affairs that Munich played for military. Just as British Prime Minister Neville Chamberlain's sincere search for "peace in our time" had only strengthened those who made war, so too had congressional use of trade barriers to aid Depression-hit American producers backfired, postwar leaders believed. Other nations had retaliated, exports had plummeted even more than imports, and the world economic catastrophe helped to spawn both Adolf Hitler's Nazi regime in Germany and aggressive militarism in Japan. Only by building a more open world could we prevent the sort of mutually destructive, beggar-thy-neighbor competition that had produced national economic disaster and international bloodshed. This meant reducing barriers to trade, and to cross-border economic transactions in general.[109]

Partly because of the president's role as chief negotiator and partly because the presidency's national constituency reduced the pressure that could be brought to bear by labor unions and specific industries seeking protection, presidents, both Democratic and Republican, became the primary force for advancing the free trade agenda. The parochial nature of the legislative branch ensured that Congress would always contain sizable numbers of protectionists. But presidents were generally successful in securing congressional support for initiatives to liberalize trade.

INTERNATIONAL TRADE NEGOTIATIONS

After entering office in 1933, President Franklin Roosevelt acted to reverse Smoot-Hawley. With the enthusiastic support of his secretary of state, Cordell Hull, Roosevelt asked the Democratic-controlled Congress to delegate to him the authority to reduce U.S. tariffs up to 50 percent in return for equal tariff concessions by other nations. Despite nearly unanimous Republican opposition, Congress passed the Trade Agreements Act of 1934, which delegated this power to the president. Armed with new authority the Roosevelt administration negotiated bilateral agreements with many nations that cut tariffs and increased the flow of trade. The increased access to foreign markets that resulted helped stimulate the U.S. economy. After the initial success of Roosevelt's negotiations, congressional grants of power to the president to negotiate mutual tariff reductions became a regular feature of U.S. trade policy.

After World War II, President Truman sought to establish more sweeping arrangements to reduce international protectionism. At the urging of the United States, twenty-three nations signed the General Agreement on Tariffs and Trade (GATT) in 1947. Since then most nations have signed the agreement. Under GATT, mutilateral negotiations aimed at reducing trade barriers were to be held at regular intervals. The signatories also agreed to the "most favored nation" principle, which committed each nation to apply tariff rates equally to all the other GATT participants. In addition, the agreement prohibited certain restrictive trade practices such as import quotas and set up procedures to mediate trade disputes and implement sanctions against violators of the agreement.

Since 1947 GATT signatories have held eight multinational trade negotiation rounds. The first five rounds produced small but significant tariff reductions. In 1962 Congress passed the Trade Expansion Act with the strong support of the Kennedy administration. The act gave the president broad authority to reduce or eliminate U.S. import duties in return for similar trade concessions from other countries. The sixth round of GATT, known as the "Kennedy Round," resulted in tariffs on industrial products being cut by an average of more than 35 percent. In addition, for the first time the GATT participants discussed nontariff barriers to trade. When the round ended in 1967, however, many industries in the United States and in other countries lobbied against further cuts in tariffs because they feared increased foreign competition.

After the Kennedy Round, dozens of bills with protectionist provisions were introduced in Congress. Few were passed, but the drive for trade barrier reduction had temporarily peaked. Congress did not renew the president's authority to participate in multilateral trade negotiations, which had expired in 1967, until it passed the Trade Act of 1974 after the next GATT round was already under way. Although this act extended the president's authority to negotiate reductions of trade barriers, it placed more restrictions on the president's power and reflected the growing pressures from U.S. domestic industries to retaliate against unfair trading practices of foreign countries. The seventh round of GATT (Tokyo Round) was less successful in reducing tariff barriers than the Kennedy Round, although it made some progress on eliminating nontariff barriers.

Throughout much of its history the U.S. economy has benefited from trade surpluses. In 1981, however, the U.S. trade position began to decline rapidly as exports failed to keep pace with imports. The following year the U.S. current account, a measure of the net flow of goods and services traded with other countries, dropped into deficit. By 1987 the current account deficit had reached $167 billion. The large current account deficit cost the U.S. economy good jobs because Americans were buying so many products manufactured overseas. In addition, because the United States had to borrow to finance the trade imbalance, the current account deficit was increasing the U.S. dependence on foreign credit and adding to the debts of the nation. *(See Table 6-3.)*

These problems focused public attention on the trade deficit and increased pressure on Congress to pass legislation to protect American industries from foreign competition. In response to

TABLE 6–3 Current Account Surplus or Deficit, 1950–1996 *(billions of dollars)*

Year	*Current account surplus or deficit (–)*[a]	*Year*	*Current account surplus or deficit (–)*[a]	*Year*	*Current account surplus or deficit (–)*[a]
1950	–1.8	1966	3.0	1982	–11.4
1951	0.9	1967	2.6	1983	–44.4
1952	0.6	1968	0.6	1984	–99.8
1953	–1.3	1969	0.4	1985	–125.4
1954	0.2	1970	2.3	1986	–151.2
1955	0.4	1971	–1.4	1987	–167.1
1956	2.7	1972	–5.8	1988	–128.2
1957	4.8	1973	7.1	1989	–102.8
1958	0.8	1974	2.0	1990	–91.7
1959	–1.3	1975	18.1	1991	–7.0
1960	2.8	1976	4.3	1992	–67.9
1961	3.8	1977	–14.3	1993	–103.9
1962	3.4	1978	–15.1	1994	–104.4
1963	4.4	1979	–0.3	1995	–105.1
1964	6.8	1980	2.3	1996[b]	–112.0
1965	5.4	1981	5.0		

SOURCE: Commerce Department, Bureau of Economic Analysis.
NOTE: a. Net total of U.S. international trade in merchandise, services, and investments. b. Estimate.

Representatives David E. Bonior (D-Mich.) and Gerald B. Solomon (R-N.Y.) lead an anti-NAFTA rally in November 1993. Despite strong opposition from labor and protectionist groups, President Bill Clinton rallied enough bipartisan support in Congress to pass the trade agreement.

the mounting U.S. trade deficit, Congress enacted the Omnibus Trade Act in 1988, which mandated retaliatory responses to unfair foreign trade practices. President Reagan's firm support of free trade prevented Congress from enacting a more protectionist trade bill.

The continuing trade deficit during the late 1980s and early 1990s, however, sustained protectionist sentiments in Congress and among the American people. With the breakup of the Soviet Union and the end of the cold war, more attention was focused on economic competition with Japan and Western Europe. Many Americans viewed the trade deficit as a sign of American economic decline relative to its major industrial allies.[110]

In 1994 the eighth round of GATT (Uruguay Round) was completed. This breakthrough agreement signed by more than one hundred nations provided for tariffs to be reduced on most manufactured items by an average of one-third. The round was the first to reduce barriers on agricultural products, protect intellectual property rights, and establish rules covering trade in services.

The most controversial aspect of the far-reaching agreement, however, was the establishment of the World Trade Organization (WTO), which would replace GATT's existing institutional structure. Some critics charged that it would damage U.S. sovereignty because its dispute resolution procedures could not be vetoed by the United States. If the United States were judged to be at fault in a trade dispute, it would have to accept the WTO's ruling or open itself up to sanctions. But supporters of the agreement argued successfully that such a mechanism was precisely what was needed to protect American commercial interests. Because of the relatively open trading posture of the United States, Americans were far more often the injured party in trade disputes. Therefore, they contended, reforms that put teeth into GATT enforcement procedures would be a great advantage to American exporters.

In 1994 President Clinton, a strong advocate of free trade, lobbied heavily for GATT. On November 29, 1994, a lame-duck House of Representatives passed legislation implementing GATT by a vote of 288–164. The Senate followed on December 1 by passing the act, 76–24. Clinton signed the legislation on December 8, concluding the eight-year effort to negotiate and approve the Uruguay Round.

North American Free Trade Agreement

Even as the eighth GATT round was proceeding, the United States embarked on negotiations with Canada and Mexico to establish a single North American free trade area. From start to finish, this was a presidential initiative.

President Bush had responded positively to a proposal by President Carlos Salinas de Gortari of Mexico to negotiate a free trade agreement.[111] But then Bush went even further, advocating in June 1990 a long-term goal of creating a free trade area encompassing the entire Western Hemisphere "stretching from the port of Anchorage to the Tierra del Fuego." The first step would be concluding a North American Free Trade Agreement (NAFTA) between Canada, Mexico, and the United States.

The idea of concluding a free trade agreement with Mexico prompted immediate resistance in Congress. Many members, especially those representing districts where older industries and union labor predominated, argued that a free trade agreement with Mexico would cost American jobs. They contended that the elimination of tariffs on goods from Mexico, a relatively poor country where workers were paid low wages, would disadvantage U.S. industry, which had much higher labor costs. They envisioned a scenario in which Mexican exports would undercut American goods in the United States and American firms would send factories south of the border to take advantage of lower wages and environmental standards.

Presidents Bush and Clinton and their free trade allies in Congress countered that the United States had many economic advantages over Mexico that would offset the lower labor costs in Mexico. They reminded critics that the elimination of Mexican trade barriers, which were higher than American trade barriers, would open completely a large and increasingly prosperous market to U.S. businesses, thereby creating jobs in the United States. They also noted that failure to establish open trading relations with Mexico could forfeit this market to competitors in the European Community and Asia.

Unlike GATT, which few American voters understood well, NAFTA had been reduced by supporters and critics to a relatively simple set of propositions. To critics, the free trade agreement meant the loss of American jobs and the erosion of American wages, under pressure from a lower-wage trading partner. To supporters, the agreement would bring all the classic benefits of free trade: more exports, more jobs, more economic growth, and less inflation. As such, the debate on NAFTA became the most emotional and hard-fought debate on trade in the postdepression era.

President Bush signed the NAFTA accord shortly before he left office in January 1993, leaving the fight for its approval in Congress to President Clinton. Clinton announced his support for the agreement, but declared that he would negotiate "side agreements" with Mexico to address concerns about environmental protection, labor, and import surges. But these side agreements did not satisfy NAFTA's critics, most of whom sought the defeat of the agreement in Congress.

President Clinton demonstrated the centrality of the presidency to the maintenance of the free trade position by mounting a bipartisan campaign for NAFTA's passage in Congress. Despite advice from some advisers in August 1993 that securing approval of NAFTA was a lost cause, Clinton skillfully rallied a bipartisan coalition containing more Republicans than Democrats to pass the agreement.[112] Clinton used every means of presidential power at his disposal to sway undecided members of Congress, including old-fashioned dealmaking in which he promised to deliver pet projects and other political favors to wavering members in exchange for their votes.

The implementing legislation and side agreements were approved 234–200 by the House on November 17, 1993. The Senate followed three days later with a 61–38 vote of approval. Clinton signed the bill December 8, and the agreement went into effect on January 1, 1994.

Fast-track Authority

The passage of NAFTA and GATT depended on a mechanism for congressional consideration of trade agreements known as "fast-track" authority. This procedure was first established by Congress as part of the Trade Act of 1974, and it was subsequently renewed several times. Using fast-track authority, a president can negotiate a trade agreement, then submit for Congress's approval a comprehensive, nonamendable piece of legislation implementing the agreement. Congress must consider that legislation within a set time period under expedited rules. Because Congress cannot amend trade agreements negotiated under fast-track authority, the president has broad power over the details of negotiation. When presidents have had this authority, it has greatly expanded their power to conclude trade agreements.

The political consideration behind the establishment of the fast-track authority is that trade agreements have become so complicated and indivisible that they cannot be altered without undermining the entire agreement. For example, presidents and their trade negotiators may make compromises in one area of trade, such as agriculture, to secure concessions from foreign countries in another, such as textiles. But after the agreement is signed, if lawmakers from agricultural states succeed in changing portions of the agreement related to farm products, the compromises on which the agreement is based can be undermined. Therefore, the fast-track procedure gives the president the latitude to negotiate complex trade agreements without having to prevail on multiple votes in Congress designed to chip away pieces of the agreement.

Despite the utility of fast-track procedures, Congress has not been willing to make this authority permanent. From 1974 until 1991, fast-track authority was extended quietly as part of broader trade legislation. In 1991, however, fast-track became a hotly contested issue in Congress. Fast-track was set to expire on June 1, unless it was extended. Under the 1988 Trade Act, which had contained the last fast-track extension, a single, two-year extension of fast-track authority could be obtained by the president as long as neither house disapproved of the president's request. Because fast-track authority has the status of a procedural rule in both houses of Congress, either house acting alone could block the extension.

Opponents of the extension focused on Bush's intention to use it to conclude a free trade agreement with Mexico, which had less support than the ongoing GATT negotiations. They also questioned whether it provided presidents with too much power over trade agreements.[113]

Fast-track authority was extended by votes of 231–192 in the House and 59–36 in the Senate. Bush concluded the NAFTA using this extension. But the debate and the relatively close votes on fast-track posed a threat to long-term presidential primacy in trade negotiations, especially since either house acting alone could deny the president fast-track authority. If presidents were unable to secure fast-track authority in the future, they probably would be unable to conclude major trade agreements.

President Clinton was able to renew fast-track authority in 1993 by comfortable votes. But this extension was only for six and a half months and only applied to GATT talks. The limited scope of the extension and the desire of most Democrats to support their new president accounted for its relatively painless enactment. The GATT agreement was concluded under the authority of this extension, but no further extension was forthcoming. As of January 1997, neither house of Congress had brought fast-track legislation to the floor.

INTERNATIONAL MONETARY RELATIONS

When one nation imports goods from another, it usually must pay for those goods in the seller's currency. The cost of the seller's currency in terms of the buyer's currency is called the "exchange rate." Exchange rates affect a country's ability to export its goods because the higher its currency is valued on international markets, the more expensive its goods will be for foreign buyers. Since a dollar that is worth less relative to foreign currencies will make U.S. goods cheaper for foreigners to buy, intervention to lower the value of the dollar is a prominent tool that presidents have used to fight trade deficits.

Bretton Woods Agreement

After World War II the United States led the world in setting up an international monetary system that established stable exchange rates conducive to free trade. Forty-four nations signed an agreement at Bretton Woods, New Hampshire, in 1944 that made gold the standard by which currencies were valued. The Bretton Woods agreement established the International Monetary Fund (IMF) to oversee adjustments in exchange rates and the World Bank to provide loans for postwar reconstruction. The intention of the United States was to build a predictable international currency system that would prevent both destabilizing fluctuations in exchange rates and deliberate currency devaluations that could threaten free trade.

Each member of the IMF was required to declare a "par" value for its currency in relation to the U.S. dollar, which was pegged to gold at $35 per troy ounce. Official exchange rates of the world's currencies were not allowed to fluctuate more than 1 percent from their par value. Because the United States held most of the world's gold reserves and the U.S. dollar's value was backed by the government's pledge to convert dollars into gold, nations used the dollar as an international trading currency and as a reserve of wealth just like gold. In effect, the United States functioned as banker to the world.[114]

The Bretton Woods arrangement functioned well during the 1940s, 1950s, and early 1960s. The stability it produced brought an enormous increase in world trade and the resurgence of economies devastated by World War II. By the mid-1960s, however, the dollar's role as an international reserve currency was causing the United States economic problems. Because other nations wanted to hold dollars to trade and back up their own currencies, dollars flowed overseas but failed to return. The result was a growing U.S. balance-of-payments deficit that weakened international confidence in the dollar and led many foreign investors to exchange their dollars for gold. U.S. gold reserves fell from more than $23 billion in 1949 to just $10 billion in 1971.

In response to this problem, on August 15, 1971, Richard Nixon stunned the world by announcing that the U.S. Treasury would no longer convert dollars into gold. The dollar's value would be allowed to "float" to a level determined by international currency markets. Since other currencies depended on the dollar, they, too, would have to float. The dollar, which had been overvalued, declined against other currencies, making U.S. goods cheaper overseas.[115]

Nixon's decision ushered in a new era of international monetary relations that required a higher degree of coordination between governments. Although several countries proposed plans to salvage the Bretton Woods system, by 1973 all major currencies were floating. Nations found that currency values could not be left entirely to market forces because the markets produced sharp fluctuations in exchange rates as investors shifted large amounts of money from currency to currency in search of higher earnings. Moreover, the market forces did not always push exchange rates in the direction that was needed to prevent trade imbalances. For example, between 1981 and 1985, despite a growing U.S. trade deficit that would have been slowed by a weaker dollar, the dollar's value increased as foreign investors converted their money to dollars to take advantage of the high interest rates, low inflation, and political stability to be found in the United States.

Managing the Value of the Dollar

Under the post–Bretton Woods system of floating exchange rates, governments have often attempted to adjust the value of their currency through intervention in the currency markets. The United States and other governments intervene in currency markets through their central banks. If U.S. policy makers decide that the value of the dollar is too high they can lower its value by selling dollars on the open market. Conversely, a weak dollar can be strengthened if the central bank shrinks the supply by buying dollars on the open market.

Intervention in currency markets is primarily the responsibility of the secretary of the Treasury, but the Fed also plays a major role. Decisions to intervene are usually made jointly by representatives of the Treasury Department and the Federal Reserve System. For major interventions, the Treasury secretary and the Fed chairman will usually consult. Treasury and the Fed independently control distinct accounts that can be used for the purpose of currency intervention. The actual transactions from both accounts are conducted by the Federal Reserve Bank of New York. The Fed, therefore, has the means to intervene in currency markets on its own initiative. But in practice, it will not do so if Treasury has an objection.[116]

Currency interventions do not technically require presidential approval. But the central role of the Treasury secretary, who serves at the pleasure of the president, ensures that the chief ex-

PRESIDENTIAL POWER IN INTERNATIONAL ECONOMICS: 1995 MEXICAN FINANCIAL CRISIS

The extent of presidential power in the area of international economics was demonstrated in early 1995 by President Clinton's response to the Mexican financial crisis. On December 20, 1994, Mexico unexpectedly devalued the peso. Concerns in the international currency markets about political instability in Mexico, and about that country's debt level and trade deficit, created strong downward pressure on the peso. The next day, the Mexican government decided to let its currency float freely. The value of the peso plummeted 40 percent within a few days.

The peso's collapse sent the American financial community into a panic. Banks that had made large loans to Mexico feared that they would take huge losses. The value of mutual funds and retirement funds that had invested in Mexico dropped sharply. Businesses in the United States that had expanded to take advantage of the prospect of increased exports to Mexico faced the possibility that Mexicans would no longer be able to afford their products and services. The Clinton administration estimated that 700,000 jobs in the United States depended on reestablishing financial stability in Mexico.

Initially, the president planned to present a financial rescue plan to Congress for its authorization. The plan would have provided $40 billion in American loans and loan guarantees to Mexico in exchange for promises of further Mexican economic reforms. Although congressional leaders of both parties voiced support for such a package, congressional vote counters doubted that the plan had enough support to pass. Many rank-and-file House members saw a Mexican financial relief plan as an unnecessary taxpayer bailout of a corrupt government and of Wall Street brokers who had made bad investments.

Facing defeat in Congress, Clinton decided to act without congressional approval. On January 31, 1995, he announced that despite Congress's reluctance to go along with a Mexican rescue plan, the United States would provide $20 billion to Mexico in short-term loans and longer-term loan guarantees. The president also announced that he and Treasury Secretary Robert E. Rubin had secured from the International Monetary Fund and other international lending sources an additional $30 billion in loans to Mexico.

The White House also issued a joint statement by Clinton and congressional leaders saying that the president "has full authority to provide this assistance." Some critics in Congress blasted the president for bypassing Congress, but most members were relieved that they would not have to cast a politically difficult vote on the issue.

The $20 billion in loans came from the Exchange Stabilization Fund (ESF), which has about $25 billion in reserves. The primary role of the fund, which was established in 1934 by the Gold Reserve Act, has been to provide a means by which the Treasury secretary, acting with the approval of the president, could stabilize the dollar on foreign exchange markets. During the Reagan and Bush administrations, the ESF had been used to provide small short-term loans to Latin American nations experiencing financial problems. For example, President Reagan had authorized an $825 million short-term loan to Mexico from the ESF in response to a 1982 peso crisis. But the Clinton rescue plan far exceeded previous uses of the ESF for bailouts of foreign currencies.

The rescue plan has been viewed as a success. Mexico began repayment on the loans early and investment capital returned quickly to the country. Mexico's early repayment combined with the fact that the United States actually made money on the loans due to their high rate of interest silenced critics who claimed the loans would never be repaid. Moreover, Clinton's use of the ESF undoubtedly established a precedent that future presidents could use to address foreign financial crises of similar magnitude. The action also reaffirmed presidential primacy and flexibility in international economic policy making.

ecutive can exercise decisive influence over the process. In addition, even with their sizable reserves, it is difficult for Treasury and the Fed to alter the value of the dollar without cooperation from the central banks of the other industrialized powers. Consequently, coordination of exchange rate policies between the major industrialized countries is usually necessary to affect currency values. The president, as chief economic manager and the official charged with negotiating with foreign countries, must oversee this coordination.

Negotiations with other nations on currency levels are usually led by the Treasury secretary and attended by representatives of the Fed. Currency levels are also frequently discussed by the president and the leaders of the G-7 nations at their annual economic summits. Negotiations between governments often have resulted in informal agreements to take concerted action to adjust exchange rates. In January 1989, for example, the major industrial nations agreed to slow the rise of the dollar, which was being pushed up near a previously agreed upon secret limit by rising interest rates in the United States that were attracting foreign capital. At the same time, West Germany wanted its currency to be held up because of fears in that country that a weaker mark would lead to inflation by increasing the costs of imports. The world's major central banks responded by buying marks with dollars, thereby holding down the dollar's rise and propping up the mark.[117]

The importance of currency intervention was illustrated dramatically in the early 1980s. The strong dollar had encouraged American consumers to buy foreign goods and made American goods too expensive overseas to compete with comparable foreign products, thus contributing to the growing U.S. trade deficit. During Reagan's first term the administration had largely ignored the dollar's value. The president maintained early in his term that the exchange markets were inherently stable. The administration believed that market fluctuations that did occur were prompted by uncertainty about government intentions. Therefore a policy that consistently avoided intervention would yield the most stable exchange rates.[118] But when the current account deficit jumped from $44.5 billion in 1983 to $99.7 billion in 1984, the Reagan administration concluded that it had to act to bring down the value of the dollar. It therefore announced in January 1985, shortly after James Baker had taken over as Treasury secretary, that the U.S. would intervene in the currency markets to bring down the value of the dollar. U.S. intervention, sometimes with the cooperation of other central banks, succeeded in dramatically lowering the value of the dollar from the peak reached in February 1985. Although the lower dollar did not produce a reduction in the U.S. current account deficit until 1988, the U.S. trade problem would have been much worse without intervention.

NOTES

1. Clinton Rossiter, *The American Presidency,* 2d ed. (New York: Harcourt Brace, 1960), 21.
2. Harold M. Barger, *The Impossible Presidency: Illusions and Realities of Executive Power* (Glenview, Ill.: Scott, Foresman, 1984), 320.
3. Quoted in Francis Russell, *The Shadow of Blooming Grove* (New York: McGraw-Hill, 1968), 559.
4. N. Gregory Mankiw, "A Quick Refresher Course in Macroeconomics," *Journal of Economic Literature* 28 (December 1990): 1647–1648.
5. Charles Morris, "It's Not the Economy, Stupid," *Atlantic Monthly,* July 1993, 50.
6. See Joseph Spiers, "Washington's Crummy Numbers," *Fortune,* May 15, 1995, 37–38; and James C. Cooper and Aaron Berstein, "Suddenly, the Economy Doesn't Measure Up," *Business Week,* July 31, 1995, 74–76.
7. Rudiger Dornbusch and Stanley Fischer, eds., *Macroeconomics,* 4th ed. (New York: McGraw-Hill, 1987), 450–451.
8. Michael P. Riccards, *A Republic, If You Can Keep It: The Foundation of the American Presidency, 1700–1800* (New York: Greenwood Press, 1987), 90.
9. Ibid., 91–97.
10. Jonathan Hughes and Louis P. Cain, *American Economic History,* 4th ed. (New York: HarperCollins, 1994), 194.
11. Riccards, *A Republic, If You Can Keep It,* 101.
12. Hughes and Cain, *American Economic History,* 200.
13. James E. Anderson, *Politics and the Economy* (Boston: Little, Brown, 1966), 9.
14. Hughes and Cain, *American Economic History,* 194.
15. Anderson, *Politics and the Economy,* 9–10.
16. Ibid., 11–12.
17. John Milton Cooper Jr., "The Great Debate," *Constitution* 6 (spring 1994): 42–43.
18. Arthur M. Johnson, *The American Economy* (New York: Free Press, 1974), 52.
19. John F. Witte, "The President vs. Congress on Tax Policy," in *The President and Economic Policy,* ed. James P. Pfiffner (Philadelphia: Institute for the Study of Human Issues, 1986), 166.
20. Emmet J. Hughes, *The Living Presidency* (Baltimore: Penguin, 1974), 216–217.
21. Louis Fisher, *The Politics of Shared Power: Congress and the Executive,* 3d ed. (Washington, D.C.: CQ Press, 1993), 177–178.
22. Anderson, *Politics and the Economy,* 123.
23. George C. Edwards III and Stephen J. Wayne, *Presidential Leadership, Politics and Policy Making,* 3d ed.(New York: St. Martin's Press, 1994), 391.
24. Herbert Stein, *Presidential Economics: The Making of Economic Policy from Roosevelt to Clinton,* 3d rev. ed. (Washington, D.C.: American Enterprise Institute, 1994), 32–33.
25. Anthony S. Campagna, *U.S. National Economic Policy, 1917–1985* (New York: Praeger, 1987), 101.
26. Richard Pious, *The American Presidency* (New York: Basic Books, 1979), 295.
27. Campagna, *U.S. National Economic Policy,* 131.
28. Ibid., 141.
29. Norman C. Thomas and Joseph A. Pika, *The Politics of the Presidency,* 4th ed. (Washington, D.C.: CQ Press, 1996), 365.
30. Campagna, *U.S. National Economic Policy,* 196.
31. Stein, *Presidential Economics,* 77.
32. Dorothy Buckton James, *The Contemporary Presidency,* 2d ed. (Indianapolis: Bobbs-Merrill, 1974), 94.
33. Campagna, *U.S. National Economic Policy,* 210–211.
34. Charles E. Jacob, "Macroeconomic Policy Choices of Postwar Presidents," in *The President and Economic Policy,* 65.
35. Campagna, *U.S. National Economic Policy,* 238–243.
36. Jacob, "Macroeconomic Policy Choices," 67.
37. Richard M. Nixon, *Six Crises* (New York: Doubleday, 1962), 309–310.
38. Jacob, "Macroeconomic Policy Choices," 67.
39. Stein, *Presidential Economics,* 106–107.
40. Campagna, *U.S. National Economic Policy,* 306–307.
41. Thomas and Pika, *Politics of the Presidency,* 371.
42. Quoted in Pious, *The American Presidency,* 297.
43. Jacob, "Macroeconomic Policy Choices," 69.
44. James, *The Contemporary Presidency,* 96.
45. Campagna, *U.S. National Economic Policy,* 351.
46. James, *The Contemporary Presidency,* 103.
47. Ibid., 106.
48. Stein, *Presidential Economics,* 214.
49. Campagna, *U.S. National Economic Policy,* 401–402.
50. Jacob, "Macroeconomic Policy Choices," 75.
51. Stein, *Presidential Economics,* 218.
52. Ibid., 228–232.
53. Jacob, "Macroeconomic Policy Choices," 74.
54. Ann Mari May, "Fiscal Policy, Monetary Policy, and the Carter Presidency," *Presidential Studies Quarterly* 23 (fall 1993): 700–701.
55. Campagna, *U.S. National Economic Policy,* 485–488.
56. Ibid., 486.
57. Stein, *Presidential Economics,* 255–256.
58. James P. Pfiffner, "The Crisis of Confidence in U.S. Economic Policy," in *The President and Economic Policy,* 10.
59. James Tobin, "Voodoo Curse, Exorcising the Legacy of Reaganomics," *Harvard International Review* (summer 1992): 10.
60. Stein, *Presidential Economics,* 420–421.
61. George Hager, "One Outcome of Budget Package: Higher Deficits on the Way," *Congressional Quarterly Weekly Report,* November 3, 1990, 3711.
62. Stephen Skowronek, *The Politics Presidents Make: Leadership from John Adams to George Bush* (Cambridge, Mass.: Harvard University Press, 1993), 438.
63. David E. Rosenbaum, "On the Economy, Bush Followed Reagan's Lead, Not His Success," *New York Times,* June 29, 1992.
64. Sidney M. Milkis and Michael Nelson, *The American Presidency: Origins and Development, 1776–1993,* 2d ed. (Washington, D.C.: CQ Press, 1994), 384.
65. Stein, *Presidential Economics,* 424–425.
66. Milkis and Nelson, *American Presidency,* 395–396.
67. George Hager and David S. Cloud, "Democrats Tie Their Fate to Clinton's Budget Bill," *Congressional Quarterly Weekly Report,* August 7, 1993, 2122–2129.
68. Edwards and Wayne, *Presidential Leadership,* 397.
69. "Clinton Praises Agreement," *Congressional Quarterly Weekly Report,* November 25, 1995, 3612.
70. George Hager, "Congress, Clinton Yield Enough to Close the Book

on Fiscal '96," *Congressional Quarterly Weekly Report,* April 27, 1996, 1155–1157.

71. Kim Quaile Hill and John Patrick Plumlee, "Presidential Success in Budgetary Policymaking: A Longitudinal Analysis," *Presidential Studies Quarterly* 12 (Spring 1982): 174.

72. Ibid., 175.

73. Pious, *The American Presidency,* 322–324.

74. Fisher, *The Politics of Shared Power,* 186.

75. Ibid., 190–191.

76. Pfiffner, "The Crisis of Confidence in U.S. Economic Policy," 2.

77. Mary H. Cooper, "Federal Budget Deficit," *Editorial Research Reports,* January 20, 1984, 48–52.

78. Ibid., 56.

79. Anderson, *Politics and the Economy,* 113.

80. Edwards and Wayne, *Presidential Leadership,* 391–392.

81. Ibid., 393.

82. Hill and Plumlee, "Presidential Success in Budgetary Policymaking," 179.

83. Campagna, *U.S. National Economic Policy,* 471.

84. Ibid., 472.

85. Stein, *Presidential Economics,* 311–312.

86. Forrest McDonald, *The American Presidency: An Intellectual History* (Lawrence: University Press of Kansas, 1994), 379–380.

87. Joseph J. DioGuardi, *Unaccountable Congress* (Washington, D.C.: Regnery Gateway, 1992), 27–28.

88. Viveca Novak, "Defective Remedy," *National Journal,* March 27, 1993, 750.

89. McDonald, *The American Presidency,* 313.

90. Fisher, *The Politics of Shared Power,* 201–202.

91. Ibid., 201.

92. Witte, "The President vs. Congress on Tax Policy," 180.

93. Ibid.

94. Godfrey Hodgson, *All Things to All Men* (New York: Simon and Schuster, 1980), 227.

95. Timothy J. Conlan, Margaret T. Wrightson, and David R. Beam, *Taxing Choices: The Politics of Tax Reform* (Washington, D.C.: Congressional Quarterly, 1990), 45–48.

96. Jean R. Schroedel, *Congress, the President and Policymaking: A Historical Analysis* (New York: Sharpe, 1994), 66–80.

97. Alberta Sbragia, "Monetary Policy and Monetary Theory: The Poverty of Choice," in *The President and Economic Policy,* 222.

98. Dornbusch and Fischer, *Macroeconomics,* 439–446.

99. Paul Peretz, "The Politics of Fiscal and Monetary Policy," in *The Politics of American Economic Policy Making,* ed. Paul Peretz (Armonk, N.Y.: Sharpe, 1987), 149.

100. Ibid., 148.

101. Clyde H. Farnsworth, "Brady Warns that Fed Could Delay Recovery," *New York Times,* June 2, 1992.

102. Pious, *The American Presidency,* 315.

103. Frederic S. Mishkin, *The Economics of Money, Banking, and Financial Markets,* 3d ed. (New York: HarperCollins, 1992), 398.

104. Michael Bradley, *Economics* (Glenview, Ill.: Scott, Foresman, 1980), 576–577.

105. Pious, *The American Presidency,* 313.

106. John M. Berry and Kathleen Day, "Worker Pay, Benefits Up 4.9% in '88, *Washington Post,* January 25, 1989, F1.

107. Jonas Prager, *Fundamentals of Money, Banking and Financial Institutions* (New York: Harper and Row, 1982), 297.

108. Erwin C. Hargrove, *The Power of the Modern Presidency* (Philadelphia: Temple University Press, 1974), 159.

109. I. M. Destler, *American Trade Politics,* 2d ed. (Washington, D.C.: Institute for International Economics, 1992), 6.

110. Stein, *Presidential Economics,* 416.

111. Destler, *American Trade Politics,* 98.

112. R. W. Apple, "A High-Stakes Gamble that Paid Off," *New York Times,* November 18, 1993, A1.

113. Destler, *American Trade Politics,* 98–100.

114. Miroslav Nincic, *United States Foreign Policy, Choices and Trade-offs* (Washington, D.C.: CQ Press, 1988), 337–338.

115. James, *The Contemporary Presidency,* 117–118.

116. Owen F. Humpage, "Institutional Aspects of U.S. Intervention," *Economic Review* 30 (first quarter, 1994): 2–6.

117. Walter S. Mossberg, "Dollar Selling Aimed at Curbing Its Rise," *Wall Street Journal,* January 12, 1989, A2.

118. Humpage, "Institutional Aspects of U.S. Intervention," 6.

SELECTED BIBLIOGRAPHY

Anderson, James E. *Politics and the Economy.* Boston: Little, Brown, 1966.

Barger, Harold M. *The Impossible Presidency: Illusions and Realities of Executive Power.* Glenview, Ill.: Scott, Foresman, 1984.

Campagna, Anthony S. *U.S. National Economic Policy, 1917–1985.* New York: Praeger, 1987.

Destler, I. M. *American Trade Politics.* 3d ed. Washington, D.C.: Institute for International Economics, 1995.

Edwards, George C., III, and Stephen J. Wayne. *Presidential Leadership: Politics and Policy Making.* 3d ed. New York: St. Martin's Press, 1994.

Fisher, Louis. *The Politics of Shared Power: Congress and the Executive.* 3d ed. Washington, D.C.: CQ Press, 1993.

Hughes, Jonathan, and Louis P. Cain. *American Economic History.* 4th ed. New York : HarperCollins, 1994.

Mishkin, Frederic S. *The Economics of Money, Banking, and Financial Markets.* 4th ed. New York: HarperCollins, 1995.

Peretz, Paul, ed. *The Politics of American Economic Policy Making.* Armonk, N.Y.: Sharpe, 1987.

Pfiffner, James P., ed. *The President and Economic Policy.* Philadelphia: Institute for the Study of Human Issues, 1986.

Pious, Richard. *The American Presidency.* New York: Basic Books, 1979.

Stein, Herbert. *Presidential Economics: The Making of Economic Policy from Roosevelt to Clinton.* 3d rev. ed. Washington, D.C.: American Enterprise Institute, 1994.

Thomas, Norman C., and Joseph A. Pika. *The Politics of the Presidency.* 4th ed. Washington, D.C.: CQ Press, 1996.

Illustration Credits and Acknowledgments

Chapter 1 Chief Executive

3 Reuters/Bettmann 8 Marilynn K. Yee, *New York Times* Pictures 10 White House 12 White House 13 *(top left)* Ken Heinen, *(top center)* White House, *(top right)* Roger Sandler, *(bottom)* Karen Ruckman 15 R. Michael Jenkins 25 John F. Kennedy Library 26 Nixon Project, National Archives 27 *Washington Star,* courtesy of the Martin Luther King, Jr. Library 36 Steve Karafyllakis 62 Library of Congress 71 Associated Press 73 U.S. Coast Guard 75 Kathleen Beall 79 Library of Congress

Chapter 2 Legislative Leader

93 R. Michael Jenkins 96 no credit 100 *(both)* Library of Congress 102 Library of Congress 111 John F. Kennedy Library 113 *(left)* courtesy of the Dwight D. Eisenhower Library, *(right)* John F. Kennedy Library 119 Gerald R. Ford Library

Chapter 3 Chief Diplomat

129 Theodore Roosevelt Collection, Harvard College Library 134 John F. Kennedy Library 138 Jimmy Carter Library 141 Library of Congress 144 no credit 146 Reuters 149 *(left)* Bill Auth, *(right)* no credit 151 (top) National Archives, *(bottom)* White House 156 Reuters/Bettmann 158 White House

Chapter 4 Commander in Chief

168 Library of Congress 169 Library of Congress 175 AP/Wide World Photos 182 George Bush Presidential Materials Project 184 United Nations Photo 187 Dwight D. Eisenhower Library 188 Library of Congress 189 Library of Congress 191 courtesy of the White House 194 Library of Congress 197 Library of Congress 198 U.S. Air Force

Chapter 5 Chief of State

211 White House 213 UPI/Bettmann 216 Library of Congress 217 *(top)* Reuters/Bettmann, *(bottom)* Ronald Reagan Library 222 Library of Congress 229 George Tames, *New York Times* 232 Jimmy Carter Library 235 Reuters 237 Nixon Project, National Archives

Chapter 6 Chief Economist

242 Library of Congress 245 Library of Congress 249 UPI/Bettmann 251 United Press International 257 Reuters/Luc Wovovitch Archive Photos 262 UPI/Bettmann 271 Bill Fitz-Patrick, White House 274 R. Michael Jenkins

Index